JOSE MARIA JAVIERRE

JOHN OF GOD
LOCO
IN GRANADA

Translated by
Benedict O'Grady O.H.

National Library of Australia Cataloguing–in–Publication entry:

Javierre, José María
[Juan de Dios loco en Granada.]
John of God loco in Granada

ISBN 0 646 39168 2.

1. John of God, Saint, 1495-1550
2. Psychiatry - History
3. Charity
4. Christian saints • Spain - Biography
I. O'Grady. Benedict
II. Brothers of St. John of God
III. Title

282.092

John of God *loco* in Granada was first published in Spanish by EDICIONES SIGUEME S.A. Salamanca, in 1996. This English translation was made and published in 2000 with the kind permission and co-operation of the original publishers

• Designed, typeset & edited by Fineline Print Pty Ltd.
• Printed by Fineline Print Pty Ltd.

AUTHOR'S FOREWORD

When I wrote about the life of St. John of God in my book that was published in Spanish under the title "San Juan de Dios – Loco en Granada" I wanted to make the life of this extraordinary man known to as wide a public as possible. Consequently, I was very pleased to learn that some English-speaking members of the Hospitaller Order of St. John of God in Australia were working on an English translation of my work. When I was advised of this initiative in 1995 I encouraged their efforts and began to look forward to the culmination of their work. Some four years later, in June 1999, the translation was placed in my hands.

I wish to express my thanks for, and appreciation of, the efforts that have been made to bring this English translation to fruition and publication. Anyone who has been involved in such translating work will know how much time and energy has to be expended to carry out such a task. I have been assured, and believe, that it was a labour of love!

I have been asked to approve the translation for a limited publication and distribution by the English-speaking Provinces of the Order. I willingly, and happily, give my approval to this publication. I trust that readers of "John of God – Loco in Granada" will, like many readers of the Spanish original, be drawn closer to a man, and saint, whom I consider to be one of the towering figures of human, and creation, history.

José María Javierre
Seville, January 2000

TRANSLATOR'S FOREWORD

When I first read José María Javierre's "San Juan de Dios – Loco en Granada" I was captivated by its content and style. So it was with pleasure that I accepted the invitation of the then Australian Provincial, Brother Joseph Smith, to translate the work with a view to its being published by the English-speaking Provinces of the Order. This was an act of some courage on my part because, although I love and savour the Spanish language, I learned it as an adult and not at my mother's knee! Since I judged Javierre's style to be a mixture of the familiar and conversational with occasional flights of poetry, I was concerned that I might not do full justice to his original narrative. However, I was easily persuaded that the great good of conveying his insights and knowledge to English-speakers who would not otherwise have access to them warranted the risk. I hope that those who read this translation will reach the same conclusion. One problem of translation stayed with me throughout my work on the book - how to translate its title. In Spanish "Loco en Granada" works well but the literal English translation, "mad in Granada", seemed too stark - after all Javierre argues that John of God's madness episode must not be seen simplistically as nothing more than a psychiatric disturbance. My final decision was to use the Spanish word 'loco' in the English title. I believe that most English-speaking readers will understand the sense of the word and the more complete English dictionaries, such as the New Oxford Dictionary of English, give 'loco' as meaning crazy or insane.

As usual with such projects as this, there are many persons whom I should thank for having, one way or another, promoted and aided the work. The first of those must be Brother Brian O'Donnell who has been the constant driving force behind the project and its realisation.

The present Provincial, Brother Peter Burke, supported the project to the other English-speaking Provincials, convincing them of its worth and gaining their agreement to financially supporting the publication by guaranteeing to take a certain number of copies.

Sister Maureen Casey O.P. edited the translation at an important stage in its development. Mr. Gavin Greenwood and Brother Damian Keane unselfishly gave their time to the somewhat tedious process of proof-reading. Mr. Michael Flannery generously supplied the photographs of Granada that have been used to illustrate the city of Granada that John of God knew, and loved, so well.

My efforts, and all those associated with me in this project, will be amply rewarded by an wider knowledge and deepened love of the man to whose following I have devoted my life as a Brother of St. John of God.

Benedict O'Grady O.H.
Sydney, 8 March 2000

CONTENTS

PROLOGUE

– Juan Ciudad. That is what they called a poor Castilian shepherd from the Oropesan (Toledo) countryside. It seems he was born in Portugal (1495), of Jewish origins. Christian by vocation, he had nothing more to support him than his hands. He was a man of the world rather than of a particular city or country. Although he served twice in the army of the King of Spain, victory did not bring him any glory. He started life poor and ended it in the same condition, without honours, without money. Juan Ciudad, a man of the world. This was his first identity.

– Juan the madman. That is what they called him much later on. He had no past that could identify him, no surrounding family to protect him. In his maturity he survived as a hawker peddling books and illustrations, sharing the misery of the lowest on the scale of life. He arrived at Granada and settled there (1538). He gave away everything, making himself the poorest, a poor madman amongst others similarly afflicted in the 'lofty' city of Granada. He lived among the insane at the hospital founded by the monarchs Ferdinand and Isabella. He learned how to share in their sufferings, he put himself in tune with God, a good Christian, amongst the poor insane.

– Juan de Dios. In good mental health and full of ardour he was released from the hospital. He placed himself at the service of the abandoned who died of cold and illness in the great city of Granada. Everyone saw them, but only Juan saw them as they truly were and his heart went out to them because in them he discovered Christ. He made no judgements and was not influenced by adverse comments. He had little education but he knew the Gospel and at once began to carry it out. He had no need of commentaries or explanations other than his altruistic creativity. In the heart of Granada he opened up a way of love, a pathway to God and of caring for the poor. That is why they began calling him Juan de Dios [John of God], as God willed, and they called him that up to the day he died (1550).

– Juan the Christian. As his surname was Ciudad [city] it would seem he was of Jewish origin, (the world was his motherland), but it was at Granada he found his place and discovered himself as a Christian. He was neither a theologian nor

a cleric, he had no annuity nor wrote any treatise. He assisted the poor by selling firewood that he gathered in the countryside and along the roadside. He appealed to the wealthy for money for those he assisted. He had no agenda other than the urgency of the love in action that he carried out for the poor. He internalised and lived the great words of Matthew (25: 31-46): "I was hungry and you fed me, I was sick and you took care of me..." He discovered Jesus, without needing to 'make himself' poor, for he was poor already. He only had to make himself the servant of the poor whom he found all around him, thus making himself Christ for them. That is why we can call him Juan the Christian.

– *Juan the Saint, Juan the Hospitaller*. He did not need anyone but he never lacked friends: God put people and brothers at his side who were able to understand him. St. John de Avila was his guide. Noble men and women helped him, covering his constant debts and supporting his works of powerful love. The poorest in Granada welcomed him as one of their own. He also had companions who took up his way of life. He died without having founded a religious order but the impelling force of his live was an example that converted some of his followers into disciples. They wanted to perpetuate his work by creating the Hospitaller Order that bears his name and, to this day, can be found throughout the world. Perhaps he was the last of the popular saints of the Church: a man of the people (Ciudad - being his surname), friend of God in the service of the most sick and needy.

– *Javierre's Juan de Dios*. Five hundred years since his birth, José María Javierre came to write the life of Juan Ciudad. It may be the greatest of his biographies. He is an historian and journalist who is attentive to the heartbeat of the life of the Church. He has written the best lives of the greatest saints of a century of saints (Teresa of Jesus, John of the Cross...). Now, from the wisdom that flows from his heart in the maturity of his life, he has given us this biography which combines history and present experience.

My friend Javierre, you have written of yourself when you write the life of your saint. You have thrown open your heart to us when you make the heart of Juan Ciudad your own – a universal man, Jewish *converso*, lonely shepherd, soldier without glory, a real Christian in the heart of the New Andalusia of 16th century Granada. Not only friends of lives of saints are going to read your work but also those who are associated with you by profession.

They include journalists, historians, all who love life including theologians like myself - your admirer who walks with you, one foot in academia and the other on the pathways of the life that you know how to describe so well when you speak to us of St. John of God. May you live long José María Javierre so as to continue to offer us your wisdom so vigorously set out in lives like this!

Xabier Pikaza

1

WHAT A MAN! "THIS JOHN OF GOD... AND OF THE NEIGHBOUR."

The people of Granada often looked up to the twin peaks of Valete and Mulhacén towering above their city. But higher than these mountains was their regard for this man who was now dying. Already in the last few years of his life they attributed a flood of miracles to him. Now that he will soon be dead what will they come up with now? Take the story about the donkey for instance.

John of God started a hospital to give refuge to the sick poor whom he discovered abandoned like so much garbage in the streets.

They tell the story that he bought a donkey to carry the hospital's dirty laundry to the banks of the River Genil for laundering. He used to tether the beast to an iron grille in front of a window at the hospital.

Well, one day as dusk was approaching, along came a thief, who untied the beast, mounted it, and disappeared down the street.

Nobody had ever warned the thief that stealing a donkey from a saint was a dangerous thing to do.

When the thief arrived at the entrance to his cave, he attempted to dismount, but could not. He was stuck fast to the donkey's back. He called out for help, but in vain. Not one of his friends or neighbours could help him. Fed up with all the braying and struggling, they left him to himself and went off to their beds. The luckless thief backed out of the doorway and with his head thrust down below the donkey's ears trotted off in sheer terror down the deserted streets of Granada. As dawn broke his mount took him straight up the road that led to the hospital where it stopped right in front of the main entrance. The thief pleaded to see Brother John of God who, when he heard of the misadventure, came out and gently patted the donkey's neck, telling the thief to dismount.

They tell dozens of tales like this one. Of course, John and his helpers did take the hospital's laundry to the river Genil. However, not a single word is recorded in the documents of the period that refer to the anecdote of the thief who was stuck fast upon the back of the anti-theft donkey. Nevertheless, popular cautionary anecdotes of this kind showed how the Granadinos kept alive the memory of their Brother John of God.

Today, those of us who have to render a truthful and accurate account of the life of John of God are faced with the task of having to effectively clean away the encrustation of such popular pious anecdotes attributed to him by his devotees.

Soon such fanciful tales will cause irreparable damage to the figure of John of God. One of the most bizarre examples of this is the one about the donkey. Little by little these tales were to fill up his biography from birth to death. They felt that they had to sprinkle holy water on each stage of his life. Thus we see the village bells ringing out on their own accord when the baby John was born. They have the Virgin Mary saving him from peril, and on one occasion had her presenting her infant Son to him; and, believe it or not, they even had him present at two places simultaneously. Even in the short time that John slept, they had angels waking him up in the middle of the night so that he could go to the bedside and comfort someone who was dying. Then they had the Archangel Raphael helping him to carry sick people. On another occasion John of God lifted up his eyes as he was washing the feet of a poor man and discovered the Lord Jesus Christ looking at him. An even more enchanting tale is that of the apparition at the little whitewashed hamlet called Gaucín which stands in the Ronda foothills. Here they have John coming across a barefoot child whom he picks up and puts upon his shoulders to carry across a stream. How weighty he is! He can barely carry him. Surely you remember the legend about the perspiring giant St. Christopher. Well, they were to say it was just like that. And that is nothing to what they were to say about his battles with the devil. Hundreds of stories circulated about him, some extravagant, others flowery in the extreme.

Spain's famous poet and playwright Lope de Vega popularised these tales by circulating them on a nation-wide scale. Lope de Vega said, *"I declare to have read about them in the works of serious authors, many of whom are historians and poets."* To this he swore and signed: *"Lope de Vega Carpio, citizen of Madrid, well-known to the Holy and General Inquisition, Apostolic Notary registered with the Roman Archives and a presbyter cleric, resident in the houses of Francos Street, and 56 years of age."* A little more than 70 years had passed since the death of John of God, when Lope put this load of amazing happenings together in his work, "The Canticle of John of God and Antón Martín". Lope de Vega declared:

3

*"neither poetry nor stories
can reduce to a number your glories."*

Well, I can at least try to do this in my present-day biography. The job of cleaning away the incredible wonders in John of God's story calls for a combination of studying precise documentation while, at the same time, maintaining a keen respect for existing tradition.

Thirty years had passed since the death of John of God, and already there was an conglomeration of these amazing events attributed to him in circulation. Then, because it would have been insensitive to contemptuously throw out all these marvels that surrounded someone of the calibre of John of God, along came a certain valiant author who carefully investigated them in order to write an authentic biography. As soon as word got out at Granada about what was happening to blessed John, those who 'knew' him protested. Two Hospitaller brothers recorded that they were reproached for "lack of concern that we Brothers of John of God must have had for the truthfulness of his life story".

They counter attacked by responding that now a book had been written about his life, customs and holiness. It was not good enough for them, contradicted his devotees, saying that the book was a very brief account and much more needed to be put down.

No less a person than Brother Francisco Fidel, the future General of the Order, received the same complaint: from Doña Sancha Guzman, the senior maid-in-waiting to the Duchess of Savoy. Doña Sancha knew John of God at Granada and had quite a lot to do with him. She said of the book presented by the Brother General that it seemed to her *"to be quite small."* Then she added, *"I am a woman who had a lot to do with the things made famous by blessed John who came to discuss matters with me. So how dare he make up a book that is such a tiny volume."* So small was it in fact that it could fit in the palm of one's hand. The lady went on to say that if it were a respectable Toledan book, it would have a spine measuring at least four and a half inches in width, even broader than that of a dictionary.

Now I want to say something confidential to my readers. I do not know whether you know John of God very well. Possibly many of you would have, as I did up to three years ago, a somewhat fuzzy idea about the saint of charity who founded hospitals and the Hospitaller congregation.

Is that all there is to him, nothing more? Well then, prepare yourself for a surprise. You will see what type of man John of God really was. You will see what a story he has to tell.

He was a brilliant person, even excessively so. He broke the mould. He was excessively human. He was excessively holy. He came to stay at Granada, a city Gómez Moreno considered to be *"unbalanced in its excellence."* Unbalanced John of God. Unbalanced Granada. How lucky the Granadinos are to have such an excessive saint, one of whom they could compose "apocryphal gospels" in order to recount his feats. Very well, now I intend to start sifting these tales in order to separate the wheat from the chaff.

What an amazing and fascinating man John of God was at Granada. Simone de Beauvoir, the lady of the mid 20th century Parisian smart set, noted one day that she had grown old, and this discovery did not please her at all. She looked in the mirror and saw her pale face furrowed with wrinkles. She rebelled against the threat that her death was imminent and that there was nothing she could do about it. A cloud of despondency overshadowed her. She wanted to take stock of her life and asked herself what more had life to offer. Her love for the celebrated philosopher Jean Paul Sartre had been so long ago. She wrote that there remained a few beauty spots she wanted to see, ranging from the snow-covered Alps to the Bay of San Francisco, from the dawn over Fujiyama to the red sunset of the Congo. Certainly, featured among her many engravings was the Andalusian shore's "golden sands of Mazagón" which she fortunately visited before it was ruined by summer tourists. It seems to me that the Parisian trend setter of my younger days forgot to include *persons*, human beings, among her existential riches – only scenic views.

I think that our real treasure is the great number of splendid men and women whom we have come across throughout the years of our lives. As we met them at some bend in the road, they left us a memory of themselves. The radiant recollection of such people is the most delightful of all views. As is so often the case, those persons who leave such a lasting remembrance with us are often quite unaware of it. This fact made me decide to select for my imaginary hall of fame persons who throughout my own life have left a profound mark upon me. Some of them held brilliant positions in public life, others, the majority of them, are simply good ordinary folk.

One such person, whom I really got to know quite well over the past three years, is John of God. So now my imaginary hall of fame includes him. John of God takes his place among the dozen or so men and women who, for me, are alive once more in the pages of history. I place each one of them in the hall of fame of my glorious heroes. Each one is a charming person who has really captivated me. I find it really worthwhile to walk alongside them as I travel the paths of this world. Yes, finding myself in the company of John of God really reconciles me with the human race.

I am sure you will come to know him too, and you will be amazed at the experience of John, hitherto undreamed of. Even the legend of the thief who rode through the streets of Granada throughout the night with his backside stuck to the donkey's back, seems worthy of a smile.

Don José María Peman, an acknowledged expert on Andalusia who has tramped through its villages and cities, has this to say: "When you come to think about it, there is only one miracle in the biography of St. John of God, and that is the miracle of charity." This author hits the nail right on the head, for charity is neither a redundant word, nor does it clash with justice.

John of God saw those who were suffering on the margin of society in that glorious Granada which the Emperor Charles V tried to create as an alternative to the magnificent Granada of the Nasrides Moorish dynasty. Possibly at that time there was a lot of cheap literature about the fall of Al-Andalus in circulation. John of God saw the plight of those who lived on the margin of society, the poor and the ill. Nobody considered them, yet there they were, on the outer of that grand society. They were the forgotten ones, the abandoned.

John, poor fellow, did not think it was his job to shake-up the social structures of the second half of the 16th century. Nor did Teresa of Calcutta have any voice or a vote at the economic sessions which are periodically held by the "G 7", those seven richest countries on the planet that lay down the economic ground rules. By means of his charitable works, John of God did not pretend he was fixing up the unjust situation that existed in his day. He simply saw the unfortunates, the cast-offs of that magnificent city: those who were thrown into the drains, covered with filth, devoured by lice and consigned to the scrap-heap of humanity. He saw the hungry, the abandoned, the vanquished and the diseased. He saw them all and decided to help them, to esteem them, to respect them and to serve them. He loved them, he gave them charity.

John of God did this with kindness and tenderness and without making any big deal out of it. Nor did he insult the affluent people who passed him by pretending not to notice anything. He dedicated himself to collecting money from the rich so he could help the poor. Yes, he did that, and he was always courteous in the way he went about begging. In that he identified himself with the friendly irony of Andalusia. I have discovered a good deal of sarcasm in the way he went about this. For instance, take the case of "The House of the Dead Man".

The people of Granada dubbed the palace of the Salazar family in the Horno de Marina "the House of the Dead Man". Prominently displayed at the entrance was the heraldic shield of the distinguished Salazars. They were of an illustrious lineage and counted many Royal Chancelley judges amongst them. They were also friends of our John, which induces us to suspect that "The House of the Dead Man" does not correspond to this palace, but rather to the one next door, that of the Roncals, or even perhaps to that of some other wealthy aristocratic family nearby. If indeed it was the Salazar's house, they nevertheless remained John's friends and protectors in spite of the joke he played upon them.

The story goes like this. John of God was wandering about one evening and stumbled upon the corpse of a poor man lying in the street. Witnesses said that "he was without a shroud and no one was going to bury him." Just another poor wretch without a mother or father, not even a dog to bark for him. John of God knocked upon the door of a rich family and when the householder arrived he asked him for enough money to bury the poor man who did not even have a shroud.

The wealthy man told him to go away. John didn't say a word, but went to where the corpse was lying, picked it up and placed it upon his shoulders and carried it back to the front door of the selfish rich man.

He put the corpse on the doorstep, then knocked upon the door again. The owner reappeared and John loudly said to him: "Brother, your obligation is as great as mine, so for God's sake give me the means so that we can both bury him."

The wealthy man became afraid when he saw the corpse left upon his doorstep. He dipped his hand into his purse and gave enough to buy a shroud and bury him.

I guess that as he handed the money over, it must have cost John of God quite an effort to stop himself from laughing.

John asked politely and graciously. He devised a slogan, a formula, which has entered into the theology of charity.

Curiously enough, this formula was invented a century and a half before by a certain "pious man" called Diego of the city of Cremona in Lombardy, Italy. Diego distributed all his belongings among the poor and to hospitals, then he sent his disciples out into the world to beg for those in need. The Cremonese, as his followers were called, asked for alms with the words, "do well for yourselves." John of God was illiterate, so he could never have known of this reference to his 14th century predecessor. Nevertheless, he came out with an identical phrase, thus saying as he begged, "brothers and sisters do good!"

"Do good by giving me what you can for the poor. If you give alms you please God, you fulfil the Christian commandment, and furthermore, you do good for yourselves." In this way he converted the poor into a bank of profitable investment, something which would seem like a tranquilliser for the affluent who do very nicely in this life, and at the same time try to assure themselves of heaven in the next. As far as John of God was concerned, this slogan was something quite recent. He needed money for his poor people who were ill, and he also knew the biblical value of almsgiving, so from there he left it up to each one's conscience to consider.

John was convinced that by assisting those who suffer, it is really Jesus Christ himself who is helped. Mother Teresa of Calcutta practiced the same theory, and this is what she has to say: "When the poor let us help them, they let us serve Jesus." Because Jesus is in them.

John set up in Granada a type of celestial bank where the deposits earned interest. Thus, as he begged, he told his benefactors, "I want you to profit through these alms." Yes, John of God changed almsgiving into a means of accruing profit.

John was always up to his eyes in debt because the expenditures of his hospital were like a bottomless well. He once wrote to a benefactor asking for a donation so he could "pay for what is owing on meat and oil, as they don't want to give me any further credit since I owe so much already. I am holding them off with the promise that I will soon be getting some money from Malaga." Then, with good humour, he lamented, "often I cannot leave the house because of the debts I owe."

John of God begged and he begged: He said, "as water extinguishes fire, likewise charity extinguishes sin." He always knew how to offer an excellent profit: "Who would not invest what one has with this blessed merchant (Christ) who offers us such a bargain?" John of God was absolutely convinced of this: "What a happy investment and profit," How true that is, for it is written in the Gospels, but only John went about the streets saying so. His words were like flames burning into the very soul of Granada.

Note well, John of God's dialectic banking slogan was no joke. He never studied any of the medieval Latin volumes that contained the accumulated wisdom of the Greek philosophers adapted to Christian thought. John's education went ahead through the movement of the charity that enlightened his heart. The sagacious Aristotle set out the "primacy of love of self" in an essentially categorical manner as a fundamental principle. We always love ourselves by providing this love to ourselves; bringing about happiness, including the most generous love of which we are capable. Thomas Aquinas confirms Aristotle's theory by applying it boldly to the love of God. We cannot love God unless we can see in him our own good. Though the brilliant exclamations of mystics might suggest something else, the truth is, love binds our happiness to the kind paternal gaze of God, in whom we are and have our being, and whom we seek. By the very fact that we are creatures of God, we love him and we love our neighbour as ourselves. The whole thing has to come from us, and it rotates as we play our part in it. As the theologian Aquinas stated: "The order of charity proceeds from nature; for it is by nature that every being loves itself more than others. Furthermore, this order of charity will continue in the next life." Or could it be that John of God's banking strategy is firmly supported upon an anthropological basis. To give alms is to love. Lovingly do well by giving alms. "What a happy investment and profit."

Four prostitutes promised John of God that they would change their lives if he would take them away from Granada to the faraway city of Toledo where they hoped to settle down. So he made preparations to take them on the journey. He also took his companion Angulo, for that seemed to be a good move. When his spiritual director, Father Avila, that most wise priest of the Andalusian clergy of his time, received the news that John of God was calmly going into brothels to rescue the poor women he reprimanded him and warned him of the dangers involved.

"Keep on your guard regarding the women you are bringing back to God's service. They are turning out to be quite a hindrance and expense to you. It would be better not to keep them there unless they get married soon or find domestic work with respectable ladies, otherwise they are going to be lost and all that you have done for them will collapse."

John knew that these prostitutes were 'the poor', just like the sick people huddled under shelters in the rubbish dumps; just like the street urchins and vagabonds; they all belonged to John of God's domain. It was worth his effort to rescue some, even if others laughed at him and deceived him. How about that journey from Granada to Toledo! Well nothing like it was ever seen before in the annals of the saints; a brother accompanying four harlots, three of whom ran away from him on the fifth day.

The question is, Why did he do it? Well we are soon going to see that they thought he was crazy, and he just let them go on thinking that. In my opinion, John of God showed a lot of wisdom for one who was crazy. Sensitive to his surroundings and visionary of the future, he will leave his mark on his times: we will see him introducing a blueprint which will be the forerunner of the modern hospital system. Within a few decades, he will take his place within the scientific movement set in motion by Galilleo and Kepler. The illiterate John of God adds to the achievements of his epoch by bringing about two innovations in the progress of healthcare – technology and love. The current studies of the history of medicine and nursing have situated the figure of John of God within their precise delineation, demolishing baroque exaggerations and recognising his merits, all brought about by his enthusiasm rather than by any strategy.

We should be ashamed that, after some four and a half centuries, so much misery still remains to be remedied upon the face of the earth. By all means, even if some day we are able to arrive at the eradication of poverty, hunger and misery, John of God will still continue to be a valid witness, devoutly supporting health progress with tender and loving attention. That is how he lifts healthcare services to a higher and more human level favourable to the mysterious presence of God. This is all going to happen at Granada, where, as they say, everyone witnessed the spectacle that blessed John put on. He was only playing a role to give them the slip, he did not care, and he went on and finished the job.

John of God thought his conduct was natural and normal. He was not going to waste any time in giving himself any airs. He remembered the scene of the judgement proposed by Jesus to his disciples. Good and bad ended up astonished when the Lord rewarded or punished them: 'because he was hungry, thirsty, imprisoned, unclothed'. Some of "you helped me, others no." Lord, when did we not come to your aid? "When you did it to the poor, you did it to me." All were astonished, those who had not fulfilled the precept of love as well as those who had. Could it be that even the compassionate had not discovered the secret?

John of God certainly had, his outrageous madness nobly sprang forth from the secret he had discovered. John was aware of that, and he certainly did not give himself any airs about it. By all appearances confused, he really knew how the dice were being cast.

I ask myself, How was it that John chose Granada to be the scene of his adventure? Granada, that unbalanced city as Gómez Moreno called it. That extravagant, yet at the same time, hidden city of Granada, eternally loved by so many, myself included. Why Granada? Only the angels that trace the pathways of the stars through celestial space know the reply to that question.

I warn my readers that the biography of John of God is going to set before them dozens of questions that are engaging and puzzling. As a rule, when my friends ask me what sort of effort it costs me to make an honest narrative of the lives of persons whose biographies I am writing, I explain that it is necessary to get into the skins of your subjects, to see with their eyes, think with their brains, feel with their senses and carefully walk in step with the heartbeat of their lives. Then, as one day follows another, the biographer will begin to become quite familiar with his subject and manage to grasp what he or she is all about, grabbing his subject by the collar as it were.

John's story is contagious and I assure you that you will be infected by it, because no one can come close to a person like John with immunity.

In my imagination I have this hall of fame where I place all the marvellous people who have enriched my life. These are my personal heroes and among them is a brilliant biochemist who dedicated himself to scientific research into the secret process of how plants transform sunlight into vital energy for our planet. Maybe you have heard of him, Professor Manuel Losada, his name sometimes appears in various publications. Losada writes that by the turn of the 20th century, we must seriously get wise to ourselves and seek the truth without hesitating to do the moral thing. This is what he has to say:

"The worrying enigmas all about us must be cleared up. The origin and evolution of the universe has to be unravelled, likewise the origin and evolution of life. But above all, the search for the sense of creation and the finality of human existence must go on. Doubt is the torch of the wise, it is not for setting fires alight, but to abolish darkness."

According to Losada, our human pathway is a steep one, but it is a pathway that is *'enlightened by reason and sweetened by love.'*

The conflagration started by John of God at Granada permits us to unravel some intellectual enigmas. The ultimate reason for our earthly presence is the perplexing question asked by each dweller upon this planet. We stumble along with the persistent existence of evil, that sad shadow which obscures our confidence in the paternal goodness of God the Creator. Inborn deficiencies, illness, natural disasters and historic pestilence, as well as egoism, evil and the cruel characteristics of our human species, pour into our minds all sorts of distressing motives. No single question rises to heaven more frequently than the repeated lament as to why we suffer evil. It is as if God the Father, the all-powerful One, permits the failures of nature. On one hand we see the rich Epicurean who enjoys the pleasures of this life, while on the other, there are so many people, poor like Lazarus, sunken in misery.

Why are there sick, physically disabled and mentally impaired people? What is the mystery behind so many *errors* of creation? To this question John of God offers a pragmatic answer. He gives no reasons, nor does he come up with any theories. He simply bends down to the poor wounded one, lifts him up, places him upon his shoulders and carries him to a refuge for rest and there he gently binds up his wounds. He has compassion.

Contemplating from our intellectual arrogance the comings and goings of John through the streets of Granada, I think that there was a hidden wisdom in John of God's agenda. It makes us think that those who are emarginated in our society are right before us now waiting for us to extend our kindness to them.

Should a formula for justice that liberates the disinherited ever eventuate, then history would record that a happy day. While waiting for this golden age to dawn, John of God simply went about his task distributing blankets to the destitute and cooking hot meals to nourish them. He opens up his basket right before our very noses.

"Give me help for the poor, do good, by giving to me..."

John of God answers the enigma of evil with love. In his own peculiar manner he unveils the meaning of creation.

Now we are going to see how God lay in wait to catch John in his net. Without any doubt he was a chosen one, a sign of contradiction. God marked him out and fastened himself upon him. An interior fire consumed John of God and he seemed to be crazy to those who lived around him.

I have an unbelieving friend who is going to read this book with interest, but he is not going to believe this. So, because he is such a good friend and is interested in the lives of people of integrity, I hereby insert a few curious items to intrigue him. Finally, after much historic research, it can be said for certain that John of God came from a family of *Conversos*, which is to say, Jewish blood flowed through his veins.

It is my good fortune that over the years I have been able to make a detailed study of three personages who lived in 16th century Spain. Now I can add a fourth one to the list. The first was John de Avila, a recognised master of spiritual direction of his day. The second, Teresa of Avila, a woman who was full of talent, goodness, grace, and I would like to add, sound common sense. Next comes John of the Cross, refined, accomplished, and an aesthetic exponent of divine love. Well, all three of them, John, Teresa and John, were all members of the *Jewish Mafia* of their epoch. All three were born into *Conversos* families, a dangerous connotation in the eyes of proud Spaniards who boasted of having pure blood running through their veins. Such people considered *Conversos* to be of a lower social class and suspect of heresy. However, it is certain that during the reigns of the Catholic Monarchs, Isabella and Ferdinand, and Emperor Charles V, the *Mafia* included dozens and dozens of illustrious persons, even persons who were champions of military, intellectual and religious exploits.

My three champions, John de Avila, Teresa of Jesus and John of the Cross, were all of Jewish extraction. Now I can add another as well, and that is John of God.

The insufficiency of documentation referring to the first part of his life made it a difficult task to trace John of God's Jewish origin. Nevertheless, the clues seemed to be compelling, and besides, the very dearth of documentation is sufficient to point the finger at this fact. Those who knew the secret conveniently engaged in a 'cover-up' in order to hide the stain, which in their eyes, obscured the standing of the future saint.

Yes, John of God also has his roots in Jewish antecedents. I ask myself, from where did so many Old Christians, as they were known, draw their aversion and sense of repugnance towards the religious relationship of Jews and Christians. The truth is simple, for we know that besides being Christians of the New Testament, we are also heirs of the Hebrew People of the Old Testament. We of the New Testament have been spiritually conceived with Jesus, our brother, in the womb of a Jewish Virgin of Nazareth named Mary. It does not seem very reasonable to cross out my three Johns, de Avila, of the Cross, of God, and my Teresa of Jesus as having impure blood, because of their kinship with Jesus Christ and his Mother. On the contrary, it would seem to give them the stamp of nobility.

Come now my incredulous friend, you certainly fit very nicely into the company of our Christian community with its Old Testament biblical precepts. You will be happy to learn of John of God's biological connection with the Jews. Maybe in some way you might even think of us believers in a more favourable light since we identify ourselves with Christ our big brother. I know you are going to ask me why John of God only stayed within the sphere of charitable activity instead of heading a violent rebellion of the outcasts, like the revolt of the slaves led by Sparticus. That was the same old complaint that his countrymen put to Jesus Christ.

Oriana Fallaci once confessed to Roberto Gervaso: *"I do not believe in God or the afterlife, but we all have a need sometimes to feel close to these two adorable fantasies."*

Well, I am sure that I can safely say that the story of John of God is going to stagger my unbelieving friend, because it is a beautiful story and absolutely true.

John of God, it seems to me, is a perfect name. However, a certain poet was able to go even one better. Poets have an ability to share in divine creation, because they have been given the gift of being able to enhance the beauty of the reality about them.

The poet I am referring to is Gerardo Diego and he gave John a second name at Granada. He called him John **of God** and **of the Neighbour.**

That is truly who he was, John of God and of the Neighbour.

2
HOW WE COME TO
KNOW JOHN OF GOD

What do we know exactly about John of God and what historic truth can be obtained by a thorough study of the documents relative to him?

Let us leave aside, perhaps somewhat regretfully, the more or less aesthetic pious legends which devotees have attached to his person over the last four centuries.

I would like to list for my readers some names that we will come across as we weave through the chapters of his story. I already know that he was a saint, but that is a horse of a different colour. It is unimportant to me whether some dazzling things pop up sooner or later when we start putting all the pieces together. However, as it is up to me to write his human story, I have to base this upon the clues left conserved in dependable documents. Such clues could be important, ordinary or honorific.

We begin, handicapped by the regrettable lack of John's personal papers. He left behind no writings in his own hand, a deficiency that makes it very difficult to get access to an historic personage. In other words, how can anyone become a saint without writing like a Cervantes?

Did John of God not write anything at all? Nothing! I suspect that he did not know how to write. But there are his letters, half a dozen of them. I will return to these later on, but John did not personally write these letters. He dictated them, then signed each one with his signature. He used an enigmatic signature that looked more like a design than letters.

Before describing these six letters, all of which provides good biographical material, I must point out that I have divided the 55–year span of John's life into two sections. The first dates from his birth until he arrived at Granada, the second is from that arrival until his death.

Born in the year 1495, John Ciudad went to Granada in 1538 when he was 43 years of age. Prior to this, he was just like any other ordinary person who lived in Spain at that period. Consequently barely any documented evidence exists that gives any trace of the perplexing obscurity of the first 43 years of his life.

The second half of his story covers the twelve years he spent at Granada. From that time onwards we find an impressive amount of documentation, for John of God had become quite famous at Granada. I will soon explain how this documentation came to be discovered and how, in the latter part of the 20th century, it enriches our knowledge of John of God. While we know hardly anything at all of the first part of his life, the second part tells us almost everything. This curious inequality of information impels us to carefully examine the clues that might lead to a new conclusion when investigating the early stages of John of God's biography. There are significant leads to follow, even though they are somewhat ambiguous.

The most precious biographical materials of John of God are the six letters he signed. They are carefully expressed and give us a valuable insight into certain episodes of his dealings with others. Above all, they illustrate his prudent psychology.

We will see that there are also suggestions that John of God wrote other letters. The six extant ones came to light when the beatification process of John of God got under way and required for examination letters and any other writings that could be attributed to him.

Of the six extant letters handed over to the tribunal only four were originals. These were later placed in the Hospitaller Order's archives. One letter arrived as a copy, because the owner preferred to hold on to the original. This copy was verified and scrupulously checked with the original to prove its authenticity.

John's letters were addressed to the following recipients:

a) Two to his friend and benefactor Gutierre Lasso de la Vega, whom he called "my dearly loved brother in Jesus Christ." Both letters were conserved by the Lasso family at their home in the town of Almagro until Don Gutierre's great-grandchildren willingly handed them over to the beatification process.

b) Three letters to his very close friend and, in a certain sense, spiritual disciple, Doña Maria de los Cobos y Mendoza, Duchess of Sessa. Here we see the tender relationship between John and this young and charming woman. He refers to her as "most noble", "virtuous lady", "my dearly beloved sister", "good Duchess", "generous and humble", such was the courtesy John rendered her, and she well deserved it. The letters he wrote to the Duchess emerged in various circumstances:

–The first was returned to the judges of the beatification process not in its original form but as a copy.

–The second did not arrive in time for the beatification process, but came to light much later in its original form. In spite of its late arrival

and omission from the published letters, its authenticity was indubitable.

—The third letter was given to the process in copy form with its authenticity signed by a notary. A lady-in-waiting to the Duchess of Sessa retained the original.

c) One to a certain Luis Bautista, who had asked his advice regarding his state in life. The original of this letter was sent in to the beatification process.

Six letters, only a handful of pages in all. The Granadino professor, Gómez Moreno, on whose research I will comment later, points out that there were three scribes, each of whom *"wrote with a very distinct hand."*

Thus John dictated his letters, but he signed them himself, using an intriguing signature that has always puzzled researches even to this day. Look at the signature and tell me if you can make anything of it.

Indubitably the three letters of the signature are a capital 'Y' and a small 'f' and small 'o' put together to make 'Yfo'. Indisputably this is the signature of John of God. What odd things one can see on paper. I once visited the private chapel of the Bishop of Cordoba. There I saw reverently conserved in a showcase a receipt that read: *"I, John of God, hereby affirm that I have received from you, Ferdinand de Castro, four ducats in alms which your wife, may she be in glory, instructed should be given to me as alms for the poor. I have placed my signature to this receipt in Granada, on the 6th of December of the year 1548 with my three letters."* (His signature is attached). Ferdinand, the citizen of Granada, would never have dreamt where that receipt for four ducats, signed by John of God, would end up.

Searching for the significance of the three letters constituting this signature can lead one into a labyrinth. However, we will attempt to decipher them at the opportune time.

Only one of the six letters signed by John bear the date on which he dictated them. The second letter to Gutierre Lasso carries the date 8 January 1550, two months prior to John's death.

Gómez Moreno put the letters into a reasonable order. He pointed out certain references that were contained in the letters themselves. For instance, the one to Luis Bautista was written long before any of the others. The two to Gutierre Lasso were written close together, so they were sent in 1550. The first and second letters to the Duchess of Sessa seem to have been written about the same time. The third letter to the Duchess must certainly have been

1. The pomegranate ('granada') is found in many forms and materials throughout the city that John of God made his home in the last years of his life.

2. The arch - about all that remains of the Elvira Gate through which John of God entered Granada for the first time.

dictated only a few days before 8 March 1550, the day John died. It can confidently be said that all six were written in the last three or four years of his life.

Once the beatification process was terminated, copies of the letters were made and then certified by a notary and dispatched to Rome. The originals were conserved in the Hospitaller Order's archives which, at that time, were situated at Antón Martín Hospital, Madrid. When the Spanish anticlerical laws known as the *Desamortización* were enacted in the 19th century, the letters were transferred to Seville. From there, early in the 20th century, they were later sent to the archives of the General Curia of the Hospitaller Order at Rome for safekeeping. With the exception of the second letter to the Duchess of Sessa, all the original letters are now conserved in these archives. The six and a half pages of the second original letter to the Duchess are conserved for veneration in the *camarín*, as the room of the Saint's relics is called, at the Basilica of St. John of God, Granada.

Although they are few, the letters dictated by John of God pour forth his feelings at a time when these were forceful and sensitive. Later I am going to quote some of the forceful expressions and wise sayings from his letters. They give us an insight into a just and sincere man who was one with the simple people and spoke their language. In order to refer to the Virgin Mary as being immaculate, he, like the common people, used the expression "always intact". In order to express gratitude for money given for his hospital he said: *"The alms you gave have already been recorded in the book of life by the angels."*

When her husband was absent he consoled the Duchess like a kind grandfather. *"There you are all alone and separated, away from the gossip of the court, at home like a chaste turtledove awaiting the good duke."*

If John wrote, or rather dictated, more letters then we have a problem. In his first letter to the Duchess of Sessa, he confides, *"I decided to write to the Count de Feria and the Duke de Arcos."* We do not know whether his decision to write passed into reality, for as we will see, he was certainly kept very busy and had little time to spare.

In some of his letters he asked for a reply, for instance when he wrote to Luis Bautista: *"Always write to me, no matter where you may be."*

21

He wrote to Gutierre Lasso requesting a letter *"from your son the Archdeacon."* Therefore we can deduce that he probably received quite a deal of correspondence. Who could say otherwise? However, given his way of life, I have my doubts. John liked to get mail from people associated with him, but I can not clearly see him dictating too many replies. If only I were wrong, maybe one day more of his lost letters might miraculously come to light.

At least some of the replies that he wrote to his spiritual director John de Avila, might possibly turn up, but how many? Well, two at least, for we do have three letters written from him to John of God and two of them say, *"I have received your letter."*

Master Avila's letters contain tantalising references to John's way of life. It is a pity that John's replies have gone missing. It would be wonderful if two, or three, or more came to light, because John took notice of what his God-given guide used to tell him.

The six letters described above correspond to John's external life, and essentially they refer to his relationship with persons who gave him material assistance.

His letters to Master Avila reflect his interior life, his intimate spirituality, his personal dialogue with the mysterious Presence who, on one cold winter's morning at Granada, overwhelmed him.

Could any lost letters come to light? Oh! that they might!

Now I would like to move ahead, since Avila's letters reflect a curious discrepancy between master and disciple. This seems incredible, given the veneration John had for his mentor who was directly instrumental in bringing about his crucial encounter with God and whom he esteemed to be rich in wisdom and sanctity.

However, the texts of Avila's letters at least allow us to test one or two distinct follow-ups. John of God was the odd man out among Avila's disciples. Avila was frightened by John's revolutionary behaviour. We are going to see that, in his absence, he imposed on John a substitute spiritual director whom he was to heed and obey. John was full of reckless yet well-disposed impulses which he found difficult to moderate with a right measure of prudence.

As a rule biographies are not recognised as a basic

component of history, yet there is one biography that presents a documented source that bestows much value upon John of God. Fortunately we have this biography at our disposal and it is worthy of inclusion as source material in our study of John of God. This makes up for the deplorable lack of references in the first stage of his life, and it also sets us upon the right track when it comes to the years he spent at Granada. Obviously, here we are speaking of a very special biography.

Méndez Salvatierra became Archbishop of Granada in February 1578 and appointed the diocesan priest, Francisco de Castro, rector of John of God Hospital. This hospital sprang up in the city as the legacy of its founder, John of God, and the Brothers of the Hospitaller Order conducted it.

John had died 28 years previously, in 1550. Now both his Order and hospitals were held in great esteem. Each hospital had a priest rector integrated into its administration. The priest resided within the building, and shared with the brothers in their ministry by giving spiritual attention to the sick and dying, It was required that: *"he had to show himself to be benevolent with the poor, to be honest, and to be charitable and of good example."* These "rectors", who could either chose to take vows, or not, in the Order, were appointed by the bishop in accordance with the papal bulls of the period.

I believe that Francisco de Castro was a priest who died at an early age in 1584, 34 years after the death of John of God whom he probably did not know personally. This does seem to be the case, although he does not specifically say so in his work. Castro probably arrived at Granada as a young man accompanying the new archbishop, Méndez Salvatierra, who, it appears, was especially charitable towards the poor. Perhaps the Archbishop recognised the right qualities in this young priest to take up the duty of rector at the hospital. Castro was well educated and, it seems, a Master of Theology. The introduction to his book refers to him as *"Master Francisco de Castro, Priest Rector of the Hospital..."*. Nevertheless, the use of this title, Master does not specify what degree he had received upon graduation.

Father Castro lived in the community of eighteen or twenty brothers at the hospital and he shared in their daily work. He describes the brothers as *"caring for the poor in the wards of the hospital. Some brothers are employed in running the house while others go out begging for alms about the city."* Castro goes on to say *"that is how a hundred and twenty beds are kept going."* He then adds that, *"sometimes it is necessary to put up three or four hundred beds."* Castro greatly admired the brothers and says so in his book:

From the very beginning this hospital had it, as a legacy from John of God, that no poor person who arrived was sent away, nor were beds limited, but everyone who came was received and even when they had no beds they were to put up stretchers. That is how they cared for them. Once they had been given the sacraments nobody died on the floor. All the helpers here are unpaid volunteers for the love of God. Thus the house is better served than anywhere else in the world, because all the workers come here to help in order to save their souls by exercising charity. Thus everyone gives of their utmost without having to be constantly supervised.

The way in which the brothers went about their duties by day and night, increased Father Castro's respect for the person of John of God:

"Everybody was pleased with the example left by John of God and many men were inspired to imitate him and to follow in his footsteps in serving the poor. They sought to serve God alone in the way of hospitality. They had no need of learning and studies for they were well endowed with the love of God, charity, humility and worldly detachment."

Master Francisco de Castro's keen intellect made him aware of the necessity of writing his book, which he called *'The History of the life and holy works of John of God'*. Castro's aim was to show the world how divine Providence raises up *"exemplary men of heroic life"* who, he adds, *"are models of Christian conduct."* Such a one was John of God:

"A humble man who was looked down on by the eyes of the worldly, but who was highly esteemed in the sight of God."

Castro set his hand to the task that lay before him, having as his purpose to let his readers learn from the example of John of God. Let us learn what? Castro utilises a word in its classic sense that I also intend to use in the same way. That word is the Spanish verb *"desentrañar"* which means 'to unravel'. In modern Spanish *desentrañar* includes the meaning *"to tear out the entrails"*, or *"to investigate the difficult aspects of a matter."* But, when it is used as a reflexive verb, it becomes *"desentrañarse"* and signifies *"to strip oneself bare of what one has, so as to give it to others."* This latter form is exactly what Father Castro wanted to convey to his readers:

"Christian reader, this then is a living example given to you by Our Lord so that you can firstly understand how to act for the welfare of

others and to take on works of charity and mercy. That does not mean simply parting with some superfluous thing to share out amongst your needy brothers and sisters, but rather pouring yourself out as much as you can and being more like a father to them."

This, Castro tells us, is also what we must do in imitation of the Lord Jesus Christ, *"who truly stripped himself bare for our sake."*

Master Castro came up against a serious difficulty when he began to gather material for John's biography. It is my guess that there were, in fact, two stumbling blocks that he encountered. He admits to the first, but remains silent on the second. The first one arises from the love and devotion that Granada had for its *blessed* John of God who had died only a few years before. In contrast with the scarcity of dependable documents relating to events in the biography we can nevertheless take as true what Castro wrote; but then *miraculous* tales were mixed up with this as a result of the popular devotion held for John of God. Castro tells us that he was *"a quiet man who rarely spoke of anything that was not charitable and for the good of the poor."* He was seen arriving at Granada as one who had come down from heaven, but Castro honestly says, *"we do not possess news of many things that could be pertinent to this story."* Then, like the conscientious historian that he was, he resolves the problem by stating the truth:

"What I cannot verify I have omitted, but the prudent reader should be able to read between the lines; for it is better that we leave out now something which could be said later, than to talk about it now without certainty."

Castro then proceeded to describe the source of his information and does so in two parts. Logically, there were those *"credible persons who knew and worked"* with John. Nevertheless, Castro reminds his readers that although it was only thirty years since the death of John of God, *"due to the fragility of time,"* those who knew him *"have made guesses, and since these cannot be verified, I therefore am unable to write about them."*

Added to this honest admission, are those close witnesses who were the contemporaries of John of God. Castro also had a real treasure at his disposal in the form of a notebook, which, unfortunately, is now lost. This mysterious notebook, on which historians have pinned so much trust, was nothing less than a written record of memoirs jotted down by a certain *"companion"* of John of God.

"We have especially made use of a notebook which one who accompanied him on all his journeys has left us. He was a man who was very much like himself in spirit. He fully and clearly wrote down in a good hand what he saw as an eye-witness."

Who was this exceptional witness who was so close to John, who was so much like him? Did the saint speak such priceless sayings to the recipient in confidence? Who was this companion who recorded all this information during his journeys with John of God? And how did Castro get hold of this notebook, which helped him so much in writing his work? The truth is, we know neither his name nor how the notebook appeared.

This companion had to be someone whom we know to have been close to John while he lived at Granada, even though we do not know his name.

Where did the notebook end up? How grateful a researcher would be if only he could get his hands on it now. I ask myself, would it have been possible that the officials of the beatification process, who probably had access to the notebook mentioned by Castro, had it bundled up with all the other documents that appertained to the beatification process. If that were the case, then there is a good chance that the notebook lies buried deep in the section reserved for the Causes of Saints in the vaults of the Vatican Archives.

Master Castro went ahead with his short yet important and conscientious work. Following the preface where he explains the providential valour of John of God's life, there is a dedication to Archbishop Salvatierra. Then there is an explanatory note in which he states his sources. Finally come the 21 chapters relating the biography of John of God from his birth to his funeral. Castro then adds a further five chapters that relate to the initial development of the Hospitaller Order. The first edition was printed in 1585 – *at Granada, in the publishing house of Antonio de Librixaó consisting of 123 well spaced pages.*

However, Master Castro did not see his book published, for he died at John of God Hospital in the winter of 1584, the year in which *"his mother and heir"*, Catalina, obtained the necessary licence to publish his work. Catalina's royal permission to print stated that it was granted by Philip II *"in the Town of Madrid, on the eighth day of the month of June of the year one thousand five hundred and eighty-four."* This licence was then inserted at the beginning of the biography along with the certification that a tax of five *blancas* per page had been paid. Also in the introductory pages was a poem in Latin honouring the Archbishop and an illustration from a crudely made, yet touching, woodcut depicting John of God kneeling before a crucifix. Then another poem lauding Salvatierra and, finally, a letter from Catalina to *"the Most Illustrious and Reverend Lord Archbishop"*, which, as could be expected, thanked him for his protection and *"for bringing this book to birth by having it printed."* Then she adds a personal touch; *"you have remedied so many necessities for me."*

Only two examples of this first edition are extant, one is in the Vatican Library and the other in the Cordoba Provincial Library. A second edition was published three years later. There is only one known copy and this is conserved in the British Library. An almost forgotten third edition was published early in the 17th century. There were several translations of Castro's work into other languages the first being in Italian in 1587.

Although the biography by Castro disappointed many of John's devotees because of its brevity and modest form, it nevertheless caught the attention of relevant persons, one of whom was Fray Luis de Granada who alluded to the relationship of John of God and John de Avila. Fray Luis said John of God *"had much to say that we would not have known had not his life been so well written."* There is not the slightest doubt that Fray Luis had read closely Castro's book. It is even possible that one of Castro's phrases had influenced him to write the biography of Master Avila. In the seventh chapter of Castro's book we read the account of the first meeting of John of God with Master Avila. Castro eulogises Avila as *"an excellent man who was resplendent in holiness, prudence and letters and whose example and teaching throughout Spain brought forth great results for the Lord"*, adding that *"his story really needs telling in its own right."*

Thereby, he left open an invitation to someone to write the life of the Master – which is precisely what Fray Luis de Granada did.

Now I must justify why I consider the biography written by Francisco de Castro to be a source document in the critical study of John of God.

There are four reasons;

– Firstly the proximity of the facts: John had died thirty years previously and Granada kept the fragrance of that admirable personality alive. Castro breathed the very atmosphere of John's presence.

– Secondly, Castro had available to him dozens, even hundreds, of persons who knew, saw and heard John speak, all were eyewitnesses. Anyone who was a young person of 20 years at Granada in the year 1538, the year of John's arrival, would have been 65 by the time Castro began writing. Such a person could have known John well.

– Furthermore, and above all, there was that notebook of the anonymous companion of John of God who accompanied him "on all his journeys," and unfortunately this is not available to me now.

– Finally, there is the critical willingness of Castro to reject doubtful witnesses when he set out to write his work.

This quality of the biography by Castro shines forth with renewed splendour when it is compared with the biographies written some thirty or fifty years later. The biographies that followed Castro were collections of legends, sham miracles and apparitions that converted John's life into a showcase of marvels. These had the effect of diminishing the rich authenticity of his person, his charity, his self-sacrificing dedication and generosity towards the needy.

Such were the so-called baroque biographies which aimed at adding more colour to the figure of St. John of God, but in fact ended up besmirching him by presenting him as an unreal eccentric.

These baroque works about John of God began early in the 17th century and endured right up to the mid-20th century. Fortunately, on the occasion of the 4th centenary of the death of St. John of God in 1950, Professor Manuel Gómez Moreno came out with an entirely new history of the Saint. Gómez Moreno went into his work like a bull in a china shop, bringing down the encrustation of plaster that had for so long obscured the genuine figure of John of God.

Gómez Moreno made an indisputably wise move when he based his work upon a renewed study of the biography written by Master Francisco de Castro, which, after three editions, had fallen into oblivion and had disappeared from the horizon. Gómez Moreno prepared a new edition of Castro, the fourth, and this was published in 1950. He enriched it with documents and an admirable commentary and added a selection of testimonies given by several witnesses at the beatification process. Gómez Moreno used the biography by Francisco de Castro as the starting point for studying the trail left by John of God.

As I have already indicated, when I set out upon the track of Castro, I came up against two serious difficulties. One of these was Castro's acknowledgment that he wanted to clarify the image of John of God by getting rid of all doubtful additions to his life-story, and thanks to Castro's unbending decision, he admirably passed that test.

I also pointed out that Castro confronted a second difficulty that he did not mention. What was it, and why am I referring to it? My readers will find this out for themselves when they have read the first few chapters of this book. I am of the opinion that Castro purposely concealed some privileged information.

In the light of what we know now, I am certain that Castro knew of John of God's Jewish origin. Furthermore, he must have known of the circumstances of John's early childhood in Portugal where, in his birthplace Montemor-O-Novo , he was called João.

Sixteenth century Catholics in Spain and Portugal regarded anyone of Jewish descent to be suspect. They thought that a *converso* would never bring happiness to the believing community, only misfortune. What is more, they would not accept the fact that a saint could ever come out of a *converso* family. John of God turned up at Granada and captured the affection of the entire city through his charitable works. Were Castro to relate in his story that *contaminated* blood circulated in *blessed* John's veins such a revelation would have caused a shocking sensation, for such an accusation would have been sufficient to destroy anyone's reputation.

Today's Christian mentality finds it incomprehensible to have an aversion to anyone's racial antecedents, after all Jesus and Mary were both Jews. However, in our modern-day mentality, we must be mindful of the complex problems that existed four centuries ago on the Iberian Peninsula.

I believe that Master Castro considered that he did not have the right to tarnish the resplendent image of John of God by revealing to the Granadinos that he was a *tainted* Jew. So, he did not do so. He simply remained silent.

When he wrote his biography of Master John of Avila, Fray Luis de Granada was faced with the same dilemma regarding the family roots of his subject. The following astute sentence shows how he overcame the problem: *"It is not worthwhile knowing about the earthly parents of the Servant of God."* Yes, dear Fray Luis, that is especially so when it is convenient for us to remain ignorant!

In order to set out upon the path of John of God's biography I am going to put all the material at our disposition in chronological order.

During the final two years of his life John of God personally dictated six letters that are available to us.

Thirty-five years after his death we get the priceless biography based upon the testimony of eyewitnesses written by Master Francisco de Castro who also utilised the notebook of memoirs jotted down by a companion who had John's confidence.

The third documented attestation came to light in a file that had lain unnoticed until recently when the patience of a researcher on John of God's life unearthed it. Since this file of documents belongs to the same period of time, it takes its place with the two aforementioned sources and comes after the letters dictated by John of God. Of course, I am giving chronological precedence to the biography by Castro, since it is an overall story of John's life and embraces the episodes referred to in the aforementioned documents.

John of God founded two hospitals at Granada. The first was small and situated in a street in the centre of the city. The second was larger and was on the slope that leads up to the Alhambra.

But the second hospital was also too small to hold the number of sick and homeless persons, and abandoned children that filled it. John needed much more space to take care of his poor people. So he and his friends dreamed of opening up another building large enough to respond to their charitable ambitions. Two influential persons were among John of God's ardent collaborators who supported this dream. They were the Archbishop, who at that time was Pedro Guerrero, and John's spiritual director, Master Avila. For this long desired third hospital, the Jeronymite Friars gave the land.

The Jeronymites were friars of the Empire, for they were under the protection of Queen Isabella and, later on, her grandson the Emperor Charles. The Jeronymites were with the Christian troops at the conquest of Granada. While they waited for the capitulation of the city, they founded their provisional monastery in the field of Santa Fe. After the conquest of Granada, Doña Isabella granted some property of the Moorish kings, the Nublo house and orchard, where the friars built a monastery. They used stones taken from the Arab fortress at the Elvira Gate. This monastery proved to be too small for their growing community, so they constructed a second monastery on a site two hundred metres away from the first. This second one was splendid and had a magnificent church. During the period when John was occupied with serving the poor, the Jeronymites were putting the finishing touches to their fine church which they intended to contain the mortal remains of El Gran Capitán, Gonzalo Fernández de Córdoba, the military leader of the conquest of Granada.

Subsequently the first monastery that the friars had abandoned fell into ruins. It seems that it was because of their friendship with Master Avila, that the Jeronymites donated the property that was to make the dream of a new John of God Hospital possible.

Thanks to the recently discovered file that was hidden away in the Archives of the Provincial Government of Granada, we now know the history of how the new hospital came about. This hospital was built from the foundations up, because the old San Hieronymo [Jerome] Monastery had completely fallen into ruins. John of God and Master Avila got an extraordinary team of friends together to organise the task of fund-raising for the venture. Avila preached lively sermons in the churches that were attended by great crowds of people. Distinguished ladies donated their jewellery and Archbishop Guerrero sought the aid of the famous architect Diego de Siloé who, some years later, left a bequest to the hospital.

The building proceeded well, but John of God died before it was completed. His followers, who were soon to be constituted into the Hospitaller Order, moved the inmates from their old hospital into the new one in 1553, three years after the death of its founder.

The hospital flourished, but in 1572 a *gift* arrived from the Pope in Rome that was to cause some unpleasantness for the brothers of John of God Hospital. Pius V had signed a bull which gave the embryonic Hospitaller Order papal protection and placed it under the jurisdiction of the bishop of each diocese where it was or would be represented. The bull specifically stated that it *"prohibited the interference of anyone"* in the work of the brothers.

This really upset the Jeronymites who considered themselves as having the right to exercise control over of the hospital, simply because they had given the land and it was built right alongside their own monastery. They took the case to court, and on 15 October 1573, they lost it in favour of the independence of the brothers.

The recently rediscovered file contains the testimony given before the judge at the tribunal by 17 witnesses. Twelve of these witnesses were men and women who were associated with the charitable work of John of God. They were very close to him personally and shared his enthusiasm. What they stated has thrown much more light upon the closing years of John's life, for they were eyewitnesses who testified only twenty years after his death.

Our fourth documented source material comes from yet another process. This time it is much more complex and further removed in time from John of God's day. The Granadinos wanted to canonise Brother John of God thereby having him officially declared a saint. They loved him and thought that sainthood was inevitable for him.

It was necessary then to meet the canonical requirements for proceeding with the proposed cause in accordance with the established norms. The process used was the same as that which endured right up to the time of the Second Vatican Council. It consisted of two parts, the first one being the Ordinary Process, and the second being the Apostolic Process. Today the proceedings for canonisation have been simplified considerably to avoid the repetition of the various proceedings.

John of God had been dead for 72 years in the year 1622 when the Ordinary Process began. It was far too late to interview people who had known him personally and still cherished memories of him. A small boy who was ten years of age at the time of his funeral in 1550 would have been 82 were he to give evidence at this Ordinary Process.

On 22 October 1622 the Procurator General of the Hospitaller Order made a formal request to the Papal Nuncio to

Spain to nominate a judge to preside over the Ordinary Process. The Prior General of the Hospitaller Order, Brother Fidel, nominated Fray Domingo de Mendoza for this responsibility. Fray Mendoza was a distinguished jurist who had previously had success in conducting the cause for the canonisation of St. Isidore the Farmer. As soon as the Papal Nuncio approved Fray Mendoza's appointment he petitioned the Cardinal Archbishop of Toledo, into whose jurisdiction Madrid fell at that time, for permission to promulgate the cause. Permission was granted and an edict was directed *"to all faithful Christians... living and staying in the towns and villages of these realms and dominions"* to manifest what they know *"about the life and miracles of the blessed John of God."*

The Ordinary Process began at Madrid on 1 November 1622. On that day Fray Mendoza listened to statements presented by 24 citizens. The process then moved to Granada, Oropesa, Montemor-O-Novo and to all the other places where anyone might be able to come forth with some reliable recollection of John of God. In all, 457 witnesses were interviewed, and naturally the majority of them, 94 in fact, came from Granada. Madrid came next in numbers with 85 witnesses presenting their testimony. Of the 457 witnesses interviewed, 89 were elderly people who had personally known John, the remainder were hearsay witness and stated that *"they had heard it said..."*

The witnesses were obliged to reply to a questionnaire of 63 questions at each place where the Ordinary Process was officially convoked. It seems incredible but, by the time the Ordinary Process ended in 1624, Fray Mendoza had waded through almost 29 thousand replies. He sorted them out and sent them to the Sacred Congregation of Rites, which was the Vatican authority that handled such matters. This brought the Ordinary Process to a conclusion. Obviously, this mountain of documented evidence is a goldmine of data about John of God awaiting research by historians.

Unfortunately, the methodology of this Ordinary Process had a certain defect. The statements of the witnesses were strictly regulated by a predetermined questionnaire that sought concrete answers. This was purposely so, in order to avoid each witness wandering off the track into rambling discourses, thereby making statements that would have been far too longwinded. It was also important that the questionnaire did not have leading questions that might influence the replies. The questionnaire in this process was aimed at getting a certain type of answer that might not necessarily be too flattering about the subject.

I have already told you about the fine and straightforward biography of John of God written by Master Francisco de Castro, and how it went through three editions, the last one being in 1613. Gómez Moreno calls the biographies that came after this date, "*baroque biographies*"; all of which were jam-packed with sham miracles, prophecies and apparitions. Readers of these works were served up a John of God shrouded in fantasy, artificiality, marvels and visions. They became used to this image of John of God being presented.

The creator of such mystification was Brother Dionisio Celi who was the Prior of the Granada Hospital. In 1621 he published his: "Miraculous life and holy works of the blessed Patriarch John of God, Portuguese, and Founder of the Sacred Religion [Order] which cares for the sick." If the title alone does not provoke suspicions of grandeur, then the text really goes beyond all reasonable limits. Celi took the biography by Castro and 'completed' it chapter by chapter, introducing fifty absurd and fantastic miraculous events that he attributed to John of God. Lope de Vega copied a couple of these prodigies and included them in his famous 'Comedia' honouring John of God. Celi's imagination overstepped the fantasies of any poet. He had bells ringing on their own accord when the infant John was born, columns of fire coming down from heaven, apparitions of Jesus, conversations with the Virgin Mary, angels visiting and helping him, battles with the Devil, miraculous cures and prophetic revelations. He pulled John of God out of his historic context and transfigured him into a kind of beneficial magician. Celi had the effrontery to fill up Castro's work with his own inventions and then present his book as "composed by Master Francisco de Castro newly augmented and emended by a religious of the same Order."

Brother Dionisio Celi's has a place in the annals of hagiography as one who is responsible for distorting the true story of John of God with suspect pious additions. Brother Dionisio Celi's luck ran out when the judges of the beatification process took up his life of John of God and drafted the questionnaire on the basis of his wild assertions. These fantastic claims by Celi were then put to the witnesses to either confirm or deny. The result was, according to Gómez Moreno, a true miracle. Every single witness, all of whom were under oath to tell the truth, rejected Brother Celi's wild inventions out of hand. The witnesses had spoken their minds and the apparitions, voices from heaven and beyond the grave, were all cast out.

As a consequence of this the biography by Celi was discredited. Nevertheless it still had an effect upon two others that were soon to come along. One of these biographies was by the Augustinian friar Antonio de Govea (1624) and the other by a minor cleric, Manuel Tríncheria (1773). Both of these works were in a more moderate vein than Celi's, but they were still somewhat fantastic.

The findings of the Ordinary Process were examined at Rome, and after they were accepted, the Apostolic Process began on 18 January 1625. This tribunal was to clarify, or rather complete, any doubtful points left open by the Ordinary Process. In effect, the Congregation of Rites set out to purge Brother Dionisio Celi's fantastic claims. At the same time the Congregation of Rites retained the information it had received from the witnesses at the Ordinary Process, without alluding to what had been obtained without reasonable justification. This Apostolic Process concluded at the end of that same year 1625.

The final success came when Urban VIII beatified Blessed John of God on 22 September 1630. His canonisation came sixty years later when Alexander VIII declared John of God a saint.

For years and years the goldmine of data lay undisturbed. Nobody had ever penetrated that immense gallery of testimony that might enrich the story of John of God. Then along came Professor Gómez Moreno who discovered the way into the goldmine and went in with the first wagons to bring out the rich treasure. Gómez Moreno then used this material when he compiled his commentary, thereby enriching his edition of the biography by Castro (1950).

Gómez Moreno says it was a Jesuit friend of his who first put him on the right track in hunting down the file that lay hidden away in the Provincial Government Archives of Granada. When the 19th century Spanish Government passed its infamous *Act of Desamortizacíon* [confiscation of Church property and the legal dissolution of religious orders], it naturally had an effect on the Hospitaller Brothers and their hospital at Granada. Not only was the hospital confiscated by the State, so too were its archives which were taken away and placed in the Archives of the Provincial Government. There they were placed with a mountain of other documents and the file of the beatification process lay forgotten with them. Today students may examine the contents of this file at the Casa de los Pisa Archives and, if they so wish, photocopy them. I am going to come back to this subject later.

This process represents the fourth section of the documented references to John of God.

With the file which up to recently had been sleeping in the archives, we now have the four elements of the repository of documents that indicate clues left by John of God:

1. His letters.
2. The biography written by Francisco de Castro which recorded memories of John only 30 years after his death.
3. The statements of 16 witnesses called upon to make statements under oath in the lawsuit brought by the Jeronymite Friars 26 years after the death of John of God.
4. The proceedings of the beatification process 80 years later.

Now I want to say something about those who have done the research I have encountered while working on this life of John of God. They all form the group of workers who labour in this field.

I mentioned how the biography of John of God by Francisco de Castro lay forgotten for nigh on three centuries, from the start of the 17th to midway through the 20th, and how it was displaced by the baroque biographies written by Dionisio Celi and Antonio Govea. These highly devotional yet well-intentioned works were packed with phoney miracles and apparitions, all of which lacked any historical basis. These fabrications disfigured the true image of John of God, and as one may well suppose, these *miraculous* biographies set the framework for the forty or so books on the life of John of God that were later published in a popular style throughout the world in various languages.

In 1950, the year of the fourth centenary of the death of John of God, Professor Gómez Moreno republished the Castro text and, through his erudite commentary on it, made a laughing stock of the baroque biographies.

About that time two learned Granadinos manifested a great love for their city. One was Gallego Burín who defended his city against the incursions of interfering town-planners; the other was Gómez Moreno who, from Madrid, lectured about subjects relating to Granada, John of God being among them.

Gómez Moreno lived to be a hundred years of age. His father was a renowned archaeologist and painter, and it was from him that he received his taste for historical research. Gómez Moreno's reputation was already well established while he was still a young professor at Madrid. In spite of a heavy workload, he still found the time to resuscitate Francisco de Castro's work to mark the fourth centenary of the death of John of God. He did not know at the time that he would be starting an avalanche of research and study that was to throw light upon the true image of John of God.

The most mysterious thing about John of God is basically the celebrated episode of *madness* that was sparked off when he heard the words of Master Avila. It was as if a volcano exploded within his soul. This *madness* has been the subject of many psychiatric studies and commentaries by renowned psychiatrists. Gómez Moreno gives us the starting point when the episode occurred and when, and how, he emerged from it, but we lack a definitive work on this piece of John of God's life-story. Since 1950 up to the present time, the work of research on this subject has made much headway.

I am placing the figure of John of God exactly within its historic context and its cultural ambience, and I have brought together the work already started by other workers in this field.

It would take from about 25 to 30 years, the first third of the 21st century, to investigate the mountain of files stored away in the archives. Who knows what treasures might come to light that would enrich the repository of documents appertaining to John of God. Possibly they might even turn up the missing notebook written by John's companion, even the lost letters; or some unsuspected testimonies which would aid future researchers to come up with a definitive biography of John of God. Who knows, perhaps a couple of tomes of some thousand pages loaded with footnotes might even eventuate. At the present moment it seems that the completion of such a study would appear to be still a long way off.

Now that I have told you what we really know about John of God, and how and from where we obtained this data, let me now say something about those who utilise this information. These are enthusiastic persons who are keen to achieve their purpose, but there is a basic problem here in as much as the disciples of John of God, his sons, the Brothers of the Hospitaller Order, are concerned. You see, they simply lack the time to pursue such pursuits because their first call is to fulfil their professional duties by day and night in serving the sick poor and those who have need of their expertise in their hospitals and institutions. The brothers simply do not get the time to search through archives for their Order's historical roots. They are well aware that when a family grows to such an extent as theirs has, it is essential to build it upon the solid rock foundation of its founder. This therefore, calls for a serious study of the founder's charism, that gift planted by God in the spirit of John of God. That is why the brothers try to find as much time as they can for this study. To do so they often deprive themselves of leisure time in order to be able to delve into the archives of the Order as a means of knowing and understanding its traditions.

Following the publication of Gómez Moreno's book with its reprint of the original version of Castro, new biographies of John of God began to appear in various languages. Cousson brought out a French version; Gabrielle Russotto and Igino Giordani, Italian; Braun, German; José Cruset, Alfredo Muñoz Hidalgo, Valentín Riesco and Juan Félix Bellido, Spanish; Brochardo Costa, Portuguese; and English, Ruben Rumbout in the United States, Norbert McMahon in Ireland [and Benedict O'Grady in Australia]. Amongst the personal interpretations that have come forth are those of the German, Wilhelm Hunerman and the Spaniard Agustín Laborde. The Italian, Gabrielle Russotto, wrote a study of the spirituality of John of God.

In 1951 Brother Rafael María Saucedo's painstaking and detailed research gave a decisive impulse to this movement when he published his findings in a series of articles entitled *Chronology applied to the life of St. John of God*, which appeared in various magazines of the Hospitaller Order. The modern method of formulating historic criteria is to set it out in strict chronological form. This is precisely what Saucedo did. So precise were his findings that very little later revision was required.

The Order's various magazines frequently publish articles about its founder. Brother Giuseppe Magliozzi, an Italian missionary St. John of God Brother in the Philippines, edited a compendium of such articles in 1992. This work contains several articles by Brothers of the Hospitaller Order and it has proved very helpful to me in preparing this present work.

It was an unforgettable experience for me when I set out to search for documents relating to John of God. I experienced a real lesson in generosity and goodness. Researching archives requires much patience and tenacity for it can go on for months, often with hours spent in fruitless effort. For that very reason, when something really worthwhile turns up, many researchers hang on to it like grim death, fearful that somebody else may lay their hands on what they have discovered and publish it. My experience in this regard was just the reverse.

As you have already seen, there is a dearth of documentation covering the first 43 years of John of God's life. By way of contrast, there is an abundance of documentation covering the last twelve years of his life which he spent at Granada, a city that takes great care to preserve any documents pertaining to its significant citizens.

I calculate that at least five to six years would be necessary to wade through all the public and private archives at Granada that are safeguarding the information we seek concerning persons and families who, in one way or another, knew John of God. That is why I needed to seek advice from someone who could set me on the right track. My helper was an octogenarian John of God Brother named Matías de Mina whose wisdom is proverbial with all who know him. An Aragonese by birth, he joined the Hospitaller Order just prior to the outbreak of the Spanish Civil War. A cultured and learned man, Brother Matías held many positions of leadership in his Order. At the age of seventy he sought, and was granted, permission by his superiors to go to Granada to research the traces of John of God.

When I first met Brother Matías he had already been investigating the archives of Granada for a dozen years. I asked him if he would help me plan a methodology that would be useful in mining the archives. Brother Matías promptly accepted my request, and soon afterwards he handed me a bundle of about a hundred folders crammed with photocopies of documents. It really took the wind right out of my sails when I discovered that these folders contained the carefully catalogued material he had gleaned during his twelve years of intensive research which he patiently carried out in the nooks and crannies of Granada. This material included:

* A copy of the biography by Francisco de Castro, carefully noted line by line, chapter by chapter.
* A card index of persons and families of the witnesses who testified at the beatification process. These were carefully classified into groups, those who personally knew John of God and those who did not.
* Clarifications of a great many locations throughout the city with some historic association with the life of John of God.

I said in amazement, "Brother Matías, I can't possibly make use of the fruit of your efforts before you have it published." Then he nonchalantly replied, "Why not?" I thought that Matías de Mina was a man who had come very close to perfectly summing up the talents of John of God. I listened to him in bewilderment as he answered my questions, such as: What was John's physique like? Who were his best friends? What was his anthropological physiognomy? For visitors to Granada, Matías de Mina was a perfect guide to the places familiar to John of God. "Brother Matías, I would be a cheat were I to utilise your unpublished research." He would hear nothing of it. "It's all yours," he said as he handed it over to me. I gratefully accepted his generous gift.

Without doubt this bundle of historic papers will see light some day in published form. At present this fund of historic documentation is conserved at the Casa de los Pisa Archives at Granada. Thus I have had the pleasure of perusing all this research as if I had been the one who had spent ten years patiently researching the intricate Granada archives of the first half of the 16th century. In fact, that is why the name Matías de Mina really should appear on this book beside my own.

José Sánches Martínez is also a St. John of God Brother dedicated to the service of the ill and needy. He carried out substantial research for his doctoral thesis at the Gregorian University, Rome. Calling his work *The Spiritual Journey of John of God*, he traced the path of John of God's profound interior transformation under the action of the Holy Spirit that lead to his specific and decisive form of charitable mission. Sánchez Martínez pinpoints this charism, peculiar to John of God, as being the mysterious action of God impelling him towards heroic service to the neighbour in need, through the self-abasement, or annihilation, of his *persona*. The author calls this process by the two Greek words used by St. Paul. He says John of God, through *kenosis* (self-renunciation), passed on to diakonia (service of the neighbour).

The book by Sánchez Martínez was published at Madrid in 1995. It had a large appendix of statements made by witnesses at the litigation bought against the John of God Brothers by the Jeronymite Friars in the year 1572. These came from previously unpublished files. I have used these as the third collection of documents referring to John of God. Originally an ideological thesis, I consider this independently published book worthy of respect in itself.

Research on John of God was carried on for years by Julián García Sánchez far from Granada. García Sánchez came across John of God in a somewhat indirect way while he was researching documents relating to the Counts of the fiefdom of Oropesa and their lands and commerce. By a happy coincidence his studies about Oropesa brought him into contact with John of God who lived at Oropesa for a longer period than he lived anywhere else. In all, John spent a total of 28 years working as a shepherd within that Toledan domain. This period was divided into two parts: 20 years in the first part and 8 in the second.

At the time of writing, García Sánchez is bringing his gigantic work on the Lords of Oropesa to a close. He has uncovered quite a lot of hitherto unknown facts, and I am grateful to him for consenting to let me make use of some of his unpublished work. The sheer volume of data he has discovered apropos the Counts of Oropesa has amazed the curators of the Spanish National Historic Archives, the Provincial Archives of Toledo, and the Toledo Municipal Council's parish records. Thanks to the documents researched by García Sánchez, a flood of light has now been shed upon the obscurity of John's infancy and younger years.

Readers are often amazed when they come across some startling news, so that is why I wanted to come clean with the credentials for my book. Nevertheless, as you can well imagine, these facts are the fruit of long hours of work — my own as well as that of others. The job has not been easy, but it has been worth while. Sometimes it went along well, at other times it began to lag. Anyway, if you perhaps think I might have tired, let me tell you, I am as sprightly and as happy as a child in a playground. Doesn't John of God deserve that? He who was able to give so much consolation surely deserves all I can give him. I discussed this matter with a learned friend and told him of my satisfaction and also the difficulties that faced me as I set out on the path in search of John of God the man of charity. My friend then reminded me of some verses of a German poet of the style of Nietzche.

Soon it is going to snow;
Although outside the sun still shines,
Yet later our epoch will fill the soul with coldness,
fear, egoism, frivolity, and threats.

Soon it is going to snow;
Happy the one who has a home, a refuge!
Happy are you if you can count upon
close friends who love you,
Who give you warmth.

Soon it is going to snow;
Woe to the homeless, the lonely, the abandoned,
the beggar, the poor!
They have no home to go to, no warm hearth.
John of God wanted to give them a home,
he struggled to give them a hearth.

Before it snows,
Before they die of cold,
Lonely and without tender care,
He went in search of a home for them.

What does John of God deserve?
All he merits is weariness.
What a glorious human being he was.

3
GRANADA

I was once invited to speak at a seminar held at Praia Grande, the ancient residence of the Portuguese kings near Sintra on the Atlantic seaboard. Those attending were all young people. I was the only oldie among them. What a couple of wonderful days we had! You could contemplate the majestic waves crashing along the beach on one side, while on the other there was the fascinating flora growing among the massive stones of Sintra.

We spoke about John of God. One young man put forward the question, "Why did John of God choose to go to Granada?"

Choose! Who did the choosing? Who chose that place to be the stage for John of God's adventure?

Clearly, it was God who chose to meet John at Granada. John was not aware of this. He had taken the right road to Granada, but his compass could have pointed him towards another track under the winds of fortune. But he took Granada.

Who got the best of this deal? Did John profit most from his welcome by Granada, or did Granada enrich itself more by accepting him?

Why Granada? I simply replied, I do not know, these things happen, along the way of life, as God wills.

I swear that the first time I experienced the magic of Granada – and that was some 50 years ago – I felt that I was in one of the three most beautiful cities in Spain, or maybe even Europe. I remember this now, but Granada has lost a great deal of its charm. I realise that architects defend their position by saying that cities are living entities, always on the move and evolving. They say cities are condemned to death unless new buildings are constructed, if that were not the case they would be left like dried butterflies in a showcase because, so they say, new buildings carry the aesthetic air of each epoch. Yes, the architects are right.

That is why urban planning carries two conditions. The first being, that new buildings in historic cities must be beautiful, artistically pleasing, and at least, discreet and acceptable. They would not be absurd eyesores if they fitted into this category. Secondly, they should always respect each city's physiognomy and character, and never rob it of its charms.

Granada today has become a stifling city, because they have blocked out the mountains. I recall that, on my first visit to

Granada so many years ago, you could walk down the Gran Via and view the pathways that led up into the Albaycín on the left and on the right you could see the massive structure of the Cathedral. When you looked straight ahead, you could plainly see the foothills. In those days I used to get the impression that the streets and alleyways simply melted away into these hills that fringe the Sierra Nevada. I thought the mountains were like a loving mother cradling her treasures, the Alhambra, the Generalife, the rivers and palaces, and yes, the very inhabitants of Granada themselves.

Possibly it is too late now for Granada to recover its lost beauty. Maybe one day that pretentious bank building constructed right behind the monument to Queen Isabella in the plaza named after her might be razed to the ground. Why was it that they had to go and plug up the Sierra Nevada, which once you could see so clearly, protecting the very heart of Granada. Nowhere on this earth is a bank so inappropriately placed. This hideous and presumptuous building with its garish mirror facade screams of the *nouveaux riche* and robs Granada of its once delightful skyline. It would not be too costly to pull it down – we see plenty of big buildings imploded on television. It is a pity that such a monstrosity was ever built at Granada.

We know exactly when John of God arrived at Granada because it coincided with a significant change in the city. Historians tell us that, since 1492, Granada has experienced two crucial changes. Granada, like every other major European city, has witnessed periodic changes. These have often occurred at intervals of some 15 to 20 years and were brought about by successive technological, economic and social advances. There is no doubt that two most significant changes occurred at Granada. The first was when it changed from a Moslem city to a Christian one after the conquest by the Catholic Monarchs. The second was in modern times, particularly during the third and fourth decades of the 20th century.

Granada's last great transformation began in 1920 and lasted until 1950. During this period its physiognomy changed to that of a modern city with a huge demographic growth bringing about an urban sprawl. Old people used to tell stories about the old rural Granada where people used to get about on donkeys. It was a Granada where you could ride the little tram for three *perrochicas* and go out to Santa Fe in the countryside for a picnic lunch. Yes, it was just three *perrochicas*, the equivalent of five cents, and that included the return fare.

The streets were bogged with mud every time it rained, and the goatherd used to let his goats wander right up to your front door, but for a couple of small coins he would move them off to annoy somebody else. Then there was the waterseller who would wash a glass and fill it up for his customer with crystal clear water from a mountain stream. When children were his customers he would give them a candy.

In those days Granada started at the Elvira Gate and ended at the Royal Gate, and from there on there was only open countryside. When the first automobiles came along, people used to scramble for safety in the open doorways to let them pass. Was there ever a drought at Granada? Never! Granada is truly the city of water. Once Granada was plagued with periodic droughts, even more so than other cities, but the Granadinos took up the challenge and opened up wells all over their city. There is an abundant subterranean water supply, but a taxidriver told me that he took no satisfaction from that. He said, "What would happen to us if something awful like an earthquake occurred? My father told me that there is a huge cavity full of water underneath Granada and it cushions Granada from earth tremors."

Those who have lived through the last transformation of Granada are now well over sixty years of age. When they pass on, their children and grandchildren will simply think that Granada has always been as it is now, a city jammed with traffic and surrounded by expanding suburbs, which that great lover of Granada, Paco Izquierdo, utterly detested, calling it *"a monstrous conglomeration of dreadfully vulgar and absurd architecture. Why should this be considered part of Granada?"*

John of God found himself immersed in the famous transformation started by the Catholic Monarchs at Granada in 1492. This transformation was continued by their grandson the Emperor Charles, and was still in full force during the first half of the 16th century. Due to a deliberate political decision, the Granada of the Nasrides Moslems was destined to become a magnificent Christian city. There was a flurry of building activity. First the Royal Chapel was finished, then the Palace of Charles V, and the

Cathedral and dozens of churches and magnificent palaces were built. However, not one of them was able to surpass the beauty of the Alhambra.

While all these new buildings were going up, gangs of labourers were paving new streets and plazas with cobblestones. This was done, not only for the purpose of enlarging the narrow Arabic houses, but also making provision for the Castilian families that poured into Granada following the conquest. When John of God arrived at Granada he saw the city embroiled in a hive of building activity.

Thanks to quite recent research, almost all the places frequented by John of God at Granada have now been identified, in spite of all the urban changes that have taken place over the intervening four centuries. Brother Matías de Mina has written a guide to the places associated with John of God. Brother Matías admits that there are a few perplexing, even doubtful, locations yet to ascertain, but such doubts are few and he has done much to dispel them. We now know practically all the Granada of John of God.

With Brother Matías as my guide, following the footprints of John of God around Granada was like an act of devotion. He stopped and gave an explanation at each place blessed by John's presence. It was as if each stop was like the bead of a rosary in his honour, and believe me, it was an utter pleasure to experience. If you exclude the outer city sprawl of Granada, the historic centre still contains the fragrance of John of God's presence and the pilgrim can really sense it.

Brother Matías made me start my pilgrimage at the Elvira Gate, the same entrance to the city used by John when he first arrived there.

Without going into every detail, one can be struck by many different sights when walking through Granada. Paco Izquierdo warned me by saying the city *"is a mixture of many odd civilisations and they ride upon each other like a toboggan."*

We climbed up the Cuesta Gomérez, which is the road that rises from the city centre and goes straight up to the Alhambra. I had to ask myself, "Why did John of God decide to establish his second hospital on this steep slope where he would have had to carry some of his sick people?" Today the road is made of asphalt and is not all that hard to climb, but it would have been another story for John of God in his day, especially in winter when the Gomérez Rise was knee deep in mud. What could he do about it? He just had to put his hospital where they gave him a house.

If we trace the confines of the city from the Elvira Gate to the Campo del Principe, and then for the same distance to the left and right, we have the area of the city that was surrounded by countryside in John of God's time. This is the same area where we now see the sites referred to in his biography. Did he ever get the time to savour the aesthetic qualities of Granada? Surely not!

The mystic friar and poet, John of the Cross, entered Granada some years after John of God; 42 years after to be exact. While he lived there he found inspiration in its stimulating beauty. The Granada locations of John of the Cross and John of God curiously coincided. However, John of God spent most of his time within the walls of the old city where the people carried out their daily lives midst pleasure and sorrow. On the other hand, John of the Cross remained in the silence of the periphery, in the foothills of the Sierra Nevada and the plains of La Vega. In solitude he sought the echoes of the creative presence of God.

John of the Cross was the Prior of the Carmelite convent, and while he was at Granada he was trying to prepare for a General Chapter of the Discalced Carmelites. He was worried that he might be recognised if he got about too much, so he refused to visit Granada's leading citizens and consequently missed out on a lot of donations for his convent. John of the Cross spent his days and nights praying in the open air, and all the while he soaked up the beauty surrounding him from the Alhambra to La Vega. Sometimes he would invite his friars to climb with him up the foothills that led to the snow capped Sierra Nevada. This is what he said: *"Today each one has to go up to the mountains, and each one has to be alone to spend this day in prayer and in communication with Our Lord."*

John of the Cross soaked himself in the beauty of Granada. He composed pages and pages in which he dealt with the mystic vicissitudes of the human soul which, while hidden, goes out to embrace the blessed happiness of a meeting with God. From the symbolism of the mountain top, John of the Cross wrote these words as he gazed down on the bustling daily life of Granada: *"Oh, souls created for greatness, and called to it, why are you holding back from this? Your ostentatious claims are contemptible and your possessions are miseries."*

In contrast with John of the Cross, the other John was up to his neck in the miseries of the city. He gave a hand to the abandoned and healed the wounds of the poor who were sick. Both Johns completed the courses marked out for them. While they seemed to be so different from each another, Granada was nevertheless the scene of activity for both, John of the Cross with its breathtaking beauty, John of God with its stinking pus.

Theoretically the work of John of God, namely his dedication to remedying the corporal and spiritual suffering of the city's inhabitants, was more risky and less acceptable. Granada really should not be seen as being sky or land, but somewhere in between. My Granadino friends pointed out this enigma to me. It goes to show how they love their city, yet they have a great sense of irony and can make a joke at their own expense. For instance, they cruelly say this against themselves. *"Look, our city possesses beauty in its natural horizon and its monuments. But still Granadinos have a lot of failings, and that is why our neighbours at Malaga have coined the phrase, 'Granada has the sky and the land, but just look at what's in between'."*

Maybe it is because the Granadinos are in between. The inhabitants of a certain part of Italy are also pretty subtle, and ironically speak of their own defects: *"When God created the world, he made Italy such a beautiful place that, in order to compensate for it, he decided to fill it with Italians."*

I do not believe it. All races like to laugh at their own defects. Antonio Machado wrote the most venomous piece of flattery about his own native city Seville: *"Seville, without the people of Seville, what a marvel that would be!"*

Paco Izquierdo considers the following witticism that the Granadinos tell of themselves to be unquestionable:

"Look, we are a people gifted with a sense of irony, but we get annoyed when others call us country bumpkins, hicks, and yokels. Or call us Moors, because we have a tendency to keep our womenfolk indoors doing housework. And we don't like to be called nincompoops just because we presume to have an ancestral culture. This sort of slinging off hurts us, but we don't mind being called miserly and stingy, for the simple reason that we are miserly and stingy."

I warn you, let only the Granadinos go on like that, for they are simply 'kidding'. Both Granada's sky and terrain are beautiful, and so too is the middle of their city. Never say a disparaging word of Granada, for on a plaque that is attached to the Gunpowder

Magazine, next to the La Vela Tower, you can read the words of the poet Icaza, which all Granadinos know by heart: "*Woman, give alms, for nothing in life is as bad as being blind in Granada.*"

Were the Granadinos as proud of their city back in the 16th century? In the days of John of God there was a nine-year-old boy who became the celebrated Dominican friar known as Luis de Granada. He was born of poor Galician immigrants who came to Granada in search of a living. His father died when he was five years old and Count Tendilla, the Governor of the Alhambra, helped his mother by taking the little boy into his home and having him educated along with his own children. The child of the poor washerwoman went on to ennoble Granada twice over, by his birth and by his appellation. Fray Luis wrote thousands of pages, and in one of his works he praises his city and gives a symbolic description of its namesake, the pomegranate, which in Spanish is called la granada:

"The Creator saw to it that it was robed in its right measurements so that it was completely covered to defend itself from the inclemency of the sun and wind. It is rather stiff and hard on the outside, but on the inside it is quite mild in order to protect the tender fruit it encloses.

And so that nobody might overlook the elegance of this fruit, he finished it off by placing a royal crown on top of it, and it seems that kings use this as a model for their own.

It seems as if the Creator wanted to show everyone that this was the queen of all fruits. It is as vivid as coral, at least in the colour of its seeds. Nothing can come close to this fruit as far as flavour and health-giving properties go, because it is pleasing to the eye, sweet to the palate, delicious to the healthy, and health-giving to the ill, and its quality lets it last the whole year through."

Why did Granada become the stage for John of God's adventure? I wonder if Granada suited John, or was it that John suited Granada? He was shown the road map to go there, God saw to that.

4

Montemor - O - Novo

1495

John of God was born in a village called Montemor-O-Novo in the heartland of Portugal. Actually, Portugal has two towns called Montemor, one called '*O Velho*', (the old), and the other '*O Novo*', (the new).

Montemor-O-Velho is 27 kilometres from Coimbra, a third of the way to the north of Portugal. It stands on the right bank of the Mondego close to where this river flows into the Atlantic at Figueira da Foz. Situated halfway along the coast between Lisbon and Porto, Montemor-O-Velho, with its wide streets, churches, convents and good harbour, has an air of prosperity about it. The town has earned a distinguished place in the noble annals of the ancient Kingdom. Historic documents tell of its valiant battle against the Caliph Abderraman who could not stand up to the valiant Abbot João, the grandson of Ramiro I of Leon.

Montemor-O-Novo is quite another story. Its inhabitants have little in common with those of Montemor-O-Novo. In Montemor-O-Novo they smilingly comment:

"*Down here in the south we are Communists.*" And what about the other Montemor? "*O they are aristocrats.*" However, are you proud of your fellow townsman saint? "*One thing does not cancel out the other, John of God was more of a Communist than we are.*"

A saint or a poet gives splendour to any town and here they boast of both. The saint was John of God who was born here at the end of the 15th century. The famous Portuguese poet Belchior Manuel Curvo Semedo e Sequeirá was born here in the 18th century.

Let us leave aristocratic Montemor-O-Velho and return to Montemor-O-Novo. It got its reputation as a hotbed of Communism as a result of its involvement in the agrarian reform and the socialist revolution that swept the country in 1974 when the Army, backed by Caetano, brought the Salazar regime to an end. When you consider the agrarian and economic structures of the Province of Alentejo, it seems inevitable that the peasants would seek to open the door to let in the sunlight of democracy. To this end they supported the Communist program.

Alentejo is the largest of Portugal's regions and occupies almost all of the southern third of the country. It borders Algarve at the southern end and Guadiana on the east with the ocean to its west. Alentejo is divided into two sections, Alentejo Alto in the

3. The shrine in Calle Elvira on the site of the bookstall that John of God set up when he first arrived at Granada.

4. The window that opens into the cell in which John of God was incarcerated during his stay in the Royal Hospital.

north and Alentejo Bajo in the south. I think it is unfair to brand Alentejo Alto, as many do, the *'land without shade'* because it does not have many large trees. If you travel into Guadiana from the Spanish border city of Badajoz, you pass through the gentle undulating hills of Ossa on which there is an abundance of vegetation as far as Montemor-O-Novo.

Halfway between Badajoz and Lisbon stands Montemor-O-Novo. It is 25 kilometres from Evora, the regional capital of Alentejo Alto (Beja is the regional capital of Alentejo Bajo). The hills begin to die out as they reach the wandering Rivers Tagus and Almanzo (also known as the Canha) which irrigate the fertile lowlands. In centuries long past, this was the scene of clashes between the Moors and Christians. The fortified castle that King Sancho I built at Montemor-O-Novo was, in those days, one of Portugal's finest.

I arrived at Montemor-O-Novo to sniff out the traces of John of God in Portugal. I was already quite aware that there are very few reliable historic records of him that could be found here. Honestly, you could count on the fingers of one hand the indisputable facts regarding the earliest years of his childhood. Here of course, he was called João. It was not until he went to Spain that his name was changed to Juan. [João and Juan, both mean John in English.]

I enjoyed my visit here, although it was an experience that would have been something like a person going to Israel and spending a day at Nazareth and Sephoris to inquire about news of the parents of Mary, a virgin engaged to a man called Joseph. Nothing certain came of it, although I must admit that I really felt the presence of John of God who, in 1495, was born at Montemor-O-Novo.

At that time, Montemor-O-Novo had a population of approximately four thousand inhabitants. This number is reached by referring to the first census made in 1530 at the command of King John III. This census recorded 1,064 families. Of course there were many children born into families, but there was also a high infant mortality rate. The three principle centres of population were Lisbon, 40,000; Oporto, 10,000; and Evora with 9,000 inhabitants.

The population of Montemor-O-Novo today is 8,000

inhabitants and the town still retains its agricultural character, olives being its principal crop. I was lucky enough to have my visit coincide with market day when all the local produce was put out for sale. The European Common Market has not been kind to Montemor-O-Novo, for it forbids it to become industrialised. Communists control its Town Council – so what do the Mayor and Councillors think about St. John of God? I was informed that they respect him and they are very much aware that St. John of God gives great lustre to their town's history. They assured me that they also appreciate and respect his sons, the St. John of God Brothers, who conduct the town's hospital for children.

Doña Jiulietta Marques is the director of a curious museum run by the Friends of Montemor-O-Novo. It contains exhibits ranging from the present day back to the town's first inhabitants in Roman times. The prehistoric inhabitants lived mainly on a hill overlooking the district, while small groups of people were scattered along the fertile banks of the Guadiana and Canha where significant relics of this ancient civilisation have been discovered. The Escoural Cave, dating to the middle of the Palaeolithic era, contains 35 galleries that conserve wall-paintings, utensils, ceramics and human remains. There are hundreds of dolmens from the Megalithic age scattered about. Seven miles along the road from Montemor-O-Novo to Lisbon is a menhir classified as a national monument.

Thousands of years later, the Romans, then the Arabs, came to Montemor-O-Novo bringing with them their own peculiar ways of life. It was during the Arab occupation that Algarve and Alentejo acquired fame throughout the Mediterranean region for their poets, geographers, historians, philosophers and mathematicians. This was a phenomenon identical with Al-Andalus, southern Spain of the Arabs. The documented history of Montemor-O-Novo began halfway through the 12th century with the vanguard of the Christian forces of the Reconquest which, gradually during the 11th and 12th centuries, came down from the north. Once they were established the Borgoña dynasty was established at Guimarães, 'O Berço da Nacionalidade'. In 1165 the knight Geraldo Sempavor (Gerald the Fearless) took Evora for King Alfonso Henriques. He also took Montemor-O-Novo, but 25 years later the Moor, Jussuf Jacub, led a raiding party and destroyed the castle at Montemor-O-Novo. King Sancho I had the castle rebuilt and a wall placed about the town. From then on it remained safe from Moorish incursions.

Montemor-O-Novo took on its own physiognomy from the 13th

to the 14ᵗʰ centuries. The town had two sections; on the heights near the Castle lived those who were protected by the town's walls, knights and their servants, Christians of 'pure blood'. Below on the lowland lived the rest of the population that spread out into the nearby fields. This was called the 'Arrabal' and contained Jews, more or less conversos, Moors and the poorest of the population.

Four parish churches were constructed to keep pace with the expansion of the homes of the wealthy in the higher section of the town. The Arrabal had to be content with little chapels and the church of the hospital dedicated to St. Andrew.

In the higher section of the town, known as Villa Alta, a gateway reminiscent of the Roman epoch led onto the Castle enclosure which was guarded by a slender medieval tower, known as the Clock Tower. In those days, when the Portuguese kings and their retinues visited Montemor-O-Novo, they stayed at the Castle which was the Lord Mayor's residence. King Sebastian conceded the title 'Noble Town' to Montemor-O-Novo and, as the chronicles record, the various kings signed many an important document when they visited the Mayoral Palace. For instance, Don Dinis petitioned the Pope from Montemor-O-Novo for permission to establish a centre of learning in Portugal which became known as the 'General Studies' and was the forerunner to Coimbra University. It was while he was at Montemor-O-Novo that Don Manuel I, called 'The Unfortunate', picked Vasco da Gama to lead the first voyage to India.

If you visit Montemor-O-Novo, it is well worth your time to go and listen to what Doña Jiulietta has to say about the town's long history. She will tell you that John of God, or João de Deus as he is called in Portugal, is the pride of Montemor-O-Novo.

John was born in the humble dwelling of his parents in the Arrabal. Who were his parents? That is the big question and it will not be long before you will understand why. The question of John's parents really puts one on the spot, because we have to accept *provisionally* about half a dozen bits of information as certain.

To start with, there is his father's name, Andrew Cidade. [Ciudad in Spanish and City in English.] You have no idea how much sweat I poured out looking this up and to what lengths I went in searching the archives.

Both the mother's Christian name and surname are

uncertain. Maybe it was Ana, or Teresa, or even Ana Teresa. Maybe it was Maria. And what about the surname? Later witnesses came up with the surname *Duarte*. However, I have my suspicions here, because these witnesses seem to have wanted to give the good woman one of Portugal's most aristocratic genealogies by means of a distinguished surname. The Duarte family is one of the most noble lineages in the Kingdom. Well, that does not matter to me so much, for I know she was the mother of a famous son.

So much vagueness arises from a basic deficiency. There is no record of John's baptism, because the parish only began keeping records in 1542. Plenty of patience is needed here since nothing was recorded before the second half of the 16th century. Yes, here we are walking on uncertain ground and there are a lot of pitfalls into which one can fall. Mercantile documents of the period show nothing concrete in regards to the town's poorer inhabitants who lived in the Arrabal. It would have been another story had the Cidades lived where the upper class of the town lived, close to the Castle.

In 1607, more than a hundred years after the birth of John of God, two Hospitaller Brothers, Juan López Piñero and Juan Pecador, came to Montemor-O-Novo. They intended to build a church over the house where John of God was born.

Fifteen years later, the clerks appointed by Rome came to Montemor-O-Novo to record the testimony of witnesses for the canonical beatification process of John of God who, by that time, had become a household name. This beatification process took place in 24 locations, including Montemor-O-Novo.

The first investigations took place 112 years after his birth, and the second 127 years. Too much time had elapsed to be able to find clear memories. Of course, there was second-hand material put forward regarding the child born to the Cidade couple. However, now we are speaking of a lapse of some two generations. But some trace could remain; it seems that it did and they found it.

Let us look at an example. Our investigators spoke with a Montemor-O-Novo resident who was somewhere between 50 and 60 years of age. That meant he was born some 60 to 50 years after the infancy of João Cidade. The grandparents, parents, uncles and aunts of our witness remembered the Cidades perfectly. And they had good reason to remember them, because certainly strange things had happened to that couple. Country folk have good memories for local events, and they pass these stories along from parent to child, at least for the first or second generation.

I would like to say that although the testimony of the witnesses was subjected to a rigorous filtering, the information that was gathered was well worth the effort expended in its collection. At least *provisionally*, let us take it that John's father's name was Andrew Cidade.

Word of John of God's achievements at Granada between 1539 and 1550 would have arrived at Montemor-O-Novo sooner or later. This news about John of God would have been sufficient to stimulate his fellow countrymen to start searching their memories in regards to the parents of the child João.

It needed a bit of working on, but I thought it well worth while to reconstruct the statements made by the witnesses at the beatification process. Their testimony has permitted us to discover the house of his birth and to unearth about half a dozen facts.

Manuel Dias put up a good case for his hometown: *"I always heard that the parents of John of God always lived in Verde Street in this town, in the houses where the holy man John of God was surely born."*

The widow Blasia who lived in the street at the right of this house agreed with Manuel Dias: *"He was born in this town, in two one-story houses with a lower floor (basement?) where this witness knows that the aforementioned father and mother lived in Verde Street in the aforementioned town."*

Manuel Dias reinforced his evidence with some information that should have clarified the matter: *"... and it is in the parish of Santa Maria del Obispo of this town, where naturally he had to be Christened."* Of course, it had to be *"naturally"*, because Santa Maria del Obispo was the mother parish of Montemor-O-Novo and the only one with a baptismal font and the authority to administer baptism.

But it should not be forgotten that the Rua Verde, the street where the Cidades lived, was situated in the Arrabal. Yet, the parish church was up in the Villa Alta section of the town and well inside the fortification walls near the Castle. The parents would have had to go up there to have their baby baptised.

Going on the certain testimony of similar witnesses, the two Hospitaller Brothers, López and Pecador, set about their work in 1607. They began with the construction of a shrine in the location where the Cidades had lived. We reverently visited this little church which over the years has been frequently renovated and beautified.

The lower part of the Rua Verde winds its way down the hill to the Arrabal, which in those days was only an open field. Today it is in the centre of Montemor-O-Novo, yet it still retains its rural character.

We now come to the "Cidades' house" and find it situated on two levels. The top level is the church, with the crypt where the original Rua Verde sloped away. This is the actual room where the baby João was born. The Hospitaller Brothers were very discreet when they set about constructing the memorial to their founder. There is nothing ostentatious about it. The crypt section opens onto a long narrow corridor that ends at a small shrine that is no more than about 10 x 3 metres in area. In this little space are placed a few austere benches. Over the altar is an image of St. John of God that is not particularly attractive. It is a simple place where the birth of a baby born to a poor family is remembered.

Due to the slope of the Rua Verde, this small birthplace is a semi-basement. It has the proportions of a room that is the scene of a legend that arose out of the imagination of a certain reverend clergyman called Joan Gomes Vasconcelos. He was 46 years of age and a native of Evora. He described the three lodgings composing the house as being "moderate and humble." Not quite so, for according to the reverend gentleman, one of the lodgings was used for servants' quarters. That tells us that they had at least one servant living in, so perhaps the Cidades were not so poor after all. What the Reverend Gomes Vasconcelos had in mind to do was bring the origins of John of God into line with some of the great saints, particularly St. Francis of Assisi. The 'Fioretti' of St. Francis relate that, towards the end of the 12th century, actually in the years 1181 and 1182, a son was born to the leading merchant of Assisi, Pietro Bernardone, who at the time was away in France on business. His wife, the noble lady Pica, fearful of the pains of childbirth, ordered her servants to carry her to the stable so she could give birth like the Blessed Virgin Mary in the stable at Bethlehem.

And so to embellish the story the Reverend Gomes likens the birth of João to those of Assisi and Bethlehem. He dropped the following gem: "While the mother was in the pains of childbirth, a poor man arrived at the door begging alms. He entered the room where the mother of the blessed Father John of God was lying in bed, and he said to her to arise and go out into the stable and give birth in the manger. She will have a son who would be the father of many and light in that kingdom." Well my good cleric, that poor man begging alms simply would have had to be an angel.

These concocted baroque myths have, little by little, slipped into the biography of John of God with the result of turning him into some sort of plaster image. What is really necessary in order to write a successful biography, is to get a good sieve and separate the wheat from the chaff.

The publication written by Gomes Vasconcelos was accepted enthusiastically, particularly by another native of Montemor-O-Novo, Luis Messía de la Cerda, a high ranking official at the Valladolid Royal Chancellery. This is what he had to say: *"I grew up truly believing that blessed John was born in a stable like St. Francis, and I can swear that this is certainly the case."* De la Cerda said he was very vexed if anyone ever doubted that what he claimed was true.

The church that was built over the site of the Cidade home eventually became the parish church of the town. By this time the population of Villa Alta near the Castle had begun to move away, and at the same time the Arrabal grew to such an extent that it became the main township.

In the summer of 1625 the church built by Brothers López and Pecador was opened. It had a splendid nave, a baroque altarpiece, and its walls were decorated with typical Portuguese polychrome blue tiles, while the ceiling was painted with oriental motifs reminiscent of those one sees in the Vatican museum. Over the main doorway is an ingenious painting depicting the birth of St. John of God, interesting, but sheer fantasy, nothing more.

One important historic relic is preserved in this church, namely the baptismal font where the baby João was baptised. Naturally, this was once in the ancient parish church of Santa Maria del Obispo up at Villa Alta, before it eventually fell into ruins along with the Castle and its surroundings. The font's octagonal form rests upon a stout support made of beautifully carved stonework with a filigree border showing dapples of colour and gold leaf. This precious piece once witnessed the pouring of the Holy Spirit upon the enigmatic little baby. I was delighted with the restored decorations of the church, especially to see beside the font, a lovely little painting of Brother John giving alms. It depicts him with a poor man at his side and how delightful and ingenious it is. Saint João, is shown here at the baptismal font where he began the journey that brought him to sainthood.

The parents of the baby João were faced with a problem, and you will know the extent of that problem when you read the next chapter. For the moment, let us accept, *provisionally*, that his name was Andrew Cidade and his wife's was Ana, Teresa or even Maria, Duarte.

Permit me here to raise reverently a lament to the guardian angels. The Lord God, ruler of the constellations of the cosmos, marks the course of each of us here below as we move upon the face of this planet earth. This is done with special care I am sure, and God sets a magnifying glass on certain persons destined for extraordinary enterprises, just as special care is given the little ones, the weak, the ordinary, because all of us are important in the providence of God. The historic adventure of John of God being already foreseen, dear guardian angels, knowing that the Lord God had put the future saint's genes into the womb of a simple Portuguese woman, why did you not take the trouble to give us some sort of clue? Then we would not have this annoyance of not knowing her baptismal name, let alone her surname. All we can do is try to find out. It is a small worry, but my dear guardian angels I would really love you to have told me. But if that is not to be – well exact information in a story about sanctity is not all that important, so let us think about it and see what turns up.

As I have my doubts, I want to set my magnifying glass upon the statements made by the local people a hundred or more years after the birth of their compatriot João.

In the first place I must say that I am partial to the statement made by our old friend Manuel Dias. Here is what the scribe wrote of it:

"He said that he knew neither the father nor the mother but he had always heard it said that the father and mother of the aforementioned John of God were old and legitimate Christians having no mixture of either the Muslim or Jewish races, nor of new Christians or any other kind of sect."

Christian, old or new! Come now Manuel Dias, we will have to look into that. You have really gone too far. You cannot back up that statement can you? Or was it that someone whispered into your ear not to meddle with the noble blood of our holy João? I ask you, and also those who may have advised you, do you think that the Jewish blood in the veins of Jesus of Nazareth and his Mother Mary is less noble than the blood of all the old Christians of Portugal or, for that matter, Castile and the *orbe terrarum*? Look here dear Manuel, we are going to have to look into this because you are being too clever by half.

Fortunately a capable witness turned up with lots of family memories. Andrew Alvares Cidade was a linen weaver, and a resident of Montemor-O-Novo. He lived in the street at the lower end of the town square. He was not too sure how old he was, but said he was more or less 63 years of age: *"This witness stated that his father was Andrew Lorenzo Cidade and throughout his life he had often heard that he was the first cousin of holy John of God."*

Now we have a living relative, whose tested evidence brings news directly from his father who, as cousin of the saint, knew the father of João, Andrew Cidade.

Anyway, our good weaver added further information linking him to the family: *"I knew Blas Cidade very well, he was the brother of the father of the holy man John of God."* The records show that, *"the aforementioned Blas Cidade, died at the age of forty, without ever having married."*

Furthermore, when he was young, our weaver had received his information from two sources, his father, the cousin of the child João, and his bachelor uncle, Blas, who was the brother of João's father. The weaver did not get his lines mixed up, he testified responsibly: *"This witness is aware that he is in the lineage of the holy man and he heard this said by his father; and also because he knew the aforementioned Blas Cidade, the brother of the father of holy John of God."*

The scribe who recorded this statement was very impressed by the quality of the witness and believed him, as he declared: If one reads all his testimony, word for word, right to the end, it is self-evident.

What a pity the biographers of John of God did not get hold of this witness and, like a lemon, squeeze every drop out of him. All we get from his statement are a few substantial facts that,

without any doubt, are quite true, but also quite inadequate:
* that the father of the child João was named Andrew Cidade;
* that he was able to live on what he owned and his property;
* that he held no public office;
* that when he was left a widower, he went to Lisbon and entered the Convent of San Francisco at Xabregas where he became a friar;
* that he died in that state.

Precious information of course, but that is all it is. What a pity! Confidentially, I must confess that I have a suspicion that something a bit shady might have occurred. Did the scribes by any chance tamper with the weaver's statement? I rather fear that they might have preferred not to record some of the facts that were presented. The scribe finished off his report with the curt sentence: *"He said nothing else."*

Is that possible for a person with family ties to the Cidade couple? The scribe was implacable and gave his own account: *"Then before the witnesses, the Vicar ordered me to read the statement made by the aforementioned Andrew Alvares Cidade that I had recorded. Then, having read it, the Vicar asked if there was anything else to either add or delete, but there was nothing because it was entirely true."*

I simply do not believe it. I cannot accept the mere opinion of a scribe who would not have the slightest idea of what the Cidade family discussed or what went on in the heart of their home. What the scribe recorded was certainly what was stated. Nevertheless, I still harbour suspicions, and they are well founded too, that everything that was said on that occasion was not written down. They cut out so much of Andrew Alvares Cidade's statement that all that was left of it was a couple of words.

Why were they cut out? Well, it was because the officials of the beatification process did not like the sworn statement that the weaver presented, since it contained facts and circumstances which these same officials had already made up their minds not to hear, for they did not want to smear the glorious image of John of God. I refer particularly to the imprudence of Manuel Dias in attributing *"uncontaminated pure blood"* to John of God by saying he was the son of *"old and legitimate Christians."*

There are signs that point to a conspiracy to tamper with history by burying certain secrets that were considered to be ignominious in those days. The good weaver, the son of a cousin of the holy man John of God, therefore his second cousin, knew the secret and they asked him not to mention it in his declaration. The scribe did not want to hear anything about it, and even though someone with the surname Cidade made the statement, he refused to record it. I must ask pardon of the guardian angels, for they have left traces, even though men have tried to erase them.

The date of the birth of the child João Cidade is uncertain, but it was probably close to what the documents, in the absence of a baptismal certificate, indicate: spring of 1495. Was it 8 March 1495? John of God died at the age of 55 years on 8 March so, by going back exactly 55 years, somebody conveniently fixed the date of his birth to be 8 March 1495.

The year 1495 was an auspicious one for Montemor-O-Novo, because that was the year King João II died and was succeeded by Manuel I who was living at the time in Montemor-O-Novo Castle. It was from here that he convoked the Royal Court. King Manuel I was called 'The Unfortunate', a name that suited him well, for he lost one wife after another. Under the sceptre of Manuel 'The Unfortunate' Portugal's fame as a world power began.

The formation of Portugal, which runs along the Atlantic coast of the Iberian Peninsula, offers pages of fascinating history. The Moslems of the 8th century saw it and wanted to occupy the north of Lusitania, the region comprising the area between the rivers Miño and Douro. They quickly took over the Douro estuary that was defended by the two cities at its entrance, Porto on the right and Cale on the left. Thus was born the territory of 'Portucale' which Princess Teresa, daughter of Alfonso VI, King of Castile and Leon, had received as her dowry when, in 1095, she married the Frenchman, Henry, son of the Duke of Burgundy who came with his knights to participate in the Reconquest. Henry and Teresa were established as the Duke and Duchess of Guimarães, a small city in the region of Portucale. They had a son, Alfonso Henriques, who valiantly fought the Moors. Alfonso broke the ties binding Portucale to Castile and proclaimed himself King of Portugal in 1139. He carried out his conquests as far south as Lisbon. Because of his origins, many French historians claim that Portugal had its origins in the adventures of Gallic knights.

Recognised by Pope Alexander II as King of Portugal, Alfonso Henriques instigated the Burgundy dynasty in Portugal. Successive kings drove out the Moors in the south and kept the Castilians at bay on the east. While this stabilised Portugal, relations with Spain were shaky and sometimes erupted into war, a notable battle being that of Aljubarrota. There were also amiable times, as for instance the relationship between Denis I and the Spanish Infanta Isabella of Aragon whom the history books call *"the saintly Queen of Coimbra"*, also, Don Pedro, with his beautiful but hapless Inés, whose dramatic love affair has been celebrated by Camoens and Montherlant.

The Burgundy dynasty disappeared in the late 14th century and gave rise to the Avis dynasty headed by the victor of the Battle of Aljubarrota, King João I. Following a difficult period of droughts, plagues and peasant revolts, Portugal began its great step forward into discovery under the leadership of the young Prince Henry, son of João I. During the reigns of João II and Manuel I, 'The Unfortunate', Portugal dominated half the world.

If we accept that John of God was born in the spring of 1495, then his birth occurred six months before Manuel, 'The Unfortunate', arrived at Montemor-O-Novo in the autumn of that same year. In the hope of making a picture that might resemble family life in the Cidade home when John was a baby, I painstakingly searched through the statements made by witnesses at the beatification process for fragments of evidence so I could place the pieces of the mosaic together. It was a mountain of work for a small result.

Notwithstanding the spider's web in which we will see his parents enmeshed the little boy João, being unaware of it, enjoyed a life like other children of his age. Fortunately the family was spared the knowledge of the grave misfortune about to befall it. Children are happy when they are protected by the love of their parents and receive from them all that they need for their sustenance. This would not be the case if they were to know otherwise. Boecio points out that the one condition lacking in order to make their happiness complete is their ability to reflect on the wellbeing that they enjoy. Maybe it is better that way, otherwise they might not want to grow up.

Some of the statements made at the Process suggested that

Andrew Cidade worked in the fields and that he owned some horses. The use of the plural here immediately makes me suspicious. In any case, Andrew probably owned a mule, a beast more typical of the simple peasant. Perhaps these horses appeared at the suggestion of what later biographers put forward, namely that the Cidades had a small shop attached to their house. Maybe the horses were used to transport merchandise to this shop.

If they did have a shop I wonder what they sold. I am not able to say that we are speaking of a normal business here, because there was a local ordinance of Montemor-O-Novo that prohibited business premises in the Arrabal. The only shops permitted were found in the Villa Alta near the Castle, because this kept the centre of commerce in the principal residential area. The inhabitants of the Arrabal had to climb the hill and enter the walled Villa Alta in order to fulfil their religious and civil obligations as well as to do their shopping.

The shape of Montemor-O-Novo began to change towards the end of the 15th century. Once the danger from marauding Arabs had disappeared, many well-to-do families, seeking more land and better living conditions, began to settle in the Arrabal beyond the town walls. The Castle slowly began to deteriorate and, after a couple of centuries of neglect, finally fell into complete ruin and remains thus to this day.

In order to satisfy the growing demands of the new and increasing population lawful shops and others that were tolerated began to spring up in the Arrabal. It was just too much trouble to climb up to the Castle every time one wanted to buy anything. The Cidade shop, if indeed it ever existed, would have been one of these. The biographies give no clues to indicate the economic situation of the Cidades. If they had been wealthy, then they would have said so, likewise if they had been miserably poor. From what one gathers, it seems that, for just ordinary simple people, their home was somewhat better than most others in the same circumstances. The biographer Castro, whose first page is less frank than history demands, immediately illustrates why I am distrustful, for it carries a cautiously worded phrase that says the child João *"was born of middle-class parents who were neither rich nor poor."*

The picture this gives of young João is that of a completely normal young boy; playing in the fields, swimming with the other boys in the river, climbing the hill up to the Castle, prancing about when a fair comes to town, and all dressed up in his Sunday best for the feast of San Sebastian. It conveys an image of our little João living a normal happy life like any other boy in the town. You might say he was just a typical country kid before the days of television.

Was he an only child? Well these writers say he was, but in fact we do not have the slightest idea regarding the conditions surrounding his upbringing.

Let us go back and look once more at the clue given by the weaver. According to him, Andrew Cidade joined the Franciscans at a convent in Lisbon after the death of his wife. In the mid-19th century a Franciscan named Friar Jerome of Bethlehem, compiled *'The Seraphic Chronicle of the Holy Province of Algarves'*. He stated in his chronicle that Andrew Cidade was exemplary in fulfilling the precepts of Christian charity both before and after he joined the Franciscan Order. Friar Jerome came to the following conclusion: *"Since virtues are hereditary through blood, this excellent father handed his charity on to his son as an inheritance."* Of course, such a generalisation is easy to make after such a long time, especially when the son was already elevated to the honours of the altar. No, we have absolutely no definite information about how this modest family lived.

I was surprised about one thing in regard to João's boyhood, and it is the only thing we know about him at this time of his life. He played the game of *Birlimbao* with the other boys in the town. He must have played all the classic games that children play, but this game of *Birlimbao* was to become fixed in his memory, for one day he was to recall it at Granada with a smile. Let us now look many years into the future.

One day he came into Granada with a bundle of firewood on his back: *He went into the plaza and everyone saw him loaded with his firewood. They had not seen him since his madness, so a good many people began gathering about him in wonder. When some of his friends saw him they began to laugh and poke fun at him saying: "What is this brother John, have you turned into a woodsman now?"* John was not in the least put out, but remembering his boyhood game, smilingly said: *"Brothers, this is a game of Birlimbao, three galleys and a flagship, in which the more you see, the less you are going to learn."*

The layabouts in the plaza at Granada were completely nonplussed. They had never heard of the game of *Birlimbao*, so John told them about it, and they listened to him eagerly.

At Montemor-O-Novo the children played *Birlimbao*. The one who led the game had to get up on the shoulders of a companion who was blindfolded. Then a third player, who acted as judge, put a riddle to them. If the one who was blindfolded answered the riddle correctly, he was the winner, and he then could get up on the shoulders of the one who lost. If he could not answer he had to give up, and so the game went on until he became exhausted. But children never get tired of such games.

I am delighted to see that even in his madness at Granada, John turns his gaze back to his boyhood game of *Birlimbao*. It is pleasant to know that the only indisputable fact we have of João's childhood is that he used to play *Birlimbao*.

Although there is no documented evidence, we do know that the young João, like most other children in Portugal, had heard stories about the new discoveries then taking place. His youthful fancy was enchanted by all he saw about him: the almond groves silhouetted against the blue sky above the Villa Alta, the open fields that were now further away from the Arrabal, and the tranquil waters of the river. At the same time other fantasies would erupt upon these peaceful images; exciting tales of valiant sailors with faces turned windward as their tall ships at full sail ploughed through the seas. He would have had dreams of golden islands, birds of paradise, naked black natives, glorious sunsets, exotic fruits and flowers, starry tropical nights. Portugal was passing through exciting times.

The maritime expeditions excited the whole country, and nowhere more so than at Montemor-O-Novo. It was here in the Castle of the Lords of Montemor-O-Novo, that King Manuel handed Vasco da Gama his commission to lead the definitive expedition to discover a route to the Indies. Some modern authors say that Vasco da Gama was actually a son of Montemor-O-Novo, but this is contested by biographers who say that it is more likely that he came from the town of Sines on the Atlantic seaboard. Besides, Sines was the home of many a brave sailor. Certainly, young João must have heard of the exploits of Vasco, but what exploits?

At the beginning of the 16th century, Spain and Portugal literally shared domination of the world, and they had the Pope's blessing for it as well. It must be said that Portugal was the first country to merit the title 'expansionist', for this is what it purposely set out to do from the 14th century, while Spain was still kept busy putting all its efforts into the Reconquest. There was always tension along Portugal's eastern border with Castile, so it looked towards the vast Atlantic on the west for its expansion and consequently launched out into exploration by sea.

Portugal's maritime aspirations were in response to the rapidly changing world. The flood of events that began with the onset of the 16th century, were to swiftly alter the face of the globe. One such event was the onset of geographic discovery which, among other things, was not fully in agreement regarding any definite decision about the Earth being globe shaped. The world used to be perceived as being perfectly horizontal, like a pancake; then it adopted the form of a sphere and turned itself around upon itself and gyrated around the sun.

The kings of Portugal and Spain placed tremendous importance on the value of pepper, mustard, ginger, tarragon, all spices of the Orient. This is somewhat curious and difficult for us to understand but, at immense risk, they mounted great maritime expeditions to go in search of these spices. They also desired gold, gems, porcelain and silk, but above all they wanted spices.

Of course gold was vital to them for the minting of money and to stimulate commerce, but what about the spices? Did they have such an appetite for tasty dishes? They had something more than an appetite, for they needed spices to conserve the meat and fish which used to go rotten when transported, since they had no refrigeration. So valuable were spices, that pepper was even used instead of money.

For centuries Venice and Genoa had utilised the route taken by Marco Polo to send their overland caravans to the Orient. Then towards the middle of the 14th century, the Ottoman Turks put an end to that by cutting this traffic off at the Balkans and Asia Minor. This created serious difficulties for the Italian merchants who saw that they had no other choice but to go to India, Mongolia and China by sea via the Mediterranean, a route that would take them through the dangers of the Arab world. At that time the Italian republics only sent their ships beyond Gibraltar to round the Iberian Peninsula in order to hug the Atlantic coastline to reach Flanders where they had commercial interests with the Hanseatic League in northern Europe. Bruges and Antwerp were their destinations, and here they traded pepper, silk, wine and fruits in return for minerals, fish and skins.

The kings of Portugal, and no less their sailors, wanted to challenge the mysterious sea. The Middle Ages left behind them a reverential fear of the ocean whose dark waters concealed the furies of howling winds, incandescent fire, frozen masses, all of which were viewed as leading to the gateway of hell. If men and ships unwisely strayed from the coast, they were simply devoured.

The Avis dynasty now ruled Portugal. After his victory over the Spaniards at Aljubarrota, João I, set about clearing the seas of North African Berbers. For years the Berbers had been the scourge of the Algarve coast. In July 1415 João I and his third son, Prince Henry, set out from Lisbon leading a fleet of two hundred vessels. The Portuguese expedition overpowered and took possession of Ceuta in mid-August. They then used this Mediterranean city as a platform to patrol the movements of the Berbers, and also as a starting point for exploration into North Africa in the hope that a new route might be discovered for the importation of spices.

Prince Henry was well aware that little Portugal did not have sufficient manpower to occupy the vast tracts of Morocco, so he decided that Ceuta would be a good base from which to set out towards the south along the African coast to the lands of gold and slaves. He has gone into history as Henry the Navigator, although he did not sail again after this expedition. Henry established a maritime base at Lagos and an observatory at Sagres. Cartographers, mathematicians, astronomers and ship builders were attracted to the Algarve coast. Under Henry's patronage they studied the wind, the ocean currents, the courses of the stars; they studied the use of the compass, the quadrant and the astrolabe and made maps based upon those traced by learned Arab scholars. A big step was made with the design and construction of new naval vessels, such as the pot-bellied Caravel with its capacity to rapidly sail long distances.

Equipped with such precious scientific instruments, Henry called on his men to overcome their superstitions, for until that time no European sailor had ever gone down the African coast beyond Cape Nun. At latitude 29° north they suddenly turned, and without going back, they sailed out into the Atlantic to set up bases on the islands of Madeira and Azores.

Portuguese navigators continued to fill in the gaps on the map of West Africa. They established small bases and marked them with obelisks that indicated the sovereignty of Portugal. The Portuguese called these columns *padroes*. Many of these stone columns remain to this day, still bearing inscriptions carved in Latin, Portuguese and Arabic. The captain of the last ship to make a landing would set up one of these *padroes*, then when another ship ventured further along the coast, its captain would erect a new *padroe* to mark Portugal's claim to the territory.

The daring and tenacity of its navigators took the ships of Portugal to the coast of Guinea, where they discovered that, instead of the coastline turning east, as the maps of the day showed, it kept running south right through the tropics. Unfortunately, when Prince Henry died in 1460, the bases along the African coast became colonies for the traffic in slaves.

Beginning in 1481, King João gave a new impulse to Portuguese expansion on land and sea. Two intrepid explorers took land routes. One was Pedro da Covilha who set out from North Africa and crossed into Arabia and from there went on until he reached the coast of India. His aim was to spy upon the commercial enterprises of the Arabs who had established markets reaching from the Eastern Mediterranean to the Orient.

The other overland explorer was Alfonso da Paiva. He penetrated into the interior of Africa in search of Ethiopia, the fabled kingdom of Prester John, the imaginary personage reputed to be a wealthy and powerful Christian ruler.

Covilha succeeded in getting the information he wanted from Chinese and Hindus who loaded their merchandise aboard Moslem vessels. From here the Arab merchants took their valuable cargo through the Persian Gulf to the Red Sea and then into the Mediterranean.

Paiva was unfortunate, for he died in the effort to reach his goal. The brave Covilha tried to make good the absence of his companion by setting out for Ethiopia. He sent word back to Lisbon that the story about the fabulous Prester John was simply a myth, but he did have an audience with the King of the Ethiopians. Covilha returned to Portugal with the valuable information that the Indian Ocean continued south to the point where it met with the Atlantic Ocean.

This information meant that the southernmost tip of Africa would allow ships to pass between the Atlantic and Indian Oceans. The Portuguese continued to explore the western coast of Africa until finally they reached the Indian Ocean and then moved up the eastern coast. This resulted in the discovery of a new sea route around Africa that would take them to their long desired trade with India.

Portugal enjoyed twenty years of naval supremacy, during which time its captains continued to set up padroes and bases. They moved into the sweltering tropics. Diogo Cao reached the mouth of the River Zaire, an achievement the Africans thought impossible for white men. A contemporary account tells the story of how an African chief who wanted to overthrow his neighbouring rivals, used a strange strategy. He covered all his men with white clay from head to toe so his enemies might mistake them for Portuguese.

In 1492 Portugal achieved its goal when Bartolomeu Dias reached the southernmost point of Africa. He was blown far off course by fierce winds and lost sight of the African coast. When he finally saw land again, he realised that he had rounded the Cape because the coast now ran northwards. He called the tip of Africa, the Cape of Storms, but King João was so pleased when he heard of this discovery, that he renamed it the Cape of Good Hope.

Due to trouble with his sailors, Dias was forced to return to Lisbon, which he did by going back the way he had come. Finally the King was able to meet this great man who had accomplished so much.

Manuel 'The Unfortunate', who succeeded his father João II, found his hero in Vasco da Gama. However Portugal could not escape the interference of Spain in its sea-lanes and it was inevitable that they would clash. This would have happened earlier had it not been for Spain's struggle in the Reconquest.

Ever since the time of Ferdinand III, *the Saint*, Spain had made some attempts to occupy points along the North African coast to make the Mediterranean safe for Spanish trade routes. Although the kings of Portugal placed an absolute embargo on any information about their naval advances, there was a real espionage ring operating that permitted the galleons of Andalusia and Biscay to voyage as far as the Portuguese enclaves in Africa where they traded for merchandise and slaves. A bitter confrontation took place over the possession of Ceuta. Spain and Portugal eventually made a pact. Portugal recognised Spanish sovereignty over the Canary Islands and Spain promised to respect the rights of Portugal along the African coast *"as far as India."* Various papal bulls that confirmed this "exclusive right" of the Portuguese to African navigation and gave Portugal its long desired sea route to India sealed this pact.

Immediately following the Reconquest of Granada, Portugal had the good fortune to have Christopher Columbus offer his navigational services. Now he was in the service of Portugal, Columbus naturally went to King João II to tell him about his dream of finding a sea route to India by navigating directly across the Atlantic. After all, Columbus was now convinced that *"the world was round."*

No one can say for sure whether the Portuguese King wanted to draw attention away from his African designs now that they were bearing fruit or whether he was just fobbing off Columbus, since he had already sent an exploratory expedition out to look for the route mentioned by the dreamer from Genoa, an expedition that never returned. In any case, Columbus was fed up with the treatment he received from the king, so he left Portugal in disgust and went to Spain. He had in mind to seek the patronage of the Catholic Monarchs and to ask them to finance his venture.

While Portugal prepared its definitive expedition to sail to India via the Cape of Good Hope, the Spanish expedition to America set sail in 1492 with Spain claiming everything that was yet to be discovered.

Two tremendous storms overtook Columbus upon his return from his first American voyage. He was forced to take the 'Niña' to the Azores and land on Portuguese territory. Columbus then went to Lisbon and appeared before King João II who received him kindly, nevertheless he suspected that the lands Columbus had discovered belonged to him by right of the papal bulls granted to Portugal.

Columbus was convinced that he would find an alternative route to India. Back in Spain, at the port of Palos de la Frontera, he sent his famous journal of his voyage to the Catholic Monarchs who were then staying at Barcelona. The Portuguese King sent an ambassador who arrived at Barcelona at the same time as Christopher Columbus. João II maintained that the islands discovered by Columbus for Spain probably belonged to Portugal.

The diplomatic quarrel gathered pace and finally ended up on the Pope's desk. The Pope at the time was the Spaniard, Alexander VI, who decided he would solve the problem by drawing a line straight through the map of the world. Beyond the meridian 46° 37', corresponding to 370 leagues East of the Cape Verde islands, all lands yet to be discovered were to belong to Spain, while on the other side of the line, they were to go to Portugal.

In June 1494, only a year before the birth of Andrew

Cidade's son at Montemor-O-Novo, the two kings of the Iberian Peninsula came together to sign the Treaty of Tordesillas. This treaty divided between them all the territories yet to be discovered. Some years later, King Francis of France sarcastically commented: *"How I would love to see pass away that sharp deal that divided the New World between my brothers the Kings of Spain and Portugal."*

There have been some biographers of John of God who, without any documented proof, have suggested that Andrew Cidade was once tempted to enlist in the crew that Vasco da Gama recruited for his Indian expedition. This is mere supposition, invented to fill the yawning gap in the information about the early years of young João and his family.

If it could be shown for sure that the childish mind of little João was occupied with exciting tales about the new discoveries, he would not, at that tender age, have been able to grasp the full measure of such adventures. During his early years in his village, John had probably made up his mind, like so many young Portuguese of that time, to join in the adventure. After all, many a young Portuguese lad at this period did just that. In fact, Portugal's rush to colonisation just about ruined the country for it drew off almost a million of its two million inhabitants.

It is only fair to say that history shows that the commercial and political thrust of Spain and Portugal included the fulfilment of the Christian precept to propagate the message of the Gospel in the newly discovered territories. From its inception, Spanish and Portuguese colonisation went hand in glove with evangelisation which at times was strongly opposed to the behaviour of the colonists. The governments and individuals of both countries considered it their duty to convert the heathens, a messianic motive that they took very seriously. In one of his letters, Columbus said to Queen Isabella: *"The main desire of Your Most Serene Majesty is the conversion of these countries to the holy faith of Christ."*

For many a young Portuguese youth, enlistment in the service of the King opened the way to security and success, both of which he would hardly find had he remained at home. Certainly this would be the case were he to come from the unpromising region of Alentejo, where there were laws that forced parents to either have their sons apprenticed to an artisan or placed in service with some nobleman. The aim of this law was good; namely to stop their sons from becoming beggars, but to make the law stick was quite another matter. That is why the prospects of João Cidade remaining at Montemor-O-Novo were very slim. He would probably have ended up in the army or navy. Well it so happened that the little boy João did leave Montemor-O-Novo .

João Cidade was only two years of age when Vasco da Gama sailed forth from Lisbon in July 1497 to begin his great adventure.

No one knows for sure, but Vasco da Gama was somewhere between 30 and 45 years of age in 1497. It seems we know more about da Gama in his earlier years. He was of a noble family and the son of a high-ranking functionary. By the time the King chose him to lead four vessels constructed under the expert supervision of Bartolomé Días, da Gama had already demonstrated his skill in seamanship. Dias warned him about the storms he had experienced in the South Atlantic, and advised him to avoid the coast of Sierra Leone by sailing westwards to avail himself of the prevailing winds that would eventually take him to the Cape of Good Hope.

On 8 July 1497, Vasco da Gama weighed anchor and put to sea with his heavily armed ships manned by 160 mariners. On board were also 12 prisoners who had been condemned to death but were given a reprieve because of the perils they were about to face. The whole of Lisbon was praying for them as they sailed away into the unknown. King Manuel gave Vasco da Gama a letter to hand to the Raja of Calcutta, their destination. The letter stated that "the men (from the West) had always desired to go to India" (by sea of course, because they had already been there by land many times before), but God "had not agreed to such a thing," and that is why it had not been successful. "Now God wills it and it would be wrong to resist that clear and manifest will."

The ships of Vasco da Gama , according to the advice given by Bartolomé Días, had made a huge curve into the Atlantic. Three months later, after a voyage of some six thousand kilometres, they anchored in Santa Helena Bay just north of the Cape of Good Hope. After rounding the Cape, Vasco da Gama planted a padrao on the eastern shore. As they pushed northwards the expedition noticed that the waters were getting warmer. When da Gama arrived at Mozambique, he came across the large Arab trading ships that plied between Africa and India. Using one of his sailors as an interpreter, da Gama was able to learn from the Arabs that much further to the north lay great ports where there was trade in spices, pearls and rubies. They finally arrived at Mombassa, the port of modern-

day Kenya. Then sailing on to Malindi, they took on board a pilot who came from Western India and he guided them through the Arabian Sea. Thanks to the monsoon winds that blew from the south-east, the European ships came to rest near Calicut (not Calcutta as they first intended) on the Malabar coast on 20 May 1498. Thanks to the information received from Covilha, the Portuguese knew that the port of Calicut was the hub of the Malabar coastal spice trade and it became the principal Portuguese base in India.

Relations between the Arab merchants and the Portuguese deteriorated rapidly. Fearful that the Portuguese were getting the upper hand in the spice trade, the Arabs poisoned the mind of Raja Zamorin against Vasco da Gama to such an extent that the Raja sought to have the Portuguese navigator put to death. However, Vasco da Gama set sail for home towards the end of August. The homeward voyage took six months, three spent in the Indian Ocean and the rest after rounding the Cape of Good Hope. After an absence of more than two years, Vasco da Gama arrived at the Bay of Lisbon in September 1499. He had navigated 45,000 kilometres, lost two of his ships and the lives of 125 men.

Upon his return, Portugal went mad with delight and Manuel I gave Vasco da Gama a splendid reception. The King bestowed upon him the title 'Admiral of the Sea of the Indies' with a grant of 300,000 silver reales. The Portuguese King informed the Catholic Monarchs saying: *"From now on, all Christianity in this part of Europe will be able to supply itself with spices and precious stones."* By the time the child João Cidade had reached four years of age, Vasco da Gama had opened up the Portuguese colonial empire. By the time João reached twenty, a dozen Portuguese navigators were to have covered 20,000 kilometres of coastline from Cape Bojador in the Atlantic to the Molucas Islands in the Pacific. Certainly, Portugal's golden age is long over, but history is like that.

Nobody in Montemor-O-Novo had the slightest idea how Andrew Cidade's son would turn out in the years to come. A hundred years later, the child was to become elevated to the rank of a hero. His biographers would adorn each step of his life story with marvels that had not the slightest basis in historical fact. What they did to John of God was to turn him into some sort of baroque plaster wonder-worker.

It is not worth getting too worked up about that; these are just simple folk tales that bring a smile to the face. They are ingenuously repeated in the lives of saints, often copied from one to the other. It is unfortunate, however, when certain authors put forward such fantasies as being true events. That is exactly what happened to John of God. Nevertheless, from what we now know, it is not too difficult to sift the wheat from the chaff.

Some of these fantastic yarns surrounding the birth of the baby João are worth a mention. You recall the tale that started in the imagination of the reverend Gomes Vasconcelos and was backed up by Doctor Messía de la Cerda. He added to the myth by inserting into it a poor pilgrim who advised the expectant mother to go down into the stable to give birth, thereby imitating Mary at Bethlehem and Signora Pica at Assisi. They also had the bells of the Montemor-O-Novo parish church ringing on their own accord to awaken the parishioners. The implication being, of course, that the people would leap out of their beds when they heard the bells joyfully pealing and rush *en masse* up to the church. They recounted that there was a holy priest called Don Cosmos who said he had seen a column of fire come to rest over the home of the Cidades in Verde Street. *"They ran down there and found the new-born baby João bathed in heavenly light, smiling and moving his little arms about."* Don Cosmos said it was just like that night in Bethlehem, the only difference being that the bells in the church tower took the place of angels. It seems that something went amiss with the pealing system, because according to this yarn, *"the bells went on ringing in the parish church for four hours."*

There was supposed to have been a peasant working at that hour in the fields beyond the Arrabal. This peasant is said to have sworn that he saw the same vision as the priest Don Cosmos. He said that he saw a column of fire descend from heaven while he was irrigating his orchard. And there is more to come. A solitary hermit up in the rugged Ossa Ranges, which can be seen from the Castle, is said to have seen a vision of angels who revealed to him the glorious plan made out by divine Providence for the newborn baby in Verde Street. Is it any wonder that there is no need to be concerned for such tales? One can understand why the baby was smiling.

I prefer to call John in his infancy, by his Portuguese name João, because it is by that name that he is honoured in his birth place. The child was to abandon Portugal and go to Spain where everyone was to call him Juan, [which of course an English-speaking reader will recognise as John]. It is with a certain sadness I find João de Deus changed to Juan de Dios, John of God. A Portuguese biographer also made the same polite lament: *"What happens to us in Portugal is that our saints go to live elsewhere."*

That seems to be the case, at least where John of God is concerned. And what about the Franciscan friar, Anthony of Padua, born at Lisbon but considered to be an Italian. This famous medieval preacher is venerated today for his prodigious life story and, because he is considered to be an expert matchmaker, is quite popular with young women eager to find a husband.

That is why I render homage to Montemor-O-Novo. A few verses by Lope de Vega spring to my mind. Lope left aside the astonishing miracles surrounding John of God, yet he honours his birthplace:

"Montemor-O-Novo whose brightest star,
before the dawn left you for afar."

I am captivated by this praise, substantiated by how the people of Montemor-O-Novo, love him, venerate him and celebrated the fifth centenary of João's birth in 1995.

And these are Communists? Yes, but in their own way.

Permit me to be so bold as to set before you something that puzzles. Was John of God really born at Montemor-O-Novo? Is there any historic proof about his birth at Montemor-O-Novo ? How is it that, at eight years of age, he disappears from there?

Notes to Chapter 4

* Although Montemor-O-Novo is disputed these days as the birthplace of John of God, nevertheless, the beatification process witnesses at Granada confirmed what Francisco de Castro stated in his 1587 biography of St. John of God: *"He was born in a village called Montemor-O-Novo which lies within the diocese of Evora in the Kingdom of Portugal."* The unanimity of the witnesses who considered him to be Portuguese would lack justification were it not the truth.

* Among the witnesses mentioned, witness 85 responded to question 6: *"This witness knows that the father and mother of the holy man John of God always lived in the street called Verde in this town of Montemor-O-Novo."* Witness 29 replied to the first question: *"This witness knows that he was Portuguese and that he was a native of the town of Montemor-O-Novo".* Witness 87 replied to the same question: *"He was Portuguese and came from the town of Montemor-O-Novo in the Kingdom of Portugal."* Witness 23 also answered question 1: *"I heard it said that he was a native of Portugal."* Witnesses 5, 17, 26, 47, all replied likewise to question 1. Only witnesses 33 and 56 replied to the same question: *"I did not know until now that he could have been Portuguese."* (*"Now"*, in this case means at the time of the beatification process.)

* I have quoted from the statements made by Manuel Dias at the beatification process held at Montemor-O-Novo on 28 March 1623: *"He lived in the house he inherited in Alfareros Street."* Andrew Cidade: *"A weaver of linen."* Blasia Dias. *"A woman who was widowed and living in Derecha Street."*

* Data and documents relating to the Cidades at Montemor-O-Novo were supplied by the researchers, A. A. Banha de Andade, 'S. João de Deus na sua terra natal', Evora 1978; and J. Chorao Lavajo, 'Montemor-O-Novo', Evora, 1991. Other historic references are from H. Raposo, *A vila-Berão do Santo, en Sao João de Deus. Homenagen de Portugal ao seu glorioso filho*, 1550-1950, Bertrand 1950.

* References to the date of John of God's birth can be found in Raphael María Saucedo's 'La Cronología aplicada en la vida de N. Padre San Juan de Dios', Paz y Caridad 11-12 (1951): 282-285; 336-343; 13-18 (1952); 56-63; 113-119; 193-204; 228-233; 285-290. To fix the global chronology of the Saint, Saucedo starts with the baptism: *"In the year 1623 when Father Domingo de Mendoza, the judge of the cause for the beatification of our Father St. John of God, had the archbishop of Evora, Don José de Melo, institute the Process in his diocese they searched in Montemor-O-Novo for the date of the Saint's baptism. However, since the parish records did not begin until 1542, this information that would have thrown so much light on the chronology was unable to be discovered. The same applies to the genealogy of the Saint."* R. M. Saucedo, 'Enayos histáticos, etc.', Paz y Caridad 12 919510 337.

* G. Magliozzi, 'Pagine juandediane', Rome, 1992, 105-108. This author unsuccessfully tried to trace the year of João's birth to 1492. He seems to have been influenced by the sentimental supposition that St. John of God might have been born on the same year as the conquest of Granada and the discovery of America.

5

A REAL DETECTIVE STORY

Montemor-O-Novo
Oropesa
Torralba de Oropesa

1503

When the little boy João was eight years old, an event took place that cast a shadow over the circumstances of his birth and the first forty years of his life.

That the event occurred is proven beyond all doubt. Don Francisco de Castro, the only authoritative guide for John of God's biographers, affirmed its validity. I have already established the dependability of Castro's writings.

I have come to the conclusion that in the first paragraph of his work Castro has pulled the wool over our eyes. I am not saying that he actually lied, but I do believe he was trying to throw us off the track, and that this was intentional. I am very aware of the gravity of my supposition and how it might appear to be extremely bold to suggest that Castro mischievously tampered with history. I beg you to permit me some margin of doubt on the matter, at least until you have finished reading this chapter, when my reasons for believing that Castro laid down a smokescreen to mislead us will be evident.

Here is the tricky sentence he wrote: "... *he grew up with them until he was eight years old, and then from there, without their knowledge, he was taken away by a cleric to the town of Oropesa.*"

What have we here? The abduction of eight year old João! He is kidnapped and taken away from Montemor-O-Novo without either the knowledge, or the authorisation, of his parents. Heaven help us, taken by a cleric too!

Castro tells us that it was 30 years before this abducted child returned to his hometown, by which time his mother and father had gone from Montemor. He was told that his mother had died of a broken heart soon after he was taken away; and that his father went off to Lisbon where he became a Franciscan friar and ended his days in the monastery. Castro is the only historian who knew the complete truth about several vexing matters that we are now going to consider.

* The birthplace of little João's parents.
* The time and reason for their going to Montemor-O-Novo.
* Their separation from their young son.
* The abduction theory and its execution.
* The suspect's identity and motive.
* The consequences of the event.
* How did João finally turn up at Oropesa more than 300 kilometres distance from Montemor-O-Novo ? The journey

normally would have been along the *Camino Real* which ran between Toledo and Lisbon, and passed through Montemor-O-Novo. This was a main road with much coming and going of muleteers, traders, friars, men and women of all sorts, Portuguese and Spaniards. These questions are not asked lightly.

I believe that I have good grounds for suspecting that Castro could have told us much more than he did. So why did he remain silent? That's the question.

The key to the answer lies in the initial misdeed, *"without their knowledge."* It would have been quite a different matter if the parents had willingly confided their son to the cleric. There are a couple of reasons why they might have done that – for instance to have him educated, or to give him a better start in life. What do you think? Castro notes that the initial evil act was *"without their knowledge"* and that's all.

Someone knew what was going on, and Castro knew too, but he said nothing. Today, five hundred years after the event, researchers are able to hunt through the archives. This research turns out to be real detective work. When I returned home after tracing John of God from Oropesa to Montemor-O-Novo, a friend of mine at Seville said he was dumbfounded to know that I was hot on the trail of John of God's origins. *"José María, you have seen John of God's tomb at Granada, so why are you so fussy about trying to prove that he was born?"* I smiled at my friend's reasoning that if John had died, he must have been born! But something kept gnawing away at the back of my mind, which I will share with you.

Let us break away from our story for a moment to note that when João was five years old and happily playing at Montemor-O-Novo, another little boy was born at Ghent in Flanders. This child would one day be the master of his world. He would live eight years longer than John of God and history was to call him Charles I of Spain and Charles V of Germany. The lives of João and Charles ran parallel to each other.

Let me explain. When João was nine, that is the year after his abduction by the strange cleric, Queen Isabella of Castile died. She was the grandmother of Prince Charles who was born in Flanders and who was to be the future Emperor. Charles came into the world right at the end of the 15th century. Four years later,

Isabella died in an austere palace at Medina del Campo on 26 November 1504.

Isabella is numbered amongst the famous women who have walked this earth. According to the historian Bernáldez, she spent her final years in severe suffering. As she lay dying she wondered about the destiny of her baby grandson who had been born at Ghent.

During her reign of thirty years, Queen Isabella experienced great pleasure and great sorrow. She finally saw a unified Spain that was free of internal conflict. She strengthened the power of the throne, and rode side by side with her husband, Ferdinand, on that unforgettable day when the Moors ceded Granada. Finally the gap in the map of Spain had been filled. She added new lands beyond the seas to her crown which continued to expand as seafarers and the *Conquistadores* pushed it further ahead. In 1504, the year of her death, Gonzalo de Cordoba annihilated the French forces at Naples. In the meantime, Isabella's husband, King Ferdinand of Aragon, was negotiating politically favourable marriages for their children – one son, the rest daughters. His desire was to unite the two Iberian nations of Spain and Portugal to bring about an effective Spanish presence in the tapestry of European alliances through the marriages of his daughters. Unfortunately, each marriage ended badly.

The Catholic Monarchs had a son late in life, Prince Juan, whom his mother Isabella used to call "my angel." Juan married the Archduchess Margarita of Austria, daughter of the Emperor Maximilian. The marriage only lasted from April to October 1497. Prince Juan died at Salamanca and was interred in a sepulchre in the church of St. Thomas which his grieving mother had had constructed at Avila. Princess Margarita was delivered of a son soon after the death of her husband, but the infant was stillborn.

The first daughter to marry was their eldest, Isabella. She married Prince Alfonso, son of King João II of Portugal, but she became a widow in 1491 after only a few months of marriage. Once recovered, at the insistence of her mother, she agreed to return to Portugal and marry King Manuel I, "The Unfortunate", the cousin of her late husband. He, handsome, kind and sensitive, had secretly been in love with the Spanish princess ever since he first saw her.

They married in September 1497 when the ships of Vasco da Gama were sailing towards India. Before da Gama returned to Portugal, Isabella died in childbirth in the summer of 1498. She left behind her the infant Prince Miguel who, at birth, inherited the entire Iberian Peninsula. He might have permanently united Spain and Portugal had events not taken a different turn. The three kingdoms of Portugal, Aragon and Castile should have united under his rule but he followed his mother Isabella into eternity before reaching the age of two. His tiny body lies next to his illustrious grandparents in the Royal Chapel at Granada. It seems a contradiction that such a tiny coffin could enclose the hopes and aspirations of Spain and Portugal. The widower, King Manuel, two years after the death of Isabella then married Maria, another daughter of the Catholic Monarchs. She, early in the summer of 1502 gave birth to a prince, Juan, who will be João III of Portugal but who will never be King of Spain, because the future Emperor King (Charles V of Germany and Charles I of Spain) had been born in Flanders.

The Catholic Monarchs' youngest daughter, the Infanta Catherine, had gone to England and married the heir to the throne, Prince Arthur, son of the eccentric and avaricious King Henry VII who decided when Catherine was prematurely widowed, that she should marry his second son once he had matured a little. So, the unfortunate Catherine became the wife of Henry VIII. He eventually repudiated her and imprisoned her for life in Kimbolton Castle.

With the deaths of the 'little angel', Juan, and the infant Miguel, the inheritance of the Catholic Monarchs fell to the second of Isabella's daughters, Juana. King Ferdinand gained diplomatic advantage by arranging her marriage to the Archduke Philip, called The Fair, son of the Emperor Maximilian of Austria and the brother of Margarita the widow of Prince João of Portugal.

Queen Isabella was to die anguishing for her married daughter in Flanders, Juana, whose happiness and that of her subjects was at stake. For Juana had four children - two daughters and two sons. Charles, the eldest of the boys, was heir to the Austrian Empire and the Throne of Spain. Juana and her husband Philip should have been happy, but that was not the case. She, "mad with love", was jealous of her husband who flirted with women throughout Europe. While her husband the Archduke Philip was away on a journey, Juana gave orders that his latest paramour be tied to a chair and that her lovely blond hair be shaven. When letters from Flanders brought this painful news to Isabella I of Spain she realised that her daughter was mad, but she needed to know if the scheming Archduke Philip was in fact pushing for royal power. However, the dying Queen Isabella did not know that Philip the Fair had suddenly died without ever tasting the fabulous power that might have been his. One fine autumn day in 1506, Philip gave a sumptuous feast at Brussels to which he invited all his cronies of the court. After eating and drinking he got up from the table, mounted a horse and rode off to play a ball game. He became so thirsty that he drank a draught of ice-cold water, which sent him into the next world. Rumour went about the court that someone had poisoned him.

At Flanders, five years after the birth of our João at Montemor-O-Novo, a baby boy was born. This child was to be King Charles I of Spain, and Emperor Charles V of Germany. He was the recipient of history's greatest bequest: the Germanic Empire from his Austrian grandfather Maximilian; and the Flemish-Burgundian inheritance from his paternal grandmother; and of course, the Spanish inheritance along with its overseas extension, from his grandparents, Isabella of Castile and Ferdinand of Aragon.

Life is full of strange ironies and misery is inherent in the human condition. Providence has called Charles to occupy the greatest throne on earth, yet the child was born in very peculiar circumstances. The medieval chronicle relates that Signora Pica went down to the stable to give birth to St. Francis. And the *miraculous* legends want us to believe that the mother of our João went into the stable to await the hour of her delivery. It happens to be a fact that the great King Emperor Charles was born in a lavatory. I beg your indulgence!

The scatterbrained Philip had already discounted the affections of his wife when, on the evening of 24 February 1500, he organised a feast in the salons of his palace, the Prinsenhof, on the outskirts of Ghent. Consumed as always by jealousy, poor Juana decided to catch her philandering husband red-handed during the festivities that he had organised for that evening. Instead of staying at home and going to bed, she presented herself at the banquet. Suddenly her labour pains began and Philip's lady friends were immediately asked to leave. Right there and then, Juana gave birth to the baby who was to be the most powerful man on earth on the hard floor of a lavatory. The Emperor's future enemies ceaselessly poked fun at him for the manner of his birth on that February night. In homage to our emperor, I once spent a morning wandering through the ruins of Prinsenhof. All that remains now is a derelict gateway and part of a wall perforated with a window that they say corresponds to the private apartments of the unfortunate Queen Juana [known in English as "Joan the Mad"].

Sleuths hot on the trail of John of God's origins have been sifting through any evidence that might produce a reasonable hypothesis for the extraordinary abduction of the little boy João. However, we have never been able to arrive at anything that we can agree upon. I hope that something will eventually turn up in an archive somewhere.

Personally, I think the most persuasive hypothesis is that proposed by my friend Brother Matías de Mina, who has been researching the trail of John of God's story for many a long year. Brother Matías simply speaks of a kidnapping, and I am inclined to think that that is the best and surest way to solve the puzzle.

In those times it was quite frequent and normal for parents to hand their children over to someone who was able to support them and offer them a future. They tried to avoid the laws that imposed upon them the responsibility to see that their children did not become beggars. They sought a solution by placing their offspring in the service of persons of good repute.

Brother Matías quietly and convincingly explained his theory to me. Perhaps he is correct. If only our friend Castro had not inserted his fatal phrase, *"without their knowledge."* This suggests that the cleric took hold of the little boy and went off with him without the parents' knowledge. Furthermore, there is nothing to suggest that this was done in accordance with the boy's wishes. Castro, who is the only one who knew the complete truth, records the many years of suffering João's parents endured, particularly his mother who, as an aged relative testified, died of a broken heart.

"My son, this you must know. Only a few days after you were taken away from this country, your mother died. It was due to the pain and sorrow that she felt from your absence. You were so little and she had no idea who was responsible, where you had gone or how. All of us know that it was this heartbreak that cut her days short and brought about her death."

"You were taken away," without the agreement of the parents. Had they agreed, then surely there would have been some sort of contact later on between themselves and their son. Since this did not happen, the child must have been kidnapped.

The hypothesis put forward by some scholars of St. John of God, offers two variations, both based upon the person of the *cleric*. One conjecture is that the *cleric* was one of those erratic students who fluttered about from university to university. He was given shelter for the night at the home of the Cidades and he probably told them he was on his way to some destination, Salamanca for instance. The parents of João took the opportunity to confide their son to his care so that he might get an education and have a better chance in life.

The other hypothesis transforms the *cleric* into a Jeronymite Friar from the monastery of Guadalupe. This hypothesis arose because there were some friars who travelled about seeking donations of clothing, money and comestibles to support the patients in the hospitals they conducted adjacent to their celebrated monastery at Guadalupe. It is remarkable that the municipal records of Montemor-O-Novo for the year 1503 show that a certain Fray Bartolomeu Chauchos arrived in the town. He came to Montemor-O-Novo furnished with documents granted him by Manuel I, as well as the written permission of the Prior of the Guadalupe Monastery, to collect donations. This hypothesis says that the friar stayed overnight with the Cidades who confided their son to his care so that he could not only see the famous sanctuary of Our Lady of Guadalupe but seek his own destiny, whether within the same monastery or as an apprentice to a shepherd.

Those who defend this latter hypothesis have fixed the itinerary that the friar and child would have taken after leaving Montemor-O-Novo on their way to the Guadalupe monastery as follows: Evora, Badajoz, Méroda, the fringe of the Sierra Montáchez, and then to Zorita for access to the Villuercas.

Suppose the Prior of the Jeronymites decided it was not convenient to keep the child in the monastery and told the alms-collecting monk to take João with him on his expedition and drop him off with a good family where he could work. Were that the case, the friar and the little boy would have gone north, crossed the Sierra Altamira near the San Vincente Gorge, bridged the Tagus at Puente del Arzobispo and, finally, arrived at Oropesa where a good suitable family accepted the child as a shepherd boy.

Let it be said, neither theory – that of the Jeronymite friar or the itinerant student – can explain away Castro's puzzling paragraph.

Firstly, the boy did not confide in his parents: he simply disappeared *"without their knowledge"*. *"They took you from us"* his uncle proclaimed many years later. Secondly, and more seriously, the welcome given to the cleric with food and lodging in the Cidade home lacks any documentary evidence. It is no more than sheer fantasy. That either a friar or a student, after accepting such charitable hospitality, kidnapped the child, is quite unbelievable.

Two more hypotheses are put forward, both implying that the boy João was willing to leave home and go with the mysterious cleric. Why was this so?

Some authors have suggested that after supper, the visitor related stories of the adventures and accomplishments of the Portuguese mariners under the leadership of King Manuel. Vasco da Gama, who has certain connections with Montemor-O-Novo, has written his own immortal page in history. Young Portuguese men flocked to take part in these heroic expeditions. Could it be that João so wanted to go off on these adventures to be a hero that when the student left the house next morning to resume his journey he clung to his side insisting that he be taken along? This reminds us of the story of Teresa and her little brother Rodrigo running away from home in search of martyrdom at the hands of the Moors.

I must add the proposition of other authors that elevates the abduction of the child João to the level of sentimentalism. Their version says the visitor spoke of abundant riches, gold and money, all just there for the taking. But these treasures were to be found a great distance away. At this time, João's mother was gravely ill and needed specialised medical attention, but the doctors lived far away in Serúbal and Lisbon and one would need a fortune to pay them. The little boy therefore decided to join the visitor on his journey in search of this treasure. Having found it, he could return and have his mother cured.

These ludicrous hypotheses are advanced in apparently serious books, but none of them merit attention. The only benefit from all these odd views about the puzzling childish flight of little João from Montemor-O-Novo is that they make one smile.

The following closes this litany of hypotheses. It is recorded that an epidemic afflicted Alentejo from 1502 to 1503. It was the first of the frequent plagues that fell upon the Iberian Peninsula throughout the 16th century. Perhaps it silently attacked the Cidades and broke up their family. It is most unlikely that the scourge of an epidemic is connected with the unplanned departure of the child João, hand in hand with an unknown visitor, heading towards some unknown destination.

There is one more thing to add to the catalogue of fantasies that have been put forward regarding the flight, or abduction, of the child João. There are extremists who bedeck the life of John of God with ludicrous miracles and, to back up their claims, have recourse to a *divine call*. They hold that he left home because he was destined to complete the great task God reserved for him in the future. They say it was something like the voice that Abraham heard when Yahweh told him to abandon the country of his forefathers.

There are others who love the tales about the knaves of Spain's Golden Age. These persons see the famous *cleric* as a rogue, a *bon viveur* who actually kidnapped the boy and carried him off to make use of him for dishonest purposes. Under the pretence of being a cripple, led by the hand of a small boy, he would hope to gain sympathy and receive alms.

To sum up: no serious historian today would give the slightest credence to what Castro said about the boy. It is obvious an artificial smokescreen, invented by Don Francisco de Castro, to deflect us from the truth

Why would a person as respectable as Castro wish to hide the truth about the infancy and early boyhood of João?

I am offering two possible explanations for consideration. Firstly, Castro was perfectly aware of the truth about young João's family at the time he was writing the biography of John of God. Castro knew the identity of his parents, their origin and the economic conditions of the home. From this he was able to know the reason for the boy's flight. *'To the Christian Reader'* was the heading Castro gave to the foreword in his biography of John of God. In this letter to his readers, Castro acknowledged that the principal source of the material for his work came from a notebook given to him by *"a companion"* of John of God. This *companion* accompanied John of God on all his journeys: this man enjoyed John of God's confidence because he was *"very much like him in spirit"*. For that reason, what he recorded was the testimony of an eyewitness. There is no doubt that the two friends would have shared many a long conversation while they were on the road in search of donations. In the evening when they stopped to rest, such conversations would have continued between the two friends on a more intimate level. John would have spoken of his family background and the loneliness of a life deprived of parents. His friend copied what he said into his private notebook. Castro eventually got to read these confidences but disdained to use this information, keeping it to himself.

"... he grew up with his parents until he was eight years old and then, without their knowledge, he was taken away from there by a cleric to the town of Oropesa."

Castro's smokescreen was so successful that no one was able to penetrate it. The mystery remained for more than four centuries ago since his book was published in 1584. What was Castro's secret? What was its mystery? What was he hiding?

Modern-day researchers have now been able to discover a crack in the mystery, through which light is filtering from the end of the tunnel. This new lead first appeared about forty years ago. I ask myself, How would the biography written by Castro have been accepted had his secret been revealed in his day? Well, that is not as important as determining the truth now coming to light. Only what can be authenticated can be accepted; what cannot be proven must go onto the margin, using the same sound principle advocated by Castro himself: *"For it is better that we leave out something now, than to speak about it without certainty."*

It will be good for us to get to the bottom of this business. Why? Because the social and religious circumstances that made Castro so cautious no longer exist. We will not let ourselves fall into the trap that caused Castro to be so much on his guard.

Those with a good knowledge of Spanish history will recall that half a century ago researchers came up with some very interesting information regarding the extent of Judaism in the identity and history of Spain. The renowned poet and historian, Américo Castro, let off a bomb when he described the Iberian race as a hotchpotch made up of *"three castes of believers, Christians, Moors and Jews"* and that the intermingling of these three castes resulted in the Spanish people of today.

This fascinating view of the reality of Spanish history provoked a famous reply from the renowned medievalist, Claudio Sánchez Albornoz. He reproached Américo Castro for forgetting the indigenous element in the essential Hispanic makeup because this was there long before the Moors and Jews. A real clash of views resulted between these two eminent experts of Spanish history and, as a result of the debate, great stimulation was given to research which has endured for some fifty years. Some of the results have had universal acceptance while others have simply gone into the files of local archives. Leading these researchers are Caro Baroja, Domínguez Ortiz, Fernández Alvarez, Millás, Cantera, López Martínez, Ruano, Suárez Fernández, Azcona, Gómez Menor and Márquez Villanueva – quite an impressive bunch.

Centuries ago, the seed of coexistence of Jews in the bosom of Spanish society grew into the typical suspicion of minorities that arises in popular majorities. There was a common disapproval of the Jewish moneylenders, no doubt because people saw them getting rich through monopolising hated occupations such as tax collecting and money lending. The accumulation of riches by the Jews stimulated much of the persecution against them under the guise of religion, but the real cause was the desire to lay hands on their wealth. Persecutions and killings brought about many *conversions* to the Christian faith. In many cases these conversions were quite evidently false, but others were sincere.

In the middle of the 14th century, Spanish Jews suffered ferocious and bloody persecutions. The last was in 1391 and it spread from Seville throughout the rest of the peninsula. Many Jewish families had come from Castile and settled in the Andalusian city of Seville from where they escaped to the north from Arab invasion when it came. In 1248, when Ferdinand III had retaken Seville, they began to return. Some continued to practice their religion, others converted to Christianity and these were called 'Conversos'. There was a significant upgrading in the economy of the City of Seville, and this included both social and political life. A hundred years later, at the end of the 14th century in the ill-fated year 1391, along came a fanatical archdeacon called Ferrán Martínez who preached frenzied sermons against the Jews. Unscrupulous Christians soon discovered that if they attacked the Jews and expelled or killed them, they were then able to take over a great amount of property and money. The incentive to such easy robbery awoke an inquisitorial force of hypocrites who hid behind the parapets of the archdeacon's theological arguments. They wrote an ignominious page of Seville's history in blood and, sad to say, this had its echo in Toledo, Madrid, Cuenca, Zaragoza and other cities throughout Spain.

A hundred years later, in the final third of the 15th century, along came the Catholic Monarchs. Rightly were they called by this title because, like all other European monarchs, they used the cement of religion as an excuse to bring about their realms. While they were at Seville planning their final assault upon the Nasrides Kingdom, the Catholic Monarchs made a resolution to defend the Christian faith with royal power. That decision went to shape Spanish life for centuries to come. They saw this to be the chain that would bind Spanish unity, so in order to achieve this purpose they needed an instrument to bring it about: the Inquisition, until then controlled by the popes. Ferdinand and Isabella appealed to Sixtus IV who agreed to give them the bull that unleashed the modern Inquisition, or as it is better known, the Spanish Inquisition. The papal confidence in the Catholic Monarchs permitted them to organise and direct the Tribunal of the Inquisition with ecclesiastic judges, although the secular arm carried out the execution of sentences. In the year 1478, an outbreak of sacrileges, violence and perversions broke out at Seville. The general population attributed these foul crimes to the *Conversos*.

There was much celebration during the sojourn of the Catholic Monarchs at Seville. At one bullfight, matadors on horseback armed with lances went into the arena to fight 20 bulls. This was the time when the voice of the Dominican Prior of the Convent of San Pablo, Fray Alonso de Hojeda, was heard ranting from the pulpits calling for *holy* vengeance upon the Jews. It made no difference to de Hojeda whether the Jews practised their faith in secret of whether they were *Conversos* whom he called false Christians. He was aided and abetted by the city's *'traditionalist'* clergy who professed how *"happy and welcome it was to have the Tribunals of the Inquisition."* Ferdinand and Isabella appointed Cardinal Archbishop Mendoza to set up the Inquisition. Mendoza wrote a catechism that only served to inflame the violent preachers. Once Ferdinand and Isabella received the papal bull, they immediately inaugurated *the Holy Tribunal of Seville.* Two years later, *the Council of the Supreme Inquisition* was inaugurated for the whole of the Spanish Kingdom. Historians of old attributed to Seville the glory of having established the first of the inquisitorial tribunal.

It was very much to the medieval taste: a mixture of political and religious interests giving prestige to the exercise of power. Firstly there were the local authorities, then came the bishops and judges, and finally the Pope, all making use of this system of *Inquisition*. There were hunts to bring anyone accused of covert ideological or moral deviations out into the open. Vigilance and defence of the supreme values is given a sacred character and put a weapon of incalculable worth in the hands of the authorities.

Everyone knows that the Inquisition worked by using the habitual methods of all European countries during that age, so it is not reasonable to attribute an exclusive litany of horrors to the *wickedness of Christians* as if they were the only ones committing them. Besides, all know that the tortures used by the Inquisition had their remote origins in the cultures of the Orient and the Mediterranean, including the Roman. Torture by fire was specifically connected with Germanic practices. However, none of this historic reasoning was of any consolation to the Jews of Seville who had the most frightening torments fall upon their heads. There were so many prisoners that they could not fit into the Convent of San Pablo so they were thrown into the cells of Triana Castle. A wave of terror passed over the whole of southern Spain and the pyres began to blaze.

Historians are not in agreement about the exact number of persons who were burnt at the stake, and it would be a good thing if some historian would conscientiously work on this subject. But it is beyond all doubt that the first burning at the stake took place at Seville in 1481.

A curious situation arose in the 15th century. Jewish life was harassed, and at times intolerably so, by the Christians who compelled the Jews to convert to Christianity. However, such conversions were always suspected, and in fact the *Conversos* were viewed to be a *fifth column* within the Christian State. Vicens Vives calculated the number of *Conversos* to be some hundreds of thousands during in the early years of the 15th century, influenced by financial relations as well as intellectual prestige. *It was very easy to accuse them of heresy if they were called Jewish swine."* The number of *Conversos* increased as the century progressed, especially when the Catholic Monarchs put Spain on a footing in preparation for a *holy war* to conquer Granada. Spain, by means of the conquest of Granada, achieved its longed for political and religious unity. Every time the Royal Court assembled high ranking nobles and ecclesiastics petitioned the Catholic Monarchs to take a stronger hand in discriminating against the Jews. Coloured symbols were introduced and Jewish females were forced to wear a blue badge on the right shoulder. The Jews were forced to live in ghettos where their religious practices were kept under strict observation.

Above all, the Christians were suspicious of the contact of Jewish *Conversos* with the Jews who were faithful to the old religion. Documents of the period show that *"many New Christians"* who had converted from Judaism still secretly practiced the rites of Judaism. That is not surprising because Talmudic Law considered null and void conversions to Christianity obtained through violence. Therefore the number of the Anuzim, those forced into Christianity, continued to increase.

"When Castile initiated its push ahead", says Fernández Alvarez, *"the Catholic Monarchs ruled a heterogeneous people composed of Christians, Moors and Jews. From that time onwards the Jews, Conversos and the Moors constituted a powder keg ready to explode unless it was constantly watched."*

In 1478 the Catholic Monarchs obtained the famous bull from Pope Sixtus IV authorising them to set up the Tribunal of the Inquisition. The first seat of the Tribunal was installed in the Convent of San Pablo, Seville. The Inquisition was ordered to conserve the purity of the Catholic faith, therefore its competency did not cover Jews or Moslems. However, Conversos could be denounced as being suspect of apostasy, that is to say, returning to their former Jewish religion and mocking Christianity. The Inquisitors began their work in Andalusia with such firmness that relatives of the victims and ecclesiastics of evangelical spirit, complained to the Pope. As a result of these complaints, the Pope threatened to abolish the Inquisition altogether. Isabella and Ferdinand then employed every means at their disposal and used their diplomatic skill to avoid the Pope's threat by letting Rome reserve the right to appoint the judges, but not before they obtained the faculty of recommending to the Pope their own candidates. Thus, on 2 August 1483, Isabella got her wish, and the Prior of the Dominican Convent of San Pablo at Seville, Fray Tomás de Torquemada, was appointed General Inquisitor of the Crown of Castile.

Torquemada extended the Tribunal to various other places and he appointed deputy inquisitors. He also promulgated the 'Institutions of the Holy Office', which, unfortunately, admitted anonymous denunciations and required the faithful to come forward to inform on anyone who was in any way suspect. Toledo was next with its own Tribunal of the Inquisition, and the other cities of the North followed soon after. This

created a wave of panic to flow through the households of many Conversos.
During the period in which Spain was gaining the last piece of Moslem territory held by the Nasrides Kingdom of Granada there was internal unease about the Jewish minority. This tension caused suspicion, not only of Jews as such, but also the *Conversos* or New Christians. The social mistrust of Conversos was a bitter blow to those families who were sincere converts. Later, many famous persons of the highest quality in politics and literature were to spring from such families. For instance, Fray Hernando de Talavera who was the confessor to the Queen Isabella and then became the first Archbishop of Granada; and then there were Luis Vives, Luis de León, Mateo Alemán, Diego Laínez, John de Avila, Teresa of Avila and John of the Cross. And what about John of God?

Ah, John of God! No Spanish historian ever mentioned that likelihood until these times. Even less so, those who have been closest to the studies and documentation relating to John of God. Someone has invented the delightful neologism *Juandediano* to describe the studies on the life and spirituality of St. John of God. They were well aware of the statements made, loudly and clearly, by the witnesses at the beatification process.

"The father and mother of the aforementioned John of God were legitimate Old Christians having no mixture of the race of the Moor, and neither Jew nor Old Christians." (Witness Manuel Dias, Montemor-O-Novo, 28 March 1623).

However, in 1962 the historian Julio Caro Baroja wrote in volume two of his *'The Jews in Modern and Contemporary Spain'* that he had discovered in the writings of a certain 17th century Portuguese Jesuit that John of God was the son of Conversos. Caro Baroja indicated that he agreed with this position.

Such a discovery raised some dust and inevitably made headlines in certain magazines in the form of the question: *'Was St. John of God a Jew?'*

Well, a similar rumpus had erupted some fifteen years earlier over the scandal caused when a similar statement was made in regards to St. Teresa of Avila. Between 1945 and 1950 the devotees of St. Teresa suffered a great shock. It was as if a fiery cross was set up on their front lawn. From Hispanic America came a work by Américo Castro whose serious research beautifully and reasonably traced through the characteristic literary style of Teresa of Avila. This pointed to her having had very close connections with New Christians – converts from Judaism to Catholicism. Another patient researcher, Narciso Alonso Cortés, sent Américo Castro a copy of an ancient file he had unearthed through diligent research in the Valladolid Royal Chancellery Archives. In black and white, this document clearly proved the Jewish descent of St. Teresa's father, and it confirmed Américo Castro's hypothesis. This news astonished both the staff at the Valladolid Archives and Américo Castro himself. They could hardly believe it. St. Teresa of Avila was of Jewish blood!

A detail indicates the degree of fright caused by this discovery. A Carmelite author by the name of Father Efrén de la Madre de Dios wrote a biography called 'The Life and Times of St. Teresa', but before he had finished his book he became aware of this startling information. Fr. Efrén became afraid that the honest truth might upset his readers, so he tried to water it down. He attempts to explain it by saying that the grandfather of St. Teresa used to do "too much" business with the Jews and this prompted him to convert from Christianity and embrace Judaism. When he read that, Américo Castro was so disgusted with such an absurd hypothesis that he wrote: "How could it be possible, and even likely, that at the end of the 15th century, when a multitude of Jews were converting to Christianity out of fear of being tortured and killed, a Toledan by the name of Sánchez quietly comes along to have himself circumcised." In a later edition of his book, Fr. Efrén admitted without dissimulation that the Saint's grandfather was a Jewish convert.

Antonio Vieira was the Jesuit mentioned by Américo Castro. Vieira was born at Lisbon in 1609 and as a child went with his parents to Brazil. He entered the Jesuit novitiate at the tender age of fourteen and was ordained priest when he was 26 years of age. At first in India, then later in Brazil, Vieira gained a reputation as a distinguished preacher and he is remembered as a great defender of the Brazilian Indians. He was a prolific author whose literary works occupy 15 volumes and are regarded as classics in the Portuguese language. When he went from Brazil to Portugal he was appointed by King João IV as Court Preacher and Royal Adviser. Until 1667 he was in the hands of the Inquisition and under house arrest because, after the death of King João IV, he had written some enigmatic predictions relating to the triumph of Portugal in the next millennium, which, according to Vieira, were to follow the resurrection of the deceased king. Because he published the fantasies of the seer Gonzalo Annes de Bandarra, his prudent superiors sent him off to Rome where he resided for six years *in patriotic convalescence*. While in Rome Vieira was given the task of promoting the cause for the beatification of the Jesuit, Ignacio de Açevado. After that he returned to Portugal and from there went back to Brazil where he died at Bahia in the summer of 1697. It was during his final years that Vieira achieved a high reputation for his literary works. The amazing nun, Sister Juana Inés de la Cruz, wrote a theological work criticising a certain sermon given by Vieira. The nun intelligently defended our human liberty, but she was publicly reprimanded for it , by the Bishop of Puebla in the later argument, which Sister Juana Inés naturally lost. While he was living in Rome Vieira became curious about some aspects of the process of the beatification of John of God by Urban VIII on 21 September 1630. Vieira resided in Rome between 1669 and 1675, the period in which the Roman Curia was preparing for the canonisation of Blessed John of God. The actual canonisation took place some 15 years later.

While he was in Rome, Vieira wanted to find out exactly what evidence had put obstacles in the way of the beatification of John of God, and were still obstructions to his canonisation. In the canonisation process of saints there is a public prosecutor, known in Canon Law as the Promoter of the Faith – and in common parlance the *Devil's Advocate*. His duty is to meticulously search for any defects in the candidate put forward for canonisation and, if there are any defects, to see that they are brought to light. As a writer, Vieira was particularly interested in knowing about the apparent "shadows" in the official picture of the figure of John of God. Experience has taught me as an author that one of the best ways to penetrate the confidential sections of a saint's life is to unravel the bits that the *Devil's Advocate* opposes.

Somebody whispered a secret to the Jesuit Vieira: namely that the process of the already 'blessed John of God 'put to one side a question that might have held back, God knows for how long, his official glorification. Those who compiled the definitive conclusions of the beatification process had swept something under the mat, namely that John of God was the son of Jews. In spite of the statements made by the witnesses, and the reports of the judges of the Roman Rota, not a single word was said about it in the Roman Curia. No one wanted to get involved with the matter. They wanted to avoid any scandal. Why? Because many Christians would have considered that John of God had come from a blemished family and, in their eyes, was also culpable. It was something that could not be erased – having been born of the same race as the Lord Jesus Christ and Mary of Nazareth, a Jew!

Vieira wrote a book while he was at Rome denouncing the hypocrisy of Christians who worshipped Jesus the Jew, while detesting the Jewish people. He called his work '*Treatise in Favour of the Hebrew Nation*', and in it he neither cut out or watered down a single paragraph of the secret details that came to light regarding John of God in the Vatican processes: "*What are we to say of the only Portuguese patriarch that the Church of God possesses? The glorious exemplar of humility and universal charity, St. John of God, belonged to this race (Hebrew).*"

John of God was already beatified when Vieira wrote this in 1674, hence he carried the title *Blessed*; however, the impulsive Jesuit presumed to apply absolute sanctity to John of God. He continues: "*Ask yourself this question (the Jewish race of St. John of God). Who in the Roman Curia does not know about it, having seen and heard it in his canonisation process? They cannot avoid it because it is considered to be without any doubt. Such is the shame of our times that they constantly conceal the parents and grandparents of the saint, as if this were to point out some sort of defect in him. After all, the Apostle Paul was proud to belong to this race.*"

Caro Baroja soundly endorses this: "*St. John of God was the son and grandson of Jews of very humble circumstances, which is to say, he belonged to a defenceless social group.*" He then goes on to remark: "*And it is paradoxical that another of the most characteristic saints of Spain's Golden Age, was in fact a poor Portuguese Jew …The Saint's surname is Ciudad, or Cidade [City in English], a common surname among the Jews.*"

Let us return to Vieira: "*John of God's methods of piety and charity have something enigmatic about them.*" This evokes a parallel that is not too bad: "*They are methods (of piety and charity) which recall to our memory events that we have read about in books concerning Russia. Also, there have been pious men in countries a long way away from Eastern Europe. In those places there were also many charitable men surrounded by a multitude of beggars ...Therefore, it seems obvious that persons like these could not have been lacking amongst Conversos."*

In the same year that Caro Baroja's book appeared, that expert exponent of Castro's work, Manuel Gómez Moreno, was interviewed for a magazine by Antonio Vázquez. Gómez Moreno spoke about the book and made the following comment:

"The only fact that that I later discovered is that John of God was of the Jewish race. I followed this up in a work by a Portuguese author who wrote that it was odd that one should speak so badly about the Jews when John of God was of this race. This made me think that the research into the strange events surrounding the saint's early childhood is indicative of the treatment handed out to the Jewish race."

While he was studying the Jewish ancestry of St. Teresa and St. John of the Cross in 1970, Gómez Menor said that, without a moment of hesitation he would add St. John of God to the list of the illustrious talented Spaniards who, to some degree, had Jewish blood running in their veins.

Gómez Menor says that John of God was born in the Toledan village of Casarrubios but we will come back to this soon.

The surname Ciudad, or Cidade in Portuguese [City], is enough to certify that John of God was Jewish. If *Conversos* went back to the practice of their Jewish faith, consequently placing themselves in a position in which the Inquisition could seize them, they would have to forfeit all their property. So, in order to throw the Holy Office off their scent, they would change their paternal names. This juggling of Jewish surnames was quite a complicated affair, but many did so in order to avoid persecution.

Gómez Menor discovered a wonderful list of place-names used as surnames by the Jews of Toledo. He noted that when they were baptised they would alter their Jewish surname in order to suppress its characteristic prefixes. So they assumed names according to their professions such as, Cirujano (Surgeon), Sastre (Tailor), Platero (Silversmith); or names peculiar to a country, for instance, Alemán (German), Navarro (Navarre), Zamorano (Zamora). Sometimes they took the names of a parish, like San Ginés, Santiago, San Román. There were patronymic names derived from some ancestor, such as Díaz or Ortiz; and topographic names derived from places where the family resided, like Alcocer, Burgos, Córdoba, Dueñas, and so forth. I was delighted to see the research undertaken by the Toledan archivist Gómez Menor, and I wished to ask him what he thought of the surname Ciudad? His answer was quite surprising.

García Sánchez, another archives ferret, will soon have something to tell us. He asserts that the surname Cidade (Ciudad) was utilised by John's father, and perhaps his grandparents, to blur the family's identity.

According to Caro Baroja, *"the converso Ciudad was a city man"*, not of the countryside. That meant there was an abundance of surnames that alluded to this character in the lineage of those belonging to this cast of city dweller: Ciudad (City), Calle (Street), Mercado (Merchant), and they had their equivalents in other languages as well. By the second half of the 15ᵗʰ century, the *'Chronicle of Don Alvaro de Luna'* recorded a Juan Ciudad as, *"a wealthy tax collector who was an insolent Converso"* and one of the leading Conversos in Toledo. Furthermore, there is the disturbing fact that the Inquisition at Toledo condemned another Juan Ciudad. So the question arises, what connection is there between the Ciudads of Toledo and the Cidades of Montemor-O-Novo?

The Hospitaller Brothers of St. John of God reacted to the fuss caused by the statements made by Caro Baroja in a more circumspect way. Caro Baroja's statements provoked replies from some of the brothers who had made a study of the events in the life of their founder. Nevertheless, such revelations did not cause even a ripple in the general community of Christians, which just goes to show how the sociological atmosphere has altered over the years. Nowadays no one is surprised at *impure blood*, that ancient concern about *"endangering the religious quality of the race."* Today such a notion is sheer absurdity.

Two Hospitaller Brothers, the Spaniard, Rafael Maria Saucedo, and the Italian, Giuseppe Magliozzi, took this matter to heart. Firstly they attacked the basis of the Jesuit Vieira's thesis, and then they attacked Caro Baroja's position.

I think that, against Vieira, they proceeded with an excess of good faith. The Jesuit presented, as his source of information, the canonical process that elevated John of God to the honours of the altar. Saucedo rummaged through the files of the process line by line without finding anything that could have given Vieira cause to make his statements. Well, there was a remote reference. The Promoter of the Faith, better known by his sobriquet *Devil's*

Advocate, demanded that he be given proof of John of God's baptism; *"to dispel any suspicion that in a country where there are infidels, he also may have been born an infidel."* This was, so he said, *"because in Portugal there are various sects, Moslems, Jews, Moors and New Christians."* However, the required proof did not exist.

Vieira was not going to let them get out of this situation so easily. In calling for proof of baptism, the trail to discover the Jewish origins of Blessed John of God was opened up. But Vieira believed that this alluded to *distinct* sources of the official process. He had received a friendly tip-off from *private circles* so he knew the secret about John of God. He knew because his source of information, well aware of the irregularity of disclosing such a sensitive matter as the Jewish origins of John of God, had whispered the secret to him. Therefore it was puerile to go searching through the files of the official process for the source of Vieira's information.

Saucedo was openly annoyed with Julio Caro Baroja. He reproached him for adducing inane arguments of a psychological character in order to confirm Vieira's theory about John of God's Jewish origins. He did not care for Caro Baroja's reference to the style of John of God's practice of piety and charity being *"stamped with the oriental seal of the Jewish Conversos."* *"Moreover,* Caro Baroja said, *"There have also been pious men in countries a long way away from Eastern Europe. In those places there were also many charitable men surrounded by a multitude of beggars, the incurably ill, cripples, and wealthy women, society ladies if you wish, who enthusiastically gave their wealth to the service of religious activities. The miracle was in the order of the day, in which the most humble and abject members of society are those who arrive at greater perfection."*

Saucedo also did not care for Julio Caro Baroja outlining a list of examples of charity and devotion similar to those of John of God. He asks: *"Where is the oriental and Judaic character of these works here?"* Saucedo was very annoyed, and it is a pity he let slip the ancient Spanish animosity towards the Jews: *"I say in passing, Jews are better known for their avarice than their generosity."* Then he went on to say: *"Furthermore, John of God could not in any way have been born into a Jewish family."* This prejudice impeded a balanced and calm in-depth examination by Saucedo. Nevertheless, a few years later Rafael Saucedo changed his opinion and let himself remain *"open to the suspicion"* that our saint might have had Jewish origins.

Granada was the city where the Catholic Monarchs signed the decree to expel the Jews on 31 March 1492. Ferdinand and Isabella gave the Jews three months to be baptised if they wanted to remain in Spain. Those who refused were forced to leave with their wives, children, servants and relatives. They could take goods with them but no gold or silver. The chronicler Bernáldez, who was no friend of the Jews, felt it a pity to see them *"exchange a house for a donkey and a vineyard for a little clothing or linen."* A hundred and fifty thousand Jews travelled the roads of Portugal and Spain that led to the Levant or to Andalusia from where they abandoned the country. Caro Baroja calculates that 240,000 remained under the guise of *Conversos*.

From around Toledo a huge number of Jewish families took the *Camino Real* that led from Castile to the Portuguese border. There were friendly relations between the cities of Castile and Portugal and much trade passed along the *Camino Real* where traffic from Madrid and Toledo met upon the heights of Torrijo and continued towards Oropesa, Navalmoral, Mérida and Badajoz. The *Camino Real* crossed the border and entered into Elvas, Extremoz, Evora, and Montemor-O-Novo to go on to Setábal and finish at Lisbon. The chroniclers of the times record that there were good relations between the two countries and that this permitted Jewish families to flow back and forth during the bitter days of the exile.

The major part of Castilian Jews, as well as those from Extremadura and Toledo, sought refuge in Portugal because the King of Portugal, João II, refused to imitate the example of the Catholic Monarchs who urged him to expel the Jews. Nevertheless the refugees soon lost the security of their refuge because the Catholic Monarchs put pressure on the Portuguese King to achieve their purpose. As the festivities for a royal marriage began in Portugal, the Jewish families in that country sent up a cry of lamentation.

Remember what I said before about the Catholic Monarchs marrying off their eldest daughter Isabel to Prince Alfonso the son of King João II of Portugal, and how she soon became a widow. Well, her parents arranged for her to marry again and in 1497 she married Manuel, cousin of the deceased Alfonso. João II had died two years previously and his grandson Manuel, who was to be called 'The Unfortunate', assumed the Portuguese throne. A year and a half later, all the formalities of his marriage with the Infanta Isabel were finalised on 11 August 1497 at Medina del Campo. One of the conditions in the marriage contract, at the insistence of the Catholic Monarchs, was to maintain the religious unity of Manuel's kingdom. They feared the influence of Jewish refugees in Portugal on Spain. Isabella and Ferdinand renewed the pressure on their neighbouring kingdom by including in the matrimonial contract a specific clause that the Portuguese King could not ignore. They told *His Most Serene Majesty* of Portugal that *"if you are in agreement"* he must expel every heretic and let not a single one remain in his kingdom and dominions. They said *"if you are in agreement"* but they gave him a deadline of just one month to comply.

Documents of the period show that King Manuel did what he could to wriggle out of this clause, but he nevertheless had to finally succumb to the pressure of his in-laws. Manuel tried to sweeten the bitter pill by exhorting the Jews to be baptised and thereby be free of the expulsion order. In any case he took his time with those who refused baptism by using a procedure that turned out to be counterproductive. A law was passed that forced Jewish families in Portugal to hand over their sons who were under fourteen years of age to be *"brought up in the faith of the Kingdom"* by Christian families throughout towns and villages of Portugal. The chronicles of the period tell of baptisms *en masse*; but they also tell accounts of horrors, of desperate Jewish parents who drowned their young sons rather than hand them over.

The chronicler Damião de Goes adds a tone that I wish to emphasise, with reference to the kidnapping that occurred in the home of the Cidades at Montemor-O-Novo. De Goes says: *"Some Jews preferred to kill their boys rather than allow them to be snatched away from them without any hope of seeing them again."* These boys were taken away from them forever.

I have mentioned that there was a lot of coming and going of Jews between Portugal and the district around Toledo. When the persecution became more severe on each side of the border both the economic and political life began to fluctuate because neither the Kings nor the Inquisition maintained a permanently strict insistence on the ordinances. For example, García Sánchez was able to find in the Oropesa Archives that there was a great deal of *"coming and going."*

We know of the case of Hernandálvarez Tamayo, an illustrious man who was Jewish by race, since his mother was a Jewish girl, residing in the Arrabal of Montemor-O-Novo. His father was probably the Count of Oropesa, who was in the habit of going down from the Castle to pass amorous nights with the beautiful Jewish girls. Hernandálvarez was a young student at Salamanca, the expenses for his education were paid secretly by his father. The secret of the Count's propensity for visiting the girls of the Arrabal was openly rumoured both up in the walled part of town and below. Hernandálvarez was exiled in 1492 and crossed from Spain to Portugal where he settled at Evora. There be bought a house and used it to give refuge to persecuted Jews. Oropesans found help there. He even set up a Talmudic school. Evidently Hernandálvarez Tamayo maintained secret contact with the Conversos who remained at Oropesa, one of them being a natural son of the Count of the Castle like himself.

When the edict of expulsion was issued, it was found to be unenforceable and the Inquisition was not able to carry out the cleansing of the Jews and Conversos who returned to Judaism in Toledo and the immense region surrounding it. Classic writers have called Toledo *"the lordly mirror of Spain."* They say that: *"Toledo is to Spain, what the heart is to the human body."* However, I see significance in the symbolism of likening Toledo to *"the heart of Spain,"* even though Gómez Menor certainly defines it as having *"a Judeo-Christian population."* The ruling class contained *Conversos* families resulting from the intermingling of Christians and convert Jews. The merchant class was entirely made up of *Conversos*. The *Conversos* founded convents and supported hospitals. A good number of Toledo's friars and men of letters were *Conversos*. Well, what did the Inquisition do to this marvellous city?

Harsh treatment began all of a sudden and, as it gathered momentum, it swept all before it, including the Toledan merchant Sánchez de Toledo, the grandfather of Teresa of Avila. Teresa's grandfather saved himself from the Inquisition by voluntarily appearing before its tribunal and confessing himself guilty of practising Jewish rites. His sentence was the minimum enforced: that of *Sambenito*, which was the term given to penitents reconciled by the Inquisition. His punishment consisted of spending seven Fridays on the city streets. It is ironic to think that, should he have been burnt at the stake, his grand daughter would never have been born and we would be left without a saint. The tribunal of the Inquisition respected neither kings nor rogues.

Little by little the raging flood of the Inquisition began to rise yet Toledo continued to protect its *Conversos*. It truly functioned as the complete *"heart of Spain"* pumping through its veins blood *"of every colour."*

The lives of the family of Ciudad-Cidade, with their son João-Juan-John, centred on the *Camino Real* which linked Madrid-Toledo-Oropesa. After a distance of five centuries, it is exciting to pursue their trail even though it is rather a tedious one and has little assurance of results. But it is well worth the effort, so let us get on with our detective work.

Notes to Chapter 5

* [In this English translation the quotes from Francisco de Castro are from the English translation of the 1587 Granada edition of *Historia de la Vida*, etc. Cf. O'Grady-Castro, op.cit., chapters 1 & 3.]
* The passage of the Jeronymite friar from Guadalupe seeking alms at Montemor-O-Novo: A. A. Banha de Arande, *S. João de Deus na sua terra natal*, Evora, 1978, 10.
* The position of Caro Baroja: J. Caro Baroja, *Los judios en la España moderna y contemporánea*, II, Madrid 1962, 238-239. The account *"Treatise in favour of the Hebrew Nation"*, directed by Padre A. Vieira to Prince Pedro, in A. Vieira, *Obras escolhidas* IV, Lisbon 1951, 121. José Sánchez, in his recent study cited, agrees with the opinion of Caro Baroja but initially showed his reservations in *San Juan de Dios, Judeo?* Paz y Caridad (1963) 397. In the same vein: Rafael Ma. Saucedo *San Juan de Dios, Judeo?*: Paz y Caridad (1963) 482-489; ibid., 558-570. Saucedo came up with this unequivocal paragraph on his hard allegation against Vieira and Caro Baroja: *"It therefore so happens that St. John of God was the son of poor old legitimate Catholics, without any spot or impurity of Moorish, New Christians or any other suspect sect, blood."* To bolster his opinion he quotes the testimony of witnesses, as reported in the notes of Chapter 4. The interview with M. Gómez Moreno appeared in Paz y Caridad (1963) 47. For Magliozzi's position, in G. Magliozzi, *Pagine Juandediane*, Rome 1992, see *'La presunta ascendenza ebrea'* (p. 115-118).
* The research of García Sánchez and Gómez Menor has an incentive of maximum interest; they work in the area of Toledo and are very familiar with the facts concerned: J. García Sánchez, San Juan de Dios en *el Señorial de Oropesa*: Beresit 4 (1992) 93-113., *el Señorial de Oropesa*, unpublished, chapter XX. José Gómez Menor, apart from his major work *El linaje familiar de santa Teresa y de san Juan de la Cruz*, (the family lineage of St. Teresa and St. John of the Cross), Toledo 1970, I have read his latest works, *Vias de carne y tiempo* (Paths of flesh and time): Monte Carmelo 100 (1992) 375-434, and *Los antepasados judaizantes...* (Jewish ancestors) Bulletin of the Royal Academy of History I, 190 (1993) 13-30.
* The marriage contract between King Manuel (the Unfortunate) and the Infanta Isabella, is from *As Gavetas de Torre de Tombo*, Lisbon 1967. The attitude of King Manuel towards the Jews, is from D. De Goes, *Chronica d'el rei d. Manuel*, Lisbon 1909.

6

CASARRUBIOS
DEL MONTE
PRESENTS A SURPRISE

Please look up Casarrubios on the map, because here you will receive your first surprise. Casarrubios is situated on the old road that used to go down from Madrid towards Torrijos-Santa Olalla where it met up with the road to Toledo to become part of the Extremadura Camino Real. When the roads were improved and widened the plan called for it to digress slightly to the left, thereby cutting off Casarrubios del Monte to the advantage of Navalcarnero. Consequently, from then to the present day, when travelling the highway from Madrid to Badajoz, one passes through Navalcarnero, leaving Casarrubios sadly alone five kilometres to the left off the highway. The once flourishing town of Casarrubios del Monte is today only a shadow of its former self. When I went to Casarrubios there was a surprise awaiting me, and I am sure there is a surprise there in store for you too.

Casarrubios del Monte is a quiet town. The ruin of its ancient castle is the only relic of Casarrubios del Monte's past glory. I asked the parish priest how many inhabitants lived in the village, and he told me there were two thousand, excluding those living in the outlying areas. This young pastor has three churches to serve: the parish church, a chapel on the outskirts, and the church of the Cistercian nuns. Mother María Evangelista founded this convent in 1633. She had a reputation for sanctity and came to Casarrubios del Monte from Valladolid with thirty nuns. They must have made a pleasant sight as they chanted their prayers, in choir, behind the screen at the rear of the high altar. Unfortunately they were all poisoned by Colza oil, which the poor things had made themselves from wild Cole seed.

Casarrubios, 48 kilometres from Toledo and 50 from Madrid, is at the centre of a dry region: only a handful of market gardens that are watered by a small creek flowing from the Guadarrama River.

There is nowhere in Spain that is not affected by the European Common Market. But, as they informed me at Casarrubios, they are still waiting to reap the benefits of industrial development. I replied that it should not be very long in arriving since they were not too far from Madrid. "We should be so lucky," they replied.

In 1959, three years before Caro Baroja came across the forgotten pages of the Portuguese Jesuit Vieira, Vidal Benito

Revuelta had published a thirty page booklet dedicated to St. John of God in a series called *'Spanish Themes'*. His booklet presented yet another puzzle in reference to our saint. This was a report about Casarrubios del Monte that was made in the 1575 census ordered by Philip II.

The year 1575 was exactly 25 years after the death of St. John of God and six years before Francisco de Castro wrote his biography. Therefore it was not too far removed in time from the events that had taken place.

The census ordered by Philip II was called *"Historic-geographic Reports on the Towns of Spain"* and consisted of a set of questions that referred to the historic origin and circumstances of each locality, both large and small. It required information about each town's boundaries, climate, produce, etc. An official of the Kingdom collected the replies given by selected individuals in each place.

The official appointed by the Crown for Casarrubios del Monte was its parish priest, Gaspar de Arévalo. He asked for replies from three elderly citizens of the town, two men and a woman..

"I, Gaspar de Arévalo, parish priest of Casarrubios, hereby report, in accordance with the questions required of this town of Casarrubios by order of the very illustrious gentleman Doctor Busto de Villegas, Governor and General Administrator of the Archdiocese of Toledo."

The three elderly persons chosen to answer the questions all had good memories. They provided some very authentic data in the oral tradition.

Question number 38 asked what they could remember: *"about any persons who came from the village who were renowned for letters or military service, or any other thing, either good or evil. Or persons who had been born there or had left it; and to relate what they may know of their deeds and sayings; and any other commendatory accounts of that which may have occurred in the aforementioned village."*

The good old folk poured out a string of famous persons, and I guess they got a bit of help from their pastor who was able to consult the parish records. They said they knew *"many valiant gentlemen in the military, some in the cavalry, others in the infantry who had served well beyond this kingdom. And there were men who were principally known for letters and the Church who had gone forth and become famous."*

They named the professors: Córdoba, Gómez del Rincón, Francisco Núñez... and physicians, humanists, writers, lawyers, judges and counsellors of Castile. Some of them are quite notable in my opinion.

Amongst those noted for sanctity and doing good works, they named Garci Ximénez and Rodrigo de Vivar, both of whom had distributed their wealth to good causes before they died. They also listed the Jesuit, Juan Bautista; the friar, Gregorio Téllez; and the nun, María Evangelista. And, although he was not born at Casarrubios del Monte, they also mentioned Saint Simón de Rojas who was confessor to Philip III and came to the town to console the King who had fallen ill on a journey and was forced through his illness to remain there for several months.

Questions were asked about those who had recently died, and the report concluded with this surprising line: *"John of God, the one who founded the famous hospital of Granada."* (There you have it in black and white!), followed by, *"There are many other learned people, some dead, others living to this day."*

Beware of the temptation to dismiss too easily these words of Don Gaspar and his three old parishioners. They were speaking only 25 years after the death of St. John of God when his fame did not extend far beyond Granada but that of his hospital certainly did.

How did the people of Casarrubios del Monte get hold of his name? Did they borrow it instead of stealing that of some other saint? My ferret-like instinct forces me to take them seriously, even though I fear it leads me into a labyrinth.

On 30 April 1981 the Casarrubios del Monte Municipal Council declared certain buildings to be *"of local historic interest."* They are the Castle, the facade and the tower of the Gothic Palace, the ruins of the old parish church of San Andrés, the church of Santa María, the church and convent of the Cistercian nuns, the hermitage of La Virgen de la Salud [Our Lady of Health] and the town's *Gothic pillory*. Please note that I have put the pillory into italics, because there is a catch here, but we will come to that later. The Council also declared to be of artistic interest, a collection of paintings; and of historic interest, the more than forty volumes of manuscripts in the Municipality Archives, without forgetting the very well kept Parish Archives. The Town Councillors have in their grasp enough stimulating material to publish a history of Casarrubios del Monte simply based upon the documentation that they already possess. Casarrubios del Monte also claims to be, among other things, the birthplace of Juan Ciudad, known as St. John of God. These are only some of the notable features of this ancient town.

Asserting Casarrubios del Monte to be the birthplace of John of God actually has some credibility. When I was there, I met José Antonio Garay, the Town Clerk, who had accepted the challenge to study and write the local history. However, he lamented: *"This Municipality agrees, but it has forgotten one fundamental concern, because how can anyone write its history without having read everything contained in these archives? The first volumes were written in the 15th and 16th centuries, and only a specialist in ancient documents would be capable of carrying out such a task. It took us more than three years to simply make an inventory of these volumes."*

With good judgement Garay started with a rough outline and, as he progressed, his enthusiasm grew. This first rough draft, collecting and sorting all the relevant material, offered a treasure of historic data and allowed him to draw up an accurate picture of the ancient fiefdom of Casarrubios del Monte and its splendid past: the Medieval inclusion of the towns of Madrid and Casarrubios within the territory of Segovia, the lawsuit with the city of Segovia, the appeal to the Crown of Aragon; its mortgage by the territory of Estella; the part played by Gonzalo Chacón in the marriage of Isabella of Castile with Ferdinand of Aragon.

Garay put a splendid assortment of records together which he dedicated: *"To the most illustrious son of Casarrubios del Monte, born about 1498 (sic), greatly deprived in his childhood and youth because, according to all indications, he was illegitimate (sic) or, as is sometimes said, the son of a Jewish man and a Christian woman (sic). In any case, he was of Casarrubios del Monte and not of Portugal as has been claimed..."*

Garay's research did not come up with any more documents that referred to the census ordered by Philip II. The young parish priest showed me an enormous cabinet in which the ancient parish records are conserved. They were brought there centuries before from the ancient parish church of San Andrés that eventually fell into ruin. They have been stored here for centuries awaiting someone like Gómez Menor to browse through them, and rightly so, for these archives belong to the Toledo Archdiocese.

About half a dozen scholars have made a study of Casarrubios del Monte's claim to be the place of John of God's roots. They have come up with two hypotheses and, when all is said and done, both could be combined with the birth of the child João in Portugal.

To begin with, the first is fantasy. But it does not cause doubts about the baby having Jewish blood. It all happened at a time when Count Alverez de Toledo, the Lord of Oropesa, had large estates at Casarrubios del Monte. The administrator of the Count's estates lived in the Casarrubios Palace, where from time to time, he would entertain guests. Perhaps the papers documenting this activity still remain in one of the forty or more huge volumes within the Municipality's archives awaiting investigation by Garay. The Count, as you know, had few scruples in begetting children outside of the matrimonial bed; so there is quite a possibility that he was responsible for the pregnancy of a certain young woman of whom was born John of God. The Count was a friend of the Lord of Montemor-O-Novo, so he sent the pregnant girl there where she could deliver his illegitimate child far away from Casarrubios del Monte. When the baby grew into a young child, the Count had him brought to, and raised on, his own Oropesan estates. I do not want to further discuss this first hypothesis, since obviously it is quite flawed.

However, the second hypothesis is more risky than the first. It is supported by a proven fact recorded by the Toledo Inquisition. Señor Garey assures me that the following can be found in the Casarrubios del Monte Municipal Archives: *"in these years"* of 1498 the Inquisition of Toledo condemned a Jew *"for having made a Christian girl pregnant."*

As we put the bits of this jigsaw puzzle together, we are able to see a picture emerging. A certain Jew from Casarrubios del Monte was in love with a Christian girl. They loved each other deeply, but it was an impossible love. The girl became pregnant and the local people knowing the story, alerted the Inquisition at Toledo. The Jewish boy was arrested, tried and condemned to be executed at Casarrubios del Monte. Was it the Chacón family, which administrated the town, that was responsible for having the young Jew arrested?

Now let us return to consider the pillory. Why?, you may ask. When I was speaking about the historic monuments that the Municipality voted to conserve, I mentioned that there's more to the pillory. That's because it also served as a scaffold.

I was taken to the outskirts of the town where there stands a grisly stone column that looks as if it were once the upright for a cross, but there was no cross here. It was a gloomy and odious stone object. *"The whole of Casarrubios del Monte has known for centuries that the father of St. John of God was hung from this pillory."*

Where are the records of this trial by the Inquisition? Who knows? Maybe they are at Toledo, or perhaps in the Municipality or parish archives.

How does the story unfold? What about the Jewish boy and the pregnant Christian girl who was taken far away to have her confinement without shame? Was perhaps her destination Montemor-O-Novo? Did she give birth to a son? Was he kidnapped when he was about eight years old? Was he taken to Casarrubios del Monte? No, it was to Oropesa where nobody could link him with the drama that befell his parents.

I suppose I must put aside these questions without any further ado but, I must say, these two enormous archives at Casarrubios del Monte make me feel very uneasy.

As you can see, we met up with some difficulties at Casarrubios del Monte. Let the traveller now go back to where the highway turns off to Casarrubios del Monte at Valmojado. A hundred kilometres further on, in the direction of Portugal, the highway starts to follow the same route as the *Camino Real* and passes through Maqueda, Santa Olalla, Talavera, and Oropesa.

Oropesa hides family secrets about John of God, concerning his father, his mother, his birth and his flight from Montemor-O-Novo. Secrets which, as far as I am concerned, Francisco de Castro knew perfectly well. But Castro kept quiet about them. He hid them behind an impenetrable smokescreen, made up of hints here and suggestions there - just sufficient to mislead us.

In all probability, Castro's enigmatic opening sentence of his biography actually corresponds with the reality.

"John was of Portuguese nationality, from a village called Montemor-O-Novo." Castro does not say that he was born there, but

that *"he was of a certain nationality"* and from a village. He adds: *"Born of middle-class parents who were neither very rich nor poor. He grew up with his parents."*

Were they legitimate, natural, or adoptive parents? Castro does not give their first names or surnames.

"Until the age of eight years."

"From there, without their knowledge."

"He was taken away...", Castro then says *"he was taken to the town of Oropesa."* Once more we are confronted by the lack of clarity as Castro snares us with incomplete and less accurate information than we require to arrive at the truth of the matter. He gives us the stuff of legends.

Castro wanted to avoid talking about John of God's parents altogether. Their identity caused inconvenience for the figure of John of God. It would not assist the requirements of any future canonical process into sainthood because in those days there were implacable objections to impurity of blood. All her life, Teresa of Jesus had kept silent that the Inquisition had punished her grandfather. Likewise, John of the Cross kept his Jewish roots secret for similar reasons.

Two to three hundred thousand Conversos, scattered throughout the Iberian peninsular, with their intermarriages, in one generation alone, caused such a number of blood mixes that any family could be at risk of being brought before an investigation of the Inquisition. Purity of blood, that is to say, certainty that no Jewish blood contaminated the genealogy of a family, became a national obsession. There was proliferation of suspicion, accusation and revenge. Present studies of the trials of the Inquisition reveal the cruel pursuit that was suffered by illustrious persons of literature, politics and religion belonging to families that might have Jewish blood, either directly or indirectly. The Conversos were subject to suspicion and, from the start, were not thought to be genuinely converted. Therefore they were considered to be linked to secret plots against Spain and the Catholic religion.

Castro wanted, at all costs, to avoid having his hero seen in such a derogatory light. He was aware that any future beatification process of John of God would be terribly complicated if this news were made public. That is why he concealed the fact of John of God's Jewish descent. He also wanted to maintain John of God's reputation for holiness at Granada, which would have suffered a devastating blow if the truth had been revealed.

Because Castro was a biographer who strictly kept to "*investigating the truth*" about his subject and writing "*what we know for certain*", he would not allow himself to lie by saying that John of God had brilliant Old Christian parents who had no mixture of impure blood. The baroque biographers who came after him were not so honest and they affirmed these qualities in John of God without the slightest scruple. Castro quietly skimmed over all references to John of God's family. I believe he was not obliged to recount what he knew. He was writing about John and preferred to keep silence about his parents.

Following up what Castro intended from the start, the Jesuit Vieira was able to sift out the facts while he was in Rome. With the same tenacity that urged him to strive for justice for the Indians in Brazil and the Jews in Portugal, Vieira sought the truth about John of God's origins. He did this by gaining the confidence of persons associated with the canonisation process, persons who knew what was happening and who whispered the truth to him.

Of course there is some sadness in finding out that neither men nor their works are ever perfect: González Moreno, a Castro enthusiast and therefore a rigorous critic, affirms that the biography written by Castro, is irreproachable from the historical point of view.

Yes, he was not deceiving us; let us just say that he was putting us off the track. Perhaps we can throw some more light on this puzzle as we move on to Oropesa.

Notes to Chapter 6

* Casarrubios del Monte: P. Madoz, *Sagra de Toledo (La)*, in *Diccionario geográfico-estudíastico-histórico de España y sus posesiones de ultramar*, XIII, Madrid 1849, 617; Id., Casarrubios del Monte, in *ibid*. VI Id., Toledo, in *ibid*. XVI.
* Benito Revuelta, *San Juan de Dios* (col. 'Temas españolas' # 395), Madrid 1959.
* Garay, *Datos para la historia de la Villa y Señorio de Casarrubios del Monte* (photocopied), Casarrubios del Monte 1984. Id., *Casarrubios del Monte, una historia desconocida* (photocopied), Casarrubios del Monte 1988. Señor Garay is the Town Clerk of Casarrubios del Monte and is at the moment arranging to publish a brief report on his research. He says he has no doubt that the coincidence of the census ordered by Philip II and the execution of the Jew directly raises the drama of John of God. It is presumed that the girl was sent far away to deliver her child, for Garay has discovered in documents relating to the lawsuit between Casarrubios del Monte and Segovia a report printed in 1618 with references to the Jew who was executed for intercourse with a Christian.
* The complete text of the declarations of Casarrubios del Monte for the census of Philip II, in C. Viñas-R. Paz, Relaciones histórico-geográficas de los pueblos de España I, Madrid 1951, 255-267.
* G. Magliozzi, *Pagine juandediane*, Rome 1992, 111, has an hypothesis that the Count sent the girl to his estate at Casarrubios del Monte to avoid the scandal of her pregnancy, then the girl gave the child to a Portuguese couple to bring up outside Spain. He sent for the boy at Montemor-O-Novo when he was 8 years old and had him placed with the family of one of his tenants. Magliozzi admits that his hypothesis is more like a *TV soap opera*. The research undertaken by García Sánchez demonstrates that the Count of Oropesa did not have possessions or interests at Casarrubios del Monte.
* Maria Luis Morales, *Juan de Dios y sus aportaciones a la asistencia hospitalaria*, Madrid 1989 (doctrinal thesis at the Complutense University [Madrid] Faculty of Medicine, photocopied), 43. Morales considers the Casarrubios del Monte document absolutely trustworthy: *"Let us consider from now on that John of God was born at Casarrubios del Monte."*

7

THE SHEPHERD

Oropesa
Torralba de Oropesa
1503 - 1522

After his abduction from Montemor-O-Novo, the child João, now called Juan, mysteriously appeared in the Spanish town of Oropesa in the Province of Toledo. He remained here for the next twenty years, passing through childhood, adolescence and into manhood. He was to spend a further eight years at Oropesa, but we will return to this later on. Of his life span of 55 years, John of God spent almost 30 of them at Oropesa which, of course, was the longest period of his life. He was at Granada for 16 years but he lived 29 years at Oropesa.

It does seem strange that Oropesa should have had no connection with Juan's family mystery. Maybe the information that Castro wanted to cover up lies concealed in some hiding place at Oropesa and is just waiting to be discovered. I nurture the hope that this may be so.

Although it is a long time since these events occurred, Oropesa still offers the possibility of being a rich source of precious information.

Viewed from the highway to Extremadura, Oropesa Castle appears like a painting of an idyllic scene of centuries long ago. From the vantage point high up in the Castle there is a great view of the picturesque countryside called the Arañuelo, so named after the spider grub that infested the district.

El Arañuelo takes in the flat lands between the River Tagus to the south and the Tiéjar to the north, a fringe in a strategic position. With Talavera and Toledo on the right and Extremadura on the left, the Arañuelo occupies the central section of the old road and conserved its position linked with the north where it was politically and religiously integrated into the province of Avila. The landscape is attractive along the banks of the river Tiétar that flows through the Arañuelo into the narrow mountain pass of the beautiful Sierra Gredos, then on to the lower Sierra Aguila where the hill known as the Puerta del Pico looks down upon Avila. There was much communication in those days between Avila, Talavera and Oropesa. Well, what occurred in its history?

From 1081 to 1085, just prior to the taking of Toledo by King Alfonso VI of Castile, Count Raymond of Burgundy, husband of Doña Urraca the daughter of the monarch who constructed the walls of Avila, crossed the Gredos Mountains from north to south. He passed over the

Tiétar and descended with his soldiers to the banks of the Tagus, a strategy that cut off the support the Moors of Badajoz had given to the Arab King of Toledo. Alfonso VI took Toledo in 1085. The Count of Burgundy, who loved building fortifications, never got paid for his part in the building of the marvellous city walls of Avila. The Count went south and settled on the hill of Oropesa, which made an ideal lookout over the Arañuelo. This strategic spot, centred between the Tagus and the Gredos, was ideal for defending the north from the waves of invading North African Almoravides in the 11th century and their successors, the Almohade Moors of the 12th. Thus the district around Oropesa became dependent on the military power of Avila for its defence.

The Arañuelo used to belong to the Diocese of Avila in respect to ecclesiastical jurisdiction. This was because Avila was a permanent base for the Castilian military forces and its Cathedral Chapter had the support of Compostella against the powerful new Archbishop of Toledo. Avila's Oropesa enclave lasted right up to the mid- 20th century, when the Archbishop of Toledo assumed it in 1955, cutting the Diocese of Avila back to the other side of the Tiétar and the Alardos narrows.

This area quickly became depopulated as the reconquest of Spain moved south: Oropesa was a village unclaimed by anyone and was without fame or glory. Alfonso X intended to repopulate it but he had little success due to the troubles that occurred during the early part of the 14th century. The Hunting Book of Alfonso XI referred to these lands as abounding with "bears and wolves."

A new age in the history of Oropesa began in the middle of the 14th century, when Enrique II bestowed the title of 'First Lord of the Town' upon García Alverez de Toledo. The First Lord took possession of Oropesa and a dozen of the surrounding villages and lands around it.

I want to pay special attention to one of these villages – Torralba. García Alverez de Toledo accompanied the king on his push to the south but, before he left, he appointed a capable governor and instructed him to build a new castle and to keep the town safe. According to the historian García Sánchez, the title Lord of Oropesa had been used before by six successive Basque lords, thus Alverez de Toledo really became the seventh. Four more lords succeeded him, the last being the twelfth Lord of Oropesa, Ferdinand III of the House of Alverez de Toledo.

This Ferdinand Alverez de Toledo was barely a child when he sent his armed followers to join the forces of Queen Isabella against Beltraneja. Once more Oropesa's strategic position rendered valuable service because it cut off communication between Beltraneja's ally, Archbishop Alfonso Carrillo of Toledo, and the city of Plasencia which at that time was the chief source of Portuguese help against the Crown of Castile.

Queen Isabella was at Seville when, on 30 August 1477, she rewarded the Lord of Oropesa by granting him the title of Count. Thus Ferdinand Alverez de Toledo became the first Count of Oropesa.

The protection of the Queen continued and the new Count proceeded to push the development of the wool trade and defend the grazing lands which were the foundation of the local economy. During his reign, in 1492, the expulsion of the Jews occurred and, with this, we come to the years of John of God's childhood.

There were two Counts of Oropesa while John of God lived there. Ferdinand who was the first Count of Oropesa, and his son Francisco who succeeded him. But before we move on to find out more about them, let us recall that Oropesa was situated on the 'Camino Real' that went from Toledo to Extremadura. By tracing a horizontal line between these two places, and a vertical one between Puente del Arzobispo and Avila, we find Oropesa as the epicentre of famous places of interest: Trujillo, Talavera, Guadalupe and Yuste – all of which radiated from Oropesa. Francisco de Toledo y Figuera, son of the second Count, was a famous Oropesan who became the 5th Viceroy of Peru.

The Counts of Oropesa became involved in the national life of Spain and transferred their residence from Oropesa to Madrid at the beginning of the 17th century. From then on they began to neglect the interests of Oropesa, which of course affected the welfare of the peasants who worked their estates. The Crown granted independence to the Count's towns and villages and was generously reimbursed for them. Manuel Joaquín, the 8th Count of Oropesa, joined the Austrian faction during the War of Succession. He was Captain General of Toledo and Prime Minister in the reign of Charles II. As he was on the losing side in the war, he felt the full force of the reprisals of Philip V who confiscated all his lands. From exile in Vienna, his son, the 11th Count, pleaded for pardon, which Philip V granted him "with royal benevolence" and returned his lands to him. The Oropesa Municipal Council was established in the early 19th century. When Doña María del Pilar, widow of the 13th Count, died without issue the right of succession to Oropesa passed to the Duke de Frías.

During his twenty years at Oropesa, John of God would scarcely have known Count Ferdinand – if he even saw him, because the first Count of Oropesa died at the beginning of autumn in 1504, when Juan had hardly been there a year.

Because of the decree signed by his protector Queen Isabella, Don Ferdinand was compelled to expel the Jews from his lands, but certainly he was not very happy about it. García Sánchez estimates that there were approximately 600 persons at Oropesa before the massacres of 1391, after which there were about 250. They lived on the outskirts of the town while the upper class, theoretically *Old Christians* and composed mainly of gentlemen farmers, servants of the Count and soldiers, lived within the town walls. The Jews, meanwhile, lived in the outlying Arrabal, separated from the rest of the town by the *Camino Real* that passed through Oropesa. This part of the town also contained some families of *Mudéjeras*, the name given to the Moslems who lived under Christian rule. Therefore the Oropesans were divided into two distinct sections, the privileged class within the town walls, and those who lived in the Arrabal, Jews and Moslems, who secretly practised their religion. The Jews contributed to swelling the Royal coffers by paying taxes and occasionally making loans. When Oropesa passed from being a royal town to that of a *señorio,* that is, under the rule of the Count, the Alvarez de Toledo family inherited this *Jewish financial protection.*

The Jews were greatly involved in the business life of Oropesa. Consequently when the order came to expel them the commerce of Oropesa was greatly damaged and, naturally, Don Ferdinand's own financial interests suffered as a result. It is also on record that Don Ferdinand had other interests in the Jewish quarter – "amorous ones." Seduced by the beauty of the young Jewish girls he used to go down from the Castle to visit them in the Arrabal and, as a result, sired quite a few illegitimate children. Yes that is so, and he had them all baptised and given names that would record their origins. He sent the boys to study at Salamanca, and amongst the natural sons he fathered were two famous friars. One was the Franciscan, Hernando de la Plaza, a cantankerous man

119

who preached against others of his race. The other was Fray Hernando de Talavera, a holy *Converso* called to great things at the side of Queen Isabella. The chronological account of the illegitimate birth of Fray Hernando interests me greatly. The account provides insufficient time between the age of the Count and the famous friar's ordination to the priesthood. In his unpublished manuscript García Sánchez shows that the presumed father of Fray Hernando de Talavera was actually not the first Count of Oropesa, but rather his grandfather Don García. This confusion in the allegation rather indicates the nonchalance of the noble masters of Oropesa Castle with regard to their sexual escapades.

The Count's affinity with the Jews had a curious underpinning within the Castle itself. The Count's first marriage was to Doña María de Mendoza who died without children. He then married Doña María Pacheco, one of the most notable women during the reign of Queen Isabella – La Católica. María Pacheco, daughter of the Marquis de Villena who was a favourite of Enrique IV, came from a Converso family. So, the Count was married to a Converso woman.

Of course, the expulsion decree did not touch the Countess. After all she was a convert, not a Jew. Married at the age of twenty, she had been a lady-in-waiting to Queen Isabella. The Countess gave birth to nine children. A son became a priest and four daughters became nuns at the Conceptionist convent. Beatriz de Silva who was a companion of the Countess when they were together serving in the household of the Queen founded this convent at Oropesa. Francisco, the firstborn son of the Countess, became the second Count of Oropesa.

Although Don Ferdinand was disgusted at the command to expel the Jews, he nevertheless derived some benefit from it. The majority of Oropesa's expelled Jews took the *Camino Real* that led directly to Portugal. When they left Oropesa their homes and properties were taken over by the Count. He distributed some of these properties amongst his favourites but he kept the best of them, including the synagogue, for himself.

The Catholic Monarchs allowed the nobility to keep the valuables of the Jews. This was the norm for the whole of Spain. It was compensation to the nobility for their loss of taxes and income due to the banishment of such a great number of Jews.

The situation became more complicated when the Jews from Oropesa reached Portugal. Some embarked for North Africa where the majority expired. But many remained in Portugal and were baptised in the hope that they might return once more to Oropesa as *Conversos*, which continued the interchange between Alentejo and the Arañuelo of Oropesa. This proceeded in such a way that the Holy Office was never quite able to work out whether the repatriated were truly *Conversos* or merely cryptic Jews. Count Ferdinand saw all this going on and he wanted them to return and he recognised that he was legally obliged to restore to them their confiscated estates.

The "coming and going" of Jewish families or *Conversos*, between Castile and Portugal, casts important light on the *secret vicissitudes* of Andrés Ciudad-Cidade and his son Juan-João, who obviously were not Martians who had just dropped out of the Cosmos, as Castro would have liked us to believe. They were real persons who had their roots in Oropesa and Montemor-O-Novo. Were they involved in any way in the "comings and goings"?

The boy Juan came from Montemor-O-Novo. It was from there that "they took him" in the year 1503 when he was eight years of age. When Don Ferdinand Alvarez De Toledo died in 1504, his son Francisco Alvarez De Toledo y Pacheco succeeded him and became the second Count of Oropesa. His father had arranged for him to marry Doña Maria de Figueroa, daughter of the Count de Feria.

Count Francisco Alvarez de Toledo y Pacheco was a fine man and a good son to his mother María Pacheco. He was a faithful vassal of the Emperor Charles V, once he put behind him his fickleness in supporting Padilla in the uprising of the Castilian *Comuneros*. Charles V was disposed to punish him by having the walls of his castle demolished. The Count obtained pardon for his error. From then on Charles relied on him and we will see the Count sending his retainers to the battles of the Emperor.

Oropesa prospered under the administration of Don Francisco, 2nd Count of Oropesa, who died in the year 1542. When the 2nd Count died, the child Juan had spent 19 of his 28 years under his command, while he only lived one year, 1503 to 1504, during the life of the 1st Count, Don Ferdinand.

No one knows whether the child Juan and the first Count ever met each other. Probably not, because this Count was not a very pleasant man nor was he disposed to mix with his vassals, especially if they were poor. Obviously the case of Juan did not attract his attention, and why should it, since, after all, he was merely a lad without a history who went out to guard sheep on the Arañuelo.

That former age of splendour has left some traces of glory at Oropesa. Travellers driving along the highway are often tempted to stop briefly and get out of their cars to admire the picturesque Castle. My advice to them is to give in to the temptation.

The first thing that attracted me was the town's enigmatic heraldic shield that I was informed dates back to a legend of medieval origin. Emblazoned upon the town's heraldic shield is the story of how Oropesa got its name. The Romans had already called it *Comedium Orbis* because it is situated *'in the middle'* of the Iberian Peninsula. Well, more or less in the middle!

Upon the heraldic shield is the image of a damsel standing on the castle battlements holding a cross in her left hand and a set of scales in her right. There is a tree opposite the cross, which refers to the Arañuelo forest, which alas, is no more. Tradition says the Arabs captured the young lady and demanded her ransom from the Knights Templar. The amount of the ransom was to be as much gold as she weighed. A giant balance was constructed and the young lady sat on one of its plates, while gold was piled upon the other. Finally both damsel and gold were evenly balanced and the beautiful captive was liberated. She was worth her weight in gold. And that is how Oropesa got its name [*oro* being Spanish for 'gold', and *pesa* meaning 'weight', consequently *Oropesa = weight in gold*].

The present population of Oropesa is 3,500 inhabitants. When you walk through its streets you can easily pick out the traces of the town's walls that divided it into two sections. The Navarro Plaza was made by demolishing the houses owned by a wealthy Jew of the Arrabal, Menahem Navarro. There are about a dozen religious houses and palaces in the town, all of which go back centuries in Oropesa's history. Today there are gift shops specialising in the sale of lace and ceramics.

In our times the Castle has been converted into a national *parador* [one of a chain of hotels run by the Spanish Department of Tourism]. With medieval grace, its fine tower rises victorious from the threat of destruction issuing from the Emperor's anger. There are still remnants of the earlier Arab Palace standing next to

Alvarez de Toledo's Castle. Of course, both palace and castle have been restored and reborn as the charming parador, which recently won the coveted 'Our Europe' tourist award.

On the morning of one Palm Sunday I had an appointment with Don Julio García Sánchez at his home in Lagartera. This village is nationally renowned on account of its skilled women who do fine embroidery and sell it from their homes. They are not exactly 'embroiderers' but rather 'needle-workers' which, as Don Julio explained to me, has a subtle difference:

"There are three essential verbs here. 'Coser' [to sew] means joining pieces together to make a whole and this is what dressmakers, seamstresses and tailors do.

'Bordar' [to embroider] originally meant to reinforce edges and the outline of the garments. This evolved into making the borders the main feature of the piece. Embroidery was all the fashion in mediaeval Europe. Embroiderers had plenty of work and there were famous schools of embroidery such as those of the Jeronymites at Guadalupe and Cisneros at Toledo. Trimming with embroidery always enhanced and widened the garment.

'Labrar' [to work] in a certain context has always been understood as a feminine activity, refrerring to the joining of cut out pieces of cloth in a pattern that incorporates designs of fauna and flora with a slight touch of colour. The embroiderers of Lagartera have been doing this work for centuries, in fact since the end of the 15th century. Queen Isabella started a lacemaking school at Alcázares in Seville. She gathered together a group of Labranderas of Moorish origin, and eventually some moved to Toledo. But the workshop of Lagartera, begun by Isabella's Moorish girls from Seville, is the only one to survive."

Lagartera is a small village and is only a stone's throw from Oropesa. Don Julián lives here in a charming cottage that is really a small museum of the special wonders of the Arañuelo. Julián is a native of the village, he is world travelled, and is an expert on the history of the Arañuelo. He showed me the treasures he keeps in his home, amongst which is a file he keeps on John of God. He has published some of the research he has carried out on John of God in the magazine *Beresith* which is published by the Toledan International Fraternity of Researchers.

Don Julián García Sánchez is a tenacious researcher with a nose like a bloodhound for sniffing out important clues to be discovered in historical documents. He has carried out research, quietly and over a period of many years, in the archives of the Oropesa Municipality, the parishes of Oropesa, Lagartera, Torralba de Oropesa, the Province of Toledo and the National Historic Archives. As a result he has located, with some certainty, the family which took in the little boy, Juan, when he arrived from Montemor-O-Novo. Here are his findings.

First of all Don Julián García Sánchez began his research from a reasonable base. He discovered that the ancient documents made very little reference to the town of Oropesa, or the Oropesa Arrabal, but called it instead "the Fiefdom of Oropesa." This means the township of Oropesa and its twelve surrounding villages that were granted by King Enrique II to *"the First Lord of the town"*, García Alverez de Toledo, in the 14th century.

You will recall that I have already mentioned a place called Torralba de Oropesa. This village is situated on the plain to the left of Oropesa and today the highway runs right through it.

I will refer now to the statements made by witnesses at Oropesa at the Beatification Process of John of God in 1623. While two witnesses declared that they had known him personally, the others said that they had not.

I note in each declaration three levels. One level is that of information given by the witness, certain or doubtful, whether firsthand knowledge or hearsay. The next level, interesting but debatable, relates to a visit which, according to local tradition, John of God made to Oropesa, (after his charitable works at Granada had already gained him a reputation for holiness), where he did exactly as he did at Granada. This makes one cautious about these stories. The third level is what the witnesses had heard from the pulpits from enthusiastic preachers narrating the life and miracles of John of God.

This latter is illustrated by the Jesuit priest, Gabriel de Vasas, who was a native of Oropesa residing in Madrid: *"When I was thirty years of age I heard Doctor Francisco Ruiz preach (at Oropesa) ...during a fiesta... the doctor told the people that they were fortunate and favoured in that Brother John of God had grown up in their village of Oropesa"*.

Preachers told the story of the saint from beginning to end even though he was not canonised. The Oropesans really made his story their own, adding their own direct knowledge of events to it and speaking about it to anyone who was willing to listen.

A wizened old man named Francisco González, contributed this gem. He said besides being John of God: *"the brother was called by another name, here they called him John of Hopefulness."* The old man's title, 'Hopefulness', would go well in a poem.

I feel that I have to correct yet another mistake of our friend Castro, whose memory I venerate and to whom researchers on John of God have so much reason to be grateful. Without the biography by Castro we would be left adrift.

I am sure this new mistake is not intentional, any more than his *'kidnapping'* from Montemor-O-Novo was. It is simply that Castro wrote his book 40 years before the Beatification Process, therefore he was completely unaware of the statements that would be made by the witnesses at Oropesa. This is what he wrote:

" *...and from there (Montemor-O-Novo), without their knowing it, he was taken by a cleric to the village of Oropesa where he lived for a long time in the house of a good man called El Mayoral."*

Well, the *"good man"* did not have the surname Mayoral at all; some biographers have conferred on him a Christian name and two surnames, Francisco Cid Mayoral.

García Sánchez says the surname Mayoral was common right throughout the Fiefdom of Oropesa. Four witnesses attributed the fostering of the Portuguese child to a certain Señor Mayoral. However, these witnesses qualified their statements with *"so they say"* and *"so one has heard."* Then in contrast to this, the remainder of the witnesses clearly and positively state that Juan was taken into the Herruz family, the head of which was a gentleman named Francisco de Herruz.

Now we meet a witness who was no less than the great-grand-daughter of Francisco de Herruz himself. She is Maria de Vergara Herruz y Navas, the daughter of Captain Francisco Herruz and 50 years of age when the scribe of the Process recorded her statement: *"She heard it said by her father, who is now deceased 14 years, but lived to be 70 years of age, that the blessed man lived in this town. Although he is not yet declared so, this witness wanted to say 'blessed' John of God, and that he was in the service of her paternal great grandfather, of whom she said (the great grandfather) was 'so-and-so' Herruz, because she does not actually know his name."*

In clarification of this Father Gabriel de Vasas, being a

Jesuit, carefully stated: *"He came from Portugal as a child of tender years and was taken in by some gentlefolk of high standing whose family belonged to the town of Oropesa and was called 'so-and-so' Herruz de Naba."*

The Jesuit went on to say this about the Herruz family: *"They employed him as a shepherd lad for the flocks. Often shepherds and shepherd boys were placed under the charge of a mayoral [overseer] who stood in for the owner [of the flock]."*

This means that our good friend Castro made his error through the use of a *paronym*: a word with two meanings. *Mayoral* with a capital M is a surname, but *mayoral* without a capital is the chief of the shepherds, in other words, the overseer. Castro mistook the profession for the surname, and subsequent biographers did likewise.

To sum up, the child Juan was taken away from Portugal and was taken in by the Herruz family. Let's see who were the members of this Herruz family with whom John of God lived for 20 years.

Don Julián García Sánchez knows all about the Herruz family. This is the great fruit of his research that he has permitted me to examine. He has drawn up a genealogical tree of four generations of Herruz.

Francisco de Herruz, "man of arms", "captain" and "servant of the King" took part in the capture of Granada. He came, apparently in flight, to Torralba de Oropesa, the village situated on the plain protected by Oropesa Castle. The story went that he was a fugitive from justice for a crime he had committed. In reality, after being tried and condemned to *'hang from the gibbet'*, his relatives paid a financial penalty and had him released. And so he came to settle here with his possessions. Francisco de Herruz was born at Trujillo in Extremadura and came to Torralba early in 1500. Here he married Catalina Nazarena, a young lady from Villacastín who was then living at Torralba. The couple had six children, the first born in 1509 and the last in 1522. All this information comes from the National Historical Archives, thanks to a document showing that Francisco's grandson, who was a Jeronymite friar, aspired to the title of 'Associate of the Holy Office', an obligation of the Inquisition.

Herruz was a *hidalgo*, the title given to a wealthy free

gentleman. He was rich and clever with few scruples when it came to business matters, so it is small wonder that he did so well. He became the Mayor of Torralba but, because of his self interest, he was unpopular. Rumours were then invented about him saying that he was the son of Moors. In spite of such rumours, his family lived comfortably and had servants. Herruz even bought two slaves and had them baptised in the parish church giving them the Christian names of Pedro and Catalina.

Herruz employed a man named Francisco whom he placed in charge of his farm and flocks. This was the overseer, or the *mayoral*.

When Juan de Herruz, Francisco's eldest child was born in 1509 our young Portuguese, João, now Juan, had already been working for six years as a shepherd lad guarding the flocks. We have no idea how the child Juan fell in with the Herruz family. If Castro had only given us some hint!

Like his father when he was young, Juan de Herruz had a military career and went on to obtain the position of the Count's major-domo at his palace. The dashing young Herruz soon gained popularity with the Count's family and the upper-class citizens of the town.

Meanwhile, the child Juan Ciudad was growing up among sheep and farm labourers, servants and slaves. From Castro we know that Juan tried to please and serve his mayoral: *"He endeavoured as a shepherd to please the good man just mentioned, for as long as he remained in his house. His employers were very fond of him and he was loved by all."* He used to have to go back and forth between the house and the flocks: *"His particular job was to fetch supplies and other things that the shepherds needed."*

Our Juan grew from eight to fifteen years of age. Meanwhile Spain was awaiting the arrival of that child called Charles who was born in Flanders at the turn of the century. His destiny was to be ruler of a considerable part of the then known world. Queen Isabella had died and King Ferdinand was guiding Spain during the time his grandson Charles was growing up. Ferdinand's Spain, now united and powerful, peacefully passed from Queen Isabella to her grandson Charles.

This was mainly thanks to Ferdinand and the gaunt Franciscan friar Jiménez de Cisneros, Archbishop of Toledo. But while these two tolerated each other, it appears that the king detested the friar and vice versa. Nevertheless both men put the interests of Spain above their personal animosities.

When Philip the Fair died, in 1506, and Juana was so mentally unbalanced that history will remember her as Joan the Mad, the six year old infant Charles, son of the unfortunate marriage, was now entitled to the crown of Castile. There was no Regent to take charge of the affairs of state until that obscure infant, born of an Austrian father and a Spanish mother, and residing far away in the pallid duchies of Flanders, would come of age.

Immediately after the death of Philip the Fair, the Archbishop of Toledo, Jiménez de Cisneros, convoked an assembly of the nobles to organise a Regency Council. He sent an urgent message to King Ferdinand of Aragon who was aboard ship at the time and halfway between Barcelona and Naples. The message asked the King to return at once and take possession of the kingdom that the Gran Capitán had conquered for the Crown of Aragon. Ferdinand was well aware of the cunning scheme of Cisneros. Ferdinand had made a pact with his archenemy Louis XII of France when Queen Isabella died, and asked him for his niece's hand in marriage. The lady in question was the eighteen year old Germana de Foix, and the Spanish King's offer to the King of France was a dowry of half the kingdom of Naples. Ferdinand was already 54 years old, but Louis XII was only too happy to send him his young niece in exchange for a French presence at Naples.

Ferdinand received the news of the death of Philip the Fair at Portofino on the Italian border and was handed the letter from Cisneros urgently recalling him to Spain as Regent. The King knew why Cisneros was in such a hurry. The infant Charles, besides having a maternal grandfather, namely Ferdinand, logically had a paternal grandfather who was none other than Maximilian I, Emperor of Austria. Maximilian was claiming the Regency of Castile as his right, until his grandson reached his majority. Ferdinand replied to Cisneros that he would finish his business at Naples as quickly as he could, then he would make haste to return to Spain.

As soon as he met his new spouse at Naples, Ferdinand returned to Castile where he arrived in mid-August 1507. He received Cisneros and gave him the Cardinal's hat that he had brought back with him from Rome. A handful of nobles, the favourites of the deceased Philip the Fair, tried to create problems by putting forward the candidature of the Emperor Maximilian as Regent of Castile, but Ferdinand promptly thwarted them.

All dressed up in his cardinal's finery, Cisneros still thought of himself as an ascetic friar. He put the income he received from the Archdiocese of Toledo aside for a glorious opportunity he anticipated. When Ferdinand returned, Cisneros handed him eight million *maravedis* [a currency of varying value] which, during the first years of his Regency, the King used to fortify Spanish bases along the North African coast. The Spaniards aimed to sweep the Moorish pirates from the Mediterranean and to free the southern ports of Spain from the constant menace of their raids. The Spanish fought with varying fortunes, they won some brilliant battles like that of Oran, and they lost some, like the terrific reverse they suffered on the island of Djerba at the entrance to the Gulf of Gabes.

At first glance we can see two divergent destinies. One is that of the pampered boy Charles in Flanders, and the other is that of the boy Juan caring for the sheep of Señor Herruz, mayor of the humble village of Torralba de Oropesa. I ask myself if their guardian angels were aware of the path mapped out for each young man by Providence. I would like it to be so, for I dare say that while these boys were sleeping at night, the angels of Charles and Juan might have got to know each other at some celestial social gathering. Two distinct destinies: Charles to be the Emperor, and Juan... who knows!

If you so wished, you could tell me that all that we know about John of God from his eighth to his twentieth year can fit into a thimble. The *mayoral Francisco*, whose surname was probably Vázquez, set little Juan to work helping the shepherds who looked after the flocks of their master, Francisco de Herruz. As a lad, Juan worked as a roustabout and I dare say that when he grew up he too became a shepherd. This period of his life is a black hole that biographers have rushed to fill from their vivid imaginations. I for one can tell you that when it comes to writing someone's life story, it is a shame to come upon a gap of twenty years. Well, at the moment it is twenty years, but we will be returning to Oropesa later when Juan will spend a further nine years there. Thanks to Castro we do know that the total number of years added up to twenty-nine. Castro indicates that Juan's work was appreciated and that, *"without parents and at a tender age"*, he tried to earn the confidence of his masters and *"served with great diligence all the time that he remained in their home."* His masters, for their part, saw nothing but good in what the boy did. *"His masters were well disposed towards him and he was loved by all..."*

Castro also quotes these words in italics but he does not say if the man, *"who was well-disposed towards him"*, was in fact the *mayoral*, his immediate overseer or Señor Herruz, his master. It seems it could well be both, and the farm labourers and other shepherds were amongst *all those* who loved him.

Now that this is established, let me remind you that we also know precious little about Our Lord Jesus Christ's first thirty years at Nazareth, other than that he grew in age and wisdom before God and men and that he was the helper of an artisan, perhaps a carpenter. The Evangelists do not say very much about Jesus, but the apocryphal writers invented prodigies, sometimes very beautiful ones, in order to enrich these silent years. In this way, the life of John of God by Castro can be said to be similar to the Gospel, while other apocryphal authors filled up the gap in John of God's life with false miracles.

There were shepherds caring for their flocks throughout the Arañuelo that spread from the fields at the foot of the Castle to the banks of the creeks that flowed into the Tiétar and upwards into the shrubby pastures of the foothills of the Sierra Aquila. This was pasture country and the work was hard. The land produced wheat, barley, olive-oil and wine, and the acorns that abounded were eagerly eaten by the sheep, goats, pigs and cows that grazed the Arañuelo. Madoz writes that hunting was good and that hares and grouse were plentiful. At times wolves came down from the mountains to these pastures. There were windmills for grinding the wheat and crushing olives for oil, and apples, cherries and plums grew profusely. Winters were freezing, summers scorching, and if the creeks dried up there was plenty of cool water to be had from the wells.

The life of a labourer or shepherd in those days was quite uneventful. Who would ever have imagined the noise of modern traffic that now rushes along the highway between the Tiétar and the Tagus. These humble people used to live in houses made of mud and rubble, a few were made of brick and all were at ground level. It was another story within the walls of the town. Here there were luxurious mansions, churches, convents and the palaces of the gentry, not to mention the Castle itself. The home of the Herruz family at Torralba de Oropesa was a splendid stone building. On days when the shepherd Juan ate in the house he would take his meals with the domestic servants in the large dining room reserved for them. Feastdays and the occasional excursion broke the monotony of the yearly activities. On the occasions when the Count rode out with his retainers to wage war, horsemen would come riding down from the hills at a gallop to join him. In the servants' dining room the main subject of conversation was about the young men from the area who had embarked for the Indies.

It requires some effort today to imagine what it was like to be a shepherd in those times. I see Juan, first as a lad, then as a man, with his leather bag at his side and blanket folded over his shoulder, with his shepherd's crook in his hand driving the flock before him. Juan sits keeping guard over the sheep, gazing up into the clouds now and then, while grazing cows passed by. Did he sing the popular songs of the day? What were his thoughts, did he fantasise, pray, think about man and God? Juan, always alone from dawn to dusk spending endless hours under the open sky, taking refuge from the occasional storm, sheltering in the shade from the heat of summer, and in winter from the snow. What went on within him? What was he thinking? What sort of shepherd was he, a rustic, or a philosophical one? Maybe he was like one of those austere biblical shepherds who were aware of God's presence at their side in a breath of the wind?

I give up! Who could possibly know what goes on in anyone's mind, let alone one who spent twenty years as a lonely shepherd. If there are still any shepherds around these days, I would image they probably have the earphones of a transistor plugged into their ears. Certainly, it would be a lifestyle vastly different from the days of long ago.

Some of the apocryphal biographies have presumed that during his early years at Oropesa, or better to say Torralba de Oropesa, Juan went to school. Don't tell me that there was a school in that humble village in the Arañuelo, a village that consisted mainly of shepherds! What school? All would have lived a Christian life and practised the Catholic faith, that is for certain. Juan learned to read, and we will later see him as a seller of books, but I have not the faintest idea where or when he learned this skill.

What went on inside Juan? Between the ages of eight and twenty, he would have experienced the vacillations, fears and anxieties that we have all experienced. There he was - in his solitude; a shepherd for twenty years under the open sky just watching the clouds pass by.

The question that remains unanswered is the one about his parents. We must ask ourselves how the relationship between John and his parents was ruptured, if indeed it was. How is it that Herruz or Francisco, the mayoral, did not search them out?

These are questions that have no answers, because we come up against Castro's sealed lips.

Juan certainly admired the second Count, Don Francisco, who governed Oropesa from 1504, the year after Juan arrived as a little boy from Montemor-O-Novo, until he left the Arañuelo in 1542.

The ancient chronicles continuously declare the virtues of Count Francisco, saying that he was virtuous, patriotic and charitable. His wife María died after only six years of marriage, leaving him with three children. She left a will bequeathing six thousand maravedis to have a hospital built. When writing his own will and testament Don Francisco added a further sum for the construction of this hospital. He ordered that the hospital be built close to the palace door; *"so that the Counts of Oropesa may never forget to hold the poor close to their hearts."* This was true, at least for Count Francisco, who throughout his life was generous to the poor. He established communal wheat silos and a bank to lend money to aid them when a terrible drought struck the Arañuelo during the first part of the 16th century. He dictated that upon his tomb this sentence should be engraved: *"Here lies buried the Count of Oropesa, Don Francisco Alvarez de Toledo, who died imploring God for mercy."*

Count Francisco knew how to get along with the Crown. He only had one bad moment, and a very dangerous one at that. When the *Comuneros* of Castile rose up against the Emperor Charles, the Count of Oropesa threw in his lot with the Castilian communes. The young Emperor forgave the Count and although he threatened to have the battlements of his castle demolished, he relented. Oropesa's historian, García Sánchez, says that henceforth Oropesa remained loyal to the Emperor and took his side in the war of succession against the Beltraneja faction, and also against the *Comuneros*.

Cardinal Cisneros died in 1517 and Charles hastened to

leave Flanders for Spain. Spain's internal turmoil, which had been going on for centuries throughout the middle ages, came to a halt between 1515 and 1522 when the new *Austrian era* opened under the sceptre of Charles V.

After uniting Navarra with the Crown of Castile, Ferdinand the Catholic began to show visible signs of fatigue. Theoretically he could have arranged for two good allies at the diplomatic table of Europe. One was his son-in-law Henry VIII of England who was married to Catherine of Aragon who was, as the chronicles of the Catholic Monarchs affirm, "the most beloved daughter of Ferdinand and an exact image of Isabella." The other was his fifteen-year-old grandson Charles, who had taken over the reign of Flanders and was the heir to the Austrian Empire. If the son-in-law and the grandson were to come to his aid, Ferdinand would be able to give a good lesson to the King of France.

Neither gave him any help whatsoever. It happened that the King of France, Luis XII, who was a personal enemy of Don Ferdinand despite his astute marriage with his niece Germana de Foix, died leaving as successor an impetuous boy who took the name of Francis I. Don Ferdinand just could not understand these young men at all. His grandson Charles had signed a pact of friendship with the French King Francis who, feeling himself safe behind the chain of the Alps, had sent a large army into the northern Italian provinces. By the time the Pope and his friends, among them Don Ferdinand, wanted to do something about it, Francis I of France had already taken Milan. Pope Leo X was terrified by the French military might so he signed a pact with Francis I. What could Don Ferdinand the Catholic do then?

Well, what he did was this – he wrote his last will and testament and promptly died. Don Ferdinand's will confirmed the unity of Spain. He established his daughter Juana as the Queen of Castile, making her and her descendants heirs to the Crown of Aragon. Consequently, the unknown sixteen year old Flemish Prince Charles, son of Philip the Fair and the unfortunate Juana, came to Spain and united the Crowns of Castile and Aragon. Ferdinand thus fulfilled a duty that was a final homage to his Isabella and to Spain, because he was displeased with both his son-in-law Philip and his grandson Charles.

He also fulfilled another duty by appointing Cardinal Jiménez de Cisneros as Regent of Castile until the arrival of Prince Charles. Both Ferdinand and Cardinal Cisneros had a mutual respect as well as a mutual antipathy.

Cisneros was sixteen years older than Ferdinand, and he was not to last much longer than him. He was Regent for only two years, 1516 to 1517.

The Cardinal had to leave the retreat where he had taken refuge. It was a fruitful retreat which gave him the opportunity to fulfil some intellectual achievements. One was to establish Alcalá University and another to bring out the Polyglot Bible. He then returned to politics, surer of himself, and more prudent and resolved.

Cisneros advised Charles to return to Spain as quickly as possible and to put down any ambitions the Flemish lords might have to curry favours from him and get him to sell positions in Castile to the highest bidder. He told Charles that he was to avoid at all costs the appointment of foreigners to posts of government in Spain.

Charles made his own arrangements. He postponed his arrival in Spain on the advice of the Flemish nobles who had a great taste for wasting the Spanish money that had arrived from America. The Prince finally started his journey in the autumn of 1517 and arrived in the Asturias on 19 September. From here he set off for Valladolid. Charles had made an appointment to meet Cisneros along the way but while the Cardinal Regent was on his way to meet the Prince he fell ill at Roa and died on 8 November, two weeks before the planned entry into Valladolid. It was a pity that the Prince's cortege took so long to arrive due to the extravagant treatment he was given by the local nobility of every town he passed through.

It was more the pity, because Charles had a great need to receive the prudent advice of the shrewd old Cardinal. Had Charles followed the Cardinal's counsel, perhaps the rebellion of the *Comuneros* might have been avoided. The new monarch made a big mistake by arriving in Spain surrounded by Flemish courtiers.

Charles's grandfather, the Emperor Maximilian, died in January 1519. There were three candidates available to rule the Empire, Henry VIII of England, Francis I of France and Charles himself. The English King was not very interested but the King of France was and announced that he was prepared to pay three million gold franks to gain election.

This feud between Charles and Francis did not simply start

with the vanity of two young rival monarchs. Charles was of the House of Hapsburg while Francis was of the House of Valois, the two ancient and habitual enemies of the central European scene. Imperial dignity brought with it a religious dignity that gave the Imperial House a certain moral superiority over the monarchies and fiefdoms of the entire Continent.

Charles was the winner, and the Spaniards could see who was going to pay the Imperial bill for their king. Charles was delighted, but his Flemish retinue became full of suspicion because so far nothing had been said about who was going to pay the costs. Their suspicions became confirmed when Charles announced at Barcelona that he would embark for Germany to accept the Empire. He said he had no time to preside over the Valencia Court, but Adrian of Utrech, the recently appointed Bishop of Tortosa, would represent him. Charles once again convoked the Court of Castile to meet at Santiago de Compostela before he was due to depart from the port of La Coruña.

Why did he convoke the Court of Castile? The Castilians were soon to find out. Charles told them that he wanted more financial help to the tune of two hundred thousand ducats to cover the expenses of his first imperial journey to Germany.

The whole of the Levant was infuriated because the King did not turn up at their Courts. A series of popular threatening movements began.

When the nobles of Castile turned up for the Castilian Court, they felt vexed to see that a foreigner was once more presiding. The hated Johannes Sauvage had died during the King's journeys and he had been replaced by the Italo-Fleming, Mercurio Gattinara. What was the use of repeatedly petitioning the King?

Gattinara, Chievres and Charles himself were very anxious to use the Royal Courts to approve taxes, but the nobles of various cities made it known that they would not cede to such a demand. Valladolid, Leon and Toledo took the first steps in a rebellion, and this began to gather pace as other towns joined them. Chievres and his Flemish company advised Charles to embark as soon as possible. The Monarch replied with a promise to the Court that he would appoint Spaniards to take over the business of government. Nevertheless, as he was about to embark, he appointed the now Cardinal Adrian of Utrecht as Governor to manage things while he was away. Who could understand what he was up to? Charles and his retinue embarked for Flanders and Germany on 20 March. It looked more like a flight and it left Spain on the point of exploding.

The rebellion that did explode has been called by history, the *'War of the Comuneros'*, since it tried to defend the interests of the communities of Castile against the pressure of royal power.

Toledo was the first city to rise up against the Cardinal Regent and his Royal Council. Segovia followed next and its inhabitants hanged the City Procurator, Rodrigo de Tordesillas, because he surrendered to the Court and the caprices of the King and his Flemish retinue. The idea of punishing weak procurators spread throughout the whole of Castile. When the unfortunate officials were not found, their effigies were burnt in public. The wise and valiant Bishop Acuña headed a rebellion at Zamora that was followed by the cities of Guadalajara, Madrid and Avila. Castile was truly burning while King Charles was on his way to Flanders. Charles made a stopover at Dover in the south of England. He then went to meet Henry VIII at Canterbury where he hoped to gain Henry's support to combat the threats of Francis I.

Adrian the Cardinal Regent, asked the nobles for their support to suppress the revolt of the cities. He sent an army from Valladolid where he resided, to put down the revolt led by the popular Juan Bravo at Segovia. The Comuneros of Toledo, led by Padilla, went to the aid of Segovia and forced the Imperialists to flee. This success encouraged Leon, Salamanca, Murcia and other cities to join the cause. Many *hidalgos* [gentleman landowners] joined forces with the Comuneros although the majority of the nobility remained loyal to the Cardinal Regent. Burgos, Palencia and Valladolid, while threatening the members of the Royal Council with punishment, nevertheless remained loyal to the King.

All of a sudden Avila found itself to be the capital of the rebellion. And what about Oropesa? Well, it could hardly avoid its historic obligation to Avila but, as García Sánchez demonstrates, it remained loyal to the Emperor.

The rebellion fell to pieces and it leaders, Padilla, Bravo and Maldonado were beheaded. They all went to their deaths gallantly. After four centuries, Spanish school children still recite the last words these chiefs of the *Comuneros* spoke at the foot of the scaffold.

When they arrived upon black draped mules at the place

of execution, the officer who read the sentence said: *"This is the justice ordered by His Majesty, that they are to be beheaded as traitors!"* Juan Bravo could not but help himself from replying: *"While you and those who command you say 'traitors', it is rather for our zeal for the public welfare and defence of Castile."*

Padilla smiled quietly at his companion: *"Señor Juan Bravo, yesterday was the day we fought like gentlemen, today is the day we die as Christians."* The first to mount the scaffold was Padilla who was the Captain General of the revolt, but Bravo asked if he could go first, saying: *"I do not want to see the greatest gentleman in Castile die."* Maldonado was the last to meet the axe, and their heads were then put on tall poles for public exhibition.

Today the names of Padilla, Bravo and Maldonado are written in letters of gold on the façade of the Palace of Justice in homage to the defenders of Spain's democratic freedom.

Did the rebellion of the Comuneros have any hidden meaning? Don Gregorio Marañon says that they were *"reactionaries"* of their time faced with the universal imperatives imposed upon the national community. Today, there is a certain sector of our young democracy that raises the flag of regional autonomy, and it cannot be taken lightly that they make their points forcefully with historic documents.

At Torralba de Oropesa there was a young man who was about to turn 28 years of age. We are certain of the following:

* Juan Ciudad worked for wages as a shepherd at a village called Torralba de Oropesa, situated in the countryside of the Arañuelo between Talavera and Extremadura, on the banks of the Tagus in the foothills of the Credos Mountains.
* He worked under the orders of Francisco, a *mayoral* [overseer] of flocks of sheep.
* The owner of the flocks was a *hidalgo* [wealthy gentleman landowner] landlord and mayor named Francisco Herruz.

The local ruler was Don Francisco, 2nd Count of Oropesa under His Majesty the Emperor Charles.

The error that named Oropesa as the place where Juan was put when he arrived from Montemor-O-Novo, has now been corrected. It was not Oropesa but Torralba de Oropesa.

Also corrected is the mistake that the head of the family

that took in the child Juan was called Francisco Mayoral, or Francisco Cid Mayoral. His true name was Francisco Herruz.

The documentation collected by García Sánchez fits exactly with the statements made by the witnesses of the Beatification Process of John of God.

How is the principal enigma of the Ciudad family to be faced? First of all, set aside the information given to us by Castro at the beginning of his biography. Make a rigorous investigation and then we will arrive at the decision to disqualify it altogether, even though we can well understand the reason why the biographer inserted it into his work. He wanted to protect the image of John of God from dark suspicions.

Secondly, the serious indications that there is a Jewish link with the Ciudads now appears to go well beyond probability. The admission that Juan was in fact the son of *Conversos*, opens up the way to fit together the pieces of the jigsaw puzzle. By incorporating the comings and goings of the Arañuelo Jews between Oropesa and the Portuguese countryside around Alentejo, we can intensify the search for documents that will clear up the mystery of the Ciudads, their presence at Montemor-O-Novo and the return of the child Juan to the Arañuelo. This would dispel the secrecy that Castro has put around them. García Sánchez says: *"Critical history cannot admit the version utilised by the rector of the Granada hospital, where he says a child just enters like an angel into a Castilian gentleman's family home. It takes a bit of working out to think that Castro, who was so objective, had fallen for this myth. The paragraph; "He grew up with his parents until he was eight years old, then without their knowing it he was taken away by a cleric to the town of Oropesa..." is no more than an artificial smokescreen to cover up the comings and goings of the Ciudad family along the road between Evora and Oropesa. This was the path frequented by the Jews of those days as they went to and from Oropesa and Evora. These Jews were natives of the town or from its neighbourhood and had been exiled or persecuted by the Toledo Inquisition."*

What are we missing then? One fine day soon something might turn up in the archives to give us a pleasant surprise, as it did half a century ago with St. Teresa of Avila's lineage. We can hope that the archives will enlighten us still more about the family and infancy of John of God. For example, the missing notebook might be discovered at Granada or Rome, that same notebook in which *"one who accompanied him* [John of God] *on all his journeys has left us"* and which served Castro as the basis for his biography. This same notebook in which the mysterious companion of John of God made records, *"fully and clearly"* as Castro says, and hastens to add, in which he *"wrote down in a good hand what he saw as an eye-witness as well as what was said by credible persons who knew and did business with him."* Where could this notebook be? In some corner of the Granada Archives, perhaps. Or maybe it will appear in Rome where it could have been sent as a precious exhibit for the Beatification Process, and where the *Monsignori* of the Roman Curia, like Castro, placed an embargo upon its use, because it made a bothersome reference to the Saint's Jewish origins. Who knows!

Notes to Chapter 7

* On Oropesa: P Madoz, *Diccionario geografico-estadístico-histórico de España* XII, Madrid 1847, 370; O. García Gil-A Fernández Arroyo, *Oropesa , señorio y condado,* Madrid 1982; J. M. Gómez Rodríguez-A. Moreno-J. M. Hernández Piña, *Oropesa y los Alvarez de Toledo,* Talavera 1985; J. García Sánchez, *Crónicas del Arañuelo* (2 vols), Toledo 1985. A. Sáinz y Suárez, *Oropesa. Gredos. Tormes. Toledo. Monograía histórico-fotografica,* Toledo 1914.
* Fundamental research on the Herruz family and the *'mayoral'* of the flocks, in J. García Sánchez, *El Señorio de Oropesa,* unpublished manuscript; Id., *San Juan de Dios en el Señorio de Oropesa*: Beresit 4 (1992) 93-113, where García Sánchez brings forward the chapter of his unpublished work; Id., *Dónde nació el beato Alonso de Orozco?*: Toletum 27 (Toledo s.f.) 109-127. The suggestion about the illegitimacy of Fray Hernando de Talavera, Id., *El Señorio de Oropesa,* chapter XX of the unpublished work, p 8.
* The basic document for locating the genealogy of Herruz is *"Información de la Genealogía y Limpieza de Jerónimo Herruz y de María Muñoz, si mujer para una familiatura del Santo Oficio en Torralba"*; Archivo Histórico Nacional, Consejo de la Inquisición, Cargos del S.O., Leg. 284 num. 6, año 1598. In studying this file I have come to the conclusion that the security checks of the FBI in the USA to see that their agents are clean of any Communist contamination are a bit of a joke when compared with the severity with which the Holy Office investigated the purity of blood of its agents .
* Rafael María Saucedo, O.H., in his *Cronológia aplicada en la vida de N. P. S. Juan de Dios*: Paz y Caridad 12 (Nov.- Dec. 1951) 338, seems to confuse Francisco Vázquez; *"He who is well remembered, major-domo to the Count of Oropesa"* with *"the House of Herruz y Navas."* There are several errors in this reference. Firstly, that the Herruz family where John of God lived was headed by Francisco Herruz García: *"Navas"*, as García Sánchez has demonstrated in the places cited, is equal to *"Montalvo"* and is a surname incorporated with *"Herruz"* through marriage over a period of several generations; the witnesses at the Beatification Process mixed the surnames because they made statements when many years had already gone by. *"Herruz is*

accompanied in fact by Navas y Montalvo." Secondly, Francisco Vázquez in no way whatsoever belonged to the Herruz nucleus. Perhaps as a farm worker he might have worked as a *mayoral* of sheep flocks. The statement at the Beatification Process calls him *"he who is well remembered,"* because he left a generous will to have Masses celebrated and alms distributed in the parish of the Assumption at Oropesa. Actually it is impossible to identify Francisco Vázquez with the nucleus of the Herruz, because the Herruz of the time of John of God lived at Torralba de Oropesa, not in the town of Oropesa. Furthermore, Francisco Vázquez held an office in the Count's household and would have been always with him at Oropesa. To understand the mix-up in the testimony of the witnesses at the Beatification Process, it should be remembered that the descendants of Herruz had already left Torralba de Oropesa so the witnesses only knew them as residents of the town of Oropesa, not of Torralba.

* Established data about the 20 years John of God lived at Torralba de Oropesa as a shepherd, plus the eight years after he returned there from Fuenterrabía, do not exist. For this reason it is meritorious, although hardly fruitful, that the biographers have tried to fill the gap intelligently. For example, J. Cruset *Una avententura iluminada. San Juan de Dios,* Madrid (4) 1977, 32-34; A. Muñoz Hidalgo, *De Juan Ciudad a Juan de Dios,* Barcelona 1990, 29-32; V. A. Riesco, *Y Dios se hice hermano,* Madrid 1994, 10-11.

* For the life of a shepherd and the significance of the *Mesta* (association of sheep farmers) in the 16th century: M. Fernández Alvarez, *La sociedad española en el siglo de Oro,* I. Madrid (2) 1989, 84-88.

* Regarding the statements made by the witnesses at the Beatification Process; it should be remembered that the questions were prepared on the basis of the biography written by Dionisio Celi and not upon the critical biography written by Francisco de Castro. Celi did not say one word, nor did he even hint, that John of God's parents were *Conversos* and it is not surprising that various witnesses agreed with this. Others, following the mentality of the period, maintained that John of God's parents were *"Old Christians"* and he had *"no mixed blood",* and Celi says: *"No one could think that a saint might have Jewish parents."* This was the way of thinking of the time.

8

HE JOINS THE ARMY, AND IS LATER DISMISSED

Torralba, Fuenterrabía, Torralba
1523

While at Torralba, was Juan offered a girl's hand in marriage? This is a suspicion that is raised by some of his biographers.

The 'offer', and also the possibility of the young man falling in love would be quite normal since he had grown up at Torralba de Oropesa from childhood to the age of 28.

We might include an alternative provocative question, How is it that Juan Ciudad never fell in love? What were the sentimental life and sexual experiences of Juan Ciudad shepherd at Torralba de Oropesa?

The documents are silent on the subject. Not because they make it disappear by slight of hand, considering it a knotty problem, but because they treat it as they have other points, with absolute silence.

Now I am going to tell you why the 'offer' of this marriageable young woman seems 'suspect'. The girl of whom they speak would be the daughter of the mayoral under whose orders Juan worked. So impressed was the mayoral with the good qualities of the young man that he offered him his daughter's hand in marriage.

Such a gesture would have been very consequential, and without doubt it would have given his career a big boost, for it would raise him up from just an ordinary shepherd to being in line for the job of mayoral. Of course, this would have opened up a vast new horizon to the young shepherd who otherwise seemed condemned, and resigned, to spending the rest of his life following the flocks.

What actually occurred was this. The post-Castro biographers took their cue from a confused witness named Francisco González who testified at the beatification process. This witness identified the mayoral of the flocks that belonged to Francisco Herruz, with a certain Francisco Mayoral who was the local Oropesa jailer. Francisco González oddly confused the turnkey with the mayoral, who was the overseer of the flocks. This witness said: "He wanted to marry one of his daughters to the aforementioned John of God." The witness confused the title 'mayoral' with the jailer's surname, Mayoral. This was a very confused witness indeed, but who could blame him? After all, it was 120 years after the event.

However, the preachers of miracle-laden panegyrics on John of God were served up yet another great opportunity on a silver tray. They used the story to praise John of God's virtues to the skies. It made no difference to them if these virtues were true or simply apocryphal. Anyway, the witness González ended his testimony with the anecdote of the marriage proposal: "John of God went away and stayed away; (the would be father-in-law) never saw him again."

There was enough ammunition here for these preachers to give plenty of sermons on the virtue of chastity in John of God who, when he was a shepherd, fled from temptation. This was just another of the many fictitious tales that successive writers invented to enhance the Saint's reputation. When these writers lacked the bread of history, they gorged themselves on the cake of fantasy.

Did Juan flee from marriage? No, he did not. He went off to war. He did not run away, he enlisted as a soldier, joining the Count's armed retinue.

It was the spring of 1523 and Juan Ciudad, who up to now had been far removed from the major conflicts of his day, stepped upon the stage where the powerful of this world play out their roles. Juan was a passive subject who had to fall in with whatever the monarchs of Spain and Portugal dictated. The ordinances against the descendants of Jews had vigorously shaken the newborn infant and someone was aware of that as soon as he left his mother's womb. Later he lived as a simple shepherd taking care of flocks on the Arañuelo pastureland until he turned 28 in March 1523. Juan would return in disgrace from his first foray into the public arena.

King Charles won the Imperial Crown when he was elected Emperor at Frankfurt, Germany. His coronation took place at Aquisgrán on 22 October 1520. A few years later Pope Clement VII was to declare at Bologna that Charles was the Emperor of the West and the successor of Charlemagne.

On his way home to Spain from Aquisgrán, Charles decided to call upon Henry VIII in England. The aim of this visit was to persuade Henry to join him against the French King, Francis I. The conduct of the three Christian monarchs of the period does not seem very exemplary. Luther had unleashed the hurricane of the Reformation, the Turks were striking the borders of Hungary and, meanwhile, Charles, Henry and Francis, were consuming the energy of their vassals in 'family squabbles'.

The first of these wars broke out as soon as Charles arrived back in Spain and heard that Francis I was already massing troops on the Spanish border. The King of France could not bear to see his rival elected as Emperor - both of them having conspired to obtain that imperial crown. Charles was the craftier of the two. He had delegated his aunt, Margarita of Austria, to carry out diplomatic operations on his behalf and he had ordered her to spend whatever money was required to obtain what he wanted.

All the electors swore 'that their votes were pure and their hands clean' but they still made use of the election to carry on the tradition of stuffing the coffers of their respective fiefdoms. In fact, they sold their vote to the highest bidder.

According to 15th century papal bulls, the dignity of electing the Emperor was in the hands of seven electors, the Archbishops of Cologne, Maguncia and Treveris, the King of Bohemia, the Duke of Saxon, the Count Palatine of the Rhine and the Margrave of Brandenburg.

The aunt of Charles, Margarita, applied plenty of money and charm to securing the post for her nephew. It was a tough fight because Pope Leo X favoured Francis I. Margarita knew that she had to play rough so she secured the support of the bankers who were probably the most powerful ones in Europe, the Fuggers of Augsburg. The Fuggers put bags and bags of gold florins at her disposal.

The banking house of Fuggers lent money to such famous debtors as Pope Leo X, Frederick of Saxony and William of Bavaria. But they were not too worried about Margarita, the lady from Burgundy with the sacks of gold florins. They knew she was borrowing on behalf of Charles who, besides being Emperor, was also King of Spain where the doors were wide open to receive shiploads of riches from the New World.

The electors met at Frankfurt on 28 June 1519. Margaret triumphed and Charles became "King of the Romans and Emperor of Germany." The Duke of Saxony explained the profound motives of the election. He pointed out that Charles, apart from being the Archduke of Austria and Prince of Germany, was also the Sovereign of Castile, Aragon, Naples and the New World. Therefore he was the only one capable of defending Christianity from the danger being presented by the Turks on both land and sea. The Saxon Duke stressed that the reason for electing Charles was the peril represented by the Turks and he failed to make any reference to the gold florins from the Fuggers' bank.

Francis I was quite aware of what was going on and he was furious. While Charles was breathing the air of imperialism in Germany and the Comuneros in Spain were in revolt Francis decided to go to war on a hypocritical excuse.

Charles and Francis were a pair of fighting cocks. Remember how when Charles's grandmother Isabella died, his grandfather Ferdinand the Catholic made a shrewd marriage with Germana de Foix, the niece of the French King, Louis XII. This marriage aimed at gaining the sympathy of the neighbouring country but it backfired and proved to be counter-productive.

The Spanish King never trusted Francis who was behind the military and diplomatic uproar that followed. It is not easy for Frenchmen and Spaniards to understand how Ferdinand of Aragon reconciled his being Catholic with being so devious. Perhaps it is from those years that the young folk of my Aragon take the sentiments of the jota [folk-song and dance] which three centuries later would support the War of Independence from France: "The Virgin of the Pilar says she does not want to be French; what she wants to be is the Commander of the Aragonese troops."

Ferdinand's marriage to the niece of the King of France did not bring him much comfort. It so happened that the most intrepid French general who fought the Spaniards on the Italian battlefields was the Duke of Nemours, Gaston de Foix. Gaston was Germana's brother so you can imagine how his sister, King Ferdinand's wife, felt about that! Early in 1512, Gaston de Foix was killed in the battle of Ravena, and it was just as well because had he survived three more years his sister would have been left without the Bay of Naples.

To be quite honest, the French could not trust King Ferdinand of Aragon either, because he was as cunning as a snake. He used the fighting that was going on all over Italy to take advantage of achieving a lifelong ambition – the incorporation of Navarre into the Crown of Spain.

In the meantime there was a sudden short-lived war. In 1512 King Ferdinand picked the feast of Santiago, Spain's patron saint, to send his troops into battle. They conquered Pamplona, the capital of Navarre. The Navarrese monarch was Queen Catherine de Foix whose spouse was a French nobleman. He was a wealthy land-owner called Jean de Albret. Queen Catherine was of the House of the Counts of Foix, lords of the ancient French province of Bearn. Her family was related to the King of France and now, of course, Queen Germana de Foix was the spouse of King Ferdinand of Aragon. The House of Foix was split by internal squabbling, with each of its branches seeking support of some sector of the Navarre nobility. The Queen could never rely on anyone except the King of France for assistance.

The French reacted at once when it was known that Ferdinand's army had taken Pamplona. King Jean de Albret led the troops of Louis XII and urged the Navarrese to rise up against the Spanish invaders. They set up a siege outside the walled city of Pamplona and bombarded its walls with artillery fire for 27 days causing severe damage. The defenders held their ground within the city's walls.

The internal quarrelling of de Albret's besieging forces left them so weak that they were unable to prevail against the reinforcements Ferdinand had sent to help Pamplona. The French surrendered to the Spaniards and fled to their own side of the Pyrenees. Ferdinand was still up to his old tricks. He travelled to all the major towns proclaiming himself King of Navarre, while at the same time recognising the forces, customs and laws of the country. He shrewdly tamed the discontented with copious gifts. He offered a truce to Louis XII who signed it in order to rid himself of the whole sorry affair. Two years later the Court at Burgos declared that Navarre was definitively annexed to the Crown of Castile.

In 1521 Francis, the son of King Louis XII, went to war to regain Navarre from Charles, the grandson of Ferdinand the Catholic. The damage caused by these two hot heads was not just in separating military forces but also dividing the strength of Christianity in their respective countries. Had they become allies they might have stemmed the onrush of Protestantism unleashed by Luther and the advance of the Turks who seriously threatened to invade Europe. Maybe Francis and Charles were just too young!

The personal squabbles between King Francis I and Emperor Charles V came about through the displeasure of the

French King at being refused the spiritual lordship of Europe implicit in the imperial dignity. Francis longed with all his juvenile impetuosity to be elected Emperor and he never forgave Charles for stealing the sceptre from his grasp. His resentment led the French King to form a pact with the Protestants and the Turks against the Emperor. From the European point of view this was an act of sheer madness.

Of course, the deep hostility that Francis had for Charles turned into a political feud fuelled by animosity and envy. Francis was surrounded, or rather I should say confined, by a ring of imperial forces; Austria and Germany to the east, Flanders to the north and Spain to the south. On several occasions Charles had tried to get the support of England's Henry VIII through a pact which would cut the French off from the west. Fortunately for Francis I, the English did not trust Charles nor did they want to put themselves within the Emperor's grasp, even though Henry's wife, Catherine of Aragon, was Charles's aunt since she was the daughter of the Catholic Monarchs and the sister of 'Joan the Mad'.

It so happened that Francis I unleashed a war in which our shepherd from Oropesa, Juan Ciudad, took part.

The French King crossed the Spanish border on 12 May 1521, using the pretext that he was going to retake the throne of Navarre for Henry Labrit, the son of Jean Albret, from whom Ferdinand the Catholic had wrested the kingdom.

Historians of the period say that Francis I made a grave error in hesitating to attack. The Emperor's troops had overthrown the Comuneros at Villalar on 23 April and were still fit enough to take on the French. If Francis had launched the attack six months earlier Don Charles would have been in danger of losing his crown. The French army poured down through the Roncal Valley and headed straight for Pamplona. The Viceroy of Navarre dispatched twelve urgent letters to the Commander-in-Chief of Castile appealing for reinforcements but these troops did not come. On 19 May, the vanguard of the French army had already arrived at the gates of Pamplona. The Spaniards retreated in the direction of Logroño, leaving only a garrison in the city. A battle ensured and the garrison defended the city for six hours before surrendering. Captain Ignacio de Loyola was wounded in this battle.

Elated with their success, the French continued advancing

towards Logroño: they confidently imagined that the Spanish companies of the Comuneros would join them. Actually, the reverse occurred: a wave of patriotism swept over the Spaniards who united to fight off the invader. When the Spanish flag flew again at Noain, a town close to Pamplona, thousands of French soldiers lay dead and the rest were prisoners. Francis I had to swallow one of the most bitter doses of defeat in his life.

A few months later, in the autumn of 1521, the French attempted to make a comeback, and under the command of General Gouffier de Bonnivet, they launched a brilliant counter-attack upon the Spanish cities of Behovia and Fuenterrabía. With cannon fire they took Fuenterrabía on 18 October and placed three thousand men within the fortifications. The villages of the Basque province of Guipúzcoa sent thousands of volunteers to lay siege to 'French' Fuenterrabía. The struggle went on for two years with its skirmishes and ambushes – the French inside, the Guipúzcoa volunteers outside.

That was the case until early in 1523 when the Emperor decided it was time to regain Fuenterrabía. Charles, with the help of his generals - he was only 23 at the time - developed a good strategy. In order to confront the French he decided to simultaneously attack on several fronts. The Emperor's plans called for the English allies to enter France through Flanders, the Germans from the eastern flank, and Charles would personally lead the Spaniards towards Fuenterrabía from the south.

The Emperor also wanted to take advantage of the fact that Francis, anxious to expel the Spanish from the north of Italy, had sent off some of his men to Milan, leaving unguarded the Spanish border at Bidasoa.

Italy was the theatre of war where the armies of Charles and Francis clashed in order to totally destroy one another. It was a pity to see this beautiful country, cradle of the most refined culture of this stage of the Renaissance, turned into an arena for ferocious clashes between two foreign armies. And for what?

The Italians were unable to agree amongst themselves and it was going to be three long centuries before they would achieve the goal of national unity. Not one of its little states or kingdoms had sufficient energy to assert itself over the rest, even though they enjoyed impressive historic prestige: the kingdom of Naples, the Duchy of Milan, the republics of Venice and Genoa, all evaded the

5. The facade of the house of the Venegas family where John of God sheltered at night when he first returned to Granada after his visit to Guadalupe.

6. The doorway leading into the vestibule of the Casa Venegas (Casa de los Tiros) where John of God first began giving accommodation to the poor of Granada.

dominance of the others. In order to avoid being dominated by the others, each little Italian state made and broke alliances with foreign nations. That is how the French, Germans, Austrians and Spaniards subjugated Italy for so long.

Charles considered that, within the imperial strategy, there was a piece of Italy that was crucial - the Duchy of Milan. This was situated at a junction of the roads that united three substantial parts of the Empire – Spain, Austria and the Netherlands. For this reason Francis I, on more than one occasion, with great tenacity, directed his armies' offensives against Milan. He knew that if he were to drive the imperial troops from the Duchy of Milan, the Emperor would see his dominions disconnected.

The Emperor, returning from the hurried ceremony at Aquisgrán and his even more hasty second visit to Henry VIII in England, entered Spain at the port of Santander on 16 July 1522, bringing with him four thousand German mercenaries and a great arsenal of the latest German artillery.

Sebastian Elcano's around-the-world voyage and the conquests of Pizarro-Cortéz in the New World were about to add lustre to the Imperial Crown.

On arrival the new Emperor wisely moved to heal the wounds caused by the rebellion of the Comuneros by granting generous pardons. This caused the nobles to toast his generosity and he appealed to their patriotism and called on them to accept levies to go against the French invaders and to retake Fuenterrabía.

Early in 1523 Charles convoked the Court at Palencia and a few months later reconvened it at Valladolid. He told the nobles that he wanted funds for the war and ordered them to supply them quickly. Among these nobles at Valladolid was the Count of Oropesa who, because of his brief flirtation with the Comuneros, was glad of the opportunity to prove his loyalty to the Emperor: *loyal... and pleased to have saved the walls of his castle from destruction.*

Our young Juan decided to enlist, but no one knows the interior impulse that caused him to make this decision. As our friend Castro says in the first biography, *"he was a young, twenty-two year old bachelor..."*. Castro was wrong. Juan was twenty-eight at the time. Then Castro goes on to tell us: *"he willingly set out for war."* His first biographer suggests a couple of motives for this: maybe he heard these from the companion who gave him so much material:

"John's motive was really a desire to see the world and enjoy freedom."

These words would have been said in confidence by Juan to his friend and companion, because Castro dares to add a comment which practically serves as a confession of Juan's sins as a soldier: *"Juan was moved by a desire... that commonly possesses those who go off to war, to rush down the wide, if arduous, road of vice."* Castro concludes by saying that Juan experienced the darker side of military adventures: " *...he passed through many troubles and fell into many dangers."*

While the Emperor Charles was preparing his troops for war he received the sad news that Pope Adrian of Utrech, his friend and tutor, had died in the autumn of 1523. Adrian of Utrech bore the title of Pope Adrian VI. As pope he was not given time to do much – he reigned only a year. At Rome they gave him a hostile reception for he was generally considered to be a 'creature' of the Emperor. The cardinals who opposed him claimed that to elect Adrian as Pope was tantamount to electing the Emperor himself. Adrian was a good man but when Renaissance Rome saw the pious and austere Pope arrive they nicknamed him the 'uncouth Dutchman' because his appearance was more like that of a monk than a prince of the Church. It appears that in that epoch they only wanted princes. Adrian made the same blunder that Charles made when he went to Spain – he brought Flemish advisers with him. They were intelligent men, but their names - Enkevoirt, Ingelwinkel, Dirk van Heeze – aroused hilarity amongst the Romans. With the death of Adrian VI we saw the last non-Italian pope until the election of John Paul II.

The conclave lasted for fifty days, then Cardinal Giulio, a member of the Medici family, was elected and took the name Clement VII.

Juan Ciudad, shepherd of Oropesa, marched off to war with other young men from Castile under the banner of their Emperor. Like most of them, he had no idea of what was in store for him. Many were to die in those cruel wars, some falling in Italy and others drowned in sea battles with the Berbers who came across from Africa to continue their piracy along the coasts of Sicily and Naples. Others would meet death in Flanders, France and Germany. Castilian families learnt to bear in silence the death of their sons on far-flung battlefields.

Had Juan been killed in action, his name would not have occupied a single line in history. Who would lose any sleep over a young shepherd who marched off when the Emperor's call was heard for the defence of Fuenterrabía and did not return?

Fortunately Juan was to return – even though he would come back in disgrace. Forty lancers departed from Oropesa Castle under the command of the hidalgo Francisco Herruz – hidalgo and master of the shepherd Juan Ciudad. Obviously Herruz was chosen by the Count because he was known as a former soldier, having been a "man of arms" and captain in the war of Granada – before being pardoned from the sentence he had received prior to his coming to Torralba.

Juan Ciudad's decision to enlist is more comprehensible when you consider that Francisco Herruz was to lead the Oropesan lancers. And so the shepherd Juan marched off with men he knew and confidence in his master who was now their captain. The adventure was beginning to look quite promising.

The general headquarters were established at Vitoria and the Emperor went there in person. Iñigo de Velasco was the Commander-in-Chief of the regular soldiers and, in accordance with the custom of the time, the number of these troops was increased by the retainers of the nobility. In all there were 24,000 Spanish troops and 3,000 mercenaries.

The Commander-in-Chief marched his columns and crossed the frontier at the River Bidasoa and began a clean up operation in French territory to serve as a rearguard of Fuenterrabía. The Spaniards spread terror as far as the Bearn, attacking castles, setting up camps, burning and pillaging villages and putting the enemy to flight. Satisfied with their incursion into enemy territory, Velasco returned with his troops to the frontier and began to bombard the walls of Fuenterrabía with the cannons that Charles had brought back from Germany. The chronicles of the period describe the consternation of the French garrison commander, Franquet, when he saw seven ships sent from France by La Rochelle destroyed and burnt by the Spanish in the Bidasoa estuary. After that defeat, the French surrendered Fuenterrabía on 25 March.

Two aspects of his first military adventure remained engraved in Juan's memory. " ...*he passed through many troubles and fell into many dangers."*

We will come to the dangers later on, but the consideration of the vices is merely conjectural. Later on, we will see John of God often confessing himself to be a sinner on account of the vices that ensnared him as a soldier. Vice went along with soldiering in those days – as it does these days, if it comes to that: death, brutality, cruelty, wine, women. Let it be far from our minds that Juan Ciudad went from one to another of these pitfalls. This was the boy who came from the fields of the Arañuelo with a clean heart and had spent more than 25 years in a religious atmosphere of friendly Castillian peasant families. Then again, it is not hard to imagine how, in the company of other soldiers, he might have been involved in the pillaging of homes and villages. That certainly would remain fixed upon his mind. Also, there was always the prevalence of obscene language and depraved conduct in army camps at night; thieving, contempt for the property of others, the rounds of prostitutes and violent brawls over any trifling matter. Then in the supreme hour of battle he would have to be prepared to thrust his lance into the body of an unknown person. Likewise, there was always the possibility of getting the same treatment himself. I wonder how he would have reacted if he had had to blast a man's chest apart with a shot from a harquebus. He would see mutilated bodies all about him, hear cries of agony, shrieks of terror, songs of victory. Then at night, he would have to throw himself down in some ditch, and, stiff with the winter's cold and with fear in his soul, try to sleep.

Juan was a soldier amongst soldiers. He was just another member of the troop who had to be loyal to it despite all the outrages it committed. I doubt if he had read it, but he could agree with what Erasmus wrote: "War is something so cruel that it is more suited to wild beasts than to man."

Perils almost cost Juan his life on two occasions. The accounts given about them leads one to suspect that, due to his familiarity with Captain Herruz, he was assigned to auxiliary services or quartermaster duties.

It so happened that one day Juan's squad had run out of provisions, so he volunteered to go and make a search amongst the houses scattered throughout the countryside. No sooner said than done!

This took place during the mop-up operations ordered by

the Commander of the French Basque country, prior to the siege of Fuenterrabía. Juan's squad had found a mare, so he promptly mounted it and galloped off into the countryside. Castro says it was a French mare so, naturally, it could not be expected to obey commands given in Spanish. Or was it that the mare was just cantankerous? We shall soon see.

Juan had hardly ridden two leagues on his mount when the mare recognised her usual surroundings and bolted towards familiar territory. Off she sped at a furious gallop making a beeline for her master's camp. Juan tugged at the reins in an effort to stop her but it was impossible and, with a sudden lunge, she threw her terrified rider to the ground. Juan hit his head on a rock when he fell, leaving himself unconscious with blood pouring from his mouth and nostrils.

He lay unconscious for more than two hours upon a rocky outcrop. The calculation of two hours is certainly his own, because what we know comes from the conversation he later had with his companions when he explained what had happened. When he regained consciousness he became aware of the pain caused by his fall. He also realised what would happen to him were he to be taken prisoner by the French. He then fervently prayed, and here is how Castro relates it:

"He fell down upon his knees and fixed his gaze upon heaven and in a voice barely audible, called upon the name of Our Lady the Virgin Mary to whom he had always been devoted, saying: 'Mother of God, come to my help. Pray to your holy Son for me so that he may save me from this peril in which I find myself, and that he may not allow my enemies to capture me.'"

This is the first time that Christian piety appears in relation to Juan and it takes the form of confidence in the Blessed Virgin Mary, *"to whom he had always been devoted."* With regard to the Lord Jesus Christ, he beseeched the Blessed Virgin to *"pray to your holy Son for me."*

Behind this simple episode – simple as far as circumstances are concerned but grave because it is obvious that Juan could have died from loss of blood as he lay bleeding upon that rocky outcrop – his spontaneous prayer was fervent and reflected years of Christian practice while he lived as a shepherd at Oropesa.

Soldier Juan Ciudad was convinced that he had received heavenly protection, and that is why he so clearly remembered the prayer he raised to heaven. When he regained consciousness he picked up a stick to serve as a crutch and limped back to where his companions were waiting for his return. Their camp was not a formal military one but, rather, a bivouac to serve them during the days of their incursion into enemy territory.

They saw him come back "in such a bad condition" that they thought that he might have stumbled across the French. He explained what happened in his episode with the 'French mare' – jokingly giving an account of it so as not to cause a fuss. His companions took good care of him, covering him with their coarse tabards to make him perspire, a treatment that appears to have worked, for Castro says "from then on he healed and was better in a few days." We do not know what intellectual and sentimental accoutrements our shepherd-become-soldier brought with him from the fields of Torralba. Consequently, one would need to be bold to suggest what thoughts and desires went through his mind during those few days of convalescence when he recognised that he may have been, for the first time as far as we know, on the brink of death.

The second danger, although less grave, nevertheless brought with it fatal consequences. The story of our shepherd almost came to an end with him hanging from a tree in the Jaizkibel foothills within sight of Fuenterrabía. The actual date of this incident is not recorded, although it seems to correspond with the first weeks of the formal siege when Commander Iñigo de Velasco set his 24,000 soldiers to surround the city of Fuenterrabía.

By its strategic position, Fuenterrabía, or Hondarribia as it is called in the Basque language, had for centuries been the theatre of sieges and assaults. Now Francis I and Charles V were engaged in giving this ancient fortress of King Sancho Abarca yet another taste of battle. At the end of the 18th century, other Frenchmen would set the castle ablaze. All that is left of the areas used as a garrison have been restored and today serve as the Parador [hotel] Castillo de Carlos V.

The eyes of our Oropesan shepherd eagerly took in the panorama of the Basque countryside with its views of Fuenterrabía, the woodland, the river, the beach and the sea. It was so vastly different from the undulating fields of the Arañuelo and the region of the Gredos Mountains.

But a dramatic incident soon awoke him from his

daydreams. The officers trusted Juan in his quartermaster duties, and the men also trusted him. That is why the captain placed him on duty to guard a pile of booty captured from the French. These spoils consisted of clothing and when it was discovered that they were missing the officer in charge was furious. I suppose the clothing would have consisted of overcoats that the soldiers wanted during the cold of winter. Perhaps some jewels also, but who knows? Juan was negligent in keeping guard over the loot and so it was stolen.

The theft did not demand great skill on the part of the perpetrators. The booty was piled up in the corner of a tent, so all that was necessary was to put an arm underneath the flap and drag the stuff out, the guard would not be suspicious of his own companions. The captain was so enraged that he ordered that the culprit be punished, and the punishment he ordered was immediate death by hanging.

Wars always rate lightly the value of life. A person can be seen as no more than a number. This was a period in history when armies lacked an established organisation. That is how a captain could arbitrarily sentence a man to be executed on the spot. But, you say, just for being careless in guarding booty? Yes, he could be hanged just for that! Let's see who this captain was.

Juan marched away from Oropesa in a detachment of 40 lancers recruited by the Count of Oropesa, who placed them under the orders of the hidalgo Francisco Herruz. When the Oropesans were integrated into the army, 24,000 strong, under General Iñigo de Velasco, we do not know if Juan remained under the direct orders of Captain Herruz. Probably he did not, because when they arrived at the front there were the inevitable readjustments to be made. I suspect that, no matter how angry Herruz might have been, he was not going to condemn his soldier to death over some precious booty – not this boy who had grown up very close to his own family. It would be quite impossible for our captain from Oropesa to give such a barbarous command. Furthermore, to hang a man under those circumstances would more or less require some sort of court martial. No, in the eyes of the hidalgo Herruz, his shepherd Juan Ciudad represented a very special type of man.

Juan knew that death was staring him in the face. Already the soldiers were beginning to carry out the command of the captain who had condemned him to death. Then, at the same time, someone who was obviously influential saw the commotion and wanted to know what was going on. When told the reason for the sentence, he persuaded the captain to rescind his order thereby saving Juan's life. This is Castro's account of the incident: *"It so happened that a kind person respected by the captain passed by and, when he found out what was going on, requested that the order not be put into effect."* This kind person said an alternative punishment should be imposed – such as a dishonourable discharge from the army: *"Once he had made his opinion known to the captain, he immediately left the camp."*

Being expelled from the army was quite a different thing from being condemned to death. The captain accepted this recommendation and Juan, who was not a professional mercenary but a volunteer in the company raised by his Count, was nevertheless thrown out of the army and that was the end of the story. Obviously he was glad to have saved his skin but no one tells us this, least of all Juan himself.

Who was this personage who so providentially saved Juan from the gibbet? A century later, the playwright Lope de Vega, in his celebrated *Comedia*, wrote that the high ranking officer who interceded on Juan's behalf while he stood there with the noose around his neck, was the Duke de Alba. There is no doubt that a lot of the success of de Vega's play was due to the flattery the author poured upon the House of Alba. In fact Lope de Vega was in the employ of the Albas, whom he called "the saviours of John of God", but that does not mean anything.

It so happened that there really was an Alba at the battle of Fuenterrabía and his presence there is recorded in the chronicles. He was a 14 year old boy named Ferdinand Alvarez de Toledo, the future 3rd Duke de Alba. In order to indulge in the cult of Mars this lad ran away to war from his grandfather's palace at Piedrahita without the latter's permission. A warrior! Certainly! As he grew older neither the teaching of Boscán or the friendship of Garcilaso were able to subdue his bellicose spirit. To this day he is remembered in the Netherlands as having being sent by Satan.

If the young Alba saved Juan Ciudad from the gibbet, we are quite happy that the friends of John of God see him the way he is depicted by Lope de Vega. But, after all, the famous playwright was merely using poetic licence, however interesting.

The more likely scenario is that the hidalgo Herruz got to

hear of the affair and speedily went to the captain concerned in order to intercede on behalf of his shepherd lad. And who other than Herruz could have been the kind person who convinced the captain to reduce the sentence from death to expulsion.

(Here I just want to put into parenthesis: The Alverez de Toledo, Counts of Oropesa, were cousins of the Alverez de Toledo, Dukes de Alba, but of a distant branch.)

On behalf of Emperor Charles V, Iñigo Velasco as the Commander-in-Chief of the army accepted the surrender of the French in the central plaza of Fuenterrabía on 25 March 1524. Clearly on that occasion the young Duke de Alba dissipated the anger of his family for his escapade.

Juan Ciudad took no part in the festivities, for he was already well halfway across Spain on his return journey to Oropesa. Was he exhausted or downhearted? Surely he must have been saddened. One author speculates that he was so embarrassed at being dismissed from the army that he tarried for some months, maybe years, before returning to Oropesa. The inference here being that he needed some time to get over the affair and to recharge his spirit. In reality, the expulsion of a volunteer from the army did not mean very much. The soldier Ciudad had no formal ties with the army. In fact his dismissal occurred only a couple of months before the rest of the Oropesan lancers returned under the Count's standard. Certainly, Juan returned home somewhat earlier due to his bitter experience but not in disgrace. Anyway, the long journey home alone would have been tiresome, especially as he would have had to sleep under the stars and beg for food.

Another commentator wonders whether it was after Fuenterrabía that Juan was awakened to a mysterious desire to consecrate his life to the service of unfortunate people. Others emphasise the unfortunate experience with the French mare as possibly being the cause of some brain damage, which later on explains some crucial moments in his biography.

Let us take a step at a time. At the moment, Juan is walking sadly, without much enthusiasm, towards Oropesa.

Notes to Chapter 8

* The proposal of marriage with the daughter of Francisco Mayoral is related by Francisco González in his testimony as a witness at the Beatification process. (J. García Sánchez, Beresit 4 (1992) 98). J. Cruset, *Una aventura iluminada. San Juan de Dios*, Madrid 4 1997, 36; and A.Muñoz Hidalgo, *De Juan Ciudad a Juan de Dios*, Barcelona 1990, 32: both have taken this up with interest but are basically in error because they have not been able to solve the enigma of 'Mayoral'. We are ignorant of the number of young women who lived in the circle of servants in the Herruz household, but it is certain that there must have been many. Francisco Herruz had daughters in 1523, but they were small children, María 6 years of age and Isabella 4, which eliminates any idea of matrimony with the 28 years old Juan.

* The age when Juan enlisted in 1523 was 28, he was born in 1495, therefore Castro is in error by saying he was 22, a mistake complicated by the baroque biographers: Celi says 21, Govea 22 and Trinchería 23 (R. M. Saucedo, *Cronológia aplicada en la vida de N. P. S. Juan de Dios*: Paz y Caridad 12 (Nov.- Dec. 1951) 338-229). G. Magliozzi, *Pagine juandediane*, Rome 1992, 120: this suggests an ingenious explanation for Castro's error; the "confidential disciple" of John of God, having heard that the emperor Charles V had called men up to the army in 1522, got mixed up with the dates later on believing John of God was then 22 years of the age instead of the year of the call-up '22.

* The captain who was chief of the 40 Oropesan lancers in the war at Fuenterrabía was not Juan Herruz , the eldest son of the hidalgo Herruz because this Juan Herruz was only 13 years of age in the spring of 1523 (J. García Sánchez, *Crónicas del Arañuelo I*, Toledo 1985, 102-103). There is a witness who clearly demonstrates the pure bloodline of Antonia Herruz, great grand daughter of the hidalgo Francisco Herruz. The National Historic Archives for 1606 states: "Francisco Herruz who was the first who came to Torralba, was a captain, and is without doubt he who went to the war in Navarre. He was with the men of the Count of Oropesa and in the book of the life of John of God there is a mention about this fact." Castro, who however mistakes the name and says Juan instead of Francisco, verifies the mention.

* Magliozzi, *Pagine juandediane*, Rome 1992, 122: here in an intelligent paragraph is presented the idea that Juan tarried intentionally on his return to Oropesa over a period of some years, so as to psychologically digest the disaster of Fuenterrabía and to overcome the shame of returning as one expelled from the army. That is how Magliozzi saves the error of Castro in his 1587 biography of John of God, chapter 2 where four years are attributed to his second stage at Oropesa instead of the 8 years shown in the chronology: R. M. Saucedo, *Cronológia aplicada en la vida de N. P. S. Juan de Dios*: 339-340.

9

THE FRESH AIR OF GREEN PASTURES

Torralba de Oropesa
1524-1532

How curious that two Spanish saints fought in the same war between Francis I and Charles V on the border between France and Spain. A war that began in the spring of 1521 and lasted until the spring of 1524. They were Ignatius of Loyola and John of God.

Ignatius, a wealthy aristocrat who moved in the circle of nobility, was a captain in the army. Juan, John of God, a poor shepherd whose companions were village farm labourers, was a soldier in the lowest ranks.

The gentleman soldier Ignatius of Loyola had his leg broken by a cannon ball during a French attack upon the city of Pamplona. He remained crippled for the rest of his life. Juan the shepherd, soldier of fortune, was cast from the back of a French mare and landed upon a rock in the Fuenterrabía hinterland. His commanding officer expelled him from the army.

Ignatius was born in 1492, the year Queen Isabella took Granada and Columbus opened the way to America. Juan was born in 1495, the year Manuel the Unfortunate chose Vasco da Gama to sail to India.

Between both births, the kings of Spain and Portugal signed the famous pontifical treaty at Tordesillas in which they agreed to share the newly discovered lands and those still waiting to be discovered.

Enlightenment was awaiting Ignatius of Loyola at Monserrat. For John of God, madness awaited him at Granada.

I can imagine the shepherd Juan sitting with his flock on the banks of the Tietar on an autumn evening in 1524. This summer Juan has had plenty of time to mull over the forceful impressions left upon his mind by his military experience on the French border.

After joining in the festivities that followed the entrance to Fuenterrabía, the remainder of the Oropesan lancers and their captain, the hidalgo Herruz, returned home sometime between April and May. The labourers of Torralba, Oropesa and the surrounding countryside, were eager to hear from the lancers about their fortunes and experiences in the war. The unfortunate incident that nearly cost the shepherd Juan his life had circulated all over the countryside. He had to repeat the story dozens of times. Juan was received home with kindness, all missed him, especially his *mayoral*. Castro relates the overseer's happiness when he saw him return, *"... because he loved him like a son, he was overjoyed."* Seeing Juan so overwhelmed from the effects of the war, it is no wonder that he was received back amongst his friends with such warmth. Now Juan could once more enjoy the pleasant autumn evenings among the blue hills.

His fellow lancers backed up Juan's personal account of his adventures and his story was decidedly not all negative. He had seen the ugly side of life, inhumanity, violence, brutality and sin. His friendly conversations included the account of how his companions cared for him and nursed him back to health after his unfortunate episode with the mare. He also spoke of the kindness of the person who mediated on his behalf, thereby saving him from the gibbet.

Juan had temporally broken the thread of his life when he went away to be a soldier, he was now a shepherd again. This was his work, this was his place. Maybe an unconscious question was already stirring within him, asking him if this was to be his place forever.

Like almost all the young labourers who left the district to answer the call to arms, Juan had joined the army and marched off to Fuenterrabía with the intention of returning to Oropesa. Very few had decided to move into the ranks of mercenary companies and stay in the regular service of the Emperor. Juan was back again working as a shepherd but he did not know for how long.

My friend José Martín Descalso, like everybody else in Torralba today, laments that he is hemmed in with asphalt and finds it very difficult to discover a green spot where he can breath fresh air. The shepherd Juan Ciudad was lucky to have plenty of green pastures where he could breath freely as he did in the years before Fuenterrabía and for another eight years afterwards.

The squabbling between Francis I and Charles V continued and produced a very serious situation that greatly appalled the Emperor's Spanish vassals.

From the start of summer in 1522, Charles V established his court permanently in Spain from where he would govern the Empire, and from where he gathered his necessary men and money. He now surrounded himself with Spanish dignitaries and he often summoned sessions of the court, although to tell the truth, it was nearly always to solicit approbation for some new financial assistance. He did not go outside Spain to marry, although he looked about to see what shining prospects might be on offer by the other European kingdoms. His wife was born in Portugal but she was far removed from Portuguese lineage and one could safely say that she was Spanish. The lady of his choice was his cousin Isabel who, like himself, was a grandchild of the Catholic Monarchs. Isabel was the daughter of Maria, Infanta of Spain. King Manuel I of Portugal had married Princess Isabel, the firstborn daughter of the Catholic Monarchs. The offspring of this marriage was the baby Manuel who, for two years, held within his tiny person the hope that the kingdoms of Spain and Portugal might be united. Unfortunately the child king died after only 21 months of life. Manuel, the widower of Isabel, married his sister-in-law Maria, who was fourth daghter of the Catholic Monarchs. They had ten children and gave the name Isabel to their infant daughter as a twofold family commemoration.

When the most powerful ruler in the world, the young Charles I of Spain and V of Germany, married his cousin Isabel of Portugal the two Iberian nations were jubilant. The Emperor waited in Seville for the nuptial cortege to arrive from Lisbon and when it did, the marriage took place in the Alcázar [fortress] of Seville in the spring of 1526. It is said that the people of Seville not only thought the new Empress was beautiful, but that she was also good. They knew how to get on! Charles was overjoyed with his bride and promised to give her a palace in the Alhambra of Granada.

In the meanwhile, both good and bad news was arriving from Italy. Since the French invaded the Duchy of Milan in 1521 the troops of the Emperor Charles were attempting to stop their advance. In March 1523, Charles asked his brother Ferdinand to send him a corps of the famous German Lansqunets, mercenaries who would fight for the highest bidder. These arrived and the Emperor was then able to reinforce his army with these mercenaries. They were placed under the command of experienced generals such as Antonio de Leiva and the Marquis de Pescara. The Spanish army overthrew the French forces outside the walls of Pavia on 24 February 1525. Francis I risked his life by leading a furious cavalry charge in the battle. His horse was wounded and he fell to the ground and was taken prisoner. On the evening of his disastrous defeat the French King sent a dispatch to his mother, Louisa de Savoy, whom he had left in Paris as Regent of the kingdom. The message was: *"Everything is lost except honour and life."*

The king was taken as a prisoner to Madrid where he was forced to sign an exacting treaty known as, 'The Peace of Madrid'. This, besides forcing the French King to abandon Milan for ever and to respect the Navarre border, obliged him to marry Doña Leonora of Austria, the sister of his rival, the Emperor Charles. The chronicles say that, before signing the peace treaty, Francis whispered to a notary that he considered it to be null and void because he was forced to sign it under duress. Charles did not trust him so, before giving him his liberty, he took the two sons of the French King prisoner and kept them as hostages at Madrid. Francis knew the princes would be well treated but as soon as he stepped onto French soil he declared, *"I am still King!"* He forgot the treaty and the promised Doña Leanor remained without a husband.

The victory of the Emperor Charles over King Francis left the rulers of the Italian states utterly confused and also worried the King of England, Henry VIII. They all feared that the growing power of the Emperor might convert him into an arbitrator over their own destinies. The person who feared him most was the Pope.

Clement VII wanted to see Italy free of foreigners. After Pavia he knew that Charles would be master of Naples and Milan. So he began secret negotiations with Francis I, recently released from prison.

Charles had optimistically written into the text of the Madrid treaty which Francis I had signed, the following clause: *"That the aforementioned Lords, Emperor and King may be and are from here onwards, good, true and loyal friends, allies and confederates."* The clause was not worth the paper it was written upon!

Francis was never more to cross Bidasoa at the border, but began searching for new alliances against the Emperor. His treachery lay, not so much in the fact that he sought to win over the Pope and the King of England, but inasmuch as he sought the help of the Turkish Sultan, Sulieman the Magnificent, as well as conspiring with the German Protestants.

Clement VII concurred with the plot because he feared the Emperor Charles would dominate the whole of Europe and have absolute power in Italy. The plot against the Emperor was therefore very attractive to the Italian magnates.

In May 1526 the Pope, Francis I and the heads of the Italian states signed a pact of alliance against the Emperor at Cognac. Because of the Pope's presence, the pact was called the Clementine League. The Pope publicly declared that Francis I was under no obligation to fulfil the conditions of the Madrid pact. The war in Italy now took a nasty turn as Charles found himself having to attack the Pope himself.

Following the death of the Marquis de Pescara, the Emperor appointed Charles de Borbon Commander-in-Chief of the Spanish forces in Italy. This French general, having fallen out with the French King and also the members of his own family, shifted his allegiance to the Emperor Charles. The new Commander-in-Chief immediately had a new corps of twelve thousand German mercenaries placed under his command.

The war began. The federation of the Clementine League laid siege to Genoa, while the Imperialists made rapid incursions from Naples and pushed on to Rome. Commander de Borbon suffered a serious problem, the Emperor did not send him enough money to pay his army of mercenaries who were stationed in the north of Italy. The mercenaries resolved the problem by looting. They furiously plundered Lombardy and part of the Genoese region. Their captains promised them paradise when they got down to Rome to sack the palaces of the Pope. It was a very attractive idea to the German soldiers, the majority of whom already were professed Protestants who considered the Pope to be an antichrist.

Borbon maintained the situation until the end of January 1527. A column of 26,000 men began the march to the south. There were Prussians, Bavarians, Sueves from the Tyrol, Spaniards, and Italian reprobates who swelled the number to 30,000 – all with an idea to plunder. They had no fear of the constant rain nor were they concerned about securing their rearguard. They moved down like a flood and arrived at the gates of Rome on 5 May. The Commander-in-Chief of the Imperial army fell in the first assault but his men decimated the army of the Pope. When the Imperialists overwhelmed the city Clement VII took refuge in nearby Castle Sant' Angelo. Rome suffered a barbaric sacking: assassinations, torment, rapes, pillage and incendiaries.

The Emperor Charles was given news of the sack of Rome at Valladolid where he was preparing for the celebrations to mark the birth of his firstborn son, Philip. He suspended the celebrations and ordered the court into mourning for the outrage and called for public prayers for the Holy Father. Charles sent a declaration to Christian princes stating that he had nothing whosoever to do with the affair and that he condemned the criminals responsible for it. He was terrified and rightly so. The armies of the 'defender of Christianity' had assaulted the city of the Pope. What would his loyal Spanish subjects say? He was soon to find out from the Franciscan Cardinal Quiñones who, although he was very devoted to the monarchy, spoke up on their behalf. The Franciscan Cardinal made a play on words, based on the similar endings of his surname [*quiñon* with a meaning pertaining to 'sharing'] and the Spanish word for 'kidneys' [riñónes] to explain to Charles that the people had the impression that he now shared two titles – that of Emperor and that of 'the General of Luther'. Charles's regrets about this impression were sincere. The chronicler Pero Mexia relates that the Emperor's letters to the Pope in Castle Sant' Angelo *show great affection, consolation and offer him his love and friendship.* Charles sent orders to his captains stating that, *"should the castle be taken, he would suitably pay for the war damage and that the Pope's person would be treated with full liberty and respect."*

Juan's military service was an experience that opened his eyes to an horizon that was far wider than the fields of the Arañuelo and the foothills of the Gredos. From now on any news that came his way about what was going on in the Emperor's military campaigns had a certain familiar ring about it. Throughout the homes of Castile there was sadness and shock at the sacrilegious sacking of Rome. They just could not imagine that the troops of their Emperor would sack the city of the Pope. It was just as well that news quickly spread throughout Castile in the summer of 1529 that the Pope and the Emperor had signed a pact of peace. What joy after so much suffering! How could a country of good Christians feel happy if the soldiers of its king went on the rampage furiously swinging their swords about in the streets of Rome? It was a nightmare.

The mercenaries of the deceased Commander Borbon had outraged the Pope, cardinals, bishops and even simple monks and nuns. Fenced in at Castle Sant' Angelo, the Pope waited in vain for the Italian lords who had signed the pact of the Clementine League to come and rescue him. For a month the Pope held out but finally he surrendered. When the captains of the invading army entered the fortress they forced the Pope to pay 400,000 ducats to the mercenaries. They then sent a dispatch off to the Emperor asking him to let them know what conditions he wanted for peace. There was much coming and going of dispatches and, as a consequence, the treaty was delayed. Clement VII was sick and tired of being forcibly retained in Castle Sant' Angelo and on Christmas eve he bribed some of the castle guards and fled to exile at Orvieto from where he began negotiations for his capitulation with the faraway Emperor.

Francis I came back upon the scene. He asked Henry VIII for English troops to join him in going into Italy to liberate the Pope from his captivity. It was a favourable occasion for the French King because now he could blame the Emperor for the outrages committed against the Sovereign Pontiff, thereby shifting the blame away from himself for starting the conflict.

Henry VIII gladly accepted the invitation of Francis I because he was anxious to gain the Pope's favour. Henry was about to begin a religious drama of his own in England. For the moment the English King converted his love affairs into affairs of state. He wanted the Pope to dissolve his marriage with Catherine of Aragon, the daughter of the Catholic Monarchs, and to permit him to marry Anne Boleyn.

The Emperor Charles signed a peace treaty with Clement VII and the two became friends. In February 1530, Clement crowned Charles, 'Emperor of the West and the successor of Charlemagne'. It seemed something like a miracle, but a period of peace actually blossomed between Charles V and Francis I. The two old enemies signed a peace treaty and the Emperor's sister, the Princess Leonora, finally married the King of France. And so the two old fighting cocks who had been enemies for so long became brothers-in-law.

Henry VIII became so enslaved to his sensuality that he was already on the slippery path to schism. This was a pity because Christianity needed his help to stem the march of German Protestantism and to cut short the menaces of the Turkish army.

Juan Ciudad would have a second taste of military life when the Emperor was to begin recruiting an army to go against Sulieman.

Facts regarding Juan Ciudad's personal life during the years he was a shepherd at Torralba de Oropesa are very scarce. This is the longest period in his biography and it is virtually silent. Nevertheless, there is an indication that his employers may have given him some sort of promotion rather than leaving him as a simple shepherd bound to his flocks.

Shepherds of the period belonged to two well-defined groups: shepherds of 'standing flocks', and shepherds of 'migrating flocks'. The shepherd's job was to guard, guide and graze the sheep. The care of flocks was done in two ways: The 'standing' flock which grazed on the owner's land or that of a rural family had shepherds who did general farming duties such as working rough land, orchards and forests, and with fenced animals. For this type of work the farmer employed shepherds who lived in the common home. They were day shepherds and followed the movements of the flock throughout the various seasons of the year but in the evening they herded the sheep into a corral and then spent their nights in the house with the other servants.

The shepherd of a 'migrating' flock followed his sheep on common land that was under the surveillance of the Crown. This was an important part of the 'Mesta', as the powerful organisation of sheep owners was called. The 'Mesta' functioned like a co-operative of sheep owners who saw to it that suitable land was found, and attended to the marketing of the meat and wool. Because it was a major contributor to the royal coffers the Catholic Monarchs gave the 'Mesta' much power. Wool was exported in sacks that were individually taxed by one ducat each if they were destined for the Netherlands and two ducats if they were for Italy. The flocks of the 'Mesta' grazed on excellent mountain pastures in summer and in sheltered lowland areas in winter. The shepherds employed by the 'Mesta' cared for thousands of sheep which they took up into the hills during the heat of summer and down to the plains of Extremadura and the Mancha in the cold of winter. The 'Mesta' commanded their own mayors and judges who chose the shepherds from amongst labourers who were robust enough to withstand the long walks and changes of weather. Because of their endurance over a period of many years of arduous outdoor work, the shepherds of the 'Mesta' were eagerly recruited as mercenaries in the Emperor's army.

Juan Ciudad was a 'standing' shepherd in the service of the *hidalgo* Herruz, and he lived in his master's homestead at Torralba de Oropesa. The Herruz family moved to the town of

Oropesa many years later and some of the descendants of the *hidalgo* held prominent positions in the Castle. Juan would take his flock in summer up to the foothills of the Gredos and in winter back again to the Arañuelo. His was a far more personal type of work than that of the shepherds of the *Mesta*. He had the security of a life with the family of the *hidalgo* Herruz and the cordiality of spending his evenings in the company of farm labourers. Even though you could say that he was a personal shepherd, his was still a very hard life and called for much sacrifice. Cervantes has Don Quixote saying that a shepherd must prepare himself from childhood because *"such work was really for weather-beaten men and servants fit for that type of work from the cradle and childhood."* Juan learnt as a child and began his work in earnest when he was only a lad.

There is another clue that both before and after Juan went to Fuenterrabía Herruz could have promoted him. He looked after his master's horses and, who knows, later on maybe those of the Count. This is a pearl of a clue because there is such a scarcity of information about Juan during this period, that even this comes as a real treasure. For example, it is of value to know of his prayer to the Blessed Virgin Mary when he survived his fall from the French mare. Although we do not have any documented proof, we can presume that during his youth at Torralba, Juan lived the normal religious practices of Castilian families of the period. When he was in dire trouble, he had recourse to Our Lady as Castro affirms: *"He called upon the name of Our Lady the Virgin Mary to whom he had always been devoted."* That is quite certain.

Now another clue lets us guess that Juan's activities exceeded his simple job as a shepherd, for in some way he also looked after horses. We will soon see that he, himself, gives us the clue to this when he first begins to feel stirrings within himself to dedicate his life to serving the needy. He looked back over his life and commented how: *"... he sadly remembered how well fed, protected and healthy the horses in the Count of Oropesa's stables were, whilst the poor were so badly off, ragged and hungry... "* The injustice of this cut him to the quick. If he was also employed in looking after horses with kindness what a contrast this would be to caring for the poor who, *"were so badly off, ragged and hungry."* These are ideas that we will leave for the moment.

For now, Juan Ciudad once more enlists under the Imperial banner.

Notes to Chapter 9

* The wounding of Ignatius de Loyola at Pamplona is well documented in all biographies of the Saint; Cf. J. I. Tellechea, *Ignacio de Loyola, solo y a pie*, Salamanca 5, 1995, 83-91.

* The discussion regarding the four years of John of God's second stage at Oropesa, which in my opinion is erroneous, is included in R. M. Saucedo's, *Cronológia aplicada en la vida de N. P. S. Juan de Dios:* Paz y Caridad 12 (Nov.- Dec. 1951) 339-340. The error came about by confusing the siege of Vienna by Sulieman in 1529 - to which the Emperor did not go - with the expedition organised by Charles V against Sulieman in 1532. I have replied to G. Magliozzi's opinion in the notes to chapter 8.

* There is an immense bibliography on the *Mesta*. For the essential lines on this subjects, see M. Fernandéz Alvarez, *La sociedad española en el siglo de Oro*, I, Madrid 1989, 84-88.

10

JUAN AT VIENNA UNDER THE EMPEROR'S BANNERS

Vienna
1532

In the spring of 1532 the call goes out again throughout the empire seeking recruits for the army. This time it is to fight against the Turk. Eight years previously, when Juan first enlisted, the appeal stirred patriotic sentiments: Emperor Charles V had sworn to retake Fuenterrabía, which had been occupied by the French. This time the bugles were sounding to summon recruits for a religious crusade against the armies of Sulieman, the Turkish Sultan. Already the Turks were on the march towards Vienna where they hoped to cause a breach in the eastern flank of Europe.

We do not know whether it was the religious content of this call to arms that influenced Juan Ciudad to enlist, but enlist he did. Perhaps there was some unconscious desire in his heart to make compensation for his previous military misadventures. It also reawakened the desire he had when he was younger to break with the monotonous life of a shepherd. This is how Castro puts it: *"His youthfulness got the better of him, as it so often does with young men who have tasted life's experiences and find it hard to settle down again."* Even if that were the case, the fact remains that our shepherd is no longer a youth - in fact he is 37 years of age.

The Emperor Charles V was absent at the time and his wife, Queen Isabel, was Regent of Castile. It was she who sent word to the Count of Oropesa to recruit men for the army. There was much excitement in the Herruz homestead when word went out seeking recruits. One result was that Juan Ciudad enlisted again. The Count, good vassal that he was, complied immediately by nominating his eldest son Fernando to be the captain of the Oropesan lancers. And that is how Juan Ciudad took part in one of the 16th century's key moments of world politics.

When Pope Clement VII had crowned the Emperor Charles two years previously, he called him "the Emperor of the West and the successor of Charlemagne." Now Charles had to live up to this title and do what was expected of him as the supreme leader responsible for the security of Christendom. The Emperor immediately called upon Christian kings and princes, both Catholic and Protestant, to ward off the Asiatic avalanche that was tumbling towards Europe. We will return to Sulieman the Magnificent in his moment of greatest glory.

Two contrary imperial powers clashed head-on. The Islamic dominion of the Sultan Sulieman and the Christian domain of the Emperor Charles.

During the first half of the 16th century three Moslem dynasties ruled the East: the Ottomans of Turkey, the Safavids of Persia and the Mughals of India. Islam, supported by these three Moslem powers, controlled the land and sea from Morocco to Hungary and from Ethiopia to Central Asia. However, there was little unity between these Islamic powers due to deep-rooted religious controversy. The Turks and Mughals professed the orthodox Sunni Islam, while the Persians adhered to the Shi'ite confession. Their internal divisions led them into constant clashes, and sometimes they even sought to make alliances with European Christians against their Moslem brothers.

The Turkish Empire had conquered Constantinople, which up to the end of the 15th century had imagined itself to be the successor to the grandeur of the Roman Empire in the East and West. When Sulieman the Magnificent came to the throne in 1520, he determined to make this dream a reality. His plan was to make inroads into Europe by sea from the Mediterranean, while at the same time penetrating inland as far as Vienna.

Not even the Hispano-Austrian Empire, or that of remote China, could equal the splendour of Sulieman's Ottoman Empire that boasted forty million subjects, fifteen thousand of whom lived in the enchanting and dazzling city of Istanbul.

The Turkish Sultan, Sulieman, disciplined his army with an iron hand. To exercise naval pressure from the Mediterranean Sulieman utilised the pirate Barbarossa, whose bases extended right along the North African coast. The famous corsair terrified the coasts of Italy and the south of Spain. Barbarossa made an alliance with Sulieman who was very satisfied to count him as an ally against Spain. Sulieman conferred on Barbarossa the title Admiral of the Ottoman Fleet and accepted him as a great vassal. The Turkish sultan did more: he sent his ships to enlarge the Berber fleet.

Reinforced with such an alliance, Barbarossa became the most powerful force in the western Mediterranean. He extended the hold he had upon Algiers and he conquered Tunis from where he boldly increased his attacks upon Italian and Spanish shipping. Barbarossa wreaked havoc from Sicily to Cadiz on the Spanish Atlantic coast. Sulieman had great success in his campaigns on land. This success was handed to him upon a silver platter by the

Hungarian nobles and, I am sorry to say, by Francis I of France and Henry VIII of England, both of whom were prepared to make an alliance with the Turks, or the devil himself, in order to damage the Emperor Charles.

Sulieman's army swept into Hungary in August 1526 and coming up from Belgrade attacked the Hungarian borders. The king of Hungary, Louis II, fell in the battle of Mohacs. The wife of the Hungarian King was Margarita of Austria, sister of the Emperor Charles and also of King Ferdinand of Austria. In the event of the death of Charles or of his renouncing the imperial crown as King of the Romans, Ferdinand of Austria would become the heir to the imperial crown of Germany. The Hungarian court elected Anna, sister of the late Louis II and wife of King Ferdinand of Austria, to be their Queen. France, England and Poland were worried about this new strengthening of the Hispano-Austrian Empire. To counteract this they incited the Hungarian nobility to elect a king of their own from among their peers, which they did in the person of 'Voivode' of Transylvania, Joannes Zapolya. Civil war broke out resulting in the crushing of Zapolya's forces by Ferdinand. Zapolya had gone to Sulieman for help and promised him that if he came to his aid he would declare Hungary a feudatory of Turkey.

Sulieman thought that this was a chance too good to miss so he attacked his friend and vassal, Zapolya, and entered Buda the capital from where he launched his army towards Vienna.

It was 1529 when Ferdinand tried as best he could to defend Vienna, but he had no other support than the four companies of Spanish veterans which constituted the Royal Guard. The Emperor tried to send some help from Italy but this effort failed.

The heroic defenders of Vienna resisted the ferocious Turkish assault. Sulieman maintained his siege of the city and returned to his base camp to assemble a war machine that, by demolishing Vienna, would advance him into the heart of Europe. The Ottoman sultan was at the point of attempting, and succeeding with, the Islamic invasion of the West.

The forces of Sulieman and the imperial ambitions of Emperor Charles clashed head on. These days scholars argue about the imperial designs of Charles V and ask what were the Emperor's intentions. Was he trying to unify the world under his command as some sort of universal monarch? Or was he just trying to act as an arbitrator between Christian princes? Distinguished jurists and thinkers of his time saw him as a man marked out by heaven, who with the Pope's consent, was to guide the flock of Christianity towards the imminent final judgement. When one considers the haste with which Charles and his men were forced to act, it seems more likely that they tried to respond to each urgency as it presented itself.

A personal or collective answer to any demand calls for a great deal of goodwill from both the individual and the populace. Should the demand, that is to say the ability to carry out the task, not stand up to the measures at hand, then the opportunity to respond is lost. On the other hand Spaniards in the time of the Emperor Charles V were at a significant point of history that presented them with an agenda full of opportunities to perform acts of heroism. Anyone who wanted to be a hero had ample opportunity to become one.

The burdens of European politics and the exploits of its navigators were stretching Spain enormously. The Comuneros of Toledo and Avila who ended up losing the civil war had demonstrated with their devotion to a handful of liberties that they would be capable of heroically establishing a Spanish presence from the Baltic to the Pacific. They would be able to say truthfully that the sun never sets in the empire of their Caesar. There is no doubt that, in the households of Spain, there was a tremendous fascination with the Emperor's way of playing politics. His image was seen as a mixture of the worldly and the divine. Young men rushed to enlist in the call-up, Juan Ciudad being an example. He renounced the quiet life of a shepherd and enlisted in the army for a second time - in spite of his previous bitter experiences.

Spaniards paid a tremendous price to support the Emperor's imperialistic ambitions. Charles V not only took the sons of the upper-class families, he also took their money.

At this time Spain should have been becoming richer with every ship that arrived back from America. But that was not so. To exercise imperial responsibility cost both lives and gold. There were not enough men or resources on the Iberian Peninsula to fulfil the imperial designs so the Emperor's generals were forced to contract mercenaries. There were also the expenses of travel, viceroys, the court and the maintenance of the prestige of the imperial sceptre. Castile was astonished to see its former modest budget blow out of all proportion. Before he went off in search of the title of emperor, Charles summoned the Spanish Courts together in the famous and polemic Convocation of Santiago. There was no alternative: in 1523 the court met at Valladolid and called for the payment of new taxes of 400,000 ducats specifically to equip the army. In 1526 Charles presided at the Court at Toledo where he was able to get 200,000,000 maravedis. The following year, 1527, he held another session at Valladolid. He did not dare state the total amount he needed because the international conflicts and wars were the forerunners of a frontal clash with the Turkish army. A year later, on June 28, he extracted 200,000 pounds from the Court of Aragon. There was a flurry of extraordinary taxes on private and public properties. But even this was not enough, so the Emperor went to the great banking houses of Germany and Flanders. These gave him the money and demanded, as guarantee, the ships of the Indies.

Extremely high interest rates soon devoured the imperial coffers. The rush of riches from America by-passed Spain and went straight up to Amsterdam and Augsburg. Halfway through the century the bankers began foreclosing on the Emperor Charles and for two years they seized everything that came out of America. In this difficult moment the Emperor had to sell Crown property and he even put his hands into the dowry of the Empress. He sold the Molucas Islands to Portugal, and had to put up the mines of Almadén as a guarantee.

Spain's economy suffered critical changes. Agriculture, industry and commerce could not keep pace with unforeseen demands. Formerly the country was shut in upon itself, now it had become a platform of world contact with hardly any unifying defences. The traditional medieval Castilian fairs fell by the wayside, and industry languished, as young men were absorbed into the army. Years of poor harvests could no longer support the high prices imposed upon the populace.

Juan Ciudad participated in the clash of the titans: the Emperor of the East against the Emperor of the West; Sulieman the Magnificent, Lord of the Turks versus Charles I of Spain and V of Germany. The field of battle was Vienna.

The two opponents had carefully prepared their armies for

battle. Since January 1532 Sulieman had been building up his Mediterranean fleet with the intention of sending it under the command of Abrihin Bajá to make a summer offensive against Sicily and Naples. Sulieman's army at Vienna numbered 300,000 soldiers who came under his personal command. The Turkish troops were equipped with the latest war machines that were capable of breaching the Christian Empire's western frontier. Sulieman laid claim to the Empire as his own, by right, as Lord of Constantinople and legitimate successor of Constantine the Great.

Charles V reacted rapidly when confronted with this news. Fortunately for him the Pope was on tenterhooks. But Charles had to take into account an attitude, at least neutral, of Francis I and Henry VIII, and get the help of the Protestant German Princes who, in due course, would be reached by Sulieman when the Turks took Vienna. Theoretically Charles V exercised command over three hundred European political units, some large, others small, nevertheless, he had to rely upon the rulers, (princes, dukes, landgraves, masters) who governed them. The population did not have the means to decide political or religious affairs for itself. If the ruler broke with Rome, then the population under his rule would join the Protestant spiritual family. That was precisely what happened in England and the Nordic countries that contained a third of the inhabitants of Europe. In those days, Europe had a population numbering about sixty million, twenty million of whom had broken with the Catholic Church. Never before had Christianity had to live through a drama of such proportions as the one unleashed by the friar Martin Luther.

The people of Vienna were alarmed at the frightening news that Sulieman's Turkish troops were on the verge of taking their city. Charles V announced that when the time was opportune, and with the consent of the electors, he would hand over the imperial crown to his brother Ferdinand to whom he had entrusted Austria and Hungary. Charles called on all to come to the defence of Vienna. The Protestant princes answered the call but not before negotiating a pact with him that was signed at Nuremberg in the summer of 1532. This put into effect a provisional equality for Protestants and Catholics who agreed that nobody would be persecuted or condemned for their religious beliefs.

The Emperor Charles sent a dispatch to the Empress in Spain telling her to ask 'his faithful Catholic vassals' for men, arms and supplies to meet this necessity. The Lord of Oropesa responded to the call. Juan Ciudad enlisted in the Count's party. It seems that the Count, Don Francisco, appointed Juan to be the personal servant of his eldest son, Don Ferdinand, whom he appointed as captain to lead the Oropesan recruits. This is how Castro tells it: *"All the time that the Count (actually it was not the Count but his son Ferdinand) was in the camp of the Emperor, John served with much diligence in his retinue."* By 'in his retinue' is meant: amongst those close to him.

Spain's answer to the Emperor's call to arms was generous: "They came together - in the service of the Emperor - the veterans and the most war-experienced nobles of Spain."

In order to hinder the movements of the Turkish navy present in the Mediterranean, the Emperor ordered the Italian admiral, Andrea Doria, to send his fleet into Greek waters. The Pope sent experienced troops and financed the acquisition of 8,000 Hungarian horses. The princes of Germany, Poland, Bohemia and Moravia all contributed, but less help came from France and England, which remained neutral.

Charles led his troops to battle and so too did Sulieman. Thus both armies converged with an emperor leading each one. Numerically the odds were against Charles, for he only had 90,000 infantrymen and 30,000 cavalry against Sulieman's army of up to 300,000 Turks, although the exact number cannot be said with any certainty. In favour of the Christian army was its large number of battle-tested irregulars whose reputation for invincibility in battle had preceded them.

What a pity some journalists did not interview John of God some evening at Granada. I think that, if he had been interviewed and asked to recount his journey from Oropesa to Vienna, he would have had a fascinating story to tell.

We do not know the exact route the Spanish troops took when they set off for Vienna. But, the Spanish and Italian troops having been summoned to come together south of Lake Garda, beyond the Po, in the estates of the Marquis del Vasto to whom Charles has entrusted the expedition, the reasonable plan would have been to embark the Spanish forces at Barcelona for Genoa.

Juan saw the sea for the first time in his life from the coast at Fuenterrabía: How would our shepherd from the Arañuelo have reacted to, not only seeing the sea, but actually voyaging on it?

They began their advance from Garda on Sunday August 4, 1532. At Trent they were given orders from the Emperor to make haste. The forced march provoked mutinies and, according to the chronicles of the period, some soldiers were shot as a result. As was customary, women joined the columns as camp followers. They passed through Brixen then went on to Innsbruck. On 19 August the foot soldiers crossed the River Inn in small boats but the horses and carriages were taken overland. Onwards they marched to Kufstein, then Rosenheim. The River Inn, at the latitude of Munich, branches to the right. At Braunau they rendezvoused with the German troops and rested there until the end of the month. The infantry followed the river as far as Passau where the Inn joins the Danube.

They arrived at Linz on the first of September. Abandoning the boats, the Marquis del Vasto placed his troops in parallel columns along the banks of the Danube from Krems to Vienna. At Krems the camp suffered great damage in a fire caused by the 'commandos' of the leader of the Hungarians, Zapolya. Del Vasto transferred his camp to the open countryside after that event. Emperor Charles had his army in battle line by the first week of September.

Early in July, Sulieman took Belgrade and went on to capture Buda, which he entered on 29 July. He received a welcome with the full honours of a conquering hero by Zapolya the leader of the Hungarians. The chronicles of the period say Zapolya gave Sulieman four beautiful horses embellished with Italian harness. He also presented the Turk with "four pretty young virgins, a Pole, a Spaniard and two Italians, all dressed in silks and jewels, their beauty admired by all." Sulieman responded to this gesture by throwing a magnificent banquet for the Turkish and Hungarian captains.

During the first week of August, 30,000 Tartars arrived to swell the ranks of the Turkish army. Sulieman then moved his troops towards Vienna turning westwards where the River Raab enters the Danube. Here he extended his line as far as Graz where by early September his forces were facing the camp of the Emperor, leaving a wide 'no man's land' between the two armies that extended from Neustadt in the east to Salzburg in the west.

Both armies eyed each other with respect from a distance. The Imperialists feared the Turkish cavalry while the Ottomans, for their part, feared the Christian army's artillery. The Emperor Charles brought reinforcement companies into Vienna, while Sulieman withdrew his troops from the siege. Charles and his officers studied the situation to see if it would be advisable to follow the enemy south and attack their camp. However, they decided to hold the line on the banks of the Danube, because while it would only take 'a fast horse three days' to travel from Linz to Graz, it would be a gigantic task to move the artillery.

The Marquis del Vasto carried out, before the gates of Vienna, a tactical exercise in the presence of the Emperor. He made his squadrons open and close ranks, representing different battle movements and demonstrating with what art they had fought in the past Italian campaigns. The Emperor was duly impressed and marvelled at the spectacle. The chronicles calculated that the total number of the Emperor's troops had grown to 260,000 men. Europe had never before seen the equal of this army: "such excellent captains and outstanding soldiers." This chronicler enthusiastically added: "Clearly, this is so when we observe the magnificence and splendour of the nations that were united there and the valiant exploits of each soldier."

The two opposing armies made incursions into the no-man's-land over a two week period during the month of September, where they fought fierce isolated battles. Sulieman knew that Charles would never venture onto level ground where the Turkish cavalry could meet and annihilate the Christian army. The Turk also feared being crushed by the formidable imperial war machine so he withdrew from the conflict. Military commentators have not been able to explain Sulieman's fears and withdrawal.

The Turks broke camp and began to retreat to Belgrade, and as the chronicler so ironically puts it; "they turned their head at every step to see if the Emperor was following them." Charles could now breath freely for he had saved Europe from the invasion of Islam. What now remained to be done was to capture Sulieman's galleons in the Mediterranean.

The Emperor triumphantly entered Vienna on 24 September and on the following day he reviewed his troops

7. A 'pensione' now occupies the site where John of God began his charitable work for the poor of Granada.

8. The cloister of the Jeronymite monastery from which Fray Diego de Linares assisted the work of John of God.

camped in the fields on the city's outskirts. The soldiers wanted to see him at close range, especially the Spaniards who, as the chronicler says, "had served him for many years."

Juan would have seen the Emperor on that occasion, "as he was painted by Titian", in his celebrated portrait at Mühlberg. Seated, as José María Pemán's poetic description has it "on that horse that, raising separately its hooves to its belly, inches forward, more concerned with the elegance of a particular step than the ones that follow."

Charles's secretary Cobos wrote to the Empress from Vienna on 27 September: "Thanks be to Our Lord, His Majesty is very well. The day before yesterday he went out into the fields to review the Spanish and Italian troops, the majority of whom had never seen him before, and that applies especially to the Spaniards. It is a great pity that the Turk had fled for, without any doubt whatsoever, the Emperor would surely have vanquished him. Your Majesty can be very happy and give thanks to Our Lord that what pleases Him has taken place and that soon we will see Your Majesties happily together again."

Charles began his return journey on 4 October, "to avoid being cut off by the snows on the Alps." The light cavalry led the way, followed by the Emperor's guard and the Spanish troops under the command of the Marquis del Vasto. Next came the Cardinal Papal Delegate, the ambassadors and bishops. The Duke de Alba, commanding the Spanish cavalry and the German infantry, closed the cavalcade which entered Italy at Mantua. At Christmas the Emperor paid his respects to the Pope at Bologna. In the springtime of 1553 Charles, his nobles and fifteen battalions of Spanish infantry boarded the galleons of Andrea Doria at Genoa to set sail for Spain. They disembarked at the port of Rosas from where the Emperor led the cavalcade to Barcelona.

We do not know whether Don Fernando, the son of the Count of Oropesa, and his faithful Juan Ciudad, were with the Emperor aboard Doria's fleet which arrived at Rosas on the Catalonian coast. For motives not disclosed, Saucedo suggests that "for some secret mission that the Emperor confided to Don Ferdinand" Juan and his master went by sea to La Coruña in the north-west of Spain. Juan has ended his second military experience under the banner of the Emperor.

Notes to Chapter 10

* That it was not the Count of Oropesa, Don Francisco, but his firstborn son, Don Fernando, who went off as captain of the company to the campaign of Vienna, has been authoritatively demonstrated by Julián García Sánchez, *Crónicas de Arañuelo I*, Toledo 1985, 107. Sánches offers as proof of this the letter written by Francisco de Toledo to Cardinal Sigüenza - irrefutable evidence. Pedro Girón, *Crónica del emperador Carlos V*, Pamplona 1964, 75, confirms this by stating that; "the eldest son of the Count of Oropesa was with the nobles who went from Spain to Germany."

* Cf. R. M. Saucedo, *Ensayos históricos. La chronología aplicada en la vida de N.P.* San Juan de Dios; Paz y Caridad 12 (1951), 339-340. Some biographers say John of God went to Vienna in 1529, but this is due to confusing the attack by Sulieman in that year with the offensive organised by Charles V in 1532 to halt the Turkish advances at the gates of Vienna. Rafael Saucedo mentions this ambiguity.

* Cf. Ramón Mendéz Pidal, *Idea imperial de Carlos V*, Madrid 1971. This study is essential to understanding the imperial ambitions of Charles V.

* There is a copious bibliography on the organisation, political circumstances and developments of the Emperor's 1532 military campaign. This is supported by Pacheco de Leiva, Martín García de Cereceda, Pedron Girón, and above all, by Prudencio de Sandoval, *Historia de la Vida y hechos del Emperador Carlos V* (3 vols.), Madrid, 1955. Also, see Salvador de Madariaga, *Carlos V*, Barcelon 1982; this should be seen in conjunction with José María Zamora, *Carlos V y los españoles*.

* Juan Ciudad's return to Spain from Vienna sets forth a query. Why did Juan and his captain, the son of the Count of Oropesa, disembark at La Coruña? Saucedo offers an answer of two elements, one of which seems to me to be quite plausible while the other not so. The first element: Juan Ciudad went in the company to Vienna more as a servant of the Count, rather than as a regular soldier. The chroniclers of the period, especially Prudencio de Sandoval, in telling of the Emperor's review before the gates of Vienna after the retreat of Sulieman, says that "besides the men of war there were many others, pages and servants of soldiers and knights, who in the moment of crisis, did no less than their masters." (Prudencio de Sandoval, *Historia de la Vida y hechos del Emperador Carlos V*.): Thus Juan accompanied his master if he sailed to La Coruña. Far less likely is the second element suggested by Saucedo: that the Emperor gave Don Fernando, the eldest son of the Count of Oropesa, a secret mission to undertake in the Netherlands which was governed by the Emperor's sister, the widow Queen of Hungary, Doña Maria de Austria. That, according to Saucedo, is why the servant Juan accompanied his master to Flanders and from there sailed to the Spanish port of La Coruña. Saucedo's hypothesis has no support whatsoever in fact and it seems unlikely that Castro would have omitted to make any allusion, no matter how lightly, to the event. Castro merely says: "Once the war was over and the Turks on the retreat, he (Juan) went back with the Count (we now know that he was the son of the Count) by sea to Spain, and disembarking at the Port of La Coruña he went to Oropesa, and Juan went with him." Cf. Castro, op.cit., ch .2. Castro's badly constructed phrase leaves in ambiguity whether Juan went down from La Coruña to Oropesa, also with his master; Castro himself dispels the doubt in the first lines of chapter 3: the one who went to Oropesa was the master, not his servant. Though neither is this absolutely clear in the cited chapter 3.

11

JUAN VISITS HIS HOME VILLAGE

La Coruña, Montemor-O-Novo
1533

The reason why Don Ferdinand, the eldest son of the Count of Oropesa, and his servant Juan Ciudad returned to Spain by ship and disembarked at the Galician port of La Coruña after the Vienna campaign, remains a mystery to this day. Maybe the answer still lies hidden away waiting to be discovered in the Oropesan archives. Was it because Ferdinand had to carry out some secret mission for the Emperor in Galicia, Flanders or the Netherlands? Who knows?

Perhaps the contingent of the Galician recruits who answered the call to arms made by the Empress to fight the Turks was so great that it warranted sending them home direct from Genoa to Galicia without stopping at Barcelona where the majority of the troops disembarked. If that were the case, then maybe some of the Castilian troops also could have accompanied the Galicians direct to Galicia for demobilisation.

All that is irrelevant, for the fact remains that Juan accompanied his master and disembarked with him at La Coruña. It was here that Juan decided to break his ties with Oropesa. He would not return to the flocks of the hidalgo Herruz because he wanted his life to take another direction.

Did he make this decision because he was now free of all obligations?

Juan is now 38, and it occurs to him to visit his birthplace, Montemor-O-Novo which he left 30 years before.

Obviously those who have studied his life have tried to figure out three things about John of God during this period of time. Why did he not return to Oropesa? Why did he choose instead to go to Montemor-O-Novo, a distance of 600 kilometres from La Coruña? Oropesa would have been a far easier journey since it was only 400 kilometres away and situated on the Camino Real. What future plans had Juan in mind when he decided to quit his life long occupation as a shepherd? These are questions that need to be addressed, because each one deserves a precise, valid answer. There are many suppositions, so let us consider them in their order.

First there is his decision not to return to Oropesa. This means he abandoned his normal occupation of shepherd and cut himself off from the people whom he had considered to be his family for thirty years. Some writers have invented the story that there was a romance between Juan and the young daughter of the *mayoral* who was the overseer of the flocks owned by Herruz. This suited those who wanted to say that Juan desired to consecrate himself to God as a celibate and this was his chance to escape from having to marry the girl. Showing the future saint to have been a romantic figure might have been a brilliant stroke but this nuptial hypothesis is devoid of foundation and had its origins in fantasy nurtured by pious sermons of baroque preachers.

The matter of Juan's decision to visit Montemor-O-Novo has its foundation in what my readers already know: that there are Jewish roots in the Cidade/Ciudad family. Our friend Castro, always very cautious when it comes to this problem of Juan's family, notes some motivations: *"John felt a great urge to visit his native country, since it seemed to him to be an easy walk from where he was. Besides, he wanted to find out about his parents and relations since he had never been back there since he left as a child."* An easier walk than the one he had so many years ago from Montemor-O-Novo to Oropesa.

The psychologist Muñoz Hidalgo suggests that when Juan disembarked at La Coruña in Galicia, he heard the Galician dialect spoken - a dialect very similar to the Portuguese language - and this sparked off memories of his infancy.

The third question is rather disquieting because it specifically asks what was in Juan's mind regarding his future life. It is my opinion that some researchers attempt to invent an answer to this question based on the well-known events of his later life. Knowing that he is to become a saint, they suggest a clear call to sanctity now, and prepare him for it, by attributing to him a deep sorrow for his sins, a longing for conversion and a desire to help the poor.

As well, Juan is now 38 which, in those days, would have been considered 'on in years' and, obviously, human and divine impulses were rising within him.

Juan's experiences at Fuenterrabía and Vienna had compared unfavourably with the serene waters of his many long years spent as a shepherd wandering the Arañuelo countryside. He had been introduced to ways of behaving that he never would have thought of when he used to roam the foothills of the Sierra Gredos. How ever would he have known then the foul language of mercenaries' curses, the suffering of prisoners, how young men, strangers to each other, killed one another. Never before had he experienced long marches, camps, mutinies, assaults, fury and blood. Never had he seen vultures feasting upon corpses, or the burning and sacking of villages. This was the terrible scourge of war. There were also memories of the triumphant clarion of victory, banners flying in the breeze, and the appearance of the Emperor before the walls of Vienna. These were all blazing images engraved forever upon his mind, images of great suffering, misery and tears, wherever he turned. These experiences were to remain with Juan for the rest of his life.

Since, in my opinion, no biographer has yet thrown light upon the spirit of John of God at this time, please allow me to attempt to fill the void of information about his interior journey. If only he had he written it all up for us in his diary, or perhaps confided it in some letters dated at this period. But neither letters nor diary exist. Let us be patient!

Within a year Juan was to leave Seville for Gibraltar, and Castro gives two clues about this, but for the moment let us keep to the external character of the subject at hand. Instead of going back to Oropesa, Juan goes to his birthplace, Montemor-O-Novo, from where he had been "taken away" thirty years previously.

Juan has some money because, as we know from the records of the Vienna Campaign, the Emperor paid off all the Spanish soldiers before striking camp. The foreign mercenaries were not so lucky.

A glance at the atlas shows us the route Juan took from La Coruña to Montemor-O-Novo. His itinerary just about transversed the entire geography and history of Portugal from north to south.

The Spanish section of his journey, from La Coruña to Tuy, passes through Santiago de Compostella. It would have been strange if Juan, travelling on foot like a pilgrim, were to pass up the chance to visit the sanctuary of Santiago. There is no documented proof of a visit by Juan to the shrine of the Apostle St. James. We only say that it is a reasonable supposition. I would like to be able to say that he went there but it would be sheer fantasy for me to invent a colloquy between him and the Apostle James. For instance, just imagine what a rash thing it would be were I to say that Juan prostrated himself before St James, Captain of the

Reconquest, because he had brought him home safely from the crusade against the Turk.

Crossing the border at Tuy, Juan entered Portugal at the River Miña. He was in no hurry and, despite not being able to speak Portuguese, he stayed for a little more than a month to recuperate after his war experiences in the Portuguese border-town of Valença on the banks of the Miña. It would be a pity if someone did not tell him that he was in the place, between the mouths of the rivers Miño and Douro, where centuries before the Duke of Burgundy had declared the territory of Portucale; and that it was from there that the long campaign to push the Arabs towards the coastline of Algarve began. It took him six to seven days to cross the Peneda Mountains before he came down to Braga on the fertile coastal plain. From there he went on to Porto and Coimbra. I wonder if anyone pointed out to him that when he crossed the river Mondego he was close to a village called Montemor-O-Velho (Old Montemor)? Moving south he passed through Alcobaça, Caldas, Bombarral and Torres Vedras, then he crossed the Tagus at either Salvaterra de Magos or Vila Franca de Xira. It was a pleasant journey of sunny days and cool evenings.

Maybe his curiosity got the better of him and urged him to go and see Lisbon. If so, he would have walked along the banks of the Canha, the old Almanzor river of his childhood, that led to Montemor-O-Novo.

Montemor-O-Novo. The village of his childhood - as our old friend the biographer Castro calls it. Castro knew the truth but again he passes up the opportunity to unveil for us the mystery surrounding João's mother and father, the Cidades. Although we have to pardon him for his good intentions, we who read him now are left confused.

Keeping this in mind, we now see the topic becoming even more complicated. As Juan strolls along he drifts into the streets of his old village where he is eventually given lodgings in one of the houses of the Arrabal, where the peasants, in those days, refused nobody. He tried to explain who he was and that he had been born there but had left very many years ago. As his name was Cidade it was not long before word of his presence had passed throughout the village even to the heights of the Castle. When he looked about and saw the churches, the houses and the countryside with the river, he tried to piece together the faint memories of his early childhood. He wondered if any of his relations were still there. Castro gives the answer:

"He asked after his parents, but his relatives did not know him on account of being so little when he left the country. Nor could they give an account of his parents since he had forgotten their names."

O come now my dear Castro, here you have really gone just a bit too far. He was an eight year old child who was extracted from his home. From then on he lived the lonely life of a shepherd, so how in the name of goodness can you really expect us to believe that he had forgotten the names of his mother and father. You are hiding this family history from us. Yes, Castro you are covering something up that you do not want us to know.

"He went from one person to another and finally came across a respected old uncle." Here Castro stops short of calling him an Old Christian in order to take away any suspicion that we might have that the family was Jewish. He contents himself with simply saying he was "a respected old uncle."

The meeting between Juan and his uncle as reported by Castro, seems quite silly. I would even say that it is incredible and more than just another smokescreen. Let us look at it more closely. The uncle recognises his nephew, and "as he spoke with John and heard him describe his parents, he recognised him by the physiognomy of his face."

As far as I am concerned, I can see Castro getting quite nervous here. He writes this page with the full intention of throwing us off the track completely. As a rule he is very precise with his words, but now he speaks of physiognomy, which is quite misleading because this word always refers to facial appearances.

Castro tells us that the uncle and nephew spoke together for the greater part of the day. I fear that Castro has invented the family history given to Juan by his uncle, a history that would bury forever the family contamination which, in the near future, would be most harmful when it came to proving the sanctity of John of God. If Granada already venerated John of God as a champion of Christian charity at the time Castro was writing it would have taken some nerve to state that the ancestry of blessed John of God was Jewish. Yes, I strongly suspect that Castro has invented the uncle story just for us.

Experts on the life of John of God recognise now that this

episode, as related by Castro, is amazing and difficult to accept. However, we cannot do anything about that.

In order to follow the footsteps of John of God, Rafael Saucedo drafted an excellent chart outlining the chronology of his life. But Saucedo glosses over this passage confessing that he cannot understand that "if the child knew of his own country, and that is undeniable, how now, thirty years later, does he go looking for it?" All the time he was living at Oropesa Juan did not attempt to go back to visit Montemor-O-Novo and no one took him back for a visit. Saucedo sensibly observes that "this is especially [notable] when one considers that relations between Spain and Portugal were very cordial at that period and that communication between both kingdoms was easy and frequent." He concluded by saying: "The enigma is this: that we have never managed to solve the problem but logic and good sense make it repugnant for the Saint's historians to relate this chapter in his life."

That was Castro's view also, but today it seems that the way set out by Saucedo's intuition, as the following paragraph shows, may help put us on the right track: "I have often suspected that what is usually called the kidnapping of the child Juan Cidade (João Cidade) and his translation to Oropesa could have been pure coincidence or could have been wrapped up in a secret in regards to his birth. Secrets of this sort were frequent enough at those times. The very name Ciudad (Cidade) is suspect."

Of course it is suspect, it points to being Jewish! And what exactly was the family history that the uncle told his nephew? We know only what Castro tells us. That João's mother died only a few days after her son was abducted: *"due to the pain and sorrow of your absence, and not knowing who had carried you off, nor to where, nor how, you being such a little boy."*

And what of the father? *"Since he was widowed and childless, your father went to Lisbon and entered a monastery, taking the habit of the great saint Francis. He finished his days in great holiness."*

This concoction of Francisco de Castro really is difficult to swallow. However, for more than four centuries it gave credibility to the parents of John of God.

I want to emphasise the clever way whereby Castro has mixed John of God's real story with this bit of fiction. He goes on with this invented story by telling us that the uncle made an offer to his nephew: "*Son, if you want to stay on here, I would deem myself very happy indeed should you care to remain with me for as long as you wish.*"

Castro proceeds to give his version of what might have occurred: "*John of God showed such great remorse and sorrow for having been the cause of his parents' death that his uncle began to weep. John stayed a little time, then profusely thanked his uncle for everything that he had done for him.*"

But Castro, saying how Juan refused the offer, puts it like this: "*Kind uncle, since God saw fit to take my parents to himself, I no longer wish to stay in this country; but rather to go in search of a way to serve Our Lord beyond my native country.*"

What is the meaning of "*beyond my native country*"? We do not know, but maybe Castro is giving us some sort of a clue to the puzzle here. Juan wants to get as far away as he could from the place where his family was known, for all Montemor-O-Novo remembered that the Cidade's had Jewish origins. When he moved away from Montemor-O-Novo and sought a future that was free of any reference to him having the contaminated blood of Conversos in his veins, that's when Juan turned his back upon his native country.

We have to thank Castro for relating the nephew's farewell to his uncle, for it indicates the feelings that had matured in Juan's heart: "*I have been so wicked and sinful and since the Lord has given me life, it is fitting that I should use it to serve him and do penance.*" He then asked for his uncle's blessing: "*Bless me, then, and pray to God that he will keep me in his hands. May Our Lord reward you for your kindness and for welcoming me into your home... Then, tearfully embracing, they took their leave of one another.*" Castro closes his narrative with the uncle's blessing: "*John, go in peace and I pray that Our Lord will truly bless your good intentions.*"

Juan left Montemor-O-Novo, not for Oropesa, but beyond his native country to seek a completely new environment far from where he was known. It is clear that those close to him at Torralba de Oropesa, the Herruz family, the *mayoral* and his fellow shepherds and farm labourers all knew the story behind the appearance of that child who was brought there from Portugal under special circumstances.

In reality, this visit to Montemor-O-Novo divides the life story of John of God into two sections, before and after. Before the visit there were the complications which doubtless the Jewish origins of his family would have caused. After the visit, a whole new horizon opens out before him. He now has the prospects of a future where nobody would question the purity of his blood. And so he leaves his native country forever.

After the death of John of God, his biographer Francisco de Castro continued to keep his image clean of any "Jewish contamination": including the story of his return to Montemor-O-Novo.

Castro leaves us without clarification of how the child João was taken away from the home of his father. We may know the truth one day if someone unearths documented proof.

Juan departed, "to go outside his native country", and went to Andalusia where, in the city of Granada, Castro wrote: *"After John's uncle blessed him, he took leave of him and set off for Andalusia."*

Notes to Chapter 11

* The first 43 years in the biography of John of God are sadly deficient of information. Some authors have attempted to fill in the gaps by writing what they imagined might have occurred. Some have followed the external aspects of his life, more or less along similar lines to each other; while others have attempted to delve into the deep psychology of John of God in order to try to discover his natural and supernatural evolution. Above all, it is this latter mentioned aspect that is the most agreeable. José Sánchez in his *Kenosis-Diakonia* (op.cit), chapter 2, # 3.3.5, has tried to fill these gaps and asks us to have confidence in what he has set out to do.

* Cf. I. Giordani, *Il santo della Caritá Ospedaliera*, Rome-Milan, 1965, 44. This gives an example of the supplementary work in regards to spiritual information at each stage of the biography of John of God. It carefully sets out to reconstruct John of God's prayer at Santiago de Compostela, in spite of the fact that there is no documented evidence of any such visit, although there is a probability that it may have occurred.

* Cf. J. F. Bellido, *El corazón de la Granada*, Bilbao 1995, 44. This author makes an absurd hypothesis about the journey to Montemor-O-Novo. He says the Count of Oropesa disembarked at La Coruña (it is well proven that it was not the Count but his eldest son who led the troops) and that he then revealed to Juan his origins and why he was taken away from Montemor-O-Novo to Oropesa. How is it then that nobody ever mentioned his origins to Juan during all the years he lived at Oropesa?

* Cf. R. M. Saucedo, *Cronológia aplicada en la vida de N. P. S. Juan de Dios:* Paz y Caridad 17 (1952) 229.

12

A STOPOVER AT SEVILLE

Seville
1534-1535

We really do not know what route Juan Ciudad took when he departed Montemor-O-Novo to go to Seville. He might have passed through the province of Extremadura and then crossed the Aracena Ranges to eventually arrive at the valley of the River Guadalquivir. Then again, he could have gone directly south towards the mouth of the River Guadiana at Ayamonte and then pass through the province of Huelva. Anyway, he eventually arrived at Seville, where, for the first time, we are fortunate to know how he felt in the depths of his soul.

When Juan arrived at Seville the tremulous compass of his life had a quivering needle and, although he was apprehensive, he was still very eager to follow its direction. Leaving Montemor-O-Novo, Juan was breaking with his past life and setting out with a clean slate in search of new unknown horizons.

His stay at Seville was short lived - no more than six to eight months. Nevertheless, it was an important external and internal component in his life-story. It was here that he found "professional" work to support himself for a while, and he also found a deeper motivation for his spirit. Until now, Juan Ciudad had no fixed plan in life - he simply drifted along with the winds of change.

As a child Juan was removed from Montemor-O-Novo and taken away to Torralba de Oropesa. The circumstances surrounding his family were obscure and when he arrived at Torralba nothing of much importance happened to him. He was assigned to the work of a farm labourer: then as a shepherd boy he was set to learn all about sheep from the older shepherds. In time, he began to earn wages as one of the shepherds. He remained so for many years, firstly for a period of twenty years, then after a break in the army, a further eight.

Juan's military experience, first at Fuentarrabía and later at Vienna, was of his own choice. The Count of Oropesa formed a company and Juan decided to enlist together with other farm workers and go under the command of the *hidalgo* Herruz to the French frontier. Juan's second military experience was under the command of Don Fernando, the eldest son of the Count. Don Fernando led the Oropesan company to join the Emperor's forces that repulsed the Turkish invasion. Juan went and returned *"without leaving home."* He never became romantically involved, nor did he decide to marry - in spite of the fictitious story invented about him having the offer of the hand of the overseer's daughter. Juan was now in sight of his fortieth year. Up until now, he had not done anything remarkable with his life. He was always commanded to do things by others who had arranged his life for him. Now we find him arriving at Seville, completely prepared to take charge of his own destiny, steering his own course in life through the clouds of uncertainty. It is during this period at Seville that Juan questions himself, and God, in an attempt to discern his life's purpose.

When Juan arrived at Seville he was delighted to find it to be a pleasant and easy going city.

Seville had its origins in ancient times when it was merely a rustic village, probably populated by the early Iberians who settled on the left bank of the Guadalquivir in the centre of a barren plane. The invasions that came upstream brought about a whirlwind of development for the people: pooling the sciences of the Mediterranean with the mysteries of the Atlantic. As the centuries passed, Seville grew into a vast kingdom extending out from the valley of its river with its backdrop of distant mountains on one side, and the open sea on the other. As the surrounding land was cultivated, the river became the city's umbilical cord to the sea. Once the caravels of Columbus had left the shores of Huelva, Seville soon became the port of embarkation for Spanish sailors who followed the Guadalquivir down to its ocean port of Sanlúcar. Juan Ciudad entered Seville in the springtime of 1534, only twelve years after Juan Sebastián Elcano - having circumnavigated the globe - moored his ship 'Victoria' there, on that famous 8th of September 1522.

Seville had made such progress during the second half of the 16th century, that it became the premier city of Spain with a universally acclaimed reputation. A royal decree issued on 14 January 1503 established the "House of Contracts" which converted Seville into the port of arrival and departure of commodities and passengers voyaging between the old and the new worlds. Industry and commerce thrived. This was especially so in those commodities of a humble nature, as for instance soap. The manufacture of soaps needed 50,000 arrobas [an arroba was 11.5 kg] of olive oil. This produced 15,000 quintales [a quintal was about 45 kg] of the finest soap which was exported to Castile, France, England, Flanders and elsewhere. Throngs of financiers and merchants from Genoa, Florence, the Netherlands, Germany and from every region of Spain, came to answer the call of the Indies [Americas]. Seville's river, which the purists always call the Betis in spite of it being named the Guadalquivir (meaning 'Great River') by the Moors, was the first stage of the journey to America. It also had a drawback: there was a sandbar at Sanlúcar where the river opened into the Atlantic. Nevertheless, this was also an advantage because it made the port secure from the attacks of pirates and assaults by hostile forces in time of war. Parts of the city developed as specific areas for the Indies traffic. Here there were stevedores, prospectors and vagabonds, all part of a great throng living in the Arenal [the quarter so called because of its sandy terrain] along the waterfront near the wharves. There were bankers, agents, and pettifogger lawyers who set up their booths around the Cathedral, all trafficking in the riches arriving from America.

Towards the end of the Middle Ages Seville was an important urban nucleus, but this did not extend very far into the surrounding countryside which was essentially agrarian; administrative services and local commerce gave the city its life and wellbeing. Then came the historic upheaval bought about by the discovery of America. Seville became incorporated in the international circle of business centres. Its port became the platform for human and material interchange with the Indies, and it became one of the most significant mercantile finance centres in the world, and certainly the most important in Spain. Naturally, industry soon began to boom.

From this time onwards the appearance of Seville began to change rapidly.

Its streets improved, monuments sprung up everywhere, literature and artistic expression flourished.

Visitors from everywhere praised the character of the *Sevillanos*: a mixture of gentleness, dignity, refinement, charm and also generosity. These citizens were conspicuous because of their distinct Spanish accent. They kept themselves to themselves, in their business and feelings, yet they were civil with everyone, a trait that made them popular with visitors to their city. At this period the Seville houses began to change their characteristic Moorish style which, besides rendering protection from the sun, were closed to curious eyes from outside. Now balconies, windows and wrought iron decorations began to appear, giving the city an appearance of distinct beauty. The Sevillanos invented a style that connected the outdoors with the indoors, introducing the custom of leaving the front door ajar in order to give the passerby a discreet glimpse of the interior patio.

The women of Seville were still reminiscent of the women of Moorish times. They kept their shawls and covered a good part of their faces. Husbands, sons and lovers now brought them gifts from faraway places: dresses and mantillas of silk, taffeta, lace, and stylish hats. These women perfumed themselves and wore adornments of gold and pearls in order to enhance their beauty. Chronicles of the period say that *"they walked very correctly and took tiny steps. Their charm and elegance was renowned throughout the kingdom."* In a coquettish fashion they would let their mantillas fall halfway over their faces and peep out from under them showing only one eye.

Spaniards from every part of the Iberian Peninsula, and foreigners from many countries, thronged to Seville. Some were on their way to the Indies, others came to settle there. They were a motley lot, blacks and whites, gentlemen and slaves, businessmen, financiers, sailors, merchants – a veritable cross-section of humanity. Cervantes derived inspiration for his writings from the various types of villains from every part of the world who turned up in the quarter of the Arenal. Gold buyers set up their scales on the very steps of the Cathedral.

A century before Juan Ciudad's arrival some megalomaniacs designed the Cathedral with its immense altarpiece and ornamentation. The college established by Maese Rodrigo had since become the University. The Catholic Monarchs had crushed the pride of the great historic families so well that, when the war of the *Comuneros* against the excesses of the Emperor Charles V erupted in Spain, there was hardly a ripple of dissent in Seville. Captain Juan de Figuera was supported by the Ponce factor, which wanted to take-over the *Alcázar* [the city's fortress] but was held back by the Medina Sidona force which brought the rebellion into submission with the consequent banishment of about a dozen nobles. Perhaps this is why Charles, the young grandson of the Catholic Monarchs, chose this city which was so far away from where he resided to be the setting for his wedding with the Infanta Isabel of Portugal. The royal wedding took place here in 1526 and its memory was still vivid in the minds of the people when Juan Ciudad, the traveller without any fixed destination, arrived in their city.

I really had to ask myself, how Juan could come to Seville without hearing the call to go to America? Perhaps he did!

Juan knew perfectly well, as did every Spaniard who arrived at the banks of the Guadalquivir, that this was where the Inquisition had its last chance to ensure that no *Conversos* embanked for the Indies. Juan had recently decided to leave behind every trace of his family's Jewish origins. As he gazed down upon a forest of masts at the wharves, even if he had had the urge to set out in the direction of America, he soon would have discovered what an impossible dream that was.

History produces some curious coincidences, as we shall now see. During these very months of 1534 to 1535, a certain priest named Juan de Avila saw frustrated his personal plan to go to America as a missionary. Avila was born in a village called Almodóvar del Campo "in the Archdiocese of Toledo", situated upon the northern slopes of the Sierra Morena. He was a distinguished lawyer, a graduate of Salamanca University and a theologian of the University of Alcalá. This zealous priest came to Seville for the wedding of the Emperor Charles and the Infanta Isabel. Researchers cannot agree upon the exact year of Padre Juan de Avila's birth, but give or take a year, he would be about the same age as our shepherd Juan Ciudad. He came to Seville determined to embark for the Indies as a missionary but his qualifications did not prevail over the difficulty of his having *Converso* ancestry. Not being of *pure blood*, he was not allowed to depart. He joined the spiritual circle led by a devout canon of the Seville Cathedral named Ferdinand de Contreras. De Contreras consoled him by saying that there was plenty for him to do in Andalusia without having to go overseas. Padre Juan de Avila clashed with the Inquisition because of certain sermons he had preached in the town of Ecija and this earned him a year in prison. When he completed his sentence, on 5 July 1533, he continued his preaching and became famous.

Juan de Avila left Seville for Cordoba in January 1535 when Juan Ciudad was staying at Seville. Neither knew the other, nor would they have seen one another because Juan de Avila lived with his distinguished clerical friends within the precincts of the Cathedral whilst the shepherd Juan Ciudad was out in the fields beyond the city walls.

But the angels who accompany men and women as they travel upon this earth, would have smiled when they saw both these Johns simultaneously present at Seville. Four years on, Avila and Ciudad will meet again in another Andalusian city, Granada. What a fruitful meeting that will be!

Juan came to Seville in search of time to reflect. He had used up his army pay that he had received at Vienna, so now it was necessary for him to find some work to earn his daily bread and lodgings. He could have offered himself as a stevedore but the bustle of life in the Arenal would have impeded the time he wanted to spend in thinking about his future. More importantly, that rowdy environment would have hindered his thoughts about God, our Master, who always accompanies and awaits us in hidden places. Juan knew all about sheep so he chose work as a shepherd, intending to stay in that job only a short time because he wanted to move on to follow the map that Providence was unrolling before him.

Castro has this to say, *"he settled down, looking after livestock on a lady's rural estate."* Who is *" this lady who owns cattle"* - Juan's employer during these months at Seville? She is Doña Leonor de Zúñiga, impetuous woman and *"first lady"* of the people of Medina and Sidonia.

These two cities achieved prominence when the citizens of Ponce attempted to join forces with the *Comuneros*. She led the Medina-Sidonians in suppressing the revolt, thereby gaining the everlasting gratitude of the Emperor Charles.

However, Juan Ciudad would never have seen the face of Doña Leonor or any of the other grand ladies of Seville or their proud husbands. He was hired by an ordinary mayoral for his board and lodging. His job was to guard a flock of sheep that grazed on the open fields along the banks of the river that surrounded the city.

Juan was happy in his work and Castro even says that *"he liked looking after livestock."* It gave him hours to spend alone in peaceful silence with his thoughts.

This time we find out what he was thinking about. Having cut lose from his past, Juan Ciudad weighed up the two fundamental experiences of his life - *"the two occupations in which Our Lord willed that he spend some time, as a shepherd, and as a soldier at war."* There is no doubt that Castro gathered this information about John of God at Granada, for he comments: *"These (two occupations) are very appropriate and useful to the spiritual life."* The "occupation of soldier" because it reminds us of the on-going battle against the classic *"enemies of the soul"*: the world, the flesh and the devil. And what of the "occupation of shepherd"? Here Juan has a foreshadowing of his immediate future. Engraved deeply upon his memory was the way in which the horses in the stables of the Count of Oropesa were pampered - *"fat, groomed, sheltered"* - in contrast with the poor farm labourers - *"lean, ragged, maltreated".* He felt this injustice intensely. He did not go around making a fuss about it, nor did he blame others, he simply asked himself the question, *"John, would it not be better for you to know how to care for, and feed, the poor of Jesus Christ rather than the beasts of the field?*

During this period, between the spring and autumn of 1534, when Juan was shepherding at Seville I can just picture him, sitting on an embankment under the sky, burnished by the sun in the morning and made sweetly melancholy by the sunset, pondering this disturbing question. He had become discontented - *"He became sad and disquieted and no longer found satisfaction in looking after sheep."* In his confusion, he prayed, sighing: *"God bring me to the time when I can do it."*

"To care for and feed the poor." But our good shepherd felt overwhelmed by questions and uncertainties: *"For at that time he was unable to see the way that the Lord would give him for His service."*

He had been given *"the will"*, the desire and the direction. The rest was but a matter of time, for Juan has been *"captured"*, overtaken by a vocation. He has a plan - to somehow *"care for and feed the poor."*

I marvel, with some pleasure, that it was while looking after sheep in the solitude of the fields of Seville that Juan felt himself to be overcome and captivated by God. He knew from whence this inner voice came and he clearly saw his future work as that of a *'shepherd'*, *"for so many poor wretched people, working hard for both their spiritual and temporal nourishment and curing their bodily ills."*

What a pity Juan did not know when he arrived in the city, that he could have taken his concerns to Padre Juan de Avila.

It happened that Juan received no wise advice while he was at Seville. He had made his own choice and so he let himself be carried along by it. Indeed, he was waiting for a providential sign to set him in the right direction. When he knew what God wanted of him he would be prompt to obey, to carry out God's will. In the meantime, he would carry on. Then, as Castro tells us, *"he had a great desire to go to Africa and see that country and spend some time there."*

At first glance the idea of going to Africa seems quite odd, but it was not without rhyme or reason to Juan. During the evenings he spent among the various groups of labourers and peasants at Seville the conversation inevitably turned to the news that was circulating throughout Spain: the Emperor's preparations for war with Tunis.

Sulieman, stopped by the Emperor's war machine on the banks of the Danube, turned away from attacking Vienna. The Turk withdrew his army to south of the Balkans, but to avenge himself for his defeat upon land, Sulieman encouraged the pirate Barbarossa to raid the Italian and Spanish coastlines. Barbarrosa complied with Sulieman's orders, causing great anguish to the dying Pope Clement VII. The unfortunate pope died in 1534 but not before sadly lamenting: *"things seem to be going so badly that soon we will be hearing the sound of the enemy's oars."*

In fact, Clement VII heard nothing, because the bow of his barque was already heading towards the eternal shore. Paul III, a member of the Farnese family, now occupied the pontifical throne. The Emperor Charles V was not too sorry when he heard that Clement VII had died. Even so, he had managed to show his sorrow for causing the nightmare of the sack of Rome and to restore his friendship and good relations with the late pontiff. Clement had lacked the courage to convoke the Council that might have nipped Luther's revolt in the bud.

Charles certainly expected a good deal from the new pope. Before his ordination as a priest, Alexander Farnese, the future Paul III, was a typical Renaissance man who lived a loose life in the Papal Court. His favourite lover was a boy called Pierluigi. When he became a cardinal, Farnese underwent a conversion and became an ascetic. He showed himself to be serious and prudent. Upon his deathbed, Clement VII recommened him as his successor. The cardinals took him at his word and the conclave lasted but a few hours. Paul III was not a handsome man.

He had wild blazing eyes, was small and obese and had a long scraggy beard. As soon as he was elected pope, Paul III demonstrated his valour. At his first consistory of cardinals he bestowed the supreme ecclesiastical title upon the English bishop, John Fisher, who was incarcerated in a dungeon by Henry VIII accused of being the confessor of his cast-off wife, Queen Catherine, whom the prelate had defended tooth and nail.

The Emperor Charles V soon received word from his secret agents in Rome that the new pope was about to convoke the long-awaited council.

The Emperor now asked the Spanish courts for men and money so he could go after the pirate Barbarrosa and catch him in his lair. Two courts were convened, one in Aragon during the spring of 1533, and the other in Castile in the autumn of 1534. During the period between the two sessions of the courts, the Emperor visited the principal cities of his kingdom.

Aragon voted to give 200,000 silver *escudos* [silver or gold coins] and Castile gave 204,000,000 *maravedis* [an ancient coin of less value than the escudo]. The Emperor sent messengers to the Pope and to the Christian princes of Europe seeking their help. During the spring of 1535, 400 ships with 300,000 men aboard assembled in the southern ports of Spain. Illustrious captains of Spain, Italy, Flanders and Portugal commanded them.

Juan Ciudad had decided to go his own way as he would be called in God's good time. For now, he felt the attraction of Africa. Maybe there was some nostalgia for the two military adventures he experienced under the banner of the Emperor, but with nothing to restrain his movements, no home or possessions to keep him in one place, he left Seville and walked to Gibraltar where he embarked for North Africa. He did not join the imperial army but remained free. He decided to dedicate his energy to serving the poor whilst being absolutely poor and free himself. It won't be long before he stumbles upon those in need of his help.

Notes to Chapter 12

* Francisco de Castro describes the psychological and spiritual situation of John of God between Montemor-O-Novo and Seville. He does this in such a way that the reader gets the sensation of listening to John of God relating the episode in person. [Cf. O'Grady-Castro, op.cit, chapters III & IV.]

* There is an immense bibliography referring to studies on Seville during the 16th century. Of particular help are those of Gonzalo Argote de Molina, *Nobeleza en Andalucía*, Seville, 1588, (re-edited Jaén 1866); Ramón Carande, *Sevilla, fortaleza y mercado*, Seville 1973; Antonio Domínguez Ortiz, *Orto y ocaso de Sevilla*, Seville 1946; Antonio García Baquero, *El río y el comercio con América*, Seville 1985; Joaquín Hazañas, *Historia de Sevilla*, Seville 1933 (re-ed. 1974); Francisco Morales Padrón, *La ciudad del Quinientos*, Seville 1977; Alonso de Zúñiga, *Anales eclesiásticos y seculares... de Sevilla*, Seville 1578 (re-ed.1893).

* For the period Juan de Avila stayed at Seville, Cf. L. Sala Balust-F. Martín Hernández, *Obras completas del santo maestro Juan de Avila*, Madrid 1970, 31-54.

13

TOILING ON THE FORTIFICATIONS OF CEUTA

Ceuta
1535-1538

Juan did come across some poor people who needed his help. They were the members of a Portuguese family consisting of father, mother and four young daughters. He met them in Gibraltar, when embarking for Ceuta, and they talked together as they travelled across the Straits of Gibraltar. When Juan first met them, they were not actually poor and they engaged him as their servant, paying him a wage. But soon the story would take a strange twist. The family would become completely destitute and it would be Juan who would be maintaining them.

But first, let us take a look at the war situation at this time. The Emperor Charles V wanted to teach the pirate Barbarossa a severe lesson because he had served as the Ottoman Emperor Sulieman's foremost ally.

The audacious pirate Khair-ad-din, called by the Christians 'Barbarossa' [red beard], was born in Greece of Albanian parents who were Turkish subjects. For fifty years he had plagued every inch of the African coastline of the Mediterranean. His home base was Algiers where he had the protection of the sultans of Constantinople. In order to compensate for the shame Sulieman suffered from the defeat inflicted upon him by Charles V at the gates of Vienna, Barbarossa made an incursion upon the Italian island of Elba and from there went on to terrorise the coast of Italy. After his capture of Tunis, Barbarossa was in a strategic position to control the Mediterranean. This posed great risks to Italian and Spanish merchant vessels plying between the ports of Sicily, Calabria and the Spanish Levant.

In 1534 Charles V decided to attack Tunis and this turned out to be the start of a long drawn-out maritime war against the Turks which endured until 1571 when the Turkish fleet was defeated in the battle of Lepanto. The Emperor called for the best of the captains of Christianity and brought them all together under his direct command. These were the Italian admiral, Andrea Doria, with his 22 galleys; Alvaro de Bazán leading the Imperial ships; Luis, brother of the Empress Isabel, heading the Portuguese fleet; García de Toledo with the Neapolitan ships; and the Marquis del Vasto commanding the infantry.

The Emperor heard Mass and received Communion in the monastery of Montserrat on 30 May. Then, leaving the Empress to govern Spain, he bid her farewell and embarked at Barcelona. The

Christian fleet reached the North African coast on 17 June. Barbarossa valiantly defended the Tunisian port of La Goleta but he was roundly defeated by the superior strength of the Christian fleet. When La Goleta fell the Emperor's forces captured 400 pieces of artillery and 40 galleys. They then marched on to Tunis which they captured on 21 July. When Tunis fell many Christian captives were liberated and, as a consequence, the myth of Barbarossa's invulnerability suffered a great blow. Barbarossa fled to Bona but was shortly uprooted from this hideaway. He then escaped to Algiers where he gathered his forces together once more and threw his lot in with his friend and master Sulieman. All this happened about the time our Juan was staying in North Africa.

The name of the Portuguese gentleman whom Juan met during the voyage to Ceuta was, according to the testimony of a witness at the beatification process, Luis de Almeida. We cannot put too much credence on this, but according to this witness, *"he was one of the most noble and prominent gentlemen of Portugal."* This gentleman, with his wife and four daughters (Castro calls the daughters maidens), had been sent into exile at Ceuta. Castro says that he was exiled *"because of certain offences, for which he had been stripped of all his property and sent to serve in that frontier [colony] for some years."*

When Almeida and Juan spoke the Portuguese gentleman told how he had been exiled, which was quite true, but he did not say that the few pieces of silver he carried in his purse were fast running out. Juan spoke of how he was simply drifting along and felt that he would like to spend a bit of time in North Africa and to find some work there to keep himself. Almeida offered him a position as a servant to himself and his family. He said he would pay him a reasonable wage and Juan accepted the offer. He was happy to have found work even before setting foot in Ceuta.

At this period Ceuta belonged to the Portuguese crown. It had been captured from the Moors by João I in 1415 and became the stepping off point for Portuguese penetration into the African continent. The Straits of Gibraltar were known as the Camino Real linking the Atlantic to the Mediterranean. Ceuta was coveted by ancient Mediterranean civilisations because of its strategic position in Africa, opposite Gibraltar. The Phoenicians and Carthaginians used Ceuta as a refuge for their ships during the first Punic War some 50 years before Christ. Roman and

Byzantine civilisations, as well as the Arab Caliphate of Cordoba, all contributed to its wealth and splendour. When the Portuguese conquered Ceuta they turned the main mosque, which the Moslems had built on the site of a Christian church constructed by Justinian in the IV century, into a cathedral. Henry the Navigator gave a statue of the Blessed Virgin Mary to Ceuta, and this became known as Our Lady of Africa. King João appointed Pedro Meneses as the first governor, and Pope Martin V appointed Bishop Amaro as the first bishop. The Portuguese put a moat about the city walls.

In 1535, word had reached Portugal from Constantinople that Ceuta was about to be attacked by the Turks. Work began on the reinforcement of the city's walls because Barbarossa had promised Sulieman that he would compensate him for the loss of Tunis by capturing Ceuta, which had crumbling walls. Sulieman saw Ceuta as the perfect stepping stone for an attack upon Spain.

João III of Portugal immediately ordered the governor of Ceuta, Nuño Alvarez de Noroña, to commence work on the fortifications in order to guarantee the port city's security. And that is how our Juan found work as a stone mason's labourer.

Why did Juan's employment with the Almeida family end in failure? It appears that the whole family fell ill, probably due to the severe change of climate combined with depression caused by being exiled from their native country. The illness quickly absorbed all Almeida's financial reserves. The unfortunate man was very ashamed that he could not support his family like his other countrymen who lived at Ceuta. Not only was he forced to stop paying Juan his salary, he appealed to him to help him in his dire situation. Castro describes it thus: *"The gentleman therefore made up his mind to go quietly to John and explain his needs to him."*

His wife and daughters had enjoyed a life of comfort in Portugal. These young ladies whom he had brought up wanting for nothing were now suffering from hunger. Almeida, ill and weak, had neither the means nor the strength to work. There was also the unimaginable social stigma of a Portuguese gentleman having to work as a labourer.

The need to repair the city's fortifications offered plenty of work for labourers. Due to its urgency, the Governor increased the labour force on the walls intended to protect the city from attack by the Berbers. Almeida, worried and desperate, asked Juan if he would seek employment on the fortifications in order to keep the family alive.

Here we have a pretty situation! The servant, instead of receiving his wages from his master, goes off and hires himself as a labourer in order to support the master and his family. Almeida made the proposition knowing quite well the strength of Juan's character, otherwise he would have been risking a sarcastic reply. Juan presented himself at the fortifications for employment as a day labourer so that in the evenings he could bring back his pay to support the family.

Almeida had no idea that his desperate situation would be significant in the plan Providence had for Juan who was drifting along, as Castro reminds us, really waiting for a sign that would lead him *"to feed and care for the poor."* The first poor that our former shepherd was to feed, would be this Portuguese family which had fallen upon sorry times.

This experience will show us that there is a lot of humour lying just below the surface of Juan Ciudad's personality. I would be pleased to think that God also smiled when Juan undertook the responsibility of earning enough money to buy food for his master's family by hauling huge rocks which, I have to admit, is not very funny at all. I suspect Juan and God are going to be amused about it some years from now.

It certainly was no joke having to lug great stones and then to wrestle them into position upon the walls. The fort of Ceuta, jutting into the water, makes an attractive picture. Ceuta, enclosed within its walled fortifications, was a little province of the Portuguese dominion. The population numbered two thousand and was governed by a council consisting of a judge, the mayor, a lawyer and six elected deputies, naturally all members of the 'upper-class'. The Governor-General held supreme authority in the colony. He commanded the military that consisted of two infantry companies with a total of 420 soldiers and a cavalry company numbering 320 men. Permanently stationed in the port were three long-boats, a forty-oared brigantine and three frigates. High on the fortifications were several light cannons called falconets and small bore artillery known as *calebrina*; mortars, small cannons and a huge one called the 'Royal'. These were ready to stave off any attack but it was questionable whether they would be enough to do the trick if Barbarossa turned up. The Governor-General was aware of this – as was the King in Portugal. That is why they decided to reinforce the existing fortifications – at least to the degree that they would be able to repel a first attack long enough for the fort to be held until reinforcements arrived.

The work was extremely arduous. Those who did it were a motley lot who had turned up in the city from many places. They were young men at a loose end, older men who were drifters, ex-soldiers, malefactors on the run from justice, and one foolish man called Juan Ciudad who was certainly hard up and in dire need of a wage. The foremen of the works shouted abuse at the labourers and never hesitated to bring their whips down upon the backs of this army of drifters and rascals. The poor wretches had to load and haul blocks of stone, to cut and chip them into shape so they would fit into place to form subterranean tunnels to carry water into the moat.

If Juan spoke with God, and certainly he would have, he would have told God that this type of work was very different from his past work as a shepherd in the fields of the Arañuelo. In the long run, all this was training him for his new *job of feeding the poor.*

Although Juan Ciudad did this work for a couple of years, only a few lines were necessary to tell about it. The work went on day after day, the only time the foremen ever stopped it was when materials ran out or when money had not arrived from Portugal. When that happened the Almeida family and Juan simply went hungry: *"They did not eat, and thus they passed time patiently doing nothing."*

Almeida had to maintain the elegance of a noble gentleman, even though he had been reduced in rank by the king as punishment. For the ashamed poor of the times it was more important to maintain one's honour than to eat. If they lacked food they hid that fact from others. The classic literary depiction of the *hidalgo* [the lean Don Quixote for instance] presents him as thin from hunger; one who, before leaving home, dusted bread crumbs upon the lapels of his coat so that those whom he met might think that he had just finished a hearty breakfast. Almeida maintained the image, but his poor wife and daughters prayed fervently that Juan would start work again soon.

The time came when, if you can believe it, Juan was assailed with the temptation to become a Moslem! How could he dream of such a thing? Juan himself was scared out of his wits by the very thought of it.

How complex is our human condition! Why should we be surprised if human sensibility should take a sudden twist? Who can describe the twists and turns of our minds when we are faced, as Juan was, with a crisis.

This is what occurred. Juan had become friendly with one of the men who shared his lot as a day labourer on the fortifications. The sequel of events needs to be stated perfectly. It seems that Juan considered himself to be personally responsible for the faith of his friend. In spite of his rigorous investigation, our biographer Castro puts the devil into the picture this time. He tells us that, seeing the good work Juan was doing in supporting the Portuguese family, the devil *"tried to impede him with his usual malice."* Very well, the devil may have been setting his evil snares, but in truth the overseers were driving the labourers on the fortification mad. Castro puts it thus: *"in both word and deed they were treating the workmen like slaves."* The first biographer goes on to say that there seemed no way to escape the appalling conditions then prevailing at Ceuta, to return to the motherland: *"They were not at liberty to flee to some other Christian land."*

The only way out of the situation seemed to be to flee to Tetuán, to 'become Moors', to reject the Christian faith and to convert to Islam. This happened to many including Juan's friend: *"without hope, seduced by the demon, he fled to become a Moor."*

When he heard about this, Juan was devastated, blaming himself for his friend's apostasy: *"So great was Juan's feeling of loss over this, that all he could do was to groan and cry."*

Juan fell into a profound state of depression. His soul was invaded by a torrent of self-reproach. He really believed that it was his fault and that God, too, would blame him for not being able to keep his friend *"within the bosom of holy Mother Church"*; that the apostasy was due to his not knowing how to support his friend *"in this little trouble..."*

I concur with what Castro asserts about the devil tempting Juan to desperation: *"It almost persuaded him to despair of his own salvation,"* pushing him to the next stage, *"That he might do the same as his companion."* Juan experienced the temptation to flee to Tetuán and convert to Islam. Satan goes too far, as Castro comments: *"But our good Lord, who had his eyes fixed upon John saw greater things for* him..." To finish this episode, God came to Juan's help, opening the eyes of his soul. *"He made him well aware of the danger in which he stood and provided him with the necessary remedy."* Providentially, *"Our Lord led him to a good and wise friar"* – a Franciscan – who helped deliver Juan from his dreadful temptation. At that time Ceuta had, besides the Cathedral, two other churches, the Dominicans being responsible for one and the Franciscans for the other.

Before we spy on the confessional of the Franciscan friar, permit me to briefly recall that prayer which Juan prayed to the Blessed Virgin Mary at Fuenterrabía when he was nearly killed after being thrown from the French mare. On that occasion the danger was physical, here at Ceuta it was spiritual.

Both of these episodes were key points that carried Juan's life ahead. Had that unfortunate episode with the mare ended with his death, then that would have been the end of the story. If the Devil had been successful in making him join the Moors, then we would have been left without a saint. But in both episodes, Juan had recourse to Our Lady and it is there that we see the theme of his tender prayer.

Castro notes that before he knelt in the confessional of the friar, Juan *"had already appealed with many tears and sighs, for the help of Our Lady the Virgin."* And of course, with her on his side, the Devil lost the game.

The friar attentively listened to Juan's confession and then gave him a remedy that was rapid and firm – to leave Ceuta immediately and return to Spain. I imagine the Franciscan would have been very impressed listening to the story of a man who worked upon the fortifications in order to sustain an impoverished Portuguese family. The advice he gave Juan was to leave the Almeidas and get aboard the ferry to Spain at once: *"Go to Spain in order to kill off that diabolical temptation."*

Juan obeyed immediately. It pained him to leave his masters, but the Almeidas understood, even though they could not imagine how they would have survived for two years without the charity of their servant. It is very touching to see that Juan begged their forgiveness for leaving them. *"He had wanted to serve them as he had done all the time that they had been there together..."* He literally begged them to let him go, and I imagine they were sorry to do so: *"weeping, they said to him that they hoped the Lord would always be pleased to aid him in whatever he did, and that in Spain he would find the help he needed."* They were truly grateful. *"And with that he took his leave of them and embarked for Gibraltar."*

What happened to the Almeidas? There is no trace of how they managed, but the *miraculous* apocryphal narratives of John of God were not going to let us escape without yet another *miracle*. They tell us that after Juan left Ceuta, the King of Portugal pardoned the Almeida family and cancelled their exile. They add that when the family returned to Portugal all their possessions were restored to them, and they regained their dignity.

This was a happy conclusion in every way but, in fact, there is no documentary evidence whatsoever for this miraculous ending.

As it turned out, Barbarossa did not attack Ceuta. Was he afraid? After taking Tunis, the Emperor Charles V made the North African coastline safe from attack. He had Muley Hassan, who had been deposed by Barbarossa, restored to the throne of Tunis. Muley Hassan signed a treaty with the Emperor that effectively made him a vassal of Spain. This gave three strategic ports to the Spanish fleet: La Goleta, Bona and Bizerta.

Barbarossa would have to think twice before he could cause any more havoc. For the time being, all were keeping their swords in hand and their powder dry.

Notes to Chapter 13

* With regard to the movements of John of God from Montemor-O-Novo and, above all with regard to his stay at Seville we are using direct references to the religious evolution of Juan as reported by Castro who, without doubt gives us what he learned about the saint at Granada. Francisco de Castro, History of the Life and Holy Works of John of God, Granada, 1585, Chapter III-V.

* Various witnesses at the beatification process testified to the assistance given by John of God to the Portuguese family:
    > Witness #2: *"I heard it publicly and truthfully said that were it not for the blessed John of God, Don Luis de Almeida, who was one of the most noble and prominent gentlemen of Portugal, his wife and four daughters, would have perished from hunger."*
    > Witness # 8: *"He knew the contents [of the question] from credible and reliable persons."*
    > Witness # 10: *"I was at Ceuta and heard it said by Jacob Megía, a practising Jew,*

who at the time worked as a draftsman on the wall and moat, that the venerable father John of God worked for some time [on the fortifications] and that he gave his daily pay to an impoverished gentleman..."

Witness #46: *"That he gave the pay he earned each day as a labourer to the father and daughters he maintained through charity."*

* All these witnesses replied to question #11 of the beatification process.
* Reliable historians, especially J. Mascarenhas and J.A. Marques de Prado, have recorded valuable information on the civil, military and religious situation of Ceuta at this period.
* The temptation of John of God to become a Moslem has been watered down by the various authors. For example; Cf. Cruset, *Una aventura iluminada. San Juan de Dios*, Madrid, 4, 1977, p75, changes it to make it appear that Juan wanted to go to Tunis to bring his friend back. Francisco de Castro, History of the Life and Holy Works of John of God, Granada, 1585, Chapter V leaves no doubt whatsoever about the matter.
* The "return" of the Almeida family to Portugal, being viewed as some sort of miracle of John of God, can be seen, for example, in I. Giordani, *Il santo della carità ospedaliera*, Rome-Milan, 1965, p59.

14

THE BOOK PEDDLER OF GIBRALTAR DECIDES TO SETTLE DOWN AT GRANADA.

Gibraltar
1538

The spurious *miracles* have been recorded, but what was missing was some sort of prodigious event to mark Juan Ciudad's journey from Ceuta to Gibraltar. So they provide us with the sudden appearance of a tempest that threatens to swamp and sink the ship; and the good man Juan plays the part of Jonah and tells everyone aboard that the whole thing is his fault because he is such a great sinner. The storm passes over and they all arrive safely at the port!

The ancients knew Ceuta and Gibraltar as the two pillars of Hercules planted to separate the south of Europe and the north of Africa. *'Non plus ultra'*, beyond here there is nothing. Today, the Spanish flag flies at Ceuta and the British one at Gibraltar but when Juan Ciudad made the journey between the pillars, the African column, Ceuta, belonged to Portugal, and the European one, Gibraltar, to Spain so these nations guarded the strait. They had mariners capable of going *'plus ultra'*, further beyond the world closed off by the two mythical columns of the Greek hero.

In the early summer of 1538, Juan disembarked at Gibraltar with his purse empty. His spare clothing now lacked his two *ferreruelos* (short capes that were essential items for any vagabond). He had had sold them just before he left Ceuta so that he could give a little money to the impoverished Almeida family. Juan was unafraid to travel without provisions, for he was ready to beg shelter anywhere, to take any sort of work and to beg for alms if necessary.

There was plenty of work available in the port of Gibraltar for him to earn his daily keep. A multitude of merchants, stevedores, sailors, and fishermen all thronged together to give the port a cosmopolitan air as they went about their ways in the shadow of the famous Rock. Geographers have never been able to decide whether the Rock of Gibraltar, which is united to the continent by an isthmus, was ever a little island or not. Certainly, the ancient classics say Hercules broke the link between Europe and Africa to join the Mediterranean with the Atlantic.

In 711 AD, the southern coastline of Spain was invaded by Tarik who gave the Rock his own name, Mount Tarik, in Arabic 'Gebel-Tarik', hence *Gebeltarik* which became Gibraltar. The first Almohade Caliph, Abd-al-Mumin, founded the city four centuries later. He built a mosque, a palace and aqueduct and enclosed the city within a stout wall that was fortified with a fortress, towers and bulwarks. Gibraltar became a important strategic position guarding the strait. Arabs, Christians and pirates coveted it. Ferdinand IV captured it, but it fell once more to the Moors whose army was led by the King of Granada, Mohamed IV. In 1462 the Castilian King, Enrique IV, retook it and used it as a base for the final assault upon the kingdom of the Nasrides Moors. The Catholic Monarchs gave Gibraltar its coat of arms: a red castle on a white field surmounted by a gold key. This symbolised what they considered to be the key to the kingdom that lay between the Mediterranean and the Atlantic. Gibraltar guarded the passage between these two seas, and no ship could pass in or out without being seen or making a stop there. When Queen Isabella died in 1504, she left the following clause in her will to exhort her successors: *"to hold fast and keep the aforementioned city [Gibraltar] and never to let it slip away from the Crown of Castile, no, not even the slightest part of it."* Today it is a different story because the British flag has flown over Gibraltar for almost three centuries.

Juan Ciudad, who was free to go anywhere he liked, had returned to Spain following the advice of the Franciscan friar, to leave Ceuta as quickly as he could. He now felt sure that he would receive some sort of providential sign about his life's work to serve, heal and feed the poor of Jesus Christ. When the time came he would be ready.

Juan soon found a job as a day labourer on the docks of Gibraltar. It was hard work, but it brought him enough money to keep himself from starving. It seems that the former shepherd, who for so many years used to watch the sun set over his flocks in the Arañuelo, actually liked this type of work which was essential to the life of Gibraltar, a bustling and rowdy port.

The first thing Juan Ciudad did in Gibraltar was to visit a church where he fell to his knees before a crucifix to pray. He was still affected by the temptation to flee to the Moors and his prayer, which has been recorded, gives us a glimpse of how close he came to slipping into apostasy: *"May you be blessed, Lord, who are so good to such a great sinner as I who deserves only punishment but you have graciously delivered me from a great deception and temptation."* He was to repeat this later for his Granada friends.

Juan recognised his weakness and was truly grateful to the Lord, promising that he would never fall away again: *"With all my strength I will endeavour to serve you, give me your grace."*

Having said that, Juan added a few words of confidence, which indicate how this prayer was bound up with his hope of a divine sign, and how he knew that this sign would be true. It also shows us how he launched himself headlong, without any safety net, into the way prepared for him: *"My Lord, with all my force I supplicate you as much as I can... have the goodness to teach me the way by which I must go to enter your service and to be your slave forever. Now grant peace and serenity to this soul who has such a desire to do this."*

In the preceding chapters we saw how the lack of documentation has impeded significant development in the study of Juan's psychological and spiritual processes. Starting with his visit to Montemor-O-Novo, and later Vienna, Castro outlined his path very well and now, at Gibraltar, he allows us to see that Juan stands alone in anticipation of what lies ahead.

We know that Juan Ciudad is to meet with the divine in Granada, the city he will eventually make his own but, at Gibraltar, he was completely unaware of this. A tremendous conversion experience is in store for him. Without warning, like a meteor, God will invade his life, completely breaking down any resistance and setting him alight like a burning coal or an explosive fire. We cannot help but marvel how, in total ignorance of it, Juan allowed himself be drawn to Granada towards his appointment with God.

Besides praying in a church on his arrival, Juan made his confession and looked for regular work.

He made a long, general confession relating to the last years of his life. The natural way Juan spoke with God and confessed shows that he had adopted the normal practices of Catholic life during his period as a shepherd in the household of Herruz at Torralba de Oropesa. Here he had the example of a good Christian Castilian family of the time. His was not an educated faith, but he was a solid, fervent believer. In his prayers he asked God for *"pardon for his sins, and that he might be able to set out on the way that he was to take to serve him."*

Unexpectedly, Juan again changed his employment. As his needs were simple, he was able to save his earnings from his wharf labouring. Wanting to be more independent and less tied down to one place, he decided on the bright idea of becoming a peddler of books, an idea he immediately put into action.

Some writers have suggested that Juan chose book selling as some sort of apostolate of the press. This shows little understanding of the matter, for he had neither the education nor the necessary formation for such an occupation. Furthermore, he filled his knapsack with a mixture of religious books and secular novels of chivalry and romance and he also sold pious objects to his customers. But what he sold was irrelevant. It was peddling, the freedom to came and go as he pleased while he earned his livelihood, that appealed to him.

At that period books were a novel and attractive merchandise in Andalusia where the people had suffered a terrible deficiency in popular education. This was partially due to the impossibility of getting children from remote farms into school, a difficulty that remained even till the middle of the 20th century, when Andalusia was forced to accept the changes of an industrialised society. Peasant families on the large estates then migrated towards urban centres. When the establishment of the school system was finally achieved on the threshold of the 21st century, the south of Spain had accomplished its dream of providing schooling for all its children.

Amongst the aged population in Andalusia, the percentage of illiteracy is staggering. Correspondingly, the number of books sold is minimal.

I know a dear old Andalusian gentleman named Don Salvador who is greatly respected in his village. One day he was dozing in his rocking chair on the patio of his house, when he sensed the presence of an unexpected visitor. Without moving from his chair, or even lifting his wide brimmed hat from his face, he asked: "Who's there?"

Not wanting to disturb him, the visitor timidly answered, "I am a salesman." He was in fact one of those good peddlers one used to see going from village to village, 50 or so years ago. "And what are you selling?" "Books," he replied. Old Salvador leant over, and somewhat surprised, got up and said in amazement, "What?"

"Books, I sell books." Grandad Salvador burst into laughter and called his wife: "María, María, come quickly, there's a man here who wants to sell us books, ha! ha! Books indeed!"

Believe it or not, Don Salvador was the proprietor of one of the largest farms in the district. As a boy his parents had sent him away to college in the capital where he learned to read and write. But, he knew books were a foreign commodity in the country.

Andalusia has paid highly for snubbing literature. From books came a great number of poets and marvellous writers who had blossomed amongst the incredible aesthetic quality of its people, the majority of whom unfortunately, in those days, were illiterate.

At the time Juan Ciudad was an itinerant bookseller, all printed materials, books, pamphlets, broad sheets, textbooks, and illustrations – were a novelty and a luxury. Andalusian peasants, few of whom knew how to read, in the evenings gathered around and listened to someone who could. The book peddlers carried in their bags great loads of intellectual works, works of piety and novels about chivalry and romance, some of which were quite risque. Pictures of saints and illustrated verse and poetry were very popular.

When Gutenburg invented the moveable metal type that revolutionised printing, printing works began to spring up all over the place, especially Cologne, Venice, Rome, Paris and Brussels. As for Spain, a Latin version of *The Ethics of Aristotle* was published at Zaragoza in 1473 and printing works sprang up everywhere, as the demand for printed products became nation-wide. Gutenburg died 27 years before the birth of Juan Ciudad but the art of printing soon spread to the New World during the very years that Juan Ciudad was peddling books. At the request of Bishop Zumárraga the famous Seville printer, Juan Cromberger, sent one of his artisans, Juan Pablos, to install the first printing press in Mexico.

Today, researchers struggle to discover the reading habits of the few literate Spaniards in the 16th century. Cultured Spaniards during the period of the Renaissance read much and they read well. We know that for certain. However, it was a different story with the simple folk who lived in and around Gibraltar. They lived in tiny villages in the countryside, or in little fishing villages along the coast. Their intellectual fare needed to be simple and attractive. Juan bought his stock from book merchants in Gibraltar whom he trusted to choose the stock he peddled. There were three types of merchandise sold in the book trade of that period.

Firstly, there were books, pamphlets and images of a religious nature. A best seller of the day was *'The Altarpiece of the Life of Christ'* by El Cartujano [the Carthusian]. Another was the devotional work, *'Flos Sanctorum'*, which was popular in homes and was usually read in conjunction with 'The Golden Legend' written by Jacabo Vorágine, an author who attributed self-invented startling miracles to each saint about whom he wrote. One day a new chapter would go into 'The Golden Legend' about Juan himself. He had no idea of this, as he added pious objects to the small religious books in his bag – a few little holy pictures of the Blessed Virgin Mary and the Infant Jesus, maybe.

Juan also would have carried books of chivalry and romance, but not the shockers of the day, 'Amadis' and 'La Celistina', this latter being discreetly subtitled 'The tragic Comedy of Calixtus and Melibea' which sold clandestinely in the streets. I wonder if anyone warned him not to carry the lecherous and frivolous, 'La lozana andaluza' [the flirty Andalusian lass]!

The third type of merchandise carried, and this was the most abundant, consisted of small 'libros del cordel' [cord books] that came out at regular intervals and were quickly bought by women at their kitchen doors. These were as popular as television soap operas are today. They got their name because they were strung together on a cord so that the peddler could hang them up on a wall for the customer's inspection. Cord books were made of poor paper and their print was as cheap as their literary contents. They specialised in anything that was sensational: current affairs, crimes, prophecies, short stories, legends, historic feats and bawdy ballads and songs.

Juan went out selling his wares in and around the Gibraltar countryside, and it appears that he did quite well for himself, for soon he had some money in his pocket. In this regard we are able to detect a smile of satisfaction upon the face of our rather straight-laced biographer, Castro, who says, "He had such good grace, and was so human and friendly, and spoke to them with such kindness and love, that many bought what they had no intention of buying."

What an affable salesman and what a pity we do not have a photograph of Juan surrounded by his customers as he makes his sales pitch about his excellent wares.

From time to time the agents of the Inquisition listened to Juan's words and gave very close attention to the books he carried in his knapsack. Fortunately for him, Protestant books used to take a few years to arrive in Spain. We need to adjust our mind to the intellectual and political circumstances that split Europe down the middle into two religious halves because of Martin Luther. The states, small ones such as the German principalities, or great ones like Spain, England and France, imposed their own religion upon their subjects in order to secure national unity. Intolerance abounded. Charles V had experienced the political consequences of Protestantism in his Germanic empire, and he told his son, Philip II, to put an end to the religious dissension that threatened Spain.

The Inquisition kept a close watch on the entrance of Lutheran books into Spain, including the works of Erasmus, eagerly welcomed by some of the professors at the Alcalá University and avidly read by intellectuals and prelates between 1515 and 1530. The great Dutch thinker had a strong influence among certain Spanish scholars who sifted through the dry text of his works in order to discover their more profound meaning. Whether it was for financial gain or to proselytise, German and Flemish books also found their way into Spain. The works of Luther and his disciples were slyly smuggled into the country, often disguised under the covers of classic works, sometimes those of the Church Fathers. These books sometimes entered hidden beneath the false bottoms of wine barrels. The Inquisition relentlessly pursued this clandestine traffic and passengers arriving in Spain had their luggage thoroughly searched. The agents of the Inquisition also searched ships anchored in Spanish ports, and they carted away anyone, foreigner or not, whom they suspected of illegal traffic in such literature. The Inquisition's efforts to stifle the availability of Protestant books increased as the century progressed. Such traffic was of grave concern to the Archbishop of Seville, Ferdinand de Valdés, a severe man from the foggy, cold and rainy region of the mountains of Asturias in the northern tip of Spain. Charles V appointed him Inquisitor General, in 1547. Valdés wasted no time in drawing up a catalogue of prohibited books that became known as the Index.

The Inquisitor Valdés instigated a violent operation against Protestant contraband. Not a soul in Seville would have suspected that a certain Julián Hernández from the Arenal quarter of the city was up to his eyes in such smuggling. In fact he was not a native of the Arenal at all, but passed himself off as such, in order to act as the agent for a doctor from Seville who had converted to Calvinism and had fled to Geneva. The guards of the Inquisition arrested him red-handed in the port of Seville with two tons of Protestant books, which had arrived from Switzerland. Hernández escaped from prison but was recaptured hiding in the Sierra Morena.

Alarmed by this incident, the Inquisitor Valdés imposed a strict censorship upon all publications of whatsoever type. Booksellers, libraries and private homes were raided and minutely searched to see whether they had any suspect literature in their possession. Valdés had heaps of Lutheran books burned. He commissioned a team of experts to prepare a new edition of the Index but all his efforts came to naught until Philip II, who was residing in Brussels at the time, signed the so-called 'Blood Law' on 13 September 1558. From then onwards, anyone who introduced, edited, possessed or wrote books in the Spanish language without the King's licence and the approval of the Royal Council would be sentenced to death.

This entire political and religious contention made no difference whatsoever to the book peddler Juan Ciudad. The stock he carried was simple and in no way controversial. We know from Castro that our peddler used to give a bit of free advice to his customers, and that he carried a few religious books among his wares: "When anyone approached to buy (profane books) he took the occasion to say to the person not to buy them but to buy instead ones that were good and devout."

Juan handed out little publications and religious pictures to the simple folk he met on his rounds. He recommended to them that they should hang up these illustrations in their homes "to constantly vivify devotion by looking at them and by the inner memory they awaken and represent" and that with the children's booklets "teach their children Christian doctrine."

Juan spent eight to ten months hawking his wares about the Gibraltar countryside, and his business was growing all the time, which would have helped him considerably: "His savings grew and he was able to get more and better books."

I wonder if Juan Ciudad ever learned to read, and if he could, to what extent? I wonder too, if he knew how to write. If he could read and write, then where did he learn those skills? We will consider these questions again later when we examine his few letters which have come down to us – which he dictated and signed.

It would be a mistake to suppose that, "Anyone who can sign, can write; anyone who can write, can read." Relying on this theory, researchers have carefully analysed signatures at the foot of judicial documents and from there have arrived at a percentage of literate signatories. However, if you have ever lived with the simple folk in a Spanish village, as I have, you will know that 'to sign' does not necessarily mean 'to write', or even read, for that matter. Rustic folk often learn to sign their name but that is as far as it goes. What they sign is something already read to them by someone in whom they trust.

It is not too much to suppose that someone among the few who could read and write at Torralba de Oropesa may have taught Juan these skills during the long years he was a shepherd there. But it would have been very little. Perhaps he read well enough to discuss and recommend good books to his customers.

The wandering bookseller now wanted to improve his business possibilities. We know he had to keep going back and forth to warehouses at Gibraltar in order to replenish his stock. *"Juan found it very tedious going about from place to place with his bundle strapped to his back,"* but he could not set up shop at Gibraltar because the market there was already cornered by his suppliers and they certainly would not welcome competition from Juan Ciudad. In addition, while he waited for the right time to come, he preferred to keep on the move and see new places.

As Providence would have it, his awaited time would soon arrive for *"He decided to go to Granada and settle down there,"* as Castro says.

We now know, but Juan did not, that there was a third reason for him to choose to go to Granada, namely that Granada was waiting for him.

Notes to Chapter 14

* The storm which was supposed to have almost swamped the ferry boat between Ceuta and Gibraltar is sheer fantasy, having had its origins in the imagination of D. Celi (op. cit). The tale has been copied by subsequent authors, amongst them I. Giordani, who repeats the parody of Juan Ciudad and the Jonah story, adding the Celi invention that the sailors wanted to throw him overboard., op. cit, p 60

* There are several studies on Gibraltar, amongst which are those of A. Fernández Palacios, J. Ma. Fernández Palacios and B. J.Gil Gómez, *Guías naturalísticas de la provincia de Cádiz*, Vol. I, *El Litoral*, Cádiz 1988, 103-118. Also, see *Visión del conjunto* in M. A. Vásquez Medel and others, *Provincia de Cádiz*, Vol. I, Seville 1984. Cf. J. Velarde, *Gibraltar y su Campo: una economía deprimida*, Barcelona 1970.

* For the sociological view of the influence of the book [in Spain] Cf. J.A. Pérez, el libro y la biblioteca, Barcelona 1952. For researchers on reading and writing in 16th century Spain, see, *El proceso y lectura durante el siglo XVI* (the reading process during the 16th century) in Cf. P. Aries, *Historia de la vida privada*, Vol. V, also *El proceso de cambio en la sociedad de los siglos XVI-XVIII* (the process of change in society during the 16th -18th centuries), Madrid 1992; M. Chevalier, *Lectura y lectories de los siglos XVI y XVII* (reading and readers of the 16th and 17th centuries), Madrid 1976. There are also interesting references from the 17th century, ie., A. Larquié, *L'alphabetisation à Madrid en* 1680: Revue d'Histoire Modern et Contemporaine, (1981), 132-157.

15

THE BOOK PEDDLER
AT THE GATES OF GRANADA

Gibraltar - Granada
1538

It was not good travelling weather when Juan set out upon his long walk to Granada, nevertheless, off he goes with his merchandise strapped upon his back. He took his time, about a month and a half, stopping at villages along the way to offer his wares for sale. Saucedo's reasonable chronology suggests that Juan Ciudad arrived at Granada in mid-December 1538. That means that he was on the road from the last days of October to the middle of December.

The cold air of the approaching winter would have made itself felt as he crossed the hills of Ronda. At that time of year there would have been torrential rain, brisk autumn days and freezing nights. Any gust of wind in that season was quite enough to raise goose bumps.

The track from Gibraltar left the seacoast at San Roque, then it turned inland through the vast La Almoraima countryside to enter Jimena de la Frontera. Each village and farmhouse along the route had stories to tell of smugglers and bandits, who as long as anyone could remember, came up from the seaports to seek refuge in the hill country. From the heights of Ronda, paths branched off leading to the four corners of Andalusia: the Straits of Gibraltar and Africa to the south; Córdoba, guarding the entry of the Betis, to the far north; Seville and Cádiz to the west; and lying to the east were Malaga and Granada. Ronda's history also recalls that the Carthaginians passed that way, and it was a flourishing city when Caesar went through there after being sharply repelled by Pompey's partisans. The Arabs loved Ronda, split as it was by the gorge of the Guadalevín, with its moss-covered steps descending to the mysterious freshness of enchanting caves.

Let us pause at Ronda to ask ourselves, What was it that lured Juan to Granada? What is its attraction? From Ronda, he could have chosen any direction so why did he choose Granada quite unaware, as he was at that time, that his appointment with the Lord was waiting for him there and calling for him to come?

First, I need to relate to you the legend of Gaucín.

I have already warned the reader that, chapter by chapter, I will ruthlessly prune away the brambles that threaten the true image of John of God. I refer to the invented miracles that the baroque biographers have attributed to him and which delighted the preachers who copied the flamboyant style of Fray Gerundio de Campazas.

This pruning is a requirement of history. Thank God for the true figure of the Saint, whose example and life have no need of embellishment. But I must confess that this *golden legend* found in the biographies just mentioned is really a gem. It is a pity that it lacks documentation.

Gaucín is a tiny village tucked away between the rivers Genal and Guadiano at the foot of the Ronda hill country. In ancient days the Romans built a fortress on the edge of a deep cutting in the foothills of the Sierra Hacho, and they called this fort the Eagle's Eyrie. The Arabs who later took it enlarged it to make a castle and before long, a village sprang up in its shelter. From the beginning of the 14th century, Gaucín was the scene of battles between Christians and Moors. It was here in the late 15th century, a few years prior to the taking of Granada, that the hero, Guzman the Good, fell.

Gaucín is a typical hill country village that relies upon cereal crops and livestock for its existence. It has picturesque nooks and crannies and springs of clear fresh water. The legend of Juan at Gaucín had good beginnings, for it figured no less, in the work of Spain's famous poet-playwright, Lope de Vega. Dionisio Celi developed it, incorporating it in his biography of John of God. From then, the legend has occupied a privileged place amongst the amazing episodes in the life of the saint.

The story goes like this. Our weary book peddler arrived at Gaucín with his knapsack upon his shoulders. It was only a tiny Andalusian village, and from a distance looked no bigger than a white handkerchief lying at the foot of the hills. At a bend along the track, Juan came across a barefooted child walking in the same direction. He wanted to put his own sandals on the little boy's feet but realised that they were too large for him. Instead, he picked the child up and carried him on his shoulders. The blessed child weighed a ton! After a short space Juan had to stop in order to catch his breath. When they arrived at a spring called La Adelfilla, not far from Gaucín, he put the child down saying, 'Let's go and get a drink.'

While Juan was bending over, getting a drink, the little boy called him: "*Juan!*" Looking up, Juan saw that the boy was breaking open a pomegranate. As the seeds burst forth the appearance of the child was transformed by dazzling light and, holding up the pomegranate which was surmounted by a cross, said to the astonished peddler, *"John of God, Granada will be your cross."*

What wonderful poetic licence! That was the intention of Lope de Vega who included the legend in a scene in his play *'John of God and Antón Martín'*. It seems quite clear that the author wanted to make sure that John of God was given a name that had celestial overtones, and at the same time, to closely link him with the city, Granada [called after the 'pomegranate', which is the English word for the fruit that Spaniards call a 'granada'].

This legend has no substance. There is no documentation to uphold it. And as for the name John of God, we will see later on how he got that, but it was well after he had settled down at Granada.

Lope goes on to fill his pages with this sentimentality. Anyway, he impressed one reader of note, namely the unforgettable Pope John XXIII, who as a young man undertook studies in critical history, and without any doubt, had a great respect for popular traditions. For example, John XXIII made a connection between the tale of John of God at Gaucín and the legend of St. Christopher. That legend relates how the strong giant, Christopher, wanted to put his physical energy at the service of the most powerful king in the world. One day he came upon a child who wanted to cross a river. So he put him on his shoulder to carry him across. But the infant weighed like a mountain. Pope John XXIII was delighted to see the St. Christopher legend repeated in regard to John of God. What a man was John XXIII! He was capable of applying to history the necessary critical discipline, while at the same time respecting popular traditions. He was the pope who reformed the Roman Breviary that the clergy, religious and many devout laity pray daily. He threw out all the unreliable biographies of saints that were really only pretty legends. Amongst those that were rejected was the story concerning the origin of devotion to Our Lady of Mount Carmel, with its nebulous legend about the prophet Elias. At the time of this reform of the breviary those who were close to Pope John XXIII assert that he said to his secretary: *"Let us go and devoutly pray the 'readings' of Our Lady of Mount Carmel, because next year they will be taken away from us."* I was delighted to discover this precious fable at Gaucín fitting in with the memoirs of John XXIII.

The good working folk of Gaucín would later place a statue of the "Holy God Child" in the castle's chapel, as a reminder of the legend of the apparition. When the French invaded Spain in 1810 they sacked the castle and threw the statue from its battlements. It was later recovered and restored to the chapel but during the 1936 Spanish Civil War it was destroyed. After the Civil War, the St. John of God Brothers at Granada donated another statue to the people of Gaucín.

The legend of Gaucín has a symbolic value for the Hospitaller Order of St. John of God. The pomegranate, surmounted by a star and a cross, now serves as the coat-of-arms for the sons of John of God who are spread throughout every continent of the world.

The itinerant bookseller continued on his journey. Except for the rough tracks that took him over the Serranía mountains, the rest of the way was easy. He passed through large towns that figured in the novels he sold about the Reconquest. He passed through Antequera, Archidona, Loja and Láchar, then on he went to Santa Fe and to the gates of Granada. The attraction of Granada was like a magnet that drew and lured Juan Cuidad onward in this most definitive journey of his life.

Juan had travelled across the whole of Andalusia to arrive at the city, the enchanting destination of travellers throughout the ages. As for myself, when I entered Granada for the first time many years ago, I was so struck by its beauty that I thought it must be one of the most beautiful cities in the world. Sadly, during the second half of the 20th century, the citizens of Granada have watched the degradation of their beautiful city that now has an ugly urban sprawl. Great damage has been done and furthermore, they have made no effort to restore its lost splendour.

However, in the mid-16th century Granada "is an unfinished city, in the process of transformation." Its population at this time was something between forty and sixty thousand, but the exact number is uncertain because it changed from year to year. There was great social inequality, and the Moorish population seethed with a discontent that was soon to erupt into the rebellion of the Alpujarras. Up in the famous neighbourhood of the Albaycín, orchards, known as *carmens*, were being transformed into beautiful gardens. Many a Moorish family had preferred to remain quietly at Granada, earning their livelihood as servants or slaves. Settlers came to Granada from far away Castile, Asturias and Galicia. Their coming changed the city's skyline. Also the clergy and religious orders of monks and friars who came to Granada immediately turned its mosques into Christian churches. Throughout the city new churches, convents and hospitals rapidly began to appear.

Granada's archbishops who succeeded the great Hernando de Talavera, while carrying out their religious duties, continued to build the cathedral, which was completed eventually two centuries later.

Granada was the military headquarters for the entire Andalusian coastline, which was constantly under the menace of Arab attack. The Captain General commanded the army from his palace up in the Alhambra.

The president of the Granada Royal Chancellery administered justice for the half of Spain that lay south of the river Tagus. The Royal Chancellery of Valladolid administered from Toledo northwards.

The three great powers in Spain, religious, military and civil, did not always get on well with one another.

The Catholic Monarchs had plans to make Granada even more famous than it was when it was the vital centre of the Moorish Nasrides kingdom, but it was a difficult dream to achieve. So greatly did they believe in it that they left orders that when they died they were to be interred there. They commissioned the building of the Royal Chapel, which was later embellished by their grandson, the Emperor Charles, who never considered himself to be greater than his grandparents.

Charles and his wife, the Empress Isabel, went to Granada for their honeymoon after their marriage at Seville. The city captivated them and Charles immediately commenced the construction of his famous palace in the grounds of the Alhambra. He promised Isabel that they would retire there when the time came for him to renounce the throne.

Charles was not to know that a terrible misfortune was to befall him, for soon afterwards, Isabel died prematurely. This took the edge off the Emperor's satisfaction in the advances of his *Conquistadores* in America.

A fever of stupendous exploits overtook Spaniards of the 16th century. If we did not already know the results, we might say that they had gone completely crazy. His Majesty the Emperor took seriously any adventurer who brought him maps, usually just drawn up, that showed some unknown land where mysterious people were supposed to live. His Majesty would listen, discuss and then fall for the captain's claims, giving him extraordinary powers, payment in advance, and bestow a title such as 'Commander', 'Governor', and 'Captain General' of these unknown lands. The adventurer then would arm a small fleet, enlist soldiers, promising them, in anticipation, a share of the spoils. Then off to sea they would go. What delusions of grandeur! History repeats itself sometimes, and the empire grew, so much that the sun never set upon it.

On the other hand, Europe constantly annoyed him. He did not trust either Henry of England or Francis of France and they did not trust him either. The Lutheran rebellion had spread profound discord in the empire.

During these years the Emperor's army clashed with that of Francis I, King of France, and the two began their third war. Truly, there was no peace to be found. Things were not going well for the Emperor Charles, because Francis had committed the villainy of aligning himself with the Turks. Sulieman again made another land attack upon the empire and this time he had Hungary on his side. And while that was going on, Barbarossa was also attacking the empire, by sea, by launching assaults along the Italian coast of Calabria. Yes, things were not going well for Charles. The Spanish soldier poet, Garcilaso, was killed in the battle of Nice. Why in the name of goodness do poets have to go off to war! The poet Garcilaso was a fine gentleman of Toledo and died so young, only 23 years of age. He has left us verses in his native Castilian language as well as in the Italian Tuscany tongue. But what more might he have left us had he not gone to war, but lived to sing:

> Flowing waters, crystal clear,
> Trees gaze down upon you here,
> With shady pastures everywhere.

> Birds fly above your field of battle,
> Among the trees the wounded stumble,
> Upon your green bosom, there they crumble.

The chronicles do not say whether the Emperor gave Garcilaso enough time to lament the empire. Anyhow, I feel it a consolation that he died in the arms of his friend the Marquise of Lombardy, Francisco de Borja [Borgia] who had questioned why he had lost so many dear friends.

Francisco de Borja was one of those persons whom our book peddler Juan Ciudad saw from a distance at Granada. It was a fleeting moment and it was on a sad occasion.

The thing that the Emperor Charles wanted above all was for the Pope to convoke a council of the universal Church. He sent messengers to Rome urging the Pope to do so as a matter of urgency. However, the Emperor was nursing a hope that was destined to be disappointed. The council would be too late to repair the damage done to religious unity by Martin Luther, the German *pope* at Wittenberg, and by His Majesty, Henry VIII, the English *pope* on the banks of the Thames.

That much is certain, because the English King was already living with his third wife, Jane Seymour who had presented him with his desired son, but who was found to be sickly. In fact, Henry VIII looked upon the infant with a certain disdain, asking himself whether he was worth such cruel pain. History was not kind to Henry, for his unfortunate son Edward was to be King of England for merely six years before dying young. Two women succeeded him as rulers of England: for five years the Catholic Queen, Mary Tudor, the daughter of the prisoner Catherine of Aragon; and for 45 years the Protestant Queen, Elizabeth I, daughter of the beheaded Ann Boleyn. The succession of his son and heir, Edward, had served Henry as a pretext for a thousand outrages, sending some of his most virtuous and valiant men to their death. Men like the Bishop of Rochester, John Fisher, was one, and another was the gentle and kind-hearted humanist Thomas More who, in his dying prayer, asked the Lord, *"for the grace to hold the world for nothing and to maintain himself happy and to hold his worst enemies as his best friends."*

Pope Paul III, like Charles, wanted to hold the council. He instructed his Nuncio in Vienna to make a journey throughout Germany and to extend invitations on his behalf to the council to the German princes and to Martin Luther himself. Luther arrogantly received the Nuncio but he promised to attend the future council.

Above all, the Pope and the Emperor wanted to convene the council as a means to unite the armies of Europe against the onslaught of the Turks, for Sulieman had once more cut into Hungary and again threatened the Austrian territories. Charles did not have enough troops of his own to be able to stem the breaches that were being opened all around Christendom. Finally, he sent 2,000 Spanish infantry to his brother Ferdinand, King of Austria-Hungary and future successor to the empire. The Germanic chronicles reported that these Spaniards were *"not men but devils. They were small and dark and, when their backs were to the wall, like bats which are impossible to catch."* They were prepared to die for the empire, these sons of Spain, but they were too few – the empire was short of soldiers.

For that very reason Paul III wanted peace between Charles V and Francis I. He thought this family squabble between the Emperor and the King of France was absurd and had gone too far. He called them both to meet him at Nice, but one at a time, to make sure that they would not encounter each other. The pope recommend that they accept a pact that had been drawn up by two ladies, the same two of the Peace of Cambray; the Queen of France and the widowed Queen of Hungary, both sisters of the Emperor. Charles and Francis signed the truce and promised to embrace in a spirit of eternal peace. Eternal indeed! It lasted but three years.

Juan Ciudad entered Granada a few days before Christmas 1538. Miguel de Cervantes has a passage in his famous novel Don Quixote that the Granada Municipality would do well to place in golden letters at each entrance to the city:

> *Don Quixote asked: "Where are you going Your Honour?" The gentleman answered, "I, sir, am going to Granada which is my motherland." Don Quixote replied, "It is indeed an exceptional motherland."*

> Juan was entering his new motherland because here he would be born anew. He has an appointment here in his "Good Motherland!"

Notes to Chapter 15

* In reference to the hills of Ronda: Cf. A. Boyd, *The Roads from Ronda*, London 1969; M. A. Ladero, *Andalucía en el siglo XV*, Madrid 1973; V. Pérez Díaz, *Pueblos y clases en el campo español*, Madrid 1974; E. Rodríguez Martínez, *La serranía de Ronda*, Malaga 1977; J. Sermet, *La España del Sur*, Barcelona 1956.

* Reference to Gaucín: See, *Gran Enciclopedia de Andalucía*, Vol. IV, Seville 1979, 1677-1678.

* The name of Guacín constitutes in itself a phenomenon in the biography of St. John of God: the legend incorporates it in the development of the Hospitaller Order. Cf. G. Russotto, *Lope de Vega e San Giovanni do Dio*, Turin 1954; this author made a study of Lope de Vega's relationship with the memory of John of God. Also see, M. De Mina, *San Juan de Dios en el teatro de Lope de Vega*, 'Labor Hospitalaria' (1953) 238, 320, 407. The first emblem of the Hospitaller Order was a basket, staff and collection box, which for a time coexisted with the pomegranate, star and cross which made reference to the Gaucín legend. Eventually the latter replaced the former as the Order's emblem. Cf. G. Magliozzi, *Pagine juandediane*, Rome 1992, 207-210. Gaucín has often appeared in literature, above all in the novel biographies of John of God, some of them quite good, such as that of A. Rodríguez, *A vida aventuroso de João Cidade*, Porto 1963. Some modern authors have attempted to make the Gaucín legend acceptable by giving it psychological interpretations: Cf. A. Muñoz Hidalgo, *De Juan Ciudad a Juan de Dios*, Barcelona 1990, 76: "My day-dreaming imagination gives life to the Child Jesus offering me a pomegranate. But between us there is a shining cross... That's what I remember in my famous dream." José Cruset, op. cit., p 82.

16

THE BOOKSELLER IN ELVIRA STREET

Granada
1538- 1539

I ask myself if Juan was happy to come to Granada, and why he chose that city without ever having seen it? For 15 years he had been travelling about Europe, and prior to that he had spent many years with his flocks along the banks of the River Tiétar. After his enlistment in the army, and his unfortunate experience at Fuenterrabía; and later on when he re-enlisted in the Emperor's Vienna campaign Juan Ciudad had seen a great many amazing places that really opened his eyes. So what did he think of Granada?

Juan entered the city by one of Granada's eighteen gates. Which one is unimportant because they all gave a favourable impression of the city. Sad to say, most were demolished in the 20th century, but such a lament might be a bit exaggerated because when I first came to Granada, half a century ago, I must say I was struck by its beauty. I appreciate the praise of the Arab poets and the verses of one of them, the experts tell us, can be read from traces of the script adorning the alcoves of the Alhambra. Granada speaks for itself, *"Allah has covered me with so much beauty that even the stars in the heavens stop to admire me."*

Nearer our own day, the romantic traveller Alexander Dumas came to Granada and wrote with even greater rhetoric, *"God created the Alhambra and Granada, because one day he got tired of his heavenly home."* That might seem a bit exaggerated, nevertheless it is not without some significance.

What really left me speechless on my first visit to Granada, was the glimpse of the sierra which formed a sublime backdrop upon the horizon as I gazed up from its streets and alleyways. Granada appeared to be gently nestling at the foot of the mountains, contrasting tenderness and strength. What a sight that was my friends!

Today, urban progress has created a vastly different picture. Those lovely views can no longer be seen from the city streets. Now you can only see the street that lies ahead of you lined with tall buildings, department stores, office blocks and banks, all putting a stop to any poetic ideas that might come to one's mind. They have robbed us of the sierra, and Granada without its sierra is no longer Granada. Of course, there still remain the Alhambra, the Generalife, the Cathedral, the Chapel of the Catholic Monarchs, the Royal Hospital and the gardens, palaces and churches. When all of these treasures were first built, they breathed the unpolluted atmosphere that surrounded them. There are those who love Granada, poets and artists like my friend Paco Iszquierdo, who raises his voice against the sacrileges of urbanisation. Alas it is in vain, because nobody seems to care, but like Paco, there are still some who seek a refuge from this dreadful urbanisation and find a quiet place to live, up in the Albayzín facing the Vela Tower.

Our book peddler Juan Ciudad arrived at Granada long before the 20th century when certain architects built their modern monstrosities.

Historians sometimes regret that they cannot interview persons of note, whose lives might move us. I know exactly what they mean. Certainly, I would be happy to interview the book peddler, Juan Ciudad, who turned up at Granada to open a bookstall. We would sit down in the shade of the plaza at the San Cristóbal lookout and have a good chat. We would gaze down upon the winding River Darro cutting its way through the city to link up a little further on with the River Genil. Beyond the left bank of the Darro, we would see the mysterious buildings of the Alhambra and the tree-lined Generaliffe. Over to the right we would gaze upon open fertile fields. Poets would pay much to contemplate such beauty, to gaze upon Granada with its backdrop of snow-covered peaks of the Sierra Nevada which, in the springtime, is set ablaze with sweet perfumed wildflowers.

I would ask Juan to fill in the missing pieces of his story so far, which covers the first 43 years of his life. I would ask what he thought of this magic city and how it compared with Innsbruck, which he visited after crossing the Alps; and Salzburg when he was on the banks of the Danube. In my opinion, Innsbruck, Salzburg and Granada are the most fortunate of cities, because their inhabitants have high mountains to guard them like the angels. Ideal cities! But nowadays, of the three, only Granada has blocked out its surrounding mountains. If only Don Quixote would appear with his lance at the ready and shout out what wretched scoundrels they are for having done this thing!

It is possible to divide Juan Ciudad's life into two sections. The years before his arrival at Granada which he lived as Juan Ciudad and which we have deciphered from the small amount of data available, and the twelve short years afterwards, as Juan de

Dios, that is, John of God. By popular choice Granada's citizens singled him out as a unique and outstanding personage and there is an abundance of documentation relating to the *John of God* segment.

We know little about the physical appearance of Juan-John when he passed from 'Ciudad' to 'de Dios – of God'. That is to say from the time he arrived at Granada. What type of man was he? What were his facial appearance and his mannerisms?

Written descriptions of the physical appearance of anyone hardly give a precise picture but they do present some sort of approximation, even if never quite convincing. Luis Alonso Schökel, an Old Testament scholar who specialises in applying intelligent scientific schemes of linguistic research to biblical episodes, says that in order to understand the visual impression of a person, we should look for literary clues instead of wearying ourselves out collecting epithets such as facial colour, whether the eyes are blue, the nose is aquiline, the forehead wide, the lips large and so forth. He maintains that if all that is put together, it is just like holding water between our fingers. Literary clues consist in the understanding of impressions that come through indirectly about a specific person. For example, when Homer wanted to describe the beauty of Helen, the beautiful lady who caused the Trojan War, he was not interested in accumulating useless phrases, but he did make good use of the clues he had at hand. Troy was a city under siege. It was on its last legs, its buildings were destroyed and the people were plague ravished and starving. Old men and women sat groaning and wailing at their cottage doors. Then they saw Helen pass by, and gazing upon her, marvelled at her beauty. It was enough to make them decide that it was worth going to war for this woman. That's how Homer described Helen of Troy. He made no mention of the colour of her eyes, skin, lips or forehead. All he ever said about Helen of Troy was that she was very beautiful, so much so, that she could compensate for the horrors of war.

Concerning John of God, when he begins his great adventure at Granada, we have the benefit of written material, paintings, and above all, one exceptional portrait that actually shows us his face.

Alternatively, I have searched in vain for hours, for some written description of the physique of our book peddler, Juan

Ciudad, and I only found one small item. This was a little paragraph in the testimony given at the beatification process by a certain old lady. She spoke of Juan's visit to Oropesa from Granada, and because I intend telling you about that journey in the right sequence, I will only comment now that its historic certainty is questionable and therefore needs to be taken with some reservation. The witness gave her testimony simply and convincingly, and we have her to thank for the tasteful and unique description of Juan: *"He was a tall well built man, with bushy eyebrows and was neither fat nor thin."*

When Juan first arrived at Granada in 1538, the city was going through one of its most exciting stages. It was only 46 years since the Catholic Monarchs had conquered Granada and the transformation from an Arab city to a Christian one was in full swing. However, time was still needed to achieve it and there was a lot of inevitable tension attached to its implementation. This stress was caused by two main factors. Firstly, the urban structure itself, and secondly, the new settlers who streamed into the city. The buildings that were going up all over Granada were a cause of both amazement and misgiving for the conquerors. The Italian born chronicler Pedro Mártir de Anglería, who was greatly admired by Queen Isabella, wrote about the embellishment of the city at that time. Anglería is noted for having introduced humanistic studies to the Spanish nobility. He came from Milan and arrived in Spain in the company of the Count de Tendilla. Ordained a priest, he was then taken into the household of the Queen who made him her chaplain and the teacher of her children. Later, she sent him as her ambassador on special missions. He gained a chair in the University of Salamanca and was made a canon of Granada Cathedral. Anglería wrote poetry, letters to the nobility, and a history of the New World that featured the exploits of Christopher Columbus, a work that merited him to be placed among the official chroniclers of the Indies. Well, having said that, let me quote from some paragraphs taken from Anglería's letter to the Archbishop of Toledo, Gonzálo de Mendoza. They demonstrate the amazement of the Christians at the time Granada was taken from the Moors:

"It is in my judgement, that of all the cities I have visited under

the sun, I have to prefer Granada. It outstrips all the others in the mildness of its climate, a most important thing to consider when choosing a place to live. I have discovered that it is neither too hot in summer nor too cold in winter. One can see the perpetual snows on the peaks of the mountains about six miles away from the city. In the month of July the snow melts and the result is the freshest of water which, when mixed with wine, is as refreshing as the snow itself. One can generally come across cool houses placed in strategic positions in respect to Saturn and the Sun. This ensures an uncommon freshness that lasts for days. It is easy to take a stroll through the luxuriant forest on the mountainside. And as far as strolls to refresh one's spirit when one is worn out by work or worries, what place can come near this for restoring one by nature? The sea encircles the marvellous city of Venice. Milan, in all its opulence, is surrounded by a plain. Florence is enclosed by mountains and suffers from shocking winters. Rome is constantly battered by the south wind, which brings with it the stifling air of Africa, and is inundated by the swamplands of the Tiber. No wonder few get to see old age there. Besides that, there is also the stifling heat of summer which makes the population listless and bored. Granada, on the other hand, is extremely healthy thanks to its river, the Darro, which runs through the city. Granada has both mountains and large fields and it enjoys a perpetual autumn. It has an abundance of cedars and attractive orchards of all manner of citrus fruits that emulate those of Hispérides. The foothills of the nearby mountains have abundant brooks and are covered with all sorts of vegetation, vineyards, myrtle woods and sweet smelling bushes. So beautifully adorned are the surroundings that one is reminded of the Elysian Fields, and as Your Grace is aware, water flows through there all the time. I personally have experienced its refreshing and health-giving effects. Its brooks that gently run between olive groves and orchards give refreshment to the tired spirit."

I know that this is a long quotation, but the compliments that Anglería pays to Granada are pertinent and also give me great pleasure. There is no doubt about it, the city instilled a sort of reverential awe into its Christian conquerors. They looked upon it with a sort of fear, seeing it to be full of nooks and crannies where oriental magic might be lurking. This odd sensation they experienced was precisely due to Granada's urban structure, with its narrow alleyways and tiny plazas tucked away amongst little houses. The contemporary traveller named Jerónimo Münzer testified to this when he wrote in his notebook:

"A Christian household occupies four or five times the space of a Moorish one. The homes of the Moors are a mass of entanglements and labyrinths that seem like the nests of swallows. Thus it can be safely said that there are some hundred thousand houses in Granada. These, as well as the shops, have doors which are very simple and are made of wood and large nails of the type often seen in Africa."

Urban reform was instigated precisely because of Granada's housing conditions as well as for sanitary reasons and the security offered by the city walls. Streets were widened and plazas enlarged. More importantly, new houses were built upon better ground than those built by the Arab population whose homes seldom measure more than about 50 square metres. The ordinances were carried out to the letter, and as a result the average house of an Old Christian usually took up the space of four or five Moslem homes.

The Catholic Monarchs made a great effort to make Christian Granada even greater than that of the Nasrides Moors. What they began was carried on, with no less zeal, by their grandson the Emperor Charles, but it was a goal difficult to achieve. The countryside remained as it was at the time Boabdil left it, but the architectural gems of the Alhambra and the Generalife represented a peak of human realisation. Antonio Gala, who extolled the Granada of the Nasrides kingdom, lamented the loss of the sweet aromas and the music that used to permeate the Alhambra during its days of splendour. Today, all that has disappeared. *"The Generalife is a garden bathed in shade and water, its architecture is made solely of water and shade. As for the Alhambra, its best buildings are those that have been pulled asunder."*

When Juan Ciudad entered Granada it was a city undergoing a building boom, and it remained so for most of what was left of the 16th century. The Catholic Monarchs had ordered the construction of a chapel for their burial, and this was embellished by their grandson the Emperor Charles. They also founded the Royal Hospital for poor pilgrims and the sick poor. The building industry was given new impetus in 1520, as the Venetian Ambassador, Andrea Navagro recorded: *"Outside the Elvira Gate there is a magnificent hospital made of cut stone and very ornate, but it is not yet finished."*

Queen Isabella wanted to erect the Cathedral upon the site where the greatest of Granada's two hundred mosques stood (most of them being small family ones). However, the first stone was not laid until 1523 and in 1530 the famous architect Diego de Siloé took over and accelerated the work.

When he was honeymooning at Granada, the Emperor Charles gave the city the plans to erect a palace within the walls of the Alhambra, a palace that would be, *"worthy of the empire."* Both he and the empress were so enchanted by Granada that they wanted to retire there, *"when many years were yet to pass."* It was because the Empress Isabel found the rooms of the Alhambra to be somewhat uncomfortable, that her husband promised her the new palace.

The Catholic Monarchs had the Royal Chancellery, which had jurisdiction of the whole of southern Spain, transferred from Ciudad Real to Granada. The Valladolid Royal Chancellery covered northern Spain. The Emperor Charles commissioned the architect who was building the Cathedral at the time, Diego de Siloé, to build the Granada Royal Chancellery.

The building of San Jerónimo Monastery was barely finished when the construction of its famous church began. The grandchildren of Gonzalo Fernández de Córdoba, *El Gran Capitán*, chose this church for his interment.

Churches, convents and lordly palaces began to spring up throughout Granada, giving the city the appearance of one huge building site. On 15 October 1501, Innocent VIII, by the stroke of a pen, issued a bull by which 24 mosques were to be transformed into parish churches. The adjustment to their architecture went into force immediately and by 1538 almost half the work was complete.

Work on cemeteries, streets, plazas and shops went ahead all over Granada. Labourers poured in to swell the workforce and among them came artisans as well as vagabonds. Students also came because the Royal College, which later became the university, was already functioning. And someone else was attracted to come to Granada – a certain itinerant bookseller.

The building boom concerns us because it is the measure of the surge of humanity that poured into the city producing those crowds that Juan will encounter soon after his arrival. The turning point in Juan Ciudad's life, his longed for *appointment with God*, will intimately involve him with these masses.

This was a time of tremendous tension for Granada, brought about by a mixture of economic, social, cultural and religious conditions. Very few places suffered such a contrast of splendour and misery as did Granada.

There is no way of exactly knowing Granada's population in this later part of the 16th century, so it is not remarkable that there are discrepancies in the reported numbers of men in the Moslem army that defended Granada. Likewise, we do not know how many Jews left Granada in 1492; nor how many Moors were expelled, or departed voluntarily, once the city was taken, or in subsequent roundups following the Alpujarras rebellion of 1500. Neither is it known how many Castilians came down to repopulate the Nazari kingdom. We do know that the diversity of population that resulted was fascinating and even explosive. More than explosive, it would be fatal, years later, when John of Austria finally defeated the remaining Moors in the cruel war of the Alpujarras in 1570.

"The explanation of experts is that, as the population appeared to increase, firstly by the Arabs, then by the Christians, this growth was used as a means of increasing the popularity of the city of Granada so it could claim to be amongst the major cities of the world. It appears that its first census took place in 1561. This attributed to Granada a population dispersed through 13,211 neighbourhoods, which would be something between the range of 50 and 60 thousand inhabitants. However, the Alpujarras War broke out at this time and 10% of the houses in the Albaycín were unoccupied. This is what I believe happened in reality: Granada benefited from an important migrant influx, reaching its height during the second half of the 15th century. That would have given it a population of something between 60,000 and 70,000. In 1492 there was a slight decrease caused by the emigration of the Moslems who could not support the Christian conquest. If this hypothesis can be proven, then Granada would have been the major city of the Iberian Peninsular." (Cortés Peña).

We know that when the Christians entered Granada, a handful of the Arab nobility refused to remain there beneath the enemy yoke. *"The majority went to Morocco and settled at Fez, where they were received with the greatest of kindness by the caliph who conferred high military rank upon them. Some of them bravely defended the North African coastline from Spanish attack during the reigns of Doña*

Juana and the Emperor Charles. *Some of them settled at Tunis while others went to Alexandria or some other major city in the east. Their grandchildren at Granada conserved their Spanish names and there were some who kept the titles to their country properties and the keys to their homes in the city of Granada."* (Lafuente Alcántara).

So attached were they to their Granada that neither Boabdil, nor his wife *"the sweet and affectionate Moraima"*, nor Zoraya, the widow of Muley el Zagal, nor the majority of the subjects of the Nasrides Kingdom, wanted to leave the city they loved. Because they feared that the Berbers might use Boabdil's presence as an excuse to revolt, the Catholic Monarchs had to urge him to abandon the Alpujarras, the territory that lies between Almería and Granada, and go to Fez.

The coexistence of Christians and Moors in the new Christian city was a prickly and complicated affair. The Castilians were generally simple Spanish folk and they did not distinguish between Moors, Turks or Jews, because they regarded all of them as persecutors of the Church.

There were Moors who, as Moslems, took advantage of the royal pardon granted to them after the conquest of Granada, thereby agreeing to convert to Christianity. They were then called Moriscos, to indicate they were converts to Catholicism. However, neither the people nor the Inquisition believed that the conversion of Moriscos was genuine. There was no way to know either, because Mohamed had granted his followers a formula called 'Taqiyya' which consisted of making a false apostasy so that Moslems could pretend to convert in order to avoid persecution.

The second classification of Moors related to the Turks, those powerful men from the east who were armed to the teeth and whose scimitars Christians feared on land and sea. Today, historians concede that the European Christian kings in the official propaganda calumniated the Turks. It presented them as being far more ferocious than they were in reality. The reason was, to entice the population to give personnel and money to cut short the Turkish advance, which seemed to be unstoppable. These 'Moor-Turks' from the far away orient were now spreading all along the North African coastline. The Moors feared most by Spaniards in the 16th century were, in fact, called Berbers and were pirates who preyed on shipping in the Mediterranean.

The piracy of the Berbers in the waters of the Mediterranean was audacious and shameless, and certainly very interesting. During the 7th century the Arabs occupied North

Africa and imposed the religion of Islam and called the place West Magreb. They used their foothold on North Africa as a springboard for the conquest of Spain.

When the Catholic Monarchs completed the conquest, the Andalusian provinces still lived in fear of Arab attacks. Queen Isabella knew that, in order to avoid them, Spain would have to form a bridgehead along the coast of Africa itself. Once the Arabs of Malaga and Granada had fled to exile in North Africa the implementation of the plan was seen to be urgent and was put into effect after the death of Queen Isabella. Expeditions were sent out, with varying success, as Cardinal Cisneros and King Ferdinand testified. Forts were set up at Mazalquivir, Orán, Bugía, Tripoli and the Rock of Gomera, and the banners of Aragon and Castile were alternatively flown above them.

Meanwhile, the Moors had abandoned their plan to assault Spain again. But they soon discovered another lucrative activity. From their hideaways along the African coast they ventured into the Mediterranean to strike shipping under the cover of darkness. They robbed jewels and provisions from Andalusian ports and took Christians captive and held them as hostages for ransom.

A shiver of fear went through the whole of Spain when it was learnt that the pirate Barbarossa was leading these raids. Terrible rumours circulated about the torments inflicted upon Christian captives in the dungeons of Algiers. In reality the rumours were exaggerated because the Moors were more interested in acquiring ransom money than in making martyrs. The friars of Castile and Aragon devised a scheme by which they would arrange with the Berber chiefs to pay for the ransom of their captives. This shady traffic became so shameless that the friars saw nothing wrong with keeping accounts with the Moors for ransom payments. There was a holy clergyman at Seville named Contreras, who to ransom captives, handed the Moors his walking stick as a down payment. The Moors accepted this as a deposit until he could make up the difference. They handed over the captives on the condition that Contreras would pay in full. Thus the deal was made and the holy man's walking stick was handed over as the deposit. This trade in captives only increased the insolence of the Moors and as a result they carried out the most hazardous and daring of raids. One pirate even attempted a raid into Italy to capture the Pope. Another managed to penetrate the country estate of the Princess Giulia Farnesio at Fondi. Giulia, who is reputed to have been one of the greatest beauties of the renaissance, fled to safety half-naked on horseback in the middle of the night.

The constant menace of the Berbers along the coast of Spain served as a strategic platform for the Turkish Emperor who was causing great concern to Charles V. It also brought with it the religious problem of Granada's Moriscos because Charles considered them to be spies and potential allies in the case of any possible invasion.

Granada was fortunate in having Queen Isabella designate Fray Hernando de Talavera as its first archbishop. We already know about Fray Hernando from the time Juan Ciudad was at Oropesa. As a result of his study in the archives, the researcher García Sánchez was able to include Hernando on the list of the illegitimate children begotten by the first Count of Oropesa and a Jewish mother. The Count even had the decency to send Hernando to Salamanca University.

Young Hernando was baptised as a Converso. He was both intelligent and kind. He became a professor at Salamanca University where he had graduated. After becoming a member of the Order of St. Jerome, called the Jeronymites, he became the prior of the Prado convent at Valladolid. Queen Isabella heard of his fame as a preacher and chose him as her personal confessor. The story is told of the first time the Queen went to him for confession when he ordered the royal penitent to fall upon her knees as an act of penance. He was a person of influence in the kingdom and became Bishop of Avila, and later accompanied the Catholic Monarchs to the war at Granada. Doña Isabella carefully chose two persons to govern Granada during the difficult years following the conquest; one was the Count de Tendilla to govern civil matters; the other, Fray Hernando, to govern religious affairs.

As first Archbishop of Granada he attempted to harmonise the coexistence of Christians and Moors. He prudently and quietly set out a scheme to permit the Moors who remained in the kingdom to convert to Christianity according to the law imposed by the Catholic Monarchs. He searched for priests who could speak Arabic so they could instruct the Moors. He even made an effort to learn their language himself. His kindness captivated the admiration of one and all. He was a tireless preacher and encouraged the faithful to participate in the divine office translated into the Castilian language. He wrote poetry of a devout nature. From his own funds the Archbishop started a school to educate 30 young Morisco boys to study the Castilian language. The manner of his approach resulted in many sincere and well-considered conversions.

Quite a different story is that of another valiant friar who appeared in Granada, also a friend of Doña Isabella. His name was Jiménez de Cisneros and he was the Archbishop of Toledo. He altered the system employed with reasonable success by Talavera. Cisneros imposed upon the Moors of Granada a time limit of two months to convert to Christianity or face the consequences. Great numbers presented themselves for mass baptisms. Under the orders of Cisneros, agents of the Inquisition confiscated four to five thousand sacred volumes of Islam and publicly burned them. The preposterous handling of the affair provoked an uprising in the Albaycín but a tragedy was avoided thanks to the intervention of Tendilla and Talavera: *"The Archbishop (Fray Hernando), known to everyone for his holiness, presented himself in the midst of the insurgents and using words of hope and warning, appeased the rage of the leaders."* (Anglería).

Talavera used the same tact with the Jews. After all, he was a *Converso* himself and knew within his own soul the drama of conscience they experienced. His great patroness Doña Isabella was now dead and his enemies wanted to denounce him to the Inquisition as a *Judaizante*, a secretly practising Jew. Fortunately, the Pope intervened from Rome just in time to save him from an ignominious condemnation.

Our book peddler, Juan, entered Granada thirty years after the death of Fray Hernando who had already been succeeded by four other archbishops, one holding the See of Granada for a long period, three only briefly. Even when Juan arrived, people still spoke of Fray Hernando Talavera in high praise of the way he treated the Moors and Jews fairly. It was quietly whispered that Fray Hernando came from a *Converso* family and that made Juan smile, because he too had a family secret which he had no intention of sharing. At Granada he did not use his surname Ciudad, but simply called himself Juan. He was known as Juan the peddler, and that served him until he set up his bookshop, which we will soon consider.

The rebellion of the Moors against compulsory baptism gathered momentum from the Albaycín to the Alpujarras, and from there spread from the Sierra Filebres to the sierras of Ronda and

Bermeja. King Ferdinand arrived with fresh troops from Seville and the Muslims were forced to capitulate. Those who refused to be baptised had no choice but to emigrate to North Africa. Those who accepted baptism, the Moriscos, were permitted to remain at Granada but they were badly treated by the Christians and subjected to hurtful ordinances. They were always suspected of secretly practising the religion of Islam and of conspiring with the Berber pirates. By a decree of Charles V, the Moriscos were forbidden to carry arms, or to speak or write in the Arabic language, even in the privacy of the family. They were forced to hand in all their Arabic books, to change their traditional dress, to keep the front door of their houses open at all times and to remove the veils from the faces of their wives.

The Moors were restless up in their warren of alleyways and houses in the Albaycín. Meanwhile, in the heights of the sierra in the district of Alpujarras, they were planning a rebellion to the death, confident that the Berbers would support them.

The beautiful city of Granada that welcomed our peddler was steeped in bitterness.

It seems the angels do not force themselves into our lives, otherwise Juan's guardian angel would have signified that *the appointment with God* for him was at Granada. The poet John Keats says that *"a thing of beauty is a joy for ever."* Juan's joy in Granada's beauty began the moment he set foot there.

We are not sure by which gate he first entered Granada, whether he carried any references with him or if his book suppliers at Gibraltar put him in touch with some wholesalers at Granada. His stocks would have been depleted by his long sales trek through so many towns and villages so he would need to replenish them.

He seems to have found premises without delay, for Castro, who rarely wasted words, limits himself to this curt mention: *"He took lodgings and set up shop at the Elvira Gate."*

At last, we know something certain about our man, who has been so elusive for so long. The location of his shop is *"at the Elvira Gate."*

Coincidently, Juan settles down in a part of the city that is occupied by Granada's suspect Moorish population. Perhaps he came across some *Converso* friend in a part of that vast city where families of Jewish or Moorish extraction could find protection. We don't know, maybe he was just lucky enough to find a little space near the Elvira Gate where there was a constant stream of builders, traders and visitors who came and went all day long through this city thoroughfare.

Halfway through the 16th century an encyclopaedia compiled by Pedro de Medina was published under the title '*Book of the greatness and marvellous things of Spain'*. It contained a delightful engraving of Granada at the time and it clearly shows the city wall with its dozens of towers and gates. I am reproducing it here.

We should never put too much faith in archaeological data in relation to city gateways, because walls are frequently demolished and renovated over the centuries. Nevertheless, the data referring to each of Granada's gateways appears to have a good basis. The city's eighteen gates have names suggestive of the traffic that passed through them: one for produce, another for sand taken from the banks of the Darro and used for building, another for the marketing of almonds.

The Elvira Gate was the main northern entrance to the city. It was called so because in ancient times when Granada was called Ilíberis, the gate opened on to the road that led to the Sierra Elvira. Medieval chronicles show that at this point on the town perimeter there was a suburb which was inhabited by Jews who supported the Arab invasion of 711 AD.

The Elvira Gate is the principal gateway in the entire wall. It was part of a small fort situated at the most frequented thoroughfare. It was made up of various components. The outside entrance was shaped in the typical Arabic horseshoe form and was crowned with battlements flanked by two brick towers. Passing through the archway there was a small space, open to the sky, where soldiers could mount guard. Beyond this, stood two arches with huge iron doors that led into an interior patio dominated by the wall. A little further on, were three smaller archways, one led to the fortified palace of the Mayor of the Albaycín; another to Elvira Street; and another to the cutting at the foot of the incline to the Albaycín.

Napoleon's army demolished the fort and all that remains today of Granada's historic gate is its exterior arch. Over the centuries many a famous entourage passed through this gateway.

Naturally, after the Catholic Monarchs had taken Granada the Elvira Gate had its fortification dismantled. The old fort became an administrative post, especially for the traffic that passed between the city centre and the outskirts. Today, the area just beyond the gate is called Triunfo Plaza, but in those days there was a military presence there and also the newly built Royal Hospital. It was an easy matter for Juan to find a small space among the openings of the old fort. At this spot today, there is a tiny chapel with a plaque commemorating the presence of John of God.

A "shop" or "bookshop" are names far too pretentious for this little nook where Juan settled down. It only measured two metres wide and five metres high, the latter being quite out of proportion since it corresponded to that of the old fort. It was barely more than a niche that provided enough space for Juan to hang up his stock and to receive one or two customers, because, Castro says, *"He took lodgings and set up shop at the Elvira Gate"* but later notes that Juan *"... reached his lodgings where he also kept his shop and the stock."* There is confusion about whether his lodgings and shop were one and the same space or not. If they were together, the tightness of rented space would have been obvious for all to see.

The colourful neighbourhood where Juan set up his bookstall was an excellent spot for his business because there was a constant stream of men and women coming and going all day long through Granada's main gate. It was also the entrance used by the official entourages of famous personalities visiting from other places.

The chronicles of the time indicate another interesting clientele, the day labourers who lingered about the gates of a city in expectation of work. This was the typical custom in Andalusia, therefore the Elvira Gate also served as a labour exchange. Juan would hang up his cord books, illustrated novels, devout images, medals and rosaries in order to attract these simple customers. In reality Juan's bookshop had the characteristics of what the Andalusians call a *chiringuito*, a flea-market stall but he did not sell odds and ends and knick-knacks.

Juan Ciudad never used his surname, just Juan, or, as Granada's witnesses testified, *"Juan el Portugués"* [John the Portuguese] because he wanted to keep his family background to himself. The Jewish and Moorish network had signs throughout Spain by which both *Conversos* and Moriscos could recognise one another, communicate confidently between themselves and give support to each other, so possibly, the Elvira Gate was suggested to Juan by someone 'in the know' before he arrived.

The Elvira was a magic street, holding a mysterious attraction. Exactly 43 years after the arrival of Juan *'the peddler'* at Granada, another Juan called *'of the Cross'* led a band of discalced friars of the religious family of Teresa of Jesus there. By coincidence, Juan de la Cruz [or as you know him best, John of the Cross] was also a *Converso*. Before settling into a permanent convent for the friars, John of the Cross was given temporary accommodation by the daughters of Teresa, herself a *Converso*, in Elvira Street!

Sadly today, Elvira Street has been reduced to a third grade street that is quite neglected by the Municipality. It runs parallel with the pretentious and broad Via de Colón which has taken away the Elvira's importance and has made it a mere back street. In reading the wise notes of Gallego Burín and the clever lines of Francisco Izquierdo in their respective guides to Granada, it seems Elvira street still carries some traces of that epoch of Moors and Christians. It was always known for its bustle and dirt, so much so that popular rhymes of that time tell of *"the well-known mire of Elvira Street."* It is still a street for artisans, with workshops in leather goods, woodwork and ceramics, and of course the shops, some quite small, others larger, but all crammed with goods.

During the first half of the 16th century, plans were drawn up to change Granada from a Moslem city into a Castilian one. This called for the lengthening of the two main thoroughfares of the Moorish city. Both met each other at the Plaza Hatabín, now called the Plaza Nueva. One was Elvira Street, which started at its gateway and went as far as the neighbourhoods of Colcha, Santa Escolástica and Santiago. It skipped through the Jewish neighbourhood of Mawrur and came out at the Molinos Gate. The other arterial thoroughfare went down to the Plaza Bibarrambla through the Zacatín where the clothing shops were situated, and followed the course of the River Darro as far as the Guadix Gate. The noble palace of the Chancellery is situated facing the Plaza Hatabín-Nueva, with its extension to the church of Santa Ana. This is one of the most rewarding sights for the visitor to Granada today, for it overlooks the Darro while above soars the Alhambra.

At the time Juan set up shop, Elvira Street served as a breakwater to help stem the deep anxieties that flowed down to Granada from the Albaycín. Most of the Moriscos had officially converted to Christianity but, as the conversions were forced upon them, in the majority of cases such a conversion was false. They lived under the prescription called *Taqiyya*, or false apostasy, a formula permitted by Mohamed. On account of this, the Christians were suspicious of all Moriscos – including those whose conversions were genuine. Then two circumstances occurred which aggravated the situation. The first was when the Moriscos staunchly defended their right to wear their traditional clothing and to speak, sing and dance in their own fashion. This obstinacy angered many others. Morisco women perfumed and tinted their hair with dye from henna flowers that they gathered in the springtime and dried in the open air. Christian women imagined that the ointment made from henna was magic, and probably satanic. The second circumstance was even worse – it was a threat. The Emperor Charles was forced to fight the Turks on land and above all, at sea because thousands of Muslims who had been expelled from Spain after the conquest of Granada were now protected by the Turks and joined their forces. It's uncertain whether the Moriscos were forming a Turkish fifth column on Spanish soil but it was suspected that, should there be an invasion along the Spanish coast, they would join the enemy. They were suspected also of passing information to the Berber pirates who raided the Mediterranean from the lairs in North Africa. Cervantes wrote a phrase in his *Conversation with Dogs* which expressed these unjustified suspicions of the Christian society: *"Spain, breeding and nurturing in her womb so many vipers like Moriscos."*

A fascinating Morisco woman also lived in Elvira Stree in Juan's time. She was the celebrated *Mora*, the Moorish woman of Ubeda. Of great age, she was considered to be very wise and a teacher of the great muftis of Islam in both the east and the west, who secretly came to visit her. It was said that she shed rays of light *"upon our venerable Koran."*

We know about the activity of the Mora, *"the old lady who was pious and influential"*, because of a visit paid to her by the famous *Mancebo* [young man] of Arévalo whose identity is unknown. According to the Aljamiada, a collection of Moorish documents, he was the son of a Christian mother. These papers say he was *"a scholarly young man, a Castilian of Arébalo, very expert and learned in Arabic, Hebrew, Greek and Latin literature."* Although the Aljamiada was written in Castilian, it curiously used Arabic characters, such as Kastile for Castile. What a gem of a lad! Probably he secretly practised his Moslem faith. The Mancebo went through Spain explaining the teachings of the Koran to the Morisco population *"in order to save the religion of his ancestors."* Saavedra, Harvey and other experts in the literature of the Aljamiada attribute two manuscripts to him. One is the celebrated *Tafçira*, studied by Asín Palacios. The *Tafçira* consists of Moslem law, gives news about the journeys of the Mancebo, and it describes his visit to *la Mora*, the Moorish woman of Ubeda. It seems strange that the old *Mora* of Ubeda, who was 93 years of age at the time the Mancebo visited her, had never left her house, was a virgin, poor, and lived alone save for the care given her by a niece. But she was very learned in the religion of Islam, so much so that the doctors of Islam have eulogised her.

In his *Tafçira* the Mancebo reflected on the hardships experienced by the Moriscos at Granada. They had to avoid attacks from the Christian population and to do this they had to abandon their traditional garments, renounce their dietary laws, use Christian names in public and only recite the Koran in secret. The *Alfaquíes* (masters) quietly went about from village to village recommending their faithful to use the Koran's Taqiyya which, as I have mentioned, permitted a false conversion and even allowed one to be baptised in order to avoid persecution. By the middle of the 16th century almost every trace of Islamic culture had vanished from Granada.

Juan, in his nook at the Elvira Gate, found himself caught up with this underground world of the Mora of Ubeda – the hidden old lady, who after the fall of the kingdom of the Nasrides Moors, symbolised the last remains of Islam at Granada. The coexistence of Christians and Moriscos ended up very badly.

Castro simply indicates that Juan did quite well in his little business as a bookseller at Granada: *"He stayed in business here..."*

A witness at John of God's beatification process, Cosme de Rojas, heard from his elders that Juan carried out his business in two ways: *"As a bookseller at his stall, and also as a peddler hawking books, rosaries and other items in a basket."*

And what about that subconscious *searching for a new horizon,* that mysterious appointment with God that he first felt within himself when he was in Seville? Juan was still waiting, and was ready for the appointment, knowing that the initiative was to come from the Other One.

In the meantime he went on happily selling books, as Castro states: *"Good John of God was busy at his trade and quite unaware."* Quite unaware of anything else, which is the same thing as saying that he was quite satisfied. But *"the Lord was about to remind him."* Castro then goes on to say that God *"set his merciful eyes upon John and elevated him to a different state of life."* Juan will take on his *different state of life.* The meeting with God is imminent.

Notes to Chapter 16

* The geographic, historic, anthropological, cultural and religious descriptions of Granada in the 16th century occupy an immense bibliography. The following can give a good overview of the period of John of God's presence there: M. Lafuente Alcántara, *Historia de Granada IV* (facsimile edition), Granada 1992; A. L. Cortés-B, Vincent, *Historia de Granada III*, Granada 1986; Pedro Mártir de Anglería, Epistolario, ed. López de Toro, Madrid 1953-1966; F. Bermúdez de Padres, *Antigüedades y excelencias de Granada* (facsimile edition), Madrid 1981; J. Bosque Maurel, *Granada la tierra y sus hombres*, Granada 1971; J. Caro Baroja, *Los moriscos del reino de Granada. Ensayo de historia social*, Madrid 1957; A. Domíngues Ortiz-B.Vincent, *Historia de los moriscos*, Madrid 1978; A. Gamir Sandoval, *Organizacíon de la defensa de la costa del reino de Granada desde su reconquista hasta finales del siglo XVI*, Granada 1947; M. García Fuentes, La Inquisición en Granada en el siglo XVI. Fuentes para su estudio, Granada 1981; P.Herrera Puga, *Granada en el siglo XVI. Aspectos sociales*, Granada 1976; M. A. Ladero Quesada, *Granada, Historia de un pa's islámico (1232-1571), Madrid 1969; R. López Guzmán, Colección de documentos para la historia del arte en Granada. Siglo XVI*, Granada 1993; A Saitta, *Dalla Granada mora alla Granada cattolica. Incroci di civilità*, Rome 1984; L. Torres Balbás, *Ciudades hispano-musulmanas*, Madrid 1971; F de P. Villa-Real, *El libro de las tradicionales de Granada* (facsimile edition), Granada 1990.

* Naturally, to focus upon the places refered to in John of God's day, as well as our own, it is helpful to make use of the better guides to the city of Granada, especially the classic ones of M. Gómez-Moreno González, Granada 2 1982; A. Gallego Burín, *Granada. Guía del viajero*, Granada 2 1982; also the rather scattered one by F. Izquierdo, *Guía secreta de Granada*, Madrid 1977.

* Indispensable to follow the path of John of God in Granada: M. De Mina Salvador, *Visitar la Granada de San Juan e Dios*, Granada 1994.

* There are several witnesses at the beatification process testifying to the stall, or shop, *"having seen"* or *"heard it said."*

* The evidence about the physical aspect of John of God was given by Ana de Miranda, widow of Salvador Moreno, witness #6 in the Oropesa process. I have also found amongst other witnesses fleeting references, none of them consistent; I would like to point out the success achieved by A. Muñoz Hidalgo, *De Juan Ciudad a Juan de Dios*, Barcelona, 1990, who from time to time throughout his book, gives descriptions of the corporal constitution of John of God; and although there is no documented proof for this, his educated guess is well adjusted to his subject. We will be treating the portraits and pictures of John of God further on; there is a selection suggested by M Gómez Moreno, *San Juan de Dios, Primicias históricas*, Madrid 1950, see his 'Floreto' 316-320.

* The large fragment by P. M. De Anglería is taken from his work cited above, *Epistolario* IX, 178-179.

* The quotes from Cortés Peña are from his *Historia de Granada*, 17-20.

* On the indelible footprints of Hernando de Talavera in the religious history of Granada, see P. Alcántara Suárez, *Vida del venerable don fray Hernando de Talavera*, Madrid 1866; A. Fernández de Madrid, *Vida de fray Hernando de Talavera, primer Arzobispo de Granada*, Madrid 1931; P. Fernández, *La España imperial. Fray Hernando de Talavera, confesor de los Reyes Católicos y primer Arzobispo de Granada*, Madrid, 1942.

* On the Mora (Moorish woman) of Ubeda, and the Mancebo (young man) of Arévalo, see L. López Baralt, *San Juan de la Cruz y Islam*, Madrid 1990, 285-328.
* A literary view of the Nasrides kingdom, in A. Gala, *Granada de los nazaríes*, Barcelona 1994; A novel view of the past Islamic Granada to the Christian Granada, Tariq Al', *A la sombra del granado*, Barcelona 1994.
* The witness Cosmé de Rojas did not personally know John of God, he was speaking from hearsay. He was #20 at the Madrid beatification process.
* Allow me to add a curious reference to the 'secrets' of Elvira Street, the text of which I have taken from the *Antigüedades y excelencias de Granada*, quoted above, folio 214 , by Bermúdez de Pedraza: the bowels of the celebrated street were designed to withstand the frequent earthquakes that hit Granada. The following is the notable text: "The remedy for these earthquakes, says Pliny, is to have many wells and deep tunnels through which the earth can breathe and exhale. And the Moors, being good philosophers, had a large well, which they called *Ayrón*, because this means very deep and wide and had no other purpose than to cushion earthquakes. When the Christians took over, the poor government could see no use for a well that did not hold water.

17

AN APPOINTMENT WITH GOD

Granada
1539

Juan was unaware that someone expected and awaited him at Granada where he would be struck with a bolt from heaven. I refer to the mysterious appointment he had agreed to, while he was at Seville, where he abandoned forever his employment as a shepherd. Juan was happy and carefree and continued to live a well-balanced and generous life, confident that God would decide where and when to give him a sign that would lead him to some kind of evangelical work for the needy, work that would satisfy his soul's yearnings.

From time to time history records events that seem to just come out of the blue, like a flash of lightning. One such mysterious and rare experience is about to strike Juan here in Granada.

Juan's tiny bookstall at the Elvira Gate allowed him to observe the life of the city that passed to and fro before his door. It would have been hard to find a better spot than here, to sense the heartbeat of Granada. This was the place where, day after day, country folk and city dwellers mingled together; Moors rubbed shoulders with Christians, aristocrats passed by in sedan chairs, and labourers loitered in the hope of being hired for work. The Elvira Gate, and its adjacent market place and plaza, were like a seismograph measuring the human shock waves of the Granadinos. This was the place where feelings were expressed, gossip abounded and news and warning quickly spread. It does not surprise me in the least that the keen prose of Father Castro leaves a certain amount of complacency that can only be guessed at in regards to our hawker now turned bookstall proprietor: "*Good John of God was busy at his trade and quite carefree.*" Yes! He was satisfied with his state and enjoying life.

Was Juan, while keeping his earlier premonitions to himself, waiting to have his way pointed out by the finger of God? Alternatively, had he put his appointment out of his mind after five years of waiting? Only now that he had set up shop at the Elvira Gate was he able to be *carefree*, as Castro laconically puts it – carefree, earning his livelihood without excessive confidence in, or concern for, the future.

Now, however, mysterious dark clouds gathering overhead ominously predict an approaching storm. The inevitable moment was here and his appointment with God was about to take place. It would take place not far away in the Campo de los

Mártires, the Martyrs' field, at the edge of the Alhambra, although Juan is unaware of this.

At the Elvira Gate, where all the news of Granada circulated, Juan heard that an interesting event was about to take place. The next day Master Juan de Avila was going to preach the occasional sermon on the feast of St. Sebastian.

Juan had arrived in Granada just before Christmas, so he had been living there for only six or seven weeks. In this time he had been imbued by the festive spirit so characteristic of Andalusia, and had had plenty of time to experience the religious or popular festivals during the early months of the new year. Granada's liturgical calendar in the 16th century specified 36 holy days of obligation besides Sundays. These feast days honoured episodes in the life of Christ, feasts dedicated to the Blessed Virgin Mary, the Apostles and martyrs, the feast of The Exaltation of the Holy Cross; even the anniversary of the Catholic Monarchs. These Masses were in thanksgiving for deliverance from the terrible epidemics of that period. The greatest of these feast days was Corpus Christi which had been celebrated from the earliest years of the century throughout the city with sermons, altars, decorated arches, dancing, bell ringing, artillery firing, lanterns and processions. Granada's celebration of Corpus Christi was only equalled by Toledo's celebration of the feast.

Today, the Campo de los Mártires has been converted into a leafy carmen, as the beautiful public and private gardens of Granada are called. It belongs to the Municipality and is used for artistic functions. It is situated outside the city and is separated from the Alhambra by a valley. For years it had been enclosed by a wall and was sadly left neglected and desolate. The Campo de los Mártires is situated upon the hill that the Arabs called Ahabul. In the time of the Arab king, Al-Ahmar, the grounds of the Campo were excavated to make silos for the preservation of provisions for the fortress. The silos had the form of a funnel with an opening through a round hole at the top. They were six meters deep with a circumference of eight metres in diameter. When the silos were no longer used to store food, the Arabs used them as dungeons for Christian captives. These unfortunates were kept in the silos at night after spending the day in forced labour. The German traveller Münzer visited the Campo in 1494 and wrote: "the prisoners underwent shocking suffering, jammed into those enormously deep and dank dungeons." Many Christians died in those hellholes, especially during the years of the siege of Granada.

As soon as the city fell, Queen Isabella had a hermitage built on the site. This hermitage was dedicated to the Holy Martyrs and was the first church built at Granada. The ground that the Arabs called the Field of Captives now became known as the Field of the Martyrs. Isabella had the church placed under the patronage of the Roman martyr St. Sebastian. Today the Bellas Artes Museum, which is adjacent to the carmen, conserves some pieces of a 16th century wooden altarpiece by Juan Ramírez from the Hermitage of the Martyrs.

Some years later, the Campo was given to the Discalced Carmelite friars to establish their first convent at Granada. A new prior arrived there in 1582. His name was Juan de la Cruz, John of the Cross. He was a mystic and a poet and it was here that he spent the most peaceful years of his life. It was also here that he composed the essential portion of his writings, including these brilliant lyrics of divine love: "Oh call of living love! How tenderly you wound my soul to its very depths." Besides having to find the time to put his verses together, Fray John of the Cross had an aqueduct constructed to bring water into the convent from the Alhambra. He then converted the parched grounds of the Hermitage into a flourishing garden and orchard. In the early 19th century when the anticlerical government of the day passed its iniquitous Desamortizacíon laws [the disbanding of the religious orders], the Government wanted to demolish the convent and sell off its property for a song. Fortunately, the Hermitage of the Martyrs fell into the hands of a Belgian family named Meersman who, not only maintained the gardens, but also introduced tropical plants. Later the property passed to the Dukes del Infantado and later still, the Convent of the Martyrs became the national botanical gardens which the Granada Municipality restored in the style of the 19th century, with a few lamentable innovations.

It is the year 1539, the eve of the feast of St. Sebastian, the 20th of January, and all is in readiness for Master Avila to preach in the Hermitage of the Martyrs. The ceremony will be held in the open air, unless it rains, where there is plenty of space in the grounds for the large crowds of Granadinos who will flock there. They recalled well that, not so long ago, during the Islamic occupation, this very field, the Campo de los Mártires, was the place where those giants of the Faith were martyred.

The news that the famous preacher Master Avila was to preach up at the Campo de los Martíres was announced throughout the city by criers ringing bells.

Juan de Avila had only been at Granada for two years, but he had already gained the confidence and friendship of the Archbishop, Don Gaspar, who had given him lodgings at his palace. Avila had assisted the Archbishop in many matters with his good advice. The two had a lot in common, and Juan de Avila knew that the Archbishop would take the opportunity to hear him preach at the Hermitage of the Martyrs.

Since 1492, Don Gaspar de Avalos had been the sixth archbishop to occupy the See of Granada. There was a very close relationship between him and the first archbishop, Fray Hernando de Talavera. Fray Hernando was his uncle who adopted him and who was his tutor. A fine uncle and teacher he was! Gaspar was born at Guadix six years before the fall of Granada. While still a youth, he was sent by his uncle to study theology at Paris and Salamanca. He later became a professor at Santa Maria College, Valladolid, and a canon at Murcia. Soon after his episcopal ordination as Bishop of Gaudix he was elected as Archbishop of Granada in 1526 and met the Emperor Charles when he visited the city that year. Don Gaspar had already completed the first ten years of his episcopal office in this present year of 1539. His achievements up to then included the establishment of the University, the Albaycín, two colleges for the sons of Moriscos, a theological college for priests and the Cathedral Chapter. If any further proof was needed of his evangelical zeal, suffice to say he desired Master Avila to be his guest.

Father Juan de Avila's reputation for wisdom and holiness was increasing from day to day. You will recall that Juan de Avila was at Seville when Juan Ciudad was there working as a shepherd. At that time, too, Juan Ciudad made up his mind to undertake another sort of work in response to an inner calling, albeit an uncertain one at the time. No one could have guessed that one day Juan de Avila would be the one to eventually guide Juan Ciudad to his destined appointment at Granada. The day arrived and the two Juans, neither one knowing the other, went up to the Campo de los Mártires, Avila to preach, Ciudad to listen.

Some witnesses at the beatification process when referring to the preacher, used phrases such as, *"the very learned and holy Master Avila"*; *"apostolic and esteemed preacher"*; *"great preacher"*; and, many added, *"of a holy life"*, at the mention of his name. Juan de Avila had achieved fame at Granada in the short space of two years, since he came from Cordoba at the end of 1536.

When Master Avila was exonerated by the Inquisition at Seville which had imprisoned him, he went to Ecija and then to Cordoba. He was renowned for his exemplary life of prayer and study and his availability, humility and patience. He dedicated much time to teaching the catechism to children and young students. He gave spiritual direction to selected souls and was an untiring preacher. He never asked for stipends, and his almsgiving was generous. No wonder the aura surrounding him pointed him out as an model priest. His enthusiastic friend, Fray Luis de Granada, wrote of Avila's sermons that, *"they were like a blunderbuss loaded with plenty of ammunition, which when fired, ended up shooting many birds."*

At first the people of Granada received Juan de Avila rather coolly, but it was not long before he won them over. The following is a rather expressive anecdote told by a certain Doctor Carleval who was a leading figure at Granada in those days. Master Avila was to preach on a certain day, so Carleval said to one of his friends: "Let us go along and see who this idiot is, how he preaches and what he has to say." Once they had heard the sermon they were so touched by his love of God that they went to listen attentively to his sermons thereafter.

Avila's next achievement was the difficult one of gaining the confidence of the canons of Granada Cathedral. In March 1538, they invited him to proclaim the papal bull on the Crusade. He preached on that occasion in the presence of the president, councillors and dignitaries of the city.

Our bookseller Juan was quite unaware of the risk he was taking when he climbed the hill to the Campo de los Mártires to listen to the sermon of Master Avila. This was the brilliant priest of whom it was said that Ignatius Loyola had been watching from afar and would like to have had him as a member of his Society of Jesus. Avila was a curious type, attracted to science and mechanics, he also wrote essays on making dams to conserve water, something that would be very useful in dry Andalusia. There were many remarkable doings and sayings in circulation about Master Juan de Avila. They even said he was considered the guardian of God's honour. Once he saw a priest celebrating Mass in a slovenly manner. As the time for the consecration approached Avila went up to the altar where the priest flippantly handled the Host. He quietly said to the careless celebrant: *"Be good to Christ, he is the son of a good Father."* Ignatius would have liked to hear that.

Our rather carefree Juan has made the decision to hear Master Avila preach his sermon. Fray Luis de Granada warns that to hear such a preacher can be dangerous: *"When he had to preach, he carefully made it a rule to be very temperate, in the real meaning of the word. It was like those who go to hunt birds. They do not set off an alarm but make sure that their falcon is hungry in readiness for the hunt because it flies better when it's hungry. That is how he was when he went up into the pulpit, not simply with dedication but with a lively hunger and a desire to win over, with his words, some soul for Christ. That is how he preached with such enthusiasm and fervour of spirit."*

Granada promised itself a memorable day, with a top rate preacher!

Before giving consideration to the sermon, let us see how the somewhat staid Castro eulogises Master Avila. For once he really lets himself go: *"That excellent and outstanding doctor of theology Master Avila was to be the preacher. He was a man resplendent in holiness and the latest studies in those days. His fame was so great throughout Spain that he was able to bring the very best out of people from all walks of life."* Castro affirms that his *"sermons were so famous that it is no wonder that he had such a great following,"* amongst whom we find our Juan, for *" the day arrived and amongst those going up to hear him was John of God."*

We know the text of the sermon preached by Master Avila that day with almost absolute certainty. The peaks of the sierra were snow-capped and there was crisp frost underfoot, so the morning was quite cold and invigorating.

Castro reproduces a few paragraphs of the sermon that, without any doubt, are those that John of God recalled later in talking with his confidants. Fortunately, Luis Sala Balust, who sadly died at an early age, studiously researched in a Roman archive the documents of Avila and discovered a text of the Master's autobiography. This document corresponds exactly to the sermon of the feast of St. Sebastian at Granada.

Our bookseller Juan had gone up to the Hermitage de los Mártires, not just to see a spectacular event. There is no doubt that he was impelled also by his religious devotion. Juan was completely unprepared to see himself, little by little, overpowered by an interior fire once the words of Master Avila began to sink into him. Castro says of Avila's sermon, that: *"everyone's attention was fixed upon his lively words."* It seemed to Juan that the words of the preacher were aimed directly at him, and *"they struck him to the very depths of his soul"*:

"Unless the Lord descended from the mount to the plain, what would have happened to us? Yes, what would have happened to us if the Lord had not divested himself of his greatness, disguising it and taking upon himself the form of our humanity so as to cleanse all mankind of its misery and filth? We would have remained in our infirmities."

The preacher drew from the Bible some examples of conversions through God's merciful grace. Then he went on to say: *"But the Lord did come down from the mountain in order to gather to himself all the cripples, blind people too, and he healed anyone who was sick."* Continuing further, he put some disquieting questions to his hearers: *"But what would have happened had he not come down? Who would have stooped down to heal the sick, to give sight to the blind, to give life to the dead? There are so many blind, lame, sick and dying people. Whatever would they do if they would not turn to the Lord for healing?"*

At this point, the hand-written manuscript of Master Avila's sermon bears the word *etcetera*, which indicates that he intended to *ad-lib* this accusation against those who refuse to turn to this healing source. Then he picks up the written text again and says: *"What would you say about a sick person who, when he saw Christ going about performing so many works of mercy and bestowing health, refused to be healed by him?"* The preacher answered his own question, *"Father, you would say, he does not want to be healthy, he enjoys being sick."*

At this point Avila presses home another question: *"Tell me, what would you say of a man taken prisoner by the Turks who refused to be repatriated once his ransom was paid?"* Again he answers himself: *"Father, he enjoys being a captive and is too fond of the master keeping him prisoner."*

Here the preacher hits his mark, *"Well my friend! I am telling you that this is absolutely true. The reason therefore that you, having Christ as the remedy, are..."* Once again Avila's sermon notes abruptly come to another two etceteras, indicating that he intended to ad-lib the decisive phrases. The researcher Sala Balust notes that *"the cues and abbreviations here reveal the youthful verve of the writer. "* The preacher aroused his hearers and denounced the misery of whoever does not listen to the divine invitation: *"It pleases you to be held captive by the sins for which Christ came down from the heights to destroy upon Calvary."*

The sermon grew into a crescendo and crashed upon his hearers like a mountain torrent: *"How miserable it would be if we who, by the Lord's mercy, are called to follow Christ for we have been called to the fullness of the faith that he gives us calling ourselves Christians, yet failing him no sooner than he elevates us to that honour. It really is something to cry about!"*

Let us pause a moment at this halfway mark of the sermon, and ask ourselves what was going on in the mind of our bookseller Juan, because, as soon as the sermon finishes, he will cause quite a rumpus.

When Master Avila's sermon notes are read in isolation some four and a half centuries later, it is evident that he put a great deal of thought into its preparation. Nevertheless, the words appear like dried flowers under a glass cover. His contemporaries said that his vitality, which made his sermons so lively, never dried up. *"As a rule they would last about two hours or more"*, and *"were spoken with gentleness and mildness, but with such a force of persuasion that it made his audience gasp for breath. He fascinated them so much that it seemed as if flaming sparks flew out of his mouth."* They said he *"had a heart of fire"* and that his sermons *"were very well prepared, and that he quoted passages from the Bible, classic philosophers and the Fathers of the Church in them."* His disciples vouched that the force of his convictions came from *"his tremendous love of Our Lord."* They also said his vitality came from the long hours he spent in prayer *"digesting his thoughts."* He prayed upon his knees and used to place his hands upon the feet of a crucifix. In fact his sermons often *"left his hearers feeling contrite, looking at one another without speaking a word, giving the impression that they all left converted and repentant of their faults."*

Our Juan stood there listening. What a pity the television camera cannot give us a close-up of the tense expression upon his face. The resolute voice of Master Avila struck again: *"Now, I beseech you, if anything at all stands between you and Christ even though you may be entangled in sharp and piercing thorns..."* Now the preacher comes down to the level of personal behaviour: *"Would you like to know what it is like to be a disciple of Jesus Christ? Well then, in the eyes of the world such a one is poor and humble and finds things difficult for himself, but I assure you, he is in fact much wealthier than anyone who is not a disciple of Christ. And do you want to know why? It is because his tears, poverty and persecution are given a sweet flavour by God who knows them far better than all who scorned them."*

Master Avila then paints a startling picture of those who refuse the divine invitation: *"Their laughter becomes tears, their riches turn to poverty, their power turns into captivity. It is all because they preferred to choose the poisonous cup of pleasures, riches and power. No sooner do they lift it to their lips than their heart seizes and they drop dead. They robbed others to become rich. They oppressed their neighbour to become powerful. They sought pleasure in bestial behaviour. So poisonous and blameworthy are these things, that no sooner than they choose to do them, than their heart burns up and dies the death that is sin and sin is the worst of all deaths."*

The preacher then proposed an examination of conscience as he concluded his sermon. His words hit Juan like a seismic shock rocking him to the very foundations of his being: *"Beware O you worldly person, you who turn away from serving God because you are selfseeking and take no heed of the most wretched of all miseries... Even if your riches are good and you are sinless; and how you pass your time is without sin; and your pleasures sinless; then remember that all these things have been given to you by God. Let them be like limpid rain drops falling upon your soul, softening it and making it acceptable to God who gives all these good things to you. Would you be like that sort of person who abuses the gifts that God gives you, ungratefully casting them like dirt into a cesspool?"*

Let us prepare ourselves for what the above is going to trigger, namely the *madness* which Master Avila's sermon unleashed upon Juan Ciudad. Castro has already told us two things. Firstly, Juan was awaiting a definitive meeting with God. That is to say, he was in the hope of what I like to call *his appointment*. And secondly, that the effects of the sermon exceeded any reasonable expectation, because the grace of God was activated in Juan: *"He put those words into effect, and in such a way that they remained fixed in the depths of his heart."* There you have two of Castro's statements on the subject.

I ask the reader to permit me the choice of procedure. God used Master Avila's sermon as a vehicle to realise his appointment with Juan. Our man is instantly drawn into a frightening whirlpool of experiences that push him to the very brink of human endurance, he becomes 'insane'.

It was as if his biological wineskin had burst and it is a wonder he was not torn apart. His appointment with God brought about a violent upheaval that apparently deranged Juan and threw him completely out of control. He became a subject for psychological analysis, or rather psychiatric, and by association, spiritual, because he now seems to be a person under the control of *apparently* frenetic impulses.

From 20 January to the middle of May, Juan repeatedly displays, "apparently" incomprehensible behaviours that reflect the disturbances taking place subconsciously in a person who previously demonstrated normal equilibrium.

Scientists of all persuasions have studied *the phenomenon of John of God* and have minutely examined how it came about, and have attempted to give some sort of 'reasonable' explanation for his 'madness'. We will wait four months until this hurricane passes over, before we examine each diagnosis, one by one.

You are aware of newspaper meteorological reports that speak of high and low pressures, and how a gyrating low pressure over the sea can result in atmospheric conditions that may form a waterspout. Since coming down from the Campo de los Mártires, Juan appeared to be severely disturbed, similar to the disturbances caused by unusual atmospheric pressures. It was as if he had been sucked up into the spiral of a gyrating waterspout.

Leaving the commentaries aside and before we scrutinise the results we will first look at the facts and at what occurs during the next four months.

Castro's words give us the first indication of the intimate process that occurred when the words of Master Avila's penetrated Juan's soul, *"They struck him to the very depths of his soul": and he "was convinced by them."*

As soon as the sermon had finished the crowd began to leave. They went down the hill to Granada by one of two possible paths. The first descended to the neighbourhood of Antequeruela Baja, passing through the Campo del Príncipe then going on to the Plaza Realejo. The other moved along Antequeruela Alta, then on down the slope called Cuesta de Gomérez until it reached the Plaza Nueva.

Among those who took the second pathway was a man who appeared to be completely deranged. He was gesticulating in a bizarre way and shouting out as he beat his chest with his fists. The crowd stood aside to let him pass, some were indifferent to him, other felt sorry for the poor wretch. Some even may have recognised him. *It is the bookseller from the Elvira Gate! What has happened to him?* They could hear only his shouts for God's mercy.

He has gone mad! There were plenty of potholes full of water in the Cuesta de Gomérez. Juan threw himself into one of these, putting his head into the muddy water, smearing mud on his face and pulling at his hair. He threw his arms about, telling everyone there that he was a sinner. Then he picked himself up again and began to run down the slope, dodging in and out of the people as he went. There were plenty of oddballs in the city, he was just another weirdo. Granada had plenty!

When Juan arrived at the Plaza Nueva where Elvira Street began, the young men lolling about in the plaza decided to poke fun at him, shouting out, *"Look at the madman!"*

Juan was now in his own neighbourhood, and almost everyone would surely have recognised who the madman was. The artisans along the street were accustomed to seeing him coming and going past the open doors of their workshops. Juan's customers, who had bought prints and leaflets from him, were shocked when they saw him rushing past them completely out of his mind.

The street kids teased him by shouting, *"Come on, look at the mad man!"* While saying this they shoved him about and made offensive gestures. They pulled ugly faces at him and screamed out for all to hear, *"Come on everybody, have a look at this madman."* Juan walked, ran and stumbled along amidst their shouts but no-one seeing this extraordinary performance did anything about it. Down the street he went until he reached the door of his humble dwelling, his little bookstall. He then went inside while the crowd at the Elvira Gate gawked at his conduct. Some broke away from what they were doing to see at closer range what was going on over at the bookseller's premises.

Juan was inside trashing the place. He threw books and leaflets out the door and handed out handfuls of holy pictures and rosaries to the dozens of grasping hands keen to get something for nothing. The bookseller had gone completely off his head!

Castro is keen to point out a certain alertness that the "supposed" madman had as he was tearing his shop to pieces: *"Books about chivalry and profane subjects he tore to pieces with his hands and teeth; those which were about the lives of saints and good doctrine he freely gave away."*

Was he so mad after all? He handed out books and pictures until the shop was completely empty. What an unexpected stunt it was for the passers by at the Elvira Gate! What next? He started to dispose of his provisions, giving away the groceries he had stored in his tiny quarters, as well as his clothing and his few odds and ends of furniture.

What next? Juan stands in the doorway of his empty shop and begins to strip off his clothes. *"Not satisfied with stripping himself of all his worldly goods, he even began to take off his clothing to give it away as well."* Castro tells us that he kept his shirt and breeches, *"to cover his nakedness."* The breeches he wore were named *zaragüelles*, a type of baggy breeches men often wore at that period.

That's the story! Juan completely divests himself of his wealth and lets go of everything he ever owned. He is as free as a bird. But is he a "mad bird"? Not so mad! *"Juan once more ran out into the streets of Granada."* He shouted and made quite a spectacle of himself. The urchins followed, and so too did some respectable persons, a great many people in fact. Everyone wanted to see what was going on.

Juan shouted out calling for mercy, God's mercy. Is that madness? He went down Elvira Street again and, turning to the right, ran up to the front of the Major Church and throwing himself to the ground shouted: *"Mercy! Mercy, Lord God, on this tremendous sinner who has offended you!"*

Granada did not have a cathedral at this time and Major was the name given to the church that served in its place. Eventually the Major Church would be called the Sagrario [sanctuary] of the Cathedral. It was built upon the site of the Nasrides' Great Mosque where the Arabs used to assemble. In 1501 it was turned into a Christian parish and was called *Santa Maria del O*, Our Lady of the O [after the great Advent 'O' antiphons in expectation of the birth of Christ]. The Major Church commemorated the exploit of Hernán Pérez del Pulgar in the days of the siege of Granada. During the night of 18 December 1490, led by a converted Moor, Pulgar and fifteen other horsemen slipped into Granada from the Christian camp that was situated near the River Darro. They penetrated as far as the Great Mosque where Pulgar pulled out from his saddlebag a great parchment with the Ave Maria written upon it. He then pinned the parchment on the door with his dagger. This bold action surprised an assembly of Moors inside the mosque and sent them scampering. Pulgar and his companions then took off at a gallop. The Moors of Granada retaliated and sent their hero, Tarfe, into the Christian camp with the parchment tied to the collar of his horse. It is said that Tarfe died there in a famous duel with Garcilaso de la Vega.

In order to convert the mosque into a parish church the architects had to cut arches into its naves. They called it the Major Church and it served as the temporary Cathedral while the permanent one was being built. This church represented the centre of the Christian city. At the beginning of the 18th century the building fell into ruins, but fifty years later it arose as the Sagrario parish of the Cathedral. Among its valuable pieces of art are the tombs of Pérez del Pulgar, Fray Hernando de Talavera and Pedro Mártir de Anglería.

On 20 January, Juan "the madman" came and threw himself down before the doors of the Major Church where he repeatedly called out in supplication: *"Mercy! Mercy, Lord God, on this tremendous sinner who has offended you!"*

There he was, semi-naked, barefooted and upon his knees in the midst of a circle of onlookers as he *"put mud on his face, and hit himself as he cried out in a loud voice begging forgiveness of his sins."*

In the gang of boys who had followed Juan after he left the Elvira Gate there was a certain twelve-year-old named Antón Rodríguez. Many years later this lad was to give his testimony as a significant witness. The various events that occurred at that time combined to implant an unforgettable image of "the madman" on his boyhood memory.

Antón Rodríguez was born at Illora, a village near the town of Loja. His family, like so many others, moved to Granada to live. He married Ana del Campo, and worked as a porter at the diocesan clergy house opposite the Major Church. He often spoke to people about what he witnessed there when he was a boy of twelve.

Antón lived to a great old age. He was one hundred years old when he gave his testimony at John of God's beatification process. The judges there showed some surprise when this extremely old man, in good health and sound mind, strode into the tribunal and stated that he personally knew "*the blessed Father John of God very well indeed.*" He stated in his testimony: "*I remember him as if it were only today.*" He related many incidents but began by telling them of the indelible impression made on him by "mad" Juan. The scribe recorded, "*This witness saw him at the Major Church of the city, surrounded by many people, he was shouting and pleading to God for mercy, and hitting himself very hard upon his chest.*"

Like the boy Antón, there were some priests from the Cathedral Chapter and church offices and some respectable citizens who also witnessed the bizarre behaviour of the unusual penitent. We do not know whether they were priests or lay persons who intervened, for Castro simply tells us: "*Some decent folk saw what a great fuss he was causing and they felt sorry for him, because they did not consider him to be insane as everyone else did. Lifting him up from the ground, they gently spoke with him and took him to where Father Avila was staying.*" By this time the whole of Granada knew that the Portuguese bookseller from the Elvira Gate had broken down after Master Avila's sermon up at the Hermitage de los Mártires. According to Antón Rodríguez, popular opinion was already divided: "*Some said he was mad, others that he was not, because what was happening to him was really the work of God.*"

Because we know the chain of events that followed, we can make sense of what occurred when Juan kept his appointment with God.

Notes to Chapter 17

* This episode covers four fifths of Castro's chapter 7, op. cit.
* Magliozzi amply defends the interesting and uncertain controversy he suggests in regard to the place and date in which John of God heard the sermon of Master Avila. Cf. G. Magliozzi, *Pagine juandediane*, Rome 1992, 127-142. From this argument it must be deducted that the 'conversion' of John of God occurred in the summer of 1538, leaving 16 May as his definitive move towards his hospitaller vocation. I have carefully studied Magliozzi's ingenious reasoning and I value his ample observations. But, I do not see him producing any documented proof to give them sufficient weight to explode the solid chronological structure set out by

Raphael M. Saucedo; Cf. R. M. Saucedo, *Cronológia aplicada en la vida de N. P. S. Juan de Dios:* Paz y Caridad 13 (1952) 13-19. I believe that there are two basic difficulties of Magliozzi that need to be answered from the dates stated by Castro and Saucedo. Firstly: that the Cathedral Chapter went in procession from the roadside shrine of San Sebastian which is situated on the low land where the Darro meets the Genil, while the great popular religious feast was celebrated up in the field of the Hermitage de los Mártires on the same day; it should not be a surprise to G. Magliozzi that the canons of the Cathedral have always gone ahead with their chapter obligations in the margin of loyal assistance, for in a certain sense, they considered themselves representatives and 'deputies' of the diocesan community, whether they be in company or alone. Anyway, they could have had a double celebration on the same day, one in chapter, the other in public. Besides, there was nothing to stop the chapter from organising another procession to the *'humilladero'* [roadside shrine] or to the hermitage on the first of August, the feast of St. Peter in Chains, if it was ordered by the norms laid down by Queen Isabella. It seems to be a more serious difficulty when it comes up against the arguments of Saucedo whose rather light treatment of giving weight to the mistake of Castro, who comes to the conclusion of the 'day of the Eleven Thousand Virgins' (21 October in the martyrology, 'St Ursula and Companions') which was the day of the interment of the Empress Isabel at Granada. But Saucedo adduces a possible solution which is very plausible; for the martyrology puts the feast of the Seven Virgins martyred in Persia, as being on 16 May, a date may have caused Castro to have mistaken the feast of the Eleven Thousand Virgins with that of the traditional Seven Persian Virgins. From the start I admit that the date given by Castro is fundamental. Juan entered Granada *"in the year of Our Lord, 1538."* Therefore, his conversion took place on 20 January 1539. To be fair to Magliozzi, I would like to point out that there is, in the declaration of witness #54 of the beatification process at Granada, the following: *"I heard it said that Master Avila had made a sermon at the wayside shrine [humilladero] of St. Sebastian which is at the poplar grove, and he was converted."*

* Cf. A. L. Cortés, *Las fiesta de Granada en el siglo XVI,* III, Granada 1986, 207-212.
* Brother Matías de Mina discovered in the *'Actas históricas'* some unedited documents on the Confraternity of San Sebastián. The official date on which the Archbishop, Gaspar de Avalos, authorised the Confraternity, was 20 May 1531. This was the second confraternity created at Granada since the conquest. Its members were mainly made up of merchants and men in industries. They paid for the cost of the feast and they maintained a hospital.
* There are traces of the presence of St. John of the Cross at his convent of los Mártires, at the 'carmen' to this day: the aqueduct which he constructed and a cedar which is thought to have been planted by him, although there is a bit of doubt here. In his *Dark Night, "And the cedars fan the air."*
* For the facts referring to Master Avila, besides the classic biographies of Luis Muñoz and Fray Luis de Granada, that of L. Sala Balust-F. Martín Hernández, *Obras completas del santo maestro Juan de Avila,* Madrid 1970-1971, is indispensable. The episode of Dr. Carleval, *ibid,* I, 72-73. L. Sala gives a fragment of the sermon preached by Master Avila on San Sebastian's day, *ibid* I. 27, he took the trouble to verify the text in the archives at Valencia and put it in the glossary of *La predica che converti Giovanni:* 'Vita Ospedaliera' (6, 1969) 174-178. Luis Muñoz, the disciple of

Master Avila, comments upon the effects of the sermon: *"Through divine grace and an extraordinary light that penetrated his soul, (Master Avila) was able to strike home at the heart of Juan..."* New edition...II, Madrid 1894, 495.

* Those witnesses who eulogised Master Avila at the Granada beatification process of John of God, were witnesses #9, #17, # 50, #56. Francisco de Castro, op. cit., relates without any exaggeration the behaviour of Juan in the streets of Granada following the sermon of Master Avila. I gave particular attention to Castro's account of the event.

18

DELIRIOUS JUAN MEETS WITH MASTER AVILA

Granada
1539

$\mathbf{W}$ell, I would prefer to take Juan's madness with a pinch of salt. I think that this was the way taken by a brave man, a very brave man indeed. Furthermore, we are dealing with an historic person and soon we will see what human feats he was capable of achieving for men and women who had found themselves pushed to the very limits of life; some to the verge of starvation, others who were crippled and diseased. You will see for yourselves what he is going to do for them, and it is my task to tell you about it. I believe you will be amazed at the story.

Juan heard the sermon of one of the most remarkable masters of the Spanish Renaissance on 20 January 1539. Father Juan de Avila was a cultured and amiable gentleman who admired the teachings of Erasmus. He founded colleges and universities that exist to this day. After he heard Master Avila's sermon, our hero dashes through the streets of Granada and provokes a public scandal by his fanatical behaviour, like a raving madman.

I write as a simple historian. It is not my task to interpret why John of God's blood suddenly boiled, or why the bonds of his spirit burst, causing him to make such a spectacle of himself in the streets. Later on, I will invite you to a round-table discussion with half a dozen prominent experts who include scripture scholars, theologians, psychologists and psychiatrists, all of whom have given much consideration to the matter.

Nevertheless, when I see him there rolling about in the filth, going completely off his head, shrieking like a fool, being urged on by the street kids, while good people simply looked on, it occurs to me that I must not for a moment deviate from documented evidence. I must not turn a blind eye, but rather think about it, and question what is happening. How does this behaviour fit within the culture of the time? Was he a fanatic?

I have no intention of sweetening the reliable chronicles of that period, regardless of how intractable and inevitable are the holy legends that emerged after the apparent *madman* had conquered the admiration and the esteem of the Granadinos. They were to turn him into something else altogether.

As the 20th century turns into the 21st, dare I ask you, my readers, who are so worldly-wise, so reasonable, so much against any sort of religious exaggeration and so incredulous before so-called miracles, to remain with me patiently until you see what happens when our good Juan calms down, for he does calm down, at least for a while.

We cannot enter the intimacy of his being, or judge the rationality of his mind at the time. All we can do is look at the evidence.

His bizarre behaviour, beginning on 20 January, continued through the following days. There really was an unbalanced person loose in the streets of Granada. But was he really mad?

When María Zambrano returned to Spain after a long absence she pleased those of us who know her by saying that, sometimes, *delirium* can seize upon a person if one dares to see God face to face.

Juan of Granada was delirious and deranged. He simply burst asunder when he met God at their mutually arranged appointment.

We will now accompany him to the lodgings of Master Avila.

Undoubtedly Master Juan de Avila had already been informed about the Portuguese bookseller who resided at the Elvira Gate, and how he had gone mad after listening to his sermon up at the Hermitage de los Mártires. He knew that the bookseller was going about the city streets confessing aloud that he was a sinner. That news was being spread all over the place like dust blown by the wind. What is more, the latest spectacle took place right in front of the Major Church, and as we know, Avila was the guest of Don Gaspar de Avalos who lodged him in one of the diocesan houses opposite this Cathedral.

In case Master Avila had not been fully aware of what was happening, some *"honourable persons"*, as Castro calls them, informed him because *"they were moved with compassion."* They asked themselves whether this was madness or not and took Juan to Master Avila and told him all about *"everything that had happened following the sermon."*

What a meeting that was! Juan de Avila and Juan Ciudad meeting face to face and looking each other in the eye. Of course, Ciudad had already seen Avila from a distance during the sermon, but he would only have been another head in that great crowd to Avila who would not have noticed him. Now they came together for the first time.

According to Luis Sala, both Juans were probably the same age, but the year of Juan de Avila's birth is uncertain. They came from vastly different cultural and social backgrounds. Avila came from a very well to do family and had studied under renowned professors at Salamanca and Alcalá. Amongst his friends he counted not only the Archbishop but also many of the lords and ladies of Granada. Ciudad, on the other hand, came from obscure parents and, as you know, was a shepherd for a great many years, then a soldier, once more a shepherd, a wanderer, labourer, hawker and finally the proprietor of a book stall.

Avila wore a cassock made of common cloth, but it was neat and clean. Ciudad, God bless him, was barefooted and dressed in a muddied shirt and breeches. His face was a mess and his eyes bloodshot.

Master Avila ordered that they were to be left alone. *"He sent outside all the people who had come with him and stayed alone with him in the room."*

Juan behaved himself like a lamb. He had calmed down and was quite at ease, nevertheless he felt somewhat in awe at being in the presence of the *man of God*. This was the preacher whose words had bitten so deeply into his very being. Juan fell upon his knees before him. We know the gist of what went on during that meeting. It touched upon details of Juan's past, present and future. Master Avila asked him to rise and the two held a long conversation. Avila listened as Ciudad told him his story.

Our Juan said three things. Firstly, he related his life story, we do not know in what detail; next he confessed his sins, *"showing great sorrow and contrition"*; and finally he begged the Master to accept him as a disciple. *"He asked if he would be his spiritual director."*

Father Avila could see that God, by means of his sermon at Los Mártires, had overwhelmed Juan. This gave weight to Juan's petition.

Just imagine the curious bag of credentials our Juan has to show since he came down from Los Mártires. We have already seen him upon his knees in the mud, shouting in misery for all to hear, teased by urchins, half-naked, barefooted and thought by everyone to be crazy. And now he informs the preacher that *"it was through him that our Lord had begun to bestow such tremendous graces upon him."*

Graces indeed! Gifts lavished upon him! Certainly, because beneath that madness lies a mysterious bond uniting him with his Lord. Castro tells us that Avila accepted Juan as his penitent. Juan, for his part, took him," *from that moment on, as his father confessor and counsellor.*" Furthermore, "*he was prepared to remain obedient to him even to the point of death.*"

It is quite obvious that Juan is completely calm now and his shouting has stopped. Avila listens to him attentively and patiently.

Many books of this period say that Master Avila was recognised as an exceptional spiritual director. They say that his direction influenced such personages as Teresa of Jesus, Ignatius de Loyola, Francisco de Borja and others of that calibre.

That piece of information was only partially true because at this time, 1539, Avila did not know these distinguished men and women. With the passage of time they certainly came to venerate him, that much I do know. Teresa of Jesus wrote a new edition of her autobiography, the '*Book of Life*', and submitted it to Master Avila for his scrutiny. The Inquisitor, Don Francisco de Soto Salazar, suggested this to her. Mother Teresa of Jesus had consulted him to see whether he might be disturbed by the extraordinary phenomena of her prayer. However, the Inquisitor recommended that she send a copy of the '*Book of Life*', to Master Avila. He, after reading it, was able to set her mind at rest. Her confessor, Father Báñez, thought that it was a waste of time to have the work reassessed. Nevertheless, Teresa wanted to make absolutely sure, so she carried out discretely the Inquisitor's advice without Báñez being aware of it because, at all costs, she wanted to avoid upsetting her confessor. Teresa was soon to experience the direction of the venerable Avila, whom all Spain considered to be a peerless master of the spiritual life. This all occurred in the sixties, 1564-1565 to be precise.

However, in 1539, Master Avila is exercising his influence strictly within the confines of Andalusia. Obviously he was already very gifted as an exceptionally capable counsellor. He understood that our Juan was driven mad, for he recognised his troubled state of mind. What was called for now was delicate intuition to discover whether, beneath all that frenzy, there might be some providential signs pointing the way for him to help the delirious bookseller from the Elvira Gate. Master Avila discerned that Juan's excessive behaviour indicated he had reached his appointment with God.

In his response Avila made no judgement about Juan's abnormal behaviour, the hidden underlying causes of which were in the depths of his penitent. He told Juan

- that he gave thanks to God because Juan had repented of his sins;
- that he would be his confessor;
- that he would be his counsellor.

"*Brother Juan, be courageous*," he advised. Have confidence in God and his divine mercy for, from now on, "*you will fight in the army of the Lord unto death.*" Then he added: "*When you feel depressed and upset by troubles and temptations, come to me.*"

He did not reproach Juan for the disturbance he caused in the streets of Granada but, on the contrary, said: "*Go now in peace and with the blessing of God and my blessing as well.*" Astonishingly, Avila let the fantasies of Juan pass by, for he literally said to him: "*Be faithful and constant in what you have started to do, and do not turn back nor give yourself over to the Devil.*"

How did Juan leave that meeting? Castro answers that he, "*was so relieved and buoyed up by that holy man's words of advice that once more he was overcome by a great urge to despise himself further and to mortify his body.*"

Two witnesses, who knew from first hand experience of the occasion when Juan and Master Avila met, affirmed without any hesitation that Master Avila had actually approved of Juan's conduct in the streets. One of these witnesses, Antón Rodríguez, whom we have met before, was a real expert on the matter, stating that the Master knew quite well what was behind the apparent madness: "*Master Avila let it be known to everyone that it was through true contrition and the work of God's hand.*"

Another witness, Bernabé Ruiz, was a surgeon who also owned vineyards and fields under cultivation at Albolote, a village near Granada. He also knew John of God personally. He particularly said in his declaration, that when he was a boy of eight, Master Avila taught him in a college at Granada. He also attended the lessons Master Avila gave on the arts when he was at Baeza.

Because of his direct knowledge of Master Avila, this witness was summoned to give a statement at his beatification process. We come across the witness Ruiz in both beatification processes, and it seems logical that he was able to give a good account of the relationship between the two Juans, because he admired them both. This is the declaration of Bernabé Ruiz: "*I heard Father Juan de Avila say: Although they hold that this Brother Juan is mad, he is saner than all of us think .*"

Thus it was that Master Avila thought the very strange religious experience that Juan has been going through in the streets of Granada, was not such a bad thing after all. Though now, we are going to see yet another outbreak of deranged behaviour in our *madman* as soon as he leaves the peaceful home of the Master. How was it that Avila showed his acceptance of Juan's nonsensical behaviour?

In the Vittorio Emmanuele National Library at Rome there is a manuscript of a sermon preached by Master Avila one October 4, the actual year is not recorded. The occasion was the feast of St. Francis of Assisi. It is a delightful sermon, even though it is rather longwinded. In those days, people had fewer distractions and were prepared to listen to a good sermon, even if it went on for ages. On this occasion the audience was composed of nuns. When he spoke about St. Francis the preacher explained the importance to be placed on self-depreciation if one really wants to understand the great riches of God:

"This is the secret that God reveals to those who do not trust in themselves. This is the secret that suffices for those who do not rely upon their own forces; the humble, yes, these are the ones who know about this secret. (Ask and you will receive, cry out and it will be given you.) To ask with humility, like little children, like a poor person covered with sores asking a rich one for alms, such a one will discover what is needed."

It seems to me that when he presented this sermon about St. Francis of Assisi Father Avila's memory must have gone back to that episode with the bookseller Juan in the streets of Granada. I say that because scarcely anyone accepts it as an honour from God to see oneself so despised and insulted.

The spiritual writings of Master Avila frequently point to Christian sanctity as contrasting God's greatness with the personal littleness of his human creatures. That is why self-disdain serves as a platform for launching the risky programs which Providence indicates to us.

I agree with Master Avila's schema. Juan's *madness* really did unveil to him the first phase of his appointment with God. Juan was struck as by a thunderbolt and left bewildered. He recognised the majesty of God and the love of Jesus Christ, and as a consequence, shouted out his misery, his littleness, his sins. He wanted to be insulted, despised, and that is exactly what Avila was saying in his sermon about St. Francis of Assisi:

"St. Francis went off to a cave. He was very happy to be alone in that gloomy place. Francis went there for solitude. Then, in that cave he began to groan and cry out his sins. 'Oh light which enlightens the blindness of my soul! What have you done to me? How have I offended you? How have I not loved you? How can I go on living without you? What do you want me to do Lord?' He was in doubt: 'Should I go out from here or should I stay here doing penance?' Then God said to him. 'You coward, go away from here.' He went out from there and dressed himself in a rough woollen habit, and he tied a belt of rope around his waist and went out into the streets. As he went along he met men and boys who had no idea what it was all about, and they called out: 'Look at the madman, look at the madman!' Before this, they had seen him dressed in fine silk, riding in triumph upon horseback in the company of young men. Now they called out: 'Look at the madman!' and began to rip his habit and throw mud on his face. The servant of God suffered it all in great patience and blessed God."

At Granada, neither could Juan remain hidden and out of sight in his tiny bookstall at the Elvira Gate. Here Master Avila was speaking about the humility of St. Francis, but he surely would have been reminded of that day when Juan went mad:

"He was very humble when he left there, and he was looked down upon and despised by all. They treated him as if he was dirt. He was so humble in his own estimation that if he had a bad thought, he would cry out: 'You think I am a good man, I am a hypocrite.' Then as he was crying, they reined blows down upon him and slapped his cheeks, but he went on lamenting the wrong that he had done. Now there was no more to say for the moment, other than if it were us, we would keep our sin under a lock with seven keys and hope than nobody came to hear of it. How humble, how little, how simple was this blessed Saint!"

In the eyes of Master Avila, this irrepressible urgency Juan felt to demonstrate his humility, self-disdain and supposed madness, is the first stage of his conversion, his appointment with God.

The second phase will come when the *madman* receives a light indicating the path by which Providence will lead him to the work to which he has been called.

That is why the Master wanted to keep Juan at close quarters, to keep a check on him, because he knew that Juan was to receive a call, of what description, he did not know.

Juan was on his own now. He had the blessing of Master Avila, and now his desire to be despised increased, or as Castro boldly puts it: *"He wanted everybody to take him for a madman, an evil man worthy only of contempt and being despised."* Juan then presents yet another of his spectacular performances, this time in the heart of Granada, the Plaza Bibarrambla.

I suggest to the reader that it would be worth the effort to compare today's map of Granada with one of the city as it was in the 16th century. It would prove helpful because, little by little, Juan will be making Granada his home, his cloister. It is going to be his own territory, the scene of his daily life.

The Archdiocesan buildings face one side of the Cathedral. Immediately behind them, in those days, was the main gateway that led into the Plaza Bibarrambla. This belongs to the historic centre of Granada, and was probably the urban space that suffered the most from the renovations that took place throughout the 16th century.

The Arabs called this thoroughfare the *'Rambla'*, which means a sandy place, because it opened out upon the sandbanks of the River Darro. In ancient days this was the place where the Arabs held feasts and jousting tournaments. In 1500, after the fall of the city to the Catholic Monarchs, the square was enlarged for pedestrians and it became a popular place to transact business deals. The Bibarrambla is situated right alongside the *Zacatín*, the arcades of Arab shops, and also the *Alcaicería*, the raw silk exchange. It was here that the Arabs had tanneries, leather workshops, dye works, and shops that sold clothing, drapery, bric-a-brac, shoes and jewellery. The Plaza Bibarrambla was truly the most popular place in Granada. On its perimeter buildings of an acceptable standard were constructed to house the law clerks and customs officers, and balconies were built on the Archdiocesan buildings and the Cathedral Chapter Hall. A fountain crowned with a lion holding the coat-of-arms of Granada, once stood in the centre of the plaza. It is said that this was a very splendid piece of work, but it was replaced with another fountain called the Gigantones [giants] in the 20th century. The people of Granada are so fond of the Plaza Bibarrambla that it is still a popular venue for all sorts of *fiestas*, both civil and religious.

Of course the buildings were there on that 20th day of January, but the plaza was unpaved and its centre was a great mire of mud and water. Juan went straight for that murky hole and threw himself into it. Thus the second scene of the street show began.

If he was trying to be embarrassed and disdained by everyone, I believe he achieved his purpose. *"When they saw this, the common folk believed that he had taken leave of his senses and lost all judgement."*

The little boy, Antón Rodríguez, who spoke to us about what he saw in front of the Major Church, saw him again in the Plaza Bibarrambla: *"He was at the Plaza Bibarrambla in this city and was rolling about in the mire, of which there was plenty because it was wintertime. He put mud all over himself and kissed the ground and beat his chest with a stone saying: 'Lord, I have sinned, have mercy on me.' And he said many other devout things like that."*

Juan wanted to be taken for the vilest man on earth. He listened to the teasing of the boys and came out of the mire and began to run about in his tattered shirt and zaragüella breeches. It was late afternoon on that cruel winter's day when he set off again in his bare feet, *"to run through the main streets of the city."*

I suppose that when night fell Juan at least took the sensible decision to go back and get under cover in his little stall at the Elvira Gate. I would like to know if he did that, although there is nothing written to explain where he slept at night during the days he was going about the streets of Granada in this frenzied state. Castro notes, with evident compassion: *"He ate little, and could not remain on his feet."* The little that he ate was given to him by kind women he met in the street.

Juan acted like this for some days. How many days? A few, not many. Street kids and ordinary folk followed him about as spectators. There were all sorts of oddballs in Granada, so they probably thought the bookseller had become one of their number in the city.

Before the towns and villages of Andalusia were hit by a sudden demographic growth due to the crisis some years ago in the rural sector, I was quite familiar with mentally ill persons wandering about all day long under the complacent gaze of the local inhabitants. Everybody knew them. We all knew the *village idiot* who was more or less a mischievous little guy. It seems unlikely that the odd spectacle put on by Juan lasted many days.

Juan invented a ploy that amused the urchins. He picked up two sticks and made a cross that he kissed. If they asked him, *"for the love of Jesus,"* to kiss the ground he would immediately get down on his knees and obey them. This is how Castro puts it: *"Even if a boy ordered him to do so, even though there was much mud."*

Now let us look carefully at what the witnesses have to say, so we can separate later legends from the known facts. I say this because some of the declarations made at the beatification process leave one suspicious that there may have been a certain manipulation of the facts. For example, Catalina de Contreras, a witness at the Granada process, said: *"... and in such a way that the gangs of boys followed the blessed father and made him kiss the ground many times: 'John of God, John of God, kiss the ground for the love of God.' Then he would do so and they said: 'trip over for God,' and he would do so."* Well, it so happens dear Doña Catalina, that even though you were only a small child at the time and personally witnessed what occurred, that could never have been. Juan 'the bookseller' never called himself John of God in those days. The appellation 'of God' was given to him at a much later date. Nevertheless, Brother Mátias de Mina, who drew up the itinerary of John of God throughout the houses, streets and plazas of Granada, has given me one of his notes defending the possibility that the appellation 'of God' may have been given to him by the simple folk of the city even before he was officially called so. "The street urchins and some adults found it amusing to bait the demented bookseller by asking him to carry on with such foolish behaviour as kissing the ground, putting mud on his head and tripping over, all for the love of God. Here we see a transposing of the words: 'do it for God' into, 'John the one who is of God', to 'John of God.'" Brother Mátias would like to think that this might have been the case.

He says, "As a consequence of all that, they eventually called him *John of God* and everyone knew him by that name. That was the name he gave when they took him to the Royal Hospital, and he brought it back with him when he was reintegrated into the daily life of Granada. When he began his work of mercy for the sick and poor the whole of Granada knew him by no other name than *John of God.*"

We have the testimony of yet another direct witness, Juan Lobo, who was a little eight year old boy when he personally witnessed *"Juan the Portuguese bookseller"* carrying on in that bizarre manner. He remembered the scene perfectly: *"This witness saw him especially when he was in the little plaza in front of the houses of Don Gabriel de Córdova. He saw that many urchins and other people were following him and they believed that he was insane. With great patience and humility he suffered all they said and did to him."*

The apartments of the Córdova family were most likely the palace where the *Gran Capitán,* Gonzalo Fernández de Córdoba, resided. Queen Isabella referred to El Gran Capitán as *"the shining mirror of all valiant knights, and the greatest captain in the whole of Spain."* Later he amazed the world with the success of his famous infantry. However the Gran Capitán fell out of favour with King Ferdinand and eventually died in this Granada residence. From 1539 the palace was passed down from one of his descendants to another until it became a convent for the Discalced Carmelite Nuns in 1584. You may recall, they used to live in Elvira Street before moving here. Today the little plaza where the boy Juan Lobo saw our Juan "taken to be insane", is now called the Plaza de las Descalzas.

There were some that looked upon Juan with compassion. Others shouted insults at him: *"They threw dirt, slime and all manner of filthy things at him."*

Juan accomplished what he had set out to do: *"He put up with it and took it all very patiently and happily just as if it were a fiesta."* He had Master Avila's approval and now he saw his wishes fulfilled *"without causing any harm to anyone,"* and that is a fact. Castro continues: *"He went on doing this for a few days, often falling exhausted and bruised from the screams, shoves and blows heaped upon him."*

Gangs of boys are capable of extreme cruelty when they come across some poor demented creature that they can tease and torment, and that is how they looked upon Juan: *"He was so convincing at feigning madness, for indeed almost everybody believed him to be mad."*

It is said that he once appealed to the street kids not to throw stones at him, but lumps of mud instead. But they did throw stones, which hit their mark sometimes striking his head. While they did not tire of their tormenting, Juan was *"offering his body to the stones with a cheerful countenance and without complaint or remonstrance."*

The problem of the "the poor madman" was soon to be solved. Two respectable gentlemen of the city came along, and when they saw what was happening to Juan, they lifted him up and took him away from the mob.

Notes to Chapter 18

* Cf. Maria Zambrano, *El hombre y lo divino*, Madrid 2 1991, 130. Zambrano explains here how God is found in the delirious.
* Up to now there is no direct account of the conversation at this first encounter between Juan de Avila and Juan Ciudad. However, Castro (op.cit., chapters 7 & 8) gives a very valuable summary which my account is faithfully based. The procedure of the events gathered by Castro in this fundamental passage of the biography of St. John of God quite clearly belongs to the conversations which the companion in whom of John of God confided, had with Castro.
* For the relationship of Teresa of Jesus with Juan de Avila, see: L. Sala Balust-F. Martín Hernández, *Obras completas del santo maestro Juan de Avila*, Madrid 1970, 320-324.
* For the declarations of the witness Antón Rodríguez, see the notes for Chapater 17.
* The declaration of Bernabé Ruiz, witness #87 in the Granada list, 65 among *"Those who knew John of God."*
* For the participation of Bernabé Ruiz in the beatification process of St. John de Avila, see: L. Sala Balust-F. Martín Hernández, (op.cit.) !, 10, Montilla process; p 283, and for the Granada process, note 308.
* The testimony of Juan Lobo, witness #1 on the Granada list. For the text of the sermon of Master Avila on St. Francis of Assisi, see L. Sala Balust-F. Martín Hernández, (op.cit.), III, 289-312. The idea of Juan de Avila on self-disdain and the value of humiliations received *"to honour God,"* was already perfectly formulated when he was a prisoner of the Inquisition at Seville from 1531 to 1532: *"Blessed be God and Father of Our Lord Jesus Christ, Father of mercies and God of all consolation in all our tribulation, in such a manner that we may be consoled in every anguish we experience; and this for the consolation through which God consoles us. For, as the tribulations of Christ abound in us, so from Christ comes our abundant consolation. Oh my dearly beloved brethren! God wants to open your eyes in order to consider how much mercy he gives to us in what the world considers misfortune. And how he honours us for looking for the honour of God, and what a high honour is achieved by the present setbacks,*

and how gentle, loving and sweet are God's open arms which he extends to us to receive those wounded in the battle for him. Without any doubt this exceeds without comparison, all the gall that sufferings can give us here... However, I do not know whether I am saying this well in calling these things suffering, for compared to those of the Cross, it seems to me that they are really like resting in a flowery bed full of roses." Ibid. I, 42.

19

JUAN 'THE MADMAN' IN THE WARD FOR THE INSANE

Granada
1539

Juan was shown pity by *"two respectable gentlemen who, taking him by the hand, led him away..."* Where did they take him? It was to the *madhouse*, the wing within the Granada Royal Hospital reserved for the mentally ill.

So here he was. If he really wanted to *"be taken for a madman."* It seems that Master Avila approved of this tactic so they both got what they wanted.

A plaque was unveiled in 1536 to commemorate the completion of the fourth and final stage of the Royal Hospital. This plaque stood out among the various emblems and initials decorating the final patio. Engraved in Latin with old German lettering, it read: *"Ferdinandus et Elisabeth, etc..."*, *"The Catholic Monarchs, Ferdinand and Isabella, ordered this building to be built from its foundations up. Although their death prevented them from seeing it finished to the roof, their grandson Charles, the invincible Emperor and King of all Spain, ordered the completion of the work that they had begun. This section was completed in the year of Our Lord 1536, the year in which, by the grace of God, the Emperor took the city and kingdom of Tunis by force and castigated the African pirates for the violence they committed."*

The construction of the Royal Hospital began soon after the taking of Granada and it was a difficult work to complete. It was one of a collection of buildings aimed at eradicating the Moorish influence and creating the new Christian city of Granada. It was built concurrently with the Royal Chapel, the Cathedral, the Palace of Charles V and the Royal Chancellery.

In the 1970's the University of Granada has cast much light on the history of the 16th century hospitals of the city – a thicket in which there remain shadowy areas.

The proliferation of medieval hospitals, both great and small, added to the antagonism caused by substituting the existing Arab institutions at Granada with Christian ones. The study of 'Andalusí' culture emphasises the authentic medical degrees of Arab doctors, such as Albucasis, Avicena el Cordobés and Averroes. However, the researchers have difficulty when it comes to pinpointing where their hospitals stood. There certainly was the hospital at Granada called the Maristán. It was built by King Muhammaud V in the year 1367 as a centre for the sick poor. It was completely destroyed in the 19th century and the only relics of its once beautiful embellishments which have survived to this day are two sculptured lions that now adorn the gardens of the Portal of the Alhambra.

The Maristán was situated on the embankment of the Darro and faced the atrium of what is now the church of the Immaculate Conception. It is believed that the Maristán was built at the same period as the hospital Sultan Qalawun was constructed at Cairo. The insane were kept at the Maristán during the reign of the Nasrides kings.

Under the administration of the Catholic Monarchs the Maristán was turned into a mint. To do this the unfortunate 'innocents', as the mentally ill were called, were turned out without assistance or a hospital, although at first they were provisionally installed at the semi-ruined House of San Lazarus. Between 1520 and 1525, Charles V ordered and financed the construction of a new building for the insane called the 'House of the Innocents'. This was to have been built adjacent to the Royal Gate and, as we will soon see, it never came to completion.

The Archives of the Granada Diputación [local Government] contain 'The Beridica Report of the Royal Hospital founded by the Catholic Monarchs in the city of Granada.' This ancient document states: "among the hospitals that their Majesties, the Catholic Monarchs, ordered to be established, was one at the Alhambra in this city. This was for the cure of sick persons who have any illness whatsoever." This document is dated 15 May 1501. However, the Catholic Monarchs added a provisional rider to their orders: "The intention of their Majesties was that the aforementioned hospital should be maintained until such time as the Royal Hospital was built, when this one is to cease and its patients transferred."

A great number of hospitals sprang up throughout the city simultaneously with this Alhambra hospital. These hospitals were maintained either by various entities or private persons. The hospital of Santa Ana, or as it was better known, the Archbishop's hospital, was founded by Fray Hernando de Talavera with the support of the Catholic Monarchs. There were others, such as the Mother of God, which was situated next to the Chancellery; the Pilgrims' Hospital, the Navas, Misericordia, Corpus Christi and Holy Cross. There were also hospitals associated with trades, such as the one for the 'Art of Silk.'

During the medieval period the whole of Spain was overrun with public administrations, a great many not disposed to economic efficiency. Soon groups of Christians with the capacity and means took it upon themselves to run works for the assistance of the sick. A curious case is that of the legendary national hero of Spain, El Cid. It is said he made 'the *first contribution' by founding a hospital for the treatment of lepers and the 'oriental' disease that invaded Europe after the crusades. 'General' or 'specialised' hospitals sprang up in the shadow of cathedrals and monasteries. These usually had the protection of kings and city councils. This multitude of hospitals lasted up to the end of the 18th century. The Cangas-Argüelles Dictionary cites more than two thousand, and of course, these were generally found in poor places, often where misery abounded. Charitable donations often ended up with greedy administrators in the employ of these hospitals. They would pocket the income, which was not always under the control of the boards of directors which usually comprised ecclesiastics or civil leaders who were far removed from everyday problems.*

The desired reform and rationalisation of hospitals went ahead very slowly. A royal proclamation was made in 1512 as a move to speed up this goal, but Valencia was the only city that carried it out. The Valencians did this by establishing a general hospital for patients suffering all types of illness, and this hospital also had a foundling home attached to it.

In order to achieve the same result at Granada, Charles V went ahead with the work his grandparents had commenced - the building of the Royal Hospital. However the work on the Granada Royal Hospital went on at an exceedingly slow pace. Ferdinand the Catholic chose the building site that was beyond the Elvira Gate where the city's charnel-house stood. The site had plenty of space for orchards and grazing lands for cattle. Work began in 1511 under the direction of the architect Master Egas. However, when King Ferdinand died only the ground floor had been built. In 1522 the Emperor Charles V placed García de Pradas in charge of the stone work and Juan de Plasencia in charge of the carpentry. After lots of ups and downs, the work was completed in 1536 and, to commemorate the event, the plaque that I have mentioned was unveiled. The building is in the form of a Greek cross with equal wings forming four squares with a patio in each. In the centre of these four patios rises a dome. Today, the Royal Hospital forms part of the campus of Granada University. It has had several architectural additions over the years, the most notable being the splendid entrance hall added in 1632.

The patients from the Alhambra hospital were transferred to the Royal Hospital. The insane inmates from the half-built House of the Innocents at the Royal Gate were also taken there.

The abandonment of the construction of the House of the Innocents and the removal of its inmates to the Royal Hospital particularly irked the Granada City Council because it forced it to renounce certain privileges that the Council had acquired. Nor were the administrators of the Royal Hospital pleased to have these unexpected and undesired guests moved there. Nevertheless, the Emperor stood his ground and, to make sure his orders were carried out, issued a royal decree in 1535 to have the innocents installed at the Granada Royal Hospital. These insane patients were lodged in the second patio, which was completely cut off from the rest of the hospital.

The *"two respectable gentlemen"* brought the deranged bookseller from the Elvira Gate to this place. It was towards the end of January that Juan became an inmate of the mental hospital.

Who received Juan *the madman* into the mental wards of the Royal Hospital? When the transfer from the Alhambra hospital to the new 'Royal' took place, the old team from the Alhambra continued their duties down at the new hospital. Soon changes in staff took place and there was an increase in the number of *visitators*, as the inspectors were called. These visitators constituted a type of trust or board of guardians.

Once the inmates from the House of the Innocents were installed at the Royal Hospital, the Emperor was disposed to add another member to represent the city on this board of inspectors. In this way he was able to pacify the City Council, for the new visitator was one of its members. The City Council was called 'The Twenty-four' because it consisted of that number of members. A new group of visitators was formed consisting of a member from the Council of Twenty-four and representatives of the Chancellery and San Jerónomo Monastery. They met at the Royal Hospital each Sunday and on feast days. They had the duty of seeing the inmates who were most in need. In that case, I presume they must have seen them all.

In 1539, the Majordomo, as the chief executive officer was called in those days, was a priest named Miguel Muñoz. He was also the hospital chaplain, and he carried out his duties conscientiously. The member of the Twenty-four on the Board of Visitators, whose duty it was to safeguard the rights of the inmates, was García de Pisa. This gentleman came from a distinguished family which, later on, will prove to be a great friend of our Juan. Later on too, the Majordomo, Doctor Muñoz, would become a bishop and also prove himself to be a staunch friend of John of God. But for the present, Juan was just another insane inmate, while the other was the director of the mental hospital.

It fell to Muñoz and García de Pisa to sign Juan in to the hospital. Of course they had already received reports of the bizarre behaviour of the Portuguese bookseller in the streets of the city.

Both Muñoz and Pisa had a particular interest in the new patient. Both of them were followers of Master Avila and they knew all about the aftermath of the sermon that he had preached up at Los Mártires. Besides, Muñoz had already seen Juan's behaviour in the streets following that event.

And who knows, maybe Master Avila may have sent a confidential note to the director regarding this poor man who was taken to the hospital by *"two respectable gentlemen."* I have my suspicions about whether the two gentlemen picked Juan up from the streets of their own accord, or whether they were sent to do this by Master Avila. Juan was indeed a pitiful sight: *"So badly treated, clothed in rags; and covered in wounds and bruises from blows and stoning."*

Muñoz ordered the infirmarians *"that they take him into care"* and provide him with the kind of attention that would help him recover and not deteriorate. Soon they were to submit him to the therapy applied to the demented in those days. How terrifying that was because, during that epoch, medicine did not know what to do with the mentally ill. That is not so strange for even at the end of the 20th century we still search for answers to serious questions with regard to psychiatric treatment. This being so, I think it would be fair to make a small introduction.

Documents of the period indicate that, due to financial difficulties and interruptions to the building work, the hospital was conducted in a mediocre, slipshod manner. Nor was the installation of the *innocents* praiseworthy. Still, neither any data of incompetence or carelessness accuses the hospital administrators. The Majordomo, Muñoz, and his immediate colleague, the medical doctor, Tapia, appear to have been conscientious and motivated by a responsible Christian attitude. Muñoz is the first Majordomo who had come to live within the Royal Hospital *"so he could attend to the corporal and spiritual needs of the patients and help them to die well."*

I want to say that, if the psychiatric treatment given to Juan consisted of blows and whippings, we should not blame the administrators of the hospital. Centuries will have to pass in order to cleanse mental illnesses of the magic and demoniac significance attributed to them from time immemorial. Specialists affirm that *"it was precisely with the arrival of the 19ᵗʰ century that we came to believe that the basis of scientific psychiatry comes through the study of the nervous system..."*

They placed Juan in the sector occupied by the *innocents* since 1535. This was *"the second large open corridor and right patio of the central building and the rooms of the northern quadrangle"* that is, some common wards and a few cells. The patients in the large wards were mixed, some were free and others were restrained; they formed a frightful and repulsive band. Those enclosed in cells lacked light and ventilation.

Juan was given the treatment. This was based upon whippings, whereby they tried to dominate the fury of the demented ones and through exorcisms to liberate the patients from some dark infernal presence.

The sector kept for the *'innocents'* in hospitals of that period meant nightmarish places populated by degraded human beings, full of shouting, shrieks, weeping and guffaws, eyes full of sadness and making obscene gestures. It was a kingdom of darkness, a cursed segment.

The initial phase of the treatment was intended to force pain upon demented persons in order that they *"might lose their frenzy and return to themselves"*: They were stripped naked and with their hands and feet bound, they *"were given a good bout of flogging,"* with a whip. This was Juan's first 'dose'. Probably they left him tied up in a cell, but later he was brought into a common ward where he witnessed *'the treatment'* of the other patients.

Juan was scared, he understood the situation perfectly. He saw the mentally ill being flogged, chained up, groaning; prisoners of fear. He could not remain silent. Castro picks up the commentary, suggesting that Juan was in control of what was going on about him: *"his illness was to be wounded for the love of Jesus Christ."*

He severely reprimanded the ward attendants who made him pay dearly for his allegation: *"Why do you treat so badly and cruelly these poor miserable people?"* They looked at him in astonishment, wondering what kind of madman this was who dared to reprimand them. Castro has Juan speaking out against the way the attendants treated the poor demented people. He called the patients *"my brothers and sisters"* and said the hospital was *"the house of God"* and they desecrated it by beating its patients: *"Would it not be better that you had compassion on them in their distress, and cleaned them and gave them food to eat with greater charity and love?"*

Juan's denouncement of the *'therapy'* of beatings added another reminder. Without doubt the majority of the Granadinos had heard about how the Emperor wanted to build the hospital in fulfilment of his grandparents' wishes; and how the work of building it was made possible thanks to the money and privileges conceded it by the Crown. Juan was barely some months at Granada but he knew about the subject and he was indignant at what we say today is the *misuse of public funds*. He demanded that the infirmarians fulfil the correct function for which the hospital was founded, asserting: *"The Catholic Monarchs bequeathed a full endowment for its management."*

Most probably, the ward attendants carried out this torture of the patients as a matter of routine and were following the instructions of the doctor. How were they to do otherwise since nobody knew any other way to control the ravings of the insane. They were completely puzzled by Juan's words and reacted by deciding that he was *"doubly mad"*, and a *"troublemaker"* at that. He had been brought here as a madman, so if he were not mad, he would be on the outside; and now he had the effrontery to reprimand them. What was their response? They inflicted a double dose of whippings upon him; administering them with greater force: *"So as to treat him more severely than the others, whom they regarded as merely mad."* Plain common sense. Juan would not stop *"rebuking them for their neglect even though he knew what would happen to him."* Nor did the infirmarians soften their treatment of him.

From his lodgings in the Archbishop's residence, Master Avila was keeping in touch with all that was going on in regards to Juan. He had accepted him as a disciple, and knew well *"the cause of his illness and madness."*

(Here I wish to make a note in parenthesis. The kindness and affection of Father Avila for Juan was not accidental. He looked suffering directly in the face, and required of his spiritual sons and daughters a personal identification with the sufferings of Christ. He expelled the prudery of a troubled nun with these blunt words: *"Do you think madam, that the Redeemer, after being so tormented and, as you know, taken down from the cross, and having entered heaven would not have some effect on his well cared for servants? Bulls that are both goaded and hobbled enter the bullring; likewise we have to go out into the world."* Goaded and hobbled, exactly: just like bulls going into the bullring...)

* Master Avila's interest was quite a surprise in the innocents' section of the hospital. Nobody ever went there to visit the inmates, and now someone turns up saying he is sent by Master Avila to see Juan the bookseller. In the same way Juan was just as surprised by the visit. He was deeply moved: "That his good father, Master Avila, would remember him and send someone to visit him while he was in that prison forgotten by all."

* The message sent by Master Avila was composed of three parts:

* That ,'obviously', he understood that the sufferings of Juan were "for the love of Jesus Christ..."

* That he should never give up or surrender, but fight on: *"like a good soldier, giving his life for his Lord and King."*

* That he be patient and humble: considering what our Redeemer suffered upon the Cross: *"when some suffering, no matter how trivial, appears."*

To these three dictums the Master's messenger added a curious reference regarding Juan's immediate future. It was as if Father Avila was there with Juan listening to him. Juan was confused by his encounter with God, which had left him suspended in mid air. He still had to 'hear' the voice that would direct him to the path his Master had chosen for him.

"Brother Juan, whilst you have the time, start testing yourself for the time when you will go out into the world to fight."

The two continued to correspond. Juan *"wept for joy"* having considered *"the Lord's mercy"* of which Master Avila *"had reminded him to console him in his troubles."*

Juan considered himself the slave of the Master, and sent back a warm reply. *"Tell my good father..."* He only asked that he pray for him: *"With this I will live content and hope that I will not lack his assistance."*

This contact between the messenger and Juan was in accordance with Master Avila's plan, for he evidently considered this to be only *"the beginning"* of his new disciple's personal adventure,*"the mad bookseller"* over whose progress and affairs the Master had to keep a very careful vigil. The Master, also, was waiting for God to clarify *"for what purpose"* he had brought down on Juan such damage from the sermon at Los Martíres.

Without further concrete facts, Castro left us a very clear indicator, *"With these and similar words the two visited each other secretly, and each understood the other."*

They visited and understood each other. Did the Master come personally to the Royal Hospital? Who knows! Visits made by messengers do not have to be cloaked in secrecy. On the other hand, every step taken by the Master, was public knowledge in Granada.

The desired enlightenment had come, after years of waiting, and Juan is entering the second stage of his encounter with God when his way forward will be made known to him right here in the Royal Hospital.

Praised be God, for marvellous things! As believers we should not be surprised that the stages upon which splendid and world-shaking events take place are humble and unusual. After all, Jesus our Saviour was born in a stable and no one ventures to belittle the protagonists of that night in Bethlehem.

Within the mental wards of the Granada hospital Juan lived as just another madman, another unfortunate inmate, ragged and dirty, unaware that the great work that would spring from his hands was about to begin. Since the messengers of Master Avila began to call upon him, he found the ward attendants regarding him with some deference. They still administered to him "therapeutic doses" of whipping; however they were milder because he was giving the infirmarians the impression that the *"madman's frenzy"* had begun to abate.

Here in the punishment cell, or in some corner of the great ward where dozens of patients were undergoing *therapy*, the mysterious presence of God once more invaded Juan's being, illuminating the inner recesses of his spirit; speaking without words. Slowly, gently, as the days and nights slipped by, Juan's future path revealed itself to him. At the appointed time, his whole being became illuminated and he understood his calling – his vocation.

I have a feeling of reverence as I contemplate Juan, destined for great things right here in the *'insane asylum'* while being scourged, destined to be *'of God'*.

I appreciate the lesson taught by this experience just as I reverence the star that indicates the birth of Christ at Bethlehem.

I am reminded too, of that filthy closet, in fact it was the convent lavatory, where John of the Cross was imprisoned and whilst there, broke into song. This happened in the spring of 1578, forty years after Juan's enlightenment – also in the springtime, but that of 1539.

John of the Cross was locked up in a lavatory measuring merely two meters in length by a meter and a half in width. The only light that filtered down to him came from a ventilator no more than a few centimetres wide in the roof. They thought this a sufficient substitute for a jail in those times. Besides the latrine, they gave him two blankets and a plank to sleep on. They then put a large lock on the door and handed the key to the jailer. John of the Cross was kept in that lavatory, converted into a punishment cell, from the middle of February until the end of August. They made one concession for the prisoner; they gave him a small bench so that, when he knelt, he could place his breviary on it. The filth of the cubicle encouraged an abundance of insects. The shirt he wore beneath his habit was already dirty when he was first put into the cell, it is not known whether the jailer allowed him to wash it, or if he was ever given a clean one to wear.

So you see my friends, it was there in his prison that John of the Cross was able to compose his spiritual Canticle, probably the most translucent love poem ever written.

Likewise, it was while he was in the mental hospital that our Juan finally met up with God. Day after day, he saw the poor patients being flogged, and in his heart he longed to do something about it: *"May Jesus Christ bring me to the time and give me the grace to have a hospital where I can gather in the abandoned poor and the mentally ill to serve them as I desire."*

He waited for his encounter with God in the mental hospital.

Juan began to act differently in front of the infirmarians and the doctor. We could conclude that Juan was following a *strategy* worked out with Master Avila in person or through his messengers.

The strategy involved altering the manner in which he spoke to them, and avoiding reproaches, thereby gaining their sympathy. The infirmarians informed the Majordomo that the patient had improved, *"showing himself calm and quiet."* The Majordomo ordered that the shackles which bound him be removed and *"they gave him liberty to wander freely about the house."* This means the entire hospital.

So Juan was able to go about the establishment, getting to know its various sectors. He served by helping in unpleasant tasks, which he did eagerly, without being asked. He scrubbed pots in the kitchen, swept floors, and cleaned the toilets. His kindness and gentle manner towards the inmates gained him much popularity within the hospital: *"The nurses took great comfort from seeing him"*; they considered his cure was a success, for *"liberated from his illness, he had recovered his senses very well."*

Nobody was able to guess what was propelling Juan towards his goal: *"That I may have a hospital..."* ; one to where he could bring in the poor, the ill, the insane to take loving care of them. He now knows that this is his future mission in the world.

Isabel, wife of the Emperor Charles V, had died at Toledo. She had been the great love of his life. All Spain participated in the mourning, but none more than Granada where they brought the Empress and where construction progressed on the magnificent palace where, it was said, the imperial couple had dreamt of creating their love nest.

Isabel was the only true love in the Emperor's life, despite his philandering and the fathering of five illegitimate children. At first Charles imagined that he was simply fulfilling the requirement of State when he accepted the Portuguese princess as his wife. However, when they met for the first time at Seville in 1526, she being 22 years of age and he 26, he immediately fell in love with her. The chronicles of the time relate: "She was beautiful, elegant, most refined and they seemed made for each other." And so, too, thought Titian, who painted her portrait in all her splendour. Isabel treated her husband with the greatest tact and she knew how to turn her 'Caesar' into a loving husband. Charles could not do enough for his Isabel, even when it came down to little details, such as arranging his beard in a way that pleased her. They say that, although the

Emperor was a small man, he carried himself in a well-proportioned manner, his only disfigurement being his conspicuous projecting lip due to a distortion of his lower jaw. Maybe you know about the spontaneous frankness of the Aragonese. I do, because I come from Aragon. Once, when I was in the town of Calatayud, a certain bold peasant turned to me and said; "Señor, keep you mouth shut, the flies in this place are very naughty."

Isabel solved that problem after her marriage by asking her husband to grow a short beard, requesting him to make sure it was a wide one. It was a means of concealing to a great degree his projecting bottom lip.

She correspondingly identified with the tastes and styles of her husband; "They shared opinions, made plans together, picked their servants and chose together persons to hold high office."

After two months of festivities associated with their wedding at Seville, the Imperial Couple decided to prolong their honeymoon and go to Granada. Here they were surrounded by a Renaissance court which, although on a lesser scale, copied Italian fashions. From then on Isabel considered as her friends such poets, musicians and painters as Garcilaso de la Vega, Boscán, Navagero, Castiglione, Juan de Valdés, and others. They all marvelled at the beauty of the Portuguese ladies who accompanied the Empress. It was in that youthful and enamoured atmosphere that Boscán composed the first Hendecasyllabic poetry in the Castilian language, and Garcilaso de la Vega wrote blazing verses: "for you I was born, for you I live, for you I die..."

Historians say that the months that the Imperial couple lived amidst the flowers and fountains of the Alhambra were the happiest of their lives, and "the beauty about them rendered homage to that of Isabel." Charles planted a Persian flower in the Alhambra gardens, a flower hitherto unknown in Spain, it was called the Carnation.

As winter approached, the Emperor decided to move the court north to Valladolid. As they left Granada, Isabel announced that she was pregnant, and in the following Spring she gave birth to her firstborn son, Philip.

It seems incredible that only a dozen years passed before the empress died at Toledo in the Spring of 1539, when the affairs of the Emperor were going through a fruitful period. He had made peace with King Francis I of France and had received the blessing of Pope Paul III to confront the two problems of Christianity, Luther and the Turks. He had invoked the general courts of Castile to be held at Toledo. The Courts made some complaints to him, recommended that he should not leave Spain so often, and that he should reduce war expenses. He bore the shower of criticism but, nevertheless, imposed a new tax. What else could be done if the imperial coffers were empty? The new tax was called "the excise" and consisted of reducing the measure or weight of some foodstuffs while maintaining the same price.

We see in this one of the forerunners of the modern taxation system.

The Emperor calmed the anxieties of the court and gave more time to hunting and enjoying the artistic interests cultivated by the Empress. Charles pampered Isabel who was pregnant for the fourth time. Her previous deliveries were difficult. The court praised how the Empress went through the pangs of birth without screaming or permitting anyone to see her pained face. It is recorded that, when giving birth to her firstborn son, the midwife recommended that she shout aloud in order to relax. *"Midwife, do not tempt me, I would rather die than scream."* That was the price she paid so that nobody would observe her pain. What a pity that a time came when it would have been better for her to scream than to die.

She died in childbirth at dawn on the first day of May, 1539, at the age of 35. The Emperor was on his way to Madrid with his son Philip when he was notified that his wife was in grave danger. Returning to Toledo at full gallop, he arrived too late. Charles did not want to see her dead body, he wanted to conserve forever the image of his beautiful Isabel as he remembered her. The interment of the Empress was to take place at Granada. Prince Philip was to lead the cortege while the Duke de Gandía would be responsible for the security of the coffin. Grief stricken, His Imperial Majesty went to mourn alone at the Jeronymite monastery at Sisla near Toledo.

The cortege took fifteen days to travel from Toledo to Granada where it arrived on 16 May.

Castro gives a curious piece of information. Juan, our *ex-madman*, who is now accepted by the ward attendants at the hospital as a voluntary helper, *"was sitting by the gate of the hospital"*, when the cortege passed by.

The funeral procession meant nothing to the insane

inmates. But the other patients counted themselves fortunate to be there at this time when they could see the spectacle as it passed by the hospital through the nearby Elvira Gate - the usual entrance to the city for important processions. They crowded together at the windows, which, unfortunately, were rather narrow. Impatiently they awaited the arrival of the procession, which is recorded as having arrived at four o'clock in the afternoon. Since Juan now had permission to freely circulate throughout the hospital, he sat himself down at the front gate along with the administrators, nurses and auxiliaries to await the procession.

All Spain was accompanying, in spirit, the funeral of the Empress. In some mysterious manner, Isabel had captured Charles's heart and she was loved throughout the entire Iberian Peninsula. Some historians hint at a romance, even *"ardent passion,"* between the beautiful Empress and the Duke de Gandía, Francisco de Borja, who was married to Leonor de Castro, one of Isabel's Portuguese ladies-in-waiting. The poets of the Renaissance court made a lot of the rumour about the love, so-called, that Borja had for the Empress during her honeymoon stay at Granada, and later at Toledo. They even said he confessed to his friend Garcilaso: *"I confess that when I look at her I am filled with rapture."* Neither he, nor she, ever said a word or acted in any way that was lacking in propriety. They simply let it be known that they had a very splendid platonic friendship. Because of this, and in harmony with his office of aide-de-camp to the Empress, Gandía had the Emperor's greatest confidence. He was entrusted with the key to the coffin and the duty of handing over Isabel's remains to the authorities at Granada.

The coffin was opened, the face of the Empress appeared: *" So hideous and disfigured that it caused fear and horror to those who saw it."* It is recorded that Francisco de Borja could only stammer: *"I cannot swear that this is the Empress, but if I swear anything, I swear that this here is her cadaver."* That gave rise to the legend of the famous phrase attributed to the future saint: *"I will never more serve a lord who is mortal."*

Granada observed three days of funeral rites. The clergy of the Royal Chancellery on the 17th; and the Royal Court which had come from Toledo, on the 18th and 19th. Cardinal de Burgos was the celebrant of the Mass on the 17th and the preacher on that occasion was the Archbishop of Granada, Gaspar de Avalos. There was no sermon preached on the 18th and 19th, so Francisco de Borja did not hear Master Avila; but Rivadeneira, Borja's biographer, relates that the Duke paid a visit to Father Juan de Avila who consoled and encouraged him *"to navigate in the dangerous seas of the court without looking back at the stones that others are in the habit of throwing because of ambition, envy and dishonesty."* Borja had an unusual bloodline. On his father's side, he was none other than the great-grandson of Pope Alexander VI, and on his mother's side, the great-grandson of King Ferdinand the Catholic. Francisco de Borja was 29 years of age when the Empress died. His wife, Leonor Castro, the Portuguese lady-in-waiting to Doña Isabel, bore him various children. He had now lost, through death, both his Empress and his friend, the poet Garcilaso, whose body had already been gathered from the battlefield at Nice. When he returned to Granada the Emperor, who was pleased with his service, appointed him Viceroy of Catalonia. The Duke de Gandía went on from there to other promotions.

The courtiers and leading citizens of Granada walked slowly in the funeral procession of the Empress. The clergy, monks and nuns, held their own ceremonies on the 21st. On Monday the 26th, Master Avila preached in the Cathedral. Apparently *"he preached a great sermon,"* to which his disciple, the *'ex-madman'* Juan, listened attentively.

Juan took advantage of these solemn days to have himself discharged from the hospital where *"he was greatly liked"*; he wanted to get on with his new way of life in response to the enlightenment he had received through *his encounter with God.*

"It determined him to put his good desires into action; that is, to serve Our Lord and the poor, to find food for them and to shelter pilgrims and the abandoned."

Juan saw his agenda very clearly. Master Avila supported him. He asked to speak with the Majordomo, his future friend and bishop-to-be, Doctor Muñoz. With kind words he showed his appreciation for the assistance he had received in the hospital: *"Brother, may Our Lord Jesus Christ repay you for the alms and charity you have given me in this house of God."* He then added that he felt *"well and cured in order to be able to work."* Then he asked for his discharge.

Muñoz signed the necessary form, saying he was sorry

that Juan could not stay *"a few more days"*, for he still saw that he was *"very thin and in bad shape from his past treatment."*

The discharge certificate signed by the Majordomo was of utmost importance, because not even well intentioned persons would accept the *'mad bookseller'* since they were convinced he was still *"in the grasp of his past illness."* Muñoz said: *"Thus you can freely go wherever you wish."* Castro adds: *"He said farewell to all in the house,"* where his cheerful service had evidently gained him favour. He left just as he had arrived: *"in his tattered and torn clothing, bareheaded and barefooted."*

I can just imagine how Juan, *'the ex-madman'* would have been smiling with delight as he stepped back on to *firm land,* in a manner of speaking. He had a strong sense of security: *"he knew"* what he wanted to do, for now he knew what God wanted of him. Indeed, he will not fail.

For Juan, the fellowship and assurance of Master Avila meant the enlightened support of a sure guide, for he considered him most reliable. Clearly, while Juan was restricted in the hospital, Father Avila had been keeping constant contact with him. Doubtless he talked with him during these days of the imperial funeral. Consequently they agreed that Juan should go to Baeza where the Master was to reside during the coming summer.

Before Juan sets out on foot to Baeza, where Master Avila will strengthen the psychological and spiritual fundamentals in the development of his new disciple, I must put on record a certain doubt: Were Master Avila and Juan, by common agreement, trying to mislead us regarding Juan's emotional explosion when he heard the Master's sermon at Los Mártires? Dare I say that they have been shielding the truth, with the ingenious tactic of making us believe that Juan *"took his time"* in *"clearly seeing"* God's plan in his life.

I have explained Juan's interior progress step by step, from his visit to Montemor-O-Novo to his arrival in Andalusia, and have used as my guide the only reliable document that corresponds to this period – the biography by Castro.

We know that since he was in Seville, Juan was moved in more ways than one to a conviction that he would receive an interior impulse, or an exterior voice, which would somehow reveal God's plan for his fulfilment of his desire to help the poor, the sick and needy, whom he had seen so badly treated and despised, in comparison with the horses of the Count of Oropesa. That is why he went off to wander the roads to Seville, and then on to Gibraltar, Ceuta, back again to Gibraltar and its surrounding villages, to finally end up at Granada. Juan was in no hurry, he simply took his time. It was all the same to him whether he was working as a stevedore on the wharves at Gibraltar, hauling rocks on the fortifications of Ceuta, earning his keep as an itinerant bookseller, then later having his stall at the Elvira Gate. All this time, Juan was waiting for the sign to indicate that he had been called to his *encounter with God*. For Juan, such an encounter was a certainty.

That is how it turned out. We have observed the unfolding of his encounter with God in two phases. Firstly, he received an emotional jolt in the form of the sermon of Master Avila: Juan is subjected to an emotional earthquake bewildering him with the majesty, goodness and mercy of God. It unhinged him in his behaviour and *maddened* him. Juan was perfectly aware that God had opened his eyes and had shown him the light. He nevertheless felt happy in spite of his apparent folly and of being treated as a madman. He was open to whatever God would indicate to him. He rid himself of all personal interests.

Locked up in the mental hospital he underwent the second phase when he experienced an overwhelming desire to look after his suffering brothers and sisters and an interior voice that determined his availability and showed him his specific field of action. He sees the poor flogged, chained, filthy and despised. God wants Juan to lovingly dedicate himself to caring for these forsaken human beings.

I have adjusted the analysis and treatment of the facts received from Castro, who neatly sets out two points: the sermon with its consequences and the mental hospital with its outcomes. The two phases, the sermon and the mental hospital, are integral elements of the encounter - *the encounter with God,* which resulted in *"the new Juan."* In the development of both phases, Juan was assisted, and helped by Master Juan de Avila who will accompany him in the years ahead and in the work of the *new Juan"*.

And what of my suspicion, my doubt, put there by a conscientious researcher, whose reference I have placed in the notes, and which I can summarise in this question: Did the *encounter,* or the invasion of Juan by God, really and completely

9. Calle Colcha - the place where John of God reconciled the two sworn enemies, Antón Martín and Pedro Velasco, who then asked to join him and so provided the nucleus of the religious family that is known today as the Hospitaller Order of St. John of God.

10. The dwelling that is called "The House of the Dead Man" in Horno Marina, where John of God is said to have left the body of a dead man to shame the master of the house into giving some financial assistance with his burial.

take place in the very first moment of the sermon at the Los Mártires? It was there that Juan simultaneously received the *illumination*, which led him to discover the greatness of God's mercy; and the *impulse* to spend his life in the service of the infirm. That means, Juan was *touched* by the Holy Spirit as he listened to the Master's sermon, seeing himself at the same time placed between God and the infirm like a bridge of divine mercy for his suffering brothers and sisters: he has to be the helping hand of God for them.

Agreeing with this hypothesis, Juan's first interview with Master Avila gave him the opportunity to tell the story of his past life and the absolute turn around that overtook him at Los Mártires. The Master committed himself to co-operate with him, in order that he could ascertain how to fulfil his vocation of charity in the service of the sick. Between the two, they drew up a plan with a double purpose, namely, that Juan *'experience'* the sufferings of the insane inmates; and that he *'learn'* the methods of practical assistance used in hospitals.

They developed their plan and we know the steps they took: Juan *"plays the madman,"* and consequently they lock him up – maybe through the spontaneous decision of the two *"honourable men"* or, who knows, through a decision taken at some distance by the Master. In the mental hospital Juan was subjected to the atrocious therapy of the lash and he observed the treatment meted out to the insane. Later, after they declared him cured, he participated in the operation of the hospital. Going from ward to ward, he studied the system of assistance. This was the first *'intensive course'* that enabled Juan to gain an overall view of hospital life. The Master had a *'second course'* in mind for him, at the monastery of Guadalupe.

What to say? I do not know, the hypothesis leaves me bewildered: Was this *'conspiracy'* of Master Avila with Juan *'really possible'* for a first step in nursing training, without raising suspicion regarding his future plans?

There is no great difference between the *instantaneous illumination* which simultaneously revealed the divine mercy to him showing him the field of charity where he is to find his place; and the *progressive illumination* which lifts him up by the majesty of God to the impelling force of his healing vocation.

Maybe, the Master and Juan have thrown us off the track by using a *'clever ruse'* to let us believe that when he went into the mental hospital *'Juan the madman'* even went along with the drift, when he already had made it his choice at the field of Los Mártires to serve the sick. I would think it strange if the Granadinos of that time, and we of ours, "were having our leg pulled".

In any case, whether he launches himself from the platform of Los Mártires or the Royal Hospital, Juan sets off. His mystical compass was right on target. Master Avila awaited him at Baeza.

Notes to Chapter 19

* In order to understand the effort undertaken during these recent years by Granadian researchers on the history of Granada's hospitals, it is enough to compare the biographical reference offered in *Historia universal de la medicina IV*, ed. Pedro Laín Entralgo, IV, Barcelona 1973, 189, which practically reduced to an article of J. Gutiérrez Galdó, *Los planes de estudio de la Facultad de Medicina de Granada en los siglos XVI, XVIII:* Actualidad Medicina XLI, 488 (1965) 643-655; the book by J. L. Valverde López, *Los servicios farmacéuticos del hospital de los Reyes Católicos de Granada*, Granada 1968; with the studies that appeared after the research of C. Féliz Lubelza, *El Hospital Real de Granada*, Granada 1973, and the collection of documents edited by R. López Guzmán, *Colección de documentos para la Historia del Arte en Granada*. Siglo XVI, Granada 1993, '*Hospitales*', p 75-121.

* For an overview of the history and architecture of the Royal Hospital: Cf. A. Gallego Burín, *Granada. Guía del viajero*, Granada 1973, 310-313. From the '*Maristán*', Casa de la Moneda (mint), ibid., 344.

* The city's 'revolt' against the Emperor's decision to put the insane (*innocents*) into the Royal Hospital was caused by server economic conditions, and besides, it was indicated that where the innocents' hospital was being built, was actually a more healthy site than that of the Royal Hospital. Cf. R. López Guzmán, op.cit, p 20.

* The mourning of the Emperor Charles and all Spain for the death of the Empress Isabel, is well documented, especially in Vol. I, of the famous *Corpus Documental de Carlos V*, and the various biographies of the Emperor. The description and commentaries of the funeral rites at Granada are in the *Relación de un testigo de la vista*, which is conserved in the library of the Duke de Gor, Granada, ms. 13: "*The reception of the cadaver of the Empress, wife of Charles V, in 1539 by the city of Granada. The cortege was presided by the Duke de Gandía.*" The author of the *Relación* has mistaken the precedence delegated by the Emperor to his son Prince Philip nevertheless the one truly responsible for the cortege was certainly Francisco de Borja, the aide-de-camp to the Empress.

* The meeting between the Duke and Master Avila was particularly told, correcting the error of Rivadeneira. Cf. L. Sala Balust-F. Martín Hernández, *Obras completas del santo maestro Juan de Avila*, op.cit., p 77. Various witnesses at the beatification process of John of God certified that the Duke met Avila on this occasion. However, none could say that the Duke heard him preaching on these dates: "The Royal Court left Granada after the funeral ceremonies, celebrated on the days of the 18th and 19th. Master Avila preached his sermon on the 20th after they left. Obviously the witness were familiar with the lifestory of Francisco de Borja written by Rivadeneira, who erroneously said Borja heard the sermon.

* The hypothesis of a 'conspiracy' between Master Avila and Juan to throw off the scent from the 'enlightenment' having occurred at the sermon at Los Mártires indicating to Juan his future work for the sick, was put forward by Cecilio Eseverri, *Historia de la enfermería e hispanoamericana*, Salamanca 2 1995, 118-125.

20

JUAN UPON THE
PSYCHOANALYST'S COUCH

It is the spring of 1539 and Juan is on his way to Baeza, invited there by Master Avila. Is he a changed person and, if so, what has changed in him? Has he already passed over from Juan Ciudad to *Juan de Dios* – John of God?

When he arrived in Granada he was recognised as a peaceful man but now all Granada knew about Juan's *madness* and how he used to go about the streets in such a sorry plight until *some good men* took him to the Royal Hospital where he was put in with the *innocents*. He spent almost five months in the hospital until *"Doctor Muñoz, granted him a certificate of mental health."*

Many people at Granada were aware that when the Portuguese bookseller was released from the mental hospital he had developed a close relationship with Master Avila under his excellent protection. For this reason they regarded the Portuguese with a certain respect, since it was said that Master Avila gave his protection because Juan's breakdown was not caused by insanity but rather by something that came from God. The doubt regarding the true nature of the *madness* has puzzled the Granadinos from 1539 until our own day.

If Juan's frenzied behaviour was madness, what about that *conversion*? I have narrated *"what was outwardly seen to have occurred, were the external consequences of what was occurring within him."* In the spring of 1539, we need to accompany him on his journey to Baeza where Avila awaits him.

But this Juan is 'something else'; he is no ordinary character. His true image is far greater than the externals of his story for we have seen him *'incandescent'*, seized in a flaming spiral. The atmosphere surrounding him since 'conversion' seemed invaded by 'metahistoric' phenomena, which could be natural or supernatural, we don't know.

"Who knows?" Here lies the key to the enigma: mad or what? Before continuing to accompany Juan on his life story 'we must' understand whether he was 'mad' or 'what'. What were the true elements of his 'conversion'? Since a lot can be gained in looking into the stages of this madness, let us follow the traces.

So, permit me to postpone, for now, the journey to Baeza. I am going to place before you the opinions of some medical doctors, psychologists, psychiatrists and theologians who have made a serious study of the *'conversion of John of God'*.

This is a kind of roundtable conference with eminent

specialists from various countries: an Italian, a German, a Frenchman, an American and a Spaniard.

"Juan's conversion after he heard Master Avila at the field of Los Mártires, was alive with drama and its effects were phenomenal like, as meteorologists say, a cold front, sometimes unleashed upon the coast of the Levant: an abrupt clash of masses of air with violently diversified temperatures that provoke a formidable condensation which falls upon the land like an uncommon, irresistible whirlwind."

A careful punctilious study of the case of 'John of God's conversion' can be verified from two different aspects, because it offers two 'faces'.

The biographer who methodically disregards the Christian faith, treats of a man seen as one submitted to unhinging psychological pressure, to the point of "going out of himself", upset; with fascinating consequences.

For anyone contemplating that episode from a religious point of view, the 'conversion' of Juan brings transcendent references that will motivate his later behaviour.

Dámaso Alonso made a methodical study of the poems of John of the Cross. This mystical poet was a believer who arrived at a personal experience of God, and as a result he wrote the 'Canticle'. The verses of Fray Juan de La Cruz [St. John of the Cross] carry a religious message which the poet both sought and confessed. But a literary problem presented itself when these verses were arranged from a strictly human perspective. Experts say it is unusual poetry and a challenge to the techniques of critical philology and poetic analysis. It is not true to say that such studies oppose the religious value of the poems of John of the Cross, nor can it be denied, nor detracted, for it is enough to say that they simply occur and are placed in parenthesis, so that the poem can conform to strict literary criteria as being a normal literary occurrence. Dámaso Alonso says this method has to be "from this inclination" to ground level, if the poetry of John of the Cross, in its transcendence, is to function "as poetry as such" on the margin of its religious contents; while at the same time being able to maintain the enduring freshness in which abides its prodigious esoteric even-handed effect. When Alonso speaks of "from this incline," he is really saying that it is simply human.

John of God's 'conversion' offers both 'sides' for examination. One from the religious side, though really, objectively, it occurs in a scenario with some protagonists, and with that are undoubtedly written in a Christian plot.

However, the stroke of the conversion, and the follies that immediately originated in the subject, stimulated a scientific study *"from this side,"* as one of the episodes at the height of "the stimulation of his personality" enriched with some very lively psychological and psychiatric material. That is why the study of the turmoil that went on within the mind of the quiet Portuguese bookseller on the morning of 20 January up in the field of Los Mártires, must be undertaken from two angles, one scientific, the other religious.

Some psychiatrists consider that there can be no doubt that Juan's conversion caused him to become mentally ill, either 'temporally', or 'permanently'.

Vallejo Nágera, analyst of a select group of famous insane persons, cautions about the care that psychiatrists must exercise when working on *"the pathologies and clinical histories of persons of the past using today's knowledge"*: accurate diagnosis calls for an abundance of substantiated facts where we see reflected the sure image of the psychotic person. If this diagnosis is supported by topics and falsities accumulated over a period of time, then the psychological structure of the person concerned simply becomes distorted and inevitably the resulting diagnosis will be erroneous.

Cesare Lombroso, one of the most important historic psychiatrists, was born at Verona, Italy, in 1835 and died at Turin in 1909. He diagnosed Juan as *"a genial madman"*, as one who fell into the pit of insanity, but fortunately it was a *temporary* insanity. In recovering from it, Lombroso says, Juan will set up nothing less than *"the modern hospital"*, thanks to the impulse of a privileged person: *"It was the first sanatorium to divide the patients into categories, the first to give shelter to the homeless, the first refuge for itinerants"*; such is the evaluation Lombroso gives to him.

Lombroso viewed the *conversion* as representing one of those *"facts"*, real data, upon which we have to investigate the natural process which impels mankind towards either good or evil: a basic principle of the school of positive criminology which, thanks to Lombroso, had a tremendous influence on penology. These intrinsic associations permitted him to bind *"the genius and insanity"* together - which reminds me of the popular saying: *"there is only a thin line between genius and madness."* Lombroso was a young man when he drew up his diagnosis of Juan's madness; yet when he came to retirement he reaffirmed the basic thesis: *"The genius has a natural tendency towards epilepsy, he carries epileptic deterioration within himself."* The event of Juan's conversion seems like a violent *"manic attack"* whose further development *"by its own impulse"* and thanks *"to the genial vigour of the subject"*, develops towards creativity with amazing results.

Of course, Lombroso's analysis does not suffice for today's psychiatrists; still, it is helpful to recall that his relationship between *"genius and epilepsy"* as an inexorable tribute which every great man or woman has to pay, lies today under the *"vitalising power of illness"*: the occurrence of Juan's *"conversion"* originated in an open *"spiral"* towards unforeseeable horizons.

Lope de Vega utilised his skilful poetic talent to summarise the conversion and its outcome in three lines:

> *And as one unhinged,*
> *like a stream made silent,*
> *frantically running bare.*

Pondering Juan's folly, Lope de Vega put his hand to an ironic application, counting on the recognised dignity characteristic of the Portuguese; that *"the Portuguese"* Juan, accepts being taken for a madman and outraged, so as to give a special value to his *"conversion"*:

> *What a pilgrim way!*
> *To arrive at God, through such self-abasement!*
> *A Portuguese humiliated, how frightful!*
> *Then suffering insulting blows that*
> *Castilians rein upon him,*
> *such a dishonourable thing is unheard of from Portuguese;*
> *because they are so honourable and valiant,*
> *and to do such would be blameworthy before God.*
> *I know not how it could have been endured:*
> *but it had to be something he shared*
> *between God and himself,*
> *for had he not been Portuguese, he might not have endured it.*

"A Portuguese humiliated, how frightful!" Granada derided the bookseller: well no, *"not all Granada"*, only the rabble and street urchins. Greater Granada held its breath, asking itself what lay beneath all this folly. The people of Assisi once wondered about St.

Francis, especially on the occasion when they saw him standing stark naked before his father and the bishop; a scene soon to repeat itself when in cord sandals, he went with Brother Rufino to preach in the villages: *"The people thought they had gone completely mad due to so much penance."*

Commentators on Freud make use of an effective illustration in order to explain his invention of psychoanalysis, saying he set up a *"telescope permitting us to observe the other side of the moon"*: that is our *"subconscious"* which lies deeply hidden below the surface and influences human behaviour.

A certain German professor, gifted with the characteristic tenacity of German researchers, dedicated many years to delving into the deep waters of John of God's personality in search of some clues that might uncover the *"psychological mystery of his conversion."* I must confess that I read, and reread, these pages of Ludwig Ruland with intense interest. They contain brave good ideas, and deserve thanks for the successive progression of the form of *'colloquy'* into which Ruland puts his work, which he entitled *"Conversations on St. John of God."* Ruland was born at Munich and became a professor at Münster University. He wrote his work at the start of World War II, but unfortunately his manuscript was destroyed during the bombing. In 1947 he recommenced his study: simulating conversations during *"long winter hours"* between a doctor of medicine, a professor of history and the superior of the sanatorium "Hospitalario" at Waldheim. The "superior" moderates the meeting. The historian puts forth John of God's biographic data based upon Francisco de Castro's work enriched by the circumstances of the period. Step by step, the doctor developed a conscientious psychiatric examination that focusses on the complete life of John of God.

I was truly captivated. They dedicated their sixth and seventh nights to the phenomena of the *conversion.* What was the result? Spoilt by a poor start, Ruland accepts this hypothesis: *"Throughout his entire life, John of God suffered the consequences of his fall at Fuenterrabía. It could well have been a fracture to the base of the cranium that may well have been only a disturbance with subdural consecutive haemorrhage. He certainly had some sort of lesion as a consequence of that unfortunate accident. He was then unable to resist the strong psychiatric consequences, given the unstable imbalance of his mental and sentimental state."*

Well! So the wretched French mare somehow left our Juan with brain damage. However, it was an erroneous proposition of Ruland's to say that, "without doubt" the cerebral lesion was received at Fuenterrabía!, and to put forward the *"hypothesis"* that this lesion unleashed *"an agitation of depressive origin"* which caused his emotions at the field of Los Mártires to erupt into *"an acute reactive psychosis."*

Let us avoid using technical terms. The impact at Fuenterrabía produced in Juan, according to the German professor, a small cerebral abscess as a consequence of the trauma. Consequently, the soldier was marked *"for the rest of his life"*: the emotional tension on his cerebral vessels caused his psychotic crisis. The sermon of Master Avila sparked off the strong emotional reaction in the hearer whose defences broke down pushing him to act *"scandalously."* However, in reality Juan had been psychologically *'touched'* all his life after the fall from the mare: *"The sermon of Master Avila was therefore, the exacerbating factor, but not the cause of a psychiatric depression of major intensity."*

I see two flaws in Ruland's approach: First of all, the *"cranial fracture,"* cause of *"an intracranial abscess,"* does not appear in the Castro narrative, the only source of the unpleasant incident with the French mare: Juan falls, hits his head, becomes unconscious, bleeds, gets up again, prays and walks away and his companions welcome him back: *"They heaped blankets upon him to make him perspire"*; and thus they took care of him, and *"as a result, he felt well within a few days."* That is all Castro has to say on the matter and it is never mentioned again.

My second disagreement: Ruland affirms that the famous *"abscess"* caused *"a disturbance"* in Juan for the rest of his life, bringing about *"an anxiety"*, a certain mental and psychical *instability* which constantly forced him to change location and work. But, neither before nor after the incident at the field of Los Mártires, does Juan appear to be insecure and indecisive. From Seville to Granada we see him alert and in touch with what is going on about him, all the while awaiting his expected sign. Moreover, he was always sure of himself, equally while he was lugging rocks on the fortifications of Ceuta, as in selling books in the Gibraltar countryside. And when the time came for him to set up his hospital at Granada, we will see him in full command of his mission.

Did the fall from the horse at Fuenterrabia cause a physical injury to Juan's cranium? There is no doubt that since early childhood, Juan was burdened with another and far more profound psychological trauma: The *"departure"* from his family home at Montemor-O-Novo. Five centuries later and lacking knowledge of the exact circumstances regarding this strange episode, it is impossible to measure today the emotional shock waves that had repercussions in Juan's *"psyche"*.

The North American psychiatrist, Ruben Rumbaut, did not hesitate to tie the phenomena of the *conversion* to the childhood trauma of João Cidade.

We friends of John of God are indebted to, and thank, this American researcher whose sympathy towards his historic patient clearly seems to be in good faith. He accepts a poetic version of the childhood ' mystery' of João at Montemor-O-Novo. Rumbaut enthused over the nocturnal conversation of the 'visitor' who was welcomed by the Cidades one night and inflamed the imagination of the child João as he told stories about the accomplishments of the great adventures. The little boy listened to him in fascination, and decided to flee from his home so that "he too, might experience such heroic adventures" and then some day return to Montemor-O-Novo in triumph.

In effect, João *"did run away"* from home. He soon found out that he had not reached the heights of the heroes: he looked after sheep, fell from a horse at Fuenterrabía, became a soldier again at the liberation of Vienna, all neither with grief nor glory, but obscure and dull. When he came back to Montemor-O-Novo, he was more than forty years of age and learnt of the disaster that had befallen his family: his mother's death and his father's grief. These calamities reawakened a subconscious remorse: Juan *"knew"* he was responsible for so much suffering and felt overcome by a *"parricide complex."* In Andalusia and Africa his psychological drama weighed upon him, until the sermon of Master Avila overwhelmed him in an acute depression with uncontrollable psychotic results.

Rumbaut maintains that Juan saved himself from a fatal collapse thanks to the good handling by Master Avila, who certainly reorientated his wild compass; and thanks, also, to his own physical and spiritual strength, he went on to dominate the dangerous symptoms and put back on track his life of service to the poor.

Rumbaut has given us a very attractive clinical composition, but unfortunately it, too, is based upon erroneous foundations. The child João did not flee from his home. If anything is clear in the ambiguous page of Francisco de Castro, it is that *"they carried him off"*, the child was taken away. As for the dreams of glory in Juan's childish fantasy, there is no trace. Nor is there any justification to suggest that either Juan or those who took him into their home at Oropesa, ever attempted to let Montemor-O-Novo have news of the boy who fled away.

For some 25 years, Jean Caradec Cousson, a French St John of God Brother, worked in close contact with doctors and experts in the field of neurology, as is customary for many John of God Brothers. He discussed certain passages of the biography of the holy founder with them, especially the startling moment of the *"conversion."* Brother Cousson's medical friends were of the opinion that Juan really did suffer a psychotic breakdown: If it is so, as Francisco de Castro says that Juan *"simulated"* madness, *"he passed himself off as being mad"*, these French specialists thought that Castro managed the data *"with the mentality of the 16th century"*, he lacked the scientific facts available today.

Brother Cousson was impressed with these comments and he decided to write a new biography based upon Castro's work. He utilised their historic information, which we know to be unsupportable, but interpreted the facts *"in conformity with the knowledge of modern medicine and psychiatry."*

Brother Cousson was able to please many of his confreres and devotees of St. John of God by telling them that, according to his specialist friends, the objective study of Juan, far from reducing the saint's merits, increased them. So he wrote his book, and prefaced it with a famous quotation of Pope Leo XIII who recommends, we must *"energetically"* strive against lies and falsehoods, we must go to *"the source"*, to the documents, thereby fulfilling the first law of history, *never to lie*; and the second, *never be afraid to tell the truth*. An exemplary approach by Brother Cousson who called his book *'John of God, from Anguish to Sanctity'*.

In effect, he interprets Juan's life as immersed in an atmosphere of real anguish due to being separated forever from the love and affection of his family when he was eight years of age and left alone without any blood ties. He spent forty years far from his hometown, with failures and all sorts of encounters, at Fuenterrabía, at Vienna. Finally he visited Montemor-O-Novo, then Ceuta and finally went into Andalusia and arrived at Granada. Cousson sees Juan beset by remorse, feeling himself responsible for the tragedy that befell his parents, his conscience tormented by the thought of being guilty of something that approached '*parricide*'. Overwhelmed by such inner torture, the sermon of Master Avila caused a nervous disturbance within him pushing him to forms of obsessive expiation. For Cousson, Juan is truly insane, not pretending to be:

"*He suffered an acute nervous breakdown, brief, wrapped in anguish; still conserving mental lucidity, but momentarily falling to inordinate and irresistible impulses. He gladly accepts this condition because it serves to offset his deep desire for expiation.*"

This analysis of Cousson's has the doubtless advantage of his long conversations with his neurologist friends, who specialised on the topic. But it also has the gravest inconvenience of exaggeration, irritatingly blowing up the slightest *reference of anguish* that we find in Juan's life. You know his vicissitudes, candidly related by me, on the basis of available documents. We have not seen these incidents in his life tied to any deep-seated remorse for some infantile crime that he may have committed in the long distant past.

The Spanish psychiatrist Victor Hernández Espinosa also works professionally in close association with the St. John of God Brothers at their San Boi psychiatric hospital at Barcelona. Equipped with an excellent academic preparation, enriched by long and valuable years of experience in teaching, he one day undertook this intriguing project: to put John of God himself on the couch, to submit him to psychoanalysis. In order to carry out his pathological examination, Hernández Espinosa had recourse to the information given in José Cruset's biography of John of God.

The psychiatrist's reflections, when published by the Brothers of the Aragon Province in their Barcelona magazine, caused quite a sensation and stimulated great interest amongst scholars of St. John of God. As I am about to proceed, strictly from the angle of human criteria, into the phenonemon of John of God's conversion, the psychiatrist Hernández Espinosa's contribution seems to me to be both attractive and thought-provoking for he establishes a parallel between psychoanalysis and religion:

"Psychoanalysis looks into the interior world, into the world of mental reality, into the unconscious fantasy; meanwhile religion refers to the world of divine or transcendent reality."

Having limited the field of 'psychological mythology', Hernández Espinosa refuses to follow, in the case of Juan, the proper analysis of the *compensatory mechanism of sublimation,* settled in *the libido;* and he applies a second *compensatory mechanism* which he calls *reparation,* a repairing psychodynamic.

Leaving aside technical terminology as much as possible, I intend to summarise this thought-provoking scheme. Since infancy Juan bore within himself a damaged *"interior world"*, because in his *"unconscious fantasy"* he considered himself responsible for an act of aggression towards objects worthy of love: his parents, whom he *'abandoned'* when he *'fled'* from his home.

In order to liberate himself from a pathological suffering equivalent to a living hell, he will have to assume the burden of *guilt* and the *reparation,* in an attempt to reconstruct these *'damaged internal objects'*, which are the replica in his own identity of the *"original objects damaged by the ambivalent conflict between love and hate."* If I have interpreted Dr. Hernández Espinosa well, Juan would have had to repair and reconstruct the *"internal replica"* of the *"external objects"*, his parents, whom he can never recover.

His guilt assumed, the repairing of the external object, his parents, requires Juan to repair the internal object, memory and image, in the unconscious fantasy he has of his parents who have disappeared. But how was he to do that?

Through the *"substitutory objects"* which symbolically represent the absent external objects: this *"symbolic reparation"* will allow him to restore the internal object and to rebuild his own integrity. Thus he will readjust his split and fragmented ego. If he does not support the repressive pain of reparation *" he will convert it repressively into persecutory or melancholic pain, with all the psychopathological suffering this implies."*

Starting with the *'conversion'*, Juan goes on to dedicate his mature years, *"his second life"*, to a work which is *"frankly reparatory"*, which Hernández Espinosa ingeniously qualifies as *"Granada-type reparation"*: that will be complete, perfect, 'paradigmatic', and fully carried 'at Granada'.

Dr. Hernández Espinosa says this is how Juan was able to

test his reparation: *"Through works and actions undertaken to make restitution, to recompose, to restore the external object; however their fundamental and primary objective is the recomposition of the damaged internal object in the unconscious fantasy; that is to say, the rebuilding of his personal integrity, his self-respect. When John of God said "the maximum charity we can have, is firstly to our own souls and then to our neighbours',"* he probably wanted to say, that charity done towards the neighbour has, as its first objective, charity towards one self. To heal the neighbour is to heal oneself; to repair the object is to repair the self. Juan Ciudad abandoned his home and his parents at eight years of age, induced by the promises of an adventurous student to whom his parents had given lodgings for the night; the reality is that he fled with the student and never more returned to see his parents."*

The psychiatrist particularly notes Juan's return to Montemor-O-Novo, years and years after his flight: *"It was there that he learned that his mother had died only twenty days after his flight from home, and that later his father also died in a friary. We know nothing of his emotional reaction, although it is easy to presume that he must have been overcome by guilt feelings and a desire to make reparation, which was now impossible to achieve without the original objects. It can only be supposed that "the maximum charity we can have, is firstly to have it for our own souls and then for our neighbours" is an insight that began to influence him here as a necessity: that of having charity towards the neighbour so as to be able to have charity towards oneself; an impelling force that moves him to repair the misery of other persons in order to repair the misery of his own soul that derives from being no longer able to restore life to his parents who, in him, had lost their only son. The few biographical facts that have come down to us regarding this man say nothing about all this. Nevertheless, it may be supposed that, humanly speaking, this was a moment of depressive crisis in the life of Juan Ciudad."*

This happened to him late in his life, after many years, but Juan did not give in to it. *"He is a man who was strong both physically and spiritually, gifted with an inner energy that constantly impelled him into action and never permitted him to fall into depression, into the void of voices without answers."*

What did he do? He began *"to show signs of reparation that clearly were directed towards external figures representative of the hurt and vanished parents whose memory lives on within himself:* he helps and protects the family of the Portuguese gentleman exiled to Ceuta.

However, his entry into an ambience of reparation happens with *"the crisis of maturity"* at Granada, when he hears Master Avila's sermon. Hernández Espinosa reproaches the German Professor Ruland for his hypothesis that *"the saint might be of a schizophrenic constitution and that the crisis at Granada was the consequence of a cerebral lesion caused when he fell from the horse"*:

"There is no doubt at all that it was a crisis of desperation with manifest signs of guilt feelings and an immediate tendency to expiatory behaviour. If it did not evolve into a depressive state, it would have had to be the germ of reparation that arose of its own accord and began to express itself plainly from the time of crisis."

Juan will begin serving the poor and sick as *"a work of reparation without ceasing, it occupies the rest of his life and ends as a bequest to posterity"*:

"His work was a forceful and continuous battle against every class of difficulty and adversity, apparently everything contrary to a miracle. The miracle of John of God is himself. His miracle was in overcoming Juan Ciudad and arriving at the converted John of God. His miracle is simply the triumph of love over depression, of the task of reparation over overwhelming guilt."

Juan reclaims his identity and recovers for himself: *"The interior peace of the reparative, in which love and recognition triumph over hate and guilt, emotional richness over misery of spirit, and the impulses of life over the impulses of death. In a certain way Juan Ciudad's mental health lets him emerge triumphantly from his crisis of depression and sets him on the path of reparation."*

The final section of the analysis reflects a certain enthusiasm of Dr. Hernández Espinosa as he sees Juan paying *"even his business debts"*, and how he accepts the *"paternal direction"* of Master Avila: *"Interior bliss is won when the debts are paid, when the persecuting pain of guilt, sublimated into depressive pain, opens up the door to atoning action that repairs the interior objects and re-establishes the original integrity of the human relationship of the child with its parents who provided nutrition and affection. This is the basic relationship of love and recognition, opposed to the psychopathic hell of hate and contempt. The charity of John of God, the doer-of-good, allows him to meet his parents again and make the reparation that brings about their internal re-creation as objects of love. In the biography of Juan Ciudad the initial meeting with Juan de Avila takes place at a time when Ciudad is at a critical time of his life. His feelings of reparative desperation have persecutory and guilt producing elements that demand the expiation of his sins. This state of mind transmutes itself into a filial relationship of love and respect with Avila that has to take over and symbolically represent the filial relationship that Juan Ciudad lost by his precocious flight from home at the age of eight years. This is the foundation of the reparative work that St. John of God carries out in the last years of his life.*

Hernández Espinosa's psychoanalysis falls short of the mark because he has overlooked the *supernatural* elements present in Juan's *conversion*. But let the doctor tell us why: "*I write as a psychoanalyst and as a psychopathologist, and for that reason I simply wish to touch upon the human aspect of St. John of God.*"

However, the "total Juan" is a mixture of both human and supernatural elements, and to overlook one is to endanger the other, that is to say, the person would end up deformed.

That is a theological observation that is discounted when specialists study the case "*from Espinoza's point of view*"; its force enlightens those who work "*from the other point of view.*" And it assists in reaching the final objective: an integrated vision "*from both points of view.*" I ask myself whether by any chance the psychoanalyst might include, as an hypothesis in his study, data from the area of religion, factual statements that influence the whole process and come from the patient himself.

I believe that this inclusion would alleviate certain glaring difficulties; as for example, the reference to guilt as not being exclusively focused on the "*damaged objects*", who were Juan's parents, but also on Jesus Christ, who is the "*object of the living faith*" in Juan's consciousness and subconsciousness. I confess that thus expanded upon, this area of guilt, that was latent in Juan right up to the time when he arrived at the field of Los Mártires, and the sequence of events outlined by Hernández Espinosa as '*substitution reparation*', do seem significant to me. They help in understanding the human quality and psychological vigour of the work which we see immediately undertaken by our '*new Juan*': Should the reader ask how I account for this I say: He was sustained by a strong desire to make reparation, and I consider this to be a valid reply. Juan is concerned about rebuilding himself and getting rid of his depression: he only wants to do good to the poor and to make present the love of Christ.

More than a 'theological observation', we could also say it is a 'tactical dissent' that opposes Dr. Hernández Espinosa's psychoanalysis with a very serious 'historic observation', which invalidates his work and brings it down like a house of cards: Juan as a child, my João, does not flee, no, he does not run away from home, nor does he abandon his parents, nor was he guilty of any family drama. Consequently, if guilt does not exist, it makes untenable an assumption of guilt. Sánchez Martínez gives the psychoanalyst a rap over the knuckles: *"If there is no historic foundation to affirm the flight from his parents' home, which fictional literature attributes to John of God, it is quite useless to go on about it, because everything about it in relation to John of God is also going to be mere fiction."* Thus pathogeny is simply turned into a psychoanalytical novel .

Perhaps not all of it is mere fiction. Who knows, maybe when he went back to Montemor-O-Novo, Juan might have been struck by a guilt complex, which in later life could have grown. While he could not feel responsible for the pain and anguished death of his parents because others, not he, had directed affairs, nevertheless, at Montemor-O-Novo he did come across traces of the great suffering they underwent *"on account of his absence."* Without writing the drama, without directing the persons on the stage, the child João *"was the cause"* of his parents suffering. There would be nothing strange about him feeling responsible for this in some way and, as a result, experiencing deep-centred guilt feelings.

Readers are aware of the tangle of information which Francisco de Castro, the sole trustee of the secrets of the Cidade household at Montemor-O-Novo, presents to us in the first page his book. The small boy's *"flight"* from home seems to be absolutely rejected: *"they carried him off,"* they abducted him. However, Castro himself adds how Juan felt when he returned many years later to his hometown: *"John of God greatly felt for the death of his parents, and especially because it seemed to him that he had been party to their sufferings and he showed this clearly by crying and speaking of his sorrow."*

Even if he was to blame indirectly, Juan nevertheless felt that he was the cause of their suffering. He was really a victim; but he felt guilty for so much suffering.

From this (human) side, students of the 'conversion' are able to reach a couple of conclusions; the sermon of Master Avila produced, with whirlwind force, a psychological impact on Juan; secondly, that the phenomenon that occurred at the field of Los Mártires demands of scholars an attentive reflection on how to explain the 'sudden outburst'. This includes those who see him as 'temporarily' mad and declare that he was *"going through a state of temporary dementia."* They look for a way to expand their findings and to explain Juan's later behaviour. Thus it is from Lombroso to Hernández Espinosa.

Now let us view it from 'the side of believers': What really did happen to Juan on that morning?

With all due respect to the scientific contributions to the subject of *Juan's conversion*, I really must confess that it makes me very happy to propose that it was a 'rare success' when viewed in the light of our Christian faith. Castro placed it in its historic perspective, he describes the supreme moment of his hero's life with delicate brush strokes: his biography contains 26 chapters, of which he dedicates three to the episode of the conversion. Castro has not the slightest doubt that this was the meeting, *the encounter with God.*

Castro calls this encounter, *"a strange conversion,"* prepared by *"Our Lord to fill (Juan) with zeal for his honour,"* and as a result will instil within him *"much sadness at the abandonment of the poor."*

Furthermore, God was not curing Juan of any psychotic imbalance: the two aims of Providence are orientated, one towards divine honour, the other towards the service of the unfortunate: This means *'conversion'* exactly. The 'encounter' had been slowly prepared from the day Juan went back to Montemor-O-Novo. It finally caught him 'off guard' while he quietly settled down as a stallholder at Granada: Juan was caught off guard because the initiative came from God who had *"turned his eyes of mercy towards him, not unmindful of the mercy he was yet to do."*

The words of the sermon *"penetrated him to the heart"* provoking a hurricane within his innermost being: *"He ran out from there as if he were beside himself".* He has known the greatness of God and his own lowliness; he is bewildered. However, in these first moments there is no evidence of loss of control, Castro indicates that Juan might have become *"mad."* He presents him as being fascinated *"before what he is to esteem"*, the greatness, the love of the Lord. He trembles with *"self-abnegation"* causing him to rush about "shouting" to *"proclaim his misery and solicit mercy."*

Juan wants *"to be held and judged by all as a madman"*. Thus they would be ready to humiliate him, and humiliate him they did: *"He skilfully gave such a good feigning of madness"*; but Castro warns explicitly, that Juan utilised *"this holy artfulness"* pretending he was a madman.

He kept it up and they took him to be mad; and his *"artfulness"*, his *subterfuge*, had the approbation of Master Avila. Juan would return soon, to go through it again. Naturally, later commentaries of a biblical and theological character sprang up after this 'historic account' by Castro.

The scenario and circumstances of the *'conversion'*, or the calling of Juan, his encounter with God, suggest relationships with parallel events in both the Old and New Testaments. Scripture scholars present us with: the vocation of Abraham, the driving force of Moses, the missions, sometimes very dangerous, confided by Yahweh to chosen men and women, such as that of Jeremiah. Castro, in the prelude to his book, even evokes the memory of the young David:

"Of whom sacred scripture speaks in chapter 17 of the First Book of Samuel, as being full of zeal for God's honour. He heard the boastful words spoken by the proud Goliath against the army of God, and having tried the arms of King Saul, he found he was unable to fight with them, so he cast them off and dressed as a shepherd with his slingshot and five pebbles in his shepherd's pouch and went out to fight the enemy face to face. With those arms and the help of the Lord in whom he trusted, he easily brought the enemy to the ground and removed the insult and peril from the people of God. Likewise, this new man..."

"This new man" is Juan the Portuguese bookseller, who strips himself and runs through the streets of Granada clad only in his breeches.

From the New Testament it seems necessary to draw an allegory from the fall of Saul on the road to Damascus. He becomes suddenly transformed and enlightened, changing from a persecutor to an apostle. I would be very pleased if Dr. Hernández Espinosa would invite St. Paul to lie down upon the couch of the psychoanalyst.

What do theologians have to contribute? They apply a special word to Juan's 'conversion', "*metanoia.*" This means a radical change, an absolute transformation in a person, who casts off the old skin to re-emerge clothed in the finery of divine grace.

The *metanoia* of Juan was brought about, according to Castro's testimony, through "*the efficacious words*" of the sermon: the vehicle "*of the grace of the Lord*', of "*its force and virtue.*" I believe it was "*effective*" enough to break down the framework of Juan's defences, casting him to the ground and forcing him to shout out "*as if he were mad.*" Castro adds: "*Everyone easily suspected that he had lost his reason.*" It is the vital germination of the divine word, the fruitful seed, and the essential creative principle: "*In such a manner that the words were fixed upon his heart and were to him efficacious, then they showed their force and virtue.*"

Who can measure the power of the divine word infused into the veins of a man, who can set limits upon it? Juan's encounter with God divided his life into two sections, 'before' and 'after'. His *conversion* drew the dividing line. He knew, and we know too, that he was 'invaded'. An irresistible 'presence' entered him, propelling him to follow Christ. Starting at the field of Los Mártires, Juan began to walk in the path of the mystics, those men and women who had been 'touched' by the flame of the Holy Spirit. He was ablaze, he will give light and heat while being consumed by it himself. They have destined him for a mission: "*Wishing to strip himself naked to follow the naked Jesus Christ and to make himself completely poor for The One who, being rich, made himself poor.*" (Castro).

It upsets me when our scientific friends try to trace the path of the torrent of lava that circulated through the veins and arteries of our man. Let us see if they can understand and suggest something to explain the 'inebriation' of the Apostles when they received the Holy Spirit on the day of Pentecost. Certainly they came out like drunkards. They were seen to be 'lit up' – out of this world.

Down through the ages we believers sometimes wander off the track. I can not explain why it is that I fall upon my knees before a portion of bread and wine as soon as the mysterious words are pronounced over it upon the altar. Mystery is hidden in the waters of baptism that is poured over the head of the newborn baby. Mystery accompanies the perfumed oils that anoint the elderly person who is dying; it is the mystery of Christ in the shared love of a young betrothed couple. A fever overtook Juan and he would never recover from it. We will see him undertaking works of mercy, yet the beats of his heart strike a sidereal space. From now on he is always going to be so close yet so distant, so different.

A man or woman like this, who is suddenly struck down by God, sometimes blazes a page in human history. We see them burn without remedy, beyond all logic, they are simply unique.

I have a friend named Viadero who gave me the Italian translation of a Greek book published in Milan entitled ,'The Mad Saints of Byzantium'. Knowing of my interest in the subject, he said: "Here are your mad ones for Christ." 'The Mad Saints of Byzantium' deals with venerable men and women in the communities of the Eastern Church. They, like St. Francis of Assisi, took the words of the Gospel literally. Smiling, he said, "here are the 'kamikaze pilots' of Christianity."

In the Eastern Church they tell delightful anecdotes of their own. But, truly, you can take my word for it, I personally know some 'demented ones' like them, mad ones for Christ, with the madness of the Cross. Tell me, if you let the Holy Spirit breathe upon your mind and take the pages of the Gospel seriously, let me know if you do not run the risk of 'blowing' your mind.

Castro asserts Juan was not mad, but "appeared to be mad."

Also appearing to be mad, was this beautiful girl who only yesterday, at the age of eighteen, came and stood before the Archbishop in the chapel of the Sisters of the Cross, and vowed that she would guard her chastity and be poor and obedient. Looking at her from the choir stalls near the altar was a little old nun of eighty-six, who, when she was eighteen, vowed to keep her chastity, be poor and obedient. The old sister had kept her vows, the young girl will complete hers. Crazy for the Cross – mad enough to send them to a psychoanalyst!

The Holy Spirit invaded Juan while he was in the field of Los Mártires. If he was not mad, why is this book, which tells of his transformation, called: "John of God the madman (el loco) of Granada." Pure strategy.

Let us leave him to begin his journey to Baeza to visit Master Avila who is expecting him. Juan is not mad.

When he returns to Granada we are going to see him

accomplish the immortal poem of mercy, verse by verse. He is not mad.

We recognise that if he is mad: then his madness is of a new variety, 'a horse of a different colour!'

Notes to Chapter 20

* The biographical data, fundamental to a psychological and psychiatric reflection upon the 'conversion' is found in Francisco de Castro, op. cit., chapters 7-9.

* For the *"dos laderas"* (two inclines) of the poetry of St. John of Cross see, D. Alonso. *La poesía de san Juan de la Cruz (desde esta ladera)*, Madrid 3, 1958.

* Cf. C. Lombroso, *L'uomo de genio in rapporto alla psichiatra, alla storia ed alléstetica*, (The man of genius in rapport with psychiatric [illness] throughout history and aesthetics), 6th edition, Turin 1864, pp 502-506.

* Upon the theme of 'genial madness' see J. A. Vallejo Nágera, *Locos egregios*, Madrid 9, 1980.

* For the 'conversations' of Professor Ruland, see Ludwig Ruland, *Gespraeche um Johannes von Gott, Würzburg* 1947, 156 pp (2nd ed. With the title *Ein armseliger Mensch-Ein Heiliger*, Frankfurt 1949.

* Cf. Ruben D. Rumbaut, *John of God, His Place in the History of Psychiatry and Medicine*, Miami 1978. Bilingual Edition, English and Spanish, both versions written by the Author.

* Cf. Jean Carandec Cousson, O.H., De l'angoisse a la sainteté. *Jean de Dieu patron des malades e des infirmiers*, Paris 1973. There is also an Italian translation, *Giovanni di Dio dall'angoscia alla santitá*, Rome 1976.

* Cf. V. Hernández Espinosa, *San Juan de Dios a la luz del psicoanálisis* (St. John of God in the Light of Psychoanalysis), published in the magazine *Información y Noticias*, Hermanos de San Juan de Dios, Barcelona, #115,1990, pp 3-34 & #116,1990, pp 103-109.

* For the critique by José Sánchez Martínez, see *Kénosis-Diakonía en el itinario espiritual de Juan de Dios*, Madrid 1995, 115. [An unpublished translation of this work by B O'Grady is available at the Hospitaller Order's Provincial Archives, Burwood, Sydney, NSW, Australia.]

About the fall from the horse at Francisco and subsequent cranial trauma, see Agustín Laborde, *El enfermero de Dios*, Granada 1973, 226, note 7: "*A severe cranial trauma that could leave its mark upon his conduct, even to the point of his extreme behaviour at the time of his conversion. I am unable, at this distance of time, to make a meticulous analysis nor to come to any agreement of his posterior conduct with his spectacular change of personality. John of God is not insane, nor is he an epileptic, as is well demonstrated by the cited cranial trauma; however it is not sufficient to push this as being categorised as an obsession, nor for the rest of his life (with posterior effects from the trauma), no other abnormal conduct is shown as to sufficiently point out any justification for such a bold supposition.*"

* For the reference to the exciting matter of the "lunatics for Christ" see *I santi folli di bisanzio*, Milan, 1990. For a global vision see I. Gorainoft's *pazzi in Cristo nella tradizione ortodossa*, Milan, 1988.

21

JUAN GOES TO THE SHRINE OF OUR LADY OF GUADALUPE AND LEARNS HOW A HOSPITAL FUNCTIONS

Baeza, Guadalupe
1539

Juan sets out to stay with Master Avila who, it seems, *"took him with him"*: so most likely, they left Granada to go to Baeza together.

His discharge from the Royal Hospital effectively brought Juan under the wing of Master Avila, his guide and only support who, through his disciples and sometimes in person, had maintained a relationship with him during the months he spent in the mental hospital.

We can extract from the small amount of data available to us that the Master and Juan *'conspired'* to draw up a plan for the ex-bookseller's future. The signs indicate that the objective of their plan was the *'sick poor'*, those suffering and forsaken persons without money or a roof over their heads. We do not know if Juan's life direction changed at the time of his conversion; or whether he heard the call to serve the marginalised while he was experiencing and contemplating the lot of a broken inmate in the hospital. However he is constant in his decision:

"May Jesus Christ eventually give me the grace to run a hospital where the abandoned poor and those suffering from mental disorders might have refuge and where I may be able to serve them as I desire."

Nothing was going to deter Juan, he *must open a hospital*. He has been entrusted with this work from above and the path ahead lies open before him. Master Avila agreed with this, and together they worked out a scheme based on the fact that Juan himself had been *"designated"* for this mission. Both *"know"* that Juan *will open a hospital.* It was for this that the event at the field of Los Mártires took place.

In some way Master Avila felt himself committed to Juan's *"wild"* project, for Providence had brought their paths together by bringing the *"madman"* to his house after the sermon.

And what does Master Avila know of Juan? Scarcely more than the knowledge afforded him by their first meetings, both before and after Juan, *"feigning madness"* was admitted to the hospital. The Master and his unexpected disciple had bravely dared to trick the whole of Granada with the scandalous spectacle of Juan's *'insanity'* in the streets; and his confinement among the mentally ill. Now Master Avila needs *"to know"* better this man whom God had placed in his hands; and *"to train him"* for the project: Where will Juan's human and Christian potency, his qualities, his faith, his intellectual capacity, and his expertise take him?

There is no doubt that these motivations impelled Master Avila to *"spend some time"* with Juan, probably keeping him at his side for as long as several months. Together they had left Granada for Baeza where the Master arranged some months of rest, both spiritual and physical, for his *"dangerous"* new disciple. Both of them will try to decipher the *"hospitaller"* vocation that God had so deeply instilled into Juan's inner being; and the Master will be able to train him in the practice of prayer and Christian ascetics. For Master Avila knows that anyone who works for the welfare of the neighbour, *"must nourish and strengthen his own soul with the necessary food."*

"There are some who, under the banner of doing good to others, leave their own souls without prayer." This is a grave error and is ruinous in the long run: *"There is no source, no matter how great, that if it is not replenished, dries up and comes to nothing."*

When the time arrived to put his new life on the right track, Juan could have no better, wiser, holier or more conscientious guide.

A circle of 'permanent' disciples surrounded the Master and left a record of the presence of Juan. *"He arrived at the city of Baeza together with Father Avila..."*

Master Avila used to come and go to the cities of Andalusia with a frequency quite unusual for those days. It seems that during the summer of 1539 he went to Cordoba to preach a sermon and this had the result of removing Doña María de Hoces from the clutches of the Precentor who had taken her as his mistress. The episode took on the character of a legend because the Precentor took law enforcement officers to lay siege to the house where Avila had hidden his penitent. The Master had to request the Chief Magistrate for *"an officer of the law and a guard of cavalry"* to escort the lady to Granada where he placed her with the family of a friend. The Cordoba Precentor then accused the Master of taking her away to be his own concubine.

Master Avila established his 'pastoral base' for some years at Baeza when he dedicated himself to the notable project of setting up the celebrated university.

He began by opening a boys' college. Juan was present at its foundation in the summer of 1539. Baeza was then going through a fascinating stage of its history.

I, like most of you, my readers, knew very little, almost nothing in fact, about Baeza. I went there when I was researching the traces of St. John of the Cross. The city captivated me and I am sure it will you too should you visit it.

The modern highways to the south now bypass Ubeda and Baeza. Heading south one must turn off from Bailén or Jaen to the left. The detour is well worth the effort.

The rivers Guadalquivir and Guadalimar flow gently through the final slopes of the Ubedan hills to widen out and flow towards Andújar and Montoro then onward to the open fields of Cordoba, Seville and Marismas to enter the ocean at Sanlúcar. Both rivers course through flat country once they pass through the valleys of the Ubedan hills. The Guadalimar stays close to the Guadalquivir and then they branch off to pass on either side of the city of Baeza which draws water from both. Antonio Machado once wrote: *"Fields of Baeza, when I cannot see you, I dream of you."* This is countryside that favours nostalgia!

There is a plaza at Baeza called the Plaza of the Lions. It is a tiny square tucked away off the main street and the noisy city traffic. When you go there, the clock turns back, because all of a sudden you find yourself in the 16th century.

The plaza is called 'of the Lions' because of its central fountain, made of marble taken, it seems, from the Roman ruins of the nearby Cástulo fortress. It is of sculptured Roman lions surmounted by an Iberian statue of a woman, traditionally considered to be Imilce, the Spanish wife of the Carthaginian, Hannibal, who crossed the Alps to Rome with 100 elephants and soldiers recruited in Spain. Her compatriots looked upon Imilce's romance with disgust because they hated being under the Carthaginian yoke. Nevertheless, over the centuries they maintained their homage for their fellow citizen, saying that while Hannibal was a fierce warrior, she seems to have known how to soften his heart.

The presence of Carthaginians, Romans, Visigoths, Moors and, finally, Christians, leaves Baeza as an historic reliquary: palaces and churches from the 15th and 16th centuries enrich the city.

Leading families of Baeza, weary of continuous squabbling among themselves during the 15th century, in the 16th century saw the city prosper thanks to its agriculture, its livestock, the exploitation of salt deposits, and the cultivation of wool and silk. Baeza had double the population of Avila and Burgos and desired to become like Salamanca. For this, it needed schools.

So Master Juan de Avila was invited to Baeza. The aristocracy of the city noted the imbalance between its material riches and the education of the people, so they decided to endow their city with good colleges, and perhaps even a university.

These followed from the corresponding Bull of Pope Paul III, issued in March 1538, that raised the ecclesiastic income to a sum of money that would sustain a centre of learning, whose program would have, from the start, the characteristics of a university. Its major patron, Rodrigo López, called Master Avila in the spring of 1539 to take these scholastic affairs into his own hands. Master Avila arrived from Granada to commence the task. Among his disciples would have been young intellectuals coming from colleges of Granada. He also brought our Juan who is going to participate in the foundational steps of the University of Baeza.

The Master prudently commenced with the groundwork; the university's faculties of education would come later. For the moment he opens junior schools, a college for boys and unlettered young men. Then, in establishing the college, he gives to Juan, his latest disciple a job, so that instead of 'sponging', he could earn his board and keep.

There is no documented evidence to support my opinion that the talented and practical Master Avila would have made good use of the months of Juan's stay at Baeza to let him learn with the boys to "better read and write", but that's my position.

Master Avila looked for a house in which to lodge his pupils and chose a director (rector) who was *"an elderly man and a good house-master."* This allowed him to continue his preaching and travels. He chose a *"master scribe, whose duty was to teach writing and arithmetic."* Furthermore, he named two *"assistants to the Rector"* for students *"who were already literate,"* and still another to teach the younger children. This is the exact timetable: *"Three hours of lessons in the morning, the last for reciting doctrine. The same for the afternoons, with Sundays free to go out into the streets."*

How long did Juan reside at Baeza under the wing of Master Avila? We do not know exactly, probably four or five months, from June-July until November, with a break, as we will soon see, spent in going to visit the monastery of Guadalupe in Extremadura.

Castro notes that in *"going to Guadalupe"* Juan would have endured great cold, as the country was then *"in the grip of winter."* This indicates that walking on foot was possible along the edge of the Villuercas Mountains, so this journey would have had to take place sometime between late September and October. When he returns from Guadalupe he will make a stopover at Baeza, before departing for Granada where we must have him not much later than Christmas, to be seated at the table of a bishop who, after January 1540, will already be far from Granada. It is impossible that Juan could have returned so early... On the other hand we know with certainty that there was *"another bishop"* who invited him much later.

It should not surprise you that a bishop will invite him to dine, because soon after his return to Granada, Juan becomes a public personality. Which bishop, and when they met, is a complicated matter into which we will look later.

Certainly he was not seen as a personage of any significance during these months at Baeza: Juan helped with the running of the house and its cleaning.

Master Avila lodged him in his own residence, called the *"house of the Chaplains"*, which was adjacent to the church of the Holy Spirit, where his college began to function. Thanks to the *"Master Scribe"*, Antonio de Vega, who also lived there, we know some details of how Juan conducted himself. De Vega assures us that he *"saw and spoke with him by day and night."*

Juan and Antonio had rooms near each other. Antonio de Vega complained to Master Avila: that Juan *"did not sleep in the bed,"* remaining awake and *" lighting his candle two or three times during the night"*, thus cutting his sleep short. Master Avila told de Vega *"to say nothing about it and to leave him alone."* De Vega put up with it *"even though it was an annoyance,"* for Juan was really bothering him. However, he *"never said a word, because Father Avila had ordered him not to."*

The schoolboys amused themselves at the cost of the big man who had joined them in the classrooms. They hit him and played tricks on him, and I wouldn't be surprised if they gave him a kick in the pants once in a while. Of course, Master Avila would smile and ask him from time to time: *"How did you get along today, did you learn anything?"* Juan replied yes or no as the case might have been. If he had been kicked, he said it was only a *"zapatilla"* (a touch of a slipper), and Father Avila used to comment: *"Something well gained, Brother Juan."*

The two engaged in an amusing conversation: *"What happened today Juan, any extraordinary gain?"*

This they counted if the little scamps had given him some slaps that *"were insulting or offensive?"*

"And when the boys whistled at him or mocked him, he became quite cheerful." It was *"a very profitable day."*

Although few, these months spent close to Master Avila were, without doubt, happy ones for Juan.

Biographers, including Castro, relate how Juan made a pilgrimage to Guadalupe out of devotion to the Blessed Virgin Mary: *"To give her thanks for her past help and mercy, and to ask her again for succour and support for the new life he was thinking of undertaking."*

Of course, he goes to Guadalupe as a pilgrim of Our Lady: *"He said that he had felt, always, her distinct favour and assistance in all his troubles and necessities."*

A pilgrim yes, but more than that, he will become an apprentice nurse. As we know, Father Avila is endowed with a keen scientific curiosity, and already he was aware of the high standing of the hospitals directed by the Jeronymite friars at Guadalupe. Juan's visit to the famous monastery was part of the plan worked out together by the master and his disciple to get the 'hospitaller vocation' under way: at Guadalupe Juan will see how a hospital functions.

There is no record that Master Avila might ever have visited Guadalupe personally. When he was a child of four, his parents went there on a pilgrimage from their village of Almondóvar. However, after he had established himself as the *"Apostle of Andalusia,"* he made a passing reference to the fact that, a long time before, when he was in the Almadén hills, he saw the Sanctuary of Guadalupe in the distance.

The trek from Baeza to Guadalupe was difficult, and no joke, since winter was fast closing in. The days required for the return journey would have been considerable, and the chronology does not tally: probably Juan did not go back to Granada as soon as some authors suggest, since the bishop reported to have invited him to supper had already been transferred away. I would say that it might have happened if the bishop was late in moving to his new diocese of León, or had returned to Granada to gather up his possessions. However, the stronger case in regard to this very long and fatiguing pilgrimage sees Juan returning to Granada by the spring of 1540 instead of Christmas 1539, and his lordship the bishop inviting him some time in May. In addition to this, as we shall see later, another bishop comes into the picture.

Irrespective of what might have been, Juan sets off on the journey from Baeza. *"A pilgrim"*, is the reply he would give to those inquiring of him on his journey; because that statement was as good as a passport in those times. Even though he has no intention of proclaiming it to the four winds, he also had another intention, his hospitaller vocation, for in Guadalupe he will find excellent lessons.

It is a matter of interest that the route most likely to have been taken by our pilgrim followed the track over the Sierra Morena, passing through what is today is La Carolina (but in those times was the territory of La Peñuela) ascending to Almodóvar del Campo, the birthplace of Master Avila. He then would have gone along the banks of the Guadiana.

The first stages, from Baeza through to Linares and on to Carboneros, would have been made during glorious autumn days. The pathways along the northern corner of the hills of Jaén, the southern parallel of the Sierra Morena, are gentle to the tread of the traveller. The countryside is gentle, gracious, serene and the horizon augers peace. The tracks run up and down steep inclines, along gentle undulations, through the trees and shrubs, and fields dotted with evergreen oaks and strawberry trees. But it is another matter when one talks of the path that ascends to the sierra. Without any previous warning the air becomes chill and the freezing sleet mercilessly slaps one's face. It becomes so dark that it is difficult to tell whether it is day or night. Castro's very brief reference suggests that Juan had a bad time of it: *"on this journey, cold and poorly clothed, he suffered many hardships since it was in the grip of winter."*

Since it did not *"rain money"*, he begged for alms just like any genuine pilgrim: *"He had to beg for food and went barefooted."* This sentence the biographer cuts short without further explanation, leaving it to the reader to guess the hardships.

11. *The gate through which John of God went to meet his clients who were too ashamed of their poverty to present themselves with the beggars and itinerants.*

12. *The courtyard of the Los Pisa family home where John of God died.*

The fantastic tales told by Celi and Govea embellish this journey with wondrous events. The reality was extremely hard. Today, the 300 kilometre journey, or 600 return, is made in comfort but it was not so in those days. The dates of the "short calendar" are not consistent with a journey of this length. We must postpone Juan's return to Granada until the spring of 1540. After the sierra, he had to travel the interminable paths of the Mancha, confront the new mountains at Altamira and the spur of the Villuercas: where the little River Guadalupe lies hidden. Here, upon its banks, so tradition says, the shepherd Gil Cordero made a discovery.

Juan begged, but not wanting to impose on anyone, he invented the 'woodgatherer system'. He collected a bundle of firewood and carried it on his shoulders to the door of a hospital if the town had one. Then, in exchange for this, he asked *"for something to eat and a place to sleep."* When he could not find a hospital, he sought to sell it to anyone willing to buy it and in this way he paid for his lodgings. Before moving off once more on his journey he shared whatever money he had left over with the poor.

He arrived exhausted. Today pilgrims go to Guadalupe in September, and I have seen them arriving there after three or four days on foot with their feet bleeding. Some wear tennis shoes, or runners, yet in spite of that, they need to receive first aid from the Red Cross, which sets up booths along the route. Our Juan arrived after, who knows how many days... fifteen?... twenty? He was in a sorry state.

The dark figure of Our Lady of Guadalupe is quite small, only 59 centimetres high, and can be dated with certainty from the end of the 13th century, taking its name from the River Guadalupe. It has a straight nose, large eyes, a classic chin and belongs to the group of Western European sitting statues of the Blessed Virgin with the Divine Infant upon her lap; as Mother of God, she supports the Infant; as queen she occupies a throne. Carved from cedar, it is polychromed, the dress is dark green and the mantle is red. She lets her left hand rest upon her knee. The original right hand was replaced by the present one in the 15th century in order to carry a sceptre: the hand that was cut off to make way for the new one, is kept in a golden urn. There are black shoes upon the feet. A golden veil falls from her head to her shoulders. Four large flowers decorate the dress. The Infant is in the same style and period as his Mother and was carved by the same artist: it measures 23 centimetres in height with the head slightly inclined towards his Mother's breast, and is clothed in a simple red tunic on which there is a stencilled design in gold. The Infant's right hand, also added in the 15th century, is of silver and in a attitude of benediction. The left hand is almost in relief, and rests on the *Book of Life* upon the knee. The feet are bare and the face is that of an adult with long curly hair falling to the shoulders.

Our Lady of Guadalupe has been lovingly venerated by her children from the 14th century to the present day. Beautifully clothed, adorned with crown and sceptre, her infant is likewise crowned; today the statue rests upon a splendid throne beneath a precious bronze canopy adorned with marble columns and variously coloured enamelled plaques depicting Franciscans, figures of saints, events of the shrine, maritime scenes, shields, flora and fauna.

Juan surely knew the story of the little Virgin long before he arrived at Guadalupe; probably he would have come here as a child with the good folk of the Arañuelo on a pilgrimage, perhaps even more than once. From Oropesa the walk meant crossing the Tagus at Puente del Arzobispo, climbing the Sierra Altamira then passing on to San Vicente. The peasants spent two days making the journey to the shrine. Juan would have been familiar with the friars, the solemn ceremonies attended by the pilgrims, and the gigantic building of the monastery. And, above all, the serious and gentle little Virgin.

Juan would have heard dozens of sermons about the ancient legend of how Gil Cordero, a herdsman on the banks where the little river Guadalupe joins the Tiétar, one day stumbled across the statue, the hidden treasure.

The inhabitants of the countryside call this sierra the "Villuercas". Writers of old described them as *"jagged mountains occupying many rough areas, but also with some parts that are delightful and calm."* Its inhabitants then, as now, were good country folk, herdsmen and shepherds who, in their search for pastures, sometimes took their flocks north to where the Tagus flows, or south along the banks of the Guadiana. Don Miguel de Unamuno's heart was in tune with *"the solitude of these lonely green valleys tucked away in the vastness of the sierra."*

Here, on the banks of the little river Guadalupe, in a small valley of the Sierra Villuercas the people of Extremadura found their treasure, the statue of the Blessed Virgin. The medieval legend situated in these places the apparition of Our Lady of Guadalupe. The discovery of the statue happened, more or less, about the middle of the 13th century. Naturally, the devotees of the Virgin want to give the statue nobility and antiquity.

Episodes of a dazzling legend follow one another like the beads of a rosary. These lovely tales, a mixture of Roman and oriental legends, shrouded the little statue in an aura of mystery and devotion. The legend picked no less a person than St. Luke as the carver of the statue. Luke, one of the four Evangelists, was chosen precisely because it was he who spoke most about Mary of Nazareth. St Luke died in Asia Minor and, so the legend goes, they brought his body and the statue to Constantinople. In the 6th century the Emperor Maurice gave the statue to Cardinal Gregory who was sent by the Pope to bring it back to Rome. Gregory was elected pope in 590, and is reputed to have had a great devotion to the statue said to have been carved by St. Luke. When Rome was in the grip of the plague, the Pope presided at special prayers before the statue appealing to Our Lady to save the people. The plague ceased immediately.

Pope Gregory the Great gave the statue of Our Lady to his friend St. Leandro, the Archbishop of Seville, and Leandro sent his brother Isadore to Rome to bring the statue to Seville. When it arrived, Leandro installed it with great solemnity in the principal church of the city, which stood where the cathedral is today. There it remained until the Arab invasion of 711 and, from the 8th century, legend blended with history; because, according to legend, the precious image suffers the same fate as many other images of that time. In order to save the sacred image some people, probably clerics, took it to the north to hide it in the hills of Extremadura.

For five centuries the little statue lay hidden in the foothills of the Villuercas. Nobody knew that the treasure lay hidden below the soil of the riverbank until a surprising thing occurred, during the reign of King Alphonsus the Wise, in the mid-13th century.

When Gil Cordero brought his cows home to put in their stalls he found that one was missing. He searched in the woods until he came to the banks of the river where he found his cow dead. He wanted to skin it, so he pulled out his knife. He made the sign of the cross with his knife upon the belly of the animal and, no sooner had he done that, than up jumped the cow full of life. In astonishment, the herdsman stood back and as he did so he saw the Blessed Virgin Mary standing among the trees. She told him to go and tell the priests at Cáceres to come to the place and dig. They would find a statue of Our Lady that they were not to take away but they were to build a hermitage on the spot. Thus was the prophecy of the Virgin, and in time the hermitage became "a church and very notable house and quite a large village."

The herdsman was given a miraculous confirmation of the apparition. When he arrived home, he found his wife desolate with grief, one of their children had died. Gil prayed to the Lady of the apparition and the child was revived. Naturally, Gil went to give the clergy the message he had received. This delightful legend appears listed in the codices of the 15th and 16th centuries and, of course, was garnished with the vivid colours characteristic of the popular imagination. Much later, in the mid-17th century, the monk Fray Juan de Santa Maria painted a series of some thirty ingenuous and expressive pictures illustrating the marvellous event.

The people of Cáceres, peasants and clergy, began to make a move. Guided by the herdsman Gil Cordero, they went to the little valley at the foot of the Villuercas and dug at the spot he indicated. When they removed the soil and rock, the statue was revealed. Nobody thought of carrying it away. They built a little chapel and enthroned the statue in it. They called it by the title of the nearby stream, the Guadalupe, which is a combination of two Arab words, guada (river) and lupe (hidden).

The 'history-legend' of the *Virgencita* [the little Virgin] fits in perfectly with similar narratives that can be traced from the 11th to the 15th centuries that historians refer to as the "cycle of shepherd apparitions." This refers to those stories that originated with the Arab invasion with the consequent hiding of so many images in the woods and mountains. As time went by, some of these were discovered by shepherds. The process stimulated popular devotion.

Now we move into documented history: because the Romanesque image of Our Lady of Guadalupe belongs to that group of sculptures called the 'Black Virgins of Western Europe' and can be traced with certainty to the 12th century.

One question remains hanging in the air: Why is the little statue black? (Although in reality only its face is black.) Experts give various explanations that are more or less debatable. The fact is that the group to which our carving belongs is *"the group of sculptures of the Black Virgins of Western Europe."* Poets and preachers apply the Canticle of Canticles to these statues: *"I am black but lovely, daughters of Jerusalem... take no notice of my dark colouring, it is the sun that has burnt me."* (1:5-6).

Isabella La Católica, Queen of Castile, Queen of Spain, fell in love with Guadalupe. She and her husband, Don Ferdinand, visited Guadalupe 20 times. Just imagine what the herdsman Gil Cordero would have thought if he knew that, when he went looking for his lost cow!

This devotion has a long history, starting with the building of the hermitage, which the local folk of Cáceres built in order to venerate the statue. This was no more than a mere hut. Nor would Gil Cordero have imagined that this would eventually grow into a great shrine.

Once the hermitage was built, pilgrims came to it from the countryside. Gil Cordero and his family acted as the custodians of the shrine and, as the number of travellers increased, other families later joined them. Word soon went far and wide about how the Virgin of Guadalupe favoured her devotees with miraculous cures. The hermitage was demolished and a small church was built. King Alphonsus XI ordered that the church be enlarged when he visited the shrine in 1330. After his victory at the Battle of Salado, in 1340, he went back to Guadalupe to offer thanksgiving. From that time onwards, Guadalupe was simply one of Talavera's surrounding villages.

Alphonsus XI fulfilled his royal word. Guadalupe began to transform itself into a large regional centre, which today spreads right around the monastery. The 14th century church was converted into this splendid complex of buildings; and the 'little house - hut' of the herdsman Gil Cordero became a flourishing and active village.

The protection and donations of Alphonsus XI opened up the first stage of the history of the monastery of Guadalupe, which was known as a 'secular priory.' It was governed by a priest who was appointed by the Cardinal Archbishop of Toledo. This priest was in charge of the spacious church built in the Toledan Mudéjar (Moorish) style, and also the land and farms surrounding the monastery. This property was called La Puebla (the village). As the pilgrimages increased, so too did the fame of the monastery. Its administration by the 'secular priors' lasted until 1389, the year when the Jeronymite friars were given charge of the monastery. A letter signed by Alphonsus XI in 1340 speaks for the first time of the settlers of Guadalupe. Guadalupe had a population of 600 when the Jeronymites first went there and it has been increasing in growth right up to the present day when it has almost 3,000 inhabitants. It is an attractive town with its old streets lined with ancient houses with wooden pillars and balconies adorned with flowers. There is the famous little medieval plaza called Los Tres Chorros (the three streams), the Angel Fountain and the Archway of Ages. The town also has new streets, and the inhabitants, apart from those who work for the monastery and for the benefit of pilgrims, are shopkeepers and craftsmen working in copper and other metals; all sorts of ceramics such as jugs, vases and dishes are offered for sale to the thousands of tourists.

The monastery began its 'golden age' with the arrival of the Jeronymite friars who remained there for four and a half centuries from 1389 until 1835.

King Juan I of Castile signed its Royal Charter and a community of 32 friars entered the monastery. The prior, besides governing the monastery, was also the temporal administrator of La Puebla and its farms. Over a period of four and a half centuries, there were a hundred priors and an average number of 130 friars in the community.

The priors governed Guadalupe with a firm hand. They put the final touches to the architecture of the monastery They built the church, organised the religious ceremonies, and the secular works. They received the pilgrims with kindness and established hospitals for them. They directed the management of the farms, which employed more than 650 full-time workers to cultivate crops and raise livestock.

They kept the friendship of kings. Guadalupe's fame spread beyond Spain to other countries. At the time of the discovery of America, Guadalupe became involved in the great adventure. Christopher Columbus was sentimentally associated with the devotion of Guadalupe and the friendship of the friars. When he was returning from his first voyage to America, his ship was struck by a terrific storm. He swore that if he were saved, he would make a pilgrimage to the shrine of Guadalupe to thank Our Lady for saving his vessel. He fulfilled his vow in the year 1493. On his second voyage to America, he was able to fulfil a promise he made to the Jeronymite friars by calling one of the newly discovered islands of the Caribbean, Guadalupe. The two adult American Indians whom he brought back with him as his servants were baptised, at his request, in the church at Guadalupe. He gave them the names of Christopher and Peter. Today the font in which they were baptised forms a fountain in the great plaza in front of the monastery.

Thus, from the commencement of the American enterprise Guadalupe had links with the New World. Hernán Cortés, Pizzaro, Balboa, Alvarado, Soto, Belalcázar, Valdiva, Ovando, all giants of Extremadura, as were their soldiers, came to venerate the Virgin of Guadalupe and extended their devotion to her in the Americas. Likewise did the missionaries, the chroniclers of the Indies and the jurists.

John of God arrived at Guadalupe at the height of the monastery's splendour: From the time of Charles V, it could be claimed that Guadalupe occupied *"the heart of the empire."* The Jeronymite friars gave lustre and distinction to the shrine. Pilgrims from all Extremadura and other regions of Spain, and foreigners came to the shrine, elevating it from an artistic locality to a sacred place: fulfilling its calendar of feasts in honour of the Blessed Virgin. There was a constant stream of children, youth, old folk, men and women all arriving with aching feet after the long walk. However, their eyes shone with happiness and reflected the secret force that emanated from the throne of the Virgin.

Poets have written many fine verses, and in the 14th century, one of them, the chancellor López de Ayala made his vow:

To thy house at Guadalupe
I promise to go as a pilgrim.

When the Cordoba poet Góngora went there, he wrote this verse in honour of the Virgin:

Fortunate hills of Guadalupe!
What is it awaiting me
Resting within thee?

Several of his contemporary saints made pilgrimages to Guadalupe before or after our Juan. Peter Alcántera, the austere penitent *"put down roots like a tree."* Teresa of Jesus came from Avila; Francis de Borja, from Valencia; the German medical doctor, Jerome Münzer; the indefatigable missionary Vincent Ferrer; the Portuguese, Beatrice de Silva, foundress of the Conceptionists; and the Archbishop of Valencia, Juan de Ribera. And Juan, almost John of God by now, but still Juan.

But our Juan did not come just as a pilgrim. Herein lies the importance of his visit, contrary to what most of his biographers suppose: besides his devotion to the Blessed Virgin Mary, Juan came here for the purpose of learning how to "take care of the sick."

Pilgrim and apprentice: probably in the whole of Spain there was no better practical school than at Guadalupe where Juan could see "how to run a hospital."

Master Avila knew this and that is why he "*set him on the right track*" to Guadalupe. Doubtless as a child, and also as a young man, Juan had come here with the peasants of the Arañuelo. He recalled those pilgrimages with nostalgia, as he now fulfilled the ritual of the popular devotion of entering the shrine upon his knees. Castro affirms: "*When he arrived at Guadalupe, he entered the church upon his knees.*"

The memories of his youth stirred within his heart filling him with emotion: "*Tearfully and with and great devotion he offered his needs to Our Lord and thanked Him for all that he had received.*"

In his thanksgiving, Juan gave due value to the 'enlightenment' he received at the field of Los Mártires. Castro tells us that "*he made his confession and received communion*", as is customary with pilgrims. He closes the narrative of the 'pilgrimage' saying: "*He spent some days there in prayer, until it seemed to him to be time to return.*"

It was more than "*some days,*" it was more likely three or four months, which would fit in with the plan he had drawn up with Master Avila.

We are not treating of any arbitrary supposition. When Juan returns to Baeza, the Master will urge him to go and commence 'his mission' at Granada; to start up his dreamed-of hospital. There is an evident connection between Juan's visit to Guadalupe and his 'new entry' to Granada: he has walked so far, not only to make a pilgrimage but also to learn. And, thank God, Guadalupe served his purpose admirably.

Protected by the peaks of the Villuercas, the monastery looks like a cross between a church and fortress. Its towers, the battlements on its walls, its slender steeples, belfries, domes, and halls are all capriciously thrown together, yet they form an harmonious composition. Stone, brick and mortar create a religious haven for monks and pilgrims. Encircling it is the village *La Puebla*, the flat arable land dotted with the shade of the revered olive trees, while above is the serenity of the deep blue sky of Extremadura.

In front of the main village plaza, the Gothic facade of the basilica rises above a flight of granite steps. Two towers flank the entrance of the basilica framing the doorways and windows, crowned by a beautiful Moorish-Gothic rose window. The monastery buildings occupy an area of 20,000 square metres. Its layout included three principal centres of attention, the basilica, the Moorish cloister and the Gothic cloister. All three sections contain a treasury of history and precious art.

The three naves of the basilica lead on to the splendid altarpiece above which is the *camarín* [chamber] in which the statue of the Virgin is enthroned. Today a tabernacle occupies the centre of the altar; it is a gem of history and art containing the exquisitely crafted cedar writing desk of King Philip II.

Besides the basilica, the design of the monastery is organised around two patios: one Mudéjar [Moorish with Christian influence], the other Gothic. The Mudéjar patio is adjacent to the northern side of the church. The ancient archival documents say this was a parade ground that was later converted into a cloister in the *Mudéjar* style: if you follow the railing into the cloister you will be overwhelmed by its peacefulness. The friars constructed it at the turn of the 14th century, uniting in the *Mudéjar* style both Christian and Islamic cultures. In the centre where a well was located centuries before, there now stands a mysterious little chapel with both Gothic and Arabic characteristics.

What is known as 'the Gothic Cloister' had a lot to do with our Juan's 'hospitaller apprenticeship'. It was built at the beginning of the 16th century, with three tiers of arches, the principal one decorated with a lacework of stone. It was constructed specifically as a school of medicine, nursing and pharmacy.

Apart from their *four main hospitals*, the friars of Guadalupe established *up to seven hospitals* in the village to care for various classes of sick pilgrims. Since Church law of that period forbade clerics to practice medicine or surgery they solicited, and obtained, permission from Pope Eugene IV to practice as medical doctors and surgeons.

About 1524, during the second priorship of Fray Juan de Siruela, the galleries of the Gothic cloister were finished and the friars established an infirmary and pharmacy which they furnished with the latest equipment of the period. A few years after receiving the papal dispensation there was a team of friar surgeons and medical doctors giving lessons to young students, thereby founding a true school of medicine, surgery and pharmacy. Together with the friars, the school also had famous secular surgeons. It is recorded that some carried out dissections and autopsies.

The two major hospitals were San Juan for male patients, and El Nuevo [the new] for females. Besides the chief medical officer and two surgeons there was a large staff of serving personnel amongst whom 'Juan the apprentice', newly arrived from Baeza, was able to find a temporary position.

The hospitals at Guadalupe, without counting the 'Enfermería de los monjes' [the monks' infirmary'] which was installed in the Gothic cloister, included ones for syphilitics, vagrants, pilgrims and foundlings. Juan would have heard the instructions given to the staff from the 'Book of Employment' which was written in 1462 and is conserved today in the monastery archives:

"*Regulations for a well-run hospital: 1. A good diet, a good bed and cleanliness. 2. A good physician who knows the patients. 3. A good administrator and charitable servants who turn the evil of suffering into something good.*"

There were eleven places in Guadalupe bearing the title 'hospital,' although some of them were actually hostels supported by the monastery.

Juan, the experienced traveller, would have arrived at the monastery in an exhausted state, scruffy, underfed, and half dead with cold: "*since he went barefooted...*", according to Castro's expressive phrase.

If he was carrying a letter signed by Master Avila, and surely he did carry one, you can imagine the look of surprise on the face of Prior Benavides.

Here we are again at a time in Juan's life story where the angels fail to help us. How happy we would be today, if Father Prior had kept that note asking him to permit Juan to spend some months at Guadalupe to serve his 'hospitaller apprenticeship.' Such a note would be of immense value to us now because it would definitively put this journey of Juan's to the monastery in its right perspective. Such a journey without the hospitaller motivation is inexplicable. Even if the Marian devotion of our pilgrim is taken into account he must, without much more delay, soon begin his work at Granada. There were plenty of shrines closer to Baeza where he could have implored the protection of the Blessed Virgin Mary. No, what was necessary was to go to the ideal school to learn how to take care of the ill, and that school was at Guadalupe. One can guess that the hand of Master Avila is behind the 'pilgrimage'.

Hopefully, some day Fray Sebastián, that fisher of pearls in the deep waters of the Guadalupe archives, might discover a note of recommendation by Master Avila! If only his guardian angel had provoked a flash of intuition in the mind of Prior Fray Benavides, urging him to safeguard that piece of paper.

When Juan arrived, Fray Francisco de Santa María y Benavides had only been Prior of the monastery for two months. He was the son of the Marshal Marquis de Frómista, of the noble family of Manrique. The pious and silly tradition of the miraculous biographies makes out that the Prior was amazed at the prodigious events that occurred when Juan arrived. One of these is depicted in a particular painting in the monastery: a caption reads: *"St. John of God, while praying to Our Lady of Guadalupe, receives an apparition of the heavenly Lady, who places her Most Holy Son into his arms, saying: 'John, clothe Jesus so that you will know how to clothe the poor'."*

My readers, you could not imagine the fantasies with which the 'baroque biographers' garnished Juan's pilgrimage to Guadalupe and his subsequent stay in the monastery. The Blessed Virgin Mary and St. Joseph crown him with thorns; a poor man, having his feet washed by Juan, is transformed into Jesus Christ.

Fray Benavides governed Guadalupe *"to the great satisfaction"* of both monks and workers; after his two years of priorship he was appointed Bishop of Cartegena de Indias [Colombia], then transferred to the See of Mondoñedo, and finally Segovia. He participated at the Council of Trent and died as Bishop-elect of Jaén.

They say that the good Prior *"clothed Juan with the habit of a donado"*, the tunic worn by the hospitaller auxiliaries: Thus dressed, 'the pilgrim' could circulate throughout the hospitals. Juan would see how that magnificent system of nursing operated. The Royal Hospital at Granada had provided him with brutal experiences at the cost of his own flesh, due to the therapeutic methods it employed. Instead, here at Guadalupe, he is given a different vision that was both scientific and charitable; a vision that is backed up by the 'School' of medicine, whose quality is considered by modern researchers to be worthy of praise. At Guadalupe, Juan was able to study a rational hospitaller organisation. Its vitality was maintained by the 'training' given in the 'Book of Employment' mentioned above. Its third point demanding *"a good administrator and charitable servants who turn the evil of suffering into something good,"* complements the first point - *" a good diet, a good bed and cleanliness"* and the second *"a good physician who knows the patients."* No doubt this would have made a deep impression on our 'hospitaller apprentice' and would have influenced him in his work later when he would have his own hospital.

I am convinced that Juan's journey to Guadalupe and his stay there needs a lot more research by those who study his life. Until now Castro and the majority of biographers, even to our own day, attribute a purely devotional character to this period of Juan's life. Why did they not give importance to what Juan 'saw' in the monastery hospitals?

* He saw the staff of attendants, 20 men in the hospital for males; and 25 women in the one for females: bakers, millers of olive oil, cooks, pantry hands, kitchen-garden workers, surgeons' assistants, and pharmacists.
* He saw equipment unknown in any other hospital in Spain; needles for sewing up wounds, files and saws for dental work, saws for bones, cupping glasses, trepans, periosteotome (to scrape the surface of bones), poultices and mercurial concoctions.
* He saw the pharmacy, and what a pharmacy! From the huge bookcases, the indefatigable archivist, Fray Sebastián, showed me a volume with this description of it by Fray Gabriel de Talavera: *"This hospital has its own garden of medicinal herbs and a famous pharmacy which is spotless and*

well stocked. It has such an abundance of medicines and great quantity of vases that I believe there is nothing like it in the whole of Spain. It is so well cared for that there are no unpleasant odours. Its medicines are so well prepared that the patients do not find them to be unpleasant and so have no aversion to them. The instruments and vessels for the preparation of the necessary medications are of silver and spotlessly clean. The medicines are generously distributed without any unnecessary cost or wastage."

* He saw the doctors making regular visits: *"Each day the doctor must make his rounds of the patients. He will visit during the hour of prime (early morning) and at two in the afternoon. He will be accompanied by the pharmacist, the nurses, surgeons, bleeders and other ministers who assist at the visit of the doctor and who will carry out their duties at the correct time: giving the sick great care and in cases of doubt, at least consoling them. The second doctor will also assist with the medications that are usually available."*

* He saw the lessons in theory and practice given to beginners: *"In the 16th century, and even more in the following centuries, the friar surgeons became fewer, the number of students increased, as also did the surgeons who at times numbered four; and at the end of the 16th century, lessons were given, not only to the students of the hospital, but also to others who came to listen to them; for the reputation of the doctors and surgeons had extended far and wide and many (students) came there to learn from such great masters."*

Juan saw this at Guadalupe: a complex sanatorium functioning at an excellent pace. The hospitals and school of Guadalupe amazed visitors, and brought forth the legitimate pride of the friars, as these lines of Fray Germán testify: *"The following saying, heard throughout Spain in the XV century, when applied to those who were skilful in surgery, reveals the universal fame of the surgical practice in the hospitals of Guadalupe: 'Not even if you spent your whole life practising anatomy at Guadalupe or Valencia...'"*

Juan saw this at Guadalupe. Tell me: if his heart was burning with the proposition to "have a hospital", would he not have had to interest himself in making the journey to Guadalupe?

Certainly, Juan spent a few months at the monastery, but this was far too short a time. He took the road back to Baeza, to give an account of what he had observed to Master Avila and to listen to him.

If it were early in the spring, his return journey would have been far less fatiguing. The Master and his disciple held many conversations: Castro, despite his ignorance of the hospitaller efficiency that Juan took away with him from Guadalupe, says: *"He (Juan) gave a report of his journey (to the master), and he received him with great joy."*

Weighing up the situation, Master Avila came to this decision: *"Brother Juan, you have to go back to Granada where Our Lord called you."*

At Granada Juan *"will have a hospital."*

Notes to Chapter 21

* Cf. L. Sala Balust-F. Martín Hernández, *Obras completas del santo maestro Juan de Avila*, I, op.cit., 64-91. Due to his rapid displacement, it is difficult to trace the positions of Master Avila during his itineraries from 1535 to 1542. Nevertheless, there is no doubt that John of God's stay with him at Baeza took place between the summer of 1539 and the spring of 1540.

* There is an immense bibliography of the history, archaeology and acclamation of Baeza. Cf. F. de Cózar, *Noticias y documentos para la historia de Baeza*, Jaén 1884; Gran enciclopedia de Andalucía, Vol. I, Seville 1979, 346-347.

* There is an erroneous declaration made by the witness Fernán Pérez Merino, a priest of Cabra, regarding the meeting between Juan and Master Avila at Baeza. This witness's testimony is reproduced in: Gómez Moreno, *San Juan de Dios, Primicias históricas,* op. Cit., see his *'Floreto'* 206. This witness "on hearsay" puts Juan de Avila at Montilla. The exact situation is explained by another witness, Lucas Coronado, who collected the notes of Antonio de Vega, a bookshop proprietor at Baeza: Gómez Moreno (Ibid, 227-228), also has a copy of this. Also see, Cf. G. Magliozzi, *Pagine juandediane*, op.cit., 46. Also, J. Sánchez Martínez, see *Kénosis-Diakonía en el itinario espiritual de Juan de Dios*, op.cit., 264; and *'Pleito'*, Archivio Dip. Granada, leg. 52/6.4.

* The parents of Juan de Avila made a pilgrimage to Guadalupe when he was a child: Cf. L. Sala Balust-F. Martín Hernández, *Obras completas del santo maestro Juan de Avila*, I, op.cit., 21: the Master *"saw from a distance"* the horizon of the Villuercas from Almadén, ibid., I, 113.

* For the history, art, science and devotions of Guadalupe, see Sebastián García Rodrígez (co-ordinator), *Guadalupe: siete siglos de fe y cultura*, Guadalupe 1993. He brought together the works of 17 experts in the material presented. Regarding the stay of John of God at Guadalupe, there is a mixture of suspect traditions with some delightful pieces of information: Cf. *San Juan de Dios en el monasterio de*

Guadalupe: Guadalupe 123 (1912) 75ff. The brief mention by Francisco de Castro, op.cit., is in chapter 10. For the medicine at Guadalupe see Sebastián García Rodrígez, op.cit., Ch. 16; pages 475-493 give a long report on the bibliography associated with the subject with sections taken direct from the monastery archives. Sebastián García Rodrígez says the Guadalupe 'School' is still an open question, and these days it is of particular interest to historians of medicine. Cf. T. Esteban Rojas, *Hospitales y escuelas de medicina en Guadalupe*, Madrid 1963; Cf. G. Beaujouan, *La medicina y la cirugía en el Monasterio de Guadalupe*, Asclepio XVII (1765) 155-170; Cf. V. Esteban, *Escuela de medicina y cirugía de Guadalupe y sus hospitales*, I. *Jornadas regionales Extremeño-Lusas de historia de la Medicina*, Plasencia 1974, 117 ff; there is a brief reference by L. Granjel and J. Riera in P. Laín Entralgo, *Historia universal de la medicina*, IV, Barcelona 1973, 187; J. I. de Arana, *Medicina en Guadalupe*, Badajoz 1990.

* I consider the sojourn at Guadalupe to be of the utmost importance in the first stages of the hospitaller work of John of God. The works that simply treat of the pilgrimage episode as devotional have a need to be revised, as documented evidence comes forth to present the visit in its true light. Juan, the future hospitaller knew this sanatorium was one of the best in Europe. On the one hand there is the shortage of documented evidence, while on the other there is the mention of a devotional nature given to it by Castro, which set research on John of God off the track. For myself, I am certain that between themselves, Master Avila and Juan planned this "foolish" trip on foot to Guadalupe when they worked out their hospitaller scheme beforehand back at Granada.

* Cf. Alfredo A. Muñoz Hidalgo, *De Juan Ciudad a Juan de Dios*, Barcelona, 1990, 115-123: Here are some very clear references to the *"Book of Employment"* which specified the offices or services to be carried out in the monastery. This author calls it *"a book of the major importance."* Also, in the recently published biography by V. A. Riesco, *Y Dios se hice hermano*, Madrid 1994, 43-48, there is some doubt about the influence of the Castro text which described the trip to Guadalupe without mentioning the stopover at Baeza. Also from Granada to Guadalupe, see J. F. Bellido, *El corazón de la Granada*, Bilbao 1995, 106-108.

* In the meanwhile, since we do not have the good fortune to possess documented evidence, I believe it would be prudent to follow Mateo de Mina's lead in the notes he gives on Guadalupe in his dossier of documents, already quoted, and conserved at the Casa de los Pisa, Granada: *"The historic fact of John of God's visit to Guadalupe, and his stay at the important hospital there for some time, would have been at the behest of Master Avila. And the vocational circumstances that the saint went through when he came out of the Granada Royal Hospital, give good grounds for believing that he had another motive to visit the famous shrine other than his devotion to Our Lady. That motive was to learn as much as he could in the practice of hospitality and to contrast this with his personal experience at the Granada Royal Hospital. Without further documentation on this, it is nevertheless interesting to observe how the director of the film 'The Man who Knew Love' (1979) treated this episode with great conviction."*

* Cf. Agustín Laborde, *El enfermero de Dios*, op.cit., 234, note 45: This author, himself a medical doctor, despite the novel character of his book, is obviously influenced by the various hospitaller centres at Guadalupe, for he says: *"we must hold to the fact that the subject of this biography would have had some medical formation as part of his learning the art of healing."* Laborde's influence is more specific when he says:

"When John of God installed his hospital at Granada, he already knew what a hospital should be like. He already knew how to distribute the patients into various sections, and he knew how to utilise medications, and he knew how to nurse and make use of diets. At least, he knew the rudiments of medicine, and that was enough for him to be efficacious, loving and committed."

* Cf. Cecilio Eseverri, *Historia de la enfermería e hispanoamericana,* op.cit., 53: This author places far more importance upon medicine and surgery than upon nursing, which he says this really got underway once the monks built the Gothic cloister as *"a new infirmary for the community."* He comments upon this in pages 124-127.

22

"GRANADA, WHERE YOU WERE CALLED BY THE LORD"

Granada
1540

An Andalusian fishermen's proverb warns that no wind is a good one *"for a boat that ignores the port to which it is heading."*

Juan set off south for Baeza in mid-May. No wind blew him, and the early mornings were bracing until the sun peeped over the horizon to warm up the day. But the compass Juan carried pointed unwaveringly towards Granada where his work awaited him

Turning left from Baeza and taking the road that borders the Sierra Mágina, one arrives at the heights of Iznalloz in the Genil basin and the kingdom of the Nasrides. In three days he reaches Deifontes, six leagues from Granada. Clearly his Master Avila has drawn up the route for him and set its goal: *"Brother Juan, it is time to return to Granada." "... where you were called by the Lord."*

Has Master Avila become caught up in Juan's madness, sending him off to Granada to create a hospital with no other means than his bare hands?

Let us put things in their right perspective. Bare hands, maybe, but with a unique faith that moves mountains. Master Avila has filled Juan's travelling bags with faith. In this vein he had said to him: *"The Lord who knows your intention and desire, will direct you how to serve him."*

A condition of 'listening' and remaining faithful is indicated by the Master: *"Keep him (the Lord) always before you in everything you do, and consider that he is watching you, so act as in the presence of such a great Lord."*

Avila clearly trusted Juan. From first sight of him playing the madman and taken from the streets of Granada, he trusted him. Now they know each other well. Avila knows that Juan is enlightened, 'touched'. He told his disciples: *"Although they hold that this brother Juan is mad, he is saner than all of us think."*

In spite of his trust, he has a lingering fear. Not of him as a person but of his naivety, his inexperience with regard to the deceptions and swindles that he will need to avoid when he begins to "construct" his dream hospital. Master Avila knew down to his finger tips the labyrinth formed by Granada's ecclesiastic and civil bureaucracies. He expects well of simple Juan and provided a support for him.

"On arrival at Granada, take the confessor whom I have told you about and he will be your spiritual father, without whose advice you are not to do anything of importance."

He gave him the name of the confessor – Father Portillo. Moreover, as he said to Juan: "*When something comes up that seems to require my advice, write to me wherever I may be, and I will give you all the help that I am obliged by charity to give, with the aid of the Lord.*"

With this, Juan said goodbye to his Master and went to Granada.

I can just imagine him sitting down on a ridge overlooking Granada resting at the end of the last leg of his journey. Castro notes that this was at daybreak: "*It was morning when he arrived at the city.*"

Since the sermon in the field of Los Mártires, it seems that Juan has begun a new life, he acts as if he were just born. He sees his life divided into two parts, the first half composed of the 45 years prior to 1540. The average age of Spaniards of that period was no more than 50 years, if we discount infant mortality. We know, but Juan didn't, that he has only ten years left for his 'second life' in which to fulfil his task of setting up a hospital. He is in his 'forties', a stage which the classics call "the serious age of man", the moment of truth. These years are going to be his 'special' ones, dedicated to 'a certain mission', to establishing in the teeming streets of Granada, a hospital, not a grand one like Guadalupe, nor as rich, nor as brilliant, but it would be a 'loving' hospital, where he can serve the poor as he desires.

He had his hands – and his heart. It was up to him to make a start. God would speak soon.

Juan arrives from the north; he goes around to the left of the Alhambra hills and enters at the city's eastern extremity where the pathways from the Sierra Nevada converge at the Molinos Gate. The river Genil, after irrigating the gardens of Güejar, advances towards Granada; but at the edge of the city two canals draw from the river: the canal Gorda, constructed in the 11th century by Abuya Far to irrigate the embankment; and the canal of El Cadí which supplied the residential area of Antequeruela, at the side of the Alhambra. From time immemorial a dozen mills driven by water of the Gorda canal gave their name to the nearby city gate of 'Los Molinos' [the mills].

Early that morning Juan attended Mass at the first available church. He then went back into the countryside to gather a bundle of firewood to take into the city to sell so he would get a few coins to pay for food and lodging.

He collected some branches, made a bundle, put it on his shoulders and, once more, passed through the Molinos Gate. He thought to go through the neighbourhood called Realejo to the centre of the city where he would quickly sell the firewood in the Plaza Nueva or the Plaza Bibarrambla.

He had only gone a few paces when he stopped. Sitting down on the bundle, he began to think things over. For the first time in his life he is beset by feelings of shame. He does not dare to go into Granada loaded with the firewood. That seems strange, since he never felt shy about going around hawking books, so why should he care about carrying other things on his back. He is not going to be worried about arriving in a threadbare shirt and tattered trousers at this stage. He pondered, going to the depths of his disturbance. Really, it wasn't being seen loaded down with firewood that frightened him. This was a serious fear – that the people will remember his antics when he played the madman in the streets, with the urchins hounding him. What if people think that he is still mad and someone tries to have him locked up again in the hospital? This possibility frightened him, it would be a complication, a waste of energies and time. He has to plan his movements. Maybe he should offer again the sacrifice of letting himself be taken for a madman. He did not want to be seen locked up again, especially with Master Avila so far away. Who would vouch for him? He became paralysed by shame and decided to remain that day in the barrio of Los Molinos. He gave the firewood away: *"to a poor widow who seemed to him to be in need."*

The next day *"very early in the morning"* he went to the church and assisted at Mass. He resolved to overcome his dread of what Granada might think, so *"he went to the foot of the sierra for another bundle of firewood."* He picked it up, went through the gate... and his courage began to waver: *"the sense of shame he had had the previous day began again."*

He stopped to rest and to summon his courage. Regaining his breath, he burst out laughing at himself. He literally treated it as a joke; and that is how Castro explains it: *"Goading himself he began to say to his body: 'You, Don Ass, who does not want to enter Granada with the firewood, of shame and pride...'"*

What a marvellous joke Juan played on himself, calling his

body *"Don Ass."* Exactly, and he put the donkey to the trot."... *Now you will get rid of the shame and pride: carry the firewood as far as the principal Plaza where everyone knows you and you will be seen and recognised, that should make you lose your sensitivity and pride."*

Juan: poor donkey.

He reached the Plaza Bibarrambla. There were witnesses who saw and recognised him. Obviously, he was prepared for any eventuality. Word of his arrival spread around the plaza, into the markets and through the neighbourhood streets: the Portuguese bookseller, the madman has returned and is now selling firewood. Even so, they bought the firewood! They plied him with questions as to where he had come from. Marvelling, joking: *"they made fun of him"*: *"What's this, Brother John? Are you a seller of firewood?"* *"What was it like in the Royal Hospital amongst the inmates?"* *"Nobody can understand you - you change jobs, first you sell books, now you sell firewood."* Castro emphasises how Juan handled the situation with good humour. *"He cheerfully took it all without any offence, moreover with a laugh he answered them and participated in their banter without losing what he had gained."*

Anyone who has not lived in an 'old fashioned' Andalusian village or town, such as it was some thirty years ago, would not know of the familiarity surrounding a mentally handicapped person who came to live in the area: we saw such people integrated in the community as someone very special and worthy of affection and respect, even if at first they were the subject of jokes at their expense. That is why many Granadinos felt pleased to see that the Plaza Bibarrambla had regained "that *'loco'* Portuguese", who only a few months ago, was put away in the mental hospital. They did not insult him, they joked, making fun of him in a good natured way. And they bought his firewood. I still enjoy the friendship of a mentally handicapped chap called Antoñito who lives in one of the neighbourhoods of Seville. Straightforward and good-hearted, he used to come to us once a week and hand us a receipt for one *duro* [25 cents] which he signed *"para el tonto"* [for the silly one].

The danger lay in the 'innocent' juvenile cruelty of the street urchins: The boys began running about Juan, shouting *"the madman"*, but this time they did not throw stones or roll him in the mud to make him dirty. Here Juan made use of a *"gentle play on words"* with the older boys *"who asked what he had been doing with his life"*; and he joked with the smaller ones, telling them about the Portuguese game of 'birlimbao': *"Three galleys and a galleon, which the longer you look, the less you know."*

I have read that the game of birlimbao has died out, but when I was in Portugal last year, I learned that it was still played by village children. It is called *berimbau,* and I suspect Castro has adapted the Portuguese word to the equivalent in Spanish: *"Berimbau, Berimbau, three galleys and a galleon."* The Portuguese also spelt the word *'virlimbau'*: the children also used it as the 'magic formula' of illusionists and magicians when they performed magic tricks. This is how the little ones play the game: Three participants are needed to play. The first, mounted on the back of the second, covers the eyes of the second with one hand and with the other hand holds up a number of fingers; the third, directs to the second the magic formula *'birimbau'* and asks how many fingers are on the hand; if the second gets it right, he wins; if incorrect, he loses; when he wins, they change places. I can just imagine how bewildered Juan left the lads of Granada when they heard him saying the *Berimbau* rhyme.

Amongst the adults in the crowd there were some who were watching Juan's movements very closely. Some were Master Avila's disciples who knew about the stay of the *'feigned madman'* at Baeza and had heard the opinion of the Master: *"Although they hold that this Brother Juan is mad, he is saner than all of us think."*

Now they will discover the truth. Was it one or two weeks that Juan employed in weighing up the situation while relying on the firewood he sold? He kept a few coins *"to support himself"* and gave away what he had left over to the poor. The 'spies' checked up on how Juan conducted himself on these nocturnal expeditions: *"At night he went looking for the poor who, ragged, wounded and ill, had been turned away from doorways."* So they decided to help him in gathering and selling firewood, as a witness relates: *"They went up with Juan behind the hermitage of San Antón the Elder, where they joined him in collecting and carrying bundles of firewood back upon their shoulders; and then they sold it, giving the proceeds as alms to the poor."* So, right at the beginning of his activities he met with the help of volunteers. Besides helping him, they let it be known to the right people in the city just how this rare specimen of a Christian was expressing his *madness.*

Juan and his team of volunteers went to the outskirts for firewood, going through the Molinos Gate to the banks of the Genil where the hermitage of San Antón was located and there they gathered their bundles. The sale of firewood in the Plaza Bibarrambla made him popular and provided him with a daily income.

Each night he made his rounds. It is useless to ask ourselves where he slept, because nobody knows, but it seems most likely that he just slept rough on the streets. All that mattered to him was to get his thoughts straight about how and where to begin.

He shared the proceeds from the sale of firewood among the beggars and the sick whom he searched out as they passed the night huddled in the doorways of palaces, church porches and rubbish dumps.

Documents of the period establish that Granada offered a terrifying spectacle of misery in stark contrast to the splendour of the privileged classes. Since the times of the Catholic Monarchs, the project of making a prosperous Christian city of Granada that would outshine that of the ousted Nasrides Moors had begun in earnest. The city attracted vast numbers of builders, financiers, artists, and bureaucrats, powerful people who managed money and knew how to live a life of luxury. Granada also attracted simple workmen who came to earn a livelihood. With them came the parasites, the beggars and rogues. Some came to Granada in good faith, others were far less noble in their aspirations, they were eager to gather the scraps left over from the banquet. This phenomenon took place simultaneously in the two extremes of Andalusia. Granada experienced the tensions associated with its new status as a Christian city, while Seville was receiving the treasures of the Indies. Cervantes wrote that the riches of America arrived at the Arenal near the Gold Tower at Seville, and so, too, did the greatest number of scoundrels on earth. Granada also: pestilent beggars, near the palaces of the wealthy, the sick, cripples, old people in tattered garments, faces lined with hunger, eyes that appeared glazed, women with starving babies, prostitutes. And that does not include the large number of honest peasant families who fled the unemployment of Castile to seek work here on the building sites. These people arrived at Granada without any means put aside in case of illness or for any other unforeseen circumstance.

There co-existed, in fact, two Granadas: the marvellous city of the wealthy, and the shadowed city of the miserable. The rich were few and powerful, the poor were an immense throng. It was a dramatic contrast and the rich preferred not to recognise it.

Certainly the civil and church authorities made some efforts to answer the urgent cases of sickness by opening up hospitals; and to ease the hunger of the most unfortunate with licences to beg that declared them to be "officially poor", as was also applied to the blind and crippled. But nothing was successful in stemming the flood of misery which, as night fell, began to circulate in the slums of Granada.

This is where Juan stayed during his first nights. These were decisive days for him because his sense of duty had matured within him: to serve as a bridge between the rich and the poor, to appeal for alms to alleviate the misery of those who were suffering dire poverty, to get close to the powerful in order to pass on help to the distressed.

Three centuries were to pass before the cry 'proletarians of the world unite' would unleash a social revolution. Juan never took it upon himself to become a union leader, which of course, was quite unthinkable at that period. In those days, intellectuals simply discussed 'ways and means' of assistance: whether or not it would be a good idea *"to gather the poor into spaces under supervision"*, where they would have shelter and be under guard.

Juan decided to go to the margin of juridical and economic controversies: he knew persons, men and women, who were hungry, ill, wounded, homeless, clothed in rags and without money. These were the persons in need of help, and the cold of the nights was giving them a foretaste of the approaching bitterness of winter. Charity compelled him. Compassion drove him on.

How strange it is that in our own time this complaint still prevails each time a champion of Christian assistance, like Angela of the Cross or Teresa of Calcutta, appears. There is never any lack of intellectuals who shake their heads negating the effectiveness of charity: *" the true solution lies in reforming social structures."* I agree; meanwhile whilst awaiting the arrival of this happy world of *"just economic structures"*, I think it best to distribute blankets to those who doss down under the bridge and to give them something good and hot to drink.

God did not give Juan a magic wand when he was up in the field of Los Martíres - *"Berimbau, Berimbau, three galleys and a ship"* - so he could change Granada's ragged masses into princes. All he received, and nothing more, was the mission to provide them with a hospital and love. But money was needed for that and only the wealthy possessed it. Juan will awaken the conscience of the rich, warning them that now is the time to avoid the disaster which befell the Rich Man in the Bible who wanted to go to help Lazarus when it was too late: *"Father Abraham! Take pity on me, and send Lazarus to dip his finger in some water and cool off my tongue, because I am in great pain in this fire!" And Abraham answered: "Remember, my son, that in your lifetime you were given all the good things, while Lazarus got all the bad things. Besides all that, there is a deep pit between us..."* (Lk. 16: 24-26).

Juan is going to serve as a bridge at Granada, while the wealthy represented by *'the Rich Man'* and the poor represented by *'Lazarus,'* still have time. Juan will take the money of the rich to help the poor, and this will be his social revolution. He now knows the beggars and during these nights he goes about visiting them where they doss down for the night.

Failing to hear him, the powerful were left feeling uncomfortable. It cost him some effort, but hear him they did; the powerful eventually listened.

The remarkable thing is : the first person to take notice of Juan and help him is a wealthy Moor, a son of noble Arabs.

Notes to Chapter 22

* The return of Juan to Granada in Francisco de Castro, op,cit., Ch.11.
* The date of Juan's return to Granada sets up a complex chronological problem, in which I consider the calculation by J. Cruset, op.cit., 105, to be incorrect because the time he sets for the return journey to Guadalupe from Baeza would be physically impossible to accomplish. This forces him to have the return from Baeza to Granada approximately at the beginning of autumn 1539, because Bishop Ramírez de Fuenleal was going to invite Juan to dinner on an memorable occasion, which I will relate further on. This bishop presided at the Royal Chancellery until 28 January 1540, and that is why Cruset of necessity situates this meeting between autumn and Christmas 1539, before the bishop's transferral. Neither Castro nor Saucedo give any date for this meeting with Bishop Ramírez de Fuenleal, who in all probability, might have returned to Granada on a visit. Anyway, the official date of the bishop's leaving should not have much of an effect upon the reasonable process of the chronology. Matía de Mina's notes in *Fondo Documental, etc.*, (op.cit., folios 210ff) speaks of: *"Two bishops of Tuy and the habit given to John of God."* He prudently warns: *"I have not been able to confirm whether Don Sebastián Ramírez de Fuenleal was already installed at Valladolid or León, but he made a journey to Granada between 1540 and 1542."* Later on we will see the reservation which Matías de Mina has in regards to the bishop who gave the habit to John of God, and the good reasons he puts

forward for this. It was not Ramírez de Fuenleal.

* I place great importance upon the parting colloquy and advice given by Master Avila at Baeza. It clearly shows the intertwining of the two in getting the hospitaller work of Juan under way. See Francisco de Castro, op.cit., Chapter 11, for the scheme the two hatched up for Juan's visit to Guadalupe.

* On the Molinos Gate, see Matía de Mina, *Visitar la Granada, etc.*, op.cit., 71. Also A. Gallego Burín *Granada. Guía del viajero*, Granada 1973, 167.

* For the reference to *'berimbau'* see Raquel Jardim de Castro, *S. João de Deus, um herói português do sec. XVI*, Lisbon 1995, 281. In his *Fondo Documental* (op.cit.,) 30. Matías de Mina says the game of *berimbau* is still played by the children of Montemor-O-Novo. Also. G. Magliozzi, *Pagine Juandediane*, op.cit., 47.

* When Castro, (op.cit., 11:5) says "He went looking for them at night as they were turned away from doorways, very cold, ragged, covered with sores and sick." Castro avoids using the word *'helados'*, meaning 'frozen', but chooses 'very cold' instead, because it was the spring of 1540 and although the nights were quite cold, they were not freezing.

* This is witness #3 at the Granada beatification process who speaks of the helpers Juan had in collecting the firewood. For the Hermitage of San Antón, see M. de Mina *Fondo Documental* (op.cit.,). Also the notes to Chapter 1 in Castro (op.cit.,). Also, witness #22, Juana de Acero, widow of Miguel del Castillo, who after the death of John of God, was a nurse in his hospital at Granada; said *"One day I saw him carrying a bundle of firewood upon his shoulders, and he looked as if he was too embarrassed to come in with it."*

* The documents of the period all agree to the splendour and misery that went side by side at Granada during the first half of the 16th century. Cf. A. Laborde, *El enfermero de Dios*, op.cit., 137, this certainly gives a good picture of the situation: *"Granada was a city of beggars, of people from other parts of the country who turned up at the last city to be captured in the hope of finding a fortune at the expense of the vanquished. They were attracted by the call of the Catholic Monarchs to colonise these last territories that had been conquered and added to the Crown. It did not take long for the truth to sink in that fortunes were not to be made very easily at Granada. Disease, hunger and the outstretched hand were as a symbol of broken humanity. Such was the last territory to be conquered. But it was also a territory of contrasts, because at Granada there was an abundance of great wealth, although it was not well distributed. It had palaces, luxury and extravagant fiestas. It had humility too, and this was found in the many convents that served as a refuge of piety. Granada had every kind of possibility for human life, from misery to luxury, from charity to disdain."*

23

A PROVIDENTIAL FRIENDSHIP BETWEEN JUAN AND THE SON OF NOBLE MOORS

Granada
1540

Sometimes it seems that God is jesting as our human caravan progresses along the routes of the planet. I like to think that God smiles while moving the pieces around on the chessboard, causing unusual movements within, and between, individuals. This produces what scientists call an *'anisomerous'* unity, formed by unequal and irregular parts.

For example, let us be grateful that Providence has bought to the most outstanding believer in Granada - our Juan – his first supporter: he is none other than a great-grandson of Moslem princes, namely the Venegas family. It was in the *zaguán* [covered porch] of the Venegas palace that Juan lodged the first group of sick people he had picked up from the streets: it was from that *zaguán* that Juan went with those whom he had gathered up to establish his first little hospital.

I must tell you how the aristocratic head of the Venegas family consented to Juan's bringing a motley lot of destitute sick people to the porch of his mansion. Since this episode has a fundamental importance in the hospitaller story I think that it would be worthwhile to recount the history of the Venegas family.

You will see that it is an exciting story, mixing heroism and intrigue. The social, political and economic situation of these first friends of Juan point to how he must introduce himself into the life of Granada; even to the extent of becoming part of the city's history.

The gentleman owner of the mansion, and Juan's first protector, was Don Miguel Aviz de Venegas. For some weeks, (we do not know for how many) in the year 1540, Don Miguel permitted Juan to use his *zaguán* as a refuge for the poor.

Venegas was descended from two lines, one Castilian, the other Moorish. This was as a result of a marriage that took place at the beginning of the 16th century, possibly sometime between 1500 to 1505.

The chief of the Castilian family of Vázquez Rengifo originally came from Genoa to settle at Avila. Like so many noble Castilians, he fought alongside the Catholic Monarchs and was killed in battle during the siege of Granada. His name was Juan. He had fought so valiantly at the gates of Málaga that the soldiers believed that they had seen in him Santiago [St. James the Greater], *"and from the reports that they gave to the king he came to be called*

Rengifo." They say the Catholic Monarchs looked kindly on his son, Don Gil, who obtained, with the title of Commander of Montiel, the governance or mayoralty of the Generalife whose gardens had passed to the royal patrimony after the conquest of Granada. Rengifo figured amongst the most prominent members of Granada's nobility.

Gil Rengifo gave the hand of his daughter María in marriage to Pedro Granada Venegas, offspring of a very remarkable Moorish family. Here is its story, which occupies an entire chapter in the general history of the Islamic Kingdom of Granada.

Upon the death of Enrique IV, King of Castile, in the year 1474, the kingdom of the Nasrides was ruled by King Muley Hacén, Emir of Granada. Muley Hacén refused to pay the tribute to the Catholic Monarchs which, up to this time, had been paid by the rulers of Granada to Castile. The Moorish king replied to the Castilian envoy: "*Go and tell your Sovereigns that the kings of Granada who paid these tributes are now all dead; and that now, Granada will make no effort to send any money to Castile, but will send scimitars and the points of lances against our enemies.*"

A bold reply, but it signed the death warrant for the kingdom of the Nasrides, because it gave an excuse for the Castilians to march against Granada. The chroniclers attributed, although certainly nobody actually heard it, the following scornful reply of King Ferdinand: "*I will pick out the seeds of this Granada [pomegranate], one by one.*" One by one he did pick them out – during the ups and downs of a large territorial war, from the frontline of Zahara in the north, to Almería in the south. But although it was constant, the conquest of Granada was a slow process taking a further twenty years.

The overthrow of the Islamic kingdom of the Nasrides was facilitated by internal divisions. This went back for centuries, aggravated by the disgust the Granadinos felt for the Emir's matrimonial behaviour. He was called 'Muley Hacén', since that is how the Castilian chronicles wrote it, but his actual Arab name was Abu-l-Hasan-Ali. He had abandoned his wife, the Sultana Aixa, and threw himself into the arms of a Christian slave called Zoraya. The Moors of African origin who had recently arrived at Granada favoured the infatuation of the Emir with Zoraya, while the nobility of Arabian origin sided with the abandoned Aixa.

The three main protagonists of the Granada court that

concern us are: Abd Alladh el Zaquir, one of Aixa's two sons whom the chronicles call Boabdil the Younger; the second, Mohamed el Zagal, brother of Muley Hacén; and the third, a Vizier [counsellor to the ruler] of Cordovan origin with Christian antecedents. The Vizier's name was Abu-l-Qasim Venegas, and he was so faithful to the Emir that he tried to assassinate the Sultana and her two sons. Yusef, the eldest son, was killed, but Aixa and Boabdil escaped just in time. This Venegas was the son of a noble Christian family from Cordoba. At the age of eight he was captured by the Arab forces, and was educated by the Nasrides king who had him married to the Princess Cetimerien, sister of the future King Yusef IV.

The diplomatic intelligence service of Ferdinand the Catholic manoeuvred intensively, utilising the internal Arab squabbling, whose factions sought his help against the other Moslem band. In fact, the crossing over of captains between the Christians and the Moslems was quite frequent; much more from the Granada side than from the Castillian because they saw that the collapse of the Nasrides kingdom was inevitable. Muley Hacén ruled the Alhambra while his troops were reinforcing Málaga. Boabdil had his loyal followers lodged in the castle at the Albaycín and at Almería on the coast.

After long and bloody trials, in the spring of 1487, the troops of Ferdinand the Catholic besieged Málaga: the last stepping stone to Granada. By this time Emir Muley Hacén and his Vizier, Qasim Venegas, were dead. Zagal his brother proclaimed himself Emir and Redwan Venegas, who was also brother of the previous Vizier, now succeeded him in this position. Obviously, they manoeuvred their faction into a permanent opposition to Boabdil, who had legitimately inherited the Emirate from his deceased father, King of Granada.

Ferdinand the Catholic had protected Boabdil who had negotiated a secret accord to surrender Granada without bloodshed. However, on the death of Muley Hacén, Boabdil and his uncle, Zagal, became reconciled and between them they set up a barrier to stop the Christian advance.

The long war for the conquest of Granada lasted almost twelve years, from the Moslem "surprise attack" on Zahara Castle until the surrender of 2 January 1492. The whole campaign was an intermingling of advances, retreats, heroism, discouragement, pacts and treachery on all sides. Queen Isabella was able to lift the morale of the Castilian troops during difficult moments. The chronicler Bernález depicted her thus: *"she wore a black hat with a border covering her head, and a scarlet cloak in the style of the Arab princes. Underneath this she wore a rich velvet gown and a tunic. She had a scarlet hood in the style worn by the noble ladies of Granada."* The presence of the Queen *"inflamed the valour of the Castilians."*

The spring of 1487 saw the Moors put up a brave resistance at the siege of Málaga. A ferocious battle ensured and Zagal commended the brave defence that the city put up under the leadership of Hamet el Zegrí. The same chronicler said: *"Don Ferdinand did not stifle the impatience of the army nor the high expectation of the Moors. He advised the Queen to come with her royal retinue. This was to lift the spirit of the soldiers and to put an end to the dangerous rumours that were going about. Isabella left Cordoba at once and soon afterwards arrived at Málaga where she reviewed the troops on horseback. She was accompanied by her daughter the Infanta, their ladies-in-waiting, many prelates and knights."*

After Málaga was taken in August, the Castilians suspended the military campaign until June of 1588. Zagal took refuge in his strongly held territories of Guadix, Baza, Almería and in the Alpujarra. Boabdil remained as lord of Granada and moved into the Alhambra. But he was still afraid of his uncle, so he renewed contact with the captains of Don Ferdinand who agreed to protect him, thus splitting the Arab forces into two factions, those of Zagal and those of Boabdil.

During the spring and summer of 1488, the Christians made a full-scale push against Guadix, Baza and Almería: there was no stopping them. The Catholic Monarchs planned to annihilate Zagal in 1489; then, after the uncle was beaten, his nephew Boabdil would hand Granada to them without much resistance.

Early in May, Don Ferdinand set out from Jaén with 40,000 infantrymen and 13,000 cavalry; he fell upon Baza, where we once more come upon the Venegas family. Zagal placed the defence of Baza under the charge of his cousin, Cid Hiaya, brother-in-law of the two Viziers Venegas, already mentioned and Abdul Qasim Redwan. Cid Hiaya was the son of Aben Zelim, Prince of Almería.

Who were these Islamic Venegas, the future protectors of John of God? Firstly let us look at the heroic stand made by Cid Hiaya of the Venegas family, in the defence of Baza. Some historians have arbitrarily put him down as a traitor. Even if that is so, it should not detract from the merit that derives from the support his descendants gave John of God. It is also true that there is a strong argument to demonstrate his loyalty.

Cid Hiaya sent to Baza 20,000 warriors, a number inferior to those who lay in siege, but they were hand picked and valiant. He brought ten thousand fighters from his Almerían domains. They were disciplined, impetuous and trained in "trickery, charging and retreating." The other ten thousand were called in by Zagal. These were Moors from the mountains of Alpujarra, Purchena and Tabernas, all ready to fight to the last man in defence of the Moslem faith. Their leaders were the most intrepid generals in the Moorish kingdom.

Cid Hiaya laid in provisions for the city and set up its defences. With the usual mixture of threats and flattery, Don Ferdinand called for the surrender of the Moors. Cid Hiaya responded, "*I hold the city to defend it, not to surrender it.*" From June to November Baza resisted: "*Cid Hiaya was effectively cut off from the rest of the world, yet he gave not the slightest indication of tiring or wavering. He attacked from various points both day and night, wounding, killing and depriving the Castilians of rest and sleep. Sometimes the armed Moorish knights went against the Castilian advances and challenged Isabella's champions with arrogant words: these accepted their challenges, offering the spectacle of a singular combat with exaggerated and romantic thrusts.*"

Don Ferdinand sent new emissaries to Cid Hiaya proposing lenient conditions of surrender. The Arab leader made a gift to the emissaries of an elaborately decked out frisky steed. The Castilian king, "resenting his arrogance", sent it back.

Rain threatened the besiegers and hunger the besieged. This was the situation when Queen Isabella came from Jaén. The royal retinue having arrived, Don Ferdinand wrote to Cid Hiaya offering to negotiate. Cid had the courtesy to come out of his walls one morning and to celebrate a tournament in open field for Doña Isabella, "*seizing the admiration of Isabella and her ladies-in-waiting and receiving the compliments of his enemies.*"

The presence of Isabella produced a miracle, *a rainbow of peace* - Pulgar writes. This had completely transformed the heart of the Moors. "*From that moment forth, not a drop of blood was spilt, nor*

13. The first courtyard of the John of God Hospital, Granada. The buildings that flanked this court-yard were occupied by John of God's hospital soon after his death.

14. *The second courtyard of the John of God Hospital, Granada. The buildings that formed this courtyard were built some years after the first section of hospital was opened and occupied.*

a teardrop fell. The explosion of gunpowder ceased as did the taunting and challenging. The rigours of war began to mitigate and calmness followed, paving the way for honourable capitulation."

Besides being a valiant captain, Cid Hiaya showed himself to be a political strategist, for he understood that the good fortune of the Nasrides kingdom had run out. It would be cruel and useless to prolong the war. The Moor leaders met and went to consult with Zagal, who was residing at Guadix, to see if he would approve of surrendering Baza, *"or if, on the contrary, he would support the fight going on to the last stand."* He was loyal to his king and was no traitor. Zagal accepted the capitulation of Baza.

Cid Hiaya did even more, riding to Guadix to seek Zagal's approval to surrender Guadix and Almería. Zagal, now old and ill, exclaimed: *"May the will of Allah be done."*

The Catholic Monarchs would be able to commence the definitive siege of Granada in 1490.

To pursue the family tree of the Venegas – *Benigas* – is difficult because of the geographic and historical extension of Al-Andalus [Andalusia]. The family appears, simultaneously, in many places and times.

The Venegas family traces very early ancestry to the 13th century. They were inserted in the Nazrides dynasty from the same origins, through the marriage of Princess Cetimerien to the Christian boy Venegas who was imprisoned and educated at the Alhambra. They considered themselves to be descended directly from Ibn-Hud, the king of the faction that disputed with Mohamed Ibn Yusuf the Islamic chiefdom of Andalusia when the Almohade empire collapsed and the Navas de Tolosa opened up the way south for the kings of Castile. The hereditary princes of Ibn Hud, settled with some possessions in the territory of Almería and with armed troops spread throughout the kingdom. They remained theoretical rivals of the Nasrides monarchs. During the 15th century they constructed the magnificent Cetti Meriem Palace at Granada, known as the House of the Almerían Princes. Standing at the foot of the Alhambra, its patios, porticoes, balconies and gardens extended as far as the Zacatín markets. The palace suffered much deterioration towards the end of the 15*th* century, when the Princes of Almería were far away from Granada taking part in the family feud that originated with the matrimonial infidelity of Muley Hacén. In the 20th century the palace fell victim to the demolition required to construct the Gran Via: today, sadly, it is useless to search for its vestiges in the alleyways that enter the Gran Via from the Calle Elvira.

Following the surrender of Baza, Queen Isabella, *La Católica,* used her talents and charms to win the sympathy of the Arab nobility who belonged to the Zagal circle, led by Cid Hiaya.

This was not just a political strategy; Doña Isabella took as granted the occupation of Granada and the absolute unity of Spain. She wanted to integrate the Arab leaders in the national unification process. Their troops were seeing the close of one epoch, as a new one began. Of course, the Queen considered the Catholic religion to be a basic and essential element of her Spain. It is recorded that with the *"occupation of Baza, Isabella exercised all her charms to gain the brave heart of Cid Hiaya and his captains and subjects."*

She offered him honours, riches, and flattered his ego. The Queen won this battle: *"in such a way that she overturned the heart of Prince Hiaya, who changed his name and religion."* Cid Hiaya *"abjured the Moslem faith,"* and was baptised in the field tent in the presence of Isabella and Ferdinand. He changed his family name and adopted that of *"Don Pedro de Granada."* His son, *"young, gallant and charmingly elegant,"* was called Don Alonso de Granada Venegas. The Catholic Monarchs granted Don Pedro the title 'Grandee of Spain' with the right to an escort. They confirmed his lordship of the territories of Almería and conferred on him a considerable income. The young Don Alonso courted and won the hand of Doña María de Mendoza, the favourite lady-in-waiting of Queen Isabella.

All the captains of Baza, with Don Pedro leading, put their swords at the service of Castile. That is why some writers consider Cid Hiaya to be a traitor. In truth, I do not see it as clearly as that. On one hand he fought in defence of the city up to the point of its inevitable collapse; and, on the other, there are the practices of the times: Cid Hiaya and Zagal now fought against Boabdil who, although an Arab, was their enemy. Nor would it surprise me if Don Ferdinand, for one, had influenced the will of Cid Hiaya. I would go even further and speculate that he also worked on Boabdil when it suited him.

Throughout 1490 and 1491, they reined themselves in and

Granada could breath freely for a while. The exploits of the captains became legends. Boabdil tried to open up a route to allow access to the ports along the coast of Almería in the hope that the Africans might send reinforcements. The subjects of Zagal and the peasants of Cid Hiaya rose up in arms. From Adra they established contact with the Berbers. King Ferdinand commissioned the Granada Venegases, father and son, to resolve the situation. Cid Hiaya, the father, attacked Adra from the land, while his son, Don Alonso, appointed general and admiral, attacked by sea. In effect, the young Don Alfonso utilised a stratagem that the chronicles took delight in narrating: *"The rebels of Adra sighted six ships covered with pennants and African flags bound for their port. Rejoicing at the closeness of these ships, they imagined that the sultans of Fez and Tremcen had responded to their call for help and had sent them reinforcements. They rushed down to the beach to welcome the sailors. Their hope and joy was confirmed increasingly when they saw the flagship drop anchor, not far off shore, and the disembarkation of a legion of Moslems led by an officer upon a horse. Although these newcomers maintained a suspicious silence one suspected that they might be the enemy in disguise. Terrible was the shock and great was their surprise when they saw them draw their swords and ferociously rush up on them, wounding and slaughtering without mercy. They were caught up in a bloody clash. The mayor enclosed himself within the fortress hoping to defend himself; however the squadron came inshore launching bombs at the castle. Just then a new force arrived by land, threatening an attack. The marine attackers were a disguised Christian troop of mudejares, Moorish converts, under the leadership of Don Alonso Granada Venegas, son of Cid Hiaya. The land troops, commanded by Cid Hiaya, combined with the soldiers from the ships to storm the castle where their enemies, who were faithful to the lost cause of Boabdil, had taken refuge. The Mayor, having lost all hope of rescue from either land or sea, surrendered."*

The Venegases, father and son, entered Granada with the Catholic Monarchs. Don Pedro received the position of *'Alguacil Mayor'* [Chief Bailiff]; his second marriage was with Beatriz de Sandoval and of this union was born a daughter, María de Granada. Don Pedro retired to Andarax where he died in 1505. His remains were brought back to Granada by his son and interred in the cemetery at the entrance to the Elvira Gate.

Don Alonso and Doña María de Mendoza had a son,

named Pedro de Granada Venegas II. This Pedro de Granada Venegas, son of Don Alonso and grandson of the first Pedro, who was called Cid Hiaya when he was a Moslem, had married Doña María Rengifo; thus uniting the two main streams of the former Moorish aristocracy: the Rengifo of Avila and the Venegas of the Nazarides dynasty.

Don Gil Vázquez Rengifo gave them two splendid wedding presents. He handed over his tenancy of the Generalife to his son-in-law, and he gave a palace to his daughter. He purchased this palace a few years prior to the wedding, and when the young couple moved in, it became known as the 'Casa de los Venegas'. Today the Granadinos call it the 'Casa de los Tiros'.

This palace was built at the beginning of the 16th century, like so many others in the 'new Christian Granada'. It occupies the land of an ancient fortress, adjacent to the walls of the Alfareros district. In modern Granada, it stands half way along the walk from the Zacatín markets to the Realejo district. A bishop who was president of the Royal Chancellery had built the mansion for himself. Sold and resold, it came into the hands of Commander Rengifo, who gave it as a dowry to his daughter who was now a lady of the Venegas clan.

The next generation, children of Venegas-Rengifo, connected themselves to the other illustrious Granada line, the Aviz. A great-grandson of Alonso Granada Venegas, and grandson of Miguel Aviz Venegas, named Miguel Venegas de Granada, was the first of his family to know John of God. This happened in 1540, when Juan was carrying out his nightly rounds and distributing among the poor the money that he had earned from selling firewood. I must point out a certain reservation that I have in this matter. The declaration of this 'grandson and great-grandson Venegas', analysed rigorously, gives the impression that, after so many years, he piously manipulates his memories. Nevertheless, the essence of his account deserves historic credibility.

The moderate summer nights gave way to the chill of autumn. Then came the cold of winter, bringing with it wind from the mountains that whipped the face with icy gusts. Juan knew that some of those who were under his nightly protection would die unless he could find a refuge for them. But where?

Admission to hospitals at Granada was difficult. It was more than difficult, it was unlikely, because there were not enough places available for the large numbers of people wanting them. There were delays due to certain unavoidable procedures and Juan knew this. For instance, admission to the Royal Hospital required the approval of the *Visitators* who had to sign the admission form *"depending on a place being available."*

The great-grandson of Alonso Granada Venegas gave an account of what occurred when he gave testimony at the beatification process held at Madrid. Aviz Venegas stated that his grandfather gave Juan permission to lodge the sick in the porch of his palace: *"Each night the house of the poor filled up as he carried them in from the streets upon his shoulders."*

It seems, from the grandson's account, that when this began, his grandfather had no idea that such a swarm of 'poor people' would turn up. No doubt he thought that one, two or maybe three, gathered in the *zaguán* would cause a minimum of disturbance.

We do not know when and how Juan begged permission of the noble Aviz Venegas; probably during his nightly rounds the porch of the palace had caught his attention; maybe someone had indicated the gentleman's generosity to him. The case is that Juan obtained permission to bring some of his poor into the zaguán of the Casa Venegas.

Today this beautiful palace is a museum that is surrounded by the urban sprawl. In those days it was in a more spacious setting. It delights me to sit in the café at the corner of the street and gaze at the facade of the palace to whose doorway "the blessed man" Juan brought his first sick people. Neither Venegas nor Juan had the slightest idea how far the waves of the whirlpool created in that porch would spread.

The little plaza, which boasts an attractive column situated in its centre, is named after Padre Suárez, a famous Jesuit born in the house adjacent to the Venegas palace. A memorial plaque proclaims: *"Spain honours one of the most illustrious sons of this city."*

Only a side section of the original facade remains: the tower with its battlements. These days the facade is disfigured by the 19th century ornamental stonework with three openings: the doorway and two balconies. Protruding from the battlements are symbolic muskets. Attached to the facade in symmetrical order, are five brackets upon which stand statues of classic heroes. Above the doorway is a 'hieroglyphic motto'; it is a heart centred between the words *"the"* and *"commands"*. Thus the message is easy to decipher, *"the heart commands."* A sword stands vertically above the heart inflicting a wound, strengthening the symbolic message. It was an impressive and devout sign for a gentleman's crest. It also augured well for the hospitaller family that Juan was going to create: *"The heart, wounded by mercy, commands."* There is no documented evidence that this motto of the Venegas belonged to the palace's previous owners.

Possibly, like the seeds of many a great work, this one sprang into life simply and without fanfare. Don Miguel Aviz Venegas, the master of the house, or someone in the family, gave shelter to Juan in the *zaguán* one night. He later appeared with a sick person on his shoulders asking permission to accommodate him. Granted permission, he began to bring in others: first one, then two, three. The servants of the household, observing this, concluded that the practice had the agreement of their master. Until one night... It is the grandson who narrates the story in a 'legendary' tone that is far too rhetorical:

"And when the grandfather of the aforementioned arrived on horseback at the portal of the aforementioned house, he found it so full of poor people who had been brought in that he could not find room to dismount. Because they blocked his way, he sent the grooms to chase them away from the porch and to send the blessed John of God away from the house."

"So full of poor people." How many? It seems improbable that Juan abused the trust of his benefactor to such an extent that he ran the risk of being thrown out. It seems even more improbable that someone arrived *"on horseback in the portal of the aforementioned house"*, without room to dismount. However, the episode had a happy ending: Juan *"who at that time was accommodating other poor people"* came out to speak with the gentleman: *"Juan gave the grandfather such holy reasons and justifications that he was obliged to ask pardon for his anger and he embraced him."*

When Don Miguel Aviz Venegas ceased being angry, both he and Juan came to an agreement that it would be better for Juan to search for a larger refuge for the throng he was bringing in at night.

The *"story handed down in his family"*, exaggerated the generous support of the grandfather, for the grandson says that *"he ordered that they give"* Juan *"another house"* for him *"to gather in the poor."* Although it is uncertain, this house seems to have been a gift.

A blessing upon the Islamic Venegas family, converted to Christianity, for providing Juan with the initial help he needed for *"opening his hospital."*

I must explain to you why the Granadinos call the house of the Granada Venegas family the 'Casa de los Tiros'. Scholars attribute the name to the 'muskets' (tiro being the Spanish word for gun-shot) that poke out from the battlements of the palace.

The explanation is convincing, nevertheless a magic city like Granada had to apply its fantasy to the Casa Venegas, shrouding it with the charm of legend. In effect, popular novels invented a fictitious story, setting it in the 18th century during the reign of Charles III.

This legend narrates that a certain Don Ferdinand, Marquis del Salar, in order to defend the honour of a young lady, challenged and killed a student in a duel. The parents of Doña Luisa de Zafra, the lady who was outraged, offered the Marquis a refuge in their home, protecting him from justice so that he might escape arrest. Of course, Luisa and the Marquis lived these eight days entranced in love. The legend was a cross between a detective and love story. Finally the Marquis, who was virtually a prisoner in the palace, our Casa Venegas, discovered one night that he was *"to be executed the following day."* He wrote a letter to farewell Doña Luisa, and fired *"two shots"* into himself. They found him seated in a chair with the lethal weapon in one hand and the letter of farewell to Doña Luis announcing his irrevocable intention in the other. He could not bear to have his ladylove's name besmirched by being involved in the degrading sentence handed down to him by the Chancellery.

The neighbours swore that they heard not one but two detonations (*"two shots"*): Granada gave the palace a new name, the *Casa de los Tiros*, the house of the shots.

The legend makes up a romantic mishmash about Doña Luisa, saying she became a nun and took the name, Sister Maria of Resignation, attributing to her a reputation of sanctity.

Notes to Chapter 23

* The documentation on the family of the Venegas - Benegas, Banigas - is spread throughout the medieval archives. Their role in the conquest of Granada has had several mentions, from both Arab and Christian sides. For a well balanced version see, M. Lafuente Alcántara, *Historia de Granada*, Vol IV, Granada 1846, facsimile edition, Granada 1992, 47, 58, 64ff. Also L. P. Harvey, *Yuse Banegas, Un moro en Granada bajo los Reyes Católicos:* Al-Andalus XXI (1956) 297-302;. This refers to an interesting manuscript in the National Library, Madrid, Res. 245, this gives an interesting account about the Mancebo of Arévalo speaks of how the Moorish lady of Ubeda put him in contact with a member of the Benegas [Venegas] family, who after the conquest continued to make use of certain liberties granted to the Benegas by the Catholic Monarchs in a 'safeguarded letter'. Cf. A. de la Torre y del Cerro, *Unos documentos de 1490 sobre Albucásim Venegas, alguacil de Granada*: Bulletin of the academy of science, *Bellas Letras y Nobles Artes de Córdoba* 38 (1933); L. Seco Lucena, *Notas para el estudio de Granada bajo la dominación Musulmana: 'Miselánea de estudios Arabes'* (1952) 33-37. For the intricate genealogical tree of Cid Hiaya and his connection with the origins of the Nasrides dynasty through the line of Ibn Selim, Yusuf IV and Mohamed VI the *vermilion king*, Cf., the historiographic schemes of the period: R. Arie, *L'Espagne musulmane au temps des nasries* (1232-1492), Paris 1973; T. F. Glick, *Cristianos y musulmanos en la España medieval*, Madrid 1991; M. A. Ladero Quesada, *Granada . Historia de un país islámico*, Madrid 1969; I. Pérez de Hita, Guerras civiles en Granada, Madrid 1983; L. Seco Lucena, *La Granada nazarí del siglo XV*, Granada 1975; M. Gaspar y Remiro, *Documentos árabes de la corte nazarí de Granada*: Revista de Archivos, Biblitecas y Museos II (1909) 330-339, 531-535.

* The interest that I gained while researching the participation of the Benegas in the first stages of the hospitaller work of St. John of God impelled me to investigate the presence of Juan Venegas de Córdoba in the island of Malta from 1599 to 1624 as a Hermit of the Grotto of St. Paul and as a Knight of Malta. The Maltese documents under the charge of John Azzopardi, curator of the Cathedral Museum of Medina Rabat, suggest that Venegas left Spain under duress due to some family dispute, maybe of a religious nature, because he concealed his origins. He found valuable contacts at Naples and Rome. Venegas was honoured at the Grotto of St. Paul in Malta. He died blind and in poverty at Rome before 1641. For information of Venegas in Malta, see G. Gatt Said, *La grotta de San Paulo a Malta*, Malta 1863; J. Azzopardi, *The Museum of St. Paul's Collegiate Church at Wignacourt College, Rabat-Malta*, Malta s.f., 355-357.

* The witness don Miguel Venegas declared at the beatification process held at Madrid, #12 (the 'Floreto' of Gómez Moreno has it as #24). Castro makes no mention whatsoever of the Venegas episode. The declaration of another member of the Venegas family spoke at the beatification process of the patronage the family gave to John of God, and refered to Doña aldonza Renjifo, daughter of Commander Renjifo.

* For the legend of the *Casa de los Tiros* see F. & P. Villa-Real, *El libro de las tradiciones de Granada*, Granada 1888 (facsimile edition Granada 1990) 118-225.

24

HIS FIRST HOSPITAL COMES TO LIFE IN THE CALLE LUCENA NEXT TO THE FISH MARKET

Granada
1540-1541

Two little old ladies were summoned. When their lordships the Archdiocesan judges called upon them to ask whether they believed that *"the blessed man John of God"* might have been holy, Luisa de Ribera, who gave her age as 98, and Lucía de la O who said she was *"only"* 95, both clearly recalled the memory of *"blessed Juan."* They remembered when he died, and both were present at his funeral. Lucía was 22 years of age at that time, while Luisa was a 25-year-old mother of a family. Of course, they remembered 'blessed Juan', how could they ever forget him.

The bright little old grandmother of 95 years of age, Luisa de la O, stated that she was a citizen of Granada and lived in the parish of San Cristóbal up in the Albaycín. She said her house was *"right at the very top, near the lookout,"* and that she had lived there since she arrived from Córdoba at the age of five. The judges asked how she lived: *"On alms,"* was her reply; *"and since Diego my husband died, may he be in blessed glory, I have remained a poor widow without any means and I live solely upon charity."*

Luisa, the elder of the two old ladies, gave her status in life: *"I have always remained unmarried."* Because of this, she had no family obligations and lived a very religious life. She claimed that her grandfather, the apothecary Antón Zabán, was a great friend of our Juan.

Despite their age, Lucía and Luisa were both very alert and clearly and shrewdly answered the questions put to them. Taking turn about they related about three dozen anecdotes concerning the *"blessed"* Portuguese who opened up a bookstall and was kindly thought of by everyone.

Both Lucía and Luisa said the hospital had its beginnings in a house that *"the blessed father Juan,"* had taken. *"Yes,"* they replied, *"we called him father, even though he was not a priest, because we regarded him as a consecrated person,"* and considered him a *"sacred person." "Well, he rented a house in the Calle Lucena."* : *"He took a house next to the fish market, at the end of Calle Lucena, which is all one and the same place."* Lucía testified. *"Next to the fish market,"* Luisa added, *"it was the first hospital that he had in this city, he gathered the poor there."* The fish market, or the Pescadería as it is called, and the Calle Lucena were considered to be *"all one and the same place."*

Juan abandoned the porch of the Casa Venegas and went to the busy barrio of the Pescadería, further down from the Major Church.

In order to have an exact idea of Juan's comings and goings, I suggest you now look up on the map either the ancient or modern city. You will notice that there are two main thoroughfares in the centre of Granada that cross at the Plaza Isabella la Católica: the horizontal way is the 'Gran Via de Colón', which continues towards the east via Pavaneras, Santa Escolastica and Santiago; the vertical way is 'Reyes Católicos' connecting in the north with the Carrera del Darro and in the south with the Puerta Real and Recogidas.

It is necessary to remember two facts when comparing modern Granada with that of long ago.

Firstly, a river existed before the Reyes Católicos thoroughfare was made: the River Darro was uncovered from the Carrera del Darro to the Puerta Real, where it twisted at an angle of 90 degrees to flow into the Genil. It was only covered at the Plaza Nueva; the river below this had four bridges uniting its banks.

Secondly, the city abruptly ended at the Puerta Real, where the walls came from the Elvira Gate by the lower end of the Plaza Bibarrambla, to avoid the Darro and go on to the Genil.

Today it is accepted that the historic centre of Granada is a block which includes the last stretch of the Gran Via, the Plaza Isabella la Católica, the Cathedral - only half built then - and the Plaza Bibarrambla. Looking at the map you will see, on the 'south-left' section of the block, a cluster of little streets connecting with the Plaza Bibarrambla at a street called Calle Pescadería. The Lucena is among this bunch of streets.

How Juan obtained that house is a mystery. It is quite a distance from the porch of the Casa Venegas, his 'night refuge' for the poor, and he had to cross the Darro.

In those days this barrio of the Pescadería was less central than it is today, because the city died out at the Puerta Real. Nevertheless, the chronicles assert that, even then, the Pescadería was a very busy place. It remains so to this day.

The Plaza Bibarrambla was the meeting point with the Zacatín, that fascinating labyrinth of artisans and shops created by the Arabs, where in spite of the sense of *pastiche*, you feel as if you are in an oriental market place. The Zacatín was once the most famous commercial centre: today there are still the workshops of artisans, but these are aimed solely at tourists.

The Pescadería, meaning fish market, besides having fish

stalls, also had vendors of meat and vegetables. It changed its location as the perimeter of the city expanded. Both Arab and Christian authorities called the area *around the Bibarrambla* 'Pescadería' specifying a reference to the streets of the barrio.

Probably Juan searched through this sector for his 'house-hospital' in order to install himself close to the larger *bunch* of beggars, rogues and scoundrels of the city, whom the barrio people called by the derogatory expression *'zurriburri'*. During the day the Pescadería offered a picturesque sight of bustling life; but at night the zone was the haunt of prostitutes and there was no lack of humanity to fill Juan's hospital.

Today the little Calle Lucena lies tucked away just off the Plaza Bibarrambla and is reached by the Calle Capuchinas between Mesones and Pescadería. Nearby, on a humble building, now a guesthouse, is a rather grubby plaque placed there by the City Council over a century ago 'certifying' that *"in this house the illustrious father of the poor, St. John of God founded his first hospital in 1547."* It puts the date in Roman numerals MDXXXXVII, but that does not necessarily mean that this was the exact year.

Possibly the erudite person whom the City Council consulted when it prepared the text for the plaque, wanted to express that this house functioned as the first hospital founded by St. John of God, *"until 1547."* Of course the little house as it is now, is a substitute. The original fell to ruins and was demolished in the late 19th century.

Juan came to this busy barrio of Pescadería on the instructions of Master Avila who had become convinced of the *'hospitaller vocation'* given by God to this 'unusual' disciple who had come into his life after the sermon in the field of Los Mártires.

As was his custom when he went to other cities and villages, Master Avila left behind him a group of disciples, priests and laity, at Granada. These had collaborated with him during his apostolate at Granada between the autumn of 1536, the probable time of his arrival, until the summer of 1539, the year when we saw him departing for Baeza *"taking with him"* our Juan. During this three year period, Avila was only absent from Granada for a short period during the summer of 1537 when he went to Córdoba to attend the funeral of his spiritual daughter, Doña Sancha Carrillo.

Gaining the absolute confidence of Archbishop Gaspar de

Avalos, whose house guest he was, Master Avila developed his apostolate in four areas, namely: catechism for children; pastoral care of college and university students, very noticeably exercising an influence over the development of the university itself; conviviality and spiritual direction of young priests; and indefatigable preaching.

He gave birth to a strong group of disciples, secular and clerical, some of whom we know he sent on missions to universities at Jerez, Coimbra and Evora.

Some priests were so attached to Master Avila that, *"moved by his sermons and discourses"*, they formed *"a school"* with him, a little 'congregation of *worker priests* and holy ones'. (The emphasis on the two words *'worker priests'* does not belong to Father Santiváñez, from whose *'History of the Jesuit Province of Andalusia'* I have taken this reference; it is my own; a little licence which I permitted myself to take, since I am a member of a fraternity called 'Sacerdotes Operarios'. Readers will understand my joy at coming across the term of this apostolic lineage from the times of Master Avila). Fray Luis de Granada noted that *"of the disciples* (of Avila) *there were some who were more familiar with him and who ate at his table in the little refectory he kept."* This was probably in the houses of the Archbishop. In 1537, Archbishop Avalos entrusted the Master with setting up an authentic *"seminary of priests, good students in arts and theology; he gave them a house and a priest as rector."*

To this *"priestly school"* of Master Avila doubtlessly belonged *"Padre Portillo"* whom the Master appointed to be Juan's *"confessor and spiritual father,"* when he sent him back from Baeza to Granada *"where you are called by the Lord."*

To his group of disciples, lay and clerical, Master Avila had confided an apostolic work directed towards the destitute homeless men and women who populated the barrio of the Pescadería.

When he arrived from Baeza, Juan had directions from Master Avila to get in touch with this patrol of his. Knowing the practical mind of Master Avila, it is easy to guess that he had already contacted his disciples and asked them to receive this new 'companion' into their company, explaining to them that, unlike themselves who gave of their spare time, Juan was to dedicate himself exclusively to the work.

The truth is that when Juan entered the Pescadería he found an excellent opportunity for charitable works.

Some of the sons of the Loarte family, of Jewish origin, were members of the 'school' of Master Avila. One of them, Gaspar, was later to become a professor of theology at Baeza University and was also to participate in the Master's tentative explorations for founding a religious order. He eventually became a Jesuit like so many of Avila's disciples.

Juan Loarte, with other companions in the group, motivated by the Master since 1537, set up the service of charitable assistance to the needy in the Pescadería: They came across *"many poor people who perished of the cold as they huddled beneath the porches of the Bibarrambla"*; *"poor people off the streets"*; *"they were hungry, thirsty and cold"*, *"they were ill"* and *"they slept on the construction site of the Major Church"*, the half-built cathedral where the scaffolding provided them with a refuge. There was a shortage of places in the hospitals. No one was surprised that on winter mornings, dead bodies were discovered as the result of the cruel night. Other unfortunates were found dead without anyone knowing *"who killed them."*

Loarte and his companions decided *"to take a house in the Pescadería"* to serve as a refuge for the destitute. *"They put out atocha"*, meaning they spread esparto grass on the floor, *"and had two lamps for light."* These charitable Christians undertook an activity that amazed the priest Benito de los Rios who, as rector of Santa Ana Hospital, was an expert in such matters. He said: *"At nightfall, either personally or being accompanied, they brought into this aforementioned house, all the persons whom they came across in the streets without shelter."*

At first they took up premises *"behind the Star Inn"* on a month's trial. *"Those who were ill and greatly in need, they placed in the aforementioned house to be cared for; and they gave them sustenance there and those who were able to go out to beg alms did so and returned at night to sleep in the aforementioned house; and thus the aforementioned house began."*

The number who went there was great; *"a great multitude of poor and very ill people."* Consequently *"it was necessary to take another much larger house in a street situated at the Pescadería."*

This was as related by the *"licentiate Don Benito"*, who belonged to the Chapter of the Royal Chapel and, for that reason, was perfectly aware of what Master Avila was doing at Granada. We are indebted to him for the emphatic information that Master Avila directed Juan to his disciples at the house in the Pescadería: *"The aforementioned Master Avila, to whom John of God was obedient and had been entrusted, sent him to carry out his charity with the poor people lodged in the aforementioned house."*

Mateo de Santa Cruz, a close disciple, *"was in the company of Master Avila all the time that the aforementioned Master (Avila) was in this city."* He stated that he knew Juan *" before he began doing his charitable works."* This was doubtless a reference to the period when Juan *"was a bookseller"*; and *"from the first time the aforementioned John of God began to give shelter."* He stated that Juan was *"under obedience to Master Avila"*, with whom *"he conversed"* and to whom *"he came to seek advice on how he was to manage."*

Thus it was that the followers of the Master at Granada *"observed"* Juan's activities when he returned from Baeza during the summertime of 1540, the time he began making his *"nightly rounds"* assisting the poor and sharing with them whatever money he earned during the day from the sale of firewood.

This 'keeping an eye' on Juan by Avila's disciples, is clearly reflected in the version of Martín Baeza, a well known merchant who said he saw Juan *"when he used to go about this city and sustained himself by bringing in firewood from the hills, where he went to pray, and the payment they gave him for the aforementioned firewood he gave to the poor."* Martín Baeza spoke thus on the *"incorporation"* of Juan into the *"Pescadería group"*. On a certain day, one of them invited *"John of God, who was going about the city"*, to dine and told him *"that he would serve God greatly if he (Juan) would enter the house (at the Pescadería) to serve the poor there."* It was fitting, for the task that Juan was undertaking showed that he was the ideal one for the group to invite. Our Juan responded saying, with a knowing smile, *"that if a certain person was to say so, he would do it."* Naturally, the *"person"* known to both, was Master Avila. According to Martín Baeza, the whole group agreed with the Master that Juan be sent *"into the house to serve the poor people."* It seems more probable that the business of *"the incorporation"* may have already been worked out between Baeza and his *"Granadino representative"* Padre Portillo, to whom, in his absence, Avila had confided Juan's direction. *"And that is how John of God started working at the Pescadería."*

With the presentation of these facts the logical answer to the question of *"where did Juan go to set up his refuge"* is that he went to the house in the Pescadería where Master Avila's disciples had already set up *"a refuge."* Castro describes the event: *"John of God was determined to truly procure the consolation and healing of the poor. He spoke with some devout persons who had helped him in his work; and with their aid and his enthusiasm, he rented a house at the Pescadería of this city."*

For me this paragraph confirms the contacts Juan had with Avila's disciples, confidential contacts that Castro did not know about. What Juan did, was to accept the responsibility for the house in a Calle Lucena at the Pescadería which had been rented by the *"Avila group."*

It is not for me to denigrate the support of Señor Miguel Venegas, who according to his grandson, continued to give his patronage to *blessed* Juan after the commotion when the poor invaded his porch. The grandson related how Juan, disregarding the feelings of the cook, one day dared to ransack the kitchen of the noble Venegas household, taking the roasts and all the bread. This time there was no row because the Poor Clare nuns of the convent of Santa Isabel la Real, that very day, sent to the Casa Venegas a gift of very tasty pastries and cakes. Consequently Juan's *theft* acquired a miraculous character.

The Venegas family continued to support Juan at his house in the Calle Lucena, and they told their aristocratic friends about the amazing friendship that they had established with the *"charity worker."* In this way a circle of 'protectors' formed: enlarging the "Avila group". They supported the 'first hospital' about to come to life in the Calle Lucena. In only a few months, the effects of Juan's presence had spread through Granada society like an oil spill, smooth but unstoppable, making possible his project of begging alms from the rich to help the poor.

There was an upsurge in enthusiasm: the disciples of Avila later recalled the contagious joy that they felt when they saw the impetus that Juan gave the house in the Calle Lucena; and the prose of the balanced Don Francisco de Castro breaks its bounds in this chapter of the biography, skipping about in wonderment.

The disciples of Avila accumulated a torrent of facts from a variety of memories. *"Juan gathered in the poor"; " had them on some* straw mats there"; " supported them with the alms he collected in the city"; " publicly begged for alms to support the aforementioned poor"; " hired himself out to carry out paid odd jobs " and "the people began coming to his house". Juan also continued the system of nightly rounds that the disciples had previously carried out: "He took out on his own back, the poor, who wanted to go out to beg seeking alms and he brought them back to the house that they might pass the night in shelter."

"Upon his shoulders": It astounded them to see how Juan "began to carry on his shoulders all kinds of poor persons that he found in the city", in and out he carried them and was able to fit in "so many needy persons and provide them with whatever he could." But Juan did not wait for them to arrive, he went looking for them: "He aided the needy and the vergonzantes [persons ashamed by the need to beg] outside the hospital", "the city had many houses of vergonzante women whom he helped with the alms given to him." He carried out these visits "with great love and charity." One of Juan's friends accompanied him and he recorded the delicate manner in which Juan "excused himself when offering alms." He used to tell these "vergonzantes" that "this was given to him out of love of God, so that they might also have it for the love of God."

"In this manner," he took care "of many particular needs and gave much alms, besides sustaining and caring for the poor in his hospital." Thanks to Castro, an excellent historian, we know that Juan worked energetically in the Calle Lucena, but not without a plan.

I am setting out the facts as Castro so fascinatingly describes them from the cascade of recollections.

In effect, the Calle Lucena, on the north-western side of the Pescadería, was an excellent location for "the forsaken poor, the sick and cripples" from all around the Bibarrambla to gather.

Juan found the floor of the house covered with straw and esparto grass, so he used the little money he had "since he had nothing more, nor any other remedy for them," to buy for his sick people "some old blankets and stretchers on which they could sleep."

He begged for alms in the Bibarrambla and beyond. He begged from the stalls in the marketplace where word of the 'hospital-refuge' had already circulated. They gave "each as they were able, willingly and with much kindness: some gave money, others scraps of bread, sometimes a whole loaf, others gave the leftovers of meat and other things from their own tables."

When he had collected *"enough alms"* Juan returned contentedly to the house and, smiling at his poor, said: *"God bless you brothers and sisters, pray to the Lord for those who have been good to you."*

He heated up what he had brought back *"and shared it out with them all."* He wanted to keep the house clean and tidy: *"After having eaten and prayed for the benefactors, on his own he washed the plates and bowls, scrubbed out the pots, then swept and cleaned the house."*

The disciples of Master Avila gave him some help but the running of the house mainly fell upon Juan's shoulders. *"There were still many people who remembered when he was mad and saw how cruelly he was treated and for that reason they did not want to come and help him; and thus he was left to do the work alone.*

What caused him the greatest effort was *"to draw from the cistern two pitchers of water."*

A priest heard him announce to his 'guests': *"Brothers and sisters, give great thanks to God who has waited so long for us to repent; think on how you have offended him. I will bring you a spiritual doctor to cure your souls, for afterwards the body will not lack a remedy. Trust in the Lord, he will provide everything."*

At Juan's invitation, *"Any priest, seeing his great charity,"* would come to the house to hear the confessions of the sick.

The real witnesses to the development of the 'refuge-hospital' which soon became too small, were the destitute: *"because he served the poor with such charity, many came."* *"The house was small and there were so many people that there was barely standing room."* Necessity demanded that a larger house be found, *"because of the reputation of Juan..."* they came in great numbers.

What follows is the testimony of Rodrigo Alonso de Isla, the major-domo of the illustrious judge of the Royal Chancellery, Don Gómez Tello Girón. Don Gómez had heard about Juan, the almsgiver, and maybe even knew him. Down he went through the Zacatín to the Plaza Bibarrambla. It was a cold evening and the freezing north wind which had descended upon Granada made his teeth chatter.

Don Gómez crossed Juan's path and noticed him with his basket slung over his shoulder to collect donations, and said, *"My good man you are feeling the cold, I see you are shivering."* He then removed his cloak saying, *"Take this, it is for you."* Juan thanked him with a smile.

Apparently, the following evening Don Gómez went back to the plaza: *"and when Juan crossed it, he was not wearing the cloak that was given to him."* Don Gómez questioned him, *"And where is your cloak?"* Looking directly into his face, Juan begged his pardon saying: *"Brother, give me another, because I gave that one to a poor man who had a greater need than I."* Don Gómez was greatly moved and promised, *"Tomorrow I will bring you another."* He did so and the two remained friends.

Notes to Chapter 24

* The declarations of Lucía de la O and Luis de Ribera were given at the Granada beatification process. Both women personally knew John of God. Lucía de la O was witness # 54, and Luis de Ribera # 57. There is no trace of the family of Lucía de la O because the records of the parish of San Cristóbal have disappeared. However, we do know something about Luis de Ribera because her grandfather was the apothecary Antón Zabán who was a close benefactor of John of God. According to Matías de Mina, Luis was 93 years of age, not 98 as stated.

* For the Pescadería and its vicissitudes , from the Moslem period until the Christian up to our own days, Cf. A. Gallego Burín *Granada. Guía del viajero,* Granada 1973, 220-273; and J. Belza y Ruiz de la Fuente, Las calles de Granada , Granada s.f., 287.

* The school of Master Avila during his stay at Granada from 1536 to 1539, his life with his disciples, apostolic activities: Cf. L. Sala Balust-F. Martín Hernández, *Obras completas del santo maestro Juan de Avila,* I, op.cit., 68-78. The quotation of J. De Santiváñez, *Historia de la provincia de Andalucía de la Compañia de Jesús* (manuscript, Granada, biblioteca de la Universidad) en L. Sala Balust-F. Martín Hernández, *Obras (ibid)* I, 74. For the work of Avila in colleges, universities and the creation of the seminary, see F. Bermúdez de Pedraz, *Historia eclesiastica, principios y progresos de la ciudad y religión católica de Granada,* Granada 1638, p 4a. C. 58, fol 211. [Translator's note: In Spain, the term 'worker priest', besides its obvious meaning, also means a priest who assists the sick or dying.]

* I consider the relationship of John of God and the disciples of Master Avila in the establishment of a refuge for beggars in the Calle Lucena to be of great interest. Also how this moved on to become Juan's first hospital. The data of this comes from the lawsuit between the Jeronymite friars and the John of God Brothers in 1572-1573: Cf. J. Sánchez Martínez, see *Kénosis-Diakonía en el itinario espiritual de Juan de Dios,* op.cit., 283: 'Apéndice documental' pp 285-420. I have used the quotations of pp. 186, 285, 303, 312, 330, 331, 344, 346, 362, 365, 374, 375, 377, 396, 397, 399.

* The relationship between John of God and the Venegas family according to the declaration of the grandson of Miguel Venegas: beatification process of Madrid, witness # 12, Miguel Avis Venegas.

* Quotations from Francisco de Castro on the first hospital of John of God, see op.cit., chapter 12.
* The episode on Tello Girón is related by witness # 17, Rodrigo Alonso de Ysla, in the lawsuit mentioned above. Cf. J. Sánchez Martínez, op.cit., 410-411.
* On the house in the Calle Lucena in its first months, at the beatification process of Granada, witness #1, (Juan Lobo, a scribe of the city of Granada), and witness #3, (Antón Rodríguez (the porter in the Archbishop's house). Juan Lobo stated: *"Because of the poor who were found dead in the streets, the blessed man took a house in the street called Lucena. From there he went out into the city and looked for the poor sleeping on the ground in the porches of the Plaza Bibarrambla, and the blessed John of God picked them up and put them upon his shoulders and carried them to the aforementioned house. It was there that he began his work. He did not have enough beds, so he carried beds that were donated to him, or he had bought with donations, upon his shoulders. He denied himself food to give it to the poor and for that reason he was very thin and jaundiced."* Antón Rodríguez testified: *"He gathered in many poor and sick people into the house he took. When they arrived he arranged to have them make their confession, then he washed their feet and kissed them. Although at first they slept on esparto grass matting, as soon as he had enough donations, he went out and obtained beds and bed clothing for the poor. The entire city admired the great charity of this servant of God, and they no longer held him to be mad, but a saint."*

25

JUAN SHOUTS THROUGH THE STREETS OF GRANADA LIKE A TOWN CRIER

Granada
1542-1544

Juan, at Granada, bestowed a prestige on almsgiving. His initiative was worthy of a modern marketing expert. It would be difficult to imagine attracting the attention of a city without the press, radio or television. Juan utilised the only instrument then available, proclamation by town crier. He went off, singing out like a street vendor, in quest of alms.

Street hawkers were common in the cities of Andalusia until the middle of the 20th century. They disappeared when our agrarian society began to be transformed into an industrial one. Farm labourers moved their families from country villages and flocked into the big cities. Sadly, many lost their jobs as rural workers only to find themselves unable to obtain employment in industry, many ending up worse off than they were before.

The street hawker generally offered rural products for sale to city families. Their call brought a breath of fresh country air into the city. It was a delightful sound, which I can still hear in my memory. Sometimes their calls resembled the delightful, pious, improvised Andalusian songs called *saetas*. The simple but cunning cadences rose to the street windows like the smell of wet earth, tempting the buyer who could be sure of obtaining a good product.

It is impossible to imagine Juan's catchcry and how he put it to music. I invited a composer friend of mine to do so. *"Impossible"* he said, *"a singing commercial for alms. I've never heard of such a thing.* Usually a request for alms is not shouted, but is spoken quietly, almost secretly. But Juan shouts it aloud, boldly 'asking' for help, but his jingle also promised a reward.

He continued to attract the city's attention to himself, which meant Juan ran the risk of jeopardising his mission. He need not have worried, because his personal manner matched perfectly the Christian sentiments expressed in his catchcry. Granada listened to him, understood the message and gave him assistance.

It is true that he was understood by the wealthy and powerful, those who had money at their disposal. The experts point out that the lives of the ruling class of that time were based on economic platforms similar to those of our own day. It was different on the international scene but the powerful applied the same importance to the investment of money as modern financiers.

At Seville and Granada it was Genoese families, linked to the commercial world and connected with banks of European status, creditors of the Emperor Charles V, who taught the budding Spanish 'capitalists' respect for the potential 'productivity' of their fortunes.

We marvel at Juan's inspiration that enabled him to condense into one spirited 'slogan' the evangelical message of Our Lord Jesus Christ 'for the rich'; accommodating this teaching to the psychology of the wealthy living at Granada.

They were wealthy men and women, affluent. At the same time they were sincere Christian believers. Money meant a lot to them, but they were disquieted by the warnings given by Our Lord Jesus Christ regarding the difficulties the rich encounter in order to enter heaven.

Juan's catchcry resolved the problem by asking them for a 'profitable donation': Give me a part of your earthly treasure for the poor, and I guarantee you a share in heavenly treasure.

Today's testy critical conscience reproaches Juan for soothing the consciences of the well to do by facilitating their access to eternal happiness without resolving earthly injustices. But Juan shrugs this off. It is not his call to organise the French Revolution in the 18th century, nor hasten the Marxist crisis of the 20th. He has to give meals, medicine and bedding to the unfortunates at his hospital in the Calle Lucena. It is for them he appeals. And the donors who give to him can rest assured of having as their guarantor the signature of Jesus in the pages of the Gospel: *"I was naked, sick, hungry... I tell you whenever you did this for one of the least important of these brothers and sisters of mine, you did it to me."*

I recall a rather cruel anecdote. A rich banker and his wife were leaving Sunday Mass. A beggar at the church door approached him pleading: *"Give me an alms sir, Jesus Christ will reward you."* The banker coldly turned away from him, but the beggar insisted: *"Give me an alms sir, Our Lord Jesus Christ and the Blessed Virgin Mary will reward you."* The banker stopped, turned around, and pulling a banknote out of his wallet smilingly said to the beggar: *"Ah, since your request has two signatories that is quite another matter."*

Juan's slogan, *"Who wants to do good for themselves!"* which he shouted and sang echoed through the streets of Granada. As

Castro transmits it, a phrase is added: *"Who wants to do good for themselves! Do good for the love of God my brothers and sisters in Jesus Christ?"*

Various witnesses who heard him repeated the gist of the formula with very slight variations: *"Do well for yourselves"; "Do well for oneself."*

The Book of Sirach reproaches the miser and praises the generous: *"What does gold serve the miser?... Son, before dying, do good to the brothers!"*

Juan asks brothers and sisters on behalf of brothers and sisters, rich brothers and sisters for poor ones. *"Do good brothers and sisters!"* Who could resist an infallible access to the territory of divine mercy: applying mercy to the needy, gaining mercy for ourselves. He offers for alms an unexpected, unsurpassable, profit: the divine gratitude, the thanks of Christ. Later he asks, *"if anyone knows of a better way to make a profit?"*

This man crying out in the streets of Granada amazed all who heard him, appealing equally on hot nights in summer as on freezing ones in winter, and appearing, *"so thin and poorly treated"*; moving those *"seeing him and the austerity of his life."*

Over his shoulder hung *"a large basket"*; and two pots fastened by a cord, ready to accept whatever food was offered to him, shouting all the while *"in a lively and vigorous way."* This impression of him remained engraved in the memory of the Granadinos.

"From the beginning, even when it was raining, he went out at dusk for at that time people were gathered in their homes. They would rush to their doors and windows in wonder to hear this novel method of begging; his voice had an appealing tone, and the virtue which the Lord had given him, touched everyone's hearts."

Above all, children who saw the charity worker were never to forget him as the following testimonies indicate.

Melchor Rodríguez was a 'silk merchant': *"This witness saw the blessed John of God begging for alms for the poor. He was barefooted and his legs were bare as far as the knees. His hair and beard had been shaved by a razor. He wore a woollen garment with sleeves, but it only came down as far as his knees. At night, no matter if it were snowing or raining, he would go out and shout aloud, 'who is going to do good for themselves brothers and sisters!' Over his shoulders he carried a large basket and two pots joined together with a cord."*

The other is already known to us, the little old beggar lady, Lucía de la O, who, with all her 95 years, still kept the memory of *"blessed Juan"* fresh in her mind: *"This witness saw the blessed father John of God more than six-hundred times begging for alms in the city, mostly at night after the* [evening] *prayer; and during the prayer and much later; and other times during the day, feet and legs bare, dressed in a woollen garment, his head and beard shaven with a razor,* [head] *uncovered to the inclemency of the weather; with a basket made of esparto grass in which he placed the bread; and one or two pots tied together in his hand. He called out in a loud voice: 'Brothers and sisters, do good for yourselves!'; and he used to collect many donations."*

It could not have been otherwise. Juan had captivated Granada. These were the same people who only a couple of years ago thought he was crazy, now they were filling his bag with clothing, and pouring victuals into his pots. One after the other, those who saw him testified: *"All who saw him were moved and they gave him many donations"*; *"and as they knew that he put the donations to good use, they gave him all the more, just to hear him was enough to move hearts"*; *"and he collected many alms."* *"They gave him alms very voluntarily, calling to him from the windows"*; *"and in the street this witness saw that they called to him and gave him a tarja."* (A tarja was an ancient form of currency made of vellum, in this case it signified a form of credit with the baker who marked the purchases which were later paid for by a benefactor on Juan's behalf.); *"everyone, knowing his holiness and charity, gave him many donations..."*

I will give you some examples, the first of which is thanks to little Francisca, who as an old lady recalled incidents from her childhood *"when at that time this witness was growing up in the house of the Señor Judge."*

Don Juan de Gamboa was a Basque from the town of Elorrio. He came as a 'royal scribe' [Crown Clerk] to the Chancellery: It is certain that Gamboa lived for a while in the house, known to us as the 'Casa de los Tiros', which Vásquez Rengifo had given to his daughter as a dowry when she married Alonso Venegas. Son of the scribe Don Juan, the Señor Judge, Don Benito López Gamboa, was captivated by the 'charity worker'. *"Little Francisca, gave alms to Brother Juan."* She recalled: *"And this witness herself gave him a real or two or whatever the Señor Judge gave her."*

Friendship was born between the judge and the charity worker: *"Other times he had him come in and they chatted a while and then he gave him a donation and he left; this was almost every day."*

Naturally, the little girl Francisca watched the man whom she regarded as having the aura of a saint: *"He used to go about in his bare feet, and his legs were bare as far as his knees. He never wore shoes, even when it was freezing, and you could stick a finger into the cracks upon his feet. His head was uncovered always and his beard shaven; he was dressed in a woollen garment which had a hood attached and he carried a large esparto grass basket over his shoulders for the collection of donations. He also carried a pot, in which food could be placed, and thus he went out into the streets, especially at night; and as he went about he called out: 'Brothers and sisters, who wants to do themselves some good?'"*

Another very special case is that of the apothecary Antón Zabán. Antón was the grandfather of the little old lady, Luisa Ribera, who at the age of 98 gave testimony with Lucía de la O. She said *"blessed Juan took a house next to the fish market."*

Luisa was between six and eight years of age when her grandfather, Antón Zabán, struck up a friendship with the charity worker Juan: she testified, *"I was a girl of six or eight years."* This seems a major account, because Luisa knows him until his death, when she herself was twenty.

Her grandfather ran the 'Plaza Bibarrambla apothecary shop'. His house was situated in the lane in front of the Major Church, and as his shop faced directly onto the plaza, he knew everybody in the neighbourhood of the Pescadería, including Juan, for the latter frequented this pharmacy to purchase medicines for his patients. The apothecary and Juan soon became friends: *"The grandfather of this witness called to the blessed Juan and every day gave him alms."* The child Luisa admired the figure of Juan, she says that *"I watched carefully what the blessed father was doing; and also I knew and saw many things."*

Among *"the things that she knew and saw"*, Luisa emphasised how Juan *"was given some shirts by charitable persons and he took them away and gave them to the poor."*

Through Luisa we know that Juan found time to spend with the boys and girls of the barrio: *"He taught Christian doctrine to the boys and girls and encouraged them to persevere with it, because it came to them from heaven. He used to say many other holy and good things."*

The two witnesses, Francisca, Judge Gamboa's granddaughter, and Luisa, the granddaughter of the chemist Antón Zabán, told of other amazing things. Juan thought nothing of loading his shoulders with sick people whom he found on the streets and who lacked the energy to walk: he transported them as far as the Calle Lucena.

Francisca: *"This witness saw the blessed father John of God pick up a poor man in the Calle San Jerónimo where the aforementioned Judge lived; and he carried him to his hospital, where he was well cared for and healed.*

Luisa: *"I saw the same thing when the blessed man met some poor person, he lifted him on his shoulders; and this witness saw him carrying such persons to his hospital two or three times."*

Luisa was the first to describe in detail the physical effort it cost Juan to transport his patients upon his shoulders: *"He lifted one to his shoulders so that the feet of the poor man fell to one side and the head to the other. Then with both hands, he seized feet and head, and carried the man bodily upon his shoulders."*

One day Juan had a poor man on his shoulders and, instead of stopping at the apothecary's shop, he went to the back door of his house, *"in the dead-end street,"* in order to collect money. Luisa narrates the touching scene: Antón desired that Juan *"might eat with him, for it was dinnertime and he was already seated at the table."* Since Juan was carrying someone, he excused himself, but later he put the sick man down in the covered porch where the women folk of Antón's household took him a meal: *"blessed Juan gave the food to him and kissed his hand."*

Then Juan went inside *"to eat with the grandfather of this witness."* Antón could hardly believe his eyes, Juan at his dinner table: *"The grandfather said that he esteemed it a greater privilege to have the blessed father as his guest than if he had the King himself there."* After the meal, Juan *"returned to kiss the poor man's hand"* and lifted him up.

Antón Zabán wanted to give Juan the gift of a shirt, *"a good one, so he could put it on and would not go out without it."* Juan accepted it but Luisa followed without him noticing and saw him *"put it on the poor man."*

Besides Francisca and Luisa, a half dozen other witnesses came forward to confirm the manner in which Juan carried the invalids he found in the Pescadería back to his hospital, himself dressed in *"a smock of coarse woollen material which can be bought for four reales"*, *"if he found some poor sick man when he was out begging he would put him upon his shoulders"*, *"if he* [the invalid] *could not walk, he would put him on his shoulders as best he could, and then he would go back to questing for alms"*; *"and this witness saw him lift someone up upon his shoulders, and many by the hand and by the arm, little by little."* Sometimes an ill person was too frail to be carried upon his shoulders, so Juan would put him *"in the basket!"* *"and he carried him to the hospital."*

Don Melchor de Avila showed his annoyance that there could be any suggestion that what he had to say could ever be doubted. He was *"a jurist of the city"* and a highly respected gentleman who showed the wisdom of his advanced years; and *"as he had a good property which sufficed both for himself and all within, he was in no way poor"*, he reinforced his declaration with straightforward words. He explained that Juan: *"If he went out questing and came across a poor sick man in the streets, for at that time there were plenty, and there were not many hospitals, and if the poor man was unable to walk, he would drop everything and pick him up and put him upon his shoulders or take him in his arms and carry him to his hospital."* Thus he stressed the point and nobody doubted it: *"This is what the witness maintains, he saw it, and it took place thus."*

The whole of Granada contemplated the spectacle of the charity worker with his basket and pots; heard his catchcry; saw him gently carrying a sick person on his shoulders, as if he were a scarf; holding the feet with one hand and the head with the other.

(I cannot contain myself, so allow me to skip ahead, even though I will write more about this when Juan is dying. My reflection right now is this: If we fix our gaze for a moment on the pearly gates at the time of Juan's death we will see the look of surprise on St. Peter's face when Juan turns up with an invalid slung across his shoulders. But not to worry, Peter will recognise the poor man's face, as that of the Lord Jesus. Yes, the sick man was Jesus Christ.)

Full of wonder, Granada took Juan as its own and helped him. And what help that was!

The house in the Calle Lucena where Juan unloaded his basket, emptied his pots and settled the patients in, was indeed small. The barrio was jam-packed with poor people.

There was the morning market haulage rumbling throughout the Pescadería; there were strollers and idlers from midday in the Bibarrambla; all day long the clamour of building on the construction site of the cathedral continued, as did the soliciting of the prostitutes; unfailingly, waves of the human undercurrent rolled up to Juan's little hospital.

He did as much as he could, but he was unable to do everything. It was impossible to cover such a broad scope.

He swept the floors, made the beds, shook-out the matting, *"distributed amongst the poor the donations that were given to him"; "he fed them, he comforted them": "And he, having eaten with them, recited prayers, giving thanks to God and for those who had given alms."*

He *"went about so thin and jaundiced,"* although always smiling and happy. This justifies a sound phrase by Castro who assures us it was Juan's stable advice to his followers: *"Brother, whoever serves God is happy, and sad is the one who serves the devil."*

The clergy of the Major Church and the clerks of the archdiocese, whose apartments, until the completion of the cathedral, faced the Plaza Bibarrambla, *"spied"* upon *"the famous"* charity worker. The Reverend Ambrosio Maldonado was able to draw up a short account that was meticulous and carefully prepared. I do not want to rob him of a single syllable, nor compromise his style, so you can see how substantial it was:

"The food that was left over was given to him for the poor. And when someone handed it to him he would put it into the basket he always carried with him saying: 'This is better for the poor,' and thus he carried it away and he returned to beg for more. And he slept little, and it was upon a board with a rock for a pillow. And his activity was always charitable and giving consolation and alms."

I do not think the Reverend Maldonado would be too happy if we took his words to be an exaggeration, for he said: *"What I have said to have occurred I have seen personally, because I conversed and had dealings with the aforementioned Juan."*

Someone asked Juan what was it all about, and he simply replied: *"It is for God that I ask, and it is for God that I give, blessed be God for everything."*

Specific witnesses spoke of the kind of programme with which Juan filled in his day, specifying that mostly he went out at night to bring in the sick: *"He spent most of the day in prayer, housework and making up the beds for the poor, scrubbing the pots, and bringing doctors and confessors into the house. He did many other things like that, as well as questing for alms in order to help the ashamed poor."*

This next account comes to us from a little girl named Francisca Venegas - born at Santa Fe of a simple family with nothing whatsoever to do with the aristocratic Venegases. Once *"she was out shopping with her mother to buy crockery"*:

"The blessed man Juan came along with a poor sick man upon his back, whom he carried upon his shoulders; and he put him down next to the fountain in the plaza, for it was summer. Then he went into the clothing shop and came out with a doublet, trousers and a shirt; and right there where he was, he took off the man's filthy rags torn in a thousand places and as black as soot; and he dipped him into the fountain and washed his body; and dressed him in a shirt, black trousers and a smock. Then he lifted him upon his shoulders again and took him back to his hospital."

With so many of Juan's 'clients' squeezed into the house, two things in particular began to become scarce – space and water. He brought water in pitchers from a cistern which, fortunately, was situated close by at the corner where the Calle Lucena met the Calle Capuchinas. Castro, and many witnesses, remembered that cistern which was of vital importance to the little hospital. The cisterns, from the times of the Arabs until a few decades ago, provided an invaluable service to Granada. Cisterns, public and private, of the Albayzín alone numbered fifty. Today the majority have been sealed off.

As I pointed out above, the city wall extended from the Elvira Gate, skirted around the Plaza Bibarrambla, then joined up with the Royal Gate where it followed the Darro as far as Bibataubín. The gateway that gave access to the Pescadería was called Bib-Almazda. Covered over by the walls within, the gateway was the barrio's cistern utilised by Juan. When the gateway was demolished, the cistern disappeared. However it has re-emerged during recent excavations when its ruins were brought to light.

This tells us that Juan made many trips and obtained water by the strength of his arms. *"He went to draw pitchers of water from the aforementioned cistern which faced the Calle Lucena near the Pescadería."*

However, he could not remedy the lack of space: *"Since the*

house was small, and the people many, there was hardly standing room."
The only solution was to extend the little hospital.

Castro gives an account of the event: *"He rented another and much larger house."* We do not know if Juan had anyone to advise and help him and are not sure if, when he *"rented another and much larger house"*, he abandoned the one in the Calle Lucena. Did he keep both?

Castro seems to indicate that he abandoned the Lucena because, according to him, Juan moved *"all his poor cripples and sick people to the new house."* However, the sense is still not clear, whether he moved, or carried *"upon his back"*, *"all"* his poor and cripples, *"who were unable to walk on their own feet."* What of the rest? Did they walk to the new house or remain at the Lucena?

One fact to take into account: Master Avila preached at Granada in the Major Church in 1542 *"during the octave of Corpus Christi."* He stayed *"some weeks"* at Granada engaged in the restoration work of the convent of the Poor Clares, where the sister of Archbishop Alvalos had arrived as abbess.

During the spring of the same year 1542, Avalos is appointed Archbishop of Santiago de Compostella: maybe his friend Master Avila wished to participate in his farewell. What is certain is that from Lent to Corpus Christi 1542, the Master visited Granada. Did he influence Juan in expanding his little hospital? Surely it was more than likely; thus his disciples confirm it, linking this *"second house"* to the one in the Calle Lucena: *"Since the number of poor people had grown to such an extent that they could not be accommodated in the aforementioned house, the aforementioned Master Avila advised John of God to take another house... which was much larger."*

Several of Avila's disciples were able to indicate the exact position of this *"extension"*: *"At the back door of the Archpriest's residence"*; a sentence that seems to indicate that it, too, was in the area of the Pescadería. The Archbishop's residence opened onto the Plaza Bibarrambla but it does not necessarily follow that the houses of other cathedral dignitaries did likewise – or, for that matter, that they were in the same neighbourhood.

For the opening of the new premises, Juan already had help at his disposal. This was encouraged, without doubt, by Master Avila: since *"he saw how the work was increasing, he endorsed it from the pulpits when he preached."* This explicit support of the Master for Juan's work marks the definitive and unreserved acceptance of the 'charity worker' by Granada's society: including the ecclesiastic hierarchy and civil authorities. Once the *'mad bookseller'*, now *'blessed Juan'*.

Half a dozen society ladies became involved in setting up the new house, which now *"had received the name of hospital"*: *"Already it had doctors and medications, and they spent more on these than all the other hospitals of this city put together."*

Perhaps the enthusiasm of Avila's followers led them to exaggerate the progress. Nevertheless it is certain that Juan was the force behind it: *"Throughout the whole city he begged for donations by day and night. With these he cared for the aforementioned poor."* The dying were assisted, for *"no poor person died without receiving the sacraments."*

Whether or not he left Lucena, or maintained it in addition to the 'extension' of the new house *"at the backdoor of the Archpriest's residence"*, Juan commenced a new stage which was truly 'hospitaller.' His long held desire: *"That Jesus Christ, may bring me to the time and give me the grace that I might have my own hospital,"* will soon be a reality.

15. The Basilica of St.John of God which preserves and honours the relics of St. John of God.

16. La Caridad by Bartolomé Esteban Murillo (1617-1682).

Notes to Chapter 25

* For John of God's catchcry, see Francisco de Castro, op.cit., Chapter 12. Numerous witnesses testified to the slogan: for example, at Granada, # 4 (Melchor Rodríguez), #54 (Lucia de la O), #64 (Francisca de la Fuente), #13 (Felipe de Alaiz), #26 (Domingo Navaro), #40 (Ioan de Salazar)...
* The quotation from the Book of Sirach (Ecclesiasticus) is 14:13.
* The following witnesses were amongst those at the Granada beatification process who testified to John of God carrying sick persons upon his shoulders: # 22 (Luis de Cambil), #13 (Felipe de Alaiz), #52 (Mercía Pérez), #61 (Diego López)... Amongst the many who spoke especially of the basket, I want to point out, # 4 (Melchor Rodríguez), #54 (Lucia de la O), #18 (Melchor de Avila).
* The notices about the doings of John of God in the Calle Lucena, besides those given by Castro, are from the testimony given by the following witnesses: # 22 (Luis de Cambil), #20 (Pedro Camacho), #15 (Lucas de Angulo), #29 (Alonso Sánchez Dávila), #37 (Francisca Venegas).
* For the catchcry of John of God used by the John of God Brothers when they went to Italy, see G. Magliozzi, op.cit., 25. An ancient Italian rhyme dating from 1584 goes as follows:

Vanno per Roma con lo sporto in colla	With basket on shoulder
certi gridano: Fate Bene Fratelli,	through Rome they go
per mendicar gli infirmi poverelli.	'Do well brothers' is their motto.
A questi non vè donna tanto avara	They beg for the impoverished ill.
che non faccia limosina e non sia	There is no woman who lacks the will,
verso di loro liberate e pie.	to refuse to give them a donation
	with willingness and devotion.

* On the statement made by the judge, Gamboa, see Matías de Mina, *Anotaciones*, op.cit., folio 88, (Gamboa). The statement is by Francisca de la Fuente, witness # 64.
* Matías de Mina has researched the background to the apothecary Antón Zabán, grandfather of Luisa Ribera and his research will be treated in the next chapter. Cf. M. de Mina, *Visitar la Granada, etc.*, op.cit., 117; also in his *Anotaciones*, op.cit., folio 230 (Casas de Antón Zabán).
* The phrase *"He who serves God is happy, he who serves the devil is miserable,"* is reproduced from the testimony of witness # 30 in the 'Floreto' of Gómez Moreno, *San Juan de Dios, Primicias historicos*, op.cit., 214.
* Cf. G. Magliozzi, *Pagine juandediane*, op.cit., 208; note 3 states that the John of God Brothers discarded the basket and staff as the emblem of their order because of the objections of the Capuchin Friars, who were recognised in the streets of Italy where they beg with a bag over their shoulders.
* The statement made by Ambrosio Maldonado appears in the records of the lawsuit of 1572-1573 between the John of God Brothers and the Jeronymite Friars: Cf. J. Sánchez, *Kénosis, etc.*, op.cit., 375.
* For the cistern at the Bib-Almazda Gate, see M. de Mina, *Visitar la Granada, etc.*, op.cit., 85. Cf., A. Gallego Burín *Granada. Guía del viajero*, op.cit., 205; the witness at the Granada beatification process, #3 (Antón Rodríguez) speaks of the visits of

John of God to the cistern to draw water.

* On the visit of Master Avila to Granada in the Lent of 1542 and the feast of Corpus Christi, Cf. L. Sala Balust-F. Martín Hernández, *Obras completas del santo maestro Juan de Avila*, I, op.cit., 90-91. The sister of Archbishop Avalos arrived at Granada from Baeza; *ibid.*, I, 91, note 64.

* The advice of Master Avila to Juan about extending the house and the support of the Master's disciples, is recorded in the above cited lawsuit and is reported by J. Sánchez, *Kénosis*, etc., op.cit., (witness Benito de los Ríos) 331-332.

* I am of the opinion that the new house *"at the backdoor of the Archpriest's house,"* is in the same area as the Pescadería, and this seems to be confirmed by the testimony given by Diego Ferrer in the above cited lawsuit: see J. Sánchez, op.cit., 344; also that of the witness Martín de Baeza, ibid,. 171, note 86; *"He took another house near the Biba Almazan (Bib-Almazda) Gate."*

26

ENTERED INTO THE WORLD OF SUFFERING

Granada
1545

Don Hernán Núñez de Espinosa was a handsome young twenty-year-old aristocrat who was well esteemed in the upper circles of Granada society. He was the heir to property worth more than 15,000 ducats and he was in love with a young noble lady. Life was sweet for young Don Hernán. He dressed in finery and participated in many festivities – especially the gala horse events, for he was a distinguished equestrian.

Like all the wealthy folk of Granada, Don Hernán heard the *catchcry* and the news of the *"charity worker who had set up a hospital in the Pescadería."* He decided that it would be good to take a donation to Juan, *"so that – on the eve of his wedding – Our Lord God might guide his forthcoming marriage."* Don Hernán even wanted to outdo *"the leading citizens in the city"* who were giving alms *"to the blessed man Juan, who had a great name in regard to charity."*

Joking with his friends, Don Hernán planned to put the charity worker's virtue to the test. He disguised himself as a poor man and went out to appeal for aid. Where would he find him? He spent some time begging alms at the Las Tablas Gate, a name they gave the Bib-Almazda not far from the Pescadería, because it was here that there were *"ten open air tables"* where butchers sold sheep and goat meat. The young scamp dressed as a workman.

We know the details of this ingenuous youthful piece of mischief thanks to the report of one of his nieces, Gracia de Espinosa. She told how *"her holy uncle, the priest Don Hernán"*, had an encounter with the charity worker that brought about in him an uneasiness that finally left him no longer engaged to his *"very high class"* lady.

"And going up to the blessed man, he said to him: *'Brother John of God, I am a man who has a great need, and if I do not find a solution, I fear falling into despair: I have to find no less than two hundred ducats. Since I can not let anyone else know, I have dared to come secretly to ask your help."* In short, the mendicant *'vergonzante'* begged Juan for 'confidential' assistance. Two hundred ducats, asked for openly on the street corner!

Juan consoled him and arranged to meet him there the following day: *"I give myself to God, brother, I have not got so much money. But God will give. Be at ease and do nothing rash, for God will provide. Wait for me here at nine o'clock tomorrow and God will have for you what is necessary to solve your necessity."*

Young Don Hernán thought it was very odd that this

extraordinary charity worker could possibly be capable of bringing along 200 ducats. So he prepared his response to Juan's goodness by putting *"two hundred ducats in a linen purse"*, the exact quantity he had begged, *"half in gold and half in silver."*

The following day he turned up for the appointment and found Juan at the Las Tablas Gate: *"He asked him if he was able to bring what he needed."* Juan replied: *"Yes, of course, and it is all here in a purse."* Don Hernán embraced him: *"Brother Juan, how great is God! I am not coming for a donation but to give one!"*

"And he brought out the linen purse holding the two hundred ducats and gave them to him. He then asked if they could go together to his hospital, for he wanted to give an account of his life: and the blessed Father threw his basket over his shoulder, and the two went off together..."

Don Hernán dedicated his donation *"so that Our Lord God might guide his marriage;"* Juan *"promised him that he would commend him to God."* Having been to the hospital *" the aforementioned Don Hernán went on his way."*

Juan's prayers and friendship altered the direction of this young gentleman's life, for he joined the group of Master Avila's disciples: *"From then onwards he was concerned for his salvation. He did much good for the poor in distributing his wealth to them; giving the greatest part of it to the blessed father John of God; to whom he attributed his conversion and with whom he discussed whether to be ordained and to pursue his studies."*

"Master Hernán Núñez" became a priest and in his day was held to be *"a learned and holy man"* one who *"from being a rich man came to live off alms"*. So little did he eat that, many years later, when the Archbishop asked Master Avila for a preacher for the Alpujarras the latter replied that he had chosen him *"a good man, Don Hernán Núñez"*: who would not be costly *"because each day he eats a few crumbs and a salad."*

Thus ends the joke that the elegant young man played on *"blessed Juan."*

Many *"prominent and honourable"* persons supported the growth of the new hospital with their good will and their donations, helping the work of the indefatigable alms-seeker: *"He began to establish a good reputation with all, and they gave him many of the things that he needed for the poor, and they gave him more than the usual alms - blankets, sheets, mattresses and clothing."*

Juan began to feel weary, but he was sure of himself and happy. One night, when he was returning home after a hard day, he came across a group of excited people standing around a dead man, making a fuss about 'someone' having to bury him. Juan went to a mansion in the Horno de Marina. There he set the cadaver down in the doorway and said, face to face, to the miserly noble of that house that: *"Brother, you have just as much an obligation to bury him as I do."* Alarmed, the rich man paid for the burial.

That is why to this day, in remembrance of Juan's 'slap of irony', we continue to call the Salazar palace the *'House of the Dead Man'*. However, it is more likely to have been one of the neighbouring family mansions, for the Salazar family was among the noble Granadinos who supported Juan and enjoyed his confidence:

"Doctor Alonso de Salazar, advocate of the Royal Audience, was a man of great letters, and because of this he received many big fees and was very wealthy and learned."

For this data on Salazar we are indebted to a law student who resided at the guesthouse run by Ana Flores who as a young lady, served as a maid in the Salazar home. The student admired Dr. Salazar who held the office of *'oidor'*, which corresponded with that of magistrate at the Chancellery.

This is not the first *'oidor'* of the Chancellery who had dealings with Juan and protected him. Previously we had Gamboa, now we come across Salazar. In the Chancellery, under the authority of a president, there were four magistrates for each of the four courts, amounting to sixteen magistrates in all. They dressed in distinctive robes and, of course, were highly respected.

The *oidor* Salazar, besides being a distinguished jurist, was *"a man of virtue and great charity"*: *"Blessed Juan often went to the house of Doctor Alonso de Salazar, where he was greatly esteemed and often given alms."* The Salazar family gave Juan this warm welcome because they were certain that the charity worker *"distributed to the poor with great charity"* everything he received – the money, food and clothing.

When benefactors visited Juan's house-hospital they saw *"established wards and patients"* (Castro); meaning, Juan was carrying out a work of organised assistance. It was very demanding to divide his energy between the running of the house and going out in quest of alms.

Inevitably people began to attribute to him apparitions and bizarre miracles: *"He who was, at first, taken to be mad was later regarded as a saint, a man of God"*, was the somewhat ironic comment of the old gentleman Pedro López de Eslava when he was interrogated by the judges of the beatification process. Old Pedro, as a child, saw blessed Juan *"even before he wore the habit"*:

"He wore very rough linen pants and a loose smock, open at the sides, which came down to his knees; the legs and feet bare; the beard and head were usually cut by a razor; no hat, nor cloak nor anything else; rain and snow; and in the scorching August heat."

Until he *"changed the habit"*, many witnesses recalled that he wore a *'capotillo'*, or short loose jacket open at the sides. According to the Covarrubias dictionary, there were *'capotillos'* of various types; the most common, the one Juan would have worn, was called *'de dos faldas'* [of two skirts, or two lapping sections]: *"A loose jacket open down both sides and covering the back and front, with an opening in the middle of the two skirts for inserting the head; it has some loose sleeves which can be folded to the shoulder when required."* The baggy breeches called *'zaragüelles'* were short pants made of *"burlap or coarse linen"* which came from France or Flanders and could be purchased cheaply.

The doings and sayings of the charity worker began to circulate throughout Granada. Sometimes they were accurate but on other occasions they needed to be checked out, like the events at Vargas. In reality the little Plaza Vargas served as the setting for Juan's meeting with two classes of demons: one ghostly, the other of flesh and blood.

One night Juan was returning from begging in his old barrio around the Elvira Gate. From a tavern staggered half a dozen drunken men who had been trying to satisfy their hunger with glasses of wine: *"Brother Alms-seeker, give us something to eat so that we won't die of hunger: we are out of work and famished as it has been raining for days."* They were doubtless carriers who hired themselves out and Juan possibly knew some of them from his book selling days. They ransacked his basket *"which he was carrying full of bread and other things..."* Thus he arrived back at the hospital that night empty handed.

Catalina de Arenas, who related this episode of the tavern, also tells how once she saw blessed Juan *"give three bread buns and two reales to a young manservant who was unemployed."* Juan took the young man to a shop and *"bought him some rope sandals and half a pound of cheese."*

There are unanswered questions, too, about who did the hospital housework. One day after Juan arrived home, emptied his basket and pots, and picked up the pitchers and went off to fetch water from the cistern. When he returned, he found the floor swept and the cleaning all done. He asked the patients who had done it and they said that nobody had. Later, it was said that angels did it – it had been noted that a couple of ladies came in without any fuss and scrubbed the pots, swept the floor, and then went on their way.

There was another odd and spectacular incident, one night, of a *"glow or fire,"* about which opinions differed: *"The poor people shouted that there was a fire in the house, so the patients got out of their beds calling out 'fire', 'the house is on fire!'" !"* ....

However, everyone heard the voice of *"blessed Juan"* calling out *" be at ease, it is already over."* The following day the lady friends of the hospital arrived and were unable to see any traces of a fire for, oddly, *"there were no ashes".* They wondered *"if a radiance shone forth from the blessed man..."*

We will return to a disturbing encounter in the little Plaza Vargas. Sometimes the demons bring the stench of sulphur into the complexities of Juan's Granada.

Today, European theologians comment with a certain sarcasm on the "constant presence" of demons in the religious life of Spain. As far as I am concerned, I have to confess that I too am somewhat disconcerted to see how the demon and his hordes chose to set up camp here in the 16th century so as to scare the living daylights out of my countrymen. When I was a young student I once attended a conference given at Munich University by that extraordinary researcher of Spanish spirituality, Sala Balust. He presented some valuable information regarding the relationship between John of God and Master Avila. He also presented the students with the teachings of the distinguished Professor Schmaus of Munich University. Afterwards, while commenting on the conference, Schmaus smiled and said: "Sala Balust's conference surprises you because he comes from Spain, a country where the devil is always at war."

I now wonder if he really was saying "a country where the devil lives?" The young students all applauded and laughed, I think somewhat unjustly; did not the devil drag Brother Martin Luther down by his broad cloak?

These days there is a dearth of documentation to justify any scientific revision of the 'satanic phenomena' of the 16th century with all its magic, hysteria and fakery. In his study of Spanish society during Spain's Golden Age, Fernández Alvarez states that "every one believed in those things, starting of course, with the possessed. The very air seemed to be full of demons; they were given determined intentions, and one saw them as always ready to intervene in the world of man, to disturb him both in things great and small."

It was inevitable that an extraordinary person like Juan the charity worker, whom Granada was beginning to credit with an aura of sanctity, should begin to have clashes with the Devil.

Castro assures us that Juan's *"battles"* with the devil *"were many, invisible and visible."* The first battle of half a dozen or so encounters took place in the little Plaza Vargas. We know of it from the testimony of Antón Rodríguez who was the porter at the Archbishop's residence. This old man expressed his veneration of John of God with these words: *"I hold him as a saint, if only I might be like his shoe."*

The municipal papers of Granada do not show a Plaza Vargas. This was the popular name given to the little space in front of the palace of the Vargas family. They lived near the street running along the banks of the Darro before purchasing the Salazar home in the Horno de Marina, which we know as the 'House of the Dead Man'.

The Vargas family, who were people of highborn lineage, included members who belonged to the *"Council of Twenty-four"* and the *"Knights of Santiago."* Antón Rodríguez only says that on many nights Juan *"was occupied in begging for the poor"*, and *"he was frightened twice by the devil."*

The first chapter of a war that would take in *"many battles"* has no explanation. Antón simply ended his declaration of the event: *"This witness knew that some robbers fell upon him (Juan) and stole his purse full of money."* So, was the diabolical fright provoked by a *mugging* by thugs? Demons indeed, but ones of flesh and blood?

It could be. But Granada was already buzzing with the news: that devils had openly attacked Juan the charity worker. They will cause him much mischief.

By tenaciously squeezing the paragraphs of Castro and the memories of the witnesses of this 'second epoch' of Juan in the barrio of the Pescadería we get a glimpse of the careful organisation that will soon become his hospital.

I write 'second epoch' or stage, 'of Juan in the barrio', and do not write 'his second house'. On the advice of Master Avila, Juan took another place *"at the backdoor of the Archpriest's residence,"* but I am not convinced that he abandoned the first house in the Calle Lucena. They seem to be in some way linked, like two dependencies of the same enterprise, 'his hospital'.

Conserving or not the linkage with the Calle Lucena, we perceive in this 'second hospital' the atmosphere of a house that functions at full efficiency. I am unable to give any documentation in regards to the distribution of people seeking 'refuge' by day and night as some biographers have indicated. However, the sick occupied the upper floor, the transients, by day or night, occupied the ground floor as a 'refuge'. This concept was certainly the brainchild of Juan for Granada.

The need for order was clearly seen. Attention to cleanliness, organisation of meals and sleeping arrangements for the night, time to pray in common, visits from doctors and priests to hear confessions are all to be, more or less, on a regular basis.

Medical historians describe the movement of patients who frequented European hospitals at that period. It would have been similar for those who came to Juan's hospital. Many would have been sufferers of syphilis whose grim appearance took on widespread proportions towards the end of the 15th century when the French army set siege to Naples, thereby giving it the epithet, *Morbus Gallicus*, the 'French disease'. This plague fell like a curse upon Europe from the turn of the 15th century. There are those who attribute it to American origin, but in fact the *buboes* continued to be called 'the French disease'. Writers of the epoch describe how *"the pustules first appear in the pubic area, then spread all over the skin of the body"* with terrible open pustulation of chancres and ulcers. They warned that contagion was spread through sexual intercourse; consequently, civil authorities ordered that hygienic precautions be taken in brothels, but it is doubtful whether this had any effect. Treatment was long-term and costly, and while the wealthy aristocracy of the court could be treated in their private mansions, the hospitals for the poor not only lacked skilled doctors but they also had very little in the way of medications. Syphilis was generally treated by applying a 'Saracene ointment' which was a high dose of mercury mixed into a fatty base. It was intended that by applying this as a hot poultice, the mercury would reach deep down into the affected areas.

An appalling lack of hygiene was prevalent among the poor and 'shelterless' whose clothing was filthy and who slept in the streets open to every manner of purulent contagion. In those times tumefaction and other diseases of the skin were undifferentiated and fell under the generic label of 'leprosy'.

We must not identify hospitals in Juan's day with our concept of a hospital, with installations under the direction of a chief medical officer who heads a team of doctors, nurses and technicians. Such medical services did not exist and the visits of doctors to poor patients were only done out of charity. Evidence shows they came when Juan called them and he paid them with money he collected through alms.

There was a tremendous social upheaval at the turn of the 15th century due to outstanding events such as the discovery of the New World, ocean voyages to the Orient, the diffusion of the printing press, the rediscovery of the ancient classics setting the way to freedom of thought. However, progress in public welfare and hospital care came much more slowly. Fortunately Juan's visit to Guadalupe had impressed on him that hospital reform could not be obtained by mere material means alone. He added the tenderness of a loving father. Juan heads the litany of hospitaller giants such as Camillus de Lellis and Vincent de Paul.

Juan relied upon two special helpers during these years at the Pescadería.

The first was a paid helper. This was a wise choice: to have a young man to accompany him in the street and to mind the house during his absence. One who was trustworthy and reliable and who stayed with him to the very end. His name was Juan de Avila which, by coincidence, was the same name as Master Avila. To avoid any confusion, Juan gave him the nickname 'Angulo' so we will call him this also. We do not know the reason for the choice of this nickname nor whether others, besides Juan, called him Angulo.

Angulo had just turned 30 when, in 1544, he first came to know our Juan and entered his service. He has left us the first impression that Juan made upon him: *"He was a man of great penitence and holy life. He used to go about this city dressed in sackcloth with a hood, and his feet were bare. He carried a basket over his shoulders for begging alms."*

Angulo was a bachelor at this time but he married a few years later in the spring of 1549. Juan took him on as 'a salaried worker', not as a disciple. He enjoyed the absolute confidence of his employer, as we will see in notable circumstances. Juan referred to him affectionately as *"my companion"* and they became great friends. He was an exemplary employee and deserved to be called Juan's friend.

The apothecary of the Plaza Bibarrambla was his other special helper. We have already met Antón Zabán, the grandfather of Luisa Ribera.

I have mentioned that the Zabán house had two entrances. The back door, which was usually used by the household, led onto the dead-end street facing the 'Major Church' at the side of the Archdiocesan residences; while the front door of the pharmacy opened onto the Plaza Bibarrambla.

This pharmacy of Antón Zabán was the centre of much activity since it was situated right in the centre of the popular neighbourhood from the Zacatín to the Pescadería.

The history of medicine presents some curious facts in regards to pharmacopoeia at this time. Ointments held prime importance and apart from being applied to wounds, were also rubbed into the skin in order to penetrate and relieve internal pain. Next in popularity came the herbal remedies, which these days we call folk remedies. There were many persons who came to Juan's hospital with suppurating sores and open wounds. Scratching, in an effort to soothe the itching caused by lice, caused much of this injury. An application of ointment gave some relief. The apothecaries were experts in the field of herbal medicine. The pharmacist did not follow an academic course – he learned his profession by traditional methods. Nor did he need prescriptions from doctors from which to mix his potions – he could respond to the consultation of his client.

Antón and his pharmacy extended valuable assistance to Juan. Our friend, Brother Matías de Mina, has carried out an extensive research into the name of the Zabán family, delving into the parish archives of Granada. He has come up with some very interesting facts. Antón was a *"rich man who favoured Juan with donations and his friendship."* He was a *'New Christian'*, which doubtlessly meant he was a Moorish *Converso*. He appears as godfather at various baptisms. He was more or less about fifteen years older than Juan, which means that he must have gone through the trauma of the reconquest of Granada. He attributed his willing conversion more to the kindness of Fray Hernando de Talavera than to the constraint imposed by Cisneros. He is one of the professionals who linked Arab culture to the Christian and were installed at the Plaza Bibarrambla, a prime key position of the city. Our little friend Luisa was the only child of his daughter Leonor who was married to Luis de Ribera (probably a clerk at the Chancellery). She said: *"I always felt attracted by the things of John of God"*, to whom *"my grandfather, Antón"*, showed such great esteem. Luisa, during the period at the Pescadería, was a *"lass of fifteen years"* and she kept her eyes wide open when Juan came into her grandfather's pharmacy and home.

Change had come to the archdiocese of Granada: Avalos has been appointed Archbishop of Santiago de Compostella. Juan relied much on episcopal benevolence which, fortunately, had been assured by his relationship with Master Avila who was respected by everyone and who, it was said, had refused a mitre. The clergy of Granada expected that he would end up as Archbishop of Granada. Certainly, Master Avila held the noteworthy Archbishop as his friend and adviser.

The new Archbishop, Hernando Niño de Guevara, was the son of noble Castilians and well regarded by the Emperor who nominated him, in the autumn of 1539, to be Bishop of Orense. He had been residing at Granada since the Christmas season of that same year: Charles V ordered him to preside at the Chancellery.

Thus an anomalous episcopal situation was produced at Granada. The diocese had its own Archbishop who during these recent years was, as we have seen, Gaspar de Avalos. However, another bishop resided in the city, exercising the presidency of the Chancellery of Granada.

The Emperor frequently had bishops appointed as presidents of the Chancelleries of Valladolid and Granada. Certain ecclesiastics, as well as Master Avila, denounced the inconveniences of such an episcopal presence in civil matters but Charles V was reluctant to renounce the services of intellectual bishops.

The transfer of Avalos to Santiago presented a golden opportunity to combine in the person of Niño de Guevara, who had already spent two years at Granada as the president of the Chancellery, the two offices of Archbishop and Chancellery President.

We will see that this solution did not last long because Niño de Guevara soon desired to return to his native Castile. In the meantime we have him here at Granada in the top positions of ecclesiastic and civil life from the spring of 1542: *"For to be President of the Chancellery, the reception ceremony took place in the Plaza Nueva, and not at the Bibarrambla where other bishops had received such homage"*: The Plaza Bibarrambla was close to the incomplete cathedral, and besides, the Archbishop's residence 'provisionally' faced this plaza.

To tell the truth, the appointment of Niño Guevara only had a temporary solution to the twofold ecclesiastic command of Granada through one prelate alone; but it was a pity that a certain Augustinian friar renounced the mitre: Tomás de Villanueva, whom Charles V greatly admired, refused to go there. Two years later, the same Fray Tomás agreed to become the Archbishop of Valencia where he also became a saint. Fray Tomás and our Juan would have been seen together at Granada.

For the Emperor Charles these years between 1540 and 1545 were difficult ones. No doubt about it, Charles I of Spain and V of Germany, was indeed the most powerful ruler on earth. He was master of an empire on a universal scale. The young men of Castile and Aragon, never to return, are showing the imperial banner on far-off horizons: Flanders, Germany, Italy and America, leaving behind them only a trickle of glory. Besides taking their sons, the Emperor squeezed money from the Spanish families.

Rightly or wrongly, Spain pushed ahead as long as the harvests were good. The 'barren years' brought disaster in the form of a harsh drought. The decade 1540-1550 was afflicted by dry years. The Emperor showed no sign of being overwhelmed by setbacks, he seemed to be superhuman. To make matters worse, the Turks had come overland and had attacked the Hungarian border; and Berber pirates were assaulting the Italian coastline of Calabria. Lacking soldiers, the Emperor Charles alone could not repair the breaches opening up all around Christendom. Pope Paul III wanted Charles to sign a peace treaty with King Francis I of

France who, every spring, felt the temptation to ally himself with the Turks. United, the Pope, the Emperor and the King of France would be able to accomplish the two great tasks needed to stabilise Europe, one military, the other spiritual. The military one was to make a definitive battle against the Turk, Sulieman, in the waters of the Mediterranean. The spiritual one was to convene the desired ecumenical council to heal the rifts in religious unity produced by Brother Martin Luther in Germany and by Henry VIII in England.

Granada, favoured by water, was saved from the disaster. The drought spread waves of famine throughout Castile.

Juan had given up his right to privacy to live in the public eye. He was seen constantly by the sick who were welcomed into his hospital, the poor people he assisted in the streets and the benefactors who helped him.

They saw him as happy, obliging and absorbed in his daily and nightly mission, sacrificing himself in a way that would frighten any 'normal' person. They saw his charitableness, boundless and absolute generosity as he begged alms and then distributed them to the first person that extended an imploring hand. Given a shirt or cape he would hand them on to any beggar to wear, even removing his own clothes to do so. They saw him at prayer, very close to God and absorbed in His mysterious presence. Juan did not help the poor in the 'stand-offish' way that we might have as we cast a few coins while passing down the street to continue on our way; Juan 'introduced himself' into the sphere of the poor; 'he lives' with them, he belonged to them.

I have spent a lot of time in examining the sensitivity of both John of God and John of the Cross and there is a notable parallelism between them.

No sooner had John of the Cross become immersed in the cloud of mysticism than he *withdrew* into the area of language, poetry, and mystical descriptions: with the idea of showing his readers the way that leads from the plain of the common existence to the mountain top.

John of God, after seeing things as they really are on the field of Los Martíres, 'withdrew' to the area of charity, of mercy, of service to the suffering: with the idea of showing us, who contemplate his adventure, the beautiful service of love.

Both were aware of the closeness of God and permeated by

the mysterious dew of His grace. Both were witnesses.

How appropriate it was that Granada ['pomegranate'], became the backdrop for Juan's charitable activity. It was as if a bursting *granada* had splattered its blood-red seeds to leave their indelible mark upon his heart.

Juan calls his hospital 'the House of God'. While just a little hospital, it is God's house, because each time he admits a sick person he is accepting Jesus Christ.

Notes to Chapter 26

* The statement about Hernán Núñez was given by Gracia de Espinosa who was witness # 11 at the Granada beatification process. She said she did not personally know John of God, but was relating what her uncle the priest Hernán Núñez had told her about himself. See M. De Mina, *Visitar la Granada, etc.,* op.cit., 91. For the remarks made regarding the *Oirdor* Salazar by the student Ferdinand Alvarez de Sotomayor, witness # 2 at the Lucena beatification process; Ibid., 110.

* Pedro López was witness # 8 at the Granada beatification process.

* Catalina de Arenas, witness # 56 at the Granada beatification process, was the daughter of the stone mason Bartolomé de Arenas *"who worked upon the Royal Hospital in this city,"* and also knew every detail of what was happening about the Elvira Gate. It was he who told her the story of Juan and the half a dozen drunks.

* The story of how the hospital was mysteriously cleaned in Juan's absence was well known at Granada, and was mentioned by the witnesses #3 (Antón Rodríguez), #13 (Felipe de Alaiz), #69 (Bartolomé de Fueros); other witnesses spoke about the *brilliance* or fire, #53 (Catalina de Contreras), #54 (Lucia de la O) #55 (Juana de Gálvez), #56 (Catalina de Arenas), #57 (Luisa de Ribera).

* The references to the diabolical attack and the robbers in the Plaza Vargas was cited by witness #3 ((Antón Rodríguez). Facts about the Vargas family, see M. De Mina, *Visitar la Granada, etc.,* op.cit., in the section on the *Anales de Granada* by Henríquez Jorquera, 103,104.

* For the hospitals, the sick and medicine of the epoch, see P. Laín Entralgo, (ed.) *Historia universal de la medicina,* IV, Barcelona 1973; also Ludwig Ruland, *Gespraeche um Johannes von Gott,* Würzburg 1947.

* 'Angulo', Juan de Avila, was called to give testimony in the lawsuit between the Jeronymite friars and the John of God Brothers. He was witness #1; see J. Sánchez, *Kenosis, etc.,* op.cit., 300. Matías de Mina has made a very fine research into Angulo and his family; see his *'Anotaciones', Fondo Documental,* op.cit. For the word 'Angulo', see G. Magliozzi, *Pagine juandediane,* op.cit., 496; this author makes an ingenious guess at the meaning behind the nickname: *"Maybe it was jokingly given to him along with his job at the hospital where he was a sort of majordomo, having in mind the Angulo who was quartermaster of the imperial army of Charles V at that time."*

* For the information about Antón Zabán and his grand daughter Luisa de Ribera, see M. De Mina *'Anotaciones', Fondo Documental,* op.cit., folios 'Zabán' and 'Luisa de Ribera'.

27

JUAN AND THE PROSTITUTES OF GRANADA

Granada
1545

Juan was summoned by the Archbishop. Don Hernando Niño de Guevara wanted to know why he was distributing alms to all sorts of persons without first determining who they were and if they were honest. The Archbishop had been informed that ruffians and prostitutes were deceiving Juan.

Juan frequently came to the Archbishop's palace to ask for various commodities and I am quite sure that they were given to him. Juan had struck up a friendship with the Archbishop's butler, Rodrígo Alonso, who has told us: *"sometimes he asked for chickens at the house of the aforementioned Archbishop, since they were given when he requested."*

Rodrígo admired Juan's work: *"Besides caring for the patients in the hospital at the Pescadería, this witness is aware that he also supplied many other necessary items to particular homes of persons who were too ashamed to beg, and he helped them with alms."* So it appears that Rodrígo happily gave Juan other items of food besides the occasional episcopal chicken.

However, Don Hernando Niño was anxious to know whether it was true that Juan distributed alms anywhere to anyone who asked him: including prostitutes.

The Archbishop sent for him and said that, *"he should look well to whom he gave alms."* Juan replied: *"They ask me for the love of God."*

Don Hernando Niño looked at him in surprise, not expecting Juan's straightforward response which explained to him his clear theory of charity: *"For this, things are given to me, and I have to share them; they ask me for the love of God, that is why I give."*

"And what if they are lying and deceiving you?"

"They should see that they are deceiving themselves, for it is not me they deceive when asking; since I am giving to all, for God."

After that the Archbishop no longer cared what happened to his chickens.

Juan had a fixed reply for anyone who reproached him with: *"Brother, look to whom you give."* It was, *"Ponder what God says about never turning your face away from anyone."*

Juan had heard this quotation from the prophet Isaiah in some sermon. Thus, he Juan *"gave to all,"* saying: *"I do not have to see why I give or to whom, but for whom it is asked."*

Granada showed itself to be generous with Juan. He had won over the city: the poor saw him as a protector, while the rich had been completely captivated by his catchcry, *"Do good for yourselves, brothers and sisters."* Above all, it was his compassion that attracted people. Juan Lobo was a lad of fifteen when these incidents occurred and he saw how his parents insisted that Juan enter their home: *"Some nights when it rained excessively he passed by on the street and the home of this witness; and out of respect for the friendship they had for the blessed man, John of God, they were moved with compassion and called him inside."* Juan resisted: *"and did not want to enter; so they asked him to come inside for the love of the Lord; so in he came, head, beard, body and his legs, all bare and soaking wet."* The family made a big fuss about drying him out, but Juan jokingly called his body *"a donkey."*

"They pleaded with him, out of love of Our Lord, that he might take a morsel of preserved fruit to make up for the great discomfort, but he did not: saying that because of its sins, this donkey did not deserve such a gift."

This made a lasting impression on the boy Juan Lobo: *"Thus, as the aforementioned maintains, he used to go about barefooted in the drenching rain or snow; with great fervour and attention to his poor people."* His constant appeal was: *"That they would send things through him to the poor."* His little donkey *"did not deserve a gift."*

This familiarity with the Lobo family demonstrates the extent to which Juan had entered into the social fabric of Granada; we see him become part of the city scene. The Lobo boy was the son of *"the lawyer Juan Lobo and his wife Leonor de Páez"*, who lived in the precinct (parish) of Santiago, certainly in a house close to the court of the Inquisition to whose juridical body the lawyer probably belonged. They were one of the many families, well off or aristocratic, who admired, welcomed and helped the *"blessed charity worker."*

One of Juan's activities shocked his wealthy friends and also perturbed Master Avila. Nothing would stand in the way when he went to help the needy. Juan discovered that the city's prostitutes also needed help.

He came across them everywhere he went – in the streets and at the doorways of the brothels. At this period Granada's red-light section extended in a curve from the Puerta Bib-Almazda on the western side of the Pescadería, avoiding the Plaza Bibarrambla, to the Puerta Bibataubín where the Darro meets the Genil.

The prostitutes plied their trade between the Puerta Real and the Puerta Bibataubín: from there dozens of prostitutes scattered their presence about the densely populated neighbourhood of the Pescadería; and at nightfall occupied the Plaza Bibarrambla.

Since the days of the Catholic Monarchs the section of Granada around the barrio of Bibataubín was popularly called *El Campillo* [the little field]. Today the Municipal Chambers are situated there and it has the sonorous name Plaza Mariana, after Mariana Pineda y Ganivet. It was once the site of a citadel dependant on the mayor of the Alhambra. Scholars say the name Bibataubín means *'of the hermits'*, alluding to the Moorish hermits who lived there outside the city gate. But, in fact, the area belonged to brigands, villains, and the pimps of the prostitutes of the locality; the citadel was a barracks for soldiers.

As I strolled through this part of the city which was 'laid out' towards the end of the 16th century by the architect Ambrosio de Vico, a jolting thought struck me. I began to wonder how 'blessed Juan', besides doing all that he was doing for the sick and the poor from his base at the Pescadería in the city centre, still found the time and energy to come down here to the Puerta Real and the Bibataubín to become involved among the labyrinth of brothels. It seemed to him little enough to help the prostitutes who went up to the Bibarrambla, but now he goes down to the warren of brothels. I can well understand how this disturbed Father Portillo enough to inform Master Avila about it. And that Avila would write to his 'venturesome' disciple:

"Keep on your guard regarding the women you are bringing back to God's service. They are turning out to be quite a hindrance and expense to you. It would be better not to keep them there unless they get married promptly or find domestic work with respectable ladies. Otherwise they are going to be lost and all that you have done for them would collapse to the ground."

Prudent and wise advice, because Juan was daring to take on too much. Just see what the witnesses relate: *"This witness lived in the neighbourhood of the public houses, and saw at that time..."*

Melchor Rodríguez, silk merchant, was known for his shop in the Zacatín: 'Melchor the Clothier'. His wife's name was María

Ruiz. While his shop was in the Zacatín, his residence was close to the red light district, probably near the Puerta Real.

As a boy of about ten or eleven years of age *"I saw"* the alms seeker and heard the comments of the barrio: How could he ever forget as an adult, the daring activities of *blessed* Juan? *"He converted the aforementioned public women and found husbands for them and made them good."*

News of Juan going into the brothels rapidly circulated all over Granada. The charity worker and his hospital were accepted by all as providing a public and religious service. They even considered him as being delegated by the community to clean up its unfortunates. But now he is mixing with prostitutes, provoking consternation and scandal. Later, there will be admiration.

Juan was to confront the social abandonment of the unfortunate women constrained to the segment of the city walls between the Puerta Real and Bibataubín. It was outside his hands to solve the economic gap between the rich and poor, nor did he have the means to eliminate from human history this permanent blemish of prostitution. He did all he possibly could, listening to the sad stories and giving economic assistance where it was accepted.

At first Juan was thought to be just another one of the rough types who came in from the taverns to frequent the prostitutes. It will be a different matter when they find out who he is.

The picture that emerges from the statements of witnesses is indeed graphic. Juan strolls in, avoiding the groups and he listens and watches from a corner. Then he chooses a woman, whom he approaches, paying the madam or the pimp. The chronicles say that they had girls, who came down from the Albaycín, as well as old harpies who arrived at Granada from all over the place. The young girl or old woman goes arm in arm with Juan to the cubicles of the interior patio, or they climb the stairs to a seedy upstairs room.

Even Castro's frugal prose appears here to be soaked in pity: *"They entered the cubicle and he bade her be seated."* Then he tried to gain her interest: *"My child, I will pay you what others give you and more besides; I beg you listen to a few words."*

That is what he said to any of the poor women. They were surely surprised by that madman and, like Castro, I would like to have witnessed their surprised reaction. *"He fell upon his knees on the ground before her"*, then he took from within his sleeve, *"a small crucifix which he carried for this purpose."* He confessed before the woman that he was a sinner; *"and with bitter tears, he begged Our Lord to pardon him."*

Today, we can imagine the scene played out in the theatre. Juan's face to face encounters with a prostitute in the half-light of a squalid stuffy Granada brothel in the mid 16th century, signifies a dramatic outburst of Christian love in the journey of an enslaved woman. Perhaps for the first time, she is close to a man who looked upon her with a pure gaze.

If we give credence to the commentaries recorded at Granada at the time of Juan's death, there were reactions of all kinds. Some women listened to him and were moved, others upbraided him for his trouble. Giving an account of the positive cases, Castro narrates how Juan *"began to speak prayerfully of the Passion of Our Lord Jesus Christ with such devotion that* (the woman) *felt herself beginning to weep."*

"My sister, think about how much you cost Our Lord and consider how he suffered for you; do not be the cause of your own perdition. Consider that he has an eternal reward for the good and eternal punishment for those who live in sin like you. Do not provoke him further so that he totally abandons you as your sins deserve, for you might fall like a hard and heavy stone to the depths of hell."

Castro also tells us that some insulted Juan by, *"calling him a scoundrel and a hypocrite."* The archaic Castilian word used by Castro was *bigardo* which has now fallen into disuse, but at the time he wrote it, it did not simply mean *"a loafer or a depraved person"*, it was also a strong expression to describe *"monks who lived undisciplined lives."*

More specifically: *"They insulted the holy man by calling him a hypocrite and other things."* Castro explains the angry reactions emphasising: *"For the major part these woman are so obstinate, lost and hardened in their sin, that generally for this reason, many servants of God abstain from having anything to do with them, even though they are saddened by their perdition."* He confirms that he actually received bad treatment: *"They called him names and insulted him and said many offensive and defaming things, charging that what he did was with evil intention."*

Juan held his ground and put up with the outbursts. It

seems that one of the clients of the brothel reproached an infuriated woman: "*Why are you so wicked and rude to one who has been so good to you?*" But Juan intervened: "*Leave them, say nothing to them, do not deprive me of my crown; for they know me and understand who I am, and they treat me as I deserve.*"

His tenacity bore fruit. He began to win them over one by one. Never before had they been treated with kindness and consideration. Above all, nobody had ever attempted to offer them a way out of their way of life. This 'madman' was offering to help them.

Was he mad? Obviously he was fulfilling a well thought out plan. The day that he selected for his visits to the brothels was carefully chosen, it was the day in the week that evoked a memory of the Lord's passion: "*Out of devotion he chose Fridays, on which our redemption was wrought, to go to the public house of the women, to see if he could snatch some soul away from the claws of the demon.*"

There was one notable witness who swore that he personally saw Juan in a brothel. The statements of this witness seemed truthful to the judges at the beatification process, and I am inclined to agree with them as well. Domingo Navaro was born in 1520 in the Basque country and was brought to Granada when he was three. A labourer all his life, he enjoyed good health and lived to be more than a hundred. Already aged and a bachelor: "*He sustained himself eating what he had from the produce of his farm, even though it was not much.*" The judges listened to him in fascination: "*What was your father's name?*" "*They say it was Juan Viscaíno.*" "*And your mother's?*" He could not recall his mother's name, because his uncle had brought him to Granada: "*This witness did not know his mother, nor did he remember her name.*"

The judges coaxed him on and he replied quietly and precisely: "*He said his age was a hundred and two years less a month.*" "*How do you live now?*" "*Due to his great age and frailty he was unable to work any more, and because of this he was now poor and was sustained by whatever charity was done to him.*" The judges allowed it to be written into the record that "*this appears to be so, due to his appearance and age.*" Domingo the Basque labourer, who was brought to the plains of the Genil, was a young man of 24 years of age in 1545. And he declared without hesitation: "*This witness was in the same public house*'. He saw "*blessed Juan*" enter: "*He went up to the woman that he chose and said to her: 'Daughter what can you earn in an hour? I will give it to you, just listen to me a while'."*

Domingo said that, before long, everyone who went to the brothels knew the routine of the charity worker: *"He pulled out a crucifix that he carried in his sleeve."*

Sometimes the women refused him but others listened to him. Our Juan had plenty of guts.

He proceeded with a clear-cut plan and made no vain promises but if a woman wanted to change her life, he showed her the way. There is no exact record of how many did so. The witnesses made statements referring to the plural: *"He converted many of them." "Those public women were converted." "He paid them what they would earn in their sinful work, and this witness testifies that many of them were converted."*

He used different methods. Some he took away to enter the 'refuge for prostitutes' founded a few years previously by the lawyer Bazán near the River Darro on the slope of Santa Inés. As far as we know, this was the only establishment dedicated to such work, for the famous *'beaterio'* [enclosed house for women who lived as religious without taking vows] of Santa Maria Egipciaca in the street now called Las Recogidas, *the recollected ones,* was yet to be founded by Archbishop Pedro de Castro towards the end of the 16th century. The 'refuge' of Santa Inés later became a Poor Clare convent and today it is a primary school situated in front of the palace of the Agreda family who were also Juan's friends.

He employed a few ex-prostitutes in his hospital. Possibly he 'hospitalised' some of them. Castro's precise narrative needs no explanation. *"Although some were so hardened in their vice that they took no notice of him, others, with the help of God, were filled with compunction and moved to penance. They said to him: Brother, God knows that I would go out of here with you to serve the poor at the hospital; but I am constrained to stay here and they will not let me go with you."*

"Constrained?" Money was owed to the brothel madam or pimp. Juan *"very happily replied"*, *"Daughter, trust in the Lord who has enlightened your soul, he will give you the remedy for the body; understand well that you are going to serve him and not to offend him. Make a firm proposal that you would rather die than turn back to sin; and wait here for me until I return soon."*

Juan was off like a shot to look for some money. He could

usually count on charitable persons to help him, for *"few were the times he had gone away without their support."* If they were unable to help, then he would *"come to an agreement"* with the madam or pimp, *"putting himself under obligation to pay the debt owed by the woman he would take away."*

Castro continues, and this is where there is a query. He took the 'rescued' women to the hospital: *"And placed them in the infirmary where there were other women who were being cared for with the same treatment, thus they could see with what deserts the world repays those who continue in that sort of life. Some had to have maggots removed from their putrid heads, others had parts of their bodies cauterised by fire, and others suffered great pain and had sections amputated leaving them hideous and repugnant."*

"To the hospital." To his own, to the Royal Hospital or to Santa Ana Hospital? If it was to his own hospital, he must have already set up a 'ward for women', about which, at this time, I saw no documented evidence whatsoever, although later he did set up a ward for women in his hospital.

Some rescued women related that *"he had placed"* them in the homes of families he trusted, some remained on as servants; but the majority held the hope of finding a dowry and a husband.

We already know that Juan asked his wealthy friends for dowries. But how did he go about introducing them to men who were prepared to formalise marriage with his proteges? One thing is certain from the following testimonies, he did find them: *"He arranged marriages for many, taking them away from sin and searched for dowries for them." "... he searched among the ladies and other wealthy persons of Granada for marriage dowries, and when he found husbands for them, he had them married."*

"This witness remembers being present at the marriages of those whom he had converted, and he gave them their trousseaus." "... he took them away and searched for husbands for them." "... and he had them married and reformed." "He had them married and gave them alms." "He took some to the principal homes and had them accepted into service, and he asked for a trousseau or dowry, then he found husbands for them."

A man who greatly aided Juan in this work was a certain Juan Fernández: *"a very Christian man and the friend of devout persons"*; he was devoted to the *"blessed charity worker"*, who had said to him that God himself would pay *"in this life and the other"* for the support he gave to poor 'rescued' women. Fernández became a 'matrimonial agent' for 'blessed Juan': *"He kept in his house (the women entrusted to him by Juan). When he (Juan) found husbands for them, the aforementioned Juan Fernández stood in as best man at their weddings; and under the recommendation of the aforementioned father John of God, he would keep a watch over them."*

Juan kept up his work of helping to rehabilitate prostitutes until the day he died: *"He took women away from the brothels and maintained them and went in search of husbands for them to marry. So great was his kindness and Christian charity that he always found enough to help and console them. The aforementioned John of God did this before he purchased the house in the Calle de los Gomeles, and after he bought it, he continued this work."*

One has to say that Juan was a brave man as these 'goings on' in the red-light district caused him many a headache. No doubt he was fooled in the brothels as he had been many times in the Pescaderia.

As the years passed he never abandoned those he protected. They continued to return to him in any sort of necessity. I have found no direct quotations from these rescued women but Castro, who had the benefit of hindsight, was able to write about the happy outcome of many of the marriages arranged by Juan for these women. He brought back dowries for them from Valladolid when he journeyed to Court:

"The first time that he went to the Court they gave him donations which he brought back, and he had sixteen married at the same time, just as today some of them can testify. Some are now widows and have lived, and are living, honest and chaste lives." There is a woman that one witness calls *"Oreiza"* and another *"Oriza."* The old lady had a sorry story. She had been a prostitute for thirty years when Juan took the poor woman away from the brothel in a woeful condition. He did what he could to make her comfortable and brought her some special meals. It appears there was nothing wrong with the grouchy old woman's taste: *"Because, one day he brought her a little beef and mutton which he took into the public house. And she said he was a lazy good-for-nothing and should bring her something better or go home."*

Believe me! Juan did not treat her like the old witch that she was: *"He brought her chicken and pheasant and other things to pacify her."* Eventually her ladyship, the queen of the red-light district, seems to have seen reason, for soon *"she was content with anything."* I suspect she munched a chicken drumstick that came from the Archbishop's poultry run!

Castro pointedly added this postscript to Juan's work to rehabilitate prostitutes: *"In this exercise and works of charity John of God suffered much mortification and anxiety, and he demonstrated the great heroic patience with which Our Lord had imbued his soul."*

Furthermore, Castro had commenced the chapter dedicated to these exploits, with an explicit reference to Juan's devotion to the passion of Christ: *"Brother John of God was very devoted to the passion of Our Lord Jesus Christ; because as the principal strength of all our remedies, he found in it great benefit and tenderness."*

Although Juan's journey to Toledo probably took place some time later, I feel obliged to bring it forward here since it comes as a sequel to his efforts in the brothels. I have never come across a similar episode in the biography of any saint.

Permit me to use old-fashioned expressions as I tell you: *"How blessed Juan took four harlots on a journey."*

There were four, seated on mules going from Granada to Toledo. Castro narrates the incident with a certain sense of amazement, calling it *"remarkable"*: and *"More to be admired than imitated."* We can understand recounting it because the journey clearly demonstrates Juan's audacity.

They deceived him. We see that the whores considered Juan a person of their background, just another of the strange types who swarm around the brothels. This one preached to them that they should be good. No doubt they admired him and were pleased by his interest. Some commented on their good fortune in his accompanying them in their search for a husband. They were confident of Juan, and they deceived him.

These four women from Toledo agreed amongst themselves to promise him that if he would take them back to Toledo, to resolve family matters, they would accept, in return, to abandon the brothel and go wherever he might place them.

He should have checked out whether they truly came from Toledo and if they had families there, or whether they were pretending in order to leave Granada in search of new opportunities.

Juan, in preparation, *"hired the necessary animals and the rest."* He set out with a couple of mules, some provisions, and his companion and employee, Angulo. The women rode the mules while Juan and Angulo walked alongside them.

Juan had absolute faith in Angulo, but that good young man had little hope that the expedition was going to be a success. Still he went along with what his master asked him to do. Obviously, the departure of such a strange convoy prompted certain expectations among the prostitutes and word circulated from the Bibarrambla to the Bibataubín.

Juan did not consult with Father Portillo beforehand, nor would it have even crossed his mind to do so. He considered it quite the normal thing to do and would go to any length to assist the needy. He never became enmeshed in any rhetorical discussions regarding the projects he set out to achieve. Whether convenient or not for him to go to Toledo, he took them there anyway. Father Portillo would hardly have admired him any the less had he known. After all, we know that a few years earlier, Master Avila had rescued his young lady Doña María de Hoces from the grasp of the lecherous Precentor of Cordova and taken her with him to Granada. The Precentor calumniated the Master by saying that he was taking her so as to live lewdly with her.

This is a case of *"a saint and four harlots"*, the latter riding mules, with Juan and Angulo escorting them on foot, setting out on the long journey from Granada towards the Sierra Morena: passing through Almagro on the way to Toledo. Castro notes that as they passed through the villages and town many people were dumbfounded to see them, nor was that all: *"The passers-by and others, seeing them* [the women] *and also two men in that habit with four women of that sort, scoffed and ridiculed them calling out many insults and saying they were rascals and similar things."*

"Of that habit," indicates that at this time, Juan and Angulo wore a certain monkish robe, I will tell you about this later. I wonder how the four women responded to the insults. Juan *"was silent and kept great patience";* but Angulo was irritated and said: *"I rue the day we set out with these ruined women, and now have to put up with such insults."*

The women were simply carrying out their plan: Taking advantage of a stopover at Almagro, one of them dropped out. Her companions ignored it not wishing to attract attention. Angulo was not so naïve and suspected that the other three would flee, too. He "grumbled" to Juan: "What madness this has been! Did I not tell you that these wretched women couldn't be trusted to do other than this? Leave them alone and let us return, for they are all the same."

Even though the weather was fine, it took eight days to travel from Granada to Toledo. When they arrived at the gates of the imperial city of Toledo, two more travellers vanished, leaving one remaining. After she had completed a visit to her family they returned to Granada. The return journey was a good deal easier since the two men and the woman were able to ride the mules. To Angulo's complaints, Juan gently replied: "Consider that if you went to Motril for four boxes of fish..." Angulo had probably made this journey several times. From Motril on the coast to the city of Granada was a considerable journey and travelling was done at night to avoid the heat of the day. Consequently Juan's anecdote had its desired effect: "... if you were to go to Motril to bring back four boxes of fish, and along the way three went bad, while the other one remained fresh, you would not throw out the good one with the three bad."

That is exactly what occurred: "For, of the four we brought with us, one remains, which shows a good intention; be patient and steadfast, we will take her back with us to Granada: trust in God, for if she stays with us, our journey will not have been in vain, nor small our gain."

One quarter of the party of four women turned out well; Juan was happy. He searched for a husband for her and gave her "a ration" from the hospital. Castro gives us to understand that he knew her when she was a widow: "At present she is a widow and has lived, and today still lives, manifesting such good example, virtue and devotion that she has given very good praise and good example of Christianity, showing well the mysterious way of Our Lord that he brought her to know him."

Years after Juan had died, this widow used to come to ask the Brothers for "her ration, saying that their father John of God used to give it to her."

A splendid adventure, that of the saint and the four harlots. Just imagine what Don Quixote would have thought and said if he was traipsing along with such an odd cortege through the Manchan plains of Campo de Calatrava.

One thing is certain, the prostitutes of Granada would never have forgotten the friendship that Juan extended to them.

Melchor Rodríguez, the silk merchant, told how when the

nobility and leading citizens with their ladies went to take the body
of Juan from the Pisa mansion for burial, they passed a group of
poor women weeping and singing a dirge:

Todo el tiempo que vivió	Throughout his lifetime,
En este bajo emisferio,	In this lowly domain,
De cometer adulterio,	From adulterous shame,
Muchas mujeres libró	Many a woman he liberated,
A estas las sustentó	And many he supported
De limosnas que le han dado:	with what he was given in alms:
Digno es de ser llorado.	He is worthy of our lamentations.

Notes to Chapter 27

* Witness #15 in the lawsuit gave the account of the chickens in Archbishop Niño de Guevara's poultry run and the reproach of Juan: Cf. J. Sánchez, *Kenosis, etc.*, op.cit., 396-397.

* Juan Lobo, witness #1 at the Granada beatification process, gave an extraordinary testimony: he declared that he was 90 years of age in 1622, which would have made him a lad of 18 in 1550. He was of a cultured family and the son of a public scribe in the city of Granada.

* On the prostitutes of Granada, see A. Gallego Burín *Granada. Guía del viajero*, op.cit., 189. For Bibataubín, see M. De Mina, *Visitar la Granada, etc.*, op.cit., 133. Also Bermúdez de Pedraza, *Historia eclesiástica de Granada*, Seville 1988, fol. 32.

* Melchor Rodríguez, Granada beatification process, witness #4.

* For the work of John of God with the prostitutes of Granada, see Francisco de Castro, op.cit., chapter 13. Witnesses to this at the Granada beatification process were #3 (Antón Rodríguez), #5 (Gabriel Maldonado), #26 (Domingo Navarro), #53 (Catalina de Contreras).

* For the information on the refuge of Santa Inés, see A. Gallego Burín *Granada. Guía del viajero*, op.cit., 341. The sanctimonious man of Arrecogías was made famous throughout Spain thanks to the theatrical play by Martín Recuerda whose protagonist is Mariana Pineda: F. Izquierdo, *Guía de Granada*, op.cit., 164.

* The following witnesses testified about the marriages arranged by John of God for the women from the brothels; # 3 (Antón Rodríguez), # 4(Melchor Rodríguez), #10 (Pedro Francisco de León), #1 (Jerónimo de Piñar), #20 (Diego Marín), #30 (Diego Gracía Moyano), #43 (María de Guevara).

* On the relationship between Juan Fernández and John of God, witness # 9 of the Granada beatification process Juan de Salazar, adds some very curious information reflecting the sacred character later given to John of God by his friends. I consider it opportune to insert part of the relationship in which Juan de Salazar answered question #31 at the process: "*Juan Fernández came from Cartegena and had a very significant business. At the time he came there was a drought and bread was unobtainable. Besides, along the route he had to take there were no places to buy provisions. So before leaving home he filled canisters with as much bread as he could*

carry, filled a container with wine, and cooked a large piece of bacon for the journey. He came across a poor man, and having discovered that he had been carried and put down by the father, John of God, pulled some bread and bacon out of his hamper and gave it to the poor man. Soon another came along, so he did the same for him. This went on and by the time the aforementioned Juan Fernández left the city, he had to go without any bread, bacon or wine trusting in the word of the aforementioned father. And so he went on his way until nightfall when he began to feel hungry, since he had neither bread, wine nor bacon. He felt sad that he was so far from his place. Then, in his confusion, he resolved to call upon blessed John of God. Then along came a man who said to him: 'Brother, do you want to have something to eat?' So the aforementioned Juan Fernández got up and said 'yes.' Then the aforementioned man said to him: 'Well, take this bread roll and eat.' Then when he was given the bread roll, he was surprised how white it was and what a delicious flavour it had. No doubt he was very fortunate, and the two talked about charity for the poor. When he had finished eating the bread roll, he asked him to dismount and he could then drink some very good red wine. Then the aforementioned Juan Fernández said he began to be worried because he had no vessel for this. So he dismounted and he took him to a nearby brook of clear running water and said to him: 'Brother, drink.' So the aforementioned dismounted and began to drink thinking that it was water and he began drinking the most sweet wine he had ever tasted. And when he arose from the brook to thank his benefactor, he discovered there was nobody there. He had no doubt that it was John of God or some angel who had been sent there by God for his kindness. All the time this witness was giving this testimony there were tears in his eyes, and he cried out to the blessed father saying that God had brought him to him."

* Witness #11 in the lawsuit, testified that Juan *"permanently"* worked for the rehabilitation of the prostitutes. Cf. J. Sánchez, op.cit., 377. The name 'Oreiza' or 'Oriza' was given respectively at the Granada beatification process by witnesses #46 (María Espinosa) and #61 (Diego López Roales). The episode of the protesting old woman, ibid., witness #9 (Juan de Salazar).

* The journey from Granada to Toledo is given in detail by Francisco de Castro, op.cit., chapter 13. Also, the witnesses at the Granada beatification process, #13 (Felipe de Alaiz), #43 (María de Guevara), #47 (Agueda Muñoz), #61 (Diego López Roales).

* The reference of the food ration given by the brothers to the surviving woman from the Toledo journey: see M. De Mina *'Anotaciones'*, *Fondo Documental*, op.cit., on chapter 13 of Castro.

* The witness at the Granada beatification process, #4 (Melchor Rodríguez) gave the exact words of the dirge (*coplas*).

28

THEY ARE NOW A TEAM

Granada
1546

The news resounded throughout Granada like a ricocheting bullet. : *"Antón Martín has forgiven Pedro Velasco."* Was it possible? *"He embraced him at the gate of the prison."*

It was like the outcome of a 'thriller' which the whole city had followed for months. *"Juan the charity worker had really done something."*

This story took on the mantle of a legend circulating throughout Spain like the reconquest novels of the past. A few years later the famous playwright Lope de Vega would include the episode in one of his plays, contributing to the variety of recollections.

Thus a tapestry of many threads has been passed on to us which makes it difficult to determine each circumstance. The declarations of the beatification process appear to me to have been influenced somewhat by the dramatic aspect of the tales related in the popular novels that hung from a cord when Juan peddled books.

Furthermore, it is aggravating that Castro does not even dedicate a single page of his biography to the first meeting between Juan and Antón Martín. He may have thought of including a special chapter on this matter, his early death preventing him from doing so.

Anyway, there are numerous documents that give a clear profile of the first two companions, or disciples, who formed with Juan, his first team. One was a murderer, the other a libertine.

The third member will be a spying calumniator and the fourth, a parsimonious banker, or better still, a skinflint. Juan cast his raft out to sea with this crew: a murderer, a libertine, a sly gossip and a miser.

The first, Antón Martín, was a lanky young braggart from Cuenca. He found employment as a procurer in the red-light district and they say he wore a red cap on his head to make himself look like a fighting cock. He had been in Granada for some months with no intention of leaving that city until he was successful in a case that he had put to the magistrates of the Chancellery. When his money ran out he survived by working as a protector of prostitutes. Handsome and resolute, he was able to impose his will in the brothel disputes that arose. His father was said to be Pedro de Aragón and therefore Antón Martín's real name was Antonio de Aragón.

It was reported that an argument broke out over women and money, with two men fighting to the death. One of them was Pedro Velasco, who came from a well-to-do Granada family, and the other was Pedro de Aragón, brother of Antón Martín. After the Pedro from Granada killed Pedro from Castile, he fled.

Antón Martín swore that he would see his brother's assassin hanged by the courts and if by any chance the judges acquitted him, he would kill him with his own hands.

With this idea he came down to Granada where Pedro Velasco had sought refuge. Once the indictment was presented, the Chancellery imprisoned Velasco to await the due process of the law. Even though the Velasco family employed its fortune and prestige to delay the carrying out of the sentence, finally it seemed that the prisoner would soon be executed. Antón Martín bragged to his friends that he would be in the front row when the spectacle took place. In the meantime he had become a brothel procurer whom the prostitutes feared and the ruffians respected.

This profile emerges mainly from reliable references on the subject. Other literary creations added colourful particulars suggesting that the meeting of Juan and Antón took place where the gibbet on which Pedro Velasco was to be hanged was already set up in the Plaza Nueva in front of the Chancellry.

The reality was less dramatic. When Juan visited the brothels and talked with the prostitutes, it was inevitable that he should come across Antón Martín. It seems that Antón, in the midst of his loose living, still maintained some of his religious feelings from his Castilian upbringing. He would have watched with interest, and a certain respect, the comings and goings of this strange religious layman who was so well thought of by the prostitutes.

On his part, Juan understood the yearning for revenge boiling away in the heart of Antón who, *"having been asked by many persons to forgive his enemy"*, angrily maintained his purpose. Some witnesses allow themselves to speculate that Juan and Antón met and talked enough to become friends. I think that Juan, more than once, got donations from Antón who, with his wins at gambling and his cut from prostitution, would have been free with easy money. And from that point of view, if they spoke, it seems certain that Juan would have tried to persuade him to pardon his enemy.

A crisis then occurred. Maria de Villavicencio personally knew John of God and, as the wife of an attorney, had dealings with the officials at the Chancellery. She definitely locates the conversation in the Calle de la Colcha, today linking the streets of Reyes Católicos and Pavaberas. It was called Colcha [quilt] because it was here that makers of quilts worked when their industry flourished at Granada. The Villavicencio woman testified: *"It was well known in this city that the blessed father John of God converted Brother Antón Martín in the Calle de la Colcha. That was the place where he fell before him on his knees holding a crucifix in his hands."*

Without being precise about the background to the scene, various witnesses repeated the details: Juan, crucifix in hand and on his knees in front of Antón *"begging him to forgive for the passion of Christ."* We know that this was not the first time that Juan humbled himself before someone. But surely no one had ever before knelt in front of Antón Martín with a crucifix in hand. Nor would they have pleaded to him *"for the sake of the passion of Christ."* Juan's actions melted the heart of Antón who felt himself overtaken by a torrent of mercy. He decided to forgive.

Juan, always a practical man, immediately grabbed him by the arm and led him to the Chancellery where before the judge Antón withdrew the charge. It appears the bureaucratic procedure was hurried along, for there were several *oidores* [magistrates] only too happy to comply with a petition from their *"friend, blessed Juan"*, without forcing the law. It seems that once the accusation was withdrawn, liberty was automatic for someone who had committed a *"crime of passion."*

Pedro Velasco was released from prison. Popular imagination, and poets, were unrestrained in describing *"the embrace"* of the former enemies Antón and Pedro, with Juan as the broker of the reconciliation. Both, Antón and Pedro, asked Juan to accept them as helpers in his hospital and they came to him for just that purpose.

But Juan's work, his charitable presence, was not confined to the walls of the 'house', or 'houses', in the Pescadería, it already reached out to the entire city, into its most hidden nooks and crannies.

Juan helped the poor and families of *'vergonzantes'* – those ashamed to beg. Until now, besides the permanent employee

Angulo, he counted on young men and women who dedicated part of their day to working in the hospital. Antón and Pedro headed the list of his 'full-time' disciples. Neither Juan nor they suspected that they had laid the first stone of what would become the immense edifice of the 'Hospitaller Order'.

We can imagine the faces of the pimps and harlots in the Bibataubín when they saw Antón Martín turning up as the assistant to the charity worker... *"This witness saw the two of them together, both barefooted and begging alms for the poor."*

At first sight three social classes coexist at Granada: the rich, the poor, and a middle class of workers and civil servants who were, more or less, distinguished persons.

The rich are extremely wealthy, their money giving them power and social standing. They included aristocrats, high ranking executives and, cultured persons all linked in some way to the arteries of imperial power. They cover various areas of public administration as servants of the Court. They lead a luxurious and lavish lifestyle with constant access to an entourage of renaissance poets, musicians, artists and high-ranking clergy.

Within this ruling class Juan finds some dozens of real friends and benefactors.

Lowest of all, the poor of Granada teem like miserable rats in the sewers of the city. They wait in hope for the crumbs that fall from the banquet tables of the affluent, and form a sad section of misery, disease, ignorance and filth. Juan goes about picking up their shattered bodies and placing them upon his shoulders.

In the middle of this scale, below the rich and above the poor, stood the majority of the capital's normal population, consisting of artisans, merchants, professionals, civil servants, stone masons, labourers and peasants. This gamut of families covered a broad spectrum of the population, which at the top end sometimes touched upon the ambience of the powerful establishment, while at the lowest it touched the anguish of the poor.

Distress followed when a sudden blow of misfortune struck the household of the higher middle class. The misfortune could be a long-term illness, the death of the head of the family, or some economic disaster. This created the *'pobres vergonzantes'* who, reduced to poverty, were too embarrassed to dare to solicit alms.

Circulating through the pages of picturesque Spanish literature are *hidalgos*, [minor nobles] who, having lost their fortune, try to keep up appearances of their former way of life. Readers might smile at them but behind their sorrowful facade is a hardness of heart from much bitter suffering. This kind of silent drama is not exclusive to past centuries.

Juan discovered in Granada that there was a network of secret *vergonzantes*: widows, orphans, ex-soldiers, labourers, families smitten with illness. Castro includes a sector called the *"pleitantes"* [litigants] those who awaited some juridical outcome at the Chancellery for it was necessary to insist in order to receive justice in those days.

Juan discretely distributed aid, material when possible, always friendly and spiritual: *"As he was able, he gave promptly and joyfully; and others he consoled with good-hearted and cheerful words, giving them confidence that God would provide. Thus all were comforted, and that is how he did things; for, astonishingly, nobody went to him for a sum, no matter how small or large, that the Lord did not enable him to remedy their needs as best he could."*

The witnesses estimate that a good part of Juan's day was spent in visiting homes of the *vergonzantes*. For *"he went out to find them"* rather than wait for them to come to him for help: *"he began to take care to search out the vergonzantes, devout spinsters, poor religious and beatas, and housewives who suffered secret needs."*

He used to request money from 'wealthy ladies' to take back to these silent women who received his visit as a gift from heaven. He exercised his tact to such an extent that he personally purchased: *" bread, meat, fish, charcoal and all the other necessities for their sustenance, so that they did not have to go out to seek them."*

He did more. He brought them work to do in their own homes: *"so they would not be idle, and could work to help and dress themselves"*: he brought them *"wool, flax, burlap and hemp which they could spin.* If necessary, he would bring a doctor to the house.

Unravelling the phrase where Castro indicates that in the circle of Juan's proteges *"in the shadows"* are included *"devout spinsters, religious and beatas"*, the German researcher Ludwig Ruland, known to us for his psychiatric analysis of 'conversion', puts forth this interesting observation. These 'beatas' at Granada are an Andalusian version of the European 'Beguines'.

This seems natural, taking into account the situation in

which the wars had placed Spain's feminine population. The Emperor had taken the young men off to fight in faraway places. Military captains came back from the Indies looking for more recruits to go away to discover new lands. Many soldiers who went were never to return to their homeland. The only way out for many a highborn young lady was to discretely enter a convent where her loneliness would be given a religious significance. Throughout Spain there were many nuns, some through vocation, and a great many through resignation. There was a shortage of men.

And how did Juan assist unmarried ladies deprived of a man for their entire life and condemned to absolute enclosure within the home? Certainly, some succumbed to the temptation to go down to the brothels. The majority silently lived out their days spinning, sewing and embroidering. Some, a minority, who lacked the courage, or a dowry, to knock on the door of a convent to become a nun, set out to walk along a curious path: *'private nuns'*, isolated in their homes or sharing an apartment of specially prepared quarters. Various towns in the Low Countries show tourists today the location of their Béguinage, where the *beatas* of the 16th century lived out their 'special' vocation; groups of women disposed to live in common the spirit and rule of one of the classic religious orders, especially united to the Augustinians, Franciscans and Dominicans. Some began by giving their material help to the friars in their kitchens and housework, as did the oblates and lay brothers. They formed *'convents or beaterios'* with distinct characteristics according to the choice of the foundress and norms dictated by the father confessor. They called themselves *beatas*, enclosed recluses. Elsewhere in Europe such women were generally called *Beguines*. The *'beaterios'* where they lived functioned under their own statutes until the papacy placed them all under the jurisdiction and guidance of a male religious order that was akin to their spirit.

I have been unable to unearth any document at Granada that might show that there was a *béguinage* here along the lines of the Flemish ones. However, if there were it should cause little surprise – given the close relationship between the Low Countries and Spain during the reign of Charles V. Nevertheless, Ruland says that the paragraph written by Castro shows that the *beatas* of Granada existed along similar lines to the Beguines, except each was isolated in her own home as a *tertiary* consecrated with a vow of chastity and the practice of poverty.

Read in this light the phrases of Castro show Juan as a sort of lay spiritual director, besides protector: *"There were Recogidas [pious women living in seclusion] maintaining virtue and recollection...; and later he used to sit down with them for a while and he would encourage their efforts and give a brief spiritual talk persuading them to increase their virtue and detest vice, and on that subject he gave them lively explanations (although simple) which to this day live in the memories of many who listened to them. He gave them hope, so that they would persevere; besides the grace they would receive from the Lord, the sustenance of their needs would not be lacking... With this he encouraged and animated them to live virtuously and serve Our Lord."*

It was bound to happen and it did. Evil persons thought evil of Juan, attributing immoral motives to the visits he made to the widows and spinsters. They spied upon him. Castro throws the blame upon Satan *"who never sleeps from making war, by himself and through his minions."*

They *"barked"* at Juan, and *"murmured about him"*, it being a juicy subject as much in the taverns as in the sacristies, suggesting he was *"mad again"*, getting about with prostitutes and *vergonzantes*; or that he was getting sexual satisfaction from these woman under the pretext of giving them assistance.

They surrounded Juan, these shameless voyeurs and sick minded spies. *"They followed him and fixed their eyes upon him when he went into houses."* Even worse, one such outrageous sticky-beak even sneaked into a house being visited by Juan; *"to pry into what he was saying and doing."*

It is impressive to see how these judgements on his intentions brought Juan into the open. He now counts on the priceless help of Antón and Pedro, whom he entrusts with taking care of the hospital *"providing them with what was necessary before he left the house"*; then he goes off to confront the streets visiting the homes of the *vergonzantes* and collecting alms *"until ten or eleven at night."*

From amongst the 'spies' he attracted his third disciple. Simón must have been a sneaky type, as references to him say that he used to go to the porches of churches carrying pieces of gossip. Some have him as being the son of a well-to-do family, others see him as no more than a vagabond. Serious documentary sources do not know him, all that we know is that he was included in Juan's first team. Nevertheless, tradition has attributed a nice legend to him, which without doubt had some foundation, for various witnesses give certainty to the essential nucleus. Simón *"spied"* on Juan's movements, trying to prove malicious suspicions. He saw with his own eyes Juan's honesty, charity and clear example and confessed to him his fault and begged him to receive him as a disciple.

Avila is his surname for certain, so I am going to call him Simón in order to avoid any confusion; for we now have a third Avila, the priest Master Avila, the faithful servant Angulo, now this Simón.

The 'Simon legend' started with the biography by Brother Dionisio Celi with its invented miracles. It tells that Juan was assisting a poor widow who had three small sons to bring up. One day Juan arrived at the widow's house carrying five bread rolls and a cruet of olive oil. Simón skulked along behind him and saw what Juan was up to. Then he received the mortal fright of seeing, all of a sudden, these words written on a wall: *"There is a flaming sword waiting to strike you for all your sins."* He was dumbfounded and Juan and the widow who heard the rumpus came along to witness the sobbing of the voyeur and his words of repentance and shame – all of which Juan answered with an indulgent smile.

There is one detail that obliges us to respect the essence of this incident. Our faithful witness, Antón Rodríguez, narrates the episode connecting it with a benefactress Doña Juana de Fusteros, *"mother or aunt of the medical doctor Fusteros"*, who used to help Juan look after his protected ones: Antón adds that he heard the noise of the stricken Simon. Juan *"came outside made the sign of the cross and lifted him up."* A little more is added by Francisca Fernández, naming without the slightest hesitation, the widow as Perea, saying that *"she was a poor but honest woman from an upright family."*

However conflicting the circumstance of the case, what the witnesses unanimously claim to be certain is that: *"Simón died a real saint"* as a Hospitaller Brother.

The vicissitudes of Juan with women, some of them gentle *vergonzantes*, others loose living, provided his fellow Granadinos with plenty of material, some laudatory, some mischievous, for stories about him.

The following three episodes are worthy examples but we must accept them with some reservations. I saw them included in the interrogation of the Process, which was based, as I have already warned, on the fantastic stories of Brother Celi.

A woman *"who was a stranger, good looking and middle-aged"*, said to him: *"Brother Juan, give me something for the love of God."* He replied: *"Sister, are you asking me for alms to serve God?"* She said she was, *"so he pulled out of his sleeve a handful of coins and gave them to her."* He then asked her *"what she intended to do."* The woman replied that she could do nothing. Blessed Juan said: *"If only you knew how to spin."* She said she did, *"but being a stranger she did not know anyone to ask about it."* Juan,*"took her to the home of a devout woman and told her that she should stay there; that he would return with some linen and more money, and that he would then take care of all her needs, but that she should not go outside."*

A particular case that caught my attention we owe to the canon archdeacon of Calahorra, Francisco Manso *"of His Majesty's Council for the Indies"*, a pompous cleric. He knew of a woman, *"a beautiful widow"*, who came to Granada to await the outcome of a verdict by the Chancellery on some business matter. Juan wanted *"her to avoid the dangers of going about the tribunals"*, so he looked about and found a suitable lodging for her, paid for it, *"and provided for what the widow needed."* One day when Juan visited her *"he found the door closed, but the woman opened it with difficulty."* Juan guessed what was going on and discovered she had *"a man hiding under her bed."* All turned out well for the lover *"came out, stood up and both (lover and widow) repented and broke off that wicked relationship."*

For her part, Doña Leonor María de Guevara heard of a woman who seemed to be very brazen and audacious and who dressed in male clothing and *"did many other outrageous things."* Juan tried to *"constrain and dissuade her from acting that way."* This came at the cost of choice food, served *'on a silver platter'*, which is to say, on the finest crockery; *"and sometimes he bought her expensive dresses, always with the motive of stopping her from sinning and avoiding the occasion of sin."*

Later in his life Juan will run through the flames of a terrible fire, carrying various patients upon his shoulders. In my opinion, it was much more remarkable that Juan emerged unscathed from the conflagration of women, without distinguishing saints from sinners, and unharmed by evil tongues.

It was his impeccable conduct that impressed a lawyer who lived at Madrid but whose father *"was a public scribe of the city of Granada."* Commenting on the praises of a certain female servant in his household; *"who had been saved from an evil life by blessed Juan,"* he said, *"The many things that this woman said about him can be believed, because once she was a woman with an evil tongue, but now all can see she is a good woman who can be trusted."*

Nobody dared to accuse Juan of making a false step.

Juan needs more and more money each day. His hospital, and the vergonzantes, drained his resources. He begged, others gave. Granada certainly was getting along well with its alms seeker.

But, once in a while, someone does resist. For example, the Genoese banker, Domingo Piola. Juan was not shy in asking and bankers were no exception. This one responded to him in the language of a moneylender, demanding what today we'd call 'a signature of guarantee', essential to get a loan. Fancy asking Juan to sign a warranty!

About this gentleman banker, born at Genoa, three researchers, all Hospitaller Brothers, after John of God's death, each has a doubt. Accordingly I give here what we know of the banker; and I will inform you about the three researchers.

All references certify that the banker was named Domingo and that he came to Granada from Genoa. The presence of Italian families was very common in Spain during the reign of Charles V. Above all at Seville and Granada, the former as the stepping-off point for America and the latter as the seat of the Chancellery. The Italians mainly came from Venice or Genoa.

On both sides of Italy, Genoa and Venice were, at that period, bases for assault on the sea, since they only had a handful of land essential for the anchorage of ships. Bounded on land by powerful republics, they had renounced expansion along the Italian peninsula and had followed the call of the sea. At the peak of the Middle Ages both cities had powerful fleets manned with experienced mariners. They were governed by a leader who was elected from the names of the illustrious families inscribed in the Golden Book.

When the new Doge was elected there was a ceremony of casting a ring into the waves, symbolising a marriage with the sea.

It seems that whenever this occurred the Sultan of the Turks would become furious. No one had a greater claim to this symbolic relationship with the seas, because Venetians and Genoese had uncovered the mysteries of the Mediterranean and fortified the Columns of Hercules opening them as the gateway to the West and the *Finis Terrae* routes which prompted the great epics of ocean exploration. Genoese soldiers and merchants fought and traded along the coasts of the Orient and everywhere they went they took Christianity with them. In the family documents of the Spinola family it is told that a crusader brought back from Palestine the sacred booty of a thorn from the crown of the Lord Jesus Christ, which was placed in the Genoese church of Santa Maria del Vigneto. The family name was changed to Spinola in honour of the sacred *spina*, the Italian for thorn. It is a nice story, but there is not much to support it. The Spinolas needed to have a lineage that went back to the mists of time, so they invented one that was fitting to the occupancy of their magnificent Genoese palace.

Accordingly Europe emerged from the Middle Ages when its states were firmly defined; but Genoa's fierce maritime independence was unshaken, until it decided to place itself in the pay of stronger countries. It hired out its fleets as well as its generals, and sold military attack plans, continually covering itself with the glitter of gold. The strategy of the Genoese inevitably brought forth a class of astute bankers who kept their accounts well protected in the vaults of renaissance palaces.

As Spain's presence in Austria increased, Genoa served well the Emperor Charles V and continued to do so for succeeding Spanish kings. Young Genoese, mainly bankers, merchants, military and naval personnel, began to pour into Spanish ports. Among the widening scope of the illustrious Spinola family are well known names such as Ambrosio Spinola who conquered Ostende and ended up being immortalised by Valazquez in his painting, 'The Lances'.

Brother Giuseppe Magliozzi, a keen and subtle researcher of John of God, like the banker, was born in Italy. He wrote about 'Domingo' and applied to him the surname Piola, 'Domingo Piola' of Genoa. Brother Giuseppe needs to tell us why he gives the banker this surname when some very well informed witnesses have stated that instead of 'Piola', his surname was really 'Espínola, which is to say 'Spinola', which also conserves its dulcet Italian sound in Spanish. The archives of Genoa hide the secret of the two surnames.

It is certain that the successive waves of Genoese 'Spinolas' turned in the direction of Spain until the 18th century: A handsome young second lieutenant called Benito Antonio Spinola of Genoa took his place in the Spanish fleet on 11 December 1713. From this branch of the family, Marcelo Spinola, who was to become the future saintly Archbishop of Seville, was born a century later.

Some day Brother Magliozzi will clarify the enigma of the surname 'Espínola'. In the meantime, let us call the Genoese banker who settled down at Granada, Domingo Piola.

I needed to explain about Piola. The witnesses called him well-to-do and wealthy. They said he was a little over fifty years of age, married, but childless. His meeting with Juan presents us with a certain aura of brilliance.

In the Zagr' Zúñiga family were persons of distinction who were friends of the Granada Venegas family. They kept memoirs of some conversations between Juan and Piola prior to the critical date. The banker joked about Juan's activities who replied to him saying: *"Do not laugh at me brother Genoese, one day they will be laughing at us."* The prophecy was to be fulfilled.

One day Juan knocked on the banker's door seeking a loan of 30 ducats which he needed urgently to pay for linen at the hospital. Piola the banker asked him, *"who is going to be the guarantor for this transaction?"* Juan put his hand into his bag and pulled out a small picture of the Infant Jesus that he placed on the table: *"Here is my guarantor."*

Possibly Juan's ingenuous confidence in the love of Christ was enough for divine grace to cause a merciful upheaval in the heart of the banker.

"At this, from the face of the Infant Jesus had come a great brightness and resplendence which exceeded the light of the sun. Seeing this, the Genoese was forced to see that it was a miracle and that God wanted him to do that good work, so he gave to the aforementioned John of God much more money than he had asked of him."

This was certainly the conversion of the banker. His wife had died a short time previously and Domingo Piola asked Juan to admit him to his group. He joined Antón, Pedro and Simón, to become the fourth disciple.

Cultured, integrated in the social circles of Granada, expert in accounting and finance, Domingo lent a priceless support to Juan. Close to Juan's side, Domingo shared, by day and night, Juan's concerns for the growth of his hospital, all the while breathing in his fervour and participating in his impetuous outbursts of charity. Years later, after Juan's death, the devotees of his memory will accumulate first hand references from the lips of Brother Domingo, *"This witness knew of that Brother Domingo... he heard him say thus to Brother Domingo... especially this witness knew of that Brother Domingo... Brother Domingo, treating of the life of the aforementioned John of God..."*

Brother Matías de Mina, whom we cannot thank enough for his tenacious and tireless research over many years in the archives of Granada, suspects that it was Domingo Piola who wrote the celebrated notebook in which the confidential information given by John of God had been gathered by *"someone"* . Castro utilised the same notebook which today has sadly gone missing but some day Brother Matías may give us the joy of coming across it...

Domingo Piola, 'in religious life' changed his name to Brother Domingo Benedicto and he led the brothers at Granada after Antón Martín: *"Brother Domingo was the Chief Infirmarian at the aforementioned Hospital which is called of John of God in that city of Granada."*

It was Brother Domingo's responsibility to defend the newborn Hospitaller Order when the Jeronymites took out a lawsuit against it. The way he did this, his conscientious management as trustee of the inheritance of the 'founder' in safeguarding the hospitaller lifestyle at the time it was threatened, his friendships and personal relationships with the witnesses he chose for *"getting the lawsuit back on its feet"*, are aspects of his biography which will illumine Juan's movements during the last years of his life. Domingo had the leading role to play in the lawsuit: *"The questions which had to be asked of the witnesses were formulated by Domingo Benedicto, the Senior Brother of the Hospital of John of God, as well as by other brothers of the aforementioned hospital. This was during the lawsuit brought about by the prior, friars and the monastery of San Geronimo of this city..."*

Domingo designated the lawyer who represents the hospital: *"At Granada, the twenty-fourth of December in the year one*

thousand, five hundred and seventy hereby written in my presence by the
notary. I, Francisco Ximenez, attorney at law in this city, am hereby
appointed by Domingo Benedicto, Senior Brother of the Hospital of John
of God in this city, as the attorney to represent it and all the brothers of the
aforementioned hospital at the trial of the lawsuit..."

Domingo prolonged the shadow of Juan so it will enrich us 'to know everything' about him and the hospital and for this, 'it is up to' Brother José Sánchez Martínez, whose work has greatly benefited so many 'friends' of John of God, to inform us.

At Toledo a little old lady named Estefanía de Vallejo remembered her childhood with Doña Mencía Carrillo whose home Juan frequented: *"The blessed man Juan entered the home of the lady where this witness grew up; he went about poorly clad, with only a rough garment and barefooted; to beg alms with a basket over his shoulders and a staff in his hand. These gentlefolk gave him large donations and esteemed him greatly, making him come into their drawing-room even though he was so shabbily dressed."*

The child, who was either adopted or a little maid servant, received little treats from Juan: *"The holy man used to pull apples and other little goodies out of his sleeve and give them to her"*. She also told the Toledo process that she was later taken into service at the Royal household; and that she remembered perfectly the visits to Madrid by Brother Domingo:

"After the death of the venerable father John of God, this witness saw Brother Domingo at Madrid, he was the companion of the aforementioned father John of God and his son in religion; and he went there to request alms from the ladies and many other prominent persons for the poor in the hospital at Granada; and they gave very generously to him because of the esteem and devotion they held for the aforementioned John of God."

Already they are a team, half a dozen *'madmen'* who were determined to stir Granada to assist the poor and ill. A man born in Pedro Velasco's home village of Guardafortuna also joined them. He was Juan García, a simple peasant who, unlike Pedro, had no money.

More men, both young and not so young, looked at the 'preposterous' enterprise started by Juan and asked themselves if they might find a place within it. One such was Luis Bautista, a young man known to Juan, but not to us, nor do we know where and when Juan first knew him. This Luis has left no other trace except the letter Juan wrote to him in reply to one of his, which we do not possess. From Juan's reply we know that they are true friends. He was a mixed up lad who drifted about, full of doubts but was quite normal, at least in sexual matters, for Juan comments to him: *"Seeing that you are so weak where women are concerned, I really do not know whether I should advise you to come here."*

The young man had consulted him on two points. The first was circumstantial: whether or not he should make a journey to Valencia: from where or for what reason we do not know. Juan leaves it to him to make up his mind. However, the other consideration was more serious because it concerned whether he should come to Granada to join the band of hospitallers.

Juan told him honestly that he would receive him as long as he took the step to *"really"* come, knowing *"to what he was coming."* He challenged him quite straightforwardly: *"If you do come here you will have to obey a lot more and perform much harder work than you have ever done before. But all is done for God, such as the long watches in caring for the poor."*

Juan knew perfectly well what a hard life he was living and he had no delusion that enthusiasm alone would save Luis from suffering. In this letter he goes over his sacrifices with a genial phrase, advising him that, if he comes, he can count on seeing himself skinned alive *"You will have your skin flayed to ribbons,"* adding,*"Remember how St. Bartholomew was flayed until the skin and sinew was severed from his back."* Juan was not joking: *"If you do come here, it is going to be just like that and you must be prepared to work and not to take it easy."*

Of course, his admission to the team would bring with it moral obligations: *"Remember that if you do come, you must be serious about it and must guard yourself against women as if they were the devil."*

As well there would be spiritual practices. *"Keep God in mind every day of your life... Always hear Mass entirely... Confess often, if it is possible... Do not go to sleep in mortal sin."*

The secret resides in living and loving in peace with God: *"Love Our Lord Jesus Christ above everything else in the world, for no matter how much you may love him, he loves you far more."*

We do not know whether Luis went to Valencia or joined the Hospitaller Brothers. The letter that Juan wrote him contains a golden phrase. *"Always be charitable for God is not present where charity is lacking,*" but added by way of explanation "*although God is everywhere.*" Juan gives us a sublime lesson: God is not present where charity is lacking.

Notes to Chapter 28

* The reference to Antón Martín's coloured cap is attributed to the witness Antonio Marrtínez, #17 in the '*Floreto*' of Gómez Moreno, *San Juan de Dios, Primicias historicos,* op.cit., 256. The *Comedia* by Lope de Vega is in Vol. V of *Comedías de vidas de santos, etc.*, in the Rivadeneyra Collection, Real Academia Española. For the figure of John of God in theatre of Lope, see Matías de Mina in Labor Hospitalaria (1953) 238, 320, 407. Also G. Russotto, *Lope de Vega e San Giovanni di Dio,* Rome 1954.

* Cf. G. Magliozzi, Pagine Juandediane, op.cit., 38, note 27 speaks of the strangeness of Castro not mentioning the 'case of Antón Martín', and attributes this to Castro's plan to add another chapter at a later date.

* Facts on Antón Martín before his conversion are scattered and scarce. The ones that are most reliable come from the Granada beatification process, witnesses 313 (Felipe de Alaiz), #18 (Melchor Dávila), #27 (Melchor Almirante), #29 (Alonso Sánchez Dávila), #55 (Juana de Gálvez), #59 (María de Villavicencio), and many more who repeated identical testimonies. The first band of John of God's followers later founded the Madrid hospital and these same witnesses testified to this also. Madrid welcomed Antón Martín who won its veneration. When he died there at Christmas 1553, not only did the whole population turn out to honour him at his funeral, a plaza in the city was named after him. A biography called *Galería Hospitalaria* (part 4) was published at Madrid in 1716. This work was half fact, half legend. A more reliable reference comes from the research carried out by Br.. Luis Ortega Lázaro, O.H., some of whose work is as follows: Cf.: *Antón Martín y su hospital en la Calle Atocha,* Madrid 1981:

"To begin with, we have to know he was called Antón Martín, Martín being the surname of his mother Elvira Martín de la Cuesta. He did not use his father's surname de Aragón, Pedro de Aragón being his father's name. In Spain it is usual to take two surnames, the first being that of the father, the second that of the mother. This became obligatory after the Law of Civil Registration in 1870.

"*Antón Martín was born on 25 March 1500 in the village of Mira in the Province of Cuenca, Spain.*

"His first work was as a guard on a watch tower on the Mediterranean coast at Valencia where constant vigil was kept to warn of the approach of Moorish pirates. He also served as a guard of the Register of Customs at the town of Requena where a custom duty had to be paid for merchandise passing between Valencia and Castile. Not much more is heard of him after this until some time later.

"Antón Martín had one brother, named Pedro de Aragón who worked for a wealthy farmer with a large holding at Guadafortuna in the Province of Granada. Pedro was a servant in the landowner's household and was trusted so much that he handled financial matters. He became amorously involved with his employer's daughter and as a result she became pregnant. Pedro did not wish to marry the girl, and was wisely advised against doing so by the parish priest, who was once married and became a cleric after the death of his wife. The priest saw that Pedro was a good lad and he had a daughter of marriageable age. Pedro seems to have been influenced by a popular ballad of the day that told the story of a poor boy who married the daughter of his rich master, and everyone used to call him a wastrel and ne'er-do-well. Pedro did not want the same to happen to him, so he chose the priest's daughter, who of course was as poor as a church mouse.

"Meanwhile, the rich girl was pregnant and without a fiancee had, because of the conventions of the day, brought shame upon her family. Vengeance came swiftly, a few days after his marriage Pedro was waylaid on the outskirts of Guadahortuna and beaten to death.

It was a ghastly crime, and even to this day, some 400 years since the event, is still spoken about in that village.

"News of the murder soon reached his brother Antón Martín. He went to Granada to demand the death penalty for the murderer or murderers of his brother. He first went to Guadahortuna to make an investigation for himself, and it was not too long before he discovered that the murderer was Pedro Velasco, brother of the disgraced girl left without a wedding. And although the murderer had fled, Antón hunted him down and had him thrown into the dungeons of the Royal Chancellery at Granada. A trial ensured and the criminal was sentenced to death by hanging."

Br. Ortega incorporates into his study interesting references and documents that go back as far as 1552, all referring to Antón Martín's activities in Madrid. The 18th century chronicler, Br Juan Sántos, dedicates chapter LXV to Antón Martín and Pedro Velasco in his *Cronología hospitalaria y resumen historial*, Madrid 1715, 244-247.

* Matías de Mina in '*Anotaciones*', *Fondo Documental*, op.cit., says witness # 58 at the Granada beatification process, María de Villavicencio, gives evidence that her daughter was the matron of honour at the wedding of Gil Vázquez Rengifo. Also two members of the Council of Twenty-four, were further witnesses, their names being Gonzalo Zegrí and Alonso de Venegas; all belonged to the circle of Juan's friends.

* On the Calle de la Colcha, the precise description also came from the same witness, María de Villavicencio, The scene was described by witness #39 at the Granada process, (Inés de Avila), and #8 at the Madrid process (Juan de Carvajal, a priest, born at Granada but living at Madrid; he was the son of the Secretary of the Granada Royal Chancellery, Martín de Carvajal).

* References to Antón Martín after his meeting with Juan, and later when he was in the Order, are very numerous; for example, the witnesses at the Granada process, #18 (Melchor de Avila), #19 (Jerónimo de Piñar), #26 (Domingo Navarro), #34 (María de la Paz), #48 (Luisa de Avila), #63 (Bartolomé Fernández de Cazorla) and others.

* About Pedro Velasco; G. Magliozzi at an international meeting of brothers and co-workers held at Rome 22 Nov. to Dec. 1995, suggested that Pedro Velasco was the author of the notebook utilised by Castro and that the same notebook might have been used in favour of the brothers at the lawsuit brought against them by the Jeronymites; and that Pedro Velasco might have been the one who gave fundamental input in favour of the brothers. Magliozzi says he probably

remained silent "*out of humility*" when it came to his own conversion. I was able to receive a copy of Magliozzi's paper by courtesy of the General Curia before its presentation. Naturally, the references at this period are less to Pedro Velasco rather than to Antón Martín. The above cited *Galería Hospitalaria* dedicates four chapters from Ch. 16 onwards to Antón Martín: describing the murder at Guadafortuna, the flight of Pedro Velasco, his capture and incarceration in the Granada prison and subsequent condemnation to death (pages 79-80).

* About Juan's assistance to the "*pobres vergonzantes*" (persons too ashamed to beg) see Francisco de Castro op.cit., Chapter 12. Also many witnesses at the Granada beatification process: #13 (Felipe de Alaiz), #34 (María de la Paz), #37 (Francisca de Venegas), #65 (Bernabé Ruiz).

* The episode about Simón de Avila was refered to by many witnesses at the Granada beatification process: #3 (Antón Rodríguez), #33 (Francisca Fernández), #45 (María Osguera), #48 (Luisa de Avila, she said Simón "*died a saint*"), #52 (Mercía Pérez).

* The three episodes "*with women*"; see the '*Floreto*' of Gómez Moreno, *San Juan de Dios, Primicias historicos,* op.cit., 246-248. The comment about the "*woman with an evil tongue*" was made by witness #23 at the Madrid beatification process, (Francisco Jiménez).

* Regarding Domingo Piola; the witness at the Jaén beatification process, Juan Fernández de Encio, said it was really Espinola. Also saying was a witness from the Martos beatification process, Juan López Quesada, who added to the interview of Juan with Piola a picturesque addendum, the annoyance caused to Piola's wife: "This witness heard it being said in the *city of Granada,* that he called upon so-and-so Espinola. He wanted to request alms and to ask for a loan in order to purchase some sheets for the poor. He needed thirty ducats for this and possibly more. When the aforementioned father John of God entered, he found the aforementioned Genoese at dinner. As he entered the room he said that it appeared he might have upset his wife. She had to leave her husband and our father John of God alone. He then spoke about what he had come for. Being asked for a guarantor, the aforementioned father John of God pulled a picture of the Infant Jesus from his sleeves and put it upon the table saying 'Brother, this is my guarantor'."

* The meeting between Juan and Piola was described at the Cordoba beatification process by the witness Sebastían de Carrasquilla who said Domingo Benedicto was the Chief Infirmarian.

* The quotations from the lawsuit brought by the Jeronymites are from J. Sánchez, *Kenosis,* op.cit., 285-297.

* Estefanía de Vallejo testified at the Toledo beatification process on 13-1-1623.

* The text of John of God's letter to Luis Bautista is found in a publication entitled *The Rule of St. Augustine and the Letters of St. John of God,* O. H. General Curia, Rome 1984.

29

IF GOD SO WILLS

Granada
1546-1547

What else has happened to our Juan at Granada up until now? The biographers tell us in an amusing way of a meeting with the Marquis de Tarifa, saying a *marquis tests an alms seeker*. But 'he of Tarifa' is no ordinary *marquis*, but *the most important personage in southern Spain* and, as a result of this episode, a warm friendship sprang up between him and Juan.

The name of Don Pedro Enríquez Afán de Ribera y Portocarrero was usually abbreviated by his contemporaries to Don Perafán de Ribera or simply, 'Duke de Alcalá'. This title he did not have when Juan knew him. Philip II bestowed it upon him ten years later and he also inherited the title, 'Count de Los Molares'. In Juan's time he simply signed his name *Marquis de Tarifa*.

Ancient chronicles and documents point out that the Riberas were a noble Galician family which, since the mid 13th century, fought alongside the king and eventually established its principal branch of the family at Seville. The 14th Lord, Don Pedro Afán, briefly fought the Moors under the command of the Catholic Monarchs. His son, Don Pedro Enríquez, married Doña Catalina de Ribera and died after the taking of Granada. During the first half of the 15th century there were two bishops in the Ribera family, Don Pedro at Lugo, and Don Diego at Segovia.

The Enríquez side of the family was related to princes and kings of Spain ranging from Saint Ferdinand III to Isabella, La Católica. They were given the highest trust that the Crown could confer upon individuals of royal lineage including admirals of Castile and governors general of Andalusia. And many times they were viceroys of Catalonia and Naples. To sum up, they were the *crème de la crème* of Spanish nobility. This was the type of person Juan rubbed shoulder with. Now, see what happens.

In the autumn of 1539 Don Fadrique Enríquez de Ribera, head of the family, died without issue. His brother Ferdinand had predeceased him. Thus Pedro, 'Perafán', son of the deceased Ferdinand and his nephew became heir. The deceased Don Fadrique left an imperishable memory at Seville. From a pilgrimage to the Holy Land, he traced the distances between the stations of the Via Crucis and created a 'Way of the Cross' from his palace towards the roadside Calvary called Cruz del Campo. Today it is held that Seville's famous Holy Week processions evolved from this practice.

His nephew Don Perefán de Ribera was highly decorated with honours: 16th Lord of the House of Ribera, 6th Count of Los Molares, 2nd Marquis de Tarifa, but the most important and illustrious, was 7th Governor General and senior notary of Andalusia. Within a few years time, after Juan's death, he would become the Duke de Alcalá, Viceroy of Catalonia and Viceroy of Naples.

Before he went to live in Catalonia Don Perafán resided in the Casa de Pilotas at Seville. This was the palace where tradition says the first Stations of the Cross began when the Via Crucis was measured out by old Don Fadrique when he returned from the Holy Land. It is because of the first Station of the Cross, 'Jesus condemned by Pilate', that the people of Seville called Fadrique's palace 'Pilate's House'.

The gigantic palace is an architectural marvel surrounded by patios and gardens. Here is where Don Perafán married Doña Leonor de Figuera, and it was here that he carried out his duties as Governor General of Andalusia. He attended to government and judiciary in time of peace, and military command during wartime. Appeals against the Governor General's decision could only be made to the King. Don Perafán travelled extensively in Andalusia and frequently visited Granada where the Royal Chancellery of southern Spain was situated. It was from Granada that he administered his possessions.

Those who knew Don Perafán, Marquis de Tarifa, praised his capacity to command, his noble spirit, his Christian piety: qualities with which he distinguished himself during his fourteen years as Viceroy of Naples. The Neapolitans and Philip II attributed to him the fame of a saint.

Don Perafán was a man of his times and did not hold strict ideas about marriage fidelity. His wife Doña Leonor bore him no children, so he procured them through other women. We know the names of three of his daughters - Catalina, Inés and María - and a son, Juan. Born in 1532, Juan de Ribera studied law at Salamanca University during the years that his father Don Perafán knew Juan the charity worker of Granada, John of God. Don Perafán pulled as many strings as he could to obtain canonical dispensations to facilitate his illegitimate son's rise to high ecclesiastic office. It was worth the effort, for Juan de Ribera ended up as Archbishop of Valencia and a canonised saint of the Church. The mother of Don

Perafán's son was a noble lady of Seville named Doña Teresa de los Pinelo.

The Governor General, Don Perafán, Marquis de Tarifa, was playing cards one evening with a group of his aristocratic friends during one of his frequent visits to Granada. He has a home of his own near the Carrera del Darro, but he much preferred to stay as a guest with his friends the Mendozas.

Some biographers of John of God have been thrown off the track by misinterpreting the word *'posada'* in the documents relating to the Marquis de Tarifa. They say, *"he resided at the Mendoza residence."* The documents use the word *'posada'* which means 'rested or stayed' and not the word *'residir'* meaning 'to reside'. But in this sense, *posada* obviously is not a verb but a noun meaning a 'residence or a house'. This residence was none less than one of Granada's noblest, that of the Mendozas.

Certainly, they too were friends of the charity worker, extremely good friends: Don Juan de Mendoza and his wife Doña Juana de Cárdenas were a couple from amongst the three most aristocratic marriages of Granada; they frequently received our Juan as if it were a visit from an archangel. Juan comes to visit them to request donations for his hospital; they would supply him not only with money, clothing and victuals, but above all their affection. We know of some of this familiarity from Estefanía Vallejo who, as we already know, was the little house maid at the Mendoza palace: even in old age Estefanía still remembered how the poor man Juan would turn up at the palace in his ragged clothes and everyone was as happy as if it were a fiesta:

"Those lords and ladies who brought up this witness, all came together to listen to him and they remained edified by what the holy Padre said and the advice he gave them."

Through Estefanía we know that the Mendozas often gave him new clothes when they saw that Juan *"was wearing something disgustingly disagreeable"*: the new clothes did not last him long, only until he saw a poor man.

Now we have established that the Marquis de Tarifa, Don Perafán de Ribera, was staying in the Mendoza home, it would be worth our while knowing something more about the owners of the palace at Granada where half a dozen gentlemen were playing cards. We can thereby test how the affection for, and admiration of,

Juan circulates through the illustrious arteries of Granada.

Don Juan de Mendoza, grandson of Iñigo López de Mendoza – 2nd Count de Tendilla and firstborn of the Tendilla whom the Catholic Monarchs appointed Governor of Granada – was the son of Bernadino de Mendoza Pacheco: a man of the sea, Don Bernadino, Governor of the fort of Tunis and Captain General of the galleys of Spain. His wife, Doña Elvira, was also of illustrious lineage.

Don Juan inherited his father's love of the sea and also his rank of Captain General of the galleys. *"From 1545 he commanded a squadron"*, confronting the Turks in the Mediterranean and capturing Berber pirates. His wife, Juana de Cárdenas, belonged to a long lineage of landed gentry, the Cárdenas and Carrillos of Albornoz. The married couple, Mendoza and Cárdenas, lived at Granada in their palace at the foot of the Alhambra on lands which had been the orchard and gardens of the kings of Granada, acquired by the Municipal Council in 1497 *"for the celebration of the happy marriage of the Prince"*, Queen Isabella's beloved son who died so prematurely; thereby giving to the barrio the name *'Campo del Principe'*, the Prince's field.

To this palace on the far eastern side of Granada near the Los Molinos Gate where he used to go during his first weeks when he gathered firewood, our alms-seeker now goes with full confidence: the Mendoza Cárdenas hold him in esteem.

What a coincidence, the very night the noble gentlemen were seated around the card-table, along comes Juan seeking alms! The servants knew that the alms-seeker is never to be refused entrance to that house: he goes into the gaming room.

All except the Marquis de Tarifa know Juan and welcomed him warmly: *"They all gave him alms, some two or three ducats, others four of five."*

Tarifa looked at them dumbfounded: *"The Marquis was amazed to see them all giving so much alms to such a man."* The witnesses openly relate: *"When he received this, Juan went on his way.* He carried in his purse *"twenty-five ducats."* Tarifa wanted to know *"how his friends at Granada"* knew so much about the alms-seeker: *"They informed the aforementioned Marquis of the tremendous charity of the blessed man."*

Don Perafán listened to them. He asked himself if all the

many praiseworthy things they said about him were true, or were they all being taken for a ride. Maybe he thought that his peremptory authority called for him to discover if he could have been tricked: "*He made an excuse as if he was going out for something else. In doubt about what they told him, he wanted to find out about it, so he arose and left the game...*"

What did he do? He took from his lodgings a cloak, a large brimmed hat, clothes that were different from those in which Juan had seen him at the gaming table: the story goes, "*he disguised himself.*" He hurried out into the street making sure that he would bump into the alms-seeker.

All Granada talked about what happened that night: how Don Perafán de Ribera begged: "*Brother Juan, I am an honourable man, a stranger and poor; I came here through a lawsuit and am suffering tremendously to maintain honour. I was informed about your charity; I pray you assist me, so that I may not come to do anything offensive to God.*" I have copied these words of Castro which literally coincide, to the letter, with other witnesses.

Juan did not hesitate for a moment, he replied, "putting his hand straight into the purse":

"*I give myself to God, this is what I have been given; take it brother, and may it help you in your need.*" He hands over the twenty-five ducats.

Luis de Valdiva, a former clerk of the Municipal Council, notes "*fifty ducats*", instead of "*the aforementioned twenty-five*": this is the only discrepancy.

Fifty or twenty-five ducats, the Marquis de Tarifa returned to the Mendoza home impressed, it was the exact amount that Juan had collected from the gentlemen at the gaming table: "*He recounted to them what had happened and showed them the money.*"

The following morning Tarifa went to the hospital: "*He began to joke with Juan and say to him: 'Brother, they say you were robbed last night'.*"

Juan: "*I give myself to God, that they did not rob me.*" The Marquis went on joking with him: "*Brother, because you are unable to deny the robbery they did to you, let me take care of it; so here take your twenty-five ducats; and a hundred and fifty gold escudos which I give you as a donation; take care next time you go out.*"

Don Perafán would have gone on fathering illegitimate children who then turned out saints; however he was charitable and generous and he supplied the food for the hospital for a period: *"He arranged for it a hundred and fifty loaves of bread, four sheep and eight fowls; and he ordered that this ration be given to it each day all the while he stayed at Granada."*

An enduring friendship sprang up between the charity worker and the Marquis. Juan captivated Don Perafán.

The Governor General of Andalusia, the most important person in southern Spain, never missed a visit to the hospital each time he arrived at Granada. The Granadinos were astounded when they saw the Marquis de Tarifa dismount his horse to walk along the streets with Juan: *"No matter wherever it was, if he saw him, he would dismount from his horse, embrace him and carry on a conversation with him. On other occasions he would go to visit the hospital and sometimes the Marquis would send someone to bring him to his house to dine with him."*

It was the sort of thing you would expect to see on the evening television news. A ragged pauper sitting down to dinner with the Governor General of Andalusia; his friend Don Perafán Enríquez de Ribera: "The Marquis let it be known, and said, that he dealt with and cherished the blessed man with particular affection."

We will see how the Marquis demonstrated his friendship to the very end: he claimed the honour of being a pallbearer at his funeral.

I must tell you about how Juan was given *"a habit to wear and a change of name"*, which was the definitive conversion of our 'charity worker' Juan, 'the Portuguese bookseller', into 'Brother John of God', 'blessed brother', 'blessed John'.

First I think that it is necessary to dedicate a word or two to the experts who have researched the background of our protagonist.

I think all readers would be interested to know something of the disputation engaged in by a dozen or so researchers into the life of St. John of God.

You, who have followed the movements of Juan up to now, understand it is risky to establish his 'chronologies': It is not easy to fix dates to the movements of this 'anarchical' man. I have had the good fortune to profit from the hard work of persons who, over the years, have patiently laboured to draw up a John of God calendar that fits the evidence of the available documentation. I allude firstly to Rafael María Saucedo who, from 1951 to 1952, published a priceless study that not only outshone previous ones, but has also proved to be a platform for precision of detail.

In this final stage of Juan's life, 1546, only four years before his death, we have to lean upon two facts that hinge upon chronology. The first, when he was given the 'habit'; the second, when he transferred his hospital from the barrio of the Pescadería to the Cuesta Gomérez. Around these two facts spin half a dozen events.

For the two, the Jeronymite 'lawsuit', which as you know occurred twenty-two years after John of God's death, gives us dates that do not agree with the chronology established by Saucedo.

Well, having been obliged to spend many a long night studying the relevant documents, I am holding fast to the Saucedo chronology. I advise the experts to read this chapter's endnotes, and what follows, to see my reasons. But, naturally, the question is open to debate.

Should any of my readers feel like arguing the chronology, which is pretty arid, they will soon see how closely it is backed up by substance, just like marrow in the bone. They should find the endnotes interesting.

Towards the end of 1546 two 'civil-ecclesiastical' events occurred at Granada. They were bought about by the transferral of his Lordship Archbishop Niño de Guevara: Charles V had appointed him president of the Council of Castile and had him elected to Patriarch of the West Indies and Bishop of Sigüenza. His new episcopal see was lower, but his honours higher.

When Don Niño left, two positions fell vacant: the Archbishopric of Granada and the Presidency of the Chancellery.

Master Avila was suggested to fulfil the vacant see of Granada but he bravely resisted it; however, he put forward the name of a friend, a classmate of his younger days at the University of Alcalá, Pedro Guerrero.

The Emperor decided to take his time in filling the vacancy at the Chancellery, possibly because he was taking the advice of those who wanted to separate the ecclesiastic hierarchy from civil command. He appointed Guerrero to be 'only' archbishop; for the Chancellery, he directed that, provisionally, the senior members of each of its composite bodies, under the provisional presidency of the most senior judge, would govern; and that a delegate would carry out a 'visitation', something in the nature of an audit and report of the personnel.

The visitator chosen was someone we have already met, Juan's old friend Don Miguel Muñoz, the priest who had held the position of 'Majordomo-Director' of the Royal Hospital when Juan was admitted there as a madman in 1539.

Muñoz, who had treated Juan kindly and gave him a clean bill of health, was a man of sturdy character. Coming from an ordinary family, he was sent to Salamanca to study under Canon Cañamares; collegiate of the celebrated 'Mayor San Bartolomé', the young man shone as a student. He graduated in canon law and soon occupied positions at the Salamancan Curia. From there he went on to the Granada Chancellery: he became chaplain of the Royal Chapel, and judge of crimes and disputes. Towards 1535 he took up his position at the Royal Hospital, where he gained a reputation for kindness and being an exemplary priest. In the spring of 1540 he was appointed Bishop of Tuy to succeed Bishop Ramírez Fuenleal who had moved to take up the episcopal see of León.

Ramírez Fuenleal did not actually carry out the pastorate of a bishop, either at Tuy or León: during his term as bishop of Tuy, he presided at the Granada Chancellery; during his term as bishop of León, he presided at the Valladolid Chancellery. His episcopal titles were honorific and he appointed vicars to govern the dioceses.

On the other hand, Miguel Muñoz 'functioned' as a bishop: making pastoral visits to his diocese, in spite *"of the country around Tuy being harsh and monstrous."* He governed his diocese until winter 1546. The Granada Chancellery fell vacant when Niño de Guevara departed, the Emperor required Muñoz to make sure he put the 'visitation' into force: it is certain that by the end of December 1546, Muñoz is already at Granada fulfilling his duty. It is also clear that soon after coming to Granada as 'visitator', Charles V appointed him to the presidency of the Valladolid Chancellery.

Therefore, from the winter of 1546 to summer of 1547, Miguel Muñoz carried out his visitation at Granada as Bishop of Tuy, President *"not of the Granada Chancellery but that of Valladolid."*

It is important to know this because at Granada they called him *"Bishop of Tuy, President."*

The visitations of the Chancellery were usually slow and conscientious, taking on the institution along with its dependencies; that is to say, the Royal Hospital and the prisons. Muñoz accomplished his task between the winter of 1546 and the summer of 1547. Charles V appointed him to report to the Royal Council towards the end of June 1547; then he had him transferred from the bishopric of Tuy to that of Cuenca, his native province. Muñoz died in the autumn of 1553 at 65 years of age. Archival documents speak highly of him and make special mention of a phrase he often used in his sermons: *"This we have told you, we know no more; pardon us; if we knew more, we would tell you more."*

Everything indicates that during his term at Granada between the winter of 1546 and the spring of the following year, Muñoz had a close relationship with Juan.

Now I know that the game of dates is in a bit of a muddle, but it is also amusing. You will recall that when Juan arrived back at Granada from Guadalupe via Baeza, some biographers hurried up his return in order that he might be in time to *"have dinner with a bishop"* who had invited him to his table. If that bishop was Ramírez Fuenleal, 'officially' prelate of Tuy but 'in effect' President of the Granada Royal Chancellery, our traveller would have had to arrive at Granada by Christmas 1539; Ramírez Fuenleal, destined for the Valladolid Chancellery, left for his new appointment during the final days of 1539 or early in 1540.

This 'rush' of Juan, Baeza-Guadalupe-Baeza-Granada, is impossible to carry out: too many hours of walking for so few days.

The solution to this conundrum is that it was not Ramírez Fuenleal at all, but some 'other bishop'. The affair seems to have something going for it, at least it was to dine or not with a bishop, the snag is that at that dinner 'a bishop' took the opportunity to 'somehow' give Juan a *habit and name*; that is to say, it was the hierarchy's blessing on the band of hospitallers under Juan's leadership.

So even if Juan had already rushed back from Guadalupe at meteoric speed, he would still have had to appear before the bishop as the well-known charity worker of Granada, director of a hospital and accompanied by the band of disciples that he led.

So, why did some biographers decide that the bishop at the meeting was Ramírez Fuenleal? Castro only gives us some hazy facts: *"And thus it happened that John of God was dining one day with a bishop of Tuy, who was at Granada at that time..."*

The Chancellery clerk, Felepe de Alay, declared to the judges of the Granada Process that, as a small boy, he was out walking with his father when they came across Brother John of God, and they asked him how was it they saw him with his new habit: *"The aforementioned father John of God said: 'Brother, it was given to me through obedience.'"* When pressed to give the reason for the change, Juan explained that *"the Lord Bishop of Tuy, who is the President, had commanded it."*

In effect, Ramírez Fuenleal was the Bishop of Tuy and President of the Royal Chancellery simultaneously.

However, he was not the only one to hold both offices, for so too did Miguel Muñoz, and he was there at a period which fits in much better with the movements of Juan at Granada.

Bishop Muñoz spent the period between 1546 and 1547 as Royal Visitator of the Granada Chancellery: he came from Tuy where he governed his diocese. The Chancellery lacked a president at this period. Muñoz came with absolute faculties. While exercising his office as Visitator at Granada he received his appointment to the presidency of the Valladolid Chancellery. That is to say, in the eyes of the people of Granada, Bishop Muñoz of Tuy was the President of the Royal Chancellery for two reasons: in the one at Granada he was exercising the faculty of President when he was appointed to the one at Valladolid. That is why he has passed into the annals of Granada as *"Bishop of Tuy and President"*, which is quite logical. Putting it like this, it seems appropriate to attribute to Don Miguel Muñoz the meeting with Juan: the dates match and so does the person.

Muñoz was living at Granada when the sermon of Master Avila 'converted' the 'Portuguese bookseller'. He heard all about Juan's bizarre behaviour in the streets; he signed for the admittance of the 'madman' to the Royal Hospital, where without doubt he was aware of the interest of Master Avila in that special patient; he issued him with the 'discharge certificate', and offered him assistance, including the offer to stay on at the hospital *"a few extra days"*, for he saw how *" very thin and ill-treated"* he was. When Muñoz moved to Tuy as bishop in the spring of 1540, Juan's hospitaller adventure was going flat out. And it is possible that Muñoz could have been the unnamed 'Chaplain Royal' who gave some money to Juan for his little house in the Calle Lucena...

When he appeared once more at Granada, Muñoz found Juan's work was going at full swing. Indeed the kind, charitable and devout bishop was very impressed and pleased with what he found his 'old friend' Juan to be doing.

He summoned him and they met. Various witnesses who came forward stated *"that on occasion he sat at his table."* That President, without any doubt, was Muñoz.

It was *"at his table"* he heard from Juan how God was merciful to the poor of Granada; he was aware of the assistance Juan was receiving, due to his fortunate friendship with the Mendozas, the magistrates and the Marquis de Tarifa.

It seemed to the bishop that Juan and his companions should be dressed *"poorly, but not shabbily."*

So Juan was sent for by the bishop to come and dine with him. We have already seen how Juan was not at all overwhelmed by the splendour of the luxurious palaces of Granada when he was invited to take his place at the tables of aristocratic families. This is something that attracts my attention, for he went there dressed in rags: anyone would think that he would have been ashamed to present himself clad like that. Anyway, he went just as he was to seek donations. His ragged appearance and stubby beard gave Juan a rustic appearance as if he did not care in the least what people thought of him: the poor were his kind of people and he was poor like them. Thus he punctually turned up at the bishop's invitation.

Juan did not know what His Excellency had in mind. The bishop, from his point of view, wanted to get Juan to agree to a couple of things. He had invited him on other occasions, it is reported. Juan was not in the least overwhelmed by the grand style of the Chancellery, where he counted many friends among the magistrates and clerks.

Even though the Catholic Monarchs had transferred the southern Chancellery from Ciudad Real to Granada in 1500, *"to make this city more noble and to better serve the people"*, the construction of the beautiful building now standing was not begun until 1531; it was at the height of its construction during the period of our Juan: the tribunal at that time was installed in the street which took its name 'Oidores' from the judges.

Juan came into the bishop's presence and was given a hearty welcome and invited to sit down and dine. Then the bishop came out with what he had in mind.

We cannot say with absolute certainty whether Don Miguel Muñoz, who as *"Bishop of Tuy, President"*, was the actual one who conferred the juridical character upon the two proposals he made to Juan who then accepted them. Nevertheless, the meeting soon took on an aspect of major importance: it signified the ecclesial reception of Juan's hospitaller initiative, which up to then he had been running on an *ad hoc* basis; and in a certain manner was the commencement of the future Hospitaller Order of Brothers.

They ate and chatted. Juan related what he had been doing. The bishop wanted to know something of Juan's past life, a subject which, according to all indications, our man tenaciously refused to discuss. To the Granadinos, he was the 'alms-seeker' who previously was called 'the Portuguese', sold books and ended up 'converted' in the Campo de los Mártires. At the insistent prompting of the bishop Juan was unable to escape from his family origins into this misty mantle. I am sure that that did not escape the biographer Don Francisco de Castro who knew Juan's Jewish secret and resolved to mislead his readers from the first page of his book. Also Bishop Muñoz, to whom Juan confided his enigma during that meeting, found an intelligent way to remain discreet.

I am not elaborating an arbitrary hypothesis. Seeing how Juan felt, the bishop all of sudden puts to Juan his question: *"What have you been calling yourself?"*

He calls himself simply *"Juan"*, as Don Miguel knows. The bishop wanted to know Juan's surname and family antecedents: and why he maintained a certain silence about his past life.

"Ciudad" is the surname... the surname of a Jewish family. Don Miguel would have been surprised; he understood the prudence of the *'Conversos'* who were integrated in the community of the faithful at Granada, where purity of blood was a requisite for so many offices and positions.

In this light, the 'official' imposition of a 'pure' surname takes on a special and deep meaning, not only religious, also civil: *"He asked him what he was called."* Then, clearly *"he said to him that he was called Juan."* And the bishop decided: *"That he should call himself Juan de Dios."*

469

"*Juan de Dios*" [John of God]. I agree with the observation of my good friend Brother Matías de Mina, who thinks that Don Miguel Muñoz 'ratified' the title that the people of Granada had already given him for some time. From the time of his 'madness' when the street boys invited the 'madman': take a fall for God, kiss the ground for God, dance for God; with Juan complying every time with their directions no matter how outlandish that they might be.

Later on they will see him "*asking alms for God*"; and "*for God*" they give it. John of God [from now on this is what we will call him], is his name and surname, bestowed on him by the people. Now the bishop confirms it by issuing '*this identity card*': "*You will call yourself John of God.*" Left behind and forgotten is the dangerous old surname 'Ciudad'.

Juan, feeling a mixture of humility and affection for the bishop, simply repeats to him the pleasant addition that he has invented to create for him a name for which he considered himself totally unworthy.

They are to call him "John of God"? He responds, meekly, confidently: "*If God so wills.*"

I believe that there are only three or four expressions in the immense collection of the lives of Christian saints so charged with faith, filial love, naturalness and tenderness: "*John of God... if God so wills.*"

Brilliant! These words go to the truth of the man's being. They are the prayer of a man of faith: "*if God so wills.*"

If it seems good to God, then I do not mind if they give me this name, if he forgives me my presumption and boldness. I am not worthy, I am only Juan, the poor one; however, I am quite happy... If God so wills.

"*Be at peace John of God.*"

"*... if God so wills.*"

The after-dinner conversation would be long. Don Miguel and John of God continued to talk. The bishop now wanted to mention a somewhat delicate matter of his own. To him it was seemly that John of God and his companions dressed poorly, since after all, they did care for the poor. However, since they had to enter the homes of distinguished persons in their quest of alms, and often meet with persons of high society, it was important that they should appear more neatly attired:

"*Brother John of God, just as you take that name from here for the rest of your life you will also take a way of dressing, since what you are wearing offends and disgusts those who have the goodness to sit you at their table.*"

Surely John was not expecting such a proposal. It would shock him. Nevertheless, he does not resist, he takes it as it comes: "*if God so wills.*" It was unimportant to him.

Obviously, if the bishop gave him a habit to wear, he would not be able to take it off and exchange it for the miserable rags of a poor man: "*John of God had the custom that when he dressed any poor man in his clothing, he would dress himself in that of the poor man.*"

Without hesitation he accepted the proposition of the bishop, who in truth had already given the matter serious thought and had made up his mind; and having made arrangements, he presented the attire:

"*And you shall wear a smock and trousers of coarse cloth and a sackcloth cloak besides, they are three things in the name of the Most Holy Trinity.*"

This shows that Bishop Muñoz had arranged a well planned meeting in which he used the liturgical formulas for clothing members of religious congregations in their habits. Castro carefully adds more details and tells us that the Bishop bought the clothes for John of God, blessed them and put them on him.

"*Then the Bishop sent out to buy (that habit), clothed him with his own hands.*"

For Castro it was important to emphasise the type of encounter that had taken place; he accepts without doubt the conviction of the sons of John of God who, after the founder's death, considered this to have been a fundamental step in the history of the Order:

"*The apparel worn by John of God, and the name that he bore, were not without mystery.*"

Even that John of God would maintain faithful to the name and habit, as he did (*"he never changed it until he died"*) was itself significant. Then when one adds the particular episcopal intervention, it appears like an action of the official Church directed at the life and plans of John of God; for evidently the initiative

471

belongs to Muñoz. John of God 'acquiesces to it voluntarily', 'he carried' name and habit to his death. He bears them conscious of what it means to have received them *"with the blessing of the bishop."*

So from that day forth, John of God wore that attire. We have the valuable testimony of the clerk Juan Lobo, who was a lad of fifteen or sixteen at the time when he saw him; and his parents were devoted friends of John: *"With the change of clothing he was given a pair of rough linen breeches that came to his knees, and a shirt of the same material. Over that he wore a very rough smock open down the sides. This also came down as far as his knees. His feet were bare and his beard and hair were usually shaved with a razor. He never wore a hat or anything else. He used to go out into the streets of this city to beg, even when it was raining or snowing. He did not return at night until about twelve o'clock. He used to call out: 'Brothers and sisters, who wants to do good for themselves?'"*

As John of God did, so did his own. Antón Martín, Pedro, Simón, Domingo, Juan García, his followers, dressed in the same clothing. And those who came afterwards, for he gathered new companions. 'Disciples' of that master of charity called John of God... *"If God so wills."*

The people in the street soon noticed the change, seeing them "in habits." They approved the new dress and asked John about it. He answered: *"Brothers and sisters, it was given to me under obedience."*

You know, as the year 1546 gave way to 1547, things began to heat up for John of God. His patients could not fit into the hospital. A larger place was needed. Companions 'of his habit' were helping him in his work. The noble families of Granada supported him. He would attempt to create a new hospital. Come what may.

This had to happen soon, for this man's time was running out. Public beggars and the poor *vergonzantes* who discretely came to seek alms, all the sorrowful ones of the city looked up to him. He now also gathered in abandoned children. And there were also the prostitutes,

"John of God", the name is like magic as it circulates throughout every corner of Granada. It is like a breath of fresh air coming down from the sierra. *"If God so wills."*

Notes to Chapter 29

* On Perafán Enríquez de Ribera and the Dukes de Alcalá: Cf. A. Ballesteros y Beretta, *Historia de España y su influencia en la historia universal*, Barcelona 1912; A. García Carraffa, *Enciclopedia heráldica y genealógica hispano americano XXXI*, Madrid 1958; A López de Haro, *Secunda parte del mobiliario genealógico de los reyes y títulos de España*, Madrid 1622; S. Montoto, *Sevilla en el Imperio*, Seville 1938; R. Robres Lluch, *San Juan de Ribera*, Barcelona 1960.

* A profile of Perafán de Ribera is given by R. M. Saucedo in *Labor Hospitalaria* #32 (1953) 149-157, about the trap which the biographers fell into regarding the word *posada*, which they took to mean an inn, whereas the word *posada* can, and in this case does mean, a residence. These biographers have not measured the magnitude of the personage of the Marquis de Tarifa; M. de Mina has pointed this out in his *'Anotaciones', Fondo Documental*, in the chapter *'Don Juan de Mendoza y Doña Juana de Cárdenas'*, and in the chapter *'Tarifa'*, where he sets out the lineage of both famous persons; he also indicated family members and about the visit in his *Visitar la Granada de San Juan de Dios*, op.cit., 145-161. Also see G. Magliozzi, Pagine Juandediane, op.cit., where he treats of the Viceroy of Naples.

* Perafán de Ribera died without a legitimate heir. His possessions and titles passed to his brother Ferdinand, the 3rd Marquis de Tarifa who was married to Doña Juana Cortés, daughter of the *Conquistador* of New Spain (Mexico). The Enríquez de Riberas went on with their tradition of engendering bastard sons and had them placed in high ecclesiastic positions, then in the mid-17th century we meet another illegitimate son, a bishop, who was born in Mexico and exercised the office of Viceroy. He was an Augustinian friar and died after his retirement in the Castilian convent of Nuesta Señora del Risco.

* Apart from the reliable account given by Francisco de Castro, op.cit., Chapter 18, there are the statements of the witnesses at the Granada beatification process: #5 (Gabriel Maldonado) and # 56 (Catalina de Arenas). Estefanía de Vallejo testified at the Toledo beatification process and was # 84: She was listed amongst those who personally knew John of God. In the same category appears the following witnesses who confirmed the episode: #3 (Antón Rodríguez), #8 (Pedro López de Eslava), #10 (Pedro Franc de León), #13 (Felipe de Alaiz), #14 (Melchor de Espinosa). #20 (Diego Marín), #25 (Melchor de Almirante), #29 (Alonso Sánchez Dávila), #32 (Baltasar Suárez), #36 (Juan Bautista Bravo), #38 (Catalina de Echaves), #40 (Tomás de Pedrosa), #87 (Miguel de las Higueras who made his statement at Jaén). Luis de Valdivia, the clerk who elevated the donation to 50 ducats, was witness #78 and made his statement at Matos on 14 January 1623.

* Don Juan Mendoza died violently, drowning at La Herradura on the Almuñécar coast when the galleys he was commanding were sailing towards Orán and were overtaken by a cyclone. Cf. C. Calero, *Aportación documental en torno al naufragio de la Armada española en La Herradura*. A synthesis of this work appears in M. de Mina, *'Anotaciones', Fondo Documental*, op.cit., chapter 56.

* For the Saucedo chronology mentioned above, Cf. R. M. Saucedo, *Cronológia aplicada en la vida de N. P. S. Juan de Dios*: Paz y Caridad 11 & 12 (1951); 13-18 (1952). The text of the statements of the witnesses in the celebrated lawsuit of the Jeronymites is edited and presented by J. Sánchez in his *Kenosis*, etc., op.cit., 285-429.

* It seems opportune to set out the dates, some inevitably incomplete, of the bishops and archbishops who had a connected with John of God at Granada: Gaspar de Avalos: Archbishop of Granada, 22-1-1529 to 29-3-1542.
  * Sebastián Ramírez de Fuenleal: President of the Granada Royal Chancellery 1-2-1538. Bishop of Tuy from 29-7- 1538; Bishop of León and President of the Valladolid Royal Chancellery 29-10-1539.
  * Miguel Muñoz; Bishop of Tuy 21-4- 1540.
  * Ferdinand Niño de Guevara: archbishop of Granada and President of the Granada Royal Chancellery.
  * Sebastián Ramírez de Fuenleal: went to be Bishop of Cuenca 25-7-1542. He abandoned the presidency of the Valladolid Royal Chancellery.
  * Miguel Muñoz; Bishop of Tuy, became President of the Valladolid Royal Chancellery.
  * Pedro Guerrero: Archbishop of Granada 28-10-1546.
  * The Granada Royal Chancellery was without a president from 1546 to 1549.
  * Miguel Muñoz, Bishop of Tuy: Royal Visitator of the Granada Royal Chancellery, in the winter of 1546.
  * Miguel Muñoz went to be the Bishop of Cuenca in June 1547. He continued as President of the Valladolid Royal Chancellery. (13-9-1553.
  * Diego de Ayala y Esquivel, President of the Granada Royal Chancellery 1549.
  * Pedro Guerrero (2-4-1576.
* Regarding the stay of Miguel Muñoz at Granada during the winter of 1546, see M. de Mina in 'Anotaciones', Fondo Documental, op.cit., Chapter 82, foglio 9 reproduces a records from the parish archives of the Sagrario - the register of baptisms, fol., 283, 27 December 1546. This shows that Miguel Muñoz, along with the Oidor (judge) Páez and the Countess de Santisteban, were the Godparents of the infant Mencía, daughter of Don Alvaro de Bazán.
* The testimony of witness #13, Felipe de Alay at the Granada beatification process is described along with that of #30 in the 'Floreto' of Gómez Moreno, San Juan de Dios, Primicias historicos, op.cit., 258. Although he said he belonged to the parish of San Juan de los Reyes, his death is registered in that of San José: Both parishes had a large number of royal clerks residing in them as well as other officials who belonged to the Royal Chancellery. Because of the convenience to the place of their employment, they established their homes in the streets of both parishes which were close to the Royal Chancellery. If Felipe de Alay died in the parish of San José it could mean that he had changed his address between 1623 and 11-1-1625 the date of his death. Cf. M. De Minas, 'Anotaciones', Fondo Documental, witness #13, op.cit.
* For the identification of Miguel Muñoz as the 'chaplain' who gave economic aid to John of God when he was starting off at the Calle Lucena, see M. De Mina, Dudas historicas en torno al obispo de Tuy que impuso el hábito a Ssan Juan de Dios: 'Juan Ciudad' #366 91991) 24.
* On the construction of the Royal Chancellery, see A. Gallego Burín Granada. Guía del viajero, op.cit., 329-336.
* The following witnesses at the Granada beatification process testified about the change of name and the reception of the habit: #1 (Juan Lobo), 33 (Antón Rodríguez), #5 (Gabriel Maldonado), #8 (Pedro López de Eslava), #29 (Alonso Sánchez Dávila), 332 (Baltasar Suárez), #55 (Juana Gálvez), #66 (Antón de

Morasca). Their statements were very touching, for example, Juana Gálvez: *"This witness saw the aforementioned John of God and Antón Martín and others, who went about their duties of service to the poor at the hospital wearing the habit. When asked why they wore these habits, they said it was because the President of the Royal Chancellery had given them to them; because the lords and the elite society wanted it so and they esteemed them greatly for it."* Gabriel Maldonado said: *"It was well known in this city that the aforementioned Bishop of Tuy, being President of the Chancellery...., and since then he changed to the habit, because prior to that all he wore was a jacket consisting of two flaps tied together that came down as far as his knees."*

* Cf. J. Santos, *Cronología hospitalaria y resumen historial*, op.cit., 544. Santos strongly emphasises the importance of the ceremony which he attributes to the initiative of Miguel Muñoz, Ibid., 230. Cf. E. Flórez, *España sagreada XXIII*, Madrid 1799, 31. This author speaks of Miguel Muñoz as the Bishop of Tuy as the same mentioned by Castro.

* For the history of the Royal Chancelleries: Cf. P. Gan Giménez, *La Real Chancillería de Granada* (1504-1834), Granada s. f.; M. S. Martín Postigo, *Los presidentes de la real Chancillería de Valladolid*, Valladolid 1985; A. A. Ruiz Rodríguez, *La real Chancillería de Granada en el siglo XVI*, Granada 1987.

30

THE HOSPITAL IN THE CUESTA GOMEREZ

Granada
1547

He called them his *"gavilancicos"*, his little nestling hawks. It is something new for John of God to be occupying himself with the care of children, both orphans and foundlings. Certainly, he did it in his own way. He came across an abandoned little creature muffled up in a bundle of old clothes where it had been left. He gathered it up and put it in his basket. Thus he gave a surprise to many an adoptive family bringing the gift of a baby, with the request that it be raised as their own. News about him taking responsibility for abandoned babies quickly spread.

Once he was requested to collect a baby girl: *"who had neither mother, father nor anyone else to care for her, so they gave her to the blessed father John of God."* When he went to fetch her *"he put her into his basket and took her to a home at Gabia"* a small rural village on the outskirts of Granada that figured importantly in the conquest of Granada.

"He gave the baby to them to bring up" and visited that family *"three times in three days"* but since he did not like the way they were treating the baby, he took it away again. Then *"he confided the baby to the care of someone in the Realejo to be raised."* This was the neighbourhood then preferred and populated by the Jews.

As the child grew up John of God realised that he would not be alive to see her married, so *"he left fifty ducats for her marriage,"* as a way of providing for her.

Because this touched me I am going to recount the story. The little one was called Ginesa. We know her story thanks to an old man who at 83 years of age tells it, and by way of conclusion says, *"This witness affirms it, because he later married the aforementioned child."*

This was Francisco de Olivares, a tailor by profession. At the age of twenty-five he married Ginesa in the parish church of San Cecilio. Old Francisco confirmed that his wife's dowry had already been paid for *"with the fifty ducats left by blessed John of God, which I withdrew with the accrued interest."*

They lived happily, bringing up their children and taking care of *"others whose parents were unknown."* They were influenced by the example of the man of charity. Francisco repeated the story of his wife, the "baby girl" protected by Brother John of God: *"Her name was Ginesa Pulido, and she is now deceased."* When Francisco saw that she was dying he asked for a place for her in the John of

God Hospital, where the Brothers stayed by her side until she died.

I confess that I was truly moved by the little story related by Ginesa's husband.

He even found time for the street urchins and would take a group of them to buy shirts at a popular shop in the Calle Tundidores: *"Since it was a clothing shop he outfitted many children there, and this was how he dressed as many as twenty at a time; and he paid for all they needed in clothing."*

Many charming anecdotes about him (more than you could count) were widely circulated.

On one of his typical journeys, John of God passed through the village of Albolete, situated four kilometres from Granada on the road to Jaén, where he would have gone seeking alms. There was a small hospital there and when he arrived he saw many people mingling about. They told him the news *"that a woman has given birth to twin boys."*

John of God entered the hospital, *"with his basket slung over his shoulder"*, *"and arriving at the poor woman who had delivered,"*: *"he gave her some alms, to help her get better."* He did more. As he departed *"he took one of the baby boys and wrapping him in a blanket, placed him in his basket and carried him back to Granada."* He then searched for a family to care for him: *"They called him Jorge."*

A Hospitaller Brother told the judges at the Beatification Process held at Ubeda that as a young man he used to quest for alms on the outskirts of Granada. In the hamlets of the flat country they used to speak about the visits of John of God. Some country homesteads belonged to rather elegant families, as did the 'Manor-house' of the Alcarón family, whose forebears were soldiers in the army of the Catholic Monarchs. This Brother heard from them the following story. It so happened that Don Alonso had gone off to war under the banner of the Emperor and his wife had not received any news of him for three months. John of God found her *"very distressed."* He consoled her, hazarding a prophecy: *"Do not be distressed, for your husband is well and within a year you will see him return victorious."*

The poor woman *"persisted in her feelings"* of sorrow. John of God had brought, hidden in his basket, a child that *"he had found abandoned in a church porch."* He had been searching for a foster home for the infant so, without a moment's hesitation, he handed the little baby over to Señora Alcarón saying: *"Have no doubt that it is your duty to bring up this gavilancico* [nestling] *for the glory and honour of Our Lord, until your husband comes back. He then handed her a large basket containing the infant."*

The story had a happy ending, for the lady *"took the baby because it had been given by such a great holy man, and she raised him until he was eighteen years of age"*: when he went off to war following in the footsteps of his adoptive father. Alcarón had arrived safely home *"within a year."*

John became famous for the interest that he took in abandoned children. An interest that, in the next case, could have had unwanted results. Instead we can smile at the happy ending.

We owe this story to Luis Ordóñez who left Granada to settle at Valladolid where he set up a business as a *'jubetero'*, a maker of mail doublets called *'jubetes'*. The *'jubón'* [doublet] extended from the shoulders to cover the waist. The *'jubete'* gave soldiers an added protection of mail, more or less the equivalent of the modern-day 'bullet-proof vest', but it was good only against lances.

It so happened, says Ordóñez, that the husband of a certain woman of Granada went away to war and stayed away for many years before returning home. In the meantime, the woman, who was having an affair, gave birth to an infant: *"Eventually the husband returned home and found that she had given birth to a baby, which was now a small child."* He wanted to kill the adulteress *"for such a betrayal."*

His wife, in fright, tried to save herself by appealing to our charity worker. She put the blame on John of God, explaining to her husband: *"Do not be so upset and troubled, for the baby you find here was a pitiful abandoned waif brought to our home by the blessed John of God. Since it was an abandoned baby he also paid me enough to raise him."* The husband locked his wife up in the house, pocketed the key, *"made sure that the woman could not speak with anyone while he was absent,"* and then set off to find John of God.

Now, according to the tradition of Granada, an unknown angel takes control of the situation. Maybe it was John of God's guardian angel, or that of the adulteress, or her husband's, or possibly even that of the innocent baby. That is the best explanation that can be found for John of God's stroke of intuition. When he saw the angry husband coming towards him, without knowing his or his wife's identity, he ventured to tackle the situation head on: *"Brother, I am well aware that you are concerned about your wife on account of the baby I left with her. The poor little waif was an orphan, so I have left enough money to pay for him each month in order to bring him up in your home, so if you do not want to have him in your home, just hand him back to me."*

The poor man was completely dumbfounded and regretted his hasty judgement: *"He begged blessed John of God to pardon him and said he wanted to keep the baby in his home and let his wife continue to raise him."*

One wonders what would have happened if the angels had taken no notice!

John of God by the year 1547 had his 'name' John of God, a 'habit' with episcopal recognition, companions and a small but growing team. His little hospital seems to have consisted of the 'house' itself together with the lower floors or cellars of nearby buildings. Because it was full to overflowing by day and night, it was urgent that 'his enterprise' be transferred to more spacious premises. The question was, where?

It would obviously have to be outside the Pescadería; for it would be impossible to find there a large enough property at a reasonable cost.

This overcrowding was not only obvious to John of God but also to his companions, his wealthy friends, the ladies who helped him, as well as the Archbishop himself. They were all equally concerned at the lack of space for so many sick and others seeking refuge.

The Archbishop had returned to Granada in November 1546. At forty-five, Pedro Guerrero, a native of La Rioja, was six years younger than John of God. Born at Leza, a little village near Logroño, Guerrero went to grammar school at Sigüenza, at that time one of Spain's most powerful dioceses. He studied arts at Alcalá and theology at Sigüenza from where, well equipped dialectally, he went to Salamanca, to the college of San Bartolomé. Together with Francisco de Vitoria he received his doctorate. Then he occupied the Chair of Thomistic Theology as associate professor. In 1535 he gained the Primary Chair of Sigüenza University located off-campus at 'San Antonio de Portaceli. Whilst preparing to take possession of the Chair of Canon Law at Cuenca, vacancies occurred in the episcopacy. The bishop of Sigüenza, Ferdinand de Valdés, went to Seville, and Niño de Guevara was transferred from Granada to Sigüenza leaving the Granada see vacant. Philip II 'invited' Master Avila to accept Granada but the Master suggested the name of his friend Guerrero: Avila stepped aside, Guerrero complied.

He arrived at Granada at a difficult time when, as we know, construction in the capital was at fever pitch. The city was invaded by public servants, soldiers, architects, builders, labourers and people from all walks of life, noble and ignoble. The Alpujarras [areas between Granada and Almería] beneath an outward show of peace, were boiling away heralding a rebellion by the Moors. Islamic and Christian cultures were not integrating or living comfortably alongside one another. Miserable mercenaries from Flanders and weary sailors from the Indies sought shelter at Granada. Government by the Alhambra was too far away to control the citizens, the Chancellery was subject to a Royal Visitation, the University had just opened, the building of the Cathedral was progressing at a very slow pace and the clergy were apathetic.

Pedro Guerrero appealed to his friend Avila to come to Granada as quickly as possible to advise him. Avila promised from Montilla that he would come when he could *"be free of some traps"* (as he used to call his commitments). He waited a year.

By Christmas 1546, the new Archbishop already knew of the charitable works of 'blessed John of God'. Poor and rich spoke about his accomplishments. He was amazed how the alms-seeker had won the goodwill of noble families. He received a thorough report from the Bishop of Tuy, Miguel Muñoz, the Visitor of the Royal Chancellery and the one responsible for John of God's name and habit. With these references, and considering the talent of Pedro Guerrero, we can deduce that he would have known John of God personally, perhaps calling him to his residence or visiting him in his hospital.

It is not certain whether the transfer from the Pescadería to the new site was either partially or fully completed when Guerrero took possession of his see. However, I believe that the dates of the arrival of the Archbishop and the transfer of the hospital coincide.

It is my opinion that John changed the location of his hospital during the winter months between the end of 1546 and the beginning of 1547. This 'classic' opinion is based on Saucedo's chronology which today is put under question due to certain declarations made by witnesses in the famous 'Jeronymite lawsuit'.

Chapter sixteen of Castro's biography is entitled, '*How they purchased for John of God a house for his Hospital.*" An excerpt of the text says "*so many people*" arrived there "*because of the fame*" of John of God and "*his immense charity*" that they were forced to expand his little hospital.

When you visit Granada, please go and take a cup of coffee in one of the cafes in the Plaza Nueva. Allow yourself to soak in the peacefulness of that place, one of the noblest spaces of our planet. Then take a deep breath and start climbing the Cuesta Gomérez that goes up to the Alhambra. Take it easy, without hurrying on the steep rise with its rustic appearance, for, unless you take it quietly, you will become very tired.

Just imagine what it would have been like for John of God with a sick person on his shoulders, climbing that muddy street on winter nights. The question arises, How was it that John of God and his brothers chose to have a hospital on top of such a steep grade? Transport for the sick and dying in those days was not by means of today's chromed ambulances, but in their arms in accordance with their times.

The choice of the house was 'possibly' due to its cost which, the documents say, was four hundred ducats.

The street climbs directly uphill from the Plaza Santa Ana to the Alhambra. There are three ways to go up to the Nasrides palaces but the Cuesta Gomérez, according to my friend Paco Izquiredo, "*is really the only proper way.*" Gently curved, the incline is cut off at the Puerta de las Granadas [Pomegranates Gate] where three arches give entrance to the woods of the Alhambra. These groves were planted with the idea of softening the military appearance of the Nazaride complex during John of God's time. The Gate was built under the orders of Charles V who had the Bib Albuxar Tower demolished. This was one of the three fortified towers that were set among the poplar groves encircling the Alhambra.

If you sit on the bank of the little brook that happily gurgles its way down the hillside you can see, at the foot of the gate, the houses that were once on the property of the hospital. The

Torres Bermejas [vermilion towers] to one side and the Alcazaba [citadel] on the other, flank the Cuesta Gomérez. Having made the effort to climb here *"you can breathe well, Granada."* Know that doses of history and works of art have been added to Granada's naturally pure atmosphere.

It must have been a terrific effort for John of God to climb up from the plaza below with a sick person clinging to his neck, especially when it rained, because then, according to sketches in ancient documents, the street became a ravine that carried off the waters of the Alhambra to the Darro.

Even so, high up here, on the edge of the channel, John had found a good place of repose for his sick people, with the Alhambra at their backs, Granada at their feet, and the sky, they can almost touch, by simply raising their hands!

They purchased this ramshackle building for John of God, situated on the last block on the left as you ascend the Cuesta Gomérez, immediately next to the Gate of the Pomegranates.

If you look at the map of the Alhambra, you will notice something that appears like a boat rigged out to sail the waters of Granada. The keel corresponds to the Alcazaba, with the Vela Tower gracefully planted upon its stern with flags fluttering in the wind. The slope of the hill which rises from the banks of the Darro owes its name to the Gomérez who were a troop of valiant Moors who came from Vélez de la Gomera on the African coast and established their camp here. They arrived to become the king's praetorian guard and always remained faithful to him. Although the history of the Nazride kingdom conceals endless treacheries within its pages, it seems that the Gomérez remained untainted by these courtly intrigues.

Shortly after the conquest of Granada a group of Franciscan nuns arrived from Castile and settled in the shadow of the Vela Tower. They made an error of choice. Around 1540 they moved to a new site in a road called Vistillas de los Angeles near the Molinos Gate. Commander Rodrigo de Ocampo, with the approval of his wife Leonor de Cáceres, built a convent for them called Our Lady of the Angels. The building (today No.39) in the Cuesta Gomérez, was left vacant for seven years until it was purchased for John of God by *"important and devout persons."*

Records are lacking regarding who made the purchase or

gave it to him. There is no way of finding the 'possible title deeds' among the mass of notarial protocols of the period. Nevertheless, the witnesses at the Jeronymite court case offered some names.

The first witness to testify was our friend Angulo, John of God's loyal employee. He said the house was *"bought for four hundred ducats,"* by *"the goodness of the Marquis de Mondéjar and many other gentlemen of the city."* We owe our thanks to Angulo for this choice piece of information about the new hospital.

Other Jeronymite court case documents speak of certain distinguished *"gentlemen and ladies"*: *"Doña Magdalena, mother of Don Pedro de Bobadilla, gave quite a considerable donation."*

Thus declared Leonor de Cáceres, Commander Rodrigo's wife, the couple who donated the convent building in the Vistillas. Doña Leonor is the same lady who suggested to her friends that the abandoned building in the Cuesta Gomérez might serve John of God as a hospital.

When the good Commander Rodrigo, who was a member of the City Council of Twenty-four, died and left Leonor a widow, she involved herself with charities. She was also contrary, and even bossy, exchanging gossip around the city inaccurately. However, she remembered facts of interest, and above all it made her very happy to attribute to her mother the glory of having helped blessed John of God in the purchase of the building on the Cuesta Gomérez. Consider this interesting paragraph:

"The aforementioned John of God... had a house rented in the street of the Pescaderia; in it he gathered the poor and had some palliasses for them; he sustained them with alms given to him in the city. John of God, being in the house in the Pescadería, Doña Francisca de Caçeres, who was the mother of this witness, went to see him. And seeing that the aforementioned John of God was in such poverty and want, she said to him that she would join with him in procuring a house for the poor. And soon they went looking for a house and they purchased one in the Calle de los Gomeles [Cuesta Gomérez]*."*

Benito de los Rios: *"Cleric and chaplain at the Chapel Royal at Granada"*, confirms the assistance given for the purchase of the building in the Cuesta Gomérez: *"This house of the aforementioned John of God was purchased with the funds which had been given to him."*

The witness, Martín de Baeza, understood that *"the aforementioned house was bought with the donations collected by the aforementioned John of God and by those which were also donated by other persons."* The priest Ambrosio Maldonado confirmed this: *"The Marquise de Mondéxar* [Mondejar], *the mother of the present Marquis... and Doña Francisca de Caçeres and other persons, seeing that the work of the aforementioned John of God should go on..."*

It is obvious, I believe, that the *Caçeres* ladies were very active in the venture. Doña Leonor might be a gossip but she knew these circumstances in detail.

The following is somewhat mischievous and is strictly without foundation. Nevertheless I am left feeling uneasy. If Doña Leonor, who donated the monastery of Nuestra Señora de los Angeles, was left the owner of the old abandoned property in the Cuesta Gomérez, did she pocket the 400 ducats which was the price paid by John of God's friends? I know that is rather a naughty thought!

Anyway, the cleric Maldonado told us that John of God paid rent for the house in the Pescadería so his friends advised him *"to purchase"* a building, which he did:

"The aforementioned John of God, with the donations from the above mentioned persons and other particular ones, purchased the aforementioned house of the Calle de los Gomeles."

We already know that Master Avila supported John of God's work from a distance. The fact that the new Archbishop, Pedro Guerrero, generously dipped into his purse for the translocation and installation *"at a cost of one thousand and five hundred ducats"*, is affirmed by another of John of God's biographers, Fray Antón de Govea. This writer I hold suspect, since he copies Dionisio Celi's apparitions and miracles, but he can be trusted with respect to normal data. Govea says, and it appears to Saucedo to be accurate: *"Many persons helped him in this change and no one gave a more generous hand than Don Pedro Guerrero."*

The recently arrived Archbishop had never witnessed anything to compare with what John of God was 'presenting' in his diocese. No wonder he hastened to cooperate!

John of God and his band saw to the transfer of the patients from the old hospital at the Pescadería to the Cuesta Gomérez. The comings and goings of those extraordinary processions crossed the heart of the city at various times during the day, always following the same route: Plaza Bibarrambla to the Calle Zacatín and the Plaza Nueva before entering the Cuesta

Gomérez. One would not have to go far in Granada to find out what was happening in John of God's life.

I maintain this translocation occurred during the early weeks of 1547, in the depth of winter. Readers are referred to the endnotes to this chapter where the polemics of specialists' chronologies are addressed.

The whole city knew the reason for the translocation and this is in perfect harmony with the testimony of witnesses at the beatification process: *"Since no more people could fit into the house at the Pescadería, he took a much larger one in the Cuesta Gomeles [Gomérez]. It was high up and on the left hand side going uphill and it was close to the Alhambra Gate."*

The 'hospital' in the Cuesta Gomérez was quite large, truly a hospital, and it immediately began to function and make good progress as such. But for John of God there were problems: the building, beds, the kitchen equipment and provisions, plus the inevitable costs of setting up the hospital, all drew heavily upon his funds.

As well, a multitude of patients came in. They were looking for John of God. Castro notes it almost with surprise: *"So great was the crowd of people who came to deal with hm that often there was scarcely enough room to stand."*

Twenty-two years after the death of John of God, the statements made at the 'Jeronymite court case' by eye-witnesses described the course of progress made at the hospital on the Cuesta Gomérez. The statements of some of his close collaborators highlighted two important characteristics peculiar to *"the hospital of John of God"* at Granada in those days. These were organisation and style.

From the point of view of organisation, John of God took a gigantic step forward at the Cuesta Gomérez, gaining for himself a place in the history of nursing and hospitality. It was here that Cesare Lombroso found the motives for including John of God in his gallery of *"madmen of genius"* and the grounds for considering him among the creators of *'the modern hospital'*: it was *"the first sanatorium which divided the patients into categories, and the first to give shelter to the homeless."*

"He arranged it in the form of a hospital, dividing illnesses and patients so that they might be cared for in separate wards themselves."

The eyewitnesses specifically emphasised that he set up

the house in the *"form of a hospital"*. This observation, so often repeated, indicates a deliberate purpose transmitted by John of God to his collaborators as a bold innovation: *"He set a section apart as a ward for women."* Not simply female patients, but also for the women, *"he rescued from the public houses."*

In order to carry out this plan, he had to make the building ready. Renovations were to cost him a great deal of money, so we are going to see him in financial difficulties despite the donations he received: *"In the aforementioned house he installed a kitchen and other services at a cost of more than four hundred ducats."*

Furthermore, *"Having purchased the aforementioned house in the Calle de los Gomeles, he worked upon it in order to put it into order... and after installations and repairs, the aforementioned John of God moved into it."*

He provided the hospital with the necessary furniture: *"he acquired beds and everything necessary"*:

"Even this witness helped him to appeal for the aforementioned beds among particular ladies, and she joined with him to buy timber for twenty-four beds."

"This witness" was, of course, Doña Leonor de Caçeres, who would not be missing when the rooms at the new hospital were being set up.

Our friend Angulo mentions, *"clothing and other necessary things for the aforementioned hospital."*

No one has left us a detailed description of the wards, nevertheless some of Castro's phrases permit us to obtain a glimpse of the itinerants lodged on the ground floor of the night refuge, where John of God greeted them *"at daybreak"*: *"He came down to visit them before they moved off; and those who needed clothing were given what had been left by the deceased."*

On arriving downstairs he also greeted *"the younger men whom he saw were healthy"*: exhorting them *"to serve the poor of Jesus Christ. He went with them into the sierra and they gathered firewood and each one brought back his bundle for the poor."*

Castro gives us to understand that John of God spent the night upstairs with the patients; *"He came out of his cell, called out in a loud voice so that all in the house could hear him"*:

"Brothers, let us give thanks to Our Lord, just as the little birds do. Then he recited the four prayers." After that it was the turn of *"the sacristan"*, who explained Christian doctrine *"from a window where*

all could hear him".

What window? The unevenness of the terrain on this steep hillside forces one to think that the stairs connecting the ground floor with the one above, must have been on the side of the building which faced the orchard from where the light entered. From this *"upstairs"* window the *"sacristan"* could make himself heard by the *"pilgrims"* or itinerants below, for whom, so it seems, benches and a fireplace, where they could cook their meals, had been installed.

The lack of money worried John of God, for it put the feeding of so many persons at risk. From Doña Ana Osorio we know of the system 'invented' to solve this problem: Benefactors took turns to pay for the food each day. Ladies, families, and the Archbishop himself participated, *"each one taking a day as they were able."* Don Gómez Tello, that magistrate who, on one occasion, gave some overcoats to John of God in the Plaza Bibarrambla now had a day in which it was his turn to supply *"a fanega of bread and meat."* [A fanega was an ancient dry measure equivalent to 55 kg].

The hospital would have been impossible to manage were it not for John of God's benefactors and the 'young men' who volunteered to help his band of disciples, whom we can now truly call 'brothers', dressed as they were in the habit chosen by the Bishop of Tuy. We know five of their names but the statements made at the Jeronymite court case added others, sometimes confusing the surnames. Nevertheless, one observes they are now a closely knit, stable group, emulating the ways of their chief - John of God:

"They went about wearing a similar habit to the one worn by the aforementioned John of God. They quested for alms in this city and went out to the surrounding places and villages, seeking alms for the hospital where they cared for and sustained the poor."

The hospital was finally organised with patients, a doctor and a 'rector' or chaplain, designated by the Archbishop, who also appointed a 'visitator' who *"made a report at the end of each year."* The witnesses referred to this *"diocesan control"* with a certain amount of ambiguity. [See notes at the end of this chapter.] These men and women became enmeshed in a tangle of references relating to the Calle Lucena, the Pescadería, the Cuesta Gomérez, and the later hospital that was established at the Jeronymite site after the death of John of God. Nevertheless, our friend Angulo, whom we can thoroughly trust, affirms that the *"diocesan visitation"* began *"from the time when the aforementioned hospital was in the Calle de los Gomeles."*

The organisation was notable, but even more so, was the 'style' which John of God gave to his hospital to which, witnesses assure us, Granada had already attributed the name, John of God Hospital.

During these early days when the little band of brothers was emerging, one of the most impressive things was the way they transported the poor and sick from the streets: *"They brought them back upon their shoulders."* Thus they continued the method used by John of God back at the Calle Lucena.

Another characteristic of the new hospital was that it eliminated the bureaucracy of admission. No patient was ever refused admission, regardless of his or her illness. This 'general' and 'expeditious' characteristic surprised the people of Granada:

"At the Granada Royal Hospital they treated infectious diseases, Santa Ana Hospital acute diseases, in Corpus Christi Hospital the wounded, and in La Caridad Hospital, women."

John of God set up his hospital as a 'general' one: *"With whatever illness they might have, they received all such poor who come to the aforementioned hospital and no one was rejected."* Thus bureaucratic red tape was eliminated and persons were received *"without any of the tedium and drawn-out procedures of obtaining letters of admission, as was the case in all the other hospitals."*

One outstanding document is the testimony of Benito de los Rios, who knew the problem down to his fingertips because he was the 'rector' - chaplain - at the Santa Ana Hospital:

"The same difficulty in receiving poor patients, which was experienced at the aforementioned hospital of Santa Ana this witness had found in other hospitals, when taking some patients to them, because they were unable to care for them in the aforementioned hospital where this witness was rector. This witness was told to send some poor person to another hospital as he could not be be cared for in the hospital where he was rector since the case was incurable. No other hospital of this city would find a place to receive the aforementioned poor person, but the hospital of John of God did. Then, taking him there they admitted him without going through formalities, not requiring permits, nor needing recommendations from doctors, nor anyone else, and they cared for him in

the best possible way." Possibly the difficulties in admitting patients to these other hospitals was the scarcity of available beds.

Carried in upon the back, or received without any rigmarole, they cared for them lovingly: *"with great charity"; "With their own hands they washed and tidied them and did all manner of charitable things."*

Benito de los Rios, the experienced 'rector' of Santa Ana Hospital, summed up in a few words the eulogies that I have copied from half a dozen witnesses.

"There should be nothing further to add since this witness himself declares what he particularly knows of the charity with which the aforementioned John of God and his companions treated the poor whom they brought in; other [than to say] *that the aforementioned John of God and his companions never sent away any sick person who might be incurable."*

For his part, Ambrosio Maldonado, *"the second rector"* at our hospital in the Cuesta Gomérez described how John of God discharged patients who were healed.

"And in convalescence and healing, the aforementioned John of God gave them clothing, coats, breeches, shirts, hose and footwear. He never took any credit for any of this, except to say that what he gave was shared out for God, because all he ever wanted was to do more for God. This witness is aware of this because he saw it happening just as he has stated. He knew and dealt with John of God and saw him doing it."

As can be seen from the reports, John of God showed, in the care and assistance of his patients, great tenderness and an exquisite respect of persons. He listened to them and heeded them. He never spoke to them in general terms, but applied to each case the best remedy possible: *"seated in the midst of all, with very great patience, he listened to the needs of each one, never sending anyone away disconsolate, but with either alms or good counsel."*

Sometimes things became complicated, since the behaviour of poor people is not automatically correct simply by the fact of their being poor. Dishonesty lurks, yesterday and today, within the pouch of the beggar as on the monitor of the financier's computer. Well, computers belong to our time; beggars remain forever and ever.

One of the prostitutes *"whom he had been taken away from the public house"*, and for whom he had now found a husband, was *"so bothersome and impatient"* that she was driving him crazy by going to him demanding help by day and night. The days were cold, she presented herself asking for clothing. John of God, who should have kept his habit, *"had given away his clothes"* and came home *"wrapped in a blanket."* He told the importunate woman *"that he had nothing to give her, that she should return another day."* The unpleasant woman flew into a rage: *"And began to abuse him saying: 'You wicked man, you sanctimonious hypocrite!'."* The whole hospital heard her swearing at him but John of God simply smiled at her and said: *"Take these two reales and skip over to the plaza and shout all that out aloud."*

She would not quieten down, but went on spitting insults at him. John of God was patient and they heard him whispering to himself: *"Of course I am going to have to pardon you, so I forgive you right here and now."*

"Of course", he has pardoned her already. The wretched woman finally came to her senses and realised the kindness and deep humility of her friend. Thus you will see her on the day of John of God's funeral: *"This same woman was there together with all the others whom he had rescued from an evil life. They called out aloud in the streets lamenting and saying how evil they were and confessing their faults and sins; saying that she had been very bad and that it was through the great goodness of John of God, his good example and holy admonitions, that she had given up sinning. These and other things made all the people weep."*

He had respect for the sick and the poor and they were aware of it. These were the ones who found themselves on the scrap heap of Granada society that barely considered them as human beings. They were trampled and crushed. Then along came John of God who candidly looked them in the eye especially when he wished to attend to something urgent such as assisting the dying and arranging for them to receive the final sacraments. At these times he stepped, with the utmost discretion, on their personal territory. One day he said to Ambrosio Maldonado, whom we have known as rector-chaplain at the Cuesta Gomérez: *"Father, hear this man's confession before you go to your dinner, and help him make a good confession."*

The old man was *"very ill and at the point of death."* From the accounts of his life he needed a good sprinkling of holy water before going to meet St. Peter face to face.

Ambrosio heard the dying man's confession, *"spending two*

hours with him," after which he went to his dinner. John of God asked him: *"Did you hear the man's confession?"*

"This witness replied to him, 'Yes'." John of God said to the chaplain, *"Well then, go back and assist him much better."*

"This witness went back to him", and patiently talked with the old man *"until nightfall."* But the old man resisted unloading his conscience. When night came, Padre Ambrosio *"returned to the Alhambra where he resided."* He had a small apartment within the Alcazaba tower, which the guards used to lock at night. *"Then, at midnight, John of God went to look for him and made the guards open the Alhambra to let him enter."* He dragged the chaplain from his bed and brought him back to the dying man, who finally gave in. Padre Ambrosio says, *"He confessed what he had omitted, and he died within the hour."*

Ambrosio Maldonado affirms that this was the basic concern of John of God: *"to save the souls of the poor who came to the aforementioned hospital."*

The house that they turned into a hospital stood on a large piece of land which today is subdivided into various residences. When the Hospitaller Brothers moved away after the death of John of God, a community of calced Carmelite friars from Valencia moved in. When the Carmelites moved to the plaza where the Municipal Council stands today the property in the Cuesta Gomérez was parcelled out little by little.

For this reason when you visit this place, you need to imagine what it was like in those bygone years. Thanks to a 17th century instruction on the execution of a will, Matías de Mina has been able to locate some features on the plan. These include, a three storey facade on the Cuesta Gomérez, a square patio with a gallery of stone columns, an interior staircase with windows facing the orchard, an upstairs section of two floors, a tower, a large storage container, a pedestal, with a washbasin fed by water which came directly from the Alhambra, and the orchard. Up to two hundred inmates resided there. From the beginning John of God speaks of *"more than a hundred and ten"*, and again *"more than a hundred and fifty persons."*

I find it difficult to imagine how John of God managed, but let him explain the situation regarding the expenses he incurred maintaining such a crowd. He complains of economic hardships, and is on the lookout for aid. The hospital was devouring ducats without mercy. Castro shows him compassion:

"So great were the expenses that he incurred in all that he did that the alms that came in from the city did not cover them. So, for this reason he ran up a debt amounting to three or four hundred ducats, so great was his charity."

"He ran into debt" with this tidy sum so he was going through a bad time. John of God himself gives a marvellous account of the services of the hospital: he lists them, obviously not to show off, but to solicit financial assistance. Here are his words:

"There are so many poor people coming here that many times even I wonder just how are we going to look after them... Really, seven or eight reales are needed daily for wood alone, as this big city is very cold, and especially so now that winter is here. So many poor people are turning up at this House of God, that there are more than a hundred and ten of them. They include both the sick and healthy, the people working here and the travellers. Furthermore, since this house is of a general nature, we make no distinctions in accepting the sick and all the other kinds of people. So here you will find cripples; maimed; persons with venereal diseases; mutes; mentally ill; paralysed; patients with skin troubles as well as aged folk and many children. That is not even counting many others such as the travellers and tramps who turn up here. We give them the use of a stove and water, salt and pots so they can cook their meals... Not a day goes by that we do not need at least four and a half ducats, sometimes even five for the running of the house. All this is just for bread, meat, poultry and firewood, since the medicines and clothing are another expense.'

John of God is poor yet he is the larder and pharmacy for Granada's poor. Soon his family will increase: *"I have more than a hundred and fifty persons to maintain..."*

It is clear he was trapped without any guarantees: *"On days when we do not receive sufficient alms to cover the items that I have just mentioned, I must get them on credit."*

There was no shortage of bad days at the hospital: *"there are also occasions when we have to fast."* Yet he was sustained by his interior peace: *"I am kept busy doing this as a captive for Jesus Christ."* Did he come to fear his work might breakdown for want of support? Apparently not, but nevertheless it was a constant worry gnawing away within his heart *"I am owing more than two hundred ducats for shirts, overcoats, shoes, sheets, and blankets..."*

He produces a spark of humour, almost black humour: *"I have so many debts that there are times when I dare not leave the house,"* no doubt afraid of meeting a creditor.

It happened early one morning. *"They gave blessed John of God a beating."* As the morning moved on, the whole of Granada was shocked to hear this startling news. The people rushed to the Plaza Nueva, curious to know the details.

In the Cuesta Gomérez a gentleman had slapped John of God. News of the incident quickly spread from the Chancellery to the Plaza Bibarrambla so that a dozen or more witnesses were able to remember what was said on that morning, and some children were told about it by their parents.

For example, the little girl Agueda Muñoz. She was the daughter of the midwife who worked in the homes within the Alhambra. She was going down from the fort with her mother *"to buy some apparel at the Alcaicería* [the silkmarket]." They knew John of God, his companions, and the people at the hospital, because they passed the front of the hospital when they travelled along the Cuesta Gomérez and through the Gate of the Pomegranates. Agueda Muñoz, and her daughter, little Agueda, adored blessed John of God; so the events of that day were never to be erased from the little girl's memory: *"When they arrived at the Cuesta Gomeles* [Gomérez] *they saw a great crowd of people causing an uproar. The mother of this witness asked what was going on, and she was told that John of God had been assaulted."*

That's not all. Another little child, Onofre Hurtado, son of one of the persons who actually participated in the event has his story. As an adult, Onofre took the second surname of his parents who were actually Don Juan de la Torre and Doña Ana de Avellaneda Hurtado of the illustrious and extensive Mendoza family.

Don Juan had married Doña Ana two or three years before the event and they lived in a delightful mansion in the Cuesta Gomérez. Both were children of couples very dear to John of God, namely Diego Hurtado de Mendoza and Leonor de Guevara who resided in the Plaza Santa Ana facing the site where the new Chancellery was being built. The Hurtado - Mendoza family venerated blessed John of God from the day in which they thought he miraculously cured their dying daughter, Maria. John of God called, seeking alms and discovered a very sad scene, with the doctors giving no hope for her recovery. Doña Leonor in her distress, pleaded with John of God to pray for the restoration of her daughter's health. John of God did so and soon, as if he had received a celestial answer, simply said: *"Yes, they are giving her back to us."*

The girl was cured and thereafter the family called her "The one borrowed from Our Lord", the *"Emprestadica."* Doña Leonor called herself *"the true sister of blessed John of God"*, who thus greeted her: *"true sister."*

The incident of the blow given to John of God in the Cuesta Gomérez happened at the front door of the Los Torres, the children of the *"true sister."*

Our witness, Onofre Hurtado, fourth of the six children in his family, was a priest and he treasured the memory of his father Don Juan who held distinguished positions such as Treasurer of the Royal Mint and member of the Granada Council of Twenty-four. Onofre said that, as a child, he heard the story of the assault at least a thousand times.

Early one morning John of God left the hospital, *"to look for something for the poor to eat."* The dim light of the early dawn forced him to watch his step so as to avoid the many potholes in the street. Several early risers from the Alhambra were already coming down the slope to do business in the city. What actually happened was that the good John of God accidentally struck his basket against a gentleman coming in the opposite direction and his elegant cape fell to the ground.

The gentleman reacted furiously: *"calling him a villainous scoundrel and other things"*. As servants and a pageboy picked up the cape and surrounded him, he continued shouting at John of God: *"Ah you scoundrel, clumsy dolt, why don't you look where you are going?"*

It did not take long for a curious crowd to gather. John of God *"with great patience"* tried to appease the furious man: *"Pardon me brother, I was not looking where I was going."* John of God had no idea how annoying it was to the gentleman *"to see himself addressed as brother"* a title that our charity worker *"used to call everyone."* This made the distinguished gentleman *"even more angry"* to be treated *"as a brother"* as this despicable beggar had dared to do,

"He struck him." John of God humbly turned his face: *"I am*

the one who has made the error and I surely deserved that, now you slap me on this other cheek."

The gentleman became even angrier at *"having been addressed as you"* since John of God used the word *"vos"* [familiar form of address]. He ordered: *"Lay into this ill-mannered villain."*

His men beat John of God knocking him to the ground. Let us say in his favour that the man was a stranger, *"a gentleman, a stranger on business and staying in this city due to a lawsuit."* He had never seen John of God before. He was utterly astonished when he heard the voice of Señor de La Torre calling out from the doorway of his house: *"What is going on Brother John of God?"* He immediately lifted him from the ground.

The gentleman had heard of *"the great works and virtues of blessed John of God"* and became frightened by what he had done: *"He fell at John's feet and said that he would not get up until he kissed them."* John of God lifted him up and embraced him, *"and with many tears they both begged one another for forgiveness."*

That day the whole of Granada *"was buzzing with the event."* Furthermore they said *"the aforementioned gentleman let it be known"* that it was out of shame that he *"left Granada abashed before completing his lawsuit"*; and that *"he sent fifty gold ducats to blessed John of God for the poor."*

He needed money but John of God had squeezed dry his city benefactors. What could he do about it?

"Not wanting to bother nor overburden Granada's citizens appealing constantly by day and night; ... he decided to leave them to have a spell for some days but he would seek donations in the villages and towns of Andalusia."

Notes to Chapter 30

* Witness # 7 (Francisco de Olivares) related the story told about Ginesa Pulido at the Granada beatification process. The item about the Olivares-Pulido wedding came from the archives of the parish of San Cecilio *'Deposorios'*, Vol. III, fol. 7.

* The account of John of God fitting out shirts for 20 children in the shop was given by Juan Hurtado, a witness at the Córdoba beatification process.

* On the Albolete twins, see M. Gómez Moreno, *San Juan de Dios, Primicias historicos,* op.cit., 278, witness # 33 in his *'Floreto'*.

* The Alarcón case refered to by the son of Alonso de Alarcón, Alonso de la Torre: witness # 3 at the Ubeda beatification process, (Francisco de Porras).

* The *jubetero*, Luis Ordóñez, made his statement at the Valladolid beatification process in January 1623: M. Gómez Moreno, adduces his testimony as anonymous without further reference other than # 26 in his *'Floreto'*, in *San Juan de Dios, Primicias historicos,* op.cit., 279.

* For the career and personality of Archbishop Pedro Guerrero, Cf. A. Marín Ocete, *El arzobispo don Pedro Guerrero y la politica conciliar española en el siglo XVI*, (2 vols.), Madrid 1970; García Villoslada, *Diccionario de historia eclesiástica de España* ,II (1972), 1065-1066; M. de Mina, *'Anotaciones'*, *Fondo Documental*, op.cit., 108-114. That Philip II invited Master Avila to take the See of Granada is affirmed by Bermúdez de Pedraza, *Historia eclesiástica de Granada*, Seville 1988, fol. 237; Avila's refusal to take up the position was cited at his beatification process; Jaén declaration by the lawyer Bernabé de Hortigosa; Madrid, declaration of the lawyer Francisco de Tejada; Cf. L. Sala Balust-F. Martín Hernández, *Obras completas del santo maestro Juan de Avila*, I, op.cit., 116 note 24.

* For a description of the interior of the Cuesta Gomérez hospital see Francisco de Castro, op.cit., Chapter 16; on the convent of Nuestra Señora de los Angeles, see A. Gallego Burín *Granada. Guía del viajero*, op.cit., 167; J. Belza y Ruiz de la Fuente, *Las calles de Granada*, Granada, op.cit., 40; F Henríquez Jorquera, *Anales de Granada*, (Ed. A. Marín Ocete) 48 (1934) 249; M. de Mina *Visitar la Granada de San Juan de Dios*, op.cit., 187-193.

* For the purchase of the Cuesta Gomérez property and the persons involved and who testified at the Jeronymite lawsuit; see J. Sánchez, *Kénosis, etc.*, op.cit., 301 (Angulo), 312 (Leonor de Cáceres), 322 (Benito de los Rios), 345 (Martín de Baeza), 375 (Ambrosio Maldonado).

* I continue my points on the chronological argument. Regarding the translocation of the hospital from the Pescadería to the Cuesta Gomérez, I consider correct the date January 1547 as set by R. M. Saucedo, *Cronológia aplicada en la vida de N. P. S. Juan de Dios*: Paz y Caridad (March-April 1952) 57-59: The way I see it, this date fits in perfectly with the basic facts, scarce as they are, in regards to the chronologies put forward by Castro and the witnesses at the beatification process. However, some strong difficulties present themselves with the declarations made at the Jeronymite court-case. According to J. Sánchez more study needs to be made about the year 1547 as the year of the translocation. Op.cit., 173. Also, G. Magliozzi, who made certain observations regarding the John of God calendar, op.cit, 105. Magliozzi said at the previously cited 1995 Roman Congress, that "Saucedo's chronological scheme no longer serves".

* Here we have the difficulties that originated with some of the witnesses at the

Jeronymite court-case, see J. Sánchez, op.cit., 285-428; this is an appendix of the testimonies made by the witnesses. Since the Granada city archives have no number for these documents, Sánchez has taken the liberty to invent his own.

Difficulty #1. The Archbishop who put up the money for the transfer of the Pescadería hospital to the Cuesta Gomérez was not Pedro Guerrero who arrived at Granada in October 1546. It was Gaspar de Avalos who paid for it before he left Granada in 1542. He along with Francisca de Cáceres, Diego de Linares and Master Avila made the decision to construct a new large definitive hospital at the Jeronymite site. This was stated by witness # 2, Leonor de Cáceres. *Analysis*

a) Before entering into the depths of the affair, it is well to say that I have a certain reservation regarding the declarations of Doña Leonor, who certainly comes over as a very pushy lady. She mixes up contradictory dates and events without showing the least uneasiness about it. Here is an example: the hospital at the Cuesta Gomérez had hardly opened when Leonor speaks about a meeting at the highest level to draw up plans for the final and largest hospital to be built near the Jeronymites. Thus Sánchez amounts to guessing at Leonor's long-winded declaration: "At the feast of Christmas (December 1541?), there was a meeting at the Alhambra between the Marquis de Mondéjar, Doña Francisca de Cáceres and her daughter, Fray Diego de Linares the Prior of San Jerónomo. They spoke of the needs of John of God's hospital. The Prior offered the proceeds of a certain bequest and all became interested and enthusiastic about the subject. They decided to call upon Master Avila so off they all went, the Marquis de Mondéjar included to talk it over with Archbishop Avalos. This meeting decided not to go ahead with extensions to the Gomérez hospital but to look for land to build a new hospital (T 2/7 f 40ff) *Ibid* 175, # 100.

Francisca de Cáceres hurried too quickly regarding the transfer from the Cuesta Gomérez to the Jeronymite site. This occurred in 1553, three years after the death of John of God.

b) In his chapter 22, Francisco de Castro gives a trustworthy account from start to end on the planning and set-up of the new hospital on the Jeronymite site shortly after John of God's death. This was in Archbishop Guerrero's time and had the backing of the civil authorities as well as ecclesiastic. Master Avila collected funds for this new hospital and gave money of his own as well. The hospital at the Jeronymite site went on quickly and was opened in 1553, even though the building was incomplete and *"doors and windows had to be quickly constructed."* Castro says the work began with 1,600 ducats (ibid) then many more donations flowed in to carry it further. Francisca de Cáceres brought the event far too much ahead of its time, saying that the first plans to go on with the work took form in 1541 under Gaspar de Avalos. This is only one of her many chronological mix-ups.

c) Antón de Govea, (op.cit.), chapter 30, notes that Archbishop Guerrero gave from his own pocket for the transfer from the Pescadería to the Cuesta Gomérez. He had just arrived at Granada in 1546. Govea gives this sum as 1,500 ducats. I see no contradiction between the two amounts: that of 1547 to Gomérez and that of 1551/1553 to the Jeronymite site. We are here treating of a prelate who was enthusiastic for the person of John of God and his work;

besides, Castro *(ibid)* says: *"They went to see Don Pedro about the matter and the Archbishop wasted no time in using every means at his disposal to remedy the situation. So off they went looking for a suitable site outside the city where the air was fresh and it would be convenient for everybody. There was a property quite close to the city which they thought would suit them admirably. The hospital is standing there today. The property belonged to the city and adjoined that of the Friars of St. Jerome on the site, so they say, where old St. Jerome's stood."* Govea says the Archbishop gave one sum for the Gomérez hospital; and Castro says the same for the one on the Jeronymite site. There can be no doubt that he actually gave much more which has not been noted by the biographers.

d) There is one fundamental fact to note. It was impossible for Archbishop Avalos to be the moving force for the transfer from the Pescadería to the Cuesta Gomérez, because of the sheer lack of time. He came to Granada in February 1542. John of God was discharged from the Royal Hospital in May 1539, and as we have seen, he spent some time in visiting and staying at Baeza-Guadalupe-Baeza and back to Granada. Then he spent time 'selling firewood'; the connection with the disciples of Master Avila; his period in the Calle Lucena; the moving into another house the Pescadería; his untiring work among the poor, and also with the wealthy who supported him, and so forth... All this took place before 1541 when he was able to purchase the property in the Cuesta Gomérez and transfer his patients there. This needs to be considered before we accept G. Magliozzi's proposal that the year of the infant João's birth was 1492 instead of 1495, and his arrival at Granada in 1537 instead of 1538. But this is quite a different argument.

Difficulty #2. The dates expressly stated by the various witnesses are more compelling in their selection.

a) The Rev. Ambrosio Maldonado, witness # 11, affirms two notable points: the first that he *"knew John of God in this place in the year thirty-six."* Furthermore, *"he knew and worked with the aforementioned John of God because this witness was the rector of the aforementioned hospital in the Cuesta Gomérez."* And the records show that *"he was provided"* as the hospital's second rector *"at the time of Don Hernando Niño"*; which meant it was sometime before 1546, the year Archbishop Niño de Guevara left Granada.

b) Leonor de Cáceres, witness #2, affirmed that Archbishop Avalos, sometime before 1542, appointed as rector (chaplain) to the hospital (before she had made reference to the Gomérez) a priest who had been the tutor of her son.

Analysis

a) Maldonado speaks of approximate dates, even though he speaks of *"some months more or less."* That date is enough: He affirms that he knew John of God *"in these parts thirty-six years ago,"* which is to say since 1536; and two years before that *"he knew Father Master Avila."* That is quite impossible because Avila only arrived at Granada at the end of 1536.

b) The reference to being the second rector of John of God's hospital is also ambiguous: he said that he was the rector *"of the hospital in the Cuesta Gomérez"*; then further on his statement explains that *"he was provided by"* as the second rector by Don Hernando Niño; but he does not expand on these two periods; which is to say that he was appointed by Niño as *"second rector"* for the hospital in the Pescadería then moved up to the one at the Cuesta Gomérez.

c) As for Doña Leonor de Cáceres, well we must fear some sort of a slip since she had a capacity for getting tangled up. Let us providentially accept that her protagonist was really her son's tutor and was also the rector at John of God's hospital. But, what hospital? She said that Don Gaspar de Avalos *"appointed him."* And at the same time mixes up all her dates referring to all the hospitals of John of God, Lucena, Pescadería, Gomérez and the Jeronymites. Furthermore, *"the tutor of her son"*, was he appointed by Avalos as rector of the Lucena or the Pescadería? There is nothing to point to him being at the Gomerez. Nothing strange about that, because Doña Leonor was very muddled regarding exact dates.

d) Anyone who makes a serious study of the declarations made at the Jeronymite court case, will soon see that the witnesses were playing around with the dates without taking too much care about them. From the list on the questionnaire we see that witnesses refered to questions #2 and #3 as *"more or less"* when fixing a date to the time John of God was doing his charity work at Granada in 1536. Sánchez (*ibid*, 197) says: *"The witnesses in general do not seem to have been too concerned when it came to stating exact dates."* And he points out that someone said they even knew John of God since 1533! Sánchez came to the conclusion that Leonor de Cáceres was a real chatterbox who just rambled on and on. Later on, Ana Osorio, witness #13, was far more prudent and was able to recall reliable evidence from her memory which was quite meritorious. Witness #15, Alonso de Eseguerra, *"knew John of God here thirty years ago,"* namely 1542, which seems quite reasonable.

e) Another statement, and one we can trust, came from witness #1, our old friend Angulo, who did not speak in riddles. He knew and worked with John of God since 1544 (six years before his death). Where did this occur? I have not the slightest doubt that it was at the Pescadería and then at the Cuesta Gomérez.

f) I do not believe that the chronological gaps of some of the witnesses at the Jeronymite affair, were made with a bad intention. They simply wanted to come to a final judgement. The court case was resolved in favour of the John of God Brothers agasinst the accusations brought against them by the Jeronymites. That is how all the references and memories of the witnesses were amassed in one dossier containing all John of God's hospitals without close attention being made to exact chronological procedure. That is why I do not believe it worthwhile to argue with the chronology outlined by Saucedo.

g) I do not place any special importance upon the references to dates made by the witnesses regarding the time Antón Martín and the rest of the first companions joined John of God's company in hospitality. Their replies betray the fact that they either did not know the exact dates or they simply tried to place them approximately. They simply said *"they saw"*, *"they knew"*, that they accompanied John of God at the Cuesta Gomérez. That in no way means that they saw or knew them prior to the Cuesta Gomérez hospital.

h) I consider it gratuitous to simply close down these efforts to get an exact lead on certain biographical points of St. John of God: There is no doubt at all that much more is hidden away in the various archives that will enrich this research. This future possibility seems to suggest respect for the hypothesis of the work.

i) I now consider we have some firm hinges to pen out the basic scheme of the John of God chronology during the final stages of his life. The two dates given us by Castro support Saucedo's chronology; although, logically, it is only partially open for correction: The conversion of John of God on 28 January 1539 and the discharge from the Royal Hospital on 16 May 1539.

* Magliozzi accepts the revision of the Saucedo chronology: *Necessidade de novos esquemas na vida de S. João de Deus*: Hospitalidade 59 (1995) 230, p.9; also Aires Gameiro, *ibid.*, 26-33.

* The quote by witness # 3 (Antón Rodríguez) at the Granada beatification process.

* Cf. G. Magliozzi, *Pagine etc*, op.cit., 144, note 2. Cf. J. Sánchez, *Kénosis etc.*, op.cit., 174 note 98 7 p. 174 note 99 which treats of the references made by witnesses at the Jeronymite court case.

* The statements made by the witness about the organisation and functioning of the Cuesta Gomérez hospital are taken from the Jeronymite lawsuit: see J. Sánchez *(ibid)*, 301-311 (Angulo); 311-316 (Leonor de Cáceres); 331-340 (Benito de los Rios); 362-372 (Mateo de Santa Cruz); 384-385 (Ambrosio Maldonado); 398-394 (Ana Osorio); 410-412 (Rodrígo Alonso de Ysla).

* For the quotes from Castro on the functioning of the Cuesta Gomérez hospital, see Francisco de Castro, op.cit., chapters 16 & 17; the episode about the furious ex-prostitute, *ibid*, chapter 17.

* For the physical appearance of the property in the Cuesta Gomérez, see M. De Mina, *Visitar la Granada de San Juan de Dios*, op.cit., 196-197.

* The personal data about John of God regarding his debts comes from the 2nd letter to Gutierre Lasso de la Vega, *Letters of St. John of God*, op.cit.

* The references to *"the genuine little sister"* of John of God and the "daughter on loan" came from witness # 43 (María de Guevara) at the Granada beatification process.

* The account of the rich stranger slapping John of God in the face comes from Francisco de Castro, op.cit, chapter 15; and from Onofre Hurtado de Mendoza, at the Granada beatification process; *"This witness did not know the holy man personally."* Many witness gave statements verifying this, amongst them: #13 (Felipe de Alaiz), #26 (Domingo Navarro), #27 (Melchor de Almirante), #29 (Alonso Sánchez Dávila), #43 (María de Guevara), 346 (Agueda Muñoz, daughter of the midwife from the Alhambra), #48 (Luisa de Avila).

* The citation about the proposition to leave Granada to collect alms elsewhere comes from Francisco de Castro, op.cit., chapter 16.

31

JOHN OF GOD SETS OUT ON A FUND-RAISING DRIVE

Granada
Málaga
Toledo, Oropesa, Salamanca

1547-1548

I am amazed how some of the noble families of Granada esteemed and loved John of God; and how he loved them. They saw him as genuine and sincere, without duplicity and engulfed by a holy madness that drove him to care for the ill and help the needy. They saw him as self-sacrificing, self-effacing and penitential. They saw him as one who had been completely overtaken by the mysterious presence of God.

Consider the La Torre family whom we met when John of God was struck in the face. The La Torres belonged to the select Mendoza clan whose family branches covered a wide section of Granada's aristocracy. The first was Diego Hurtado de Mendoza, married to Leonor de Guevara, John of God's *"true sister."* Besides being of the nobility, they were also very wealthy. They lived in a palace at the Plaza Santa Ana facing the worksite of the new Chancellery. Living with them was their unmarried daughter María, the young lady rescued from a fatal illness due to the intervention of John of God, and henceforth called *"our borrowed one."*

The second couple was Juan de La Torre and his wife Ana de Avellaneda whose palace was in the Cuesta Gomérez. It was La Torre who rushed to the defence of our alms-seeker when he was set upon by the furious *"gentleman stranger."* The third was Juan de Guevara whose wife was Marina de La Torre Mendoza.

The aristocrats of Granada, following the custom of the period, frequently married within the clan sometimes making it very difficult to sort out the surnames.

Nevertheless, we have been able to reconstruct the amiable relationship that John of God had with the 'Hurtado-Mendoza-La Torre' families through the statements many of them made at the beatification process. María Guevara, 'the borrowed one', Diego's daughter; Leonor María de Guevara, Diego's grand-daughter; Juan La Torre and Onofre Hurtado de Mendoza - brothers, despite their different surnames - sons of Juan de La Torre and Ana Avellaneda give delightful details about John of God's visits to the family.

Diego and Leonor had a private oratory in their palace. Years later, the children heard their parents lauding John of God's fame as a saint and his preference for the home of Diego and Leonor where *"he could go into the oratory to kneel and pray."*

They were *"great friends of blessed John of God."* He went to them when enormous needs were pressing upon him, asking *"for bigger and bigger donations."* When notified of an urgency, a group of powerful persons, *"the Marquis de Cenete, the Marquis de Cerralbo"* and the Marquis de Tarifa who was *"very fond"* of John of God, met with him together with the Archbishop Don Pedro. I imagine they had lunch, played cards, and chatted... and *"listened to the compelling requests of the 'alms-seeker': "They used to give him a great number of donations."*

John of God frequently rested for a while in one or another of these three homes when he had finished his nightly rounds of alms giving. *"He came in, wet through and fatigued with hunger."* At his usual time of calling, *"they put between two plates a little gift, something warm for his supper."*

With the supper, as encouragement, they placed *"upon a bureau a donation for the poor."* What a delightful form of blackmail! He only received the donation if he ate the supper he was served. *"He said grace and gave thanks to God, then he took the covers off the plates and ate the food they set before him."*

"He accepted the donation and said to my father: 'May God be with you brother'; and my father replied; 'You go with the same, Brother John of God.'"

John of God visited them with absolute freedom and confidence. He used to arrive saying: *"Brothers and sisters, we need this or that, please give it to the poor, which is the same as giving it to God."*

One freezing winter's day, John of God lamented to Don Juan La Torre: *"Brother, what am I to do as I am unable to provide these poor people with firewood and they are suffering so much from the cold?"* It was a shrewd question, an indirect way of begging. John of God excelled at gathering firewood himself, he had been doing it for a long time near the Los Molinos Gate. The clear hint he now gave to La Torre was aimed at the wood lying about on the ground in his olive grove. It was just a matter of picking it up and bundling it for firewood. La Torre understood, smiled and replied: *"Brother, give each poor man who is able to come some rope and a bread roll and send them into the olive grove to gather up the firewood and tie it into bundles."* John of God returned four days later to thank his benefactor for giving him *"enough firewood to last for more than ten days."*

The La Torre family knew John of God's plans, his

difficulties and the days when he had nothing to eat: *"When they saw how weakened he was through fasting "* they procured food and *"gifted him with it."*

María Guevara, *"the borrowed one"*, added some poignant memories of her childhood: *"When I was a very little girl, the aforementioned Brother John of God, took me in his arms, and gave me gifts, he called me 'the borrowed one'...."* Recalling the freezing winter nights in which she saw him come in without shoes, *"his feet frozen by the snow,"* she thought he should put them *"on a very hot brazier to thaw out..."* The little girl was full of admiration for him.

Juan La Torre junior added another important detail. His father, and no doubt the other members of the family, belonged to the circle of Master Avila, *"who used to teach them Latin and other wholesome subjects."*

If you do not know them, what a pity. I am speaking of the 'alms-seekers' whom the Hospitaller Order used to send out to the villages and towns to collect donations for the sick and poor. They did not resolve anything like the huge budgetry problems which today's great hospitals face. However, these 'alms-seekers' fulfilled a marvellous mission. By stimulating personal charity by contact, they gave far more than they received. They let others participate in their spiritual richness. At Jerez I knew a dear old brother who was admired by the entire city, as he trudged the suburbs. Of course, Blessed John of God exercised this office of 'alms-seeker' before his sons.

Having established his hospital in the Cuesta Gomérez he not only increased the number of bed patients but he took in itinerants and foundlings. The only thing that did not increase was finance to support the work. We might wish to avoid using the usual cliché but, in his case, he really did give *the shirt off his back."* He is the shirtless one of children's fables.

The solution that came to him to relieve the financial situation was to go away to beg in the villages and towns. This had two things in its favour. His name was already circulating in Andalusia, even in far-flung regions, and his reputation for good works would predispose many donors in his favour.

A second advantage would be the recommendation he could expect from his benefactors at Granada who would notify their relatives and friends in other towns.

John of God would soon cross the Despeñaperros Gorge into Castile with his staff and basket in hand. But for now, he begins in Andalusia.

The journeys of John of God, the alms-seeker, show us that he had planned his strategy well and did not set out 'haphazardly'. He set out with the support of the recommendations of the excellent friends he had made during his years at Granada.

They are aristocratic families whose branches extended throughout the entire realm. John of God's access to such noble personages was facilitated by the influence of Master Avila who remained in the background.

During the three years from 1536 to 1539 which Master Avila spent working at Granada at the side of Archbishop Gaspar de Avalos, he took as close disciples a group of young men who were sons of families that belonged to the cream of Granada's society. The Master always gave prime importance to the intellectual and Christian formation of youth, that is why, at Granada, he gave care and attention to the colleges established around the nascent University. When he went to Baeza to take charge of the college for boys, opened as the first stage of Baeza University, he had left functioning at Granada a team of disciples dedicated to assisting the sick in the Calle Lucena in the neighbourhood of the Pescadería. This was the trial hospital whose 'administration' had been handed over to John of God when he returned from Guadalupe in the summer of 1540.

That was more than ten years ago and the boys who were ten to fifteen years of age then were now young men between twenty and twenty-four. Some had married and others were bachelors, and now they occupied relatively distinguished positions. Their admiration for Master Avila had increased their esteem for John of God whom they, and their parents, loved and helped.

They certainly backed John of God's drive for funds in the cities of Andalusia; advising their relatives and friends when he was due to arrive in one or another city. The network of recommendations continued to grow, thanks to the connections of the various interrelated clans.

There is one significant family supporting the journeyings

of John of God through Andalusia. Later on, they will give him protection when he ventures across the ravine of Despeñaperros to visit the Royal Court.

The central figure was none other than the grandson of El Gran Capitán, Gonzalo Fernández de Córdoba, who from his youth was inscribed in the circle of Master Avila and who supported the charitable work of John of God.

Thanks to the young Gonzalo, a charming woman enters into the circle of John of God's friends. Her presence enriches the final years of our hero with delightful sentiments. It is clear that John of God finds himself captivated by his *'Duquesita'*, his little Duchess as he calls her, dedicating to her precious compliments. I ask myself if John of God had fallen in love during the final part of his life? Neither hail nor shine withered his heart; in spite of all that he had to suffer. We will see that the life of this young woman was beset with difficulties and John of God was like a good father to her.

My great friends of the 16th century, champions of sanctity, also had similar intimate experiences, doubtlessly bestowed from on high as a smile from God on their austerities. Teresa of Jesus was sixty years of age, almost an old lady for those times, when she found herself entrapped by an unexpected love for a man who was only twenty-nine. Teresa was not afraid. She had definitively given herself to Jesus Christ over the past twenty years and was immersed in intimate dialogue with her Lover, accepting the labours of new foundations as an answer to the mercies given her by God. Furthermore "a new love of man" could not be born of her unless he was a person who was also immersed in the mystery, and was a collaborator in her Carmelite Order. Such is the opinion of Fray Jerónimo Gracían, who says she did not take on the task just to hide the blaze of affections that suddenly sprang up within her soul. Love is not necessarily surrounded by puzzling confusion, it happens like a miraculous torrent upon the warm and human heart of the nun Teresa.

Even more astonishing is the case of John of the Cross. At the age of thirty this penitential friar was smitten by a young 25-year-old novice named Ana of Jesus, a beautiful, intelligent, mystical woman and so attractive that St. Teresa considered her to be a fundamental component for her reform. She was right, for Ana gained the admiration of Europe for Teresa's Carmel.

Fascinating Ana in her youth at Plasencia was called *"the Queen."* She was in love with God. Fray John of the Cross, whom I am told was short and skinny, was not a fascinating type but he was in love with God. To my way of thinking, it is no wonder that the two fell in love with each other. I mean they were not gazing into each others' eyes, but were looking in the same direction. Ana of Jesus Lobera and John of the Cross Yepes are two splendid figures of 16th century Spanish mysticism.

Master Avila made no secret of his affection for at least half a dozen women who closely participated in his life. For instance, few were closer to him than Doña Sancha Carrillo and the Duchess de Feria. The Master consciously ignored clerical criticisms which was quite reasonable since the nobility sometimes practised lives of luxury and scandal: *"Your Ladyship knows quite well"*, so he says in one of his letters, *"just how ill informed they are in the palaces of the highborn regarding servants of God."*

Master Avila and John of God came and went at all hours in the noble homes of the Andalusian nobility. Avila brought an air of austerity to their palaces whilst John of God took many donations from them!

There is no documented record concerning John of God's travels between Granada and Baeza, Montilla and Córdoba between 1542 and 1547 to visit Master Avila. We do know of the arrival of the Master at Granada at least between the spring of 1543 and early 1548, the last visit being in response to the wish of his friend Archbishop Pedro Guerrero. We also know for certain that John of God *"left to give a rest"* to his benefactors at Granada, and *"left to quest alms from some lords in Andalusia."* But, once again I bemoan the loss of that notebook in which *"the companion of his journeys"* jotted down the names, places and dates pertaining to John of God's travels. At least we do have some very precious details about his visit to Málaga in 1547.

Let us continue the story of young Gonzalo, the grandson of El Gran Capitán and husband of the *Duquesita* who captivated John of God, María Sarmiento de los Cobos Mendoza, Duchess of Sessa.

El Gran Capitán Gonzalo Fernández de Córdoba was twice married. His first wife died leaving him childless, while his second wife, Doña María Manrique, bore him three daughters of whom María died in infancy, Beatrice died as a young woman, and Elvira, the only surviving daughter, became the heir to El Gran Capitán.

Elvira inherited three immense treasures. These were the glorious military reputation of her father, model of heroes; possessions and the titles of nobility; one of which was the dukedom of Sessa.

Between the spring and the winter of 1503, El Gran Capitán decimated the French army sent by Luis XII into Italy to conquer the kingdom of Naples. He won, on 28 April, the battle of Ceriñola in which the French commander, the Duke of Nemours, was killed. As a gallant gesture Gonzalo de Córdoba granted him a solemn funeral.

Then on 27 December, on the banks of the river Garellano (Garigliano), El Gran Capitán annihilated the French forces. A little later, King Ferdinand, widower of Isabella La Católica and Regent during the minority of his grandson the future Charles V, arrived in Italy fearful that Don Gonzalo Fernández de Córdoba might want to elevate himself to become King of Naples. Ferdinand demanded that the victorious Gran Captain present him with the legendary 'Accounts' regarding the expenses of the campaign. They are uncertain, those malicious entries invented by the legend ("*A hundred million in lances, spades, picks and mattocks; ten thousand ducats in gloves...; fifty thousand ducats in liquor for the troops...*") But if, as it is said, Gonzalo presented Don Ferdinand a ledger of this tone: "*In friars, monks and the poor to pray to God for the prosperity of the King's army, 200,736 ducats and 9 reales; and in spies 700,494 ducats...*" then Don Ferdinand took the lesson well. Having proved the fidelity of his famous soldier, he made him Master of Santiago and conceded to him the dukedom of Sessa on 25 February 1507.

Thus it was that Don Gonzalo and Doña María Manrique became the first Duke and Duchess of Sessa, a title that commemorated the victorious Italian campaigns of El Gran Capitán.

Sessa today is called Sessa Aurunca in memory of the ancient tribe of the Aurinci who founded it three thousand years ago. It is a city in Campania with a population of 30,000. It is an episcopal see and has a Romanesque cathedral. In the nearby hills are vineyards from where, for centuries, the wine of Felerno was sent to imperial Rome.

Elvira the daughter of Don Gonzalo, 2nd Duke of Sessa married her cousin Luis Fernández de Córdoba who had half a dozen illustrious titles: Count of Cabra, Lord of Baena, Viscount of Iznallor... with his marriage the houses of Sessa and de Cabra were joined together.

Likewise the four children of the marriage, grandchildren of El Gran Capitán, were heirs to quite a number of honours and positions, the larger number going to the firstborn, Gonzalo who bore his grandfather's name.

El Gran Capitán's widow, Doña María Manrique, died in 1527 and was interred in the main chapel of the church of San Jerónimo at Granada. Before her death the illustrious lady made excellent provision for her grandson Gonzalo's formation. It is practically certain that the seventeen year old Gonzalo belonged to the circle of young men under the direct influence of Master Avila, which explains why"since his youth" he practiced assistance to the poor and sick. He married in 1539 at twenty-one years of age and was one of the first noble Granadinos who accompanied the hospitaller adventure of John of God. Castro certifies this, calling him by his title *"Third Duke of Sessa"*:

"Among all the gentry of Andalusia and Castile, he who most aided him in his necessities was the Duke of Sessa; who since his youth had taken into account his poor and hospital, and accomplished as much as he could for him at Granada: and besides this, he made it possible for him to give on all major feastdays of the year, shoes and shirts for the poor to wear; and his wife the Duchess did likewise.

His wife is 'our' Duchess. Gonzalo married the charming seventeen year old Doña María Sarmiento. She did not have as many distinguished titles as her husband, but she did have a magnificent dowry in ready cash, thanks to her father who belonged to the close personal inner circle of Charles V. Her mother was one of the shining lights amongst the ladies of the Royal Court.

Her father was Don Francisco de los Cobos, senior secretary to the Emperor Charles V. He was born at Ubeda, son of a simple rural gentleman. When he was fifteen, one of his uncles, who belonged to the group of Queen Isabella's accountants, took him with him to Granada. He then travelled about from one city to another with the mobile Court. A keen and energetic young man,

Francisco caught the attention of the Chief Accountant of Granada, Ferdinand de Zafra, who incorporated him in 'the permanent staff' of the administration. Cobos would advance for the next twenty-five years until a royal *cédula* [certificate] appointed him as the successor of the deceased Zafra.

From then on Francisco's career was upward bound. He was appointed to the Council of Twenty-four and, before long, became the right-hand man to Lope Conchillos, the Royal Secretary for the Affairs of the Indies.

Upon the death of King Ferdinand, the civil servant Cobos, now forty years of age, received a boost to his career. Instead of remaining in the service of the Regent Cardinal Cisneros, he went off to Flanders to join the team of the new king, Charles V. Cobos had one of the very few Spanish surnames among the bevy of Flemish officials whom Charles 'imported' into Spain.

In the spring of 1518, Cobos succeeded Lope Conchillos and on all his journeys occupied a place at the side of the king, who upon discovering his potential in finances admitted him to the Order of Santiago. He appointed him as royal emissary to the *Cortes*, as well as making him successor to the chamberlain, Chievres. This Flemish demagogue was famous for his mania for 'requisitioning' the gold doubloons, called *'de a dos'*, because they carried two [dos] heads or images of Don Ferdinand. They were minted during his reign. The chamberlain's pursuit of doubloons was so pronounced that they practically disappeared from circulation; and if, by luck, some Castilian found a doubloon, the chronicles say that he used to salute it with this ironic ditty: *"God save you, you double headed ducat, for if Señor Chievres comes across you, it will be the end of you."*

Naturally the succession of Chievres by Cobos was well accepted by the Court. From then on he accompanies Charles V on all his imperial journeys and manages ticklish negotiations with Italian and German bankers whose loans threatened to ruin the Emperor. Cobos accumulated titles of honour, some graciously conceded by the crown, others bought by him for a good many doubloons. These acquisitions enabled Cobos to move ahead in his political and economic ventures, so he could now take his place among the first ranks of the aristocracy, to which, of course, he could not aspire previously due to his humble family origins.

The highest honour came with his investiture in the

Military Order of Santiago, along with two other high honours that of Major Commander of Castile and Major Commander of León, equivalent to a patent of nobility. For this, Cobos negotiated and purchased from the family of Gómez de Fuensalida of Málaga, then holders of the title 'Commander of the Bastions of León', the transfer of the title, and from that he rose to 'Chief Commander of León'.

Already 'Commander', 'Imperial Secretary', 'Member of the Emperor's Council', he now married, in the autumn of 1522, María de Mendoza y Pimental, daughter of the Count and Countess of Rivadavia. Doña María gave birth to her firstborn in 1523 while her husband was away with the Emperor at the reconquest of Fuenterrabía. Coincidently, this was where Juan Ciudad, the obscure shepherd turned soldier, was undergoing a bitter experience.

Another child was born to them at Valladolid a year later. It was a daughter – María Sarmiento de Mendoza y de los Cobos, the future Duchess of Sessa.

Cobos had a palace built at Ubeda and another princely residence at Valladolid, then capital of the Empire. The pope granted privileges for *"the chapel of the Cobos at Ubeda"*, allowing it to be the family sepulchre. Cobos selected as architects and builders Siloé, Jamete and Vandelvira who brought forth *"a major piece of work of the Spanish Renaissance."*

Incorporated by Charles V into the team responsible for international policy, Cobos accompanied the Emperor to Vienna where his army was facing the Turk Sulieman. Another coincidence! Juan Ciudad was also present here when the Emperor reviewed his troops. When the Empress Isabel went to meet the Emperor at Barcelona on his return, there, in her retinue, was the lady-in-waiting named María Mendoza, wife of Francisco de los Cobos. With her were her two children Diego and María Sarmiento.

Doña María stayed quietly at Valladolid with her two children Diego and María Sarmiento while her husband the 'Chief Commander', elevated to a key position in imperial fiscal affairs and policy, went from one place to another in the Emperor's retinue. Don Francisco was only able to escape away to visit his family at Valladolid when the agenda of Charles V permitted it. So great was the Emperor's confidence in Cobos that he appointed him to be *"Secretary to Prince Philip"* thus laying the foundation for his future status as counsellor.

As for his wife Doña María and her children, the Empress honoured them by appointing both mother and daughter as ladies-in-waiting, and the son as page. But she, Doña María, hardly ever left Valladolid where she occupied herself in bringing up her two children and embellishing her palace. This was already recognised as a princely residence, since Prince Philip was usually the guest of Doña María, that is to say, the Cobos, when he stayed at Valladolid.

The little girl María grew up comely and happy and, of course, she attracted the attention of the young men who were with Prince Philip who was always accompanied by a large group of important persons to whom Charles V and Doña Isabel had entrusted the protocol and education of the future monarch. The Empress Isabel trusted in the discretion of Doña Leonor de Mascarenhas, a Portuguese lady appointed to be his nurse. Along with the boy prince were also young noblemen selected to play and study with him. Some were boys of his own age, others a little older, such as his special friend the Portuguese, Ruy Gómez de Silver, who came to Castile with the nurse in Empress Isabel's retinue.

It especially interests me to point out that among these youths surrounding the Prince, there was a certain lad whose Christian and surname denoted him as the grandson of El Gran Capitán. Gonzalo Fernández de Córdoba spent his time alternatively between Cabra, Baeza, Granada and at the Court. He directed his love to the young girl María de los Cobos Mendoza, who besides being beautiful, was desirable because of her parents' connections. In reality, the girl did not offer herself to him out of love. Between the families there was an 'arranged match'.

He was twenty-five, she was fifteen when Gonzalo and María contracted matrimony on 6 February 1539. From Madrid they moved down to Baena where their palace pleased them more than the one at Cabra. Baena was also handy to Granada and the good roads that passed through it made it convenient for Gonzalo to travel up to the Court. Gonzalo also would have been pleased to acquaint his wife with the enchantment of Granada and to present her to his friends: among whom, since 1540, that 'phenonemon of charity' called *"blessed Juan"* had occupied a significant place. This explains why, when Castro describes the alms that Gonzalo Duke of Sessa gave to John of God, he emphasises: *"The same was received from his wife the Duchess, who gave him many donations and favoured him in a great manner."*

Castro notes the generosity of the aid given by the Duke and Duchess when our alms-seeker set out to beg beyond Granada, allowing us to suppose that John of God not only saw these two when they were staying at Granada, but also when he visited them at their palace in Baena.

He was very fond of the young Duke and Duchess, and they were also very fond of him. In fact, as we shall see, our saintly John of God was enchanted by the Duchess and she, in turn, loved him.

This outline of John of God's friendships indicates that it was absolutely essential that our alms-seeker follow the 'national' routes.

Let us see how he carried out his trip to Málaga. The title 'Chief Commander', sought by Don Francisco de los Cobos to give him entrance to the ranks of the nobility, was purchased by him from a family at Málaga called Gómez de Fuensalida Lasso de la Vega.

Its chief, Don Gutierre, had fought in the reconquest of Málaga (1487) and at Granada in (1492), gaining for himself the category of 'Counsellor of State' to the Catholic Monarchs and the Order of Commander of the Bastions of León. Don Gutierre transferred to Don Francisco de los Cobos, with the endorsement of Charles V, the title 'Commander'.

In addition to the agreed price, Gómez de Fuensalida required Cobos to obtain a knighthood of Santiago for his grandson, Gutierre Lasso. These agreements created ties of friendship between the Cobos and the Fuensalida Lasso families; so much so that the young Duke and Duchess of Sessa and Gutierre Lasso, who belonged to the generation whose lives were touched by John of God, maintained a friendship and contact with each other which the researcher, Keniston, calls 'intimate'.

Probably, the Sessas, Gonzalo and María, were the ones who referred John of God to this Málaga family or maybe they took the opportunity of some visit made by Gutierre Lasso to Granada to introduce him to John of God.

Lasso wholeheartedly received John of God at Málaga on two occasions. His wife, Doña Guiomar, and their four children took advantage of the presence of this human phenomenon called John of God. They treated him as well as he would allow them, and no more than that. He came for one thing, a donation, and a donation he took away. He refers to the time as their guests, *"On the two occasions I have visited your city you have given me a very warm welcome and shown great good will towards me."*

Gutierre Lasso exercised the office of judge (regidor) in the Municipality of Málaga. He and Guiomar had four children. Luis was the eldest and heir to the estate, then Ana, Gómez and Isabel. Luis and Isabel were about to marry and their betrothed were also brother and sister. Gómez was studying for the priesthood and was already assured of a position as a canon of Málaga Cathedral. Ana, who had married at the tender age of twelve, was left a widow only two years later. She entered the convent of Santa Clara, leaving her infant son to the care of the family. A tradition says John of God visited her there and presented her with a wooden cross.

When John of God stayed with the devout and charitable Lasso family, Gutierre helped him collect donations from distinguished Málaga families and he also took him to meet Bishop Manrique who was a Dominican friar. Two things, in particular he noticed. Gutierre possessed slaves among his servants, for at that time there were two thousand Moorish slaves in the city; and that it was important for him to heartily extend aid to the poor and sick. So, John of God profited greatly from his two visits to Málaga, both of which took place in 1547. He wrote delightful letters to his friend Gutierre when he returned to Granada: *"This letter is to let you know that, thanks to God, I reached here in good health and with more than fifty ducats. Together with what you have there, that should make a hundred ducats."*

What an excellent result! The gold ducat weighed three and a half grams. We get some idea of its purchasing power when we recall that 400 ducats were paid for the premises in the Cuesta Gomérez. So it was good that he brought back a hundred ducats from Málaga.

However, John of God rapidly found himself in trouble again: *"No sooner had I arrived back, I had to borrow thirty or more ducats."* The hospital was devouring his resources: *"Neither the sum* that you are holding nor the amount that I brought back is enough, since I have more than a hundred and fifty people to maintain. Even so, God is looking after everybody."

The amount *"that you are holding"* referred to money and donations in kind which John of God had left entrusted to Gutierre. His letter urgently requested his friend at Málaga to send him the money as soon as possible: *"Send the twenty-five ducats to me as soon as you can because I owe these and many more and my creditors are waiting for me to pay."*

To assure Gutierre that the money would be safe with the bearer, John of God wrote: *"I am unable to write any more at present because the muleteer is in a hurry to get away."* Then he wrote some instruction that only he and Gutierre knew regarding the deposit: *"You will recall that one evening whilst we were strolling in the orange grove I handed it you in a small linen purse."* He asks Gutierre to put something extra in with the amount: *"You can raise something more, it is all necessary."*

In exchange, he offers to receive into his hospital any patients that Lasso might send him. Then he adds a list of persons to whom he wishes to be remembered: *"Please remember me to your very noble, virtuous and generous wife, the slave of Our Lord Jesus Christ... Give my best wishes to your son the Archdeacon as well, for we used to go out seeking blessed alms together. Please tell him to write to me soon. Remember me to all your sons and daughters and anyone else whom you may think of at Málaga, and also give my respects and best wishes to the Bishop."*

Since the Lassos had acquainted him with their family matters, he speaks of the forthcoming wedding of the eldest son and the ordination of the archdeacon: *"Our Lord knows better than anyone what he is going to do with your sons and daughters, and you have to accept what Our Lord Jesus Christ does and see it is for the best."*

Possibly John of God submitted his plan to cross the gorge of the Despeñaperros to seek donations to Master Avila while he was at Granada from early in the year until the summer of 1548. Avila himself may have coerced him to go up to the Court. The Emperor was going to travel in Europe with his imperial retinue, confidently leaving Spanish home affairs to his son Prince Philip who had just turned twenty-one and was holding his Court at Valladolid.

John of God's aristocratic friends at Granada had connections with important persons at the Court and they all supported his intention to go there and gave him warm recommendations.

Unfortunately the little Duchess of Sessa's influential father, Don Francisco de los Cobos, had died the previous year, having enjoyed right up to his last moments the favour of both Emperor and Prince. When Charles departed for Flanders he had left Cobos, together with Cardinal Tavera and the Duke de Alba, as the three counsellors to Prince Philip. Moreover, Cobos had to tackle the dangerous financial affairs of state. Early in 1543, Don Francisco saw the marriage of his son Diego and at the end of that same year participated in the nuptial festivities of Prince Philip and Doña María of Portugal, the unfortunate princess who, within eighteen months, was to die in childbirth. Between 1544 and 1547, Cobos spent much of his free time creating the Royal Archives of Simancas as well as having the thorny task of extracting from the German bankers new loans for the empire. Towards the end of 1546 his health failed and in February the following year, the Emperor wrote to him granting his request to retire to Ubeda where *"his health should respond to the fresh air."* He died there in May with his wife and children, Diego and María Sarmiento, at his bedside.

Consequently John of God has lost valuable support at Court but Doña María de Mendoza had handed over the palace at Valladolid to the service of the Prince and the exercise of charitable works. Widowed, her lady friends saw her shunning the pomp and ceremony of the Court which she formerly enjoyed. During the absences of the Prince Doña María lodged in her palace persons who came to the Court with petitions for charitable causes. When Prince Philip came to stay at the palace she lodged her proteges in one or other of the houses purchased by her late husband.

Doña María gave a small room to John of God: he needed no more when he came, as he did, with messages from her daughter. Fortunately for him, her son-in-law, the Duke Gonzalo, was in Valladolid assembling the group of nobles who have to escort Prince Philip on his approaching journey to Flanders.

The fields of Castile were in the grip of one of the most ferocious droughts of the 16th century. *"The sterile years"* were going from bad to worse. No one knew where the Spanish people found the energy needed to continue beneath the banners of the

Emperor Charles V without weakening. It will be the stuff of adventures. In America, the horizon of the New World was widening, while at the same time, in the heart of Europe the infantry regiments of the Emperor were attempting to check the onslaught of the Protestant princes who intended to attack the city of Trent where the first session of the Council was about to open.

While this was happening, the Emperor left the regency of Spain to Prince Philip, with his chosen band of counsellors and a list of advice for good government. It was a pity that the young Prince Regent, with the horrible years of drought that the country was suffering, had to convince the Court to send subsidies to his father, who is losing resources and men in the face of multiple enemies of his empire. The Spaniards know that Charles is giving priority to his responsibility, for, at Mühlberg, he gloriously won the battle and stayed in the saddle for twenty hours, despite a cruel attack of gout.

Charles was aging, nevertheless he still found the energy to carry on a romantic affair at Regensburg with Barbara Blomberg and fathered a son named Juan. This is the future Don Juan of Austria who was eighteen years younger than his half-brother Philip. The Emperor, tormented by gout, realised that his strength was failing and that he was living a life well beyond the physical capabilities of his age. While the bishops at Trent were arguing about the Eucharist and the Sacrament of Penance, Maurice of Saxony invaded the south of Germany and in a surprise attack almost captured the Emperor: Charles narrowly escaped during a night in May, wearing only his nightshirt. He fled through the alpine valleys to Innsbruk. Heaven help him had they caught him! To prevent future surprises, the Emperor asked his son Philip to go to Flanders because he wanted those states to recognise him as the heir. He planned to take him to the German Diet too, where he would also present the Prince as heir to the imperial crown. But this plan was to go awry.

On 19 January 1548, Charles sent his son a dispatch from Augsburg giving advice about how he was to govern with skill when the time arrived and instructions he wanted carried out before he left for Flanders.

Firstly, he and his retinue were to carefully study the protocol for action in Flanders and Germany where the Prince will make sure that he takes the leading role.

Secondly, he was to leave the Court at Valladolid organised *"on the Burgundy model"*, with assignments of tasks and relevant duties.

And finally, he was to make preparations for the royal wedding to take place at Valladolid at the beginning of autumn, between the Infanta María and her cousin Maximilian of Austria, both of whom will become Regents of Spain during Philip's absence in Europe.

So it is that throughout the spring of 1548, the Valladolid court will be a cauldron of activity with nervous courtesans seeing to wedding preparations, rehearsals of ceremony and new appointments.

Enter from Granada our alms-seeker, John of God, with basket over his shoulder, bare footed and bare headed!

John of God left Granada on the long journey to Valladolid. He detoured from his route both ways, taking himself off the main road in order to visit villages and cities where he could beg. I suspect he knew he would be absent for three, five or six months. Castro says it was for nine months, but I believe he counted incorrectly. Experts have determined the number of 'leagues' of that period as being equivalent to six hundred kilometres which would take up to fifty days each way, leaving him a good margin of days or hours in which to beg.

Master Avila and the friends at Granada were confident that John of God would return with abundant funds to solve the hospital's economic problems. But they overlooked his open handed ways of sharing out whatever he had to anybody in need.

He went away peacefully, leaving the hospital in the good hands of Antón Martín whom he had appointed his second-in-charge, his 'adjutant'. We can openly call him Brother Antón now, since the whole of Granada was doing so. The little team of 'disciples', in fact, formed a true religious community. Outside the hospital there were benefactors who gave donations in cash and kind and 'volunteers', men and women, who came to give a hand in the care of the patients. There are those, in the hospital, who receive a salary and work fixed hours, some living in. These are the cleaners, cooks, general hands, a sacristan and some nurses... and others, such as our friend the 'faithful employee' Angulo. However the essential running of the place fell to the brothers who were attracted by the marvellous example of John of God, totally dedicating their lives to the unstinting service of the hospital. Castro distinguishes, with absolute clarity, between *"servants and the brothers"* when he writes about this period.

Brother Antón Martín is temporarily responsibe for the hospital at Granada and for the leadership of the brothers. We only have clues with regard to the number then remaining, perhaps twelve, fifteen or twenty. Still lacking, was the 'rule' that is characteristic of religious congregations, and they did not take 'vows' yet. Pius V will give them a juridical structure after John of God's death. Yet the brothers did wear a habit; and were recognised by its style. In those early years they wore a mixture of odd materials which today would seem strange, *"material of burlap or coarse linen"* (*angeo* or *anjeo* apparently having come from the Anjou region of France), *"buriel"* [kersey] a grey or reddish woollen cloth made of dense and coarse woollen yarn, but somewhat finer than serge; *"sayal"* [sackcloth].

The important thing was that the habit, apart from discretely keeping *"them clean"* according to the advice of the bishop, gave them a sign of their identity. They were not in the juridical sense friars, but, yes, they were 'brothers'.

With the habit, slung over their shoulders went the basket, their own characteristic sign, symbol of their permanent activity as 'alms-seeker' brothers, those who beg to support the poor, the ill and the sustenance of a hospital. They have been dubbed with a nickname by the ordinary people; *"the Brothers of the basket."*

Traditionally considered to be authentic, we still conserve two of these baskets: the one which belonged to John of God that is to be found in the *camarín*, [relics room] of his basilica at Granada; the other, which belonged to one of his first disciples, is held at the Casa de los Pisa Museum, Granada. Both baskets are displayed in gilded wooden showcases bearing the classification *"hempen basket of the Covarrubias Treasury"*: *"simply woven from fibres of esparto grass and wider than high."*

John of God and his brothers, besides using the basket, utilised wickerwork boxes, knapsacks and the famous pots, made in the Moorish style with handles to allow them to be either carried by hand or over the shoulder on straps.

We know that John of God also used a staff to assist himself on his journeys beyond Granada but we will speak of it when he visits Toledo.

He left Brother Antón Martín in charge, but who accompanied John of God on this long journey and when did he - or they - actually depart from Granada?

We only have approximations for answers. The month of his commencement would probably have been April 1548. On 6 April, John of God attended the funeral, at Granada, of his confessor. It is not Padre Portillo but one, Domingo Alvarado, a Mercedarian friar who had died. John of God accompanied the remains *"crying aloud with great fervour and tears."* So certainly he did not leave Granada prior to April 6.

Some prestigious authors 'say' that he was accompanied by Pedro Velasco, the former 'enemy' of Antón Martín, who now, like him, wears the habit and carries the basket. But Castro's details of the journey are written "in the singular", indicating that John of God travelled alone: *"He underwent great hardships"*; Doña María de Mendoza *"gave him lodging"*; also *"she gave him large donations"*; *"he shared it with them"*; *"his arrival which was... they informed the King about him* (it was the Prince of course); *"They introduced him into the palace."*

We continually lament the loss of the 'notebook'. It is recorded that he went to Toledo, Oropesa and Salamanca, and of course Valladolid, the goal of his journey, but did he visit them on the way or on his return journey?

On his return he once more crossed the Despeñaperros gorge and entered Andalusia. Here he visited Córdoba, Cabra, Alcaudete and Alcalá la Real before concluding his journey at Granada.

To cross through the gorge known today as Despeñaperros, John of God would have had the option of taking one of two routes down from the plateau along the Caminio Real of Andalusia. Caravans came down from Valdepeñas to Viso del Marqués, where they tackled the sierra; or, alternatively, from Manzanares turning to the left, going towards Torre de Juan Abad to come out in front of Beas. Either of the two itineraries would take him to Toledo.

I do not ask what John of God would have thought of his first view of the Imperial City, nor if in crossing the Sierra Morena he saw more than the rough stones of the road and the bright sky above, for, it seems to me, he is 'a man of essentials'. By that I mean he paid little attention to the scenery about him, whether it was natural or man made. His main concern was to care for the sick and assist the poor and to obtain money to carry it out. All the rest is incidental.

Toledo offered him a rest and consolation. A well-earned rest after many days, crossing mountains, rivers and plains. Consolation, because he did things there in his own way. Having been well received, he felt a desire to open up his first 'branch' hospital modelled on the lines of the one he had established at Granada: *"He found the citizens willing and inclined to help the poor."* When he returns to Granada, John of God gave impetus to this Toledan project.

In the beatification process, witnesses at Toledo made highly emotional statements when they spoke of this remarkable person. Toledo, situated halfway between Granada and Valladolid, was at this time the third city in Spain with the highest density of aristocrats. The noble families passed the news between their various branches from city to city, and *blessed* John of God was news indeed.

It was here that he came within the orbit of a distinguished lady of that city, Doña Leonor de Mendoza. She belonged to the extensive imperial Mendoza clan and was related to our Duchess of Sessa. Doña Leonor was married to Alvarez Ponce de León, a leading citizen and Chief Notary of Castile and *Regidor* of Toledo. Doña Leonor longed to have a family, but was unable to fulfil this desire. She was also devout and charitable. Among the witnesses there were two who, in their youth, had lived as servants in her palace and they both later became priests. Another was a servant girl who became a Franciscan nun at the convent of Santa Isabel la Real. This is a good indication of the Christian qualities of the household. All three spoke of their mistress with the highest praise: *"Such a servant of God, and of such a distinguished lineage, she would say nothing that was not true"*; *"a person of great quality and nobility"*; *"a holy and most noble woman."* Thus they spoke, reinforcing their certainty that the stories they heard spoken about her were true.

News of an event circulated throughout the city: *"all Toledo knew of it."* I consider these to be credible witnesses. As children they used to play with the lady's little grandchildren, she was still alive then.

It so happened that Doña Leonor invited John of God to stay at her palace, but he declined. She, *"using all her powers of persuasion"* was able *"to entice him to dine some days."* She desired children and confided her grief to him and was advised to trust in God: *"He will fulfil your desire."*

When John of God was leaving Toledo a few days later, Doña Leonor asked him for a memento. As he departed he handed his walking stick to her. *"Soon afterwards she conceived and had a number of children"*: Doña Leonor gave birth to a son and two daughters.

My gynaecologist friend, who read this story, commented that this does not necessarily mean it was 'a miracle', but simply a case of the spermatozoon of Alvarez finally finding the ovaries of Doña Leonor!

Anyhow, the whole of Toledo believed that the staff of John of God brought good fortune to births, some of which were recommended to Doña Leonor. I am quoting some phrases from a simple citizen called Díaz Getino: *"Isabel Gaona, the wife of this witness, sent for the aforementioned staff during a difficult birth. She had been in labour for three days and, God be praised, when they brought it to her she quickly gave birth. She attributes this to the blessed padre, who prayed for her, and to having been touched by the aforementioned staff, through which Our Lord brought about such a good result."*

Doña Leonor had *"a wooden case lined with velvet made for the staff."* However, with so much passing about from one person to another, it soon began to show signs of wear. Those who used it from then on, had pieces of silver-plate inserted upon it, and before long the whole staff was completely covered.

Toledo never forgot. Years later when she was a widow, Doña Leonor bequeathed *"her houses, her goods, her jewels"* to the Hospitaller Brothers so that they could build a hospital; and she requested they inter her in their chapel of Corpus Christi.

She also gave them the staff. A combination of complex circumstances brought it from Toledo to Granada, where it was deposited in the Pisa Museum.

There are other staffs said to have been used by John of God in the Pisa Museum, in the Granada Basilica and at Seville. It seems reasonable that he should have used more than one.

At this time, the mid-16th century, Madrid was no more

than a small town whose geographic position was convenient for the accommodation of the Court from time to time. Twenty years were to pass before the notable 'bureaucratic king', Philip II, wanting to effectively modernise the administration of the kingdom, would build up a great city on this crossroad situated right in heart of Spain.

Even though we lack documented proof, I think that we have here the reason why Madrid did not attract John of God. He thought it more reasonable to continue his journey avoiding Madrid and turning left to pass through Salamanca on his way to Valladolid.

This put him on the way to 'his Oropesa'. This time, inevitably, as he entered the Arañuelo and made out the lordly profile of the castle from the flat land of the Tiétar, the familiar countryside must have strongly struck John of God's heart and saturated him with familiar aromas.

John of God Ciudad had left Oropesa with the armed retinue of the Duke for the imperial campaign of Vienna in 1532, sixteen years before. The young men who were his companions in those days were now aged between thirty-five and forty and he was over fifty. They recognised each other, the Herruz, 'his' family, and the shepherds and farm labourers, friends of his childhood and youth. The fields, the churches, the ducal palace, were all familiar.

Oropesa would have heard about the achievements of a 'holy hospitaller' who cared for the poor and sick at Granada. Now they see him arriving, just as he had been described to them. An old lady at the Process, Ana Miranda, who saw him then when she was a girl, gives an almost photographic description of him: *"This witness remembers very well that he was a tall man with bushy eyebrows, a strong beard, and that he was neither fat nor slim but was well built."*

Of course they regarded him as an *"exemplary man with the reputation of a saint."* His basket slung over his shoulder, he began with one hand to beg alms and with the other to hand them out: *"He was dressed in a rough woollen smock and carried a basket over his shoulder. He came to this town and went along the streets from house to house. His feet were bare and he had no head covering. He called out in a loud voice: 'Do good for yourselves.' Whatever he was given he gave away again at the prison and the hospital of this town. Whenever he heard about any poor men and women living at home, he would give assistance to them there. He gave everything in the name of God, and he did the same thing in the villages that are around this town."*

Perhaps John of God felt that he had an outstanding debt to fulfil with regard to the people who had welcomed him as a child.

Someone at Oropesa during these days coined a new surname for John: *"Juan Esperaendiós"* – John Hoping-in-God.

The references indicate that, when they talked around the family hearth, the farm labourers of Oropesa often recalled the man who left there one day to become famous for his charity.

Two old men contributed their testimony to the Process. Both had identical Christian and surnames, Francisco González, one of ninety-nine years, the other a hundred: in order to distinguish them, at Oropesa they called the hundred year old Francisco González *"el Viejo"* [the old man], while the other, with his mere ninety-nine years, was called *"el Joven"* [the young man]." Both perfectly recalled John of God the charity worker passing through Oropesa. They declared they had derived *"many great benefits"* from his example of holiness *"combined with alms, as much as in food as in money"* and *"the alms which he collected he gave to the hospital of this village and needy persons in it."* They summed him up as *"a man of tremendous charity, zeal and love of God."*

The two Franciscos, Ana Miranda, and practically all the statements made at Oropesa, exalt the care that John of God gave to a sick woman, Ana La Torre, *"She was the sister of Juan La Torre, the sword maker, who lived in the lane called Matadero Viejo. She had a wounded leg."* It was seriously wounded, ulcerated and *"its stench was almost unsupportable."*

Here they attributed to John of God the same astonishing behaviour of other healers of similar illnesses. He applied his lips to the wound of the sick woman sucking out the pus and spitting it out. They were certain that the resulting cure was miraculous. Perhaps the miracle already lay in the loving care that John of God gave to the afflicted lady.

It was inevitable that as the years went by legends arose as vestiges of John of God's visit and I have accorded them a certain respect. For example, the mulberry tree that he could have planted in the ancient home of the Herruz family, now part of the cloister of the convent of the Oblate Sisters of Christ the Priest. They also attribute to him the carving of a statue of the Child Jesus, placed over the porch of the convent. García Sánchez, with some courtesy, describes historical doubts about these traditions that, to him, go beyond reason. What is certain is that, "John of God left here to set out for various adventures..."

At Salamanca the people were startled when they saw him because they were unaccustomed to seeing anyone behaving like John of God. Two aspects of his behaviour caused admiration in the city. The first, his method of collecting alms: "*He went about the city by day and night carrying a crucifix in his hand and calling out: 'Do good for yourselves brothers and sisters.'*" This 'catchcry', used for years in the streets of Granada, caused wonder here where they had never heard anything like it. The witnesses testify that he went into the homes where there were impoverished *vergonzantes*: "*Many needy people secretly went to him and among them were some honourable persons.*"

He took the sick people he found to San Bernardo Hospital, leading them by the hand or, if they were unable to walk, carrying them on his back. One exploit circulated throughout the whole city. The hospital reserved for syphilitics, Santa María, refused to take a patient because there was no bed for him: John of God asked them to give the man to him. He then carried him to San Bernardo's where he asked that the afflicted man might occupy the place where he was staying.

With what care, "*humility and love*" he treated the patients. Accordingly the Salamancans emphasised that: "*He lovingly cleaned them.*" "*Many people came only to see how he cared for the aforementioned poor.*"

From the sieve maker, Jerónimo, comes a significant detail expressly put forward, but rarely mentioned in the documents. My perception is that it is typical of John of God's good humour and cheerfulness. Señor Jerónimo relates that John seemed quite jovial as, "*laughingly*" "*he went among the patients taking care of them, dressing them in their clothes, massaging them and turning them in their beds to make them comfortable,*" and finishes by saying: "*Laughingly and with extraordinary love and charity, it seemed that he did not desire anything more than that the patients be cheered up.*"

Nothing in John of God's biography gives the impression that he would seek to dramatise his actions, give himself airs, or cause admiration in those who saw him. He was self-possessed, happy, "*a man of laughter...*"

No wonder the Salamancans thought he was admirable: *"When he passed through the streets they came out to see him and kissed his habit."*

Two quick observations: Here he also assisted prostitutes, including one whom *"he rescued"* by providing her *"with what he could manage from his alms."* And here too *"demons attacked him"*; at least that is what those who were close to him said: *"They beat him at night and left him black and blue. When he was asked what had happened to him so as to leave him so bruised, 'God wills it', he replied."*

During the days John of God spent at Salamanca, or later at Valladolid, a youth, a future famous painter, sketched his likeness without him being aware of it. The young man collected sketches of faces that seemed to him to be gifted with special vigour. He put these in his sketchbook to provide him with artistic inspiration for later portraits, or simply to practice sketching from real life examples of natural features. It is a happy coincidence that the young apprentice artist was impressed by the face of John of God because, thanks to this chance encounter, we possess a faithful portrait of him.

The young man was the seventeen-year-old Alonso Sánchez Coello, who was soon to go to Flanders under a scholarship of the King João III of Portugal to study under the Flemish masters. Son of a Valencian family, his father was the village schoolmaster at Benifairó but he settled permanently in the Portuguese city of Castel Rodrigo, some hundred kilometres from Salamanca.

We do not know how young Coello *"saw the alms-seeker worker face to face"*. Nor are we sure whether he knew him at Salamanca or some weeks later at Valladolid. Maybe Alonso Coello, an artist by vocation, was spending some time at Salamanca where he surely spent months with masters and colleagues. He could also have gone to Valladolid where the Court was ablaze with the festivities for the royal wedding and the preparations for the European journey of Prince Philip.

What is absolutely certain is that the young man *'saw John of God'* whose face interested him so much that he incorporated the drawing in his sketchbook and kept it.

The years passed and Alonso Sánchez Coello became famous and was appointed Royal portrait painter. He was esteemed by Philip II who furnished him with lodgings within the royal mansion, the Court already having been installed at Madrid. Some twenty years after the death of John of God, Brother Domingo Benedicto (our old friend the Genoese banker Domingo Piola) commissioned Coello to paint a portrait of John of God. Coello was delighted to accept and in order to work the canvas, used *his sketch from nature* taken from life that day when he saw John of God, thereby giving us a faithful portrait.

'It is,' John of God... how fascinating!

Notes to Chapter 31

* The episode of the intertwined relationships of the Hurtado-Mendoza-Guevara-La Torre families are proven in the statements made at the Granada beatification process. Among the witnesses who personally knew John of God: # 43, María de Guevara: of those who did not personally know him: Juan La Torre, Onofre Hurtado de Mendoza, Leonor María de Guevara (Leonor Guevara's grand daughter). There are ample notices of later events of the family in M. de Mina, '*Anotaciones'*, *Fondo Documental*, op.cit..

* For a description of the church of San Jerónimo, see A. Gallego Burín *Granada. Guía del viajero*, op.cit., 248 ff.; F Henríquez Jorquera, *Anales de Granada*, (Ed. A. Marín Ocete) 48 (1934) 230; M. de Mina *Visitar la Granada de San Juan de Dios*, op.cit., 247-285.

* The quotation of Master Avila, see L. Sala Balust-F. Martín Hernández, *Obras completas del santo maestro Juan de Avila*, V, op.cit., 704, letter # 214.

* On the support of the Duchess of Sessa of John of God, see Francisco de Castro, op.cit., chapter 16 and elsewhere.

* About Francisco de los Cobos, Cf. H. Keniston, *Francisco de los Cobos, Secretario de Carlos V*, Madrid 1980.

* The journeys of John of God to Málaga and his association with Gutierre Lasso, Cf. Benito Romero, O.H., *Gutierre Lasso de la Vega, Regidor de Málaga:* Paz y Caridad #232 (1979) 23; this has been amplified by G. Magliozzi in *Un amico a Málaga*, Rome 1995. The relationship of de Cobos with Fuensalida, see . H. Keniston, op.cit., passim. The quotes from *The Letters of St. John of God* (op.cit.), correspond to the first of the two addressed to Gutierre Lasso. The second was sent just prior to his death.

* For the presence of Master Avila during the first half of 1548, see L. Sala Balust-F. Martín Hernández, *Obras, etc.*, op.cit., I, 117; V, 34.

* The appointment of Antón Martín as being responsible for the Cuesta Gomérez hospital during John of God's journey to Court, see Francisco de Castro, op.cit, chapter 16. For the persons employed, volunteers, etc., ibid, chapter 23. Also in the documents of the Jeronymite lawsuit, see J. Sánchez, *Kénosis, etc.*, op.cit., 298-300. About the brothers see Francisco de Castro, op.cit., chapter 23; also the testimony of Angulo, J. Sánchez, *Kénosis, etc.*, op.cit., 304.

* How communities of the period did not strictly adhere to profession of the vows see G. Russotto, *Spiritualità Ospedaliera*, I, (1958) Rome, 119-120; the imposition came with the issuing of the papal bull *Lubricum vitae genus*, of 17 November 1568.
* References to the basket of John of God are in Francisco de Castro, op.cit., chapter 15 and receiving the slap in the face, chapter 17.
* The funeral of Fray Domingo Alvarado and the sorrow of John of God on that occasion, see M. Gómez Moreno, *San Juan de Dios, Primicias historicos*, op.cit., 169. For the curious document *Catálogo de os obispos de Jaén y anales eclesiásticos desde obispado*, elaborated by Martin de Ximena, Madrid 1654, 473.
* There is no documented justification to say that Pedro Velasco accompanied John of God to Valladolid, although many biographies say this was so, starting with that of J. Santos, *Galería Hospitalaria* IV, 85. Because Antón Martín was left in charge, they presumed that Pedro Velasco must have been chosen to accompany John of God. Among authors who have guessed that Pedro Velasco was John of God's companion of this journey are: I. Giordani, *Il santo della carità ospedaliera*, Rome 1965, 228; J. Cruset, *El hombre que supo amar*, Madrid 1977, 136; V. Riesco, *Y Dios se hizo hermano*, Madrid 1994, 91. [B. O'Grady, *Champion of Charity*, Sydney, 1972, 162.]
* Did John of God call in at Cabra-Baena on his way to Valladolid and carry letters from the Duchess of Sessa to her mother? Probably, but: a) Not necessarily these letters, because her parents already were well aware of the relationship between John of God and their daughter. b) Was he carrying other letters of recommendation from other persons at Granada? c) There seems no doubt he went to Córdoba on the way back to inform Master Avila about his journey, and it is only a short distance from Córdoba to Cabra-Baena on the road to Granada.
* The stay at Toledo and the episode about Doña Leonor de Mendoza was stated by several witnesses at the Toledo beatification process: The priest Juan Ruiz; the priest Marcos Rodrígues; the poor Clare nun Francisca Girón de Velasco; and Juan Díez Getino. All of these answered question #57 of the beatification process. With the usual reserve, I take reference from A. Govea, (op.cit.), chapter XLI, 208; and J. Santos (op.cit,), Vol. I, 347. Regarding the story of the staff, see J. Ciudad Gómez, *Noticias historicas sobre el báculo de San Juan de Dios*, Granada 1978. The little maid Estefanía de Vallejo who served in the Granada palace of the Mendoza-Cárdenas family was taken to Madrid then to Toledo by her mistress Doña Elvira Carrillo: she knew the widow Doña Leonor and saw the staff and knew its story. She testified to this at the Toledo beatification process on 13 January 1623.
* The scarce but nevertheless valid documentation accruing from the Oropesa beatification process of 20 January 1623 permits an assurance that results erroneously to put John of God's visit to Oropesa from his pilgrimage to Guadalupe in 1539. There was sense in such a distraction because he urgently had to return to Baeza where Master Avila was awaiting him to set him upon his hospitaller calling. On the other hand, on either his going or return from Valladolid, that is to say this journey, the pieces fall into perfect place because he went to Oropesa then as part of his fund-raising activity.
* John of God at Oropesa: see A. Govea, (op.cit.), chap. XVI, 76, this position for me unequivocally the return visit from Guadalupe. The statements made at the Oropesa beatification process of 20 Jan. 1623 correspond to the following witnesses: 'Old' Francisco González and 'Young' Francisco González, María de

Vergara Herruz y Navas, Pedro Ramírez, Ana de Miranda, Lucas Hernández, Francisco Moreno; see M. Gómez Moreno, *San Juan de Dios, Primicias historicos,* op.cit., 195-198, here part of the statements are presented. J. García Sánchez, *El Señorio de Oropesa,* unpublished manuscript; Id., *San Juan de Dios en el Señorio de Oropesa:* Beresit (1992) 97 note 31. He is surprised that the quotations of Gómez Moreno do not perfectly coincide with the copy of the declarations which M. De Minas, *'Anotaciones', Fondo Documental,* (op.cit.) reasonably welcomes. The cause of the discrepancy is that Gómez Moreno, pp 105-106, has based himself upon only one of the declarations corresponding to the two old Francisco González, 'the old and the young.' The observations of J. García Sánchez about the mulberry tree planted by John of God, are in his above mentioned work, pp 110-111.

* The judge appointed to the Salamanca beatification process, cites amongst others, 4 old persons: 31 Dec. 1622 , Pedro Hernández, carpenter, 91 years of age; 2 Jan. 1623, Jerónimo Hernández, sieve maker, *"more then ninety years of age"*; 3 Jan. 1623, Marcos de Arroyo, upholsterer, *"more then ninety years of age"*; 14 Jan. 1623, María Hernández, widow *"bedridden and crippled"* who declared in her home before the notary that *"she knew John of God in this city more than seventy years ago."* That is exactly 74 years exactly. She was born sometime between 1532 and 1534, so she was 14 or 16 years old when John of God visited Salamanca.

* Cf. P. Madoz, *Diccionario geografico-estadístico-histórico de España XIII,* (1848), 638: According to Madoz there were 36 small hospitals at Salamanca in ancient times which then cut down for male patients at Santa María la Blanca, San Gregorio, Caballo Blanco and the Amparo. At the time of Bishop Tavira they were unified under the name of 'Santisima Trinidad' which is said to have been founded by the Catholic Monarchs. Within this hospital was a ward called San Bernado with 22 beds *"for practice of the art of medicine"*

* On the portrait of John of God by Alonso Sánchez Coello: see M. de Mina, *Juan de Dios al vivid y el pintor Alonso Sánchez Coello:* 'Información y Noticias' XXII, 127 (1993) 3-14. The priest Juan Sánchez Coello, son of the painter, declared as a witness at the Toledo beatification process definitive words which the clerk recorded: *"As for the veneration of the blessed padre John of God, he said that he holds to be a venerable person, a servant of God and worthy to be esteemed and venerated as such. He knows that in order to do this, Alonso Sánchez Coello, painter at the Royal Chamber of His Majesty, renowned at the Court, made a sketch of the person of John of God while he was alive. This was sketched and signed by the hand of the aforementioned Alonso Sánchez Coello who put it in one of his books saying these words: 'Brother Domingo Benedicto of the Hospital of John of God took away the same portrait of John of God to Granada.' The witness testified under the same oath: 'It was truly done by the hand of the aforementioned Alonso Sánchez Coello, and he did it from memory using a book in which he kept sketches upon parchment, and I truly have seen this.'"*

* Brother Matía de Mina whose research has thrown so much light upon the portrait, comments upon the statement made by the painter's son: "The witness was aware that there were portraits being made out of reverence for the servant of God. However, he especially points out that while John of God was still alive, he had his portrait painted by Alonso Sánchez Coello and proven as such by his own hand and signature. He did this portrait using the sketches he made and to which he added these words: 'Brother Domingo Benedicto of the Hospital of John of God , took away the same portrait of John of God to Granada.' From this he

infers (reaffirming) that John of God, while he was still living, had been sketched by the hand of his father Alonso Sánchez Coello. The same witness, still under oath, affirms that the hand writing adjacent to the sketch is also that of Alonso Sánchez Coello; and that this writing and drawing were done in a book of parchment which he kept, along with written references and he says that he truly saw this."

32

JOHN OF GOD GOES TO VALLADOLID, HAS AN AUDIENCE WITH PRINCE PHILIP, THEN VISITS THE DUCHESS OF SESSA

Valladolid
Córdoba
Baena
Granada
1548

They see one another, face to face. What a great scene.

Towards the end of this month of May the Prince will reach twenty-one years of age. No one dares to comment on his slender physique although his frioends say as much amongst themselves. They look on him with marvelling eyes because they know that destiny ordains that he will be a man of grandeur – in fact he already is, since his father, Charles, is in poor health. He will be the beloved Lord of the universe – as a Flemish painter has already depicted, him dressed in ruffles and armor with sword in belt and sceptre in hand.

It is before the beginning of Winter and the prince, surrounded by his retinue, will soon go up the Catalan coast to join the fleet of Andrea Doria to go to Genoa and then proceed, as military commander, to Milan. From there he will proceed to Mantua, and then on to Innsbruck, finishing up at Brussels where the emperor, his father, awaits him. Five years from now Philip will come into his legacy of lands rich with gold and the countries of Flanders and Brabante, as well as the crowns of Castile and Aragon. The open seas and the lands of the New World will be his.

Don Philip could not understand, and would not understand, what manner of man this was who stood before him. All he saw was a monkish figure – advanced in years, balding, with bronzed face and bare of foot. The Prince thinks, Why couldn't they've attired him properly? And prepared him for an audience with me. He had consented to receive him on the insistence of a certain nobleman and others who spoke to him of this charitable John.

The meeting seemed likely to serve no significant purpose. Phillip was experienced when it came to dealing with friars – at least with friars who were intellectual, brilliant and erudite; as he was with clerics, bishops, archbishops and distinguished cardinals.

But this poor man was not of such a class. How is it that they have not dressed him in decent attire in order to come to see me!

Ah, it would be nice to hear what John of God thought of the Prince but if he said anything, then regrettably, it lies buried away in that lost note book!

John of God was not over impressed with Valladolid. He had come from Granada which was, after all, no village and previously he had gazed on sights from Vienna to La Coruña, from Fuenterrabía to Ceuta. He knew the cities of Seville, Cádiz, Toledo. He was no country bumpkin and he came for one thing only - his poor and sick people.

Doña María Mendoza lived in a majestic palace and of course he was impressed by that, at least from the outside because we do not know if he ever saw inside. You will recall that Doña María has only been a widow for some months, Cobos having died in the spring of the previous year. She welcomed John of God and, as Castro says in the biography, arranged for his accommodation and meals: *"All the time he resided at Valladolid, this lady gave him lodgings and meals."*

However, *"lodgings"* need not mean that she brought him into her palace, for she possessed other houses in the city where she lodged friends and pilgrims. She would arrange such lodgings for none other than Mother Teresa of Jesus many years later.

In no way did the family of Doña María Mendoza suffer financial loss with the death of her husband, Cobos, who had arranged carefully for her welfare. At the peak of his political power, the Emperor's invaluable secretary had chosen a wife of distinguished lineage. María de Mendoza was the daughter of the Military Governor of Galicia, Juan Hurtado de Mendoza and María Sarmiento, third Countess de Rivadavia. She had two brothers. One was a bishop and the other a rake. Alvaro, the bishop, occupied the See of Avila at the time Teresa began the adventure of her reform of the Carmelites. The bishop's mother knew Mother Teresa of Jesus, and so too did her playboy son Bernardino who never married but in his old age feared death and turned to religion. He gave Mother Teresa a farm at Valladolid to open a convent but the property was on the banks of a river and proved unsuitable. However Doña María Mendoza came to the rescue of the nuns and lent them one of her houses as temporary accommodation while she found them a suitable permanent residence.

While Cobos was still living, Doña María had been the principal lady, admired and esteemed by the nobles of the Court, but once widowed she renounced the vanities of Court life and devoted herself to charitable projects, especially helping nuns and friars, thereby amazing the Court. It delighted her to welcome the alms-seeker from Granada recommended by her daughter, the

Duchess of Sessa and her husband, Gonzalo. Because Prince Philip and his bevy of noble gentlemen were staying in her palace, she was unable to accommodate John of God there.

Cobos had been very proud of this palace built on his wife's family property. The architect was Luis de Vega and the greatest artisans had constructed for him a lordly building of such grandeur that Philip III chose it as the 'Royal Residence' in the early 17th century when the Court resided at Valladolid.

However, during the mid 16th century the Court was continually on the move, and each time Prince Philip came to Valladolid he preferred to stay at the palace of the Cobos, a choice recommended by his father the Emperor Charles as a sign of appreciation to the memory of his faithful Secretary of State. The nobility of the realm still held Doña María Mendoza in the highest esteem and some even envied her position as the Prince's 'landlady'. This wise and talented lady became John of God's guide through the court etiquette at Valladolid.

I have already said that this was scarcely a propitious time for Prince Philip to hear of affiars that did not touch on the splendour of the Royal Court, but *"They gave news of him to the King (to the Prince), and informed him about the things that John of God did."*

John of God brought with him greetings from Granada for other noblemen, such as Count de Tendilla; and other *"lords who knew him."* The first chief of the House of Tendilla was Iñigo López de Mendoza who was appointed by the Catholic Monarchs to be Governor of the Alhambra and the City after the conquest of Granada. After his marriage he became the Marquis de Mondéjar and his title resounded in the Court like the sound of a fanfare of silver trumpets. His many grandchildren were supporters of John of God's hospital on the Cuesta Gomérez, and they often spoke about him. No wonder Tendilla became his sponsor at Valladolid. So did many other nobles. Doña María Mendoza, *"gave him a great amount of alms which he distributed to the poor who were vergonzantes."* John of God, at this high level, acts as an authentic specialist of hospitality and gives social assistance: *"He did this exceedingly well, going to look for these poor men and women in their own dwellings and giving them food just as he did at Granada."* In the meantime, Tendilla *"and others"* were busy arranging the day and hour for his audience with the Prince.

It is possible that John of God's friend, Bishop Miguel

Muñoz, presided at the Royal Chancellry of Valladolid at this time. He would probably have pondered to himself, *"Thank goodness I gave him that habit, otherwise he would turn up to see the Prince dressed in filthy rags like a Granada beggar."*

They arranged for John of God to be presented at the glittering Imperial Court presided over by Don Philip the Prince Regent. A Flemish artist had finished a portrait of him dressed in regal finery and armour, his sword at his side and his septre in his hand. We cannot say for certain whether John of God's visit coincided with the impending royal wedding. It was the Emperor's desire that when Philip left for Flanders his nephew the Archduke Maximilian, who was to marry his daughter, the Infanta María, should occupy the Regency. María was Prince Philip's sister and the Emperor ordered from Germany that the celebration of the wedding should take place in the summer of 1548.

At Valladolid John of God must have noticed the contrast between the royal splendour and the poor and destitute of the Imperial City. We know very well that he never developed any social theory, nor did he attempt to change the course of the world. It was up to him to assist the marginated by obtaining money for them from the wealthy. John of God probably escaped the royal wedding because it eventually had to be postponed until the middle of September because the bridegroom did not arrive at Valladolid until then because of illness. Probably John of God was presented to the Prince in early July. When John of God had spoken with the Prince and had obtained what he wanted, the merrymaking courtiers soon lost interest in him.

Castro incorporated into his biography the dialogue that someone circulated at the time. Perhaps he heard it from John of God himself, or from Doña María Mendoza, or perhaps Tendilla. The story goes that the meeting took place *"in the palace."* John of God, there by rightful invitation and not mere chance, was ushered into the presence of Prince Philip whom we hope showed the charity worker some sign of welcome, a smile perhaps.

Here is Castro's version of the audience. *"My Lord, I usually call everyone 'brothers in Jesus Christ'. You are my King and Lord and I have to obey you. How do you command me to address you?"* Possibly nobody had ever spoken that way to the Prince before. He disconcertedly replied, *"Juan, call me how you wish."* I think Don

Philip said these words kindly, for the poor alms-seeker does not deserve a sarcastic retort.

John of God, recognising that Philip is not yet King, replied, "*I shall call you good Prince,*" and continues, "*May God give you a good beginning in your reign and a good steadfast hand to govern; then afterwards, a good ending so you save yourself and gain heaven.*"

We salute our alms-seeker who came to beg, but who views things and speaks from God's side. His simple words are very powerful. Putting aside his own needs, he lovingly reminds the Prince of the fundamental truth that his reign merits God's blessing not just human applause. Some historians say that, amongst other mottos, Philip II chose for himself, one: "*Nec soli impar*", equal to the sun. John of God's words brought him down from the clouds and set his feet on the ground of truth.

Castro only adds: "*He spoke with him for a good while.*" We are told nothing more. He finishes off his narrative thus, "*And afterwards, he (the Prince) gave an order that he be given alms,* [from] *himself and his sisters the Infantas.*" In fact, following the interview John of God "*went every day to visit the Infantas*" Doña Juana and Doña María. It was the last mentioned who was preparing for her approaching wedding. Castro says they were generous with their donations: "*They and their ladies-in-waiting presented him with a good quantity of jewels and alms.*"

The phrase that the Prince "*gave an order that he be given alms,* [from] *himself and his sisters the Infantas,*" seems to be somewhat carefully constructed. What it really says is that Philip gave an order "*to give him alms.*" Who had to give them? "*He and his sisters,*" which means that Philip was not simply passing the matter over to the Infantas, but ordered that John of God be given his alms, too. When I read it that way, it seems to me to hold more substance and the Prince appears in a far better light than if he had simply left the matter to his sisters thereby missing out himself on following the advice of one of his most valiant subjects.

The benefactors at the Royal Court were startled by the fact that John of God, following his custom, "*took alms with one hand and gave them out with the other*": "*He distributed them to the needy poor there at Valladolid.*" They were astonished and commented on this amongst themselves. It amazed them that he came from so far away to seek alms for his hospital only to give them away to the poor at Valladolid.

Finally they asked him: *"Brother John of God, why do you not save the money and take it back to your own poor at Granada?"* His reply shows the quality of this man, *"Brother, giving it away here or giving it away at Granada, all is done for God who is everywhere."*

For him, the place where Christ lives is in the person of the poor. What is the difference, giving at Valladolid or Granada?

Fortunately, Doña María Mendoza and Count de Tendilla found a means whereby John of God could take a good amount of money back to the hospital at Granada. They *"and other nobles"* signed *"bills of exchange"*, letters of credit, (bank cheques), *"to be redeemed at Granada."* They pulled the reins on his charitable impulses and he had to graciously fall into line.

Did he find the return journey a strain? Of course! Castro describes John of God's fatigue on returning, which would have been equal to his forward journey, but now tiredness was pressing upon him. Above all, his feet were worse off, *"He travelled in his bare feet, suffering tremendously from the rough and torturous roads which cracked and cut them in many places as he stumbled over stones."* Only when he had reached his southern destination would our weatherworn traveller rest.

One of the witnesses at the Beatification Process said he spent nights of his journey sheltering in hospitals along the way. There he used to hand over the donations he had collected during that day. He never received any medical attention, but he simply started off once more the next day regardless of the irritation he suffered from chafing: *"He suffered a lot of chafing due to the rough and bulky attire rubbing his shirtless body."*

It would have been dangerous had John of God set out in winter, with gales and rain. It is quite frightening to imagine him crossing the Sierra Morena between the months of November and February. Still it was far from being a pleasant journey even in summer under the scorching sun, and more so since he did not wear a head covering of any description. Castro indicates that his friends at Granada were shocked by the state he was in: *"When he arrived the skin was peeling off his face, neck and head, due to his being bareheaded in the intense sunlight as he journeyed."*

John of God had halted twice whilst returning. It is certain he detoured after crossing over the Sierra Morena to Córdoba where he wanted to meet up with Master Avila. They had discussed the route of the return journey to Granada and planned this meeting so, when he arrived at Córdoba, he went to where the Master was staying. That's all we know, just that John of God visited the Master, probably to give an account of what he had done - an 'external' account and, above all, an 'interior' one, concerning his spiritual state and his interior frame of mind.

Only recently, the Master had left Granada to go to Constantina, a city east of Córdoba where the Duchess de Feria was about to give birth and had requested his attendance.

It was the custom for Spanish ladies of the aristocracy in the 16th century to invite persons renowned for sanctity to come into their homes to pray to God for a successful delivery. We know for instance, that Teresa of Jesus came close to death at Alba de Torres because the Provincial of the Carmelites ordered her to accompany the 'young Duchess de Alba', daughter-in-law of the 'old Duchess', during her confinement. This was to satisfy a whim of the old aristocrat, who venerated the foundress and considered her presence a heavenly guarantee of blessings. Infirm and indisposed, Mother Teresa went to Alba. As soon as she arrived there, someone notified Teresa that the young Duchess had successfully given birth to a son prematurely. Mother Teresa ironically commented, *"Blessed be God! Now it will not be necessary for this saint to be there!"*

Master Avila thought it very important to satisfy the request of the Duchess de Feria, for he had been responsible for a sincere conversion in her life from one of frivolity to religious fervour. The Duke and the Duchess had joined the circle of Master Avila's disciples three years earlier when they invited him to their castle at Zafra, precisely on that occasion to be present when the young Duchess gave birth to her first-born. Their lavish wedding had been the talk of all Andalusia. The newlyweds had passed through Córdoba *"in a carriage totally covered with silver without a piece of wood to be seen. This caused wonderment to some and scandal to others because of the enormous cost and ostentation."* One of Master Avila's disciples asked him how could he possibly go to visit *"that profane woman who went through here in a silver carriage."* The Master replied: *"Pray to God that she falls upon her knees at my feet, and later on I may be able to help her be rid of the carriage and even more."*

Within three years, the Albas had changed their lives and

were seen to be following the evangelical counsels. That is why the Master went to Constantina so quickly when the news reached him during August of 1548. It had been a rapid visit, for by the first week of September he was back at Córdoba to meet with John of God.

They talked and the Master became alarmed. John of God reported: *"He then ordered me to leave and return to Granada."*

There were three things that worried Master Avila. The first was the hardship being suffered by the traveller, so he considered it important that he return to Granada, at once, to be cared for by his companions. As well, he had been away from Granada for far too many months and the running of the hospital could suffer as a result, notwithstanding the responsible care undertaken by Antón Martín during his absence. Finally, the Master feared that John of God would soon get himself hopelessly involved with Córdoba's poor and sick.

It seems John of God acted like a charity robot producing funds as soon as any needy person approached. He tells us how he discovered, while *"wandering through the city"*, the disastrous situation of a family. *"As I was walking down the street I came across a family in dire need. There were two young maidens caring for their bedridden invalid parents and they had been doing this for ten years. They were clad in rags, covered in lice and lying on a heap of straw for a bed. I did what I could for them but, since I was in a hurry to keep an appointment with Master Avila, I was unable to do as much as I would have wished for them."*

However Master Avila stepped in and sent him back to Granada for his own good.

On his way, he stopped off at Cabra and Baena taking lots of news to the Duchess of Sessa. Both Cabra and Baeza castles belonged to the firstborn son of Gonzalo Fernández de Córdoba whose personal fortune was one of the greatest in Spain. Although the large ducal residence at Cabra was luxurious, the Fernández de Córdoba family always preferred the palace at Baena for family reunions and habitual residence. Baena was a small city but conveniently situated with respect to the southern roads to the Court.

The towns of Baena and Cabra are ten and eleven leagues respectively from Córdoba – that is sixty and nearly seventy kilometres. They constituted the axis of the marquisate of Cabra, a territory that formed an arch at the foot of the Subbéticas hills which abounded then, as now, in olives, cereals, vineyards and pastures but where irigation was poor. The fiefdom of Baena and the county of Cabra fell into the hands of Fernández de Córdoba towards the mid-15th century, when the marshal Don Diego formally obtained the grants from the Crown of Castile. The wealth and prestige of the house of Fernández de Córdoba greatly increased with the marriage of the Gran Capitán's daughter Elvira, Duchess of Sessa, with her cousin Luis, of the Egabrense branch of the family. This explains how the grandson Gonzalo, the third Duke of Sessa, was able to bring such a phenomenal fortune to his marriage with María Sarmiento, the daughter of los Cobos.

Many things were troubling our little Duchess when John of God met her at her Baena castle. She *"was sad and lonely"*, as the song has it. Lonely, because her husband was absent, her mother was far away, and her father had died just over a year ago. She was sad because she was childless, having lost one infant only hours after its birth. She had had no more. She grieved for this and had lost hope, for she had been married ten years. The political family of the Fernández de Córdoba, that of her husband, was embittered towards her because of the horrible question of an heir and a fortune.

John of God appeared on this melancholy scene like a ray of sunshine to cheer up the sad and lonely young Duchess. The young and distraught María Sarmiento seized upon the merciful kindness of Brother John of God like a lifebuoy in a shipwreck. He offers her the opportunity to collaborate with him in aiding the poor. He provides her with the motivation to start living again, to give meaning to the emptiness of her life. Thus he assists her as she and her husband previously had assisted him.

It so happened that the Fernández de Córdoba clan held great hopes when they planned the marriage of Gonzalo with María Sarmiento. The Córdobas were far wealthier than the Cobos, but they were more interested in accruing the prestige to be gained by having someone so close to the Emperor, far closer than anyone else. The Fernández de Córdoba clan made Pedro de Córdoba, Gonzalo's uncle, the direct agent for negotiating the match, and in return they promised him a relevant administrative appointment, that of chief accountant of income.

The betrothal took place on 30 November 1538 in the Royal Palace at Toledo. Cardinal Tavera blessed the young couple before such an assembly of nobility that the Emperor, who was short of stature, had to stand up and ask the courtiers to *"let him see."* That evening Cobos gave a feast that passed into the chronicles and there followed days of bull fights and jousting.

Two long years dragged out between the betrothal and the official wedding ceremony. This was because María Sarmiento's family knew that Gonzalo *"had contracted a secret betrothal with another girl."* His uncle Pedro urgently strove to break off this secret engagement by forcing closer ties with María Sarmiento. The Emperor's intervention forced Gonzalo, who *"obeyed"*, but demonstrated to his fiancée María Sarmiento a sullen resentment, as if the pretty girl had been guilty of the intrigues of the family. The Cardinal Archbishop of Toledo, assisted by six bishops at Almudena, celebrated the wedding near Madrid on 6 February 1541. Present were Prince Philip and a great many nobles. The wedding feast was opulent and guests danced to the sound of trumpets, flutes and tambourines. There were salvos of artillery, games, competitions and masquerades. While the impressive festivities took place the young spouses outwardly appeared happy but underneath there was inner turmoil.

Gonzalo and María Sarmiento spent three months at Madrid accompanied by Doña María and some other nobles before going down to Baena where the Duchess had set up her home at the castle where, *"at times,"* her husband Gonzalo also resided and frequently took her to Granada.

At first the marriage seemed to be satisfactory and María Sarmiento did everything possible to please her husband. She became pregnant and gave birth to a son, but sadly the infant died only a short time afterwards. Gonzalo had already begun his long absences, combining life as a noble gentleman companion in the retinue of Prince Philip with sporadic war expeditions.

The Duchess was alone and sad at Baena where her political in-laws detested her existence. Egged on by the terrible Doña Felipa, Gonzalo's aunt, the Córdobas even attempted to supplant the Duchess in the financial management of the duchy. Cobos, fearful for his daughter because of the bitterness being shown to her, took the matter directly to the Emperor. There are papers in the archives where this significant phrase can be read,

"The time came when the Emperor commanded, (the Duke of Sessa) to go back to his wife and live a married life with her and love her very much." He was far too optimistic, as you will see, and although María Sarmiento dearly wanted children she was unable to have any more.

Little Duchess, sad and lonely, was brought much news from Valladolid, including some confidential message connected with her husband, the contents of which we do not know.

John of God knew that, during the month of October, Prince Philip was due to leave for Europe with Gonzalo in his retinue. Furthermore, the Duchess would not see her husband until the royal expedition returned from Flanders and Germany some three years hence.

John of God's confidential message would have been either from her husband Gonzalo or about his conduct. Perhaps Gonzalo confided something to him, some promise for his wife. John of God speaks of Gonzalo to the Duchess in very positive terms, calling him *"generous"*, *"good gentleman"* and even *"virtuous."* Maybe in accentuating the positive qualities of the Duke, John of God was trying to soften the anxiety of the Duchess. He did his best to cheer her up and confided to her that Gonzalo would return safe and sound, *"in soul and body"*:

" When he comes back, if God so wills, you will ask him about what I have told you and you will see if it is true."

Thus John of God consoled the Duchess, handing her the letter. In respect to her good mother, Doña María de Mendoza, he was happy to pass on good news of her to her daughter. There was also a 'family reunion': On arrival John of God had found the Duchess accompanied by her two uncles, brothers of her mother: Alvaro the future Bishop of Avila, and Bernadino, the black sheep of the Mendoza family. They had come to Baena to spend a little while with her to comfort her over the loss of her father. They attentively listened to John of God's account of the attentions he had received from the nobles of the Court - thanks to the invaluable help of Doña María. They then returned to Valladolid.

Thanking the Duchess for the donations she had given him, John of God resumed his return journey to Granada, thinking of her as the classic perfect wife described in the Bible as she prayed for the absent husband, kept absolute fidelity, gave alms and ran the household, directing servants and officials. The Duchess was considerate and treated her servants and tenants well, *"some were old, some young, and there were orphans and widows,"* always caring for their welfare.

In summary, Brother Matías de Mina, who has done so much research on John of God, says that when he was departing from the castle at Baena he was overcome by tenderness, and thought of the young duchess Mária. *"Alone and separated like a chaste turtledove"*. A thought provoked by a flock of turtledoves flying overhead!

John of God returned to Granada but along the way he made two more stopovers. The first was at Alcaudete, four leagues from Baena. Here, the castle of the Mendoza-Carillo family at Alcaudete was one of great style. Charles V conferred on it the status of a county. A member of this branch of the Mendoza family was a certain young cousin of the Duchess of Sessa named Francisca, daughter of Don Bernadino, a brother of Count Tendilla. Francisca was very ill and spent long periods at the castle so that the country air might benefit her weak lungs. Her father and his wife Elvira and their other children lived at Granada where they, like the rest of the Mendoza clan, were such great benefactors of John of God.

Francisca was a young woman who had a certain air of mysticism about her and was very generous, characteristics which are sometimes the fruit of premature illness. John of God's affection for her was comparable only to his affection for the Duchess. These are his exact words spoken upon her death. *"Our Lord gave her a very special grace to do lots of kind things for the poor whilst she lived in this world. She never refused help to anyone asking for it out of the love of God."*

Francisca also knew how to give *"good words, good example and good doctrine"* to such an extent that John of God wrote about her to the Duchess: *"A very big book, indeed, would be needed to write down every thing she did,"* adding that *"nobody ever left her house downhearted. To this can be added the good advice and example that this happy young lady used to give."*

Nothing would stop John of God from calling in at the Alcaudete castle to visit Francisca when he heard that she was gravely ill. Only two months after his visit he was informed of the young lady's death – she was barely twenty.

This stopover also resulted in donations in kind which is appropriate where country folk live off the produce of the land. Naturally he could not carry away sacks of grain but he arranged to have these deposited in the town's community silo.

The next stop was four leagues further along the road at Alcalá la Real where there was a garrison in which the Castilian army barracked troops. These were ready to be called, should the need arise, to Granada where there had been some brief clashes between Moors and Christians. We do not know whether John of God had any particular friends here, but more than likely he did. In any case the stopover would give him the opportunity to gather his strength to tackle the final seven leagues to Granada. As it was, he fell ill and had to spend four days in the local hospital where he rested after a fashion, but that did not stop him from helping the poor about him. He gave away the little money that he had on him and even borrowed three ducats to help the poor. John of God was now penniless.

It is as well that Doña María Mendoza and the Count de Tendilla were alert enough to see that he would give away everything he received at Valladolid and made provision for Granada by promissory notes and letters of credit. Had he carried all away in cash he certainly would have arrived at his hospital without a single ducat.

John of God did not stay long at Alcalá, nor did he make an effort to collect donations there because of some local political unrest: *"The leading citizens had revolted against the Governor."*

Granada at last! They were all awaiting him. *"When he arrived back, they greeted him with tremendous jubilation."* He arrived exhausted but still trying to keep up a good appearance. Everyone greeted him, *'the citizens of Granada were relieved to see him because they esteemed him greatly."* John of God represented something fine for the city. He was a common treasure like the Sierra Nevada or the Albaycín and he belonged like the landscape of the Alhambra and the Royal Chapel. He, their charity worker, was a real blessing upon the city.

His poor people and the patients at the hospital had awaited his return more than anybody else and were overjoyed to see him again. The greater part of Granada's emarginated population knew him and longed for his homecoming especially the families of the *vergonzantes*, who because they were so ashamed to be seen begging, had been deprived, in his absence, of the discreet gifts that he took to them in their homes.

His wealthy benefactors were also expecting his return. He relied so much upon them, especially for their contacts at the Court. The Granada nobility was keen to know how he got on at the Royal Court. They eagerly plied him with questions about his conversation with Prince Philip and were curious to know what financial assistance the Prince had given him for the hospital. They also wanted to know who else had helped him at Valladolid.

None were happier to have him back among them than Antón Martín and the other brothers, his companions and fellow workers. They shared his work, his sacrifices, his ideal of seeing Jesus Christ in the person of the poor. They now had him home in their hospital and could care for him. His physical condition was shocking, his feet were callused and had deep ugly gashes in them, his face, neck and arms were weather-beaten.

Of course, his creditors were especially happy to see him return. They knew he was good and honest, not too regular in paying on time, but a good payer nevertheless. We do not know who these creditors were, but his reputation was saved thanks to the shrewdness of Doña María Mendoza and the Count de Tendilla. Had they not shown such foresight it is certain that John of God would have come back to Granada empty handed.

Notes to Chapter 32

* For references to Doña María de Mendoza, see Keniston, *Francisco de los Cobos, Secretario de Carlos V*, op.cit, passim. Also, M. de Mina, *'Anotaciones', Fondo Documental*, op.cit., Archive of Los Pisa, Granada, Don Francisco de lo Cobos y Molina, Doña María de Mendoza Sarmiento.

* The history of the Discalced Carmelites' monastery at Valladolid, see Santa Teresa in *Obras Completas* (edited by Efrén de la Madre de Dios and Otgar Steggick) Madrid 1977, 'Libro de las Fundaciones' pp 545-547.

* The intervention of the Count de Tendilla and others before the Prince, see Francisco de Castro op.cit., chapter 16; also M. de Mina, *'Anotaciones', etc.*, 'Felipe II'; J. Cruset, *El hombre que supo amar*, op.cit., 187, these also plays down the value of the conversation with Prince Philip. The following witnesses at the Granada beatification process testified to the presence of John of God in Valladolid and his audience with the prince: #9 (Juan de Salazar, a child at the time, but a reliable witness); #11 (Francisco Ruiz); #13 (Felipe de Alayz); # 16 (Melchor de Avila); #22 (Luis de Cambril); #26 (Domingo Navarro); #32 (Baltasar Suárez); #42 (Hernando Niño de Aguillar); #71 (Juan de Prado); #78 (Luis de Valdiva); #87 (Miguel de las Higueras).

* The observations regarding the fatigue of the journey come from Francisco de Castro, op.cit., chapter 16. The account of the stopover at Córdoba to visit Master Avila is recorded in the 1st letter to the Duchess of Sessa, *Letters of St. John of God* (op.cit.).

* The same letter gives details of the visits to Alcaudete and Alcalá la Real.

* For the information of dates and details of the persons refered to at this stage, see M. de Mina, *'Anotaciones', etc., 'Notes to the first and second letters to the Duchess of Sessa'*. The hostility of the members of the Cobos- Fernández de Córdoba family as a result of the marriage of the Duke and Duchess of Sessa (Gonzalo and Master Avila Sarmiento), see Keniston, *Francisco de los Cobos*, etc., op.cit., pp 208-209, 222-225, 228-231.

* Doña Francisca de Mendoza Carvajal and her husband Alfonso Fernández de Córdoba were the title holders of the duchy and owners of the ducal palace at Alcaudete. They were the parents of the children Martín Alfonso and Antonio. Don Alfonso was Governor of the town of Orán, he wanted his sons to join the naval expedition under the command of Don Juan de Mendoza which ended in shipwreck at Herradura on 19 Oct. 1562: Cf. M. de Mina *Visitar la Granada de San Juan de Dios*, op.cit., 148, 152. In regards to the revolt against the Governor of Alcalá la Real: this was due to his ostentatious performance in central administration, which was nevertheless very effective.

33

HE ENJOYED THE PASTRIES
OF BAENA

Granada
1548-1549

At the beginning of the winter of 1548 the image of 'blessed John of God' loaded with the sick on his shoulders on the way to the hospital on the Cuesta Gomérez had returned to Granada. But it was *"with much effort because he went about thin and unwell,"* after the enormous trek to Valladolid via Salamanca and back. He had been barefooted, had eaten poorly, suffered the summer's heat on his bare shaven head, and all this had seriously damaged his physical condition.

John of God continues his work at Granada just as he had done in past years: *"One day a poor sick man was lying on the ground in the Plaza Nueva near where they sell pancakes. The man was unable to move, then the blessed father came along with his basket and picking him up put him over his shoulders and took him back to his hospital."*

Alonso de la Peña, while reporting this episode to us, wants to emphasise that it was his usual way of acting: "I saw him doing this same thing at other times, because it was his custom to do so."

John of God's physical forces were deteriorating fast. "A most amazing thing occurred one dark freezing night in winter." Just where the Zacatín opens into the Plaza Nueva, John of God found *"a poor man moaning to himself"* because of the rain and cold. *"He was ill and unable, without help, to find a place to lodge."* John of God picked him up and supporting himself with his staff began to climb up the Cuesta Gomérez, *"carrying his basket and with the poor man on his shoulders."* A torrent was rushing down from the Alhambra because, once more, a rainstorm had converted the Cuesta Gomérez into a gully. John of God had tremendous difficulty pushing against the rush of water. He slipped and fell into the mire, taking the poor man and his basket with him.

Hearing the sound of the rain and the poor man splashing about, a certain neighbour peered through his downstairs window where, to his dismay, he saw and heard the blessed charity worker beating his legs with his staff and whimsically scolding his body calling it a "donkey". Castro reproduces the story, making use of the phrases taken from the witness, who reported the episode to everyone so that they would see how beautifully and cheerfully John of God overcame his weary body.

"So, Sir Donkey, you stubborn, lazy, weak, clumsy good-for-nothing; haven't you eaten today? Well, if you have eaten why aren't you

working? Can't you see that these poor folk for whom you work, have need of meals? Can't you see that this man you're carrying is dying, so why have you stopped now?"

It makes us smile to hear him call his body a good-for-nothing donkey that is causing his master so much trouble! Not only that, the basket was full of provisions he had collected in the city for his poor folk's supper. He got to his feet as best he could, even though *"he was up to his knees in water"*, and continued up the hill.

John of God was quite unaware that he had been overheard scolding himself. The next day the witness went to see him and inquired, *"Brother John of God, how did you get on after your fall last night?"* Completely taken by surprise, *"he brushed it aside"* as something of no significance.

Soon after his return to Granada, John of God set about completing some business from his journey into Castile.

Considering that he had been given such an attentive welcome, he planned to establish at Toledo 'a hospital' along similar lines to the one at Granada. Doubtlessly he would have spoken about, and given much thought to, the project.

Now, he decided to send one of his 'brothers', to start the work, which was to flourish a few years later. We know the name of the brother he sent – Ferdinand. However, the exact details of how he opened this establishment have not come down to us. Originally, it was really a 'xenodochium', a night shelter for itinerants.

However, the nucleus of the story of this foundation turns out to be astounding. Blas Ortiz, a canon of Toledo Cathedral and the Vicar General of the diocese where Cardinal Tavera was Archbishop, published in 1549 a summary guide to the Toledo Cathedral. He speaks about John of God when he treats of the hospitals. He drew up a brief but extraordinary biography that carries facts from John of God's lifetime!

"At Granada there is a man who lives in Christian simplicity and poverty, whose name is John and his surname is 'of God'. He is of humble birth and is not versed in letters or doctrine, but he has cultivated Christian charity with extraordinary zeal, occupying himself entirely in relieving the poor. He maintains and assists about 200 poor people who are deprived of basic necessities and are afflicted with various diseases.

His mode of life is like that of the Cynics. He wears a rough well-worn habit and carries a large basket over his shoulders. This is not full of worldly riches, but is open to accept alms for the poor. He walks barefooted and bareheaded. His humble appearance is accompanied by an interior humility that he prefers to any human wealth or power. He speaks with frankness and without any arrogance to the nobility from whom he solicits alms for the poor."

The 'Cynics' who dressed as they pleased and despised conventionalities were philosophers of the Greek school of Antisthenes, symbolised by Diogines who lived in a barrel in the open air:

According to Canon Ortiz, this marvellous John of God *"came to Toledo to collect alms last year"*, which is to say, 1548, *"having recognised the good disposition of the people towards helping the poor as befits a Christian. He saw for himself and tested the charity of the Toledans, so he decided"*, says the Canon, *"to send a certain Fernando"*, who introduced to Toledo what John of God practiced at Granada. Thus speaks the Canon: *"During the day he went about the city streets and plazas quietly collecting alms from people. During the night he went about the same streets shouting like a rooster at daybreak calling mortals to their daily duties. He constantly and untiringly went about well after sunset when everyone retires to their homes calling out to remind them to help the poor."*

The *"hospital of Fernando"* had been recently inaugurated, but the Canon gives no further details except to call it a "xenodochium"; that is, an asylum or refuge for transients and the emarginated.

Sifting through the material of my research on John of God like those who search for glow-worms in the night I came across little episodes like the following:

Luisa de la Cruz belonged to that group of *"vergonzantes"* families at Granada cared for by John of God. Luisa was left a widow with five children. The eldest of them was a lad who *"served in the galleys of His Majesty,"* and had the misfortune of being captured by the Moors. John of God *"fed and sustained that family with the alms that he collected."*

When John of God spoke with Prince Philip at Valladolid, he took the opportunity to tell him about the case of the young man *"taken in the territories of the Moors."* The Prince responded by ordering that the price of the young man's ransom be added to his donation. The captive eventually returned to his mother, so further good came from John of God's audience with the Prince, about which I had had some reservations.

Poor John of God! As poor as his poor people, now that the money from cashing the promissory notes he had brought from Valladolid had run out.

While he was at Alcalá la Real he fell into the trap of borrowing three ducats to help a poor struggling family.

Castro notes that the bank drafts given to him by Doña María de Mendoza and the Count de Tendilla *"only paid part of the debts that he owed."*

He was in debt for 400 ducats. What would he do, if *"his heart were not to break to see people suffering want and being unable to remedy it?"* It grieved him to be loaded down with debts; for it was impossible to be free of them *"since he gave what he had till it hurt."*

He still assisted "the poor *vergonzantes* and the women he helped to get married", the prostitutes whom he rescued from the Bibataubín red light district. "They had all missed him very much," naturally: "because they had no other father nor anyone else to help them."

His way out was to ask for help and have recourse to his dear *Duquesita* of Sessa.

He did not write a letter to the Duchess simply to ask her for money. Because he loved her and knew that she was sad, he wanted to console her. In addition, he wanted to thank her for the concern she showed him when he passed through Baena on his way home from the Court.

John of God dictated his letters to a professional letter writer, but he signed them with his own mysterious signature. This letter gives the impression that he did not stop to take a breath between one paragraph and the next. In reality he sent with his letter his own heartbeat, and what a heart it was! Doña María Sarmiento could read in this letter just how much love John of God had for her.

John of God sent the letter by the hand of his salaried assistant Angulo, whom he calls *"my companion"*. The address stated: *"This letter is to be given to the very noble and virtuous lady*

Doña Maria de Mendoza, Duchess of Sessa." John of God carefully added to his saluation an accolade of her husband: *"wife of His Lordship the generous Don Gonzalo Fernandez de Cordoba, Duke of Sessa, a virtuous and good knight of Our Lord Jesus Christ... whom he desires to serve."* This last phrase was to assure the Duchess that her husband was in the service of Jesus Christ.

As some persons might place a cross at the head of the page, John of God wrote a little invocation in homage to the Blessed Virgin Mary: *"In the name of Our Lord Jesus Christ and Our Lady the Immaculate Virgin Mary."*

Mary ever virgin, pure, immaculate! John of God's description is like that of a medieval knight proclaiming the splendour of his lady to all.

He tells the Duchess about his stopovers at Alcaudete and Alcalá la Real on his way to Granada. He particularly thanks her for her good wishes and the donation she gave him when she farewelled him: *"The angels have already recorded in the Book of Life the alms that you gave me."* Concerning the gifts the Dutchess had given him we read: *"I put the ring to good use and from its proceeds I was able to clothe two poor invalids and buy them a blanket." "I put the alb and candlesticks in your name upon the altar as soon as I could, so now you are sharing in all the Masses and prayers being said there. I pray that Our Lord Jesus Christ will reward you in heaven for this. May God reward you and your whole household for the warm welcome you gave me."*

John of God spoke of the cause of her sadness, the Duke's absence, and tries to revive her confidence by telling her that *"he will return home safe and sound in soul and body."* He alludes to the confidences that he brought back to her from the Duke at Valladolid. It appears that some tongue has been sowing some wicked seeds of friction between the Duchess and her husband. John of God angrily raises his voice about this and assures her: *"Put your trust in Jesus Christ alone! Woe to the person who only relies on humans, for whether he likes it or not, humans are going to let him down, but Jesus Christ will never do that, because he is always faithful and constant. Everything perishes except good works."*

We are ignorant of the underlying cause of this matter that touched upon the conjugal life of the Duchess. John of God lets a surge of tenderness escape him and I think he writes beautifully: *"O good Duchess, there you are all alone in that castle cut off from the goings on of the Court. You are just a chaste turtledove waiting for your* generous and humble husband, the good Duke."

He assured her that her husband benefited from how she spent her time *"praying, giving alms and continuously doing charitable deeds. May Jesus Christ guard him in body and keep his soul from danger and sin."* He added, especially for her: *"May it please God to bring him home to you soon and bless you with children. Since you always love and serve God, he is going to give you the offspring you yearn for, so they too may serve him."*

The reality was otherwise, for the Duchess was never blest with children. Thirty years later, after the death of her husband in 1578, Doña María Sarmiento founded a convent of Dominican nuns at Granada. She established the Convent of Piety and entered its community in the final years of her life. She suffered for almost her entire married life from the avaricious schemes of her in-laws, the Fernández de Córdoba.

John of God's letter to the *"chaste little turtledove"* who was all alone in her castle in the Cabra countryside, or at Baena, is bejewelled with beautiful words of glowing praise of his little Duquesita: *"Good Duchess, always keep a foot in the stirrup when you go to bed, because we have to face the fact that the war against the world, the flesh and the devil is continuous. We always have to be on our guard since we do not know the hour when our soul is going to be called away. We will be judged just as we are found."*

He recommended prayers and devout practices to her, before asking for her help. He really left that part to Angulo who knew exactly what was needed and would be able to inform her personally, so all he said was: *"I am renovating the whole house which is terribly run down and sprouting leaks all over the place. This work is causing me a lot of hardship."*

To meet the expenses of this renovation work John of God also sent Angulo into Extremadura where Master Avila was the guest of the Count de Feria and the Duke de Arcos whilst giving a series of sermons at Zafra Castle. Referring to Master Avila, John of God told the Duchess that *"he will be able to put in a good word for me so that they might send along some help which might get me out of this tight spot."*

Angulo had to receive his wages, and he needed money to make the journey to deliver John of God's message to Master Avila. The Duchess is asked to help him out in this matter, too. He asked her for a ducat to cover the costs of Angulo's travelling expenses to

Zafra, and three more, for a cause that had given him great concern. Angulo had instructions to give these three ducats to a poor family of invalids whom he had met at Córdoba on his way back from Valladolid. Being in a hurry at the time he could not spend long with them because, as he says in the letter: *"Master Avila told me to go back to Granada at once, so I hastily arranged with certain people to take care of these poor persons. Well, they either forgot or were unwilling or unable to do anything more about it."* These unfortunates had written to him from Córdoba to give him this sad news, so he told to the Duchess, *"What I read in the letter broke my heart."* He now proposed that she *"gain the benefit of this alms"* and provide the three ducats so that the two poor young women caring for their invalid parents *"may buy two blankets and a dress each."*

Of course he was confident the Duchess would accede to his request, and jokingly tells her, *"I had to give my last reale to Angulo so that he could make this journey. When I pay the workers, some of the poor people here have to go without eating."*

John of God, being well aware of the alms that the Duchess charitably distributed to the poor at Baena, wrote, *"Your obligation to those depending upon you is greater than that of strangers, but giving here or giving there, you are the one who really gains."* I can almost hear him laughing as he adds the following: *"The greater the number of Moors, the greater is the reward, as the saying goes."* [This was a colloquial saying that meant 'the greater the effort, the greater the reward.']

If the Duchess was unable to give Angulo the required four ducats, he was to sell two cahices [an ancient measure] of wheat that was being stored for him at the community silo in Alcaudete before continuing on his way. In either case, he asked the Duchess to send a short letter with Angulo telling him what had happened in regard to the donation of four ducats.

John of God was always pleading for donations and in this beautiful letter to the little Duchess, he repeats the latest reasons for his lack of shame in asking, knowing that *"to give to the poor"* means an assured gain to the one who gives:

"I am always troubling you my sister, but I trust to God that some fine day your soul will be relieved of all this... If we really considered God's great mercy we would never cease doing good whilst we may. We give to the poor only what he gives to us, yet he has promised to repay us

a hundred times as much in the life hereafter. Oh what a happy investment and profit! Who would not invest what he has with this blessed merchant who offers us such a bargain?... Just as water extinguishes fire, so too does charity extinguish sin."

What a happy investment and what profit! Charity kills sin. These two firm principles are the rock upon which John of God based his life.

The children were the ones whose eyes would widen with surprise when John of God walked unannounced into the homes, where he could confidently visit at any time.

Take for example, Inés, Luisa and Melchor who were the three little children of Doña Constanza Alvarez and the jurist, Diego de Avila, who was a member of the Council of Twenty-four. These three lived well into old age and testified at the Process, still remembering what happened when they were fifteen, thirteen and ten years of age respectively. Inés later married a Zegrí, who was descended from wealthy converted Moors. The Zegrí-Avila family inherited from Inés a reverence for John of God, and their son Juan Zegrí was a friend of Domingo Piola the Genovese banker who was won over by John of God and joined his band of brothers.

As children, Inés, Luisa and Melchor, saw how their father "dealt with John of God". "He was always welcomed and made to come in to have a meal. This witness saw him come in out of the heat and all he ate was a piece of bread and nothing else. What was left over he carried away for the poor."

Inés added an interesting detail: *"The father of this witness said to him; 'Come on eat up!' The poor will also be given it as well.'"*

Likewise, many children at Granada knew that remarkably good man, whose impression remained upon them for their whole lives: you remember Luisa the little grand-daughter of Antón Zabán the apothecary of the Plaza Bibarrambla, recalled that she was astonished to see John of God, *"take off his shirt and give it to a poor man."*

And now for the devil and demons! Care must be taken to keep in mind the mentality of the 16th century, realising that these anecdotes belong to that period and contain the sensibility of those days.

For Spaniards of the 16th century it was inconceivable that

Satan would not attempt to interfere in the life of John of God, just as he will in the lives of Teresa of Jesus and John of the Cross.

They attributed two types of diabolic intervention in the life of John of God. The visible and the invisible.

The warfare started in 1545, with the episode that occurred in little Plaza Vargas when *"they took John of God's money purse."* Nobody could explain whether they were thieves or demons. It did not take long for Granada to suspect that demons had started attacking their charity worker.

The first of the biographers to take this seriously was our friend Castro who was convinced that Satan was silently and slyly attacking John of God.

Castro already warns that the stench of the devil was at Ceuta endangering that young man who charitably worked as a labourer in order to assist the Portuguese family in reduced circumstances with what he earned: *"The demon, seeing the results that this good work was producing, both for the ones benefiting from it and the one doing it, tried with his usual malice to impede him."* It was then that he was tempted to become a Moslem.

At Granada, Satan already knew that he had come up against a champion. Documents of the period are the first to bring forward these attempts. The devil, one night, appeared before John of God in the form of a poor man and begged him saying: *"Give me alms."* Since *"he gave for God,"* John of God wanted to know, *"In whose name do you ask?"* The devil, unable to mention the holy name of God, remained silent and disappeared.

"And further along, in another street, he came back and stood before him saying 'Why did you not give me alms?'" John of God said, *"Because you did not ask for the love of Jesus Christ, I could not give it."*

This incident related by Castro gives us the idea that John of God suspected the trap set for him in the guise of a poor man: Then the devil became enraged, *"The man punched him in the stomach making him stagger a few paces backwards, then he disappeared."*

The playwright Lope de Vega expands the dialogue of John of God and Satan in a poetic, ironic and subtle form:

"Give me alms."

John of God puts the conditions before him, *"In whose name?"*

The demon insists: *"Give it to me and be quiet."*

"For whom?"

"How careful you are! Give me alms."

"I don't want to, unless you tell me for whom."

"It's enough to ask for it."

"It is no good unless you tell me first. Say for whom and you will see then how I will give it."

Furiously the devil attacked him verbally and the two contestants deliver to each other a string of insults. Satan calls John of God "an ignoramus, a villain, a madman and a rascal shepherd." John of God calls Satan "vile, lewd, rebellious to God, evil faced, drunkard." The row gets hotter when Satan threatens him:

"I am going to give you..."

John of God did not bite his tongue:

"What are you going to give me, vile rabbit?"

Lope's play can be quite funny. At one stage, the devil in disguise meets John of God and haughtily defines himself: "I am the sun."

John of God retorts,"You are a pumpkin cooked in infernal fire."

A pumpkin fritter, the devil! Any actor, playing the part must surely chuckle to himself at that!

The warfare grew stronger. I still warn the reader that I am utilising in these events a nonchalant tone, taking into account our modern mentality when interpreting the tales of diabolical happenings of the 16th century. Today psychologists and psychiatrists give reasonable explanations to the demonic obsession that originated in the 'twilight zone' of dreamt events. However, it is quite clear that the documented references are authentic, as related in the notes at the end of this chapter.

The attacks by the demon reached their climax on the 'night'of Doctor Beltrán' as it is called. Antonio Beltrán was a distinguished physician married to Elena de Ribas. At the time they were the parents of three children (a further three were born after the death of John of God). The doctor lived "next door to the church of Santa Ana" in the little plaza adjacent to the Plaza Nueva at the foot of the Alhambra where the Darro enters the heart of the city.

One dark winter's night John of God, with his basket slung across his shoulders, came along to collect alms from his usual benefactors living along the banks of the Darro. These were wealthy families and he was surer of finding the head of the family at home after nightfall.

John of God advanced along the riverbank looking for a laneway leading up to the Cuesta Gomérez. All of a sudden "a pig rushed up and crashed into his legs making him fall down." His attempts to get up were useless, for the pig "*nuzzled him for almost an hour knocking him down and trampling him.*"

I am quoting this story from Castro. The witnesses made it quite clear in their statements: "*The demon in the body of a pig, crashed into his legs making him fall over.*" The attack endured for "*a long while*", "*it trampled him into the mud and treated him badly.*" Soon the extraordinary uproar was heard in the house of Doctor Beltrán alongside the church of Santa Ana: "*They ran out of the house to help him.*" The spectacle made an impression on them, seeing blessed John of God "*exhausted and covered with mire*", and his basket, staff and alms all scattered: "*and asking him what had happened, he said that he knew no more than that they had pushed him and caused him to fall into the mud.*" They wanted to take him into the doctor's house, but "*he did not want to, but wished they would take him to be with his poor people.*"

They took him up to the hospital, "*where, because of what had happened, he was indisposed*" for several days, "*very ill in bed*"; probably the pummelling he took left him with marks on his face, because of which he avoided going out into the street. But "*persons from the city came to see him*", "*they visited him*", "*they spoke about it*" throughout Granada. As usual, Castro tells it formally: "*His face took more than a month to heal from the mauling and bites.*"

That is how contemporary documents related the event. Today we simply ask ourselves whether the devil was no more than a pig. Why make more of it? Do not pigs sometimes attack persons?

The wilderness squeezed in between the bend of the Darro and the towering hill of the Alhambra, at night presents an appropriate scenario for devilry and apparitions. Based on the previous event, other demonic interventions against John of God circulated from mouth to mouth. One story told how the devil tempted him to throw himself off the Santa Ana Bridge: "*Just as the blessed father did everything they* [the urchins in the Bibarrambla] *told* him to do, like falling over for God, then he would do it, even should he be loaded; and if they said that he should kiss the ground, he did that obeying at once, and also if he [the demon] said to him, according to this witness, that he should throw himself off the bridge; he made no reply but blessed himself and went on his way." Because naturally the demon would not dare ask him to do so "for God."

The students of university professor 'Master Juan Latino' were given a case drawn from the event in front of the home of Doctor Beltrán. This 'Master Latino' was born the son of black slaves at the ducal castle of Baena, "where they served before the taking of Granada." They came to Granada with the household of Fernández de Córdoba. As a boy Juan used to devour the contents of the schoolbooks of young Gonzalo, the future Duke of Sessa. The son of slaves learned so much Latin that he was called Juan Latino and eventually gained a chair at the university. Juan Latino venerated John of God and told his students about the time "when he (John of God) was coming back one night carrying a poor man on his shoulders taking him to his hospital, a demon in the form of a dog jumped out at him and made him fall two or three times and attacked him. John, seeing himself in this affliction, invoked the name of God and it vanished like whirlwind."

In this very ticklish subject of diabolical interventions, I prefer to limit myself to three cases which Castro puts in relation to John of God's intense prayer when he retired to his little room at the hospital, alone, recollected, face to face with the superior forces which stealthily lurk along our way.

One night, the workers of the hospital heard John of God "groaning loudly as if being beaten by someone." They went to investigate. They found him kneeling "very exhausted, covered in sweat." They heard him saying: "Jesus deliver me from Satan. Jesus be with me." From the window which faced the street, "they saw fleeing, a very frightful figure, the devil. They lifted Brother John of God up and placed him in an infirmary, where he remained for eight days, very hurt and exhausted by what had occurred."

In "the same little room" John of God was "kneeling in prayer with the door closed" when a beautiful woman stood before him. This was a temptation used by the devil with certain venerable men of ancient times. John of God loudly said that since she had entered through a closed door, she must have been the devil. With this the figure vanished.

Another day, they also heard him cry out in his room: *"Jesus Christ, Son of the living God, help me!"* Rushing in, *"they found him kneeling and holding a crucifix."* The devil had lifted him up into the air and then dropped him to the ground *"causing him great injury."*

The truth is that, apart from the ignominy of the pig, the diabolical interferences did little to distract John of God from his charitable work. The poor and the needy leave little margin for psychological niceties.

The loyal co-worker, Angulo, returned from his journey to Baena where he delivered John of God's letter to the young Duchess. He also went to Zafra where he delivered letters to the Duke de Feria and the Count de Arcos. This would have been on his way back at the beginning of that very severe winter of 1548.

Naturally, the Duchess had given Angulo the four ducats requested by John of God; one for the expenses of the journey and three for the unfortunate women at Córdoba.

In another letter to his Duchess John of God writes that it was a pity that Angulo, on his return from Zafra, was unable to call at Baena where Doña María was to have given him not only a letter for John of God, but also some important alms.

This second letter to the Duchess was written only a short time after the first. Angulo had barely arrived back when John of God sent him off again to consult with her. The young lady was an expert in the administration of goods, since she governed the rural estates of her absent husband. Angulo consults her on an urgent matter: whether to sell in the country the two cahices of wheat that she held in keeping at the communal silo of Alcaudete, or whether it would be better to take them to be sold at Granada where, without doubt, they would bring a higher price.

If the latter suggestion were the case, he would have transport costs and since as usual, he was penniless, he meekly approaches the Duchess to see what she would advise:

"This is to let you know how I am keeping and to let you know all about my troubles, needs and worries which are mounting up daily, but especially so, right at this moment. Bills keep pouring in every day and so too are the poor who arrive here in great numbers. Many are turning up in rags, barefooted with sores and covered in lice. It is so bad that we have to keep a man or two doing nothing else but keeping the copper

boiling to delouse them. It looks as if this will have to go on right through winter, even up to next May. My sister, this is just the sort of thing that makes my troubles grow daily."

Since John of God dictated his letters, he just let his troubles pour forth. Then he skips from his woes to lament the death of one of his greatest and cherished benefactresses, the cousin of the Duchess, the young Doña Francisca whom he visited after Baena at the ducal castle of Alcaudete. He had found her gravely ill; now she had died at only twenty years of age. John of God grieves her loss: "Our Lord Jesus Christ wished to take her to himself where she will be well, happy and at rest."

He would never forget her charity: "She did so much good to everyone, both by the advice she gave and the alms she distributed... Rich and poor alike, everyone who knew her, is saddened by her death. I more than anyone else, for I have far greater cause to feel her loss, because she always comforted and advised me."

His financial obligations, he explains in his letter, are not only for the maintenance of the poor and sick, but for repair work on the building: "I am renovating the whole hospital and now that I have started the job, it really has me worried."

This makes me wonder whether "this work" was due to a certain collapse of masonry which, at a date of which we are uncertain, caused damage to the building in the Cuesta Gomérez. This information came to light during the statements made by various witnesses at the Jeronymite court case.

Whatever happened, John of God saw that he needed to reinforce and renovate the building if he was to continue caring for his patients. That is why he decided "to go quickly to Andalusia as far as Zafra and Seville." Master Avila advised him that he should go personally to Zafra rather than send letters to the Duke de Feria and the Count de Arcos. John of God understood why: "Unless the man is before you, he is soon forgotten." Thus the urgency to convert the wheat he had stored away at Alcaudete into money; he asks the Duchess how to go about it: "I am sending Angulo off to either sell the wheat or bring it back, acording to whatever you think is best."

The transportation was an additional cost, but no doubt the Duchess would pay for it: "You see to it my sister, whatever you think might be best." In any case, he gave Angulo the power to carry out the entire transaction.

I find this second letter to the Duchess very sad for it

shows how greatly John of God suffered during the final years of his life. Of course, the letter is full of Christian reflections, spiritual thoughts and wise advice that he gently gives to the Duchess, his dear Duquesita. He mentions all the persons who held positions in the service of the Duchess, the Majordomo, the ladies and maids, the chaplain, the gentlemen and servants. He wanted to be remembered to them all, but he makes a special mention of *"Doña Isabella the musician."* He suggests to the Duchess that she could utilise Angulo's visit to take up a collection: *"Please ask your very kind housekeeper and all the other ladies and maidens whether they might have some little gold or silver trinket that they might like to send along for the poor."* John of God was an incorrigible beggar for alms.

In Andalusia there was then, and still is today, a tasty delicacy called 'tostadas de mollete', which my readers probably would know better as Danish pastries. The Duchess had some of these prepared when John of God visited the Baena castle. How they enjoyed them!

John of God remembers them as he closes this second letter: "Good Duchess, I often remember the gifts you made me in Cabra and Baena and the pastries you gave me." He says the word 'migajón' which literally means, a large piece and not a 'miga' a small piece, a crumb. The pastries were oval shaped and made of flaky pastry.

If you visit Andalusia, ask for breakfast coffee and 'tostadas de mollete' with whipped cream. You will thank me for the advice. John of God found them delicious!

Notes to Chapter 33

* The observations of the deteriorated physical condition of John of God belong to Francisco de Castro (op.cit.), chapter 17. The case near the 'pancake stall' was related by witness #23 at the Granada beatification process, Alonso de la Peña: *"This witness was only nine or ten years of age at the time of John of God's death."* De la Peña held several public positions in the city.
* At least half a dozen witnesses at the Granada beatification process related the episode in the Cuesta Gomérez: #33 (Antón Rodríguez); #34 (María de la Paz); #49 9 Melchora Quixada); #56 (Luisa de Ribera); #63 (Bartolomé Fernández de Cazorla); and also in the Castro (op.cit.,) work, chapter 17.
* The document referring to the foundation of the Toledo hospital was published by J. García Soriano, *La primmer mention impress de San Juan de Dios y de su Obra Hospitalaria*: 'La Caridad' Vol. I, 9 (1941) 257-262; I took it from the volume of B. Ortiz, *Sum Toletani graphica descriptio*, Toledo 1949. García Soriano also found a manuscript translation of the book in Castilian in the Spanish National Library with the inscription Méndez Salvatierra. 9168. There is some confusion regarding the chronology of the work by Ortiz: N. Antonio, Bibliotheca Hispana Nova I, 229, first published at Toledo in 1544; García Soriano draws attention to the fact that no examples of this edition have been found: "If the famous and faithful biography is not mistaken in the year"; it is mistaken: Ortiz is unable to relate the visit of John of God to 1544 because he made it in 1548; therefore the existing edition carries the date 1549, Toledo 'apud I. Ayala'. García Soriano distrusts the version in the National Library because it puts the death of Cardinal Tavera in 1535 whereas Tavera died on 1 August 1545; he also sees an error in the date 1546 which the translator attributes to the work: when in 1549 Ortiz finished and published his work, it started off in the time of Tavera which was before 1545, and was completed when Cardinal Martínez Silíceo was primate (1546-1557). Blas Ortiz was a writer of merit, who the year before this wrote a work called *Itinerarium Adriani VI P.M. ab Hispania*, Toledo 1548. Gomez Moreno in his *San Juan de Dios, Primicias etc.*, (op.cit.), 165-167, reproduces the García Soriano version. García Soriano suspects that the Ferdinand mentioned in the document could coincide with the gentleman named Hernán Núñez, the young man moved by the example of John of God at the Gate de los Tablas: he left his fiancee and joined the team of Master Avila (Cf. Supra, chap 26): I think this is stretching things a bit too far, nevertheless, there is a Master Hernán Núñez inscribed in the circle of Juan de Avila, but not among the Brothers of John of God. [An English version is found in B. O'Grady's *Champion of Charity* (op.cit.) 162-164, 169].
* Francisco López Chico, a witness at the Toledo beatification process who for 20 years lived at Granada, related the incident of the widow Luisa de la Cruz and her son the prisoner of the Moors. He gives as his direct source the evidence of Clara de Caves, daughter of Luisa and sister of the young man. This was stated at Toledo 17 Dec. 1622.
* For the needs and giving of alms at Valladolid see Francisco de Castro (op.cit.), Ch.16.
* The biography of the Duchess of Sessa, from birth to her death in March 1604, Cf. M. de Mina *Visitar la Granada de San Juan de Dios*, op.cit., 282-285.
* The Avila children figure in the "witnesses personally known to John of God." In

the Granada beatification process; #18 (Melchor), #39 (Inés), #48 (Luisa). The duty of the 'Jurado', magistrate, was known since the time of the Catholic Monarchs as 'Hombre Bueno' (good man), the defender of the people before the authorities of the Municipal Council; the first 'Royal Ordinances' fixed the number of 'jurados' at Granada to twenty. It was a position that held great honour and privilege. See chapters 25 & 26 for references to the apothecary Antón Zabán and his little grand-daughter.

* The basic source of the satanic persecutions of John of God comes from Francisco de Castro (op.cit.), chapters 14 & 18. The case near the house of Dr. Beltrán comes from the Granada beatification process: Lucia de la O, Francisca de la Fuente, Domingo Navarro, Melchor de Avila, Baltasar Suárez, Gabriel Suárez, Gabriel Maldonado ("in the morning it was known all over the city, and everyone knew about it and they went to see the blessed father John of God..."). The play by Lope de Vega: *Comedia famosa de Juan de Dios y Antón Martín*, Madrid 1618. The witness at the Granada beatification process Luisa de Avila spoke about the temptation to suicide from the bridge of Santa Ana. Castro (ibid) speaks of the fire in the house in the Calle Lucena, chapter 12: also by the Granada beatification process witnesses #53 (Catalina de Contreras), #54 (Juana de Gálvez), #56 (Catalina de Arenas) #57 (Francisca de Venegas).

* The declarations of Leonor de Cáceres about the wing of the hospital in the Cuesta Gomérez crumbling to the ground, is from the Jeronymite lawsuit, witness #2: Cf. J. Sánchez in his Kenosis, etc., op.cit., 311ff. Having studied the testimony of the aforementioned witness in the Jeronymite case, I have come to the conclusion that she was indeed a charitable woman; however, she made wild and stupid claims, even to including John of God in her own family and that her mother Doña Francisca de Cáceres was the foundress of the Hospitaller Order; her imagination even included certain persons who lived at different times into her rambling fantasy filled account. Her evidence cannot be relied upon without a severe critical examination, but it has value in showing how lightly she presented the facts regarding the priorship of Fray Diego de Linares at San Jerónimo's, and about the various Archbishops of Granada. From the circumstances related in the text is it easy to deduce that the dates of the two letters written to the Duchess of Sessa could not be those shown by Saucedo: autumn-winter 1547; but autumn-winter 1548. M. de Mina, '*Anotaciones*', *Fondo Documental*, op.cit., Archive of Los Pisa, Granada, *Notas a las cartas*, prolongs the date to February through to mid March 1549. G. Magliozzi, *Lo firmo con queste mie tre lettere*, Rome 1995, 112, puts the second letter at the end of 1549: because, according to the testimony of Cristóbal de Castro, Francisca Mendoza died when "she was about 22 years of age", and since she was born in 1527 it would have to be 1549 when she died. However, "about" is not a definite date, so if she was 21, then from 1527 it would be 1548.

34

A TRUE PROFILE OF THE MAN

Granada
1549

It came about that John of God seemed like an adventurer to the children of Granada. They would have seen him as a somewhat ragged friar, sometimes begging for alms, sometimes carrying a sick man on his shoulders. They heard their elders speaking about the prodigious life of the alms-seeker. After seventy years had passed, the judges at the Beatification Process investigated whether John of God could move on to becoming a saint. Niña Francisca Perea, an old lady of over ninety, was only ten years of age when she saw blessed John of God coming into her home. The Pereas, Diego and Ana, were noble people whose parents originally came from Galicia to Granada, when the city capitulated to Ferdinand and Isabella. Francisca was with her mother Ana when she handed a washbowl to John of God to wash his hands; then when they were warmed up they brought in a slice of brown bread spread with bacon. He tasted a small piece of the sandwich and smilingly asked permission to keep the slice in his basket: *"For my poor folk,"* he said with a smile and a chuckle.

On another day he arrived accompanied by two women, one young, the other elderly, both with plenty of 'makeup' on their faces. Francisca heard John of God ask Don Diego if he could trouble him to give these women accommodation for a couple of days *"while I find lodgings for them."* Don Diego looked at his wife Ana, and Francisca noticed that her father and mother looked quite seriously at each other. Both then gave a slight inclination of their heads, indicating they would take them in. The two were invited to stay and Francisca's mother prepared their meals. Francisca asked her father why blessed John of God brought these women to their house and he replied that *"he took them from the public house because they decided to be good."*

John of God smiled at the little girl and patted her on the head. Francisca asked her mother her if she might go with her one day to the hospital. She went and Francisca always remembered that Brother John of God was ill, *"lying on a mat which served him as a bed."* The ninety-year-old Francisca told the judges that she would never forget John of God even if a hundred years were to pass!

If you wander through the streets of Granada, make sure you pause at the Corral del Carbón. Tourists who walk up the road called Reyes Católicos from the Plaza del Ayuntamiento towards the Plaza Isabella la Católica, may not notice, that a little to the right is a superb nook, an Arabic patio built centuries ago as a warehouse and store – a public granary – where the Moslems spent hours "bargaining and trading." Its gateway will amaze you with its grand arch festooned with ornamental brickwork and stucco lettering. My Arabic friends tell me this reads: *"There is only one God, God is one; he never begot nor was he ever begotten, nor did he have any companion."* Above is a lintel with three openings, the centre one beautifully surrounded by Arabic script. The patio is called *'del Carbón'* [of coal] because, at the time of the Catholic Monarchs, it was used to store the coal that had to be brought into Granada. In John of God's day, it became a theatre for plays: what an excellent backdrop!

Adjacent to the Corral del Carbón is the Plaza Tovar where stands a magnificent building called 'Duques de Abrantes'. In spite of dozens of restorations its porticos still conserve traces of Arabic decoration and Islamic art which, in the 16th century, was incorporated into its Christian architecture.

The genealogical tree of the Abrantes is entwined with the noble Bobadilla family, who were great friends of John of God and whom he often visited.

This part of the city was on the left bank of the Darro, the same side as the Cuesta Gomérez, so obviously, it was an easy walk for our alms-seeker. It faced a bridge, appropriately called the Coal Bridge, which gave access to the Zacatín and the Plaza Bibarrambla.

John of God was always received at the door of the Bobadilla home by *"an excited crowd of children,"* for, besides the children of the master of the house, there were those of the servants: These youngsters, as adults, and into old age, were to remember the mystical figure of the charity worker, who took their attention and amused them *"with smiles and little gifts"*: small things like fruit, that he pulled out of his basket.

Such was the happy image John of God left in the houses of his benefactors. One might think that his work for the poorest of the marginated would make him go about with a grim face and ponderous manner. It was not so, and it is important to me to put these testimonies together so that we can see more clearly *"who he was and how he was."* The sieve maker at Salamanca, the old man named Jerónimo, saw John of God caring for the sick. He sums him up by saying, *"Laughter poured from his mouth'.*

So, he was jovial, simple, never dramatising his worries. Nevertheless, he was responsible, firm and conscientious: *"A man with a sense of humour."*

The upheaval that John of God experienced after the sermon in the Campo de los Mártires impelled him into external manifestations that remind us of the *fiorelli* of St. Francis of Assisi. The famous *'fiorelli'* [little flowers] of St. Francis of Assisi relate how he went out with Brother Rufino in search of happiness; and they were held to be mad. As we saw, Castro notes how John of God put up with insults, stoning and mud slinging, not only *"with great patience,"* but also *"with great joy."* We know that John of God never gave any impression of bitterness, gloom or ill humour. No matter what happened, he was seen as being full of interior joy, and sometimes jubilant. At the time of his discharge from the Royal Hospital, *"when there were still some who thought him to be mad"*, a mischievous boy, just to amuse himself, gave John of God a shove pitching him into a pool in the centre of the patio of the Palace of the Inquisition where John had gone to seek alms, *"He came out of the water laughing and joking."*

Recall too, the good humour with which John of God laughed off the insults of the enraged prostitute: *"You wicked man and sanctimonious hypocrite!"* All he said was: *"Here, take these two reales and go and shout that out in the plaza."*

The royal scribe Felipe de Alays also found him to be *"very happy and clapping his hands together"* and often humming; He always saluted him, *"Good on you Padre!"* John of God would smile and say, *"The one who serves God is happy, the one who serves the devil is sad."*

What was going on beneath his charitable kind and happy appearance? What energy was flowing through John of God's veins? Who was he, what was he?

At least it is very much in harmony with the spirit of the time that John of God's physical, psychological and spiritual attributes caused them to consider him an 'adventurer'.

Certainly every Portuguese and Spaniard born at the end of the 15th century must have felt a sense of wonder as explorers, soldiers, sailors and colonisers went out to every point of the planet. It has been said that, *"adventure was the disease of the 16th century."*

The magic call did not affect Juan Ciudad any more than it did other young men of his day. Any shepherd or farm labourer at Oropesa could join the Emperor's army or cross the Atlantic to wander the limitless horizons of the recently discovered Indies. Juan fulfilled his military duty at Fuenterrabía and Vienna without too much enthusiasm and with mediocre results. He went on to become an itinerant bookseller but neither did this offer him exciting prospects.

The final 'adventure' began in the field of Los Mártires when he obeyed an 'illumination' within the margin of normal psychological parameters. John of God, who supplanted Juan Ciudad, did not carry out in the streets of Granada the requisites of an 'adventurer'. He is *something* else, a phenomenon with a very complex make-up requiring special insight to analyse.

Let me point out that all three of the hospitaller champions of the 16th century experienced military service. Before John of God's time, there was a Venetian patrician called Jerome Emiliano who had been a soldier and a political prisoner and had experienced the horrors of the plague of 1518. He felt called to open hospitals in the North of Italy with his brothers known as the 'Somaschi' named from their headquarters in the city of Somasca. Jerome died of the plague in 1537.

In 1550, the year of John of God's death, Camillus di Lellis was born in the Italian hills of Abruzzi. He was a lively and unrestrained young man, also a soldier, who became a Capuchin friar. He left that Order through illness, but under the tutelage of Philip Neri he directed his energies towards the creation of great hospitals. Camillus died in 1614.

John of God started something new. Neither he nor his brothers were clerics or priests, but simply Christians who, later on, were made into a 'religious family', subject to the jurisdiction of the bishop.

Legends inevitably flourished about his person, because propitious circumstances favoured it. On the one hand there was the general mood in Spain that was aroused to exaltation by the feats carried out by heroes overseas. No one was surprised to find so close to home, a superman, and one who manifested gestures like those of faraway places. Simple folk showed a credulity that was open to all manner of marvels.

On the other hand, the figure of John of God suddenly burst forth into Granada like 'a madman' singled out by the finger of God for the defence and protection of the unfortunate. He incited curiosity about his origins and background. Soon there began to circulate a spurious biography that mixed his actual heroic actions with certain prodigies intended to adorn each step of his life with a halo.

We have much for which to thank Francisco de Castro who rigorously selected only information that was certain. We have much to lament concerning the material that Brother Dionisio Celi inserted in John of God's story as the truth 36 years later when he manipulatively 'completed' Castro's book with fictitious miracles and apparitions. Brother Celi became the source used by Govea and subsequent biographers.

Today this causes a tremendous amount of work in applying meticulous means to sift little by little the real story of John of God. Researchers have conscientiously been doing this over the past fifty years so that now we have a 'very real' profile. We smile at those who, while in good faith, were nevertheless naive enough to set their hands to 'embellish' his statue. We have no grounds for being scandalised about legends and popular exaggerations because often they have a basis in fact, even with their fashionable adornment.

I gleaned the following from the various notes relating to diabolical attacks. The story goes that John of God, while praying in his cell, noticed the presence of a provocative woman. Doubtless this image was a psychological effect caused by the work he was doing to help prostitutes, for the good simple folk quickly gave it a bodily form within this setting. The old lady Francisca Fernández, who for most of her life had worked as a dressmaker, talked with her needlework companions and related the event this way:

"One day the blessed father was coming down from the Alhambra and came to the Alemeda where a beautiful woman dressed in silk was walking. She came up to the blessed father and told him that she loved him tremendously and wanted to marry him if he wished to do so. The blessed father blest himself with the sign of the Cross and said: 'God help me, I most certainly do not want to.' She then disappeared in a puff of mist. This was observed by a man who was using a crowbar to loosen some soil..."

In respect to the complete life of John of God, we have no right to interpret his intimate life experiences. He leaves a few, not many, significant peep-holes through which, today, we can catch glimpses of his spiritual panorama. But we need to contain our enthusiasm, no matter how much John of God may merit it, because Andalusians have a reputation for exaggeration, to which must be added that *"anything is possible at Granada."* José María Pemán says the Arabic-Andalusian folk songs known as *Casidas* are typical of this exaggerated approach to life. He gave the example of one that tells the tale of a young man and the girl he loves. This folk song from Granada describes how the young lady was given a sash that was big enough to go round a palm tree, to wear. The poet exaggerates this to say that her waist was only the size of a wasp's: *"Yesterday afternoon you were wearing a sash that I measured with a guitar string and it went around fourteen times."* Thus the song goes on, adding an extra time around the waist with each verse! Pemán applies this psychology, which exceeds all limits, to the 'mystical' John of God. He has the spirituality of John of God in Spain's Golden age, *"pouring forth from the channels of his mad sanctity."* I think this is unnecessary exaggeration and we need to measure calmly the truth about him.

The poet Lope de Vega considered it impossible,
"How to reduce your glories to numbers,
neither verses nor stories are able."
And that is how it was with our saint, John of God.

Our interest in John of God's physical appearance is helped by some valuable data that has come down to us especially in the examination of his remains, the descriptions related or written by those who knew him and his portraits. Fortunately, there are these three ways open to us to come close to his physical figure.

It seems necessary to know his physical aspect... Dante guarantees that the face shows the colour of the heart (*"lo viso mostra la color del core"*).

The mortal remains identified as John of God's are kept in the silver urn that stands in the *Camarín*, [relics room] of the St. John of God basilica at Granada – that magnificent temple built in the mid-18th century. His body was first buried in the crypt of a chapel – that of the Pisa family – in the Minim friars' church of Our Lady of the Victory, and unfortunately, was submitted to the customary removal of fragments for reliquaries. As a result, only a handful of bones repose in the urn in the Camarín. That is why the last official recognition of the relics yielded scant material for sketching the bone structure of the saint. Medical experts state that he must have been of robust and slim build and, according to the experts, his height can be estimated as being one metre, seventy-two centimetres (approximately 5' 7").

Neither the oral or written reports of these experts give us a proper image of the person they describe. It is quite impossible to discover from the remains what may have been the colour of his eyes or the measurements of his nose. However, from the description of at least half a dozen eyewitnesses, we can glean a fairly good idea of his general appearance and bearing.

These reports I consider quickly rather than substantially, from three fundamental documented sources. Firstly, the witnesses at the Jeronymite court case, many of whom belonged to the closest circle of John of God's friends, including Angulo, who made their statements only 24 years after his death. The second accounts are diffused through the pages of Castro's biography where he categorically states: *"I prepared this work, not withstanding the short period of time since John of God left this world and that there are still plenty of people living today who remember him."* The third is the plethora of evidence that emerged from the Beatification Process, much of which was presented by *"eyewitnesses who personally knew John of God."* You have seen in the previous chapters of this book, the unmeasured richness they contain.

He was not a religious rebel, 'a protester' in the usual sense. For John of God was not a hothead nor did he attack the prevailing system. He served others with love, distributing food, applying medicines and offering shelter. He dispensed charity.

So, yes, he is certainly a revolutionary. But he did not make speeches or harangue people. As he entered the luxurious palaces of the nobility of Granada his very appearance was enough to compel a resolute examination of social conscience.

They tell us about his person: *"He always went barefooted."* At Salamanca they saw him *"with a good beard,"* at other times, *"he shaved his head and beard with a razor,"* but not always, because sometimes he went for months without shaving. *"He was tall with bushy eyebrows"*; *"He went bareheaded, for throughout the year he never wore a cap or hat"*; *"He was neither fat nor thin, but well built."* People recalled a vigorous, strong man of robust complexion, and surmised about his penitence and frequent fasting. Only one witness claimed, he was *"little, lean and of slight appearance,"* an opinion contrary to the majority.

John of God presented himself as an *agent provocateur* before Granada's high society, which, as the privileged class of that period, was dedicated to the refined cultivation of the body, and an obsession with physical appearances. The imaginary perfect woman was blond and green eyed. Her large pale hands had well-manicured fingernails. She was very slim, with firm small breasts, she had a tight waist and small feet. Men preferred their hair to be light chestnut and to be tall of stature. It annoyed them intensely when they heard themselves described by foreign travellers as *"small, dark skinned, with black hair."*

John of God could have been mistaken for one of the poor wretches who slept at night under the porticoes of the Plaza Bibarrambla. At the same time he could go into palaces where, dressed in rags and not fitting in, he brought the cry of the hungry into the household.

You will recall the trousers of *"coarse linen"* and the *"rough smock"*, open at the sides, that he wore until Bishop Muñoz gave him a habit that put an end to his exchanging his coat for the grubby rags of a beggar. The bishop forbade him to give his habit and shirt to the poor. John of God *"accepted without any murmur"* the austere habit bestowed by episcopal decision. When *"he first put on"* this habit he became something more. *"He dressed neatly"*, as Muñoz so rightly explains, *"to sit down at the table with distinguished persons."*

With basket and staff in hand, and two pots tied together with a cord slung from his shoulders, is how Granada saw John of God in its streets.

We can also view his portrait for a faithful likeness of his face.

I remind you about the young artist Alonso Sánchez Coello who at Salamanca, or Valladolid, 'saw' John of God, whose face had impressed him so much that he shetched it – whether hastily or carefully, we do not know.

More than twenty years were to pass before the Hospitaller Brothers of John of God wanted to have his portrait. Domingo Piola, now known in the Order as Brother Domingo Benedicto, went to Madrid *"to seek donations for the poor in the hospital at Granada."* Naturally, he relied on the support of families who were friends of John of God and had settled in the capital, including María Mendoza, Leonor Mendoza *"and other leading lords and ladies."* At this time, 1570, Alonso Sánchez Coello was heralded as a famous painter of royal portraits. At the Court at Toledo he had painted for Philip II, before the court moved from Toledo to Madrid in the spring of 1561. The king reserved for his Painter of the Royal Chamber a studio adjacent to the palace. A triumph for Coello.

Coello heard the ladies of the court talking about the heroism of John of God. This moved him to look through his old sketchbooks to find the drawings he had made so many years before. We do not know whether the initiative to paint this portrait first came from the ladies of the Court, or Brother Domingo at Granada. It had to be one or the other but, in any case, Coello went ahead determined to paint his portrait in oils. The artist, who had a reputation of always being short of cash, could have been glad of the money for the commission. When the portrait was completed Brother Domingo took it back to Granada – but not before Coello had written a manifest showing that, *"Brother Domingo Benedicto, brother of the hospital of John of God at Granada, took the painting of the same John of God back with him."*

Later on, the portrait was taken to Madrid from Granada, probably to place it on show at some festivity to honour him, but an excellent copy remained in the Granada Basilica. The original was pillaged from the Antón Martín Hospital during the *Desamortización*, as the period of the anticlerical government of 1825 was called. Like all the belongings of religious orders, it was confiscated by the Government. Some sensible person in the local government administration handed the portrait over for storage to the Brothers at San Rafael Hospital at Madrid, where later on, after an intensive search, it was found again.

Here is a curious detail that would make John of God smile.

In the endnotes to this chapter you are informed about the official recognition of the relics of St. John of God, which were verified on 22 January 1995. The experts took the opportunity to examine the bones, especially the skull, and submit them to the treatment of a computer. They discovered some curious traces of sinusitis, of chronic colds, and a bump from the famous fall from the French mule at Fuenterrabia. We still don't know what an analysis of his DNA might produce!

Among other things, the scientific experts decided to match the measurements of John of God's skull made by the computer, with the portrait painted by Sánchez Coello. It was a perfect match, which gives even a further seal of authenticity to the painting. Obviously, 'it is' John of God.

What sort of person does the portrait depict? Study the photograph: *"Oval face, with wide open eyes, not very dark, fine eyebrows and well spread, marked and rigid nose, full and expressive mouth, large forehead due to receding hairline, chestnut hair closely cropped, a little moustache which drooped down to his beard, also cut short and dressed in a tunic with a hood. The face stands out clearly from a dark background and has an expression that is both enigmatic and serene at the same time. It is a happy face and when studied closely seems to show forth the intense charity within his being."*

Dr. María Kusche, who gives the above description of the portrait, specialises in the works of Sánchez Coello and notes a significant point. The artist left aside the veneration of the saint, simply treating his facial features, *"with force, realism and pliability."* Coello intended to *"capture his personality by strongly highlighting"* the features of the face. Coello was a painter of *"detail and firmness"* and he has left us a very fine human figure, somewhat absorbed in the mystery. Admirable!

Today the Coello portrait is considered to be the 'authentic and official' portrait of John of God. It has had a notable influence on subsequent iconography. The first to copy the Coello work was Pedro de Raxis - scholars are uncertain whether it was Pedro senior or his son. Coello has John of God with his eyes showing concern and uncertainty looking upon the world, while De Raxis has them raised towards heaven from where he received courage and consolation. A dozen or so first-rate artists have represented John of God in various attitudes and scenarios, taking the Coello portrait as their model with its youngish oval face, almost horizontal eyelashes, large nose and close-cropped hair. Of course they have added a habit which more or less corresponded to the *"coarse smock"* and hood he used to wear: Murillo, Zurbarán, Ribera, Risueño... Marvellous!

Before all the others, I want to place the 'first drawn image' of John of God. I wonder whether the anonymous sketcher knew of the portrait by Coello, because if he did, he wanted 'to revenge himself' on the refinements of Coello. You will find it among the illustrations of this book. I want you to look at it because, unless you see it, it will be useless talking about it. It appeared in the 1579 Castilian version of that famous 'bull' of Pope Pius V whose juridical declaration pronounced the yet unnamed Hospitaller Order as 'coming of age'. The pope promulgated this bull in January 1572 – at the same as the Jeronymites were bringing a court case against the Hospitaller Brothers.

The Castilian version of the pontifical bull carried this little woodcut depicting John of God kneeling before a crucifix. Both the crucifix and John of God are the same size. In 1585, Castro's biography included this picture - without any acknowledgment. The drawing is crude yet severely authentic and it seems to have inspired devotion and love... and awe. You can see how truly devout it is, reverential, depicting John of God in an attitude of prayer, devotion, poverty and charity. Coello perfumed John of God with the typical oils of a painter of the Royal Chamber, making his figure sublime. This anonymous xylographer puts John of God in the centre of the actual scenario where he fulfilled his mission.

For me, the authentic image of John of God depicted in this

crude little anonymous woodcut is of far more value than the masterpiece painted by Coello. Why do I say that? I say that because this design, for all its simplicity, is so devout and 'brutal' and seems to depict just how John of God must have felt within himself.

What was John of God like interiorly? He had experienced a decisive cataclysm starting from the event which changed his life by pointing him towards a mission. Without this enlightenment which struck him on 20 January in the field of los Mártires', his enigma would be incomprehensible.

From then on John of God was a man 'possessed', invaded. Here is the big question. Can a human being be seized with impunity by the divine tempest? If, when the gale of God comes upon him, can anyone save himself from delirium? The sublime possession conditions two movements in a person, within and without. The relationship with God which seems profoundly and permanently directed towards the mysterious presence in the depths of his or her spirit, from there radiates outwards, to the environment of those who are to be the beneficiaries of the entrusted mission.

The simple spectators of the phenomenon took him to be mad, to have gone beyond the normal, to have lost his 'mind'. This amazement of the spectators was prophesised in the Old Testament in the Book of Wisdom. We are "foolish" who used to consider their behaviour "foolish." The 'madman' of Granada is within the usual parameters. But he has been elevated to another dimension. He is invaded.

Why the Holy Spirit seized him from among so many belongs to the mysterious synopsis of human destiny.

John of God's life thereafter went beyond the reasonable bounds that delineate our behaviour. Up to then he had been an ordinary citizen. According to the few sketchy facts of his biography, he showed himself to be normal and good-natured, correct, very kind and helpful, whether as the overseer of his flocks, or with the Emperor who called for soldiers, or with the impoverished Portuguese family exiled to Ceuta. He was a pleasant pedlar of books and prints. But from the time of the illumination...

The Bible gives us cases like his. Abraham heard the divine call to leave his home and land. Abraham listened and obeyed. The Apostles, those special friends of Jesus, were struck by a rushing wind from heaven which *"filled them with the Holy Spirit."* They came out of the Cenacle as changed men. Those who saw them mocked them saying, *"they were drunk."* Saul was struck down on the road to Damascus and was, *"dazzled by a blinding heavenly brightness"* and he heard the voice that said,

"You will be told what you are to do." The long history of the Church of the New Testament is full of events similar to that which John of God experienced. He suddenly found himself facing God on God's ground, and was cleansed, possessed and missioned.

In reality, John of God's internal and external behaviours were in harmony because his gaze was now fixed upon the presence of God within his being. The only exterior thing that concerned him was his duty, the mission that had been confided to him. A mission which embraced the poor, the ill, the suffering, all who were in need of love and charity. John of God had been missioned to share out mercy.

Let me confess that I have taken time to find out how today's Brothers of the Hospitaller Order think about their founder. I studied their magazines, their books and the results of their assemblies. I saw them at work in the houses where they continue to carry out the commandment to share mercy. They walk in the path of John of God whose spirit rests upon them.

In a television interview I did with Brother Matías de Mina, he told me not only *"how John of God was"* exteriorly, but also 'interiorly'.

John of God must be studied in the light of *"how he understands and fulfils the message of the Gospel of Jesus Christ. John of God principally carried out his work of spiritual and corporal mercy for the poor and sick in the hospital. And to do that well, he went out in search of doctors, apothecaries, nurses, and others who would give their services out of love for Our Lord Jesus Christ. He found priests to teach them Christian doctrine and administer the sacraments to them."*

Brother Matías recited before the cameras, the litany of theological, moral, and ascetic virtues accomplished by John of God, who *"saw Jesus Christ in each sick person."* He knew how *"to remove the human elements that hide the divine presence."* Matías finished by telling the following incident, demonstrating his consideration and courtesy.

"A litigant in a lawsuit told him of his financial ruin; John of God heard what he had to say, then went off to see the judge at the Royal Chancellery who had handled the case. He asked the judge if what the man said was true and he replied that it was. John of God went back to the 'vergonzante' and told him what he planned to do. He took him to the building site where the Cathedral was under construction. He showed the man a hole in the wall that was covered by a stone, and told him that he would leave a daily ration for him there. That way he could avoid the indiscreet glances of others who might see him coming to ask for it."

The existence of the interior 'illumination' of John of God hinges upon the instrumentality of the words of Master Avila.

We have already left behind the pages about John of God's conversion, which can be interpreted in two ways. It could be a purely human phenomenon scientifically explainable by psychologists and psychiatrists. Or, as believers in God would hold, there can be extraordinary interventions of grace at key moments of a person's life.

If the Holy Spirit invaded John of God while he was listening to Avila's sermon, I believe it would not be unusual for the same Spirit to tune them both into the same wavelength. This can be seen easily when the Master consented to let John of God continue to carry on with his 'mad act' when he went out into the street. That sealed it! He was soon picked up and hustled off to the Royal Hospital where he underwent the cruel 'therapy' of the lash.

At their first interview, John of God must have expressed to the Master just how the 'illumination' he received had opened up a new relationship between himself, God and the neighbour. Today we would say he was programming himself for the service of the disinherited: the poor, the sick and the marginated.

Master Avila must have thought carefully about God crossing John of God's path with his own. Avila kept a close eye on his movements, instructing him and introducing him to the circle of his own disciples who would help him in his work. He opened the way for John of God to have access to the Archbishop, the civil authorities and the noble families of Granada.

The two saw each other at every possible opportunity, although there is only documented evidence of three visits to Granada by Master Avila between 1539 and 1550. One of these visits took place in 1542 between Lent and Corpus Christi, another in the spring of 1543, and the longest when Archbishop Guerrero invited him to Granada early in 1548.

On the other hand, as always, we lack documentation that pinpoints the movements of John of God that would tell us how often he walked to Baeza and Montilla to see his Master. There are clues that he made journeys other than those I have mentioned and there are others he lamented he was unable to make, such as his planned trip to Zafra. It seems that during his journeys around Andalusia he visited the Master at Montilla, because some of Avila's disciples said they saw him there. I made a very careful study of these statements originating from the 'Avila circle', because they really wanted to acclaim the apostolic zeal of St. John de Avila, which of course is quite laudable. Some of Avila's disciples even went so far as to attribute the foundation of the Granada John of God Hospital to him. He was, of course, there right from the start, but in the capacity of a collaborator of the brothers. This was clearly established by the formal statements made at the Jeronymite lawsuit.

The simple truth is that among the 'champions' of the 16th century, influenced by Master Avila – among them his friends Francisco de Borja, Ignacio de Loyola, Teresa of Jesus, Juan de Ribera, and possibly Pedro de Alcántara – there was no one as close to him, nor as obedient as, John of God. There cannot be the slightest doubt of that. In spite of that, at times, John of God went beyond the boundaries of prudence, occcasionally, getting 'out of hand'.

You will recall that Avila sent him a letter attempting to restrain him when he found out about his trips to the brothels of the Bibataubín red-light district.

Did the Master and John of God keep up a frequent correspondence? Not too much, I am inclined to think.

When the Master tried to allay John of God's scruples by saying, *"do not think that you are pestering me by writing at length,"* I think that he was referring to the length of the letter rather than the frequency of his correspondence.

Three letters from Master Avila to John of God exist, but, unfortunately, there are none of John of God's to the Master, a great pity, because these letters would be a true mirror of his interior life.

Master Avila's epistles are a treasury of Christian spirituality, a treasure-trove of boundless riches. I was surprised to read the praise Fray Luis de Granada had for Avila's letters for he was, himself, adept at using the language of spiritual experiences: "*When they wish to write something very well, intelligent men go over it a thousand times beforehand. They read it carefully, adding something or taking something away. They give thought to each word (Demostenes was not free from doing that and he was a master of eloquence, because it was said his orations could oil a lamp). And, that being so, the letters of this Father [Avila] are such that they do not cost him any more effort than when he first puts his hand to them.*"

Likewise, with an open heart, Master Avila wrote to John of God, demonstrating his sincerest friendship: "*Our Lord wants me to guide you, and he has united us in brotherhood and love one for one anther... I do not want you saying that you do not deserve to be my son, because that is what you are to me. By the same token it would be silly of me to say that I did not deserve to be your father.*"

Replying to a letter John of God wrote him saying that he feared to bother the Master, Avila replied: "*Do not think that you are pestering me by writing at length. No letter can seem to be too long between such good friends. I ask you to remember that I really look forward to hearing from you because it makes me glad to know how you are getting along. So then, if you really don't want to annoy me, don't be slow to show it. That could cost you something, because love is manifested by deeds and not words; and it costs us a lot more to put into practice for those we love.*"

This genuine friendship of the master for his disciple gave Avila the confidence to advise him of pitfalls. He insisted that he should be obedient to Padre Portillo, whom he had placed as his confessor in his absence - "*God has not called you to rule but to be ruled.*" The Master reproached John of God for falling into debt too much: "*I think it would be all right for you to go and look for help from those Lords of Castile at Court. Yes, go ahead, but do not run up any debts while you are there.*"

No further debts were run up while John of God was away on his journey to Valladolid. Avila knew that he would hand out any alms he received and return to Granada without a single ducat. What saved him was the shrewdness of Doña María Mendoza and her promissory notes.

The Master closed his last letter with these tender words: "*At the moment I am unable to send you any clothing, but I will make it up to you by celebrating some Masses for you. That should suit you far better.*"

Father Avila's letters to John of God carry a brief catechesis of practical Christianity: *"I have a great fear that the devil might try to make you think that your own opinion is sufficient, because you could be deceived that way"*; *"A man who is full of his own opinion has no need of a demon to tempt him, because he is his own demon"*; *"It would not profit you at all to pull everybody else out of the mire and end up getting stuck in it yourself"*; *"A good and loyal servant must gain five more talents with the five entrusted to him."* *"Find the time to pray. Go to daily Mass and on Sundays listen to a sermon."* *"Watch your step that in doing good for others, you may do evil to yourself. Never deprive your soul of its nourishment, otherwise it would starve, become sad and turn bad. What, then would all the good you do for others profit you? What, then will anyone gain by winning the whole world and forfeiting his life?"*

In his third letter, it seems that the master has a premonition of John of God's approaching death: *"You have so little time left, so call upon Our Lord with all you heart."* He insists that John of God act with circumspection: *"Without prudence man falls into a thousand things that displease God... That is why a foolish man must sooner or later learn that once is enough to make a fool of himself and he would remember it for the rest of his life. If a dog is thrashed it will not go back to the place where it was punished. No bird will be caught again in the same trap."*

Above all the Master warns John of God to be especially on his guard in dealings with women. This was by no means some sort of anti-feminist position, because Avila had many women present in the circle of his friends. What really frightened him was when he heard about John of God's visits to the brothels: *"Find the time to pray. Go to Mass every day and listen to a sermon on Sundays. It would not profit you at all to pull others out of the mire and end up getting stuck in it yourself. That is why I repeat, make sure that you set time apart for prayer, go to daily Mass and listen to the Sunday sermon. Watch out for yourself as far as women are concerned. You already know how the devil can use them to trip up and trap God's servants. Remember how David sinned through desiring one. Also how his son Solomon did the same on account of many, even losing his mind to the extent of filling up God's Temple with idols. We should be fearful of falling since we are even more fragile than they were. So let us learn from the mistakes of others. Don't fool yourself by saying that you just want to be helpful, because when prudence is lacking, there is danger lurking behind even good desires. Helping someone else counts for nothing if one's own soul is wounded in the process."*

The advice was serious and it would be good to know whether it referred to something that John of God had written to him in a letter. A letter which, sad to say, we do not have.

Something strange happened to John of God, but we do not know its nature.

Not one of the specialists I have seen, who analyses this rare passage of the third letter of the master with its somewhat dramatic flavour, can tell us what happened. I am quoting this curious text as follows, but John of God's letter to Master Avila, which has been lost, would have filled in the details. Some person of flesh and blood, 'tempted' John of God, offering to free him of all his debts. Whether male or female or to what purpose we do not know.

"That person, who said he would pay your debts if you quit the other things you do, must be the very devil in human form. He was trying to deceive you by telling you that there was no sin in it. His aim was to make you lose the vocation to which you have been called by God. This is what St. Paul has to say about it: 'Lead a life worthy of the vocation to which you were called.' For instance, should God want me to serve him as an administrator, and I for my part would rather be a swineherd than do that, then I would be sinning against him. I would be accountable to him for not following his call. So Brother, if some person appears before you in shining splendour saying that he is an angel of God and says this to you, he is none other than the devil himself. Tell him that you never want to leave the path that God has set you upon. God tells us in the Gospel that 'anyone who stands firm to the end, will be saved.' Read that passage often and God will keep you from all harm. Amen."

Good for you, Brother John. Stick to what you are doing to the very end.

He loved Jesus Christ above all things and 'saw him present' in the underprivileged. John of God did what he could, in truth leaving no stone unturned. Today this adherence to the humanity of Christ is called 'Christocentricity'.

By living Christocentric spirituality, Jesus Christ is the clear motive of John of God's actions, his solidarity with the poor, going beyond any philanthropic approach. He placed unlimited confidence in the heart of Jesus and it appears this is where found his abode.

John of God knew that in practising charity he, *"put himself alongside the suffering Christ."* These days we foolishly translate into cold formulas some thoughts that seem 'too sentimental'. But Pius XI in his splendid encyclical, *'Quas Primas'*, set out theological reflections that opened up a wealth of spiritual treasures flowing from the unifying presence of the person of Christ. Jesus knew, in every moment of his life that we, his brothers and sisters, form with him the historic caravan of the centuries. That is to say 'he had us in mind', therefore he saved us, thus he redeemed us. Therefore, we must make ourselves present to him in his life in Palastine with sentiments of love and *compassion* and accompany him in his agony in Gethsemane, in the Praetorium, on the way to Calvary and upon the Cross. This *participating presence* was John of God's every night, as he carried some sick person on his shoulders.

To the Blessed Virgin Mary, John of God paid a most beautiful compliment calling her, *"Our Lady the Virgin Mary always entire."* By calling the Immaculate Virgin *"entire"* he released a torrent of endearment.

He was a man of prayer: Castro emphasises this. *"He was busy during the day and prayed at night."* Witnesses recorded seeing him, *"with his rosary beads in his hand,"* or *"carrying a crucifix."* They said, *"His words were modest, humble and he always had the name of God upon his lips."*

He was seen to be a penitent, submitting himself to mortification that would have been *"a great deal for any healthy and sound body to endure."* He put up with his lot, eating little, except when some friendly family forced him. In his hospital he was content, *"to eat simple dishes, which usually consisted of a baked onion."* He fasted frequently and did penance, sleeping roughly *"on a mat on the ground with a stone for his head to rest on"* or *"covering himself with a piece of old blanket; and sometimes he slept on a trolley which used to belong to a cripple... in a narrow space beneath the stairs."*

He had friends and was very content: *"He went to the patients and comforted them with words of encouragement. He washed them and showed them kindness. This was his usual way of doing things, and he always had a smiling and cheerful face. It was easy to see with what joy he carried out these duties. He always received everyone with great love."*

His reputation for holiness circulated throughout Granada,

causing everyone to look at him in amazement. Like a crystal vase his life was transparent, people saw him for what he was. Therefore they all liked him, in fact, loved him, *"He was the apple of the eye of all who lived at Granada,"* where he tried to help everyone, *"as if he himself was quite well off."*

There were also those who loved him from a distance. These had the good fortune to be the recipients of his letters. He wrote a total of six, four of which I have referred to already. In addition, he wrote another to both Gutierre Lasso and the Duchess of Sessa.

If he wrote others, and he almost certainly did, there were probably not too many. Some would have been sent to Master Avila for his 'advice on matters of conscience' and for his 'consultation'. Five of the six were presented when the Beatification Process was in session. Four are conserved in their original text, and the other two are authentic copies. They are brief, in all, only a total of 22 hand-written pages. Five of them are conserved in the archives of the General Curia of the Hospitaller Order in Rome while one of the letters to the Duchess of Sessa is conserved in the 'Camarín' of the Granada Basilica.

Earlier I pointed out that he 'probably' never learned how to write. Experts in calligraphy say that the same scribe wrote three of the four original letters, the text indicating that John of God dictated them at some speed without hesitation and straight from his heart withour the slightest pretence at literary style.

The signature, which he placed on his letters, presents an exciting enigma.

I have cited and copied substantial fragments from John of God's letters and have constantly turned to the biography by Castro and to quotations of many witnesses.

The mode of speaking and writing in the 16th and 17th centuries is quaint to our ears. Often the roundabout manner, punctuation, accents, or the absence thereof, create difficulties in understanding the meaning of a phrase.

I confess that I have liberally transcribed the texts but only as far as their graphic style is concerned. I quoted the phrases of the text with absolute fidelity, literally. However, I have facilitated their reading by changing the odd letter, completing full stops and commas to comply with modern tastes and adding some accents. I have made certain that none of these touch-ups have abused the original ancient text, and at the same time I have endeavoured to maintain the aroma of their archaic flavour.

I am not disturbed by having liberally harmonised the ancient script to make it intelligent for you, our modern readers.

John of God signed his letters but in trying to decipher his signature we enter into the detective's world. Why did he not sign his 'official' name given to him by Bishop Muñoz, John of God? Even if he could not write, at least he could have learned how to put down some recognisable traces of his complete name.

Furthermore, that name of his seemed to him so 'sacred', so 'excessive', that when he heard it said by others, or dictated it himself, he always added some words of his own, as if begging pardon of the Lord, as well as of those whom he was addressing: *"John of God, if God so wills it."*

The three letters forming the signature that appears at the end of each dictated letter make it evident that they are his. A receipt for a donation is also signed at the bottom with the same letters: *"Signed in my name at Granada on 6 December 1548, with these my three letters."* They are identical to those on the letters.

Now please look attentively at the three letters of 'his signature'. They were written by his hand and are placed at the end of each of the four extant original letters – you recall that two other letters are copies of originals – so with the receipt and the four originals, we have five examples of John of God's signature.

His three letters, in these five signatures, besides being writings, are 'drawings'; of trembling features awkwardly drawn. It was an effort for him to make them identical but he was consistent – they are always alike. They were written somewhat out of proportion to the measurement of the document.

Each signature comprises three letters. The first is a 'Y' with the tail, typically for those days, facing the right, not to the left as it does today. It has a horizontal dash, which can indicate, or be an abbreviation for, devotion to the Cross. If it is an abbreviation, it would seem to indicate reading 'Yo' [I].

The second letter is more controversial. Handwriting experts are in doubt as to whether it is a 'P' an 'F' or an 'S'. The letter 'S' of the period was written the way that we now usually write 'F' by hand. John of God also attached a horizontal line for devotion, or as an abbreviation; if for the latter, we all know that many words can be 'abbreviated'.

The third is clearly an 'O', if not a letter, then certainly, a circular symbol. It is an intriguing question how we are to interpret this signature which constitutes the only three letters of his writing. The many interpretations by the experts 'up to now' are as follows:

The first few would have to be rejected because they would require John of God to have mastered the Latin language, which is unthinkable.

- *"Yohannes Feci Opus"* - *'John did this'*, *which is to say "I John am responsibe for this writing."*
- *"Yohannes (Caritatis) Fratrum Ordinis"* - *"John of the Brothers of the Order of Charity."*
- *"Yohannes Frater Omnium"* - *"John everybody's brother."*

In all three cases it is necessary to substitute the 'I' or the 'J' of John (Iuan-Juan) for a 'Y'. It is difficult to believe that any informed person would accept this explanation since the 'Hospitaller Order' did not have juridical form at the time of John of God's death.

Other interpretations place emphasis upon the initial "Yo" [I]:

- *"Yo firmo"* [I sign], *leaving the final 'O' as a sort of full stop.*
- *"Yo Fray Cero"* [I Friar Zero] - *the 'O' being converted into a zero: a popular interpretation, but far too 'affected' for the likes of John of God; besides he never used the title 'Fray'* [friar].
- *"Yo Siervo"* [I servant], *with the second letter 'S', not 'F; and the full stop, the intention being that he is the servant (siervo) or slave (sclavo* [esclavo]) *of the sick. This formula permits variations of the 'O' giving this final letter the symbolism of 'Eucharist':* *"Yo Siervo de la Eucaristía"* (I, *the servant of the Eucharist), therefore* "Siervo de Dios"

[Servant of God].
- *"Yo Siervo Omilde"* - *'I the humble servant'*.
- *"Yo Siervo Oropesa"* - It would be very odd were he to refer to his years as a shepherd.

If the 'Y' is accepted as a 'J', we have:
- *"Juan Fernández Oropesa"*- Why Fernández? For *'Ferruz'*, or *'Herruz'*, his employer at Oropesa.
- *"Juan Trabajo Obediencia"* [John Work Obedience], this converts the 'F' or 'S' into a 'T'.

I will note three interpretations based upon historic factors.

a) The first is the protocol for using a regular character when signing before a notary. During the second half of the 16th century, documents carried the signature *"Yo... otorgo"* [I consent to], or *"Yo... soy testigo"* [I am a witness]. This perfectly explains the 'Y' [I], but still leaves the next two letters unexplained.

b) Perhaps John of God signed as a 'foreigner', a Portuguese living in Spain: *"Yo del Foro Odioso"* [I of the Odious Forum]. This was a type of identity card that distinguished foreigners from citizens. Those born in the country were classified as being *"del Foro Favorable"* (of the Favourable Forum), and foreigners were of the *"Foro Odioso."* But to apply this qualification to his signature was a statement that he, a foreigner, was carrying out an illegal transaction. It was also convenient for John of God to put behind him such recognition, for, besides being 'Portuguese', some might find out he was a 'Jew'.

c) Giuseppe Magliozzi, a keen researcher on John of God, proposed the brilliant theory that John of God took as his signature the initials 'Y' and 'F', those of the Catholic Monarchs Isabella [Ysabella] and Ferdinand, founders of the Granada Royal Hospital where he was admitted as a *madman*. He saw these letters repeatedly occurring on the Gothic frieze decorating the patio of the hospital chapel. Offended at seeing the terrible treatment the patients were receiving, which was very much against the desired ideal of the Monarchs, John of God, in order to make amends, chose as his monograme the initials 'Y' and 'F'. He added an 'O' as an abbreviation for 'obedeciendo' [obeying] or rather, John of God 'obeys'. He realised that the instructions left by the Catholic Monarchs when they established the hospital, were applied to the ideals of assistance, but he saw these being trampled underfoot by the administration of the Granada Royal Hospital.

I have left the most probable interpretation to last. Even here, there is cause for doubt that the signature of John of God carried with its letters a direct reference to Our Lord Jesus Christ, with an abbreviation similar to those used by Christians of the early Church.

The signature of John of God would therefore be an anagram of Christ, composed, since the early days of the Church, of the Greek letters 'X' and 'P'. John of God adds to these a horizontal line suggesting a cross and an 'O' at the end signifying his presence as "*obediente*" [obedient] or "*omilde*" [humble].

Thus, the signature would have the value of an invocation like that of Christopher Columbus who signed himself "*XPO ferens*", bearer of Christ.

Still, how do you explain the substitution of the initial 'X' with a 'Y'? Raquel Jardim, Countess of Nova Goa, solves the difficulty by saying that John of God substituted the Greek 'X' for the Merovingian 'X', of the ancient Franks, which was written as 'Y'. So far, no researching archivist has been able to decipher the mystery!

Do John of God's letters reflect his intimate life, spirituality, character, disposition and his affinity with the mysterious presence of God? They do, up to a certain point, because we are treating of 'straightforward' letters *written for a specific purpose.*

Writing to young Luis Bautista, we see how he answers the question asked by this vacillating immature candidate for John of God's work of charity. He answers him kindly and frankly. As he speaks to the young man he throws some light on his own experiences, "*I am so often negligent and betray him (God) even though I am truly sorry for this, it should make me even more sorry.*"

The text of the letter to Luis Bautista contains some very good advice for a program of evangelical perfection, and we can see John of God's own life reflected therein. In the first he even surprised himself for having written it: "*Always have charity, for where there is no charity there is no God.*"

In another, the young man is reminded that he should

come with his mind made up to spend the rest of his life in the work: *"Remember how St. Bartholomew was flayed until the skin and sinew was torn from his body. If you do come here, it is going to be like that."* John of God had invested charity with mercy, and we know only too well that he placed no limits upon the duties he undertook. He truly shed his own *"skin and sinew."*

The other five letters are 'hurriedly' written and openly ask for aid at worrying times of urgent necessity, from two of his greatest friends – Gutierre Lasso at Málaga and his dear *Duquesita*. Clearly these letters carry ascetic reflections, spiritual advice and devotional practices. He speaks of the elementary but very solid ideas about Christian formation that he had learned during the years of his childhood and youth at Oropesa. But each phrase indicates how impressively strong was the 'illumination' that he had experienced and endured. This would never be dimmed. John of God lives what I dare to call a *latreutic attitude*, one of permanent adoration of God. We can glean this from the way his letters close:

"Your lesser and disobedient brother John of God, dying should God so will, yet remaining silent and hoping in God. My desire is for the salvation of all, as much as my own. Amen Jesus" What humility, what confidence and what thoughtfulness lie behind these words!

John of God passes on the divine mercy which he has received to the sufferers, who are the 'abode' of Jesus Christ, who 'lives' within the person of the poor, a discovery he made when his eyes were opened at the time of his illumination.

To *"stay with them"* was the same as identifying oneself with Christ. John of God accepted his own annihilation, his *'kenosis'*. Just as Christ humbled himself, so he did too and, with Christ, he undertook his work of service and redemption. Sánchez in his doctrinal thesis describes correctly the dynamic unity with which the Holy Spirit guided John of God's personal path, as *"annihilation to service."* This unification situated John of God *"within poverty and suffering."* He does not live there in isolation but he *"belongs"* and enters into the redemptive state where Jesus Christ *"experiences"* the sacrifice of salvation.

For me, John of God's 'illumination' runs parallel to that of John of the Cross. Both men were 'enraptured' and dazzled. John of the Cross emerged from the mysterious cloud to teach believers the way to climb the spiritual mountain of prayer. John of God *"re-emerged"* to submerge himself in the lives of the suffering, bringing

God's mercy to them. What Valentín Riesco calls John of God's *"essential harmony"* came from this fusion of himself with Christ in the poor.

More than harmony came to him. There was an abundant harvest of charismatic attitudes. His respect for the person of the sick, his attention to the whole person, 'body and soul', his acceptance and affability towards others gave him an abounding and profound capacity to make friends, to give and receive friendship.

He did not know who, or what, he was but the 'angels' were certainly at his side. Maybe he knew that, for he was surely a man in the same team as the good angels, wherever they stood in relation to him - before, behind, on his left or on his right.

There was a story, half legend-half fact, that spread throughout Granada. In the chapel of Santa Caridad at Seville is a masterpiece by Murillo that depicts John of God carrying a sick man upon his shoulders and collapsing beneath the weight. The Archangel Raphael is helping him. In the background the night is dark and John of God is unaware of the angelic assistance.

Who was this man of mercy who carried poor unfortunates upon his shoulders?

Neither he or his patients ever found out but the Archangel knew and always remained with John of God whose eyes only see the suffering brother or sister, a fact that astounded Lope de Vega:

The poor he loved intensely, it was such a great grace,
That if an angel and a beggar he might meet face to face,
The angel he would leave and the poor man he'd embrace.

Notes to Chapter 34

* Francisca de Perea was witness #41 at the Granada beatification process and she spoke in the section of witnesses who personally knew John of God. For the Perea family see M. de Mina *Visitar la Granada de San Juan de Dios*, op.cit., 228-231: They lived in a house next to the Royal Chancellery where the jail was later built *"next to the palace of Los Pisa."* For the couple Pedro and Magdalena Bobadilla, see M. de Mina, *'Anotaciones'*, *Fondo Documental*, op.cit., Archive of Los Pisa, Granada, *Familia Bobadilla*. For the sieve maker who was a witness at the Jeronymite case, see the end notes to chapter 21.
* For the fall of John of God in the pond at the palace of the Inquisition, see Francisco de Castro, op.cit., chapter 15. For the furious prostitute, ibid. Felipe de Alays was witness #13 at the Granada beatification process (M. Gomez Moreno,

San Juan de Dios, Primicias etc., op.cit., 'Floreto' 214).

* Orators and writers frequently call John of God an 'adventurer'; valid for all, G. Antropius, *La Spiritualité de l'Orde Hospitalier de Saint Jean de Dieu*, Paris 1950, 80: *"The life of St. John of God is an immense adventure..."*

* José María Pemán, to who belongs the references on *"Andalusian exaggeration"* said this in his discourse at the Literary Contest celebrated at Granada on 12 June 1950 on the occasion of the 4th centenary of the death of John of God: *Cf. La Caridad*, special edition, Mondragón, (Guipúzcoa) 1950. Special edition: *Juegos florales* IV C. De la muerte, Madrid 1951.

* Certain vicissitudes regarding the body and relics of John of God are in M. Gomez Moreno, *San Juan de Dios, Primicias etc.*, op.cit., 297-308. The intervention - 'intention to steal' by Fray Dionisio Celi: see J. Sánchez, *Kénosis*, etc., op.cit., 41 #53. For the history and description of the basilica of St. John of God at Granada see A. Gallego Burín *Granada*, op.cit., 295-297. The latest identification of the relics was made on 22 Jan. 1995 during the celebrations of the 5th centenary of the birth of John of God. Present were Archbishop Méndez Aseno of Granada, the Prior General of the Hospitaller Order, Br. Pacual Piles, and the General Council: J. J. Hernández, *Solemne apertura de la urna de los restos de San Juan de Dios:* (monthly supplement to the magazine 'Juan Ciudad', Feb. 1995) 206.

* Matías de Mina has classified 89 witnesses who personally knew John of God, in his *'Anotaciones'*, *Fondo Documental*, op.cit., Archive of Los Pisa, Granada, notes have been made regarding each witness.

* Many witnesses gave evidence to the physical appearance of John of God and to give them would be indeterminable. The only discordant voice came from Antón Rodríguez, the porter at the Archbishop's house who spoke simultaneously of John of God and Antón Martín: Cf. M. Gomez Moreno *San Juan de Dios, Primicias etc.*, op.cit., 'Floreto' #256. Antón de Govea, Vida y muerte, etc., 14; "Tall in body, robust and bearded and of such a stamp that showed he was an energetic man."

* About the habit given by Bishop Muñoz, see R. M. Saucedo, *Ensayos, etc.*, op.cit., 'Paz y Caridad' 18 (1952) 288-290, he is correct (except where he says it was given by Bishop Ramíroz de Fuenleal): *"It was not a religious habit, but simply a decent set of clothes similar to those used by peasants of that period. It was a short jacket, closed at the front and back and open at the sides which came as far down as the knees."* Did it have a hood? Saucedo thinks it did as there are statements saying so from brothers at the Granada hospital in later years.

* The statement relating to the portrait by Sánchez Coello and the journey of Domingo Benedicto to the Court came from the testimony of the witness Estefanía de Vallejo, Toledo beatification process #14. A son of Alonso Sánchez Coello, Juan who was a priest, also testified at the Toledo beatification process on 2 March 1623, he certified to the authenticity of the portrait: see Notes to Chapter 31. Matías de Mina incorporates into his report on the portrait (ibid). A study by Dr. María Kusche author of the work *Sánchez Coello, Hofmaler Philip II, en Vision oder Wirklichkeit. Die Spanische Malerei der Neuzeit*, Munich 1991 the same author describes the portrait in the article *La vera efigies de San Juan de Dios:* Informaciones y Noticias XXII, 127 (1993), 10.

* There is an unpublished study on artistic representations of John of God belonging to the geographer Juan Miguel Larios; *Iconografía de San Juan de Dios en Andalusía*: Typewritten doctrinal thesis by Antonio Moreno Garrido, Department

of History and Art, Faculty of Philosophy and Letters, Granada University, 1995. The thesis comprises eight volumes and four with a repertoire of iconography; from a collection of almost a thousand, 800 are reproduced. Larios gives a complete bibliography on the subject and indicates other important works prior to his own: that of Walter Rother, *Der heiligen Johannes von Gott, apostel der Barmherzigkeit i der bildenen Kunst, en Der Hospitalorden des hooligan Johannes von Gott*, under the direction of G. Schawab, Munich 1932. Larios highlights the interest in the subject by authors who have touched upon it, Russotto, Saucedo and Gómez Moreno at the 1950 fourth centenary of the death of John of God. There was a catalogue issued at the Expositión Iconogáfica held at Granada to mark the 5th centenary of the birth of St. John of God. This exhibition was opened by Prof. Eduardo Quesada as commissioner on 19 Jan. 1996. According to Prof. Larios, the iconography of John of God reflects the basic aspects of the protagonist: his personal asceticism - spirit of penance and sacrifice - and his service of mercy to the sick. Larios's thesis includes the study of symbols in reference to John of God; pomegranate, cross, basket, staff, etc.

* Brother Matías de Mina's TV interview about John of God, appeared on Channel Sur TV, 13 Dec. 1995.
* There is no doubt that Master Avila was aware that John of God was providentially entrusted to him. The phrase by Fray Luis de Granada comes from his *Vida del Padre Maestro Juan de Avila*, in *Obras del Padre Maestro Juan de Avila*, Vol. XIV, Madrid, 1588. G. Magliozzi, *Pagine*, etc., op.cit., 61; he gathers together statements made by disciples of Master Avila and exaggerates the dependence of John of God upon the Master. For the visits of Padre Avila to Granada, see L. Sala Balust-F. Martín Hernández, *Obras completas del santo maestro Juan de Avila, V*, op.cit., for 1542 pp 90-91; for 1543 p 95; for 1548, pp 117-120. Cf. Joaquin Sánchez, *Influencia espiritual del maestro Juan de Avila en San Juan de Dios:* La Caridad 221, (1963) 150-160.
* The letters of Master Avila to John of God see L. Sala Balust-F. Martín Hernández, *Obras completas del santo maestro Juan de Avila*, V: 1st, pp 267-268; 2nd pp 268-270; 3rd pp 518-620. To get an idea of the interest Avila had for the care of the sick, see letter #80, '*A una doncella*', ibid., 370.
* The idea that John of God found a home in the heart of Christ comes from V. Riesco, *Y Dios se hizo hermano*, Madrid 1994, 96. The quote from the encyclical by Pius XI *Quas Primas*, for the institution of the feast of Christ the King, Holy Year 1925: AAS 17 (1925) 593-610. John of God at prayer, see Francisco de Castro op.cit., chapter 18; as a penitent, ibid, chapter 17. Explicit references to his prayer and penance was made at the Granada beatification process by the witnesses: #13 (Felipe de Alayz), #20 (Diego Marín), #25 (Bartolomé de la Cruz), #39 (Inés de Avila), #59 (Inés Núñez). María Guevara gave several details of a night when John of God took refuge in her house: "*He came along with a band of poor people and when they left him, the mother of this witness shut the doors and having given him something to eat, he enclosed himself in the oratory of the house of this witness; and this witness and other people in the house testified, that they saw that he had rolled his trousers up at the knee and was kneeling on the brick floor praying the whole night; except for a hour when he he was able to sleep, he spent all the rest of the time in prayer.*"
* Five letters of John of God were conserved in the Archives of Antón Martín Hospital, Madrid. Copies were made and verified by notaries and sent to the

Rome beatification process. With the passing of the Desamortización Law (suppression of religious orders and confiscation of Church property) in Spain, the letters were sent to Rome early in the 20th century. (Cr. J. Sánchez, *Kénosis*, etc., op.cit., 148-149). The first time they were published was as an annex to A. Govea's *Vida y muerte, etc.*, op.cit. M. García Bravo, Cartas de san Juan de Dios, Rome 1987, this carries a small description of the contents of the letters. There are various editions of the letters, all more or less well produced, but worth special mention is that of O. Marcos, *Cartas y escritos de nuestro glorioso padre San Juan de Dios*, Madrid 1939; also the edition issued by the General Curia of the Hospitaller Order in 1987 (op.cit.). M. Gomez Moreno in his *San Juan de Dios, Primicias etc.*, (op.cit.), pp 129-162. Also, with a later study, J. Cruset, *El Hombre*, etc., op.cit., 143-170. G. Magliozzi - S. Izzo, *San Giovanni di Dio. Lettere*, Rome 1981, G. Magliozzi *Pagine, etc.*, (op.cit.), 455. 458-504. V. Riesco, *Letra viva. Cartas y escritos de San Juan de Dios*, Madrid 1965; J. Gameiro, *Cartas de S. João de Deus e de sue de S. João de Avila*, Braga 1983. O. Marcus discovered the 6th letter in the Granada Basilica and published it under the title *Carta que el Gran Patriarca S. Juan de Dios escribió...*, Granada 1933. Since then it has been incorporated in other editions. Marcus also published the receipt which was discovered in the Episcopal palace, Córdoba, *Espiritualidad de la Orden*: Espiritualidad Hospitalaria (1964) 20.

* For the research on John of God's signature, see G. Russotto, *San Giovanni di Dio e il suo ordine ospedaliero*, Rome 1963, 9-16. Also several magazine articles in various idioms.

* The letters of John of God serve as a permanent source of refection upon their spirituality. Br. Pascual Piles , as Prior General, wrote an unpublished manuscript commenting upon the letters: "*Spirituality of St. John of God taken from his letters*"; Spiritual Exercises, Sant Antoni de Vilamajor, 3-10 Aug. 1994: Cf. G. Russotto, *Spiritualità ospedaliera*, op.cit., his *San Giovanni di Dio e il sup ordine ospedaliero*, Vol. I, op.cit. Cf. G. Antropius, *La Spiritualità dell'Ordine Ospedaliera do S. Giovanni di Dio*, Milan 1951. Cf. J. L. Redrado *Institutos religiosos hoy*, Madrid 1972 209-223. Cf. M. Pajares, *El hombre que sufre, fruente de espiritualidad*, typewritten manuscript. Madrid, Secretariado Interprovincial; of great interest is *Rasgos fundamentales de la espiritualidad del Hermano Hospitaliero de San Juan de Dios*, in "Encuentro de formadores de la península Iberica", Ciempozuelos, July 1991. The Meeting of the St. John of God Brothers and their Co-workers, 27 Nov.- 2 Dec. 1995 in which several papers were given on this subject. Cf. C. Salvaderi, *Incontri con S. Giovanni di Dio*, Turin 1959. Cf. J. Sánchez in his *Kenosis*, etc., op.cit., 149-164, with special reference to the letter to Luis Bautista. Cf. G. Magliozzi, *Un amico a Málaga*, op.cit.

35

THE FIRE AT THE ROYAL HOSPITAL

Granada
1549-1550

Up in Santa Inés - one of the charming little narrow lanes running between the Albaycín and the street beside the Darro – lived the illustrious Agredas family that could boast of its prominent magistrates and jurists. Their splendid villa stands to this day and is full of memories of John of God because it was one place he visited frequently with sick persons on his back on his way to the hospital in the Cuesta Gomérez.

Today as you stroll from the Albaycín to the Alhambra, there is a glorious sense of peace and beauty. It would be quite a different matter if you were carrying someone on your back through those streets long ago. You would certainly need to stop at Santa Inés before climbing up the Cuesta Gomérez .

Before crossing the Darro, John of God usually rested on a bench in the zagúan [covered porch] of the Agreda palace.

The palace is now a girls' primary school. Its front has been renovated but the central patio, staircase, verandahs, rooms and the roof remain almost intact and the bench still exists.

The Agredas came from Soria to Granada early in the 16th century, their forebears probably having participated in the reconquest of the city. It was a traditional juridical family that served their Majesties in important offices as lawyers, law officers, members of the Council of Twenty-four, financiers, canons, and magistrates. Just about everything! They also increased their family fortune by marrying into aristocratic families.

After resting in the porch, John of God would go in and ask for alms. He enjoyed the company of these good friends who welcomed him kindly.

A remarkable thing occurred, to which various witnesses attested at the Beatification Process. One day when John of God was chatting with the Agredas, as he waited for them to bring him food or money, he nonchalantly took a piece of charcoal and drew some lines, on the wall. Amazed at what he had drawn, they asked him, "Why did you sketch a sword?"

In reply he said: *"There will never be a lack of justice in that house,"* because *"they were born to be ministers of justice."* The sword, symbol of justice, was to remain with the Agreda grandees.

These little details passed into Granada's folklaw after his death. The witnesses swore that John of God drew the sword and they noted, above all, that his prophecy came to pass: *"Judges in the*

Ministry of Justice are never lacking among the descendants of the Agredas as well as governors and others in juridical positions. The names of all persons holding important juridical offices in that family would fill a large piece of paper."

A verse referring to the history of the bench, written in the 17th century, has survived the passage of time and runs thus: *"This bench served the Saint as a bed many times... On this same site the Saint sketched a sword."*

It is understandable that John of God began to lose his strength. He was greatly fatigued by his long walks, the continuous coming and going to collect alms and care for the sick. Something was bound to happen!

But before I proceed with that, I want to mention a few little episodes which, occurred during these final years and for which the witnesses at the Beatification Process had solid references as happened with the reported *"prophesy of the sword"* just related.

Our straightforward Castro collected various premonitions attributed to John of God.

One morning he met up with a patient and warned him that the devil was ready to carry off his soul. He listed a load of sins that he had committed, reminding him, *"that he had married a second time while his first wife was still living."* We are told that the patient *"was astonished, saying that nobody in the world knew about it except himself. He asked that a confessor be brought and he made his confession to a friar of St. Francis and received the Most Holy Sacrament before dying with great repentance and devotion."*

There was a woman, also a patient at the hospital, who was hearing loud voices that were making her demented. She screamed out that *"that they were calling her into the Plaza Bibarrambla."* John of God's intuition told him that a demon had entered her heart. So he told her that he knew she *"had been living as a concubine for ten years."* He then *"persuaded her with many kind words, encouraging her to ask God for pardon and confess her sins. She did so and died as a good Christian."*

Another day he told a nurse *"to go to a ward and place a candle in the hand of a little boy"* for he was dying: *"The nurse went and found it so."* The child then expired.

Sadly, John of God began to speak with persons *"very*

devoted to him" of his own death. *"He said he would die between a Friday and a Saturday."* We will see.

Francisco de Castro, when he was the rector of John of God Hospital thirty years after the death of its founder, picked up another important thing that John of God said. This was that *"he was to have many of his habit [brothers] in the ministry of the poor throughout the world, and thus it will come to be fulfilled..."*

I believe it Padre Castro, for you would have known. *"Throughout the world."*

The wanderings of John of God through the streets and plazas of Granada were endless. There was hardly a family that had not run into the alms-seeker. If you follow the lines of his crisscrossing on a map of Granada, you will see how he covered the entire city. Every district had memories of him but certain locations are 'his own', still permeated with his presence. They include the Plaza Nueva, Plaza Santa Ana, the Zacatín, Plaza Bibarrambla, Calle Elvira, the Pescadería, the Cuesta Gomérez and the Bibataubín. There is also the 'sacred' Campo de los Martíres and the open air Cenacle for his own 'Pentecost'. The Los Molinos Gate where he brought in his first loads of firewood. The Albaycín where *"Moors and rascals gathered about him to poke fun at him"* and insult him: *"Tell us good man, what miracles has Christ done?"* His reply was not what they expected. His reply was to ask them if they would not consider his patience with them to be something of a miracle, *"my not becoming angry with your treating me so badly and being offensive to me."*

What a shame there are no documents to record all his sorties into the surrounding area of Granada, and, to a lesser degree, to other Andalusian cities. Nor are there any documents that tell of his journeys, probably quite frequent, to Baena and Cabra, where he was helped affectionately by his *Duquesita* and all the Fernández de Córdobas and the Mendozas. As for other prominent persons and families, their friendship with John of God remains hidden. The Marquess de Ardales, wife of Guzman, Viceroy of Orán, had recently given birth and she would not agree to allow "any titled lord" to be her child's godfather. She wanted John of God, who was staying there at Cabra where the Ardales had their palace. Surely, John of God did not return to Granada empty-handed after that!

Cut into two parts by the Darro, which rapidly flowed towards the Genil, Granada was created by the convergence of two civilizations, the Arab and the Christian. Granada had been an Arab city, and there still remained deep traces of Islam which had thrived for "seven hundred years, five months and thirteen days." The Catholic Monarchs and Charles V took to themselves the duty of bestowing on the 'new Granada' a splendor that emulated that which had been achieved by the Moslems who likened it to "a huge vase of rubies and emeralds."

The heroic Christianity of John of God put spiritual breath into the difficult birth of the new Granada. Meanwhile Pedro Machuca and Diego de Siloé were opening up the urban scene to the influence of the renaissance. They were supported by the noble families whose fathers had participated in the Italian campaigns. John of God introduced charity and mercy into the veins of the city's heart.

It can be historically demonstrated that the Granadinos understood and supported the evangelical witness of the great charity worker, not withstanding the desires of the Moors that will explode into a great drama fifteen years after his death. But Granada surrendered itself to John of God, inscribing his name on the honour role of its sons, native born or adopted, who gave it splendour in the 16th century: Luis de Granada, John de Avila, Diego Hurtado de Mendoza, Alvaro de Bazán, John of the Cross, Francisco Suárez, Jiménez de Quesaba. Recalling the legacy of such illustrious persons, the Granadinos have the custom of displaying a false modesty aimed at eliciting the sayings that celebrate the beauty of Granada. They themselves call it an "unfortunate jumble." But, take no notice, their critics do not trouble them. They adore Granada, the adorable.

But more adorable, more divine, because of John of God the charity worker.

As the year 1549 advanced John of God's health began to deteriorate. He tried to carry on with his usual routine, but his journeys had left their mark on him. It is as though he is being swept ahead by an evil wind. A doctor in attendance on him today would be quite unhappy with his lifestyle, diet, sleeping habits and penance.

Already he has set up a strategy by which his sons will shortly support and carry on his hospital, look after his *vergonzantes* and the night refuge.

The night refuge, attached to the hospital in the Cuesta Gomérez, developed and functioned efficiently. I see it as a forerunner of what, four and a half centuries later, Mother Teresa of Calcutta and our modern night refuges would be doing. Castro called it a *"thing of great assistance"* which, until then, was unknown:

"He set up the kitchen for beggars and pilgrims whom he usually brought in to shelter from the cold and to sleep at night. It was very roomy and so well equipped that it comfortably accommodated more than two hundred poor persons who enjoyed the warmth of the fire which stood in its midst. Everyone had a bench on which to sleep, some on mattresses and others on metal trestles and still others on mats, when there was the need."

He was weary but serene: *"No one ever saw him upset nor heard a cross word pass his lips."* He amazed those who saw him putting up with *"the greatest injuries and affronts,"* he was *"always peaceful and happy."* No matter what happened, John of God remained calm; a smile on his *"laughing face."*

When the grand-daughter of the apothecary Antón was seventeen, the following event took place in the interior patio of her grandfather's house where she was "doing needlework." *"As usual, the blessed father, John of God, came in to seek alms."*

He was accompanied by *"two or three persons"* amongst whom was *"a grumbling roguish young man about twenty years of age."* John of God had promised that in this house, they would hear something that would cheer them up.

The apothecary's wife gave John of God "a silver reale." This goaded the young man into anger and he began to yell out against the poor alms-seeker: *"Look at what this cheat does, what they say about him, and the alms they give him."* Without any further ado, he grabbed the coin and struck John of God a blow. *"Give me another slap if you want to brother,"* John of God said, as he turned the other cheek.

All those who witnessed this *"were angry with the rascal"* and lunged towards him. He ran outside. *"Wishing to give him a good thrashing for the great outrage"* they chased after him into the street shouting, *"Scoundrel, thief, bad Christian!"* John of God, *"clasping Antón Zabán, pleaded that they might let him go; and that they not do any harm to the one who did well to castigate his little donkey which well deserved what it got."* But the servants went on chasing the rascal down the street *"crying out 'stop the rogue!' who disappeared at the Chapel Royal."*

Afterwards, Antón insisted that John of God *"return home and dine with him."*

I view the city of Avila as a treasure trove in which is kept the mystic fragrance of Teresa of Jesus and John of the Cross. I know the folk who live at Avila have every right to live a normal life just like any other modern city on the planet. Nevertheless, it would delight me to see it today, in the style and manner of the 16th century, making it an oasis of peace in the turbulent currents of the times.

I was invited to a conference for historians at Avila where I was to give a talk on the spirituality of John of God comparing it with the 'masters', both male and female, of that region. I suspected that the organisers of the seminar wanted to test the strength of John of God's mysticism to see if it matched that of Teresa and John of the Cross.

Surprisingly, I opened up my heart at Avila telling of my personal close friendship, which has developed in recent years, with John of God.

I thought to explain my research on John of God's 'illumination' from the point of view of 'the psychiatrist's couch' before viewing the question 'from the side of Christianity'.

Let's get down to basics. The goal and aim of the spiritual masters "on the mountain top" or "within the seventh mystic mansion" was to live in the mystery where the love of man blazes in God's glory.

The most accurate biographer of John of God, Francisco de Castro, certifies that *"in all his works he strived to see that they resulted in our Lord's honour and glory."* Through the revelation of the 'illumination' he looked for this "honour and glory" in his own particular way of exercising charity.

The Holy Spirit showed John of God where he would discover Jesus. It was to be where Jesus resided, in the sick, the hungry, the naked, the thirsty, as a prisoner, 'there' he is, 'there' he resides. I know the Gospel tells us this, but does it sink in? Do we really see it? John of God saw it and believed it and decided to put himself with Christ, to stay with him at his side, to carry him on his back, healing his wounds, giving him food and drink.

He lived permanently 'contemplating', by day and night, the mysterious presence – closely attached to Christ, twenty-four hours a day.

Teresa of Jesus wrote that when the soul arrives at the seventh mansion it opens itself up to the rapture of the Most Holy Trinity by means of the grace of mystical marriage: *"The soul remains, I am saying the spirit of this soul, is made one with God."* The soul has arrived at its centre, it reaches lasting peace, nothing disturbs it, nothing distracts it, events brush against it without breaking its order. The subject can work and be occupied without abandoning contemplation. One loves and assists with the will and heart of God himself. One leaves oneself so as to be totally inserted in the mystery of Christ and his Church.

This too is where John of God lived, in the mystery of Christ and his Church "with those who are suffering."

Don Baldmero in his conscientious study of the 'universal call to Christian perfection', speaks of 'privileged Christian experiences': "God wishes to make known the echo of the message of salvation and life, through the medium of prophetic men and women. It is God's wish to actively incarnate the mystery that he has revealed and offered in his Church, his Word, his Eucharist, in his other charisms and in his everlasting charity. These are the impressive witnesses of God."

My dear Don Baldmero, these few lines of yours which I have just copied, tell us to the very letter, the spiritual core of John of God, "the impressive witness."

All Granada wanted to help John of God during this, his final stage. They even organised groups of auxiliaries for the hospital: *"Thus did the Silversmiths' Guild."* This was stated by an old man named Antón Rodríguez who said he was *"now somewhat crippled and waiting for God to take him."* He said that during Holy Week the silversmiths decided to donate to the hospital all the money they received during the penitential procession. As soon as the procession was over, the members of the Silversmiths' Guild went up to the hospital where John of God healed the wounds left by the lashes they inflicted upon themselves. It was already midnight *"when they gave him the money they had collected."* He thanked them *"with devout and kind words full of charity, calling them all his brothers."*

The hospital *"open to everyone"* was where the ill were nursed and the healthy were given help. The hospital in the Cuesta Gomérez was a sensational success, never turning any man or woman away as Castro attests: *"Every sort of illness; fevers, skin diseases and injuries. There were cripples, incurables, the wounded and homeless, poor children and others that he brought in after they had been abandoned at the door; the insane and the mentally retarded."*

He also received all sorts of help from individuals giving a hand or bringing in foodstuffs or money... Thus the hospital came to be considered *"of common benefit"* to the city. Those with 'vocations' were arriving to join the ranks of the brothers.

Furthermore we hear about the sensitive manner in which John of God assisted the *'vergonzantes'*, those persons and families who had fallen on hard times and kept their misery to themselves without daring to ask their society for help. *"He favoured and greatly helped honest women who were in need, maidens, orphans and widows."*

He also assisted gentlemen without asking them for references. At the Alhóndiga Zaida [the grain exchange] *"This witness saw a man dressed in black who appeared to be honest, but he was suffering necessity because he was a litigant in a lawsuit. The aforementioned blessed father John of God, took from his basket a great deal of money and put it into the man's hand consoling him with kind words so that he was very contented."*

Rather than refuse help if there was not enough ready cash for some urgent necessity; *"he gave a letter for some gentleman or devout person, who might aid that need."*

As I was concluding my examination of the documents I realised that at the beginning of this book I referred to the story of the little donkey that kept the thief stuck to its back throughout the night, as a legend. Yet five witnesses swore that the story was true. Surely, all five could not have been joking.

They spoke candidly about this case, one even saying that the whole of Granada was amused when they heard about it. Another claimed the unlucky thief *"was forced to spend the whole night without dismounting from the donkey."* *"He went about the streets without being able to get off its back,"* was the way another told it. The fourth witness explained how *"Brother John of God gave alms to the scoundrel and then sent him on his way with a blessing."* The fifth witness actually named *"Pedro de Marchena"* as the servant who, at that early hour, met the burro and its jockey at the door of the hospital.

Well there you have it! I have discharged my conscience as a critical historian by handing over this portion of the documentation to you.

I want to point out to you something that is very important to John of God's hospitaller legacy. Three years after his death a splendid new hospital was *"constructed for him."* Why "constructed for him"? It was to bear his name, John of God Hospital, and it was to pass into history as the final stage of his Cuesta Gomérez hospital.

In regards to chronological events, we recognise that historians need to situate events for us with the greatest possible exactitude so I refer again to the transfer of the Calle Lucena hospital to the Cuesta Gomérez.

Because even after the expansion of the Lucena hospital in the barrio of the Pescadería, it was still too cramped, John of God had to move to the Cuesta Gomérez, which, in turn, also proved to be too small. Consequently he and his benefactors, especially Master Avila and a band of ladies, decided to draw up a plan to construct a new, big, comfortable hospital. There is no doubt about this and it was well planned.

I repeat here my conviction that the witnesses at the Jeronymite court case confused the dates and used them to suit their own purpose. These witnesses collaborated in the trial because the Hospitaller Brothers called on them to testify on their behalf. I also mentioned that the testimony of the witness, Doña Leonor de Caçeres, needs very careful scrutiny.

Mateo de Santa Cruz gave some important information at the trial regarding the relationship between John of God and Master Avila. Don Mateo calmly said that *"the poor whom the aforementioned John of God kept in the aforementioned Calle de los Gomeles [Cuesta Gomérez] were all moved down to the new hospital"* and added that *"this witness could not remember exactly whether the aforementioned John of God was already dead at the time."* For goodness sake! What are they saying? John of God was already three years in the tomb. Everybody knew that. I have studied the statements made by many of John of God's helpers and twelve years after his death these same witnesses testified again at this trial in which the hospital was defending itself against the interference of the Jeronymites.

I basically hold fast to the story related by Francisco de Castro who dedicated the whole of his 24th chapter to *"what occurred after the death of John of God."*

Antón Martín founded a hospital at Madrid, where the Hospitaller Brothers *"carried their baskets under their arm and not over their shoulder, because they thought they might cause them to bump into the many gentlefolk and important persons with whom they had to meet."* Isn't that a nice little detail! Castro said that the brothers, together with Archbishop Guerrero, decided to build the new hospital. They went ahead and built it with the aid of a great many excellent benefactors. Castro does not refer to Doña Leonor but he does mention Master Avila, both of whom certainly worked towards this goal.

I have good reason to value the information given by Castro because, after all, the new hospital was where he lived as chaplain and where he wrote his book. Yes, he was living right there among the brothers at a time when the hospital had been functioning for only 27 years.

Early in the summer of 1549 a tremendous disaster struck. About eleven o'clock in the morning of Wednesday 3 June the alarm went up throughout the entire city. From the Albaycín to the Vega, people were shouting, *"the Royal Hospital is on fire!"*

A stream of people poured out of the Plaza Nueva and rushed along the Calle Elvira to the gateway opposite the hospital. Others came along the road from the Bibarrambla and the Pescadería, while more came from the narrow alleyways behind the Cathedral building site. Everyone was yelling, *"The Hospital is on fire!"*

Witnesses of the conflagration said people were terrified by the huge column of smoke and the enormous bursts of flames. The citizens of Granada were incredulous that the huge fortress-like building, constructed with stones hauled from Alfacar, could possibly have taken fire.

What had happened? As is usually the case in such events,

the fire started with an accident. The administrators were celebrating a special occasion with a couple of dozen guests who had been invited to a banquet. The guest of honour was Doña Magdalena de Bobadilla. You can be quite sure that during the period when Don Miguel Muñoz administered the hospital, he would never have approved of spending the hospital's scarce resources on banquets! After he left that position Muñoz strongly protested about such practices and even took the matter to the Royal Court.

The Bobadilla family was very generous in its aid to the Royal Hospital and that was why Alonso de Rojas, who succeeded Muñoz as Senior Chaplain, ordered a sumptuous banquet for his guests. The pièce de résistance was *"a calf stuffed with game birds"* roasted on a spit. There are documents to show that the Senior Chaplain's roast calf was *"crammed full with capons, hens, partridges and other exotic game birds."* According to the gastronomy of the time, this was a highly prized dish and was enough to make any mouth water. Even if there were about two dozen guests, this menu would have constituted a very generous portion to each.

Towards eleven o'clock the kitchen hands were ordered to heap more fuel on the fire to accelerate the roast. Then the accident happened. A witness reported a curious detail: *"There was a great fire burning, then along came a madman who threw a canister of oil upon it."* This report seems to indicate that patients were given work to do in the hospital, as our Juan Ciudad had done some years before. The kitchenhand must have decided that some oil would help to improve the fire. The idea worked only too well, for not only did the wood alight, so too did everything else in sight. The flames rose to the height of the kitchen's wooden ceiling *"setting its panels aflame."*

It is easy to imagine how men and women would have fled in sheer terror from the kitchen. Apparently the fire spread quickly and dense smoke shot up the building's ventilators and flames soon followed.

There was a great panic as people ran about screaming. Outside, dozens, hundreds and then thousands of spectators arrived to see the calamity. Records of the day say that *"master carpenters and stonemasons"* were urgently sent for. One of these masons was Juan de Ratia who brought his apprentice with him. It was this young man who gave us an eyewitness account of the event: *"With his own eyes this witness saw how the hospital had such great timber beams, many made of an entire pine, and how these caught fire causing the greatest conflagration this city has ever seen."*

All the church bells rang wildly alerting the whole of Granada to the tragedy. A huge crowd gathered to watch *"the tremendous force of the fire"* from the Field of Triumph at the front of the hospital. The records show that carpenters, ironworkers, stonemasons and various nobles of the Court, including the Marquis de Cerralbo, who later became the Governor of Granada, "did not dare enter"; although the same documents state they attempted to do so but were driven back by the dense smoke which almost asphyxiated them. A water bucket brigade began to work but it had no effect on such an enormous blaze.

The Marquis de Cerralbo decided that the only reasonable solution was to isolate the burning area to stop the fire from passing to the other sections of the hospital. He called upon the officials of the Alhambra to send down the "fire brigade" which they always kept at the ready. He also sent for artillery pieces to blast a firebreak between the blazing section and the rest of the hospital.

Cannons were immediately dispatched from the Alcazaba fortress. They were pulled through the Gate of the Pomegranates, then rumbled down the Cuesta Gomérez at full speed where they crossed the Plaza Nueva and went up the Calle Elvira to the Field of Triumph.

Two women who were present in the crowd watching the fire from this vantage-point remembered the event. They were young at the time, only girls of fifteen and sixteen, but they clearly remembered the military officers issuing an order *"that all pregnant women and all the children be moved away for fear of the artillery."* What a strange order!

A disquieting question now arises. Just how many patients were in the burning section of the hospital? Records made after the event give no indication as to the number. Fortunately there would have been probably no more than about forty or fifty. If the fire had occurred a couple of months earlier, the hospital would have been at its full capacity. Three quarters of its capacity was unoccupied during the summer months. Existing documentation shows that, halfway through the 16th century, the Royal Hospital had two categories of patients in residence. There were the insane who were kept there permanently, and those "diseased with buboes" as syphilis was then called. Venereal disease was prevalent at Granada in those days. The syphilitic patients were given mercuric therapy twice annually at times dictated by the economy, because mercury was very expensive. One session of this mercuric therapy took place in the spring, the other in the autumn. When the therapeutic course was completed the hospital closed down the wards used by those who were "diseased with buboes." This part of the hospital then went into recess until the next session in the spring or autumn.

Since the incendiary occurred during the first week of July, the only patients in residence were the mentally ill. They lived in the big building and occupied the galleries surrounding the second patio on the right-hand side of the hospital. These 'Innocents', as the mentally ill were called, were John of God's companions when he was locked away in this place ten years previously. If any of his fellow inmates were still alive, he would have recognised their faces.

It did not take John of God long to hear of the disaster. At this hour of the morning he was usually occupied visiting the patients at the hospital in the Cuesta Gomérez and listening to the instructions of doctors. Someone came running up from the Plaza Nueva to tell him what had happened. In any case he would have heard the canons of the Alcazaba rumbling past the front of the hospital about the same time. Without a moment's hesitation he ran as fast as he could to the Elvira Gate.

I have resisted the urge to draw a dramatic picture honouring our charity worker, even though the sudden appearance of John of God upon the scene was fixed in the memories of those who witnessed it. Let us just leave the lively description of the incendiary to those persons who narrated how *"blessed John of God"* faced the situation.

The official documents only give bureaucratic data about the damage caused by the fire. The same official records state that the servants tried to evacuate the inmates before they ran for safety themselves. Still, from what witnesses described of the horrifying scene, it can be seen that those responsible for the hospital were so petrified that they were powerless to do anything to quell the flames. They simply became lost among the terrible confusion of the crowd outside.

John of God arrived amidst all this chaos and, as we would expect, he immediately acted without giving a moment's thought to heroics. When he saw the blazing hospital, all he could think of was the plight of the inmates inside. He knew he had to get them out, and what happened next had the whole of Granada holding its breath as he took centre stage putting his life on the line.

Of course he was recognised immediately as he pushed his way through the crowd and ran straight for the door and disappeared inside. Word spread quickly about who the 'daredevil' was.

A calm study of the reports reveals various nuances and contradictions sometimes within the same declaration: There were eyewitnesses who described themselves as *"being there when it happened"* claiming *"this witness testifies what he saw with his own eyes"* or *"this witness saw"* and *"this witness saw him"* and thus *"they related what they saw"*.

"The father of this witness came back and took the mother of this witness and herself to see the fire. They saw it, and this witness saw the blessed father John of God moving about on the roof." Thus began the testimony of another trustworthy witness, our reliable María Guevara whose mother Doña Leonor was called by John of God *"my true sister."* The one who said he used to *"take her by the hand."* It was also said, *"this witness heard her tell everybody that she saw the blessed father John of God."* As the years passed it is likely that fantasy began to excite popular devotion by adding incredible details to this event.

It is important to remember, when putting John of God's feat in its right context, that he knew every nook and cranny of the Royal Hospital. He knew his way about as he entered the patio of the Innocents on the right and ran up the stairs to where the poor mental patients were huddled together in terror. Perhaps, by this time only smoke had entered the wards above this second patio and the flames had yet to appear. John of God rounded the patients up, and carrying some, directed the rest towards the exit. Witnesses saw him coming out and returning several times, each time bringing more to safety. Eventually, he saved them all and not a single life was lost.

A greater risk followed as he returned to try to save as much property as he could. He hurled clothing and personal belongings from the windows into the street below. He was even seen to throw beds out as well. From below they saw him, *"jumping about like a grasshopper along the roof and under the eaves."* They shouted out for him to come down *"and to get away from such a great danger."*

The eyewitnesses repeatedly saw flames whipping about him: *"The fire grew so great that it surrounded him; and this witness and others thought that it had engulfed him. Everyone felt extremely sad and sorry for him."*

John of God was seen once more dashing about inside, and some witnesses said the minutes seemed to pass like an eternity so that all thought that he had been killed.

Luis de Ribera heard the Governor, the Marquis de Cerralbo, shouting: *"Search for the blessed father John of God. He is far more important and useful to us than ten hospitals. But because the fire was so great, nobody took any notice of what he said."*

A great cry of jubilation went up from the crowd and people blessed themselves with the sign of the Cross, when again he was seen appearing in the doorway. To the amazement of all, his habit was unscorched, which as you can imagine, was later attributed to be a miracle. It seems reasonable to me to attribute good sense to John of God not to have crazily rushed about to save the mental patients, but carefully to pick his way to avoid the flames. Surely we can accept and understand the people of Granada who called this event a miracle, having seen John of God on the roof *"without falling and without being burnt."* Some witnesses added that they saw *"his eyelashes and eyebrows had been singed."* Obviously the flames would have caused that and the dense smoke would have severely irritated his eyes.

The fire took several days to completely die down. John of God wanted to hide from the praise that everyone showered upon him: *"Everybody admired him and wanted to get close to him, thanking God because the fire had not struck him down nor harmed him in any way. He was untouched except for having his eyebrows and eyelashes singed."*

The Council of Twenty-four appointed Diego de Siloé, *"a knowledgeable and experienced person"* to make a report on the material damage caused by the calamity. When Siloé submitted his report it stated that the repairs to the structure of the Royal Hospital would take a long time to carry out and be very costly.

The hospital in the Cuesta Gomérez continued on its

normal way with John of God well and truly in control. Each day he allotted time to carrying out a special work of charity for some poor person, a patient or family or someone else in need. Autumn was coming to an end and winter with its chilly air was fast approaching. Granada seemed to have a premonition that John of God was not going to be with them much longer. He was admired and loved in that city as no one else had ever been admired and loved.

John of God, with all the admiration and love bestowed on him, was no longer able to cope with all the things that usually filled his day. Although Granada contributed generously to his charitable work, his hospital was devouring money at a fearful rate. The patients, the itinerants and the foundlings and John of God's other social services all depended on donations. As well as the daily costs of running the hospital, as we know, he was assisting all the flotsam of a resplendent city. There were also the 'beatas', whom he helped. These were poor religious women who, although they had not enclosed themselves within a monastery, lived a nun's life and had to earn their livelihood by doing needlework and other handcrafts at home.

Now the whole city began to notice that his strength was failing and all were concerned for his wellbeing. But, if he just took things a bit easier and quieter, he would be forgetting that inner 'voice' which he heard on that significant day which pointed the way ahead for him and started him on his indefatigable exercise of charity.

John of God was still heavily in debt. Significantly he admitted that he was too afraid to venture out into the streets in case he bumped into a creditor, during this winter of 1549-1550. He dictated a letter to his friend Gutierre Lasso at Málaga telling him about his debts, and speaking of the consolation he received from him. *"Writing to you, really cheers me up, since I feel as if I am actually speaking with you and telling you all my troubles as I know you share them with me."*

This second letter of John of God's to Lasso carries the date 8 January 1550. It was an unusually cold winter that year and his 'wider' family, the poor and the patients, were particularly feeling the cold: *"There are so many poor people turning up here that it often makes me afraid about how I am going to care for them."* Then he relates an impressive list of items to his friend at Málaga: *"Seven or eight reales are needed daily for firewood alone, because this big city is very cold, and especially so now that winter is here. There are so many poor people arriving here at this House of God."*

He lists again the types of patients he receives but he is particularly worried about the itinerants who come to be nourished at his kitchen: *"There are so many pilgrims and itinerants arriving here. We give them the use of a stove and supply them with water, salt and pots so they can cook their meals."* He points out that this extra cost upsets the balance of his budget, because *"there is no income for this."*

As well as depending on donations, John of God had to borrow money and he also had to buy items on credit: *"I am owing more than two hundred ducats for shirts, overcoats, shoes, sheets, and blankets, and many other things that are necessary."* He confesses that when there are not enough funds to cover the running costs they simply go hungry. *"It makes me very sad to see so many of my poor suffering brothers and sister, my neighbours, in such great need both in body and soul, and yet I am unable to help them."*

Nevertheless, there was not the slightest hint that John of God lacked confidence in divine assistance. This letter to his friend is full of Christian sentiments of trust: *"But Jesus Christ provides everything."* These following lines give a clear glimpse into his great intimacy. *"I put my trust in Jesus Christ alone and I am certain that he will bring me out of this mess because he knows what is in my heart. I have always said that a man is cursed who puts his trust in men rather than in Jesus Christ. Like it or not, he is going to be let down by men, but Jesus Christ is faithful and constant. Yes, Jesus Christ provides for everything. May everlasting thanks be given to him. Amen Jesus."*

This letter to Gutierre Lasso was born out of urgency. John of God needed to get some money sent up from Málaga. He had been named the beneficiary of the legacy of a patient who died at the Gomerez hospital. It was a vineyard at Málaga: *"He left certain goods and a vineyard to this house."* It appears that the annual rent from this property would yield very little and it would barely be worth the trouble to send anyone to Málaga to collect it.

John of God asked Gutierre Lasso to sell the property and to send the proceeds to him at Granada. *"I will buy some clothing for the poor with the money that he brings back to me, and they shall pray to God for the soul of him who left the bequest. I will also use it to pay what is owing on meat and oil, as they don't want to give me any further credit since I owe so much already. I am holding them off with the promise that*

I will soon be getting some money from Málaga."

He ended his letter as always by sending his best wishes to Gutierre's family and to the Bishop. Halfway through this hurriedly dictated letter, he says something that does not seem to fit the logic of the rest of the letter. He introduces to his friend a precious confidence in reference to his Christian faith and practice. I thought it would be worthwhile dividing this paragraph into sections in order to savour it better.

John of God first asks Gutierre to pray for him: *"Never cease praying to Jesus Christ for me so that he may grant me grace and strength, without which I could never resist nor overcome the world, the flesh and the devil."* These are the three classic enemies of the soul, and he would have first learned this when he was a child attending church at Torralba de Oropesa.

Then he continues to enumerate the virtues that he considers to be of priority. *"Ask that he would grant me humility, patience and charity towards my neighbour,"* and that *"he grant me the grace to truly confess all my sins and obey my confessor, scorning my own self-opinion for the love of Jesus Christ."* John of God sincerely and seriously considered himself a sinner:

To this spontaneous piece of self-revelation he adds a profession of faith. It is a significant paragraph for at this time in history, the sparks of heresy were coming in from Germany and England: *"I do firmly and sincerely accept and believe what holy Mother Church professes and believes. I stand firm on that, sealing and locking it with my key."* This well-turned expression of John of God's faith is enough to merit a smile, because it is so forceful. Just imagine him sealing and locking his creed with his key, which is what he called his faith.

In conclusion John of God says he desires the salvation of Gutierre's soul, and he quotes a popular verse:

"In this life of misery
Salvation must be sought.
Good living is the key,
All else is really naught."

He finishes with what could be called his 'identity card': *"Your disobedient little brother John of God, dying should God so will it, nevertheless remaining silent. My hope is in God and I desire the salvation of everyone just as much as my own. Amen Jesus."* He then adds his signature to the letter.

Archbishop Guerrero summoned John of God to his palace. He had something he wanted to say to him and he wanted to say it to his face.

Castro uses an odd word in his book to describe John of God at this period of his life. He says he "disjointed himself" as a consequence of his striving "to remedy the troubles of so many people." What really put him out of joint was his practice of going out to seek alms in the freezing cold of a bitter winter. Although he concealed his own bitter sufferings from others, everyone could see that he was becoming "*so thin and weakened.*"

His rescue of others from the fire at the Royal Hospital had increased his fame, which spread even to distant villages. They concocted legends about him that lauded his heroism and marked him out as a miracle worker. Sometimes these tales had some basis in actuality, but at today's distance from the events it is impossible for us to sift fiction from fact.

Somebody produced an anecdote about a man whose neighbour was so desperately poor and depressed that he decided to hang himself. He went out into a field at daybreak, but whom should he meet but John of God who took the rope out of his hand. After dissuading the miserable and suicidal man, he promised to help him in the support of his children.

Someone else said it was certain that "*on more than one occasion*" while blessed John of God was washing his patient's feet, he was surprised to see the stigmata of the Passion of Christ on them. When he raised his eyes, he saw the patient transformed into the Lord Jesus who said to him: "*John of God, when you wash the feet of the poor you wash mine.*"

What was proven fact, verified by various persons, was the manner in which John of God directly aided the families of *vergonzantes*. He gave money or provisions to these decent folk who had fallen on hard times. Often he left these things "*in places he had indicated, such as a secret cavity.*"

Two women, one of them the sister-in-law of the master carpenter Mateo Gutiérrez, saw John of God one winter's day "pitifully soaked to the skin." Recognising them, he accepted their invitation to go into their house. They asked him to take his habit off because "it was soaked through and through" and they gave him a blanket to keep himself warm by the fire while they put the wet habit over a heater full of hot coals to dry it. Both women said a marvellous thing occurred: *"sweet smelling vapours arose from the habit and filled the whole house."*

Yes, Granada had placed a halo over its charity worker. The pity was he only had a short time to live. It seems clear that John of God took little care of his own health. He simply carried on as if he still had the same strength as before

An unfortunate episode occurred when winter was well under way and *"it was raining heavily up in the sierra."* The rain melted the snow swelling the River Genil to a dangerous level. The river begins high up in the Sierra Nevada where seven springs empty into a small stream. From there it winds its way towards the north before the tranquil little stream widens to tumble down towards Granada where it widens again and runs parallel with the city. Today, it has been channelled to save it from flooding, but that was not the case in the winter that we are talking about now. Then it swelled alarmingly and brought down enough debris to block the archways under the city bridge and, as Castro notes, it eventually *"rose so high it covered the bridge."*

Someone told John of God that *"the swollen river was bringing down plenty of logs and wood in its torrent, even whole trees."* What that meant to John of God was free firewood, a commodity so necessary to heat his hospital. Never shy or lazy, he rounded up all the *"hardier men in the place"* and off they went *"to a little island in the river that had not yet been covered by the floodwaters."* They used *"a huge tanner's hook"* to grapple the branches and trees out of the raging torrent. This tanner's hook was something like the talons of an eagle and it served well the purpose of bringing wood in from the flooded river. This was a real windfall for John of God who wanted to *"provide light and heat for his poor folk."*

There was a certain danger in doing this and they got off the island *"which was only formed of sand"* just in time, before it was covered by the river.

Now, in the midst of all this, Archbishop Guerrero calls him to his palace.

This call did not come as a surprise because the Archbishop had given donations to John of God on previous occasions. So off he went, but he was in for a surprise on this occasion because Don Pedro wanted to scold him. A gentle ticking off, but a serious one nevertheless.

There are always interfering busybodies, whether in good faith or with sour grapes, who set themselves up as guardians of morals. Sometimes they are consumed by envy and are just too ready to accuse others in order to tarnish their image. These meddlesome persons took their tittle-tattle, which this time concerned John of God, to the Archbishop. They went about their accusations in a roundabout way, as such persons usually do, because they did not want to openly accuse a man of such reputation. In every age there are pests like these. They praised the charity worker, while at the same time they denounced him to the Archbishop. They accused John of God of grave irregularities at the hospital using carefully chosen words, beginning with praise before attacking the one they accused.

Thanks to Francisco de Castro we know in detail, exactly what they said to the Archbishop. Castro puts it in the form of a dialogue and it's nice to know that these busybodies fell on their own swords.

John of God began the interview confidently: *"What do you want of me good father and prelate?"* Don Pedro began: *"Brother John of God, it has come to my knowledge..."* and then he went on with a list of complaints. He cited them one by one starting with the claim that the hospital *"was full of malingerers who were quite capable of doing work and who should not be staying there but rather move out and find jobs for themselves."* Worse still, the hospital was sheltering women of bad repute, *"who were dishonest."* I have no doubt that these interferring busybodies rolled their eyes in sanctimonious horror at what was happening. They would like to have gone on and on with their gossip, but they said they wanted to have these disreputable types sent away from the hospital to save John of God's reputation.

Poor John of God was flabbergasted. He listened humbly and attentively to what the Archbishop said, then he gave a straightforward Christian reply. I have broken this down in order to highlight it: *"My Father, good Prelate, it is I alone who am the wicked, incorrigible and useless one."* John of God was not going to throw the blame onto anyone else, he took full responsibility himself: *"I alone deserve to be thrown out of the House of God."*

Consider here Lord Archbishop, how John of God has now resolutely introduced a dialectic element into this dialogue. You see, the hospital is not yours to say who comes and goes from it. Much less does it concern those busybodies, because the hospital belongs to God, it is the house of God.

John of God continues his defence of the poor: *"The poor folk staying at the hospital are good and I know of no vice in them."* Then he launches straight into the heart of the matter: *"There can be no reason at all to throw these abandoned and afflicted people out of their house, because every day God lets his sun shine upon the good and bad alike."* A house that belongs to God, the house of God, is something that concerns the poor children of God. Could he have made a clearer or more impeccable a reply?

Archbishop Guerrero had been a master of theology for many years, but at none of the universities of Sigüenza, Alcalá or Salamanca had he ever heard any professor give a finer or clearer theological reasoning than that which he had just heard from the charity worker. The Archbishop recognised *"the paternal love and tender affection John of God had for his poor people, even going so far as to take upon himself the faults imputed to them."* Don Pedro Guerrero gave him his blessing: *"Brother John, go in peace. I give you permission to do exactly as you wish in your hospital and do so as if it were your own home."*

Notes to Chapter 35

* In reference to the sword painted by John of God: among the witnesses were two religious who did not know him personally, nevertheless they were good witnesses. One was Fray Luis de Santisteban at Jerez, the other was Fray Juan Hurtado at Córdoba. Padre Hurtado was a Dominican and was born at Granada and could recall what was said of John of God there. He gave his testimony at Córdoba on 4 Jan. 1523. He related the journey of John of God to Cabra to be the godfather of the daughter of the Marquise de Ardales. For a description of the Agreda palace see A. Gallego Burín Granada, op.cit., 341. About the Agreda family see M. de Mina, *'Anotaciones'*, *Fondo Documental*, op.cit., Archive of Los Pisa, Granada, Los caballeros Agreda.

* The 'premonitions' are narrated by Francisco de Castro, op.cit., chapter 18. The insults made to John of God were part of the tesimony of Fray Juan Hurtado, Córdoba beatification process, 4 Jan 1523.

* For the description of the night refuge at the Cuesta Gomérez see Francisco de Castro, op.cit., chapter 14. The case of the attack by the lout upon John of God was part of the testimony of Luisa de Zabán, witness #57 at the Granada beatification process.

* The quote from Baldomero Jiménez Duque comes from his book *Mística: la experiencia del Misterio*, Valencia 1995, 188.

* The episode at the Alhóndiga Zaida [the grain exchange] was related by witness #3 at the Granada beatification process, Melchor Rodríguez. The five witnesses who spoke about the stolen donkey testified at the Granada beatification process: #3 (Antón Rodríguez), #31 (Cristóbal de Herrera), #32 (Baltasar Suárez), #45 (María Oseguera), #47 (Juana Ponce de León). For "Pedro de Marchena" according to M. de Mina, 'Anotaciones', Fondo Documental, op.cit. Also Francisco de Castro op.cit., chapter 15; also various documents belonging to the John of God Hospital, Granada.

* Sánchez Martínez, Kénosis, etc., op.cit., as author of this doctrinal thesis and editor of the first stages of the Jeronymite lawsuit, repeatedly alludes to the research regarding the development of the Granada John of God Hospital. The result of this research was presented at a symposium titled 'Spanish Monks and Monasteries' at San Lorenzo del Escorial from 1-5 Sept. 1995. The text of his subject is on pages 357-401 of the printed report. Sánchez Martínez said he would sooner or later clear the backlog of witnesses at the trial. This would place the declarations in their true value. It is understood that certain contrasting has shaken confidence in the facts given by Castro. I believe it is going too far, because who would believe that a torrent of mixed up dates pouring forth from Leonor de Cárceres would contradict Castro, the chaplain-historian of the same hospital. I believe the soluition of the conflict does not stand in the readiness, maybe after the Lucena hospital and before the purchace of the Cuesta Gomérez one, somebody (could it have been Master Avila?) thought of building a huge hospital on the Jeronymite site but was voted down and told to wait for a better time to carry out such a project. They did not have the means available between 1540 and 1547 to carry out such a grandiose scheme so consequently the Cuesta Gomérez property was decided upon. I am sure that when Sánchez finishes his research we will get to the truth of the matter. As far as I am concerned we have a fundamental fact: the Lucena hospital could not have possibly been transferred during the time of Archbishop Avalos for everything else concurs with this. A summary of the chronological changes is given by G. Magliozzi in his *Lo firma con queste mie tre lettere*, Rome 1995. 47-73, 75-98.

* Féliz Lubelza, *El Hospital Real de Granada*, Granada 1979; & M. L. Morales Zaragoza, *Juan de Dios y sus aportaciones al la Asistencia Hospitaliera*, Madrid 1989 (typewritten thesis, Faculty of Medicine, Complutense University, Madrid), gives the episode and its antecedents in the history of the Royal Hospital. C. Féliz Lubelza, adduces this from the Book of the Juntas de la Diputación [minutes of the Municipal Council] (Granada 1549) which states: "Last Wednesday of the third day of this month of July, the upstairs apartments of the Royal Hospital were destroyed by fire." It is certain that the Señora Bobadilla in whose honour the feast was being held, was not Magdalena, the daughter of Don Pedro Bobadilla, who would have been only four years of age at the time, but was her mother, Magdalena de Guzmán who took the surname of her husband when she married: see M. de Mina, *'Anotaciones', Fondo Documental*, op.cit., Archive of Los Pisa, Granada, "Magdalena de Bobadilla." Also Francisco de Castro, op.cit., chapter 14; Castro gives a brief but rather colourful description of the episode. My guide was the testimony of witnesses at the Granada beatification process: #1 (Juan Lobo), #2 (Pedro de Moya), #3 (Antón Rodrígues), #5 (Gabriel Maldonado), #8 (Pedro López de Eslava), #9 (Juan de Salazar), #10 (Pedro Franco de León), #12 (Marcos

de Perea), #16 (Marcos de Perea), #26 (Domingo Navarro), #29 (Alonso Sánchez Dávila), #31 (Crisóbal de Herrera), #2 (Baltasar Suárez), #33 (Francisca Fernández), #34 (María de la Paz), #35 (Elvira Diáz), #39 (Inés de Avila), #43 (María de Guevara), #45 (María Oseguera), #48 (Luisa de Avila), #49 (Melchora Quixada), #54 (Luisa de la O), #56 (Catalina de Arenas), #57 (Luisa de Ribera), #58 (María de Villavicencio), #59 (Inés Núñez), #64 (Francisca de la Fuente), #65 (Master Bernabé Ruiz). The two women who refered to the military commander telling pregnant woman and children to get away from the sound of the cannons, were Inés de Avila and María Oseguera. Luisa Ribera reported hearing the Corregidor (Governor), the Marquis de Cerralbo, shouting out. The apprentice to the master mason Juan de Ratia was Antón Rodríguez. Cf. C. Féliz Lubelza, El Hospital Real de Granada, op.cit., 173; the reports of the Council are stated here.

* In reference to John of God's breakdown in health see Francisco de Castro, chapter 20. The case of the attempted suicide comes from Alonso Fernández Galiano at the Córdoba beatification process (section of witnesses who did not know John of God). The apparition of Christ in the washing of the feet comes from the priest Alonso Lasso de la Vega, a witness at the Lucena beatification process, 30 Jan. 1623. Others gave similar statements. The episode of the woman and the sister-in-law of Mateo Gutiérrez, came from Bartolomé de Espinisa, Granada beatification process 23 Feb. 1623, (section of witnesses who did not know John of God). The testimony of the gathering of branches and trees from the swollen Genil comes from Baltazar Suárez , witness #23 at the Granada beatification process (witnesses who personally knew John of God); witness # 66, Antón de Morasca

* The accusation against John of God made to the Archbishop and the dialogue that followed comes from Francisco de Castro, see chapter 20. Also witness #3 at the Granada beatification process, Antón Rodríguez explicitly referred to this.

36

JOHN OF GOD ATTEMPTS TO RESCUE A BOY FROM DROWNING AND ENDS UP WITH PNEUMONIA

Granada
1550

The Genil will be the death of John of God. Maybe I am unfair in blaming this beautiful river so cherished by the Granadinos, a nourishing vein of water that gives vitality to a good portion of the fields of Andalusia from east to west. Of course the Guadalquivir gets most of the praise, the Arabs called it the 'Rio Grande', the great river of a fertile basin. The Genil, on account of the quantity of water it brings down from the Sierra Nevada, holds first place among its tributaries. This gave rise to an ancient saying of the Andalusian peasants, *"The Guadalquivir has the fame, but it gets its water from the Genil."*

It so happens that the winter floods brought down branches and trunks from the Sierra Nevada – just the very firewood that John of God needed to warm the patients in his hospital. He was not content to stay at home while all this firewood was being dumped along the riverbank. He considered it an obligation to keep gathering it.

With his energy failing, back he goes to where he will succumb, immersed in the frozen river, to be taken home to die amongst his own people.

My friend, how lovely it is to spend time walking along the banks on either side of the river. Up and down, on one side or the other of the bridge. In John of God's day, there was only the one crossing, a bridge with five Roman arches.

The Darro tumbles along the side of the Alhambra, dividing the residential erea into two. Granada ended here where the Darro empties its waters into the Genil. The Genil rushes down from the Sierra Nevada to become a raging torrent threatening to flood the city before breaking its banks along the lowlands. These days its bed is encased in cement to eliminate the danger of flooding and we can scarcely recognise the landscape of yesteryear where the Genil hastened on its course through Granada.

The Arabs, being a desert people, went wild with delight when they first saw the waters of Granada. Their literature speaks of the city having a thousand rivers with the Sannil (Genil) the greatest. They claimed its waters and fish had curative properties, even magical. Its source is in the freezing body of water fed by springs and brooks at the base of Mount Veleta for its run, with noble force, down to Granada. Poets have described the Genil as hugging the city by its waist. No longer can this be said because asphalt has covered hectares of gardens creating barriers along both sides and even closing one of the five arches. A few years ago the Mayor thought they would have to open a passage for the water by blasting the logjam free of debris.

What were once market gardens and almond groves are today delightful gardens and pathways, of the Salón, Bomba and the Violón.

On notable occasions the Granadinos used to cross the river to visit various places including the convent of the Basilian monks, the hermitage of San Sebastián, which was a Nasrides hermitage and the Genil Fortress, the famous 'Garden of the Queen', purchased from the Sultana Moraima by Isabella La Católica.

This is no place to come to in the middle of winter which it would have been when John of God dived into the river to save a boy. It was early February 1550. I want to describe what that month is like. Come in the fullness of summer, for then you will see young lovers and old folk quietly strolling along these banks. You may even be invited to share a jug of sangria and roast *perdisesasás* – roast potatoes with salt and pepper.

Summer may be fine but I assure you that the early days of winter are magnificent. It is a pity that the highrise units hide from their dwellers the peaks of the Sierra Nevada. At dawn the sun announces the birth of a new day by reflecting its rays across its craggy peaks. Then, like a skier who triumphantly reaches the highest point on the snowline, it rises in a blinding blaze of light similar to its coming out of the sea in a Botticelli painting.

I know Granada also has long dry spells and interminable summers in contrast to the ferocious blizzards when the winter winds come roaring down like beasts abandoning their immense caves. Such is life. The Genil surges down from the Sierra in a tremendous flood, produced by the thawing of the snow and the abundant rains.

We do not know the time, for certain, but it was probably at the break of dawn. John of God, with some of his helpers, came down from the Cuesta Gomérez to the river. He was quite unaware that he was going down there for the last time.

Arriving at the riverbank were "many other poor folk" who also came for firewood. Everyone was getting to work, energetically pulling the piled up branches and logs from the water.

A shriek rang out! *"A boy had carelessly gone into the river over his depth and the current knocked him down and he was carried away."* Men and women began to shout but nobody dared dive into the torrent. John of God did not hesitate, *"to save the boy, he went in deep."*

It proved useless and impossible. The boy drowned. The current had carried him away quickly before John of God could do anything to help him. John of God came out defeated and sad, as Castro attests, *"He was overwhelmed with sadness by it."*

One witness gave a more vivid description of the event. He is a credible witness who reconstructs the scene with likely elements saying that the boy was *"eager, but not very bright."* He had come with of John of God *"wanting to sell the firewood"*; and was close to him when he was hit by the torrent and swept away: *"Blessed John of God, who saw that, threw himself in to save him; both were carried away through one of the arches of the bridge over the Genil."* The water covered him. John of God went in and grasped the boy bringing him to the bank, but he was already dead.

Alonso de Troya's evidence concurs with that of Castro - the freezing water had sapped all the energy from John of God: *"Through being so soaked, he caught the illness from which he died."* It appears they had to carry him back to the Cuesta Gomeles on their shoulders. They made him as comfortable as they could in the hospital where he too became a patient.

Medical historians certify that a case of pneumonia in a body as exhausted as his was, certainly would have been fatal in those days. Six or seven days with a high fever would be enough to consume him. And consume him it did.

His brothers, his friends, the patients, everybody... they all knew that John of God was going to die. He knew it himself. He wanted to dictate a letter. It was to his little Duchess, a final adiós:

"The great love I have always had for you and your humble husband, the good Duke, means that I always have you in mind... I felt I should write this letter, good Duchess, in view of the fact that I do not know if I will ever return to see and talk with you again."

Adiós to his chaste little turtle dove. He leaves her in good hands: *"May Jesus Christ see and talk with you for me."*

It is easy to imagine how shaken everyone at the hospital in the Cuesta Gomérez would have been seeing John of God dying. Granada was shaken.

He dictated his letter: *"The pain caused by my illness is so great that I can hardly speak."* His fatigue even made it difficult to dictate: *"I am not at all sure whether I shall be able to finish this letter."* He continues to speak with the Duchess, dictating cordial paragraphs, kind words, and he gives her two pieces of advice, because he loves her and because he is grateful: *"I owe you for having always helped and supported me with your blessed alms and charity in my undertakings and needs, so as to provide the poor of this holy house of God and many others outside."* So grateful is he that if he should recover his health, he would make it a point to go and see her: *"If I should be restored to health I shall come and see you."*

He had already planned to visit her at Christmas, but that was not to be. Knowing that, he sends her his devout desires by letter: *"Unworthy sinner that I am, I send you my blessing: May God who made and created you, grant you the grace with which you may be saved."*

And now he promises her a gift, which he has prepared for her in case of his death, leaving it in the charge of his employee Angulo, *"who has gone to the Court."* He also takes the opportunity, why not, of asking the Duchess, since he can no longer do so, to take care of the co-worker because *"he and his wife will be very poor."*

It was an unusual gift, a piece of red cloth - *"keep it carefully to remind you of the precious blood of Our Lord Jesus Christ... there is no greater contemplation than the passion of Jesus Christ."* The little piece of cloth had *"three letters embroidered upon it in golden thread."* John of God says *"this is my coat of arms."* He adds: *"I have been guarding this since I first went into battle with the world."*

Who embroidered the piece of cloth? How long had he kept it? Had anyone ever see it before? Not a single clue remains. He could have kept it from the stock he carried when he was a bookseller. Then again, he could have received it from one of his friends.

He explains the symbolic meaning of the three letters as being for, faith *"according to the Church"*; charity, *"first have charity for one's own soul, then for our neighbours "*; and hope, *"in Jesus Christ alone."*

It was embroided with gold thread: *"The letters are in gold. Just as gold, which is a very precious metal, must first be extracted from the earth in which it is found and then refined and purified with fire so that it can shine and have the right colour before it has its true value, so also the soul, which is a very precious jewel."*

Yes, the three embroidered letters symbolise the three theological virtues: *"This cloth has four corners for the four virtues"*, the cardinal virtues. Prudence *"teaches us to act prudently and wisely, seeking the advice of those who are older."* Justice, *"allots to each person what is his and gives to God everything that is of God and to the world that which is of the world."* Temperance, demands *"moderation and sobriety in our use of food, drink and clothing,"* while Fortitude *"greets trial, tribulation and sickness with a smiling face."*

On the reverse is an X-shaped cross that which *"each person who wants to be saved must bear personally in the way God wishes for him and grants him the grace"* He then makes further use of the number three which makes up his letters, declaring, *"We owe God three things: love, service and reverence."* We have to spend time each day *"in prayer, work, and care for your bodily needs... just as a muleteer feeds and looks after his beast so that he can make use of it, so we should give our bodies what they need so that we have the strength to serve Jesus Christ."*

Finally, he reminds the Duchess to keep in mind: *"the hour of death, which none of us can escape; the pain and suffering of hell and the glory and beatitude of paradise."*

He explained these three points of doctrine that had been taught to him with the same composure and conviction employed by the parish priest of Oropesa and Master Avila, saying: *"As regards the first: think how death consumes and destroys everything this miserable world gives us and allows us to take with us nothing but a piece of torn and roughly sewn linen. As regards the second: think how, if we die in mortal sin, we must go and pay for such a fleeting pleasure and momentary enjoyment in the fires of hell - which last forever. As regards the third: reflect on the glory and beatitude that Jesus Christ has reserved for those who serve him and that no eye has seen, nor ear heard, nor heart of man conceived."*

I wondered whether 'the piece of red cloth' actually existed, or if it was instead a spiritual analogy that John of God concocted from his imagination as he dictated this letter to his Duquesita. I don't know, but it appears to be more real and not

17. John of God, above the entrance to the St. John of God hospital, Granada, 1609. The
anonymous sculptor strove to depict the saint in the style of habit that he and the early Brothers
wore.

18. John of God saving patients from the fire at the Royal Hospital. The work is by the Granadino artist M.Gómez Moreno (1880). Courtesy of the Museo de Bellas Artes de Granada.

simply poetic fiction. In either case, if these three letters evoke his enigmatic signature, then there is a certain relationship between his autograph and the cloth.

John of God tires and interrupts his dictation with the final recommendation: "*Above all my sister, always have charity, for this is the mother of all the virtues.*"

He confides to her how intensely he suffers: "*My sister, I am in such pain that I cannot write any more now,*" and indicates that he "*shall rest for a little while, because I want to write you a long letter.*" He will write more if he can. However, suspecting his death is not far away, he concludes: "*I do not know if we shall meet again. May Jesus Christ be with you and all those with you.*"

My Granada friends, fine intellectuals, really love their city, and know its ups and downs intimately. They can explain the secrets of that "unfortunate hodgepodge," the architectural monstrosities that Pepe Guevara condemned to the pillory with the fascinating, caricaturing cartoons by Martinmorales. I divert a little to string together praises for what lies deep within Granada, quietly noticing how pleased it makes the Granadinos when one speaks of the object of their deep love.

The city's inhabitants have a complex psychology with contradictory characteristics. Why not, since it is so ancient and such a 'sleeping beauty'.

The same can be said for its soul, Granada has contradictions woven into the fabric of its mountainous backdrop, its ambience and climate. The tourists are impressed by the sarcastic nicknames the locals have given to the Plaza Nueva, which they call a 'microwave' in summer and a 'refrigerator' in winter. Obviously an exaggeration – but the point is made.

It's a city full of surprises. One time it can be seen as beautiful, perfumed, even laughing, a "hidden water that weeps." But it's a different picture when the weather turns bad, when snow falls on the mountains and ceaseless rain pours onto the plains and a gale, that only demons could conjure up, batters the place for three days and nights in a row.

In modern times, the population manages to defend itself against the inclemency of the weather but halfway through the 16th century it was a different matter. A sudden outburst of the plague or a flooding of the Genil always brought in its wake a great many victims and it was in such a winter that the river claimed John of God.

I believe that John of God's long trek from Granada to the Court at Valladolid and back again was a major factor in undermining his health. But it was the freezing water of the Genil that dealt the final blow. John of God, and all of Granada, knew he was dying.

Courage was a constant quality of John of God. This could be witnessed each night as he brought in the poor and sick; as he went into the blazing Royal Hospital and now, this time, as he dived into the freezing waters of the river. Those who see heroic acts always admire valour. The ancient Greeks said that in order to understand how to be brave we must understand *"what is worthy of fear and what is not."* John of God only had one fear, and that was of failing to exercise the charitable mission to which he had been called. That is why his bravery was a household word.

Now, confined to his bed in the Los Gomeles hospital, the Granadinos saw him as a giant of a man who had come to the end of his life's journey. A constant stream of visitors came to see him. Antón Martín and the brothers carried on the running of the hospital, getting some experience in managing without their 'Elder Brother'. They would have been downcast at the thought of losing John of God and they knew that this was imminent.

I will not permit myself to relate 'possible' ideas and sentiments about these last days of John of God, as this would seem to me to violate a sacred territory. We know of his letter to the Duchess of Sessa and also that he had two major worries.

Firstly, there were his debts. He wanted to have written down the names of those to whom he owed money and the amounts owing. Since he alone knew about them, it might put the reputation and future of the hospital in jeopardy if he left them unattended to, and this was one worry.

Castro notes that *"he was racked with cold tremors and a high temperature"* and the high fever frightened the brothers. However, although they tried everything possible, they could not dissuade him from going out. He rose from his sick bed and *"called for a man who would write for him; and went through the city from house to house to those to whom he was indebted. He went to establish who they were and the quality of the debts, and what he owed; and some had forgotten his debts to them; and thus he put in order everything he owed."*

What a man! John of God is a person of absolute honesty. Concerning the alms that had been given him, for God, he left to the angels, who would note them in the 'Book of Life'. But with regard to the loans that he had promised to repay these were to be discharged by the hospital, according to the written record.

To emphasise his determination to repay, he ordered the debts be copied *"in another book... thus they made two"*. One he tucked away in his bed, to keep with him: and we will discover his intentions later. The copy, *"he ordered to be kept in the hospital so that, if God took him, and one should be lost, then the other would be in safe keeping, and what he owed would be paid, having made that clear."*

Having covered his concern, he succumbed to the fever and was now *"unable to manage."* Nevertheless, while he still had a spark of breath, he attended to his second great concern, his children, the poor, for he was father of his poor. He utilised two means to take care of them. He sent them messages through a third person, and he solicited alms from the persons who came to visit him, amongst them, many *"nobles and citizens"* who were curious about the nature of his illness. These he impressed and they responded to him completely. As well, *"they encouraged his companion Antón Martín so that he would take over in the absence of John of God."*

I must warn you, my dear John of God. Someone who will complicate your departure from this world is on her way to see you. She is Doña Ana Osorio, *"a lady of excellent Christian example"*, and she loves you very much.

Notes to Chapter 36

* For the boy who was drowned, see Francisco de Castro, chapter 20. Alonso de Troya made his statement at the Granada beatification process in the section of 'de oidos' [hearsay].
* John of God getting out of bed to go into the city to fulfil his debts is reported by Francisco de Castro (ibid) chapter 20. Also the last activity from his bedside. Melchor Rodríguez, witness #4 at the Granada beatification process, said "he heard it at the time that blessed John of God had visited his creditors."

37

HONOURED AFTER HIS DEATH

Granada
1550

Doña Ana Osorio wanted to take care of John of God and nurse him back to health; even though the whole of Granada knew he was dying. She was not taking John of God to her palace to die. He wanted to be with his poor folk right up to his last breath. Death should come to him on a rough bed of the Cuesta Gomérez hospital, where a trail of people were coming and going to see him and to ask after him. Granada was concerned. Should the noble lady Osorio have taken him or not?

Ana Osorio's husband was García de Pisa, a member of *the Council of Twenty-four,* and the entire Pisa Osorio family adored John of God. Their palace was one of the sheltering stops for the alms-seeker who called there when overcome by fatigue. Here too, he looked for provisional accommodation for women he rescued from prostitution and he sought abundant sums of money here, when he was extremely hard pushed. The palace-home of Los Pisa occupied a strategic position for John of God's comings and going, just as did that of the Agredas in the little street of Santa Inés. It stood next to the building site of the new Royal Chancellery and its front door was only a few steps to the bridge over the Darro at the Plaza Santa Ana. This made it a convenient stopping place to rest a while when he came down from the Albaycín before tackling the steep climb of the Cuesta Gomeles. It was convenient, too, for meeting poor *vergonzantes,* whom he saved from the embarrassment of having to go up to the Cuesta Gomérez.

Living with Don García, his wife Doña Ana and their children, was an elderly aunt, Doña Catalina, the widowed sister of Don García's father. They were very fine people and both Ana and Catalina *"esteemed and reverenced the blessed John of God because they knew of his great charity and holiness."*

They heard the news of John of God's grave illness from a neighbour, Ana Heredia, the wife of Diego Perea. This couple was friendly with the family and lived only a short distance away in a house that was shortly to be demolished to make way for the new jail being built next to the Royal Chancellery. Señora Perea, her daughters and the housekeeper of the Pisa palace, María Morales, all went up to the hospital to visit John of God and were horrified to see him in such a grave condition.

We possess Doña Ana Osorio's testimony of how she found John of God when she went up to the Cuesta Gomérez, *"He was just lying where they had put him down upon some boards with his basket at his head."* John of God had permitted himself the alleviation of substituting his basket for the stone or block of wood he usually used as a headrest.

Doña Ana knew immediately that in this place the patient was surely condemned to die: *"the little fresh air that reached him there, together with being crowded by the poor, deprived him of any chance of resting a little."*

Without a moment's hesitation, Doña Ana resolved to take him down to her home *"where he could be put to bed and given everything he needed"* in the way of nursing and medication.

To John of God the proposal should have sounded like heavenly music, but he simply smiled and said that *"they should not take him away from his poor folk"* because he wished *"to die among them and be buried."*

Doña Ana knew perfectly well that nothing in the world would make him agree to be moved, so insistence was useless. But she also knew how to find a solution. Doña Ana immediately had recourse to her friend, the Archbishop. She wrote a note to Don Pedro Guerrero notifying him of John of God's grave situation and asking him to order the ill man *"by obedience"* to go to her house. Don Pedro responded immediately, *"In virtue of holy obedience he ordered him to go".*

John of God, my dear dying John of God, try to understand: Doña Ana and the Archbishop, whom you call *"my good father and prelate"*, desire with all their heart, to bring you back to health, healed and saved from death. If you go to another barrio, you die to them and to all Granada, you die to the infinite multitude, your poor people, your patients, the holy recluses your *beatas*, your *vergonzantes* and their families, your prostitutes.

Ana and the Archbishop want your cure so that you can carry on. They do not know the day and hour fixed for you in the calendar of divine providence. If you go with them down to the other side of the riverbank, you know for certain you will die outside your hospital. Besides, it would be less trouble than having to take you down to your burial from the steep and narrow Cuesta Gomérez.

John of God saw it would be fitting to obey since *"he had preached obedience to all."* He declared he was *"beaten"* by what *"they so rightly asked him, for the love of God."*

Doña Ana sent a sedan chair and carriers up to the hospital. John of God was to make the trip down the Cuesta Gomérez to the Pisa palace like a real gentleman. A dying gentleman, none the less.

Neither the Archbishop, nor Doña Ana, not even John of God himself, had the faintest idea of the uproar that was going to erupt when the patients at the hospital heard word that their *'blessed father'* was leaving them. Our friend Castro, always fairly straightforward in his descriptions, gives the details thus: *"John of God was positioned in the chair..."* The patients *"who were able"* got up and *"encircled him"*. *"They wanted to obstruct his departure "because of the great love that they had for him."* However, they were resigned to accept *"without unfortunate resistance and trouble,"* using the only weapons at their disposal, namely *"sighing and weeping."*

"The men and women commenced to carry on with such shrieking and moaning, that even the strongest-hearted broke out in tears."

I can guess how disconcerted were Doña Ana, her friends, companions and servants. John of God, seeing his *"afflicted and weeping"* people, spoke to them:

"My brothers and sisters, God knows that I want to die here amongst you." He had no doubt at all that his hour had come. He made his farewell: *"God is better served, that I might fulfil his will and die without seeing you."*

He embraced them one by one, while they came to ask his blessing *"each one singly."*

"Remain in peace my children; and if we do not see each other any more, pray to your Lord for me".

"At these words they continued howling and saying pitiful things," so much so, that John of God, week and feverish, slumped unconscious into the chair. Castro's simple comment on this pathetic situation was: *"his patients loved him."*

When John of God *"regained consciousness"* Doña Ana, alarmed that the parting might end up in uproar, ordered them to depart at once, *"so as not to give him any more suffering." "They carried him to her home."*

What a situation! Here we have John of God the alms-seeker spending the last few days of his life in the home of one of the noblest families of Granada. They generously give him the best

19. The statue of St. John of God by Filippo della Valle (1698-1770), St. Peter's Basilica, Rome.

20. *John of God with the Virgin and Child, by Andrea Gennaroli (1650), behind the main altar of the Order's hospital on the Tiber Island, Rome.*

treatment and most loving attention. Placed *"by obedience"* under the care of Doña Ana, he offers no resistance: *"He lets them do to him as they will, and he does whatever they tell him to do."*

They removed his tattered habit and dressed him in a nightshirt before putting him to bed in an upstairs room that had a window that looked out upon the peaks of the Sierra Nevada. They brought in a doctor with medications, *"and everything else necessary."* Doña Ana saw to it that the patient lacked nothing because she was determined *"to cure him."*

Because the Pisa-Osorio family, nobles of Granada, had the good fortune of having John of God with them at the time of his final journey, their names and that of their palace remain forever tied to the memory of the blessed charity worker.

We first knew the Member of the Council of Twenty-four, Don García de Pisa, some time back – in 1539 when he was representing the Council in the Board of Trustees of the Royal Hospital, with Don Miguel Muñoz. He signed the admission form for the extraordinary bookseller known as Juan the Portuguese *'gone mad'*. It is logical that Don García would have followed attentively the progress of the *'madman'* turned charity worker, given that his palace was frequently utilised as a base for John of God's charitable activities.

Don García's wife, Ana Osorio, esteemed John of God from the first moment she met him, which according to her own reckoning was sometime between 1542 and 1543, when: *"using holy and devout words he went about this city begging in public by day and night."* Both husband and wife assisted the alms-seeker to establish himself and their home was always open to him.

The Pisa family originally came from Almagro in Campo de Calatrava, which later became the Province of Ciudad Real. Their ancestral home was in the parish of San Bartolomé, but they held the right to be buried in the chapel of San Andrés in the same parish. The family belonged to the group of Conversos, Jewish converts, of which there were many in Ciudad Real. They had to put up with much persecution in the period around 1492 when the Jews were expelled from Spain, but they were saved with the help of the Inquisition in 1495. From then on the family prospered in its financial activities and slowly but surely became integrated among the Old Christians.

Towards the end of the 15th century a certain Don García who was married to María Rodríguez, became head of the family. Their eldest son, Juan Rodrígues de Pisa, appears to have been a judge at the Ciudad

Real Chancellery. He later moved to the Royal Chancellery at Granada where he belonged to His Majesty's Council and occupied the Chair of Oidor (judge) being a deputy to the Cortes and appointed to the Council of Twenty-four. He began his duties as a justice in 1513. Judge Rodríguez de Pisa began to build his new home at the same time as the Royal Chancellery on the site next-door to it which was only a stone's throw from the Santa Ana bridge. His son García inherited the Casa de los Pisa.

A simple entrance in the Gothic style of a central balcony with stone eaves, the Pisa palace had a patio surrounded by marble pillars which supported ornate verandahs of wood. A marble fountain stood in the centre of the patio which lead to large decorative rooms. The staircase to the floor above was covered with a carved wooden ceiling in the Moorish style while the stone banisters were Gothic.

Doña Ana turned one of the upstairs rooms into a sickroom for John of God.

Her husband, García de Pisa, was the eldest son of Juan Rodríguez de Pisa who rose to one of the highest positions in the Kingdom when he was appointed to the Royal Chancellery of Valladolid in 1535. Don García 's wife, Ana, presented him with many children, at least nine, who will conserve *"with enough solicitude"* the surnames *"Pisa-Osorio."* Don García took his father's place as a member of the Council of Twenty-four - that is *regidor* of the city; a position which placed his wife Doña Ana in the cream of Granada's social life. She was of an aristocratic family that came from Galicia when the Catholic Monarchs mustered support from all the aristocracy for the conquest of Granada. Alonso de Osorio records he was under the command of the Gran Capitán at the taking of Jaén, Cazorla and Málaga.

Thus John of God the charity worker, protector of beggars and the sick poor, and loved by one of the great patrician families of Granada, came to die in their home without a word of complaint. Surely before passing into the next world, John of God should do something for the noble families who had always supported his hospital. Without their aid his charitable program would have crumbled. After all, it was their money that he used. It all happened in centuries gone by, but despite the French Revolution and Karl Marx, it is still happening right now as we move into the 21st century. In spite of everything, the world is still divided into rich and poor. Will the rich ever be generous enough to lubricate the gears of society in a just distribution of the world's goods? Let us hope so. The wealthy of Granada supported John of God who quietly mixed with perfumed ladies and gallant gentlemen with the same ease as he moved amongst the marginated. As far as John of God was concerned, an impoverished brother or sister was equal to any highborn brother or sister. The only thing that mattered to him was the heart: *"In whose name do you ask? In whose name do you give?"* You remember the success he had in the zaguán [porch] of the Casa Venegas. Now it was about to end in an upstairs room at the Casa de los Pisa... Venegas and Pisa, two very aristocratic surnames.

The priest, Bernabé Ruiz, notes the date when they carried him there, *"the end of February in the year fifteen hundred and fifty: he was at the Casa de los Pisa for nine or ten days, then he died."*

If it was a week, or if it was ten days, John of God's stay in the Casa de los Pisa gave Granada cause for concern. Rich and poor alike, the whole city wanted to *"come to see him."* Doña Ana was forced to take control.

We get a hint of the religious tension the family experienced during these days, thanks to the statements given years later by friends, servants, and various of the children of the Pisa Osorio family. Two servants especially, who lived in the palace, recalled those days: María de Morales, the housekeeper who had been in the family's service most of her life, and her assistant Francisca Espinosa.

Eight of Doña Ana's nine children were already born, their ages ranging from the youngest, three year old Catalina, to Juan, the first born, who would have been between twelve and fifteen. Naturally these five boys and three girls would have been excited to see *"the holy man who was cared for in their home."* Cristóbal, who later became a priest, said he went into the sickroom to see and speak with him. One day, he and his little sister, María, looked into his room and saw him *"kneeling in the bed just as if he were on the ground".* They asked him *"why are you doing that since you are so thin and weakened by illness?"* John of God replied that *"he could manage and he wanted to do it."* These were words that little children could understand, for they remained engraved on their memory.

Aunt Doña Catalina was the one whom Doña Ana preferred to help her care for the ill man. She was the sister of Don García's father, Don Juan Rodríguez, and when she was widowed she came to live with her nephew. Doña Catalina kept a discreet vigil, opening and shutting the door of the sickroom.

Doña Ana kept the crowds of visitors away to make sure that the patient would not be disturbed. Had she allowed a train of visitors to enter, their fussing and weeping would have distressed him. The first persons she forbade to enter were the poor, John of God's treasured friends. To see them all around his bed *"would upset him"*. Now that he could not do anything *"to help them"* he wept. Regretfully, Doña Ana ordered her servants not to allow any beggar upstairs. It would not be long before she would also forbid distinguished persons, the wealthy benefactors of the charity worker, who were upset when they came there: *"He was visited by many leading persons, lords and ladies, all fussing and insisting that the most be done for him."*

John of God was crushed by so much eulogising, *"none of which pleased him"* even though he appreciated *"the charity that motivated them."* Doña Ana strictly forbade anyone to enter.

You had no idea, dear John of God, how Granada was holding its breath in anticipation of your impending death. There are not many times in history when someone is accepted by the entire world as everybody's friend; someone whom we see going beyond the barriers which divide the world, frontiers of wealth, colour of skin, civil or ecclesiastic honours. You were such a one at Granada in the mid 16th century. In our own time, the mid 20th century, we saw a case similar to your own, when Pope John XXIII died. Everybody loved him, absolutely everybody. When it was announced that he had cancer we were all kept in suspense for three entire days and nights. Everyone was concerned, even if you got into a taxi the driver would comment on it. Pope John was a short fat man, but he had an ear that could listen to jokes about its owner. O yes he could, and he had an immense heart which accepted everyone. He had a special love of good simple folk. Your own death, John of God, evokes that of John XXIII. His terminal illness, some four hundred years after yours, caused folk to think more of human kindness. Like you, even before he died, John XXIII had become the protagonist of legends. If only you knew what things Granada was saying about you right at that moment as your life was fast ebbing away. A legend has been born. Yes, you are a legend in your own lifetime. With your death you gave your biographers a really difficult task to sift all the chaff of legend from the wheat of fact. The same thing happened to John XXIII. They pieced together a number of lovely stories about him, too. As far as the People of God, the ordinary man and woman in the street were concerned, John XXIII was already canonised. They acclaimed him for his life, regardless of the fact that the tribunals had yet to finish their work.

How come he has not been canonised? One summer's day Pope John was walking in the gardens of Castelgandolfo. He got lost and no one could find him. The police went through the vast gardens on their motorbikes and finally a patrol found him. Was he worried? Not in the least. He had simply wandered here and there without any fixed destination in mind. As he roamed through the gardens he came across some bricklayers repairing a wall and at that time they were having their lunch. The workmen saw him coming and one said, "Look, it's the Pope!" When he drew level with them he greeted them and said, "Aren't you going to invite me to join you in a glass of wine?" Sitting on a rock the Pope joined the workmen. "Just a moment, I will have to clean a glass," said one of the men. He put a little wine into a dirty glass, rinsed it about with his fingers, just the way things are done in a country village. With that, he filled the glass. At that very moment the police arrived. The Pope invited them to join them for a glass of wine. It was the most democratic toast in the history of the papacy. Why shouldn't he be canonised?

These are the stories they tell about him, whether they are true or not, who knows! They certainly fit in with his style. And your style John of God also fits in with the exaggerations which the folk of Granada talk about now that you are dying. For example, when you went to the river for firewood. Your obsession for firewood was enough to have you tumbling into the freezing waters of the Genil trying to fish it out and ending up with a fatal pneumonia. Everybody knows that you went down to the river every winter to get firewood. That is what the priest Francisco de Narváez stated: "it was the eve of the feast of Saint Thomas the Apostle, the twentieth of December. It had been snowing a lot that day and was still snowing, when along came John of God. He was barefooted and had his habit tucked up with a piece of rope. He was very determined to get on top of the wood to bring it out to give to some poor widows. Those who were looking out of the windows felt sorry for him because even horses could not go out in that snow. They shouted out to him, begging him, for the love of God, not to go out in that blizzard because it was so dangerous. But he just went on and collected a bundle of wood. As he brought it back he fell into a deep ditch which was covered over with snow and all one could see was his head and the bundle of wood. At that moment a man came by, and there being nobody else about in that field, it must have been his guardian angel. He said: "What's this, Brother John of God?" He put out his hand and pulled the servant of God out, giving thanks to His Divine Majesty. John of God was happy and the firewood was dry with not a flake of snow upon it. Some women in a shack, doing laundry, saw all this. They were amazed at such a great miracle.

Father Narváez went on to say that when his footprints were followed, he saw that he had taken the firewood to the house of some poor widows next to the parish church of San Nicolás. "They were sleeping on the floor and perishing from the cold."

Well now, my dear John of God, I am now wearing my historian's hat, so tell me how we can distinguish between happenings that are proven on the one hand, and exaggerated legends on the other, when they deliver unlikely stories like this. That's right, they have concocted this tale to show your holy mania in bringing charity to the suffering. They call you 'blessed' and truly you were blessed to them.

It attracts my attention that hardly any references are made by either Castro or the witnesses at the Beatification Process to John of God's companions, *"his brothers of the habit"* who worked so closely with him during these years. Doubtless, this silence was due to their desire to throw as much light as possible onto the protagonist.

Of course, Antón Martín and the other brothers are close to John of God's bed.

They were the first at his bedside in the hospital and again at the sickroom at the Pisa palace.

They are his heirs. John of God hands on to them the torch of charity without grandiose speeches. Nor does he give them rules or directives but something far more valuable, his spirit and example. They will carry on, the whole world will know them as, 'Hospitaller Brothers,' the Brothers of John of God.

The Archbishop, Don Pedro Guerrero comes to visit. Doña Ana allows this visitor to pass freely, what else could she do?

Ana herself would attend to him personally once she recognised that John of God was not going to be restored to health, but was dying.

It seems simple, and in our days normal, that Archbishop Don Pedro wants to see John of God. What less could the Archbishop of Granada do than to show kindness to a man of his calibre, who throughout the winters and summers of the past ten years had exercised charity. In the eyes of the Archbishop, John of

God held the position of a champion – he was at the forefront of the faithful in Granada. Coming to visit him before he dies is a sign of his affection and gratitude. Don Pedro, as pastor of the diocese, knows well that he must 'thank' John of God for his example of evangelical charity.

It's true to say, that over the past fifty years, not a single bishop had left his palace to visit a dying man, to greet him with love, let alone to thank him. What a disgrace!

Thank God customs have changed these days! Today, the bishop has been converted into a father and a close friend. Before we always saw him as austere and from afar, covered with liturgical pomp, inaccessible and even threatening. So much so, that those who were attached to the episcopal office used to apply the saying of old soldiers: *"a mule and the chief – the further away you are, the safer you are."* And that, even up to fifty years ago.

We are now going back four centuries, to the full splendour of the Renaissance when bishops, besides receiving the holy oils, had the same status as the feudal lords with lands and castles.

How could it occur to him to go down to the bedside of a poor humble dying man. But it did occur to the Archbishop. It is true that Pedro Guerrero was 'special'; and 'special' too, is our dying John of God. Arriving at the Casa de los Pisa, the Archbishop went upstairs to see him.

John of God was surprised but he welcomed him saying, *"My father and good pastor."* The Archbishop greeted him warmly *"with words and consolation"* assuring him, *"Brother John of God, if there is anything worrying you, let me know about it so I can set it right."*

You will recall that John of God had kept a book with a copy of his debts. He had the idea of handing it over to someone to settle the hospital's accounts. And who better than the Archbishop? *"Three things give me concern my father."*

Let the reader know that I am not changing a syllable, I take this verbatim from the Castro narrative.

"The first, the little that I have served Our Lord, having received so much." The prelate replied: *"My brother, you say that you have not served Our Lord, take confidence in his mercy; he will supply with the merits of his Passion what you are lacking."*

Let me interrupt just for a moment, to picture the scene of the Archbishop sitting by John of God's bed. Look who comes to see you, Brother John of God.

"The other thing, the poor whom I entrust to you, my father; and

the people who have given up sinfulness and an evil life; and the vergonzantes." Don Pedro assured him: *"I will take care of them all, as I am obliged."*

The third... John of God does not vacillate, he got straight to the point, *"The third thing is these debts I owe."*

"And putting the book into his hand", that he had been keeping in his bed: *"These are the debts I owe, which I made for Jesus Christ."* He handed him the book *"in which they were noted down."* I'm sure that Archbishop Don Pedro would have smiled: *"As for the debts you owe, I take them from now on into my charge so as to pay them, I promise you to do so just as you yourself would do."*

Having received from John of God *"the three concerns he had been guarding"*, the Archbishop blessed him: *"Be calm now, nobody is going to worry you except to take care of you and commend you to Our Lord."*

Don Pedro's Christian action towards John of God, puts him in the same category as the charity worker.

Don Pedro Guerrero was preparing to make a journey to Italy, where he eventually became one of the leading lights at the Council of Trent. In his diocesan duties he proved himself to be an Archbishop of evangelical qualities, a reformer of customs and altogether charitable. Of course John of God would have respected the Archbishop even had he been a man of mediocre qualities, but that certainly was not the case. He knew Don Pedro's personal virtue and that was the reason why he called him with all his heart, "my father and good pastor." Through the means of this bishop, "his bishop", John of God had joined his life with the Church of Jesus Christ. This faith was powerfully illustrated in the letter he sent to Gutierre Lasso: "I stand firm on that, sealing and locking it with my key." Even in Granada John of God knew of the religious troubles erupting in Europe. Pope Paul III had died only four months earlier, on 10 November 1549. He was the pope who was disgusted with the Emperor Charles for closing the first stage of the Council of Trent. Charles went to war against the armies of the Protestant princes, while at the same time he sought to establish a platform to restore the unity of the Church, which had miserably broken down. He proposed the provisional formula for the 'Interim Council' (whilst a new Council was being convoked). The Protestant theologians would accept the pontifical authority under certain conditions which included authorising priests to marry and that the Council continue its sittings in the frontier city of Trent and not at Bologna where the Pope had gone to reside. The Pope refused these conditions and, being fed up with the Emperor, called the Council. Now in the depths of winter, while John of God was throwing himself into the freezing waters of the Genil in order to retrieve firewood for the patients at his hospital, a new pope has been elected in Rome. Julius III became Pope on 8 February 1550 and immediately announced that he wanted to convoke a new stage of the Council of Trent. So off to Trent went Don Pedro Guerrero, Archbishop of Granada. It was twelve years before the Council closed its final session and during that long period Guerrero had gained universal prestige. Some of the papers he presented were prepared by his friend Master Avila to make way for a sure path for religious reform.

The fields of Spain will produce good harvests during the decade beginning in 1550 as if, midway through the century, they would like to favour the Emperor, who had lifted the burdens that he had imposed on his subjects to bolster the empire's military presence. Charles V had suffered a great disillusionment that paved the way for his abdication. You remember that when John of God was at Valladolid, Prince Philip was preparing to go to Flanders and Germany, and going with him was our friend Gonzalo, Duke of Sessa. The first thing in the Emperor's plans was for the States of Flanders to swear loyalty to his heir Prince Philip. The next thing he wanted was for the German Diet to proclaim Philip successor to the Imperial Crown. The Flemish rallied around the Prince to proclaim him as their future king but the Germans did not. They refused him the inheritance of the Empire. They preferred Philip's nephew, Maximilian, the youngest son of Ferdinand, because they considered father and son as Germanic – something that they certainly did not attribute to Charles V. Thus Charles's empire was cut right down the middle with Central Europe on one side in favour of the Hapsburgs, while the Spanish sphere was for Philip. The Emperor continued for six more years until the winter of 1556 when he sought refuge in the monastery at Yuste. The sceptre of the Empire was handed over to his brother Ferdinand, while the crown of Spain went to his son Philip.

I have not the slightest doubt that John of God was happy to see the Archbishop. *"He received great consolation from the visit of the prelate, and in what he had promised"* – to pay his debts and to take care of his poor.

Thus, the Archbishop was the executor of John of God's

last will and testament.

John of God kissed his hand *"and received his blessing."* They took their final farewell of each other. The Archbishop had given his word, he left the Pisa palace at once and *"set out for the hospital,"* where he went to assure the brothers that now, with John of God gone, they could count on him as their father.

In a certain way, the biography of John of God enters a second stage in the story of his sons, the Brothers.

Just as we light candles taking new light from the paschal candle, so John of God left a blazing torch, the mandate of mercy, from which the brothers will distribute thousands of candles throughout the entire world.

It is my guess that when Archbishop Guerrero went to the hospital after farewelling John of God, he announced the commencement of the desired 'great hospital' which would be spacious enough to accommodate comfortably *"all the patients"* and which would carry the name 'John of God Hospital'. The assistance of the whole subculture of misery in Granada, necessitated its building. Don Pedro Guerrero, while at the Cuesta Gomérez, probably addressed Antón Martín and the brothers concerning this, as well as the worries entrusted to him, the outstanding debts, which according to the declarations of the Beatification Process, *"His Excellency paid religiously."*

Brother John of God, now you can die in peace. It will take three and a half years to build but, mid-summer 1553, they will take your patients from the Cuesta Gomérez to the beautiful new building on the Jeronymite site, an event that would have made you very happy.

Meanwhile, Brother Antón Martín will travel to Madrid to seek alms following your example: *"He brought back many blankets, bed linen, clothing and other donations in cash."* It occurred to the gentry of Madrid how good it would be to have in the capital another house similar to that of the Cuesta Gomérez . They won over Brother Antón, who made Brother Domingo, the former Genoese banker, who now no longer called himself Piola but Domingo Benedicto, the head of the new hospital. The construction of the Madrid building went ahead. It was *"grand and prominent"* where *"so many sick and poor persons were received"* and found shelter and kindness. The whole of Madrid praised Brother

Antón Martín *"for his holy works of hospitality and penance."*

Thus was born, from the seed of John of God's first band of brothers, the Hospitaller Order, which will become a tree with generous branches which give shelter today, to sufferers all over the globe.

You know Brother John of God, that at the end of the 20th century, the fifth centenary of your birth was celebrated. The whole world came out to celebrate it and bless your memory and to honour your sons, your Hospitaller Brothers. Just look at your family. Without making any fuss, it daily repeats your charitable activity. One and a half thousand brothers working in 242 hospitaller centres in 45 countries, of different races and languages: From Australia to Zambia, from Bolivia to Japan, from England to New Zealand, you will hear the surprising names of places where St. John of God foundations are found throughout the world.

It did not worry your brothers to put themselves in the world's trouble spots. They first put their professional experience to service as medics during the Alpujarras uprising of the Moors. Don Juan of Austria was so impressed by their work that he made them responsible for the sickbays of his ships in the naval battle at Lepanto. From then on the brothers served permanently in Spain's naval infirmaries. Furthermore, in fulfilling their works dedicated to health services, some have become saints, others even achieving martyrdom. There is now a litany behind your name. The Hospitaller Order has a long complex history, always exemplary. It's amazing, John of God, how the Brothers make your absent heart pulsate with the energies you infuse into your Order from heaven!

Don Gregorio Marañon, a brilliant doctor who recently died in Spain, had a reputation similar to that of the *Alfaquíes*, those Moorish men of science you also knew at Granada. We cite him to you with such respect that we never fail to give him his title Don. Don Gregorio Marañon, when speaking about you, commented that today it is not possible to assist the sick without at the same time creating science because, clearly, scientific progress constantly affects the health system. Don Marañon, as a good humanist, sensitive to the interweavings of history, said, *"If John of God were to come back to life, he would be wearing an hygienic white coat and be bending over a microscope."* How nice, here is another one who, after Bishop Muñoz, has a new habit in which to dress John of God! I know that his sons do wear white coats, since they keep up to date with sophisticated scientific progress. For example, they make use of a 'cardiac pump' which avoids a great number of heart transplants. Their hospitals began to install 'highways' of facts and images to help with diagnosis. The use of the Internet immediately puts them in touch with the latest developments in any part of the world. These examples can go on and on, there's a new invention coming out every week! Through the positive structures and organisation of their hospitaller centres the brothers meet the challenges of the new diseases plaguing us today, afflictions with horrific names like Alzheimer's disease, AIDS, Ebola virus, genetic deformity and drug addiction. The list goes on. There are psychiatric disturbances caused by the concentration of people in our cities like anthills, chronic illnesses, industrial unrest and delinquency. This is today's battlefield for the Brothers of John of God. This is their barrio of the Pescadería, their Plaza Bibarrambla, their Babataubin district.

Recently, your brothers chose the ways and means to guide the Hospitaller Order as it moves into the third millennium. The present Prior General, Brother Pascual Piles, outlined a sound survey of the Order's present style which is based upon a tripod of fidelities: to the Gospel, to the Founder and to the times in which we live. He praised the scientific progress and encouraged the brothers to carry out their program of humanisation. This comes about by the way they lovingly meet those who need hospitaller assistance in today's dehumanised world in which human beings are treated as if they were machines. He said: "We brothers are called to witness to the God who loves to be in relationship with the human." John of God, you know your brothers want to act just as you did when you were in our world.

The catalogue of issues effecting us today is not a light one, as Brother Piles pointed out. He listed, "abortion; interventions in fertility; prenatal diagnosis; palliative care; quality of life; euthanasia. There is the management of the mentally ill or intellectually handicapped; the subject of freedom; the repercussions of drugs, the caring of persons with AIDS and their relatives. These are some of the subjects which move us in the ambience of hospitality and keep us constantly on our toes."

John of God, I assure you that you can justifiably be proud of your brothers. Last summer I spent a few days with a group of young brothers on the Atlantic coast. These were the cubs of the Hospitaller Order, lads ranging between 20 and 25 years of age, all of whom decided to dedicate their lives in the same way as you did. Thanks to them, and many more like them, this doubting world will fall on the side of happiness, thereby giving an answer to the question asked by Teilhard de Chardin: "If we could but see the *heap of suffering upon the earth. What an astronomical amount of it there is! And if all the suffering could be put up against all the happiness, who knows which one will fall heaviest upon the scales?"*

The Archbishop, Don Pedro, after speaking with John of God and accepting to be the executor of the *"three things worrying him,"* left the Casa de los Pisa to go to the hospital in the Cuesta Gomérez; but Castro does not mention whether he blessed him and administered the sacraments to him.

It seems strange to me that Castro should have forgotten the fact. Three witnesses came forward and without hesitation, testified that the Archbishop in person *"said Mass, heard his confession, gave him communion and administered the final anointing to blessed John of God"*; *"He said Mass, heard his confession and gave him communion and the anointing,"* one claiming, *"it was well known in this city..."*

It is very odd that Castro puts the last sacraments received by John of God after *"the Archbishop left"*: *"John of God's condition deteriorated further and he received the sacrament of Penance (even though he frequently did so). They brought Our Lord to him and he adored Him, because illness prevented him from receiving."*

We have to believe Castro, who was able to know the facts by direct reference to the children of the Pisa Osorio family.

I wish to complain that it did not occur to the first brothers to write down their own experiences and recollections. They were unaffected men, and it did not occur to them that, as time went by, others would consider their achievments to be so valuable. They carried on the work without permitting themselves the vanity of looking at their audience. This was especially so at this time when John of God was dying. I am lamenting because *"he called his companion Antón Martín"* who was left as chief of the brothers and who went, many times, to be at John's side while he stayed at the Casa de los Pisa. But when he was sent for at the last hour, when John of God *"became worse"*, all we have of this final testament is contained in two lines: *"He entrusted to him the poor, the orphans and the vergonzantes; advising him, with many devout words, concerning what he would have to do."*

John of God *"knew that the time had come when he was to*

depart." You will see what he did.

Before attending to his death, we must at least ask one question. What did John of God, his person and his journey, mean to the Christianity of his time?

While the young Portuguese Juan Ciudad was looking after sheep on the banks of the Tiétar in the fields of the Arañuelo, a violent upheaval was occurring on the stage of central Europe. The foundations of Christianity were beginning to crumble, and as we all know, the unity of the family of believers was to be split forever.

The ferment of the Protestant Reformation came out of the climate created in Italy and Germany in the mid 15th century thanks to the scholars of the Eastern Church who fled to Europe after the fall of Constantinople. Through their attachment to literature and classic art, they gave rise to humanism; and it was through their new concept of the world, life and politics, that the Renaissance got under way.

From Florence, that wonderful city, artistic and literary humanism passed to Rome. There the Popes welcomed and patronised their development to the delight of the princely circles that surrounded the Pontifical Curia. They substituted theatre, literary galas, patronage of artists and the building of monuments for religious feasts, events and concerns.

The Papal Court exchanged the mysterious presence of the eternal God for the sensuous perfume of temporal beauty. The enthusiasm of the humanists, who were dedicated to certain superficial aspects of Christian piety, concealed the profound ideological change hidden within the seeds of the movement. The Renaissance substituted the modern 'anthropologically centred' concept that puts man at the heart of the universe for the medieval 'theocentricity' that placed the concept of God as the centrepoint and core of creation. Thus the way was opened for the ultimate expressions of the new age of secularisation which is characteristic of our own day. You will recall that the Renaissance modified 'the map of the planetary system'. The Earth was supplanted by the Sun as its centre. What a good symbol this was for humankind in its own environment as it journeys towards the clouds. The problem arose when many thinkers included in 'the clouds' their own values of religion that they declared to be outmoded, no longer of service and therefore, superseded.

Luther had plenty to motivate him in denouncing the scandals of papal Rome. The number of believers who either silently or loudly longed for a reform to blow upon the embers of the Faith was legion. From today's viewpoint, both Catholic and Protestant religious historians can look back and understand how political and economic motives influenced the religious rupture. A furious gale blew up which shook dozens of theologians, German princes, the Emperor and the Pope himself. The Council of Trent arrived too late. For better or worse, no 15th century Christian was free of the outcome. The path of every great person of that epoch was conditioned, at least influenced, by the Lutheran tension. Even John of God.

Had John of God remained a simple Portuguese hawker who came to Granada to sell books and prints, the 'Protestant conflict' and the 'humanist infiltration' might have lightly touched him, nothing more, even though there were limitations imposed on the circulation of publications.

However, from the beginning of the 'illumination' which occurred in the field of Los Mártires, John of God's path was strewn with esoteric significance which surpassed him and whose historic value he was not even aware of himself. Under the guidance of Master Avila, he fulfilled the vocation to which he was called. He practised charity towards his suffering brothers and sisters. With the eyes of faith, John of God saw in them 'Jesus Christ, his suffering brother'. He used to love saying 'God lives', even better 'I give myself to God', as he fulfilled the tasks set out before him.

When we look at this from the distance of four and a half centuries, we see his image inserted into the historical scene opening up quite a margin for stimulating thought. His position is so impressive that it has a valid freshness that is essentially permanent. This is because it maintains a connection between humanistic and Christian values that became disassociated when the 15th century passed into the 16th shattering European religious unity.

I simply want to point out two methods of study. The first being strictly theological. John of God placed himself within the heart of the Gospel which traditionally recognised charity as "the essence of Christ's message." God is love, and we believe that the Trinitarian mystery immersed him in loving relationships. Jesus was sent to us as the greatest expression of love, and we human beings must feel that we are brothers and sisters in love. John of God transported love from the sacred levels of faith to the concrete circumstances about him. He converted himself into love and mercy. How? He did it by applying himself "to actualise love" by loving the person of the Lord Jesus Christ in suffering humanity. For John of God, each poor man or woman, patient, 'vergonzante', prostitute, is Jesus Christ. He clearly identified the person of Christ and the person of the sufferer, putting the two of them within the same skin. "Love-charity" belongs to the theological essence of Christianity. "Love-mercy" gives to charity an historical leaning appropriate to the Church militant.

I want to combine this with my second study proposal, adjusted to fit in with the actual temporal parameters of the 16ᵗʰ century which boiled up around the Lutheran controversy.

How many headaches arose around the disputes on justification! Whether it was by faith or by works; by gratuitous acceptance of the sinner thanks to Christ, or by playing about with human freedom.

Nowadays our theologians are astonished when they look at many of these disputes. John Paul II recalled that Luther taught that "faith in Jesus Christ justifies us because believing in Christ we believe in that which is of Christ." Cardinal Willebrands emphasised that Luther's ideas were not always correctly expressed and came to consider Luther as "a common master in the field of justification."

Indeed, the 'merciful' way John of God acted overcame the dialectic contraposition of faith and works. He placed 'faith' in 'works of mercy'; and he reconstructed the bridge which leads to mystery, by placing Christ 'within' suffering humanity and identifying the Son of God with those who begged for bread, blankets, and especially love. For John of God, faith and works were united. If renaissance humanism displaced divine values so as to affirm human values, then John of God went ahead and filled the gap by means of mercy. In drawing near to this mystery we are helped 'to keep our balance'. This was his personal 'revolution'. He had no need of taunting like Savonarola, nor to raise a hand against the ecclesiastic hierarchy, which, at that time, was extremely dangerous. His conduct pointed out a permanent reproach, and yet he ended up a saint.

He saw that he was dying: we shall see what happened.

He asked *"to be left alone,"* knowing that his hour was close by. What was the hour of his death?

They were keeping vigil. Doña Ana would have the children and servants close by in the room next door to the sickroom where blessed Brother John of God lay. She took charge herself, who would doubt it, making sure there would be silence in his vicinity; and that nothing was lacking in his care. Everyone knows that John of God is dying.

The fact that so many family members, relatives and friends of the family, all of whom were John of God's friends, crowded into the adjoining room waiting in silence, complicated the historic reconstruction of his last hours. It meant that there were many different accounts of what occurred and not all of them are in agreement.

To the passing of John of God, Castro dedicates twenty lines that appear disconnected and imprecise. The data fluctuates and does not tally. Why, I do not know. It seems so odd that a biographer would have neglected to reconstruct meticulously these last minutes of his protagonist. I will try to open a path in this thicket of memories.

Concerning the day and hour of his death, the day is perfectly recorded as, *"the eighth day of March of the year fifteen hundred and fifty."* However, the hour poses some small problems. I mentioned before that there was a certain prediction attributed to John of God saying that he would die between a Friday and a Saturday. Friday is traditionally dedicated to the memory of the Passion of Christ, and Saturday to the Blessed Virgin Mary, two favourite devotions of the 'blessed charity worker'.

To gather confidence, Castro adds that in effect John of God died *"half an hour after midnight"* on Friday the seventh and Saturday the eighth of March 1550. Castro's account appears in chapter 18 of his book. Then in chapter 20, when he tells of the death of John of God he uses the expression: *"It was the beginning of Saturday, half an hour after Matins."*

Was the hour of Matins exactly at midnight? Some monasteries certainly had the custom of rising to say Matins at midnight. That was what occurred when John of the Cross died. Fray John of the Cross lay dying at Ubeda on the night of Friday 13 December 1591. He asked what time it was and the brother Infirmarian replied: *"It is half past eleven."* John of the Cross said, *"The hour is close by, call the fathers."* The friars came in with their candles alight in order to chant Matins and the dying saint joined them in reciting the psalms. Again he asked for the time, they told him it was 12 o'clock to which he replied, *"At midnight I will be standing before God, saying Matins."*

That is how it turned out, for John of the Cross died at 12 o'clock that night between Friday and Saturday. It was during the first minutes of Saturday 14 December that he left them *"to recite Matins in heaven"* just as he said. In the meantime the friars of the convent were reciting their Matins here on Earth.

I have related this incident to you because some authors have written that the death of John of God occurred at *"daybreak of Saturday."* They base this upon the fact that Matins was not always recited at midnight but at dawn, between four and five o'clock. But naturally, that depended upon the horarium of the individual convent.

Historians of technology affirm that the first mechanical clock, *"the prototype of all future machines for counting time, was divided into 24 hours equal to sixty minutes,"* and was made early in the 14th century. The mechanical clock took the place of the ancient clocks that relied upon the sun, oil, sand, and wheels, all of which are described in historic documents. It is certain that by the end of the 10th century the monk from Aurillac in France who became the future Pope Silvester II applied the 'weight mechanism' to clocks. In 1370 Henry von Mick constructed a marvellous pendulum clock for the tower of Paris Castle. Even before the 15th century when monks wanted to know the hour of midnight to recite their Matins, they did not have to see the first rays of dawn in order to do so.

So, midnight passes and we begin to count the hours of a new day. Therefore, let us take it that Castro was right. John of God died *"half an hour after"* the commencement of Saturday 8 March. Or, if you prefer, one o'clock less thirty minutes!

A tangle of contradictory data is presented to us in the accounts given by those who were present at the time of John of God's death. Castro gives the impression that *"there was a crowd"*:

"There were present at his death many important ladies and four priests, and all were left tremendously moved by it and thanked Our Lord for such a manner of death."

This does not fit in – so many persons around the bed when John of God died. It does not fit in with the statements of various witnesses at the Beatification Process, who were close to the Pisas and who obviously had the confidence of the family. It also does not fit in with the actual purpose of Doña Ana who, to defend the privacy of the patient, forbade excessive visitors.

I think Castro's phrase does not refer to the 'presence' of ladies and priests *"when John of God expired"*, but 'later', 'afterwards' thereby understanding 'death' in the wider meaning of the word, *"until they interred him."* Above all, he told of an astonishing phenonemon which we will look at but which Castro himself thought to be quite implausible, so he tried to play it down.

But the witnesses turned out to be of a different opinion. I did some rigorous work on these, and I wish to say as an honest critic, it was hardly with any enthusiasm. If the reader wishes to follow this up, I have placed the corresponding references of each witness in the notes at the end of this chapter.

Here is the account. On the evening of Friday 7 March, John of God's condition deteriorated; he knew that his hour had arrived. He said this to Doña Ana and to other members of the family, probably the old aunt Catalina, who were present in his room; and he indicated to them by word and gesture that he wished to be left alone: "*He revealed to them that he was about to die.*" Respecting his wish, they left him alone. John of God remained in his bed dressed in the nightshirt. At someone's suggestion "*they tidy him*" before leaving.

Because John of God remains alone, no one sees his movements, nor hears his words. What he did is deduced from the state in which they soon found him.

It would have been an enormous effort for him to rise and get out of bed, remove the nightshirt and put on his habit. No doubt, when John of God was put to bed in the nightshirt, Doña Ana would have washed, or ordered to be washed, the dilapidated habit, which would have been returned to his room within sight, for the habit represented his exterior sign of identity. That is why he wanted to die in his habit.

He took a small crucifix that was probably standing by the lampstand near the wall of the room and knelt down next to the bed and prayed before it. And that is exactly as they found him: "*Kneeling on the floor with a crucifix in his hands, his head was somewhat inclined towards the feet of Christ as if he was going to kiss them.*" This crucifix exists to this day.

It was only logical that Doña Ana and those with her, as night drew on, would mount a guard to discreetly keep vigil at John of God's room without noise or disturbance. The old aunt Catalina "*pulled the door ajar and seeing him on his knees thought that he was praying so she crept away and closed the door of the room.*" It can be certain that either she or Doña Ana repeated this checking various times.

Just after midnight, they became concerned that the dying man might be in need of something, so they decided to enter. There he was upon his knees, dressed in his habit with a crucifix clasped in his hands: *"His head was somewhat inclined towards the feet of Christ as if he was going to kiss them"*, I repeat this delightful expression proving that John of God was dead.

There had been no sound of stertorous breathing, he was found in an attitude of devotion, his body had neither changed nor had it fallen over. They thought it strange to see it like that. The family was very moved – they were all there, but no one was to touch the rigid body.

Doña Ana sent word to her friends Diego de Perea and Ana Heredia who lived close by. Ana Heredia came immediately and it was from her daughter Francisca that we know a detail, that the cover on the bed *"from which John of God had risen so as to die, was green."* The old aunt, Doña Catalina Osorio, who without doubt, would have retired to rest, was awakened. She came prepared to pray, *"in her dressing gown and a white shawl."* Together they entered the room and *"saw he was dead, upon his knees, with a crucifix in his hands, dressed in his habit."*

John of God had died. The news rapidly circulated, firstly around the Plaza Santa Ana and the Cuesta Gomérez, then before dawn, the whole of Granada knew of it.

Friends and the curious soon began arriving. At first Doña Ana agreed to let the visitors into the room to see for themselves the sight of John of God, upright on his knees. Those who saw it exchanged expressions of wonderment.

Within a short while there was such a crowd pressing into the porch of the Pisa palace that order had to be established for entry: *"This witness and some others wanted to enter to see the blessed body, but there being so many people who had come there, and as it was before dawn, they were unable to enter the house."*

I suppose that Doña Ana and her husband Don García permitted their close friends and the highest dignitaries to enter, but even then their visit would have been a hurried one: *"This witness and other close friends of the House of Pisa had come to see him, but they were not permitted to stay long, because the whole city had turned up. So great was the number of people who came to see a thing as marvellous as this, that this witness and other close friends of theirs had difficulty in getting up to see him."*

The repeated statements in the Beatification Process show the tumult was noted by everyone: *"So great was the concourse of* people who had arrived, that this witness was very lucky indeed to have been able to enter to see him."

Someone, whom we already know, tells us that by 7 o'clock in the morning the queue of visitors *"had reached as far as Santa Ana."* I refer to the young girl Agueda Muñoz, daughter of the Alhambra midwife. She went along holding her mother's hand and the two of them stood in the queue and saw a pipe band coming out of the Pisa palace. It had gone there *"to honour blessed John of God with its dirges."* A certain Saraiva, leader of the pipe band and attendant at the Alhambra Governor's dining room, was known to the midwife Doña Agueda. He came over to the mother and daughter and said *"that they had already left the blessed man John of God as he was."*

Before telling you about the juridical and forensic verdict stated by the *"magistrates of the Court"* I wish to note the presence of some of our other friends. I am thinking, for example, of Luisa Ribera, the little grand daughter of the Bibarrambla apothecary Antón Zabán: *"The father and grandfather of this witness heard the noise going on, even though it was at daybreak or a little time before. They got up and both of them went to the Casa de los Pisa. There they saw him out of bed, kneeling in the middle of the room, dressed in his habit and a crucifix in his hands, his head inclined towards Christ in an attitude of prayer. Then they left for home in tears."*

I am also thinking of Lucia de la O, who went to see him with her mother: *"They were unable to enter because there were so many people queued right up to the door of Santa Ana."*

The *"Señor Oidor [justice] Gamboa"*, a constant admirer of John of God says, *"I went there to see him and at the house they told me how they found the blessed father John of God dead upon his knees with a crucifix in his hands. He was out of bed in the middle of the room."*

How could I miss out on the family of María Guevara, 'the borrowed one' and her mother Doña Leonor, *"the true sister"?* In the absence of her husband, her father-in-law Don Juan de la Torre and her brother Don Juan de Guevara accompanied her.

There were so many people that Diego López Roales, *"was unable to get into the patio"* of the Casa de los Pisa; *"he was only able to get into the zaguán"*:

"So great was the number of distinguished persons, clerics and religious who went there, that it was impossible to see him because of the crowd. The City Councillors, and their Lordships the Judges had arrived to see the blessed man."

We have to open the way for the juridical authority.

It was up to them to intervene, in a forensic capacity, given the rumour about the extraordinary manner in which the body of John of God was found: *"Kneeling with a crucifix in the hands and having been like that for more than six hours."*

The witnesses vary the length of time between four and six hours. *"It appears that he had been dead many hours before the arrival of the judges and the magistrates of the Court of the Royal Chancellery; they said that he was kneeling on the ground; that they should pick him up, and they should put him on the bed."*

We have the names of those magistrates who intervened. *"Their lordships the Magistrates of the Court were Lebrija and Sedeño."* They came, *"ordering that he be placed in a coffin and taken away for burial."* When those waiting to see the body in *"a kneeling position"* knew that the magistrates *"had put an end to it"*, they felt penalised; and accused Lebrija and Sedeño of acting *"inadvisably"* and without respect.

I wonder whether the complaint about a lack of respect was in reference to the body of John of God, or whether it was directed at the people who had been queuing for ages in order to see the deceased? They almost speak of profanation, which raises another question. Was it because they were forced to straighten the leg bones, since it was several hours after death.

I consulted medical friends: Would the rigidity of the body upon its knees create problems after four, five or six hours? There were many questions to answer before they replied, questions about his position, whether he was leaning on anything, his physical description and the state of the weather.

Is it normal for a body to remain rigid without falling over after death and after what period of time would it prove impossible to straighten his legs and lay him out for burial? These were some of my questions.

Various eyewitnesses were positive that the body was absolutely unsupported.

It was thought that, being kept fresh, four or five hours of rigidity would not make it impossible to do what was necessary without too much difficulty.

"I believe Castro's narrative has misled our advisers, *"if it were cold, they would be unable to lay him out."*

That is why I consider that the continuation of the body on its knees for a number of hours is unlikely. I leave aside so many witnesses that were in agreement, and reduce the time to fifteen minutes:

"Something really worthy of admiration occurred: after dying his body remained fixed on its knees without falling, for a space of a quarter of an hour".

Even so, I think it would have been a real effort for them, *"They thought it best to lay him out rather than let him grow cold upon his knees."* According to my medical friends, Castro does not wish to attribute an unequivocal marvel to the fact that the cadaver remained rigid upon its knees.

In any case the whole of Granada considered that what occurred was a miracle. We have a great number of witnesses coming forward to affirm that it was not just fifteen minutes, but more like, four to six hours, that John of God's body remained in this devout position after death.

Someone I respect smilingly said to me, *"After all, death brought a lot of respect to John of God, who so many times carried upon his shoulders the sick, dying and cadavers."*

Neither the city nor the Pisa family would ever forget what occurred. After many years, that simple dear old soul, Catalina de Arenas, testified to the Beatification Process that she was *"more or less ninety years of age"*, the daughter of a quarry worker, the widow of a shoemaker, *"poor and without property"*, but well cared for by her daughter, María. Honest old Catalina turned her memory back to the time when John of God died. She said she was twenty at the time and the entire city was impressed by his death. Here are her simple words: *"The whole of Granada was upset at the death of the blessed father John of God. Everyone was sad at losing such a significant servant of God who was of such importance to the poor who would miss the tremendous help he gave them. Of course the consolation he gave to the dying goes without saying. He clearly showed evidence of his holiness by the way he died out of bed upon his knees on the floor of his room, with a crucifix in his hands. He was wearing his habit and his head was inclined towards the feet of the blessed Christ."*

Many years had passed. For the Pisa family, with Doña Ana leading, the memory of the event would never be erased. The Pisa-Osorio children preserved *"the presence of blessed John of God"* as a sacred heritage. Francisca Villarreal was a servant of the priest Don Cristóbal and his sister Doña María and lived in their house. She remembered the two old ladies who were in the service of their parents' home, the housekeeper María Morales and her assistant Francisca Espinosa. Villareal related how the children of Doña Ana venerated the sickroom, which they turned into an oratory. They guarded the key *"letting nobody enter unless they were satisfied about their life and behaviour."* With regard to Brother Juan, *"This witness had always seen him and held him to be holy and blessed, and this witness still holds this view."*

They interred him; the whole city of Granada interred him. John of God belonged to the city and to everyone in it. He belonged to all. Thus they were all there to say farewell to him.

Large crowds also came in from the outlying villages. A crowd like this could only be seen on the great feast of Corpus Christi, and just as they walked in the Corpus Christi procession for the mystery of Christ, they now escorted the body of John of God, who is also a Christian mystery. They knew perfectly well that a simple man like him could not give as much for his neighbour as he did, without God's presence in him.

The procession began about nine in the morning. The pallbearers were four knights, well known to us as friends of John of God. They were none other than Tarifa, Cerralbo, Bobadilla and Guevara who carried the coffin when it was brought down into the zaguán at the entrance of the Pisa palace.

During the last two or three hours, after the body was laid out, Doña Ana had it arranged upon a *"beautifully decorated"* bed in the main parlour where,*"during this period"* friars and the clergy celebrated Mass and said prayers.

The crowd pressed tightly from *"the Santa Ana Bridge"* to the Casa Pisa. Juan Lobo, as a seventeen-year-old youth, agilely climbed up a railing of the bridge to see as much as the bends of the river permitted. The crowd *"covered the whole Carrera del Darro"*, the street running alongside the river. Juan Lobo was told when the procession had arrived as far as the church of the Minims, and the head of the procession was turning into the Calle San Juan de los Reyes. Not another soul could fit into the Plaza de la Victoria.

Once the coffin had gone out the door of the Casa Pisa a discreet contest took place, for the nobles wanted to continue with the coffin on their shoulders. But the Minim friars *"claimed it from them."* The burial was to take place in the Pisa family vault in their church, therefore it was their right to transport the body. The noble gentlemen ceded; and the Marquis de Cerralbo, who as Governor of the city, then went to take his place at the head of the Councillors who were all there. At intervals, the Minim friars let members of other religious orders take turns.

The funeral procession followed the road along the bank of the Darro passing the Arab baths, the church of San Pedro, the other bridge then on to the Convent de la Victoria *"which adjoins the Guadix Gate, where the city ends."*

All Granada was there, the Archbishop came with his Chapter, the Mayor and the Members of the Council of Twenty-four, the members of the Royal Chancellery, the confraternities *"in order of precedence"*, friars of each religious order, dignitaries, judges, magistrates, university professors, a huge crowd, and all were carrying crosses, banners and candles. Bells peeled from the belfries of all the parish churches and monasteries. The witness Cristóbal de Azaña stated that *"the bells tolled right through the funeral and they peeled with such a great clamour that it seemed as if they had changed into rational beings to show how they felt."*

My dear John of God, the thing you would have loved to see was that none of your own people were missing. They were all there: Your poor, your patients, your 'vergonzantes'; even the Moors with their hoods were there "weeping and speaking in their own language about the great charity worker and his good example." They were all saying, " a thousand blessings be upon you." There were the young women you helped with dowries, the widows, the women you helped to get married, "an immense multitude of people" which seemed to "swamp the whole city." There were also your prostitutes, amongst them that one who insulted you. You surely remember her, you told her to go out into the plaza and shout out your sins. They were all here now, saying good things about you and weeping. Just look, there at the head of the procession is the Captain General, the Marquis de Mondéjar, who came down from the Alhambra expressly for this. Halfway in the procession is the bier carrying your body, and right behind the Cathedral Chapter and before the City Aldermen, they had to prevent a disaster when the crowd surged forward in an attempt to touch your coffin. Some even pulled out daggers and knives to cut pieces from your coffin to keep as relics. Candles and torches blazed everywhere. "Granada has never seen the like."

The children had been taught *"to sing some verses"*:

John of God,
If God were willing,
From this world is now departing,
Deserving is he of our weeping.

And they repeated their refrain.

Many a woman he freed from vice,
He sustained them
With the alms he gave,
Deserving is he of weeping.

They continued to sing the ballad:

God accomplished his marvels,
for while dead he is still kneeling,
with a crucifix they found him.
Deserving is he of our weeping.

This is how it was, Granada was left orphaned, as Francisco Ruiz said, *"The city was abandoned and orphaned."*

When the cortege reached the church, because of the crowds, it could hardly enter the little plaza where the friars came out to receive the body.

Following Mass and prayers, the coffin was lowered into the crypt where it was placed *"in the vault of the Pisa chapel."* Outside, the crowd suddenly fell silent.

*J*ohn of God, *you would be pleased with Granada today, at least on the outside. Internally, the human race remains just the same. We give ourselves airs, but the heart beats its humble rhythm. The city is beautiful in spite of urban development that has blocked out the view of the Sierra Nevada with gigantic monstrosities of concrete and brick.*

What beauty there was long ago! I usually tell this to whoever asks:

"There is a series of hills descending from the Sierra Nevada. Christians and Arabs created beautiful spaces among these hills, giving them poetic sounding names like Generalife, Alhambra, Sacro Monte,

Albaycín. There are the celebrated grand villas known as 'carmenes', pools where silence and peace would move your soul filling you with mysterious harmony. It is still possible to get away from the hustle and bustle of Granada's traffic that goes absolutely crazy during certain hours of the day. Only a few years ago some of the main roads of central Granada opened to views of the Sierra Nevada. What a shame that now the clear air, bright sky, snow-capped peaks, secret waterways, have all been denied to Granada."

Today, we appreciate the many verses dedicated to Granada by the Arab poets who were obliged to emigrate a few years before your arrival there. One of them called Granada "a feast for the eyes, elevating the soul" (al-Sagundi). For Ibn al-Zaqqaq, "it is a delight to live here." Ibn Quzman confessed that "upon entering Granada it was as if a weight was lifted from my heart." More than anything else, they sang the praises of the water, the shade, the rivers and the trees of al-Andaluz. Ibn Jafaya: "Eternal paradise is nowhere but in your abode, and if I had the choice, here is where I would stay." John of God, you know what this poor man, who was forced to leave it all behind and flee to the arid desert, meant.

Granada is something precious, a pearl!

It seems I should ask John of God, "Do we practise charity?"

With a certain sense of shame I have to confess to him that we have not eliminated plagues from the planet, the scourge of hunger for example. Inequality between individuals and nations is still very apparent. But, we are striving for justice, besides taking care of social welfare and there are 1,500 Hospitaller Brothers, his sons, spread throughout our world..

One little thing that might disconcert him, is that instead of asking for help *"for the love of God,"* we now raise funds through fetes, lotteries and concerts which the ladies auxiliaries organise so well, "for the love of God."

Speaking personally, I can say that John of God's life has given me a glimmer of light concerning the obscure mystery of evil. I ask God the Father, being good and powerful, why the sorrowful Passion, why the pains and weeping?

At the side of John of God, I wonder, if maybe suffering 'exists on the side', so that we can show love and give kindness and consolation whenever any suffering person comes to us.

The loving kindness that John of God gave them in their affliction meant far more to them than what he put in their hands. It may well be that persons suffer, so that we can care for them.

John of God, I need to say it is not always clear what we should do. Sometimes your poor can also be cheats and deceive us. I have a certain friend on the street corner who begs alms. He lost an eye in a traffic accident and I wanted to buy him a glass eye. We gave him money three times to buy a glass eye. After the third time, he disappeared for a month, spent all the money and then came back without the eye! What I ask you is this, would you see Jesus beneath the skin of every sick person and identify the poor with the suffering of Jesus Christ?

I am asking you, "Is that old drunk who turns up every Saturday spinning a yarn, is he then 'this' Jesus? If Jesus 'is' my old drunk, what about my cheating friend with the glass eye?"

How do we define the significance of the goodness exercised by John of God 'within the whole of the cosmos'? Each time our astronomers use a new space telescope, they delve into the heart of the universe only to find it teeming with thousands of new galaxies. Thanks to 'Hubble' we now speak of between forty and fifty thousand galaxies, each with hundreds of thousands of stars. Our planet is like a tiny grain of sand. Shall it be, then, important to love, to practise charity?

A 'crazy' type like John of God, whether mad or not, is very special, having within him the soul of a poet who says that grace can be found in anyone who loves you anywhere on the planet.

So, John of God, poet, mad or sane, you know your love gave meaning to the cosmos, yet you knew nothing about the Hubble telescope or the fifty thousand stars. You do now!

While I was sorting through papers relating to John of God, I received word that one of the key thinkers of our century, Emile Cioran, had died in Paris. He has been dubbed, unjustly, 'the philosopher of despair'.

So many 'poor persons' like Cioran, walk the pathways of the world of humanity. Cioran was financially poor, especially when he first became an exile from his native city of Rasina in Romania where he spent a happy childhood. Indeed he was poor also, "with the burden of his intellectual yearning" after so many years of searching without finding the way.

John of God belonged to a different race of poor persons, marginated people with souls in living flesh.

I did two things before leaving Granada. Firstly I remained quietly alone for a while in the upstairs room of the Pisa palace where John of God died.

I'm not sure how I came to think about the ancient Church father Ignatius of Antioch, who lived in those times when Christians were cruelly thrown to lions. He said that if a Christian wanted to offer the Gospel of Jesus to those about him, what counted was *"generosity and greatness of soul rather than persuasive words."*

The supreme lesson of John of God was born of his greatness of soul.

(I must confess that I dared to ask John of God, if it wasn't too much of an effort, to put that famous notebook which was written *"by his companion who recorded his actions and words"* under the nose of someone in the archives of Granada or Rome! Please, leave it about for us to pick up! That would be more than enough to make him smile at our obstinate efforts to reconstruct his life story, step by step. We would feel very happy if we could put it all together, at first hand.)

The other thing I did was to steal one of the miniature pomegranates from the bush which grows in the patio of the Pisa palace.

I didn't actually steal it. I did ask permission. I fancied to keep it with me, for it was a nice little souvenir that grew in the shade of John of God.

A wise and close friend of mine, the late Xavier Zubiri, used to accuse me of fantasising when I spoke about eternal life with words more in keeping with our earthly life. Maybe, his reproach was legitimate, you can judge for yourself. To finish this book, I want to imagine an important meeting.

If, in the heavenly realm, I were to continue to practice as a journalist, I would interview St. Peter, the well-known keeper of the pearly gates. I would ask him what his reaction was that time, when half an hour after midnight on 8 March 1550, he welcomed a man carrying a sick man on his back, supporting him around the neck, with his right hand keeping the head steady, and his left hand supporting the feet.

I can well imagine the expression that came on Peter's face when he recognised the face of the sick man as that of the Lord Jesus Christ.

Notes to Chapter 37

* In regards to the use of the Casa de los Pisa as the meeting place for the *'vergonzantes'* (persons too embarrassed or ashamed to beg) with John of God: This was testified at the Madrid Beatification Process by the witness Francisca de Villarreal on 1 March 1623 who heard it from the children of Doña Ana Osorio and the house servants: *"He helped as best he could poor persons who were 'vergonzantes', and even though many came with great necessities, none left disheartened... gentlemen needing help in some law case, likewise widows and other persons whom he helped, would come to ask his assistance. He said 'God will give and it will be remedied, come back on such and such a day,' which he would state. It seemed miraculous, but on the day he said, they came back and he punctually gave them the required alms."*

* For the account of the exit from the hospital in the Cuesta Gomérez, see Francisco de Castro, op. cit., chapter 20: Castro omits the reference to the intervention of Archbishop Guerrero in the petition of Ana Osorio; an intervention firmly help up by the witnesses at the Granada Beatification Process: #8 (Pedro López Esclava), #10 (Pedro Franco de León), #11 (Francisco Ruiz), #15 (Lucas Angulo), #20 (Diego Marín), #26 (Domingo Navarro), #29 (Alonso Sánchez Dávila), #45 (María Oseguera).

* The quotations relating to the period John of God was at the Casa de los Pisa are either from Francisco de Castro, op. cit., chapter 20, or from the witnesses mentioned in this chapter.

* The Jewish antecedents of the Pisa de Almagro family, cf. L. R. Villegas Díaz, *'Sobre judeoconversos manchegos, unas apreciaciones'*, in *Encuentro en Sefarad*, Ciudad real 1987, 175-188; Villegas refers himself to the work by M. A. Ladero *Judeo conversos andaluces en el siglo XV* etc., Jaén 1984, 27-55; also A. A. Vázquez Cano, *Los Pissas: Revista de Centro de Estudios Históricos de Granada y su Reino, Vol IV* (1914) 157-170.

* About the Casa de los Pisa (Pisa palace) see A. Gallego Burín *Granada*, op.cit., 339-340. Also, for the family tree of the Pisas' see M. de Mina, *'Anotaciones', Fondo Documental*, op.cit., Archive of Los Pisa, Granada, *La familia Pisa*; aslo M. De Mina *Visitar la Granada* etc., op. cit., 264.

* Master Bernabé Ruiz declared as witness # 65 at the Granada Beatification Process. The account of the conversation between the dying John of God and the little boy Cristóbal was given by the priest don Cristóbal and Catalina de Narzáez, at the Madrid Beatification Process on 25 Jan. 1623. The same Catalina de Narzáez heard from her uncle Master Francisco the 'legend' of how John of God fell with his bundle of firewood into the snow-covered hole.

* For the juridical, assistential and spiritual development of the Hospitaller Order, Cf. G. Russotto, O.H., *San Giovanni di Dio e il suo Ordine Ospedaliero*, op. Cit.; aslo A. Pazzini, *Assistenza e ospedali, etc.*, op. Cit. For the story of the Hospitaller

Order in the navy and army, see S. Clavijo, *La Orden Hospitalaria de San Juan de Dios en la Marina de Guerra de España, Presencia y Nexo*, Madrid 1950. The phrase by G. Marañon, in Raiz y decoro de España, Madrid 1933, 147. [Also Benedict O'Grady, *A History of the Spanish Congregation of the Hospitaller Order of St. John of God from the 16th to the 19th Century*, (manuscript photocopied), General Curia of the O.H., Rome 1995, also available at the O.H. Provincial Office, Burwood, Sydney, NSW, Australia.]

* The words of Brother Pascual Piles were spoken at an assembly held at Brescia, Italy, on 1 June 1994, an English version was published by the O.H. General Curia; *A New Evangelisation for a New Hospitality.*

* The three witnesses who said the Archbishop administered the last sacraments to John of God testified this at the Granada Beatification Process , they were: #55 (Juana de Gálvez), #56 (Catalina de Arenas), #57 (Luisa Bribera). Besides these three witnesses whose words I have reproduced in the text, were further witnesses: #5 (Gabriel Maldonado), #19 (Pedro Franco de León), #13 (Felipe de Alayz), #19 (Jerónomo de Piñar), #28 (Diego de Morales), #34 (María de la Paz), #41 (Francisca de Perea). Such an overwhelming number of witnesses is enough to verify the Archbishop administering the sacraments to John of God. Some of the witnesses also said *"everyone in Granada knew it."*

* The idea of John Paul II on the doctrine of justification in Luther belongs to a public discourse and was recorded by '*L'Oservatore Romano'*, 17 Nov. 1980, p 6. The conference given by Cardinal Willebrands was given on 4 July 1970 at Evian-les-Bains and is published in '*La Documentation Catholique'* #1569 (6 Sept. 1970) 761-767.

* Regarding the historic and spiritual significance of John of God, see V. Riesco, *Y Dios se hizo hermano*, op. cit., 139-153; also J. Sánchez Martínez, *Kenosis* etc., op. cit., passim.

* The doubt as to the exact hour of John of God's death comes from G. Magliozzi, *Pagine, Juandediane*, op. cit., 168-170.

* The viaticum of John of God, see Francisco de Castro, op. Cit., chapter 20. Also A. Laborde, *El enfermero de Dios*, op.cit., 218-220. J. Cruset, *El Hombre*, etc., op.cit., 191-193. A. Muñoz Hidalgo, *De Juan Ciudad a Juan de Dios*, op. cit., 222-223, he speaks of an apparition of the Blessed Virgin Mary which cannot be sustained. V. A. Riesco, *Y Dios, etc.*, op. cit., 154-170. J. F. Bellido, *El corazón de la Granada*, op. cit., 192, here also is an alleged apparition of the Blessed Virgin Mary, and this author says John of God confided this with Doña Ana Osorio, a statement impossible to sustain with what the witnesses testified.

* The following are documented references for each detail of the chronicle which narrates the events of the evening of 7 March to the morning of the 8th.

  • The priest Cristóbal, son of Doña Ana Osorio, confided this information to Mateo del Espino Aguado who declared this at the Lucena Beatification Process on 28 March 1623. Espino had a cousin named Luis who was married to Mariana, a granddaughter of Ana Osorio, therefore a niece of the priest Cristóbal who told Espino how John of God wanted to be left alone. Various witnesses at the Granada Beatification Process made similar statements, including members of the Osorio family: #10 (Pedro Franco de León), #13 (Felipe de Alayz), #29 (Alonso Sánchez Dávila).

  • Regarding the position in which the body of John of God was found: The priest

Bernabé Ruiz swore to this at the Granada Beatification Process where he was witness # 65. Other witnesses who testified likewise were: #3 (Antón Rodríguez), #4 (Melchor Rodríguez), #10 (Pedro Franco de León), #13 (Felipe de Alayz), #19 (Jerónimo de Piñar), #41 (Francisca de Perea), #61 (Diego López Roales), and others.

- We know the movements of the old aunt Doña Catalina outside the sickroom from the testimony of Francisca de Perea (witness #41 at the Granada Beatification Process). She also gave other details on how Doña Catalina took care of the patient. Another woman, Elvira Díaz (witness #35 at the Granada Beatification Process) also spoke of the green bedspread.
- Agueda Muñoz testified on 10 Fe. 1623 as witness # 16 at the Granada Beatification Process. The pipe band was composed of an instrument called a *chirimía* which was a wooden wind instrument like a clarinet, seven centimetres long with ten holes and a reed mouthpiece.
- Luisa Ribera made her statement at the Granada Beatification Process where she was witness #57; also Lucia de la O, witness #54; Francisca de la Fuente, witness #64, spoke about the *oidor* (judge) Gamboa.
- The following witnesses at the Granada Beatification Process spoke about the magistrates being present to witness the placing of the body in the coffin: #3 (Antón Rodríguez), #26 (Domingo Navarro), #35 (Elvira Díaz), #37 (Francisca de Venegas).
- The *Licenciado* (lawyer) Alonso Suárez Sedeño appears among the register of the Royal Chancellery as a Councillor of the Court since 1548; Doctor Sancho de Librija first appears as a 'councillor for criminal cases' proposed for the position of Councillor of the Court; cf. P. Gau Gímenez. *La Real Chancillería de Granada (1505-1834),* Granada 1980, 266-337.
- I purposely excluded in the text an ironic remark in Castro's narration, which puts a final phrase into the mouth of the dying John of God: *"Jesus, Jesus, into your hands I commend my soul."* Surely, if John of God was alone in his room, how could anyone have heard this exclamation?
- I have not mentioned that five or six witnesses spoke about a *"fragrant odour"* in John of God's room as also about the rest of the Casa de los Pisa. We know that in similar circumstances places are perfumed for obvious reasons, also there are times when it is simply an imagined phenomenon. Catalina de Arenas testified on 20 March 1523 as witness # 56 at the Granada Beatification Process. Francisca de Vilarreal was among 'the witness who did not personally know John of God', she testified at the Madrid Beatification Process on 1 March 1623.

* For the interment and obsequies of John of God see Francisco de Castro, chapter 21. The statements of the witnesses coincide with slight differences in their presentation. From the Granada Beatification Process we know the following: witness #1 (Juan Lobo, was the boy who saw it from the Santa Ana bridge), #3 (Antón Rodríguez), #5 (Gabriel Maldonado), #6 (Cristóbal de Azaña), #8 Pedro López de Eslava), #34 (María de la Paz who supplied the folksong sung by the children), #35 (Elvira Diáz), #46 (Agueda Muñoz), #56 (Catalina de Arenas), #57 (Luisa de Ribera), #59 (Inés Núñez, she said people came in from outlying villages), #61 (Diego López Roales), #62 (María de Godoy), #65 (Bernabé Ruiz).